Everyone loves *The Slipper*

"Ms. Wilde's great sense of pace, her flair for local color, her use of real-life celebrity names and her sense of humor . . . make this romance so entertaining."

The New York Times Book Review

"Jennifer Wilde's new novel *The Slipper* is wonderful! Super! The Great Cinderella Novel of the Year."

Romantic Times

"The kind of storytelling you thoroughly enjoyed reading years ago . . . Jennifer Wilde is a consummate writer. . . . It's a very special novel."

Rave Reviews

"Entertaining!"

Publishers Weekly

Library of Congress Catalog Card Number: 87-7034

ISBN 0-345-35643-8

This edition published by arrangement with McGraw-Hill Book Company, a division of McGraw-Hill, Inc.

Manufactured in the United States of America

First Ballantine Books Edition: September 1988

For my mother,
who always believed in dreams
and helped make my own
become a reality

1

The girls in their white summer dresses sat in a row, young,
excited, full of dreams. The girl with the long dark-gold hair
was by far the prettiest, but she seemed totally unaware of it.
Her hands were clasped together nervously in her lap and her
blue eyes were apprehensive as, at the podium, Mr. James, the
principal, droned on and on about the virtues of this particular
graduating class. On the other side of the platform the boys sat
stiffly, uncomfortable in their dark suits and ties. Caps and gowns
had been ordered from a firm in Wichita but had failed to arrive
in time, which may well have been a blessing as the robes were
wool and the Kansas sun beat down without mercy on this last
day of May, 1955. Friends and relatives who had come to share
these moments of glory shifted impatiently on the hard metal
folding chairs set up on the school lawn and wished the principal
weren't so windy, wished he'd curtail the platitudes, announce
the scholarships and get *on* with it.

Carol Martin brushed a heavy wave of dark-gold hair from
her temple and clasped her hands together again. Would he ever
stop blathering? Would he ever make that announcement that
was going to change her life? She gazed at the sea of faces there
on the lawn and spotted Uncle Edgar, disgruntled and uninter-
ested, clearly here against his will. Aunt Jessie sat beside him,
prim and very proper, doing her duty. In her heart Carol knew

that neither of them would miss her when she left. They had taken her in ten years ago when her parents had been killed in an automobile accident in Albuquerque, New Mexico, and they had duly raised her and seen to her needs and fulfilled their responsibilities as upright, God-fearing citizens, but they had never loved her.

Not really, she thought. Uncle Edgar loved only his drugstore, devoting all his time and energy to the business. Aunt Jessie was obsessed with keeping her house clean and tidy, an example to all good Kansas wives. Their niece had always been an outsider, never mistreated, true, but never fully accepted either. Ever since she had come to live with them—a skinny seven-year-old orphan back then, frightened and bowed with grief—she had felt herself an intruder. She wouldn't be a bother to them much longer now. If only Mr. James would stop pontificating and make the announcement.

Looking away from her relatives, Carol noticed a stranger sitting in the back row and wondered who he might be. His clothes, his entire demeanor proclaimed him an alien in the midst of these middle-class farmers and small-town businessmen. His dark auburn hair was sleek, stylishly brushed, a shade too long. His tanned face was attractively weathered, his eyes dark brown, and a rather wry smile played on his wide, full lips. He wore polished brown loafers, trim brown slacks, a cream linen shirt and a bronze silk tie. His brown-and-tan checked sport coat was superbly tailored, obviously expensive and obviously not purchased at J. C. Penney's, the only major store in town. A beautiful gold watch gleamed on his left wrist. As Carol studied him, he glanced surreptitiously at the watch and arched one fine dark brow, and then he looked up and his eyes met hers and Carol blushed faintly and gazed down at the hands in her lap. The man was quite old, forty at least, and she wasn't at all interested. The only thing of any interest now was that all-important announcement. How many more platitudes could Mr. James mouth about this fine nation, these fine young people, the glorious future ahead of them?

"As you know," he said at last, "each year the Norman Philips Scholarship is awarded to one young man and one young woman who have maintained the highest level of grades and attendance throughout their sojourn at Joseph Henry High School. It is now my privilege to present these scholarships to

two remarkable young people who have been a shining example to their classmates during the past three years.''

He paused. He beamed. Carol caught her breath. She had been waiting three years for this moment, three years of constant study, of perfect attendance, of almost perfect grades—one B in Latin in her sophomore year, the rest straight A's. Hours and hours of studying, poring over the books, sweating through exams, always afraid she might slip up, make an error, put down the wrong answer. Tension. Stress. Determination. She knew that she had to escape this small, stifling town, these good, simple, narrow-minded people, and the Norman Philips Scholarship would provide the means. There was a great, glamorous world out there beyond the cornfields, and she meant to explore it and savor all its fascinations. Carol brushed her soft white skirt and straightened her shoulders as Mr. James cleared his throat.

''And the winners are—'' The principal paused again, still beaming, and Carol thought she might faint. ''Mister John Huddleston!'' he exclaimed dramatically. ''And Miss Janette Anderson!''

''No!'' Carol cried.

She was on her feet. She had no idea how she came to be standing. Everyone was staring at her. Her heart was pounding. She felt dizzy. She felt she was in the middle of a very bad dream. She shook her head repeatedly, and then she sobbed and turned and stumbled down the steps on the side of the platform and fled up the aisle between the rows of spectators. People were speaking in shocked whispers and everyone was still staring, Uncle Edgar, Aunt Jessie, the handsome older man in the expensive clothes. A large black-haired woman wearing a fuchsia dress and a white carnation corsage jumped to her feet and pursued the girl, catching her by the arm as Carol cleared the back row.

''Carol!'' the woman cried. ''Oh, Carol, I'm so sorry! I'm so sorry, darling. I know how hard you worked. I know what this meant to—''

''One B!'' Carol sobbed. ''One lousy B when I was in the tenth grade, and Janette Anderson gets the scholarship! She doesn't need it! Her father owns the hardware store. He's rich!''

Mrs. Epperson was sobbing herself. She was the speech teacher, and Carol had been her favorite student for the past three years, a bright, gifted, incredibly intuitive young girl who

stood out like a diamond among the shuffling farm boys and plump, giggling hoydens who populated her classes. Carol had had the lead in the class play a month ago and was the only student Mrs. Epperson had ever taught who might actually *amount* to something, given the right breaks, and now . . . Mrs. Epperson gasped as Carol pulled her arm free.

"It isn't fair!" Carol exclaimed.

"Life isn't, my darling. Life is many things, but it's rarely fair—"

Carol didn't hear the rest of the words. She rushed across the lawn in her high-heeled white pumps and across the football field where, almost every afternoon, sweaty jocks strutted and swaggered and vied for the attention of girls in fresh lipstick and fluffy sweaters and tight skirts who huddled on the weathered wooden bleachers and hooted encouragement. Carol had never been one of those girls. There had never been time. There had been time for nothing but the books, the algebra problems, the science projects, the French verbs. And what good had it done her? What good? She left the school grounds and crossed the street and moved hurriedly, blindly through the streets of the small town that had been a prison to her for the past ten years.

An hour later, without really knowing how she got there, she found herself curled up on the ground, surrounded by tall green stalks, in one of the interminable cornfields that surrounded the town. Her soft white dress was soiled. The heel on one of her pumps had broken off. Her cheeks were pale, stained with tears that had already dried. She was numb. The anguish inside was so great that she could no longer even feel it. All her hopes, all her dreams had been shattered in one brief moment, and there was no reason to go on living.

Janette Anderson, who was overweight and had pimples and a rich father, had won the scholarship, and Janette didn't even care about going to college. She had no ambition, no aspirations. All she cared about was getting married and having babies and living a safe, secure, mundane life in Ellsworth, Kansas, as had her parents before her. She would marry a nice, dull boy and he would go into the hardware business with her father and they would live in a nice, comfortable house and become proud parents, and Janette would cook three meals a day and keep house and join the PTA and never know, never care about all those exciting things happening in the rest of the world. It would be

enough for her. It was enough for most people. Never, never would it be enough for Carol, but, at seventeen, she was doomed. Doomed.

Another hour passed and then another. The sky had darkened to gray and a soft violet haze filled the air when she finally stood up and brushed the dust from her skirt. Still numb, her face white, her blue eyes filled with bleak resignation, she walked down the rows of corn, limping a little because of the broken heel. Clearing the corn, she crossed the narrow strip of barren ground and stepped onto the road. A horn blared deafeningly. There was an ear-splitting screech, the sound of tires desperately gripping the road and leaving rubber. Carol barely glanced up as the huge car swerved violently, missing her by inches. She watched with total lack of interest as it shot across the road and slammed to a jerking halt. The man she had seen earlier at commencement flung open the door, climbed out and stalked angrily toward her, his face ashen.

"Have you lost your mind!" he roared. "Stepping out onto the road like that, right in front of me—I almost killed you!"

"I wish you had," she said in a dull voice.

"My God!" The man raked the fingers of his right hand through thick auburn waves, his eyes glazed with shock. "If I hadn't been damned quick you'd be dead now! I'd have hit you!"

"You'd have done me a favor," she said.

"Jesus!"

The man shook his head and took a deep breath and made a valiant effort to control himself. Carol was tall, but he seemed to loom over her. He must be at least six feet three, she thought idly. He had taken off the expensive sport coat. His bronze tie had been tugged loose. His cream linen shirt had short sleeves. His shoulders were quite broad, his arms well muscled. Even though he was probably well over forty and old enough to be her father, Carol had to admit that he was good-looking. Better-looking than Mr. Matthews, the history teacher all the girls flirted with. Certainly better-looking than the boys with calflike eyes and sweaty palms who were always trying to get her to go to the Pike Drive-In with them.

The man sighed, raking fingers through his hair again, and then he really looked at her for the first time. His dark-brown eyes filled with interest. There was nothing calflike about them.

"You," he said. "The girl who—"

"The girl who made a fool of herself in front of the whole of Ellsworth," Carol said bitterly.

"Are you all right?" he inquired. Although husky, his voice was soft, a kind voice.

"I'm fine," she said coldly.

The suggestion of a grin played on his full lips. Something like amusement gleamed in those dark-brown eyes.

"I don't suppose you have a drink on you?" he said.

"I don't suppose I do."

"I could use one right now. Could I ever."

"You're out of luck," she informed him. "The only place in Ellsworth you can buy a drink is Jake's Bar and Grill. It's a sleazy dive, hardly the sort of place for a man who wears fine clothes and drives a Cadillac."

"A Cadillac I almost wrecked, thanks to you."

"I'm sorry," Carol said.

"Are you?" he asked.

"Not really. I wish you'd killed me."

"Ah, youth," he said. "You're seventeen years old. Everything is high drama at seventeen, and the drama is generally earth-shaking tragedy. Ibsen or Strindberg or Tennessee Williams, rarely Noël Coward. You don't really want to die."

"I most certainly do!"

The grin came into full play. It was a most engaging grin. Carol knew she must seem ridiculous to him, must seem a silly, self-dramatizing child, but how could anyone his age expect to know how she felt? He was sleek and poised and had clearly never known heart-wrenching disappointment. One of those people to whom everything came easy—and in abundance. He had remarkable good looks, charm, wealth. Intelligence, too, Carol admitted. Most people in Ellsworth had never even heard of Ibsen or Strindberg.

"How do you know I'm seventeen?" she asked tartly.

"I know quite a lot about you," he informed her. "After you dashed off like that, disrupting the oh-so-solemn exercises, I made it a point to find out about you. I talked to your speech teacher, Mrs. Epperson. She's a great admirer of yours."

"Why—why would you be interested in me?"

"I have my reasons," he said.

He might be over forty and terribly suave, but he was just like

the horny youths of Ellsworth. He wanted to get into her pants. She despised him. She despised the whole world.

"I see," she said.

"I doubt that you do, my child, but we'll leave it for the moment. Come on, I'll drive you home."

"I'm not going home. I can't go home—not ever again."

"You read Thomas Wolfe, too? A young man's writer, Wolfe. One idolizes him at twenty. At forty, alas, one finds him overwrought, excessive and shockingly self-indulgent. Like youth itself," he added.

"You're making fun of me."

"Would I do that? You can't go home, and I take it you're not going to the dance at the gym tonight. Can't say that I blame you—all those crepe paper streamers, all those balloons, that rock and roll band with the singer in the inevitable pink jacket caterwauling about Peggy Sue and blue suede shoes. Frightfully depressing under the circumstances."

Carol scowled. She'd never met anyone who talked like him. He smiled and curled his fingers around her elbow, guiding her toward the car.

"We'll drive on a ways," he said. "Maybe we'll find a bridge."

"A bridge?"

"So you can jump off. Of course it would be much more dramatic to step in front of a train, like Anna Karenina, or take poison, like poor Madame Bovary, but I fear a bridge will have to suffice. I believe there's one a few miles this side of Wichita. Quite high, too, if memory serves."

"You *are* making fun of me!"

"Come along, Carol."

"Go to hell."

"I probably shall, eventually. Right now I intend to go someplace quiet and dimly lit where I can have a very tall drink. You're underage, of course, but you could use a drink yourself and I imagine they'll bend the rules. Perhaps you'd prefer a milkshake?"

Carol didn't bother to reply. She climbed obediently into the car, knowing full well that he intended to get her drunk and have his way with her. It didn't matter. Nothing would ever matter again. He started the motor, pulled back onto the road, and they were cruising along at a steady speed, the motor purr-

ing gently, night falling fast now. He turned on the headlights, and they cut into the shadows like two pale silver spears. She felt another sob welling in her throat. She fought it back and closed her eyes. A fresh tear trailed slowly down her cheek. The man made no attempt at conversation. He drove the powerful car with casual ease, his hands resting lightly on the steering wheel. Carol could smell expensive cloth and lime shaving lotion and the faint, musky scent of male flesh. It wasn't at all unpleasant. Every girl had to lose her virginity eventually. It might as well be to someone who knew what he was doing.

Twenty-five minutes later he slowed the car and pulled into the drive of a low, dark building with a discreet blue neon sign glowing over the recessed front door. Carol sat up, smoothing down her skirt. Her companion eased into an empty parking space and cut off the motor. He looked at her for a long moment, then got out and came around to open the door for her. She felt apprehensive now, hesitating as his hand closed over hers. He tugged gently on her hand, pulling her out of the car. The night air was cool. Pale yellow-gold light spilled out of windows, making soft squares in front of the building. Crickets rasped. Carol could smell crushed milkweed.

"What—what is this place?" she asked nervously.

"In my day it used to be called a roadhouse. Discreetly located several miles outside the city, far away from prying eyes. Discreetly run by a staff who keep their eyes lowered and ask no questions. Soft music on the jukebox. A small, intimate dance floor. Secluded booths and tables. Excessively high prices to keep out the riffraff."

"I—I can't go in there. My dress is all rumpled and soiled. I've lost the heel on one of my shoes."

"Your dress is fine. You can take off your shoes."

"But—"

"No one will say a word," he assured her.

Carol hesitated again and then, feeling very bold, pulled off her shoes and tossed them into the car. The man smiled and closed the car door and led her toward the recessed entrance. The neon light cast pale blue shadows over her skirt as they passed beneath it. A maître d' in dark jacket greeted them and led them toward a booth in back of the large, dim room. "Moonglow" was playing quietly on the jukebox, and a single couple danced on the floor, the woman in clinging red silk jersey, the

man in business suit and horn-rimmed glasses. No one paid the least attention to Carol's wilted white dress and stockinged feet.

"Scotch and soda," her companion told the waiter who came promptly over to their booth, "and—uh—I think a glass of white wine for the lady. We'll order dinner later."

The waiter nodded and departed. The room was all shadowy, candles burning in tiny red glass jars on all the tables and booths, no direct lighting whatsoever. It was quite wicked-looking, Carol thought, like something out of an Ida Lupino movie. She felt quite wicked herself and, yes, excited, too, despite the anguish inside. She looked at the man sitting across from her, his handsome face thoughtful now.

"What were you doing at commencement?" she asked. "Are you related to one of the seniors?"

He shook his head. "You might say I was there in an official capacity. My wife usually takes care of the duties, but she left for Europe early this year, and I was stuck with the job."

"Official capacity? Job? I don't—"

"I'm Norman Philips, Carol."

She could feel the color leaving her cheeks.

"Junior," he added. "It was my father who established the scholarships for students of his old alma mater. I drove up from Wichita to present the checks to the scholarship winners."

Carol didn't say anything. The waiter brought their drinks. She looked at the glass of white wine. Although she had never had an alcoholic beverage in her life, she took up the glass and downed half of it in one gulp. Norman Philips looked alarmed.

"Hey," he said. "Take it easy. That's not soda. You're supposed to sip it."

"Fuck you," she said.

She had never used that word before. It felt strange on her lips.

"I'm not the one who selects the scholarship winners, Carol. In fact, I have nothing to do with it. I understand they're selected by members of the school board."

"And Janette Anderson's mother is on the board. Fuck her, too."

She finished the wine in another gulp, and Norman Philips shook his head and signaled the waiter and ordered another. He took a sip of his scotch and studied her with dark-brown eyes. Carol felt dizzy, felt she might burst into tears again, and she

mustn't do that, must have some pride. When the waiter brought
her second glass of wine she toyed with the stem and stared
down at it and listened to "Moonglow" and cried in spite of
herself, quietly, tears flowing down her cheeks. Philips waited
patiently and, when she was finished, handed her a clean white
handkerchief.

"Ready for dinner?" he inquired.

"I—I suppose so. I might as well get a good meal out of
this."

He looked askance at that, but he made no comment. He
ordered their meal without consulting her, and it was strange
and exotic. Carol had never tasted shad roe before or asparagus
with hollandaise sauce, either. There were so many things she
had never had, never done, but that was going to change, she
vowed. Somehow, some way, she was going to get out of Kansas
and start living in earnest, and if she had to be bad, she'd just
be bad. Mr. Philips was a very wealthy man, and there was
much he could teach her.

"Mrs. Epperson told me you're a superlative young actress,"
he said over dessert. "She said your performance in *Stage Door*
last month was brilliant, worthy of a professional. I wish I'd
been there to see it."

"It was a silly class play by a bunch of high school students.
I seriously doubt you'd have enjoyed it."

"You're a very beautiful girl, Carol."

"My cheekbones are too high. My mouth is too full. I'm too
tall."

"Very beautiful," he repeated, "and Mrs. Epperson is right—
there's a luminous quality about you, an undeniable presence. I
noticed you up there on the platform long before you made your
dramatic exit."

"Did you?"

"You stood out. I couldn't keep my eyes off you. The sun
was shining on your hair. Your hair was like dark golden wheat."

His husky voice seemed to caress each word. Oh yes, he
wanted to get into her pants. He wasn't stiff in his jeans, didn't
have damp palms like boys at school, and he wouldn't paw,
wouldn't plead, but he wanted her. Every female instinct told
her that, and Carol felt a curious sense of power that was entirely
new. She found it vaguely alarming. Something had happened
to her back there in the cornfield. Somehow she had changed.

She was a good girl, a virgin, had never even considered going all the way, but now . . . now she was utterly intrigued by this man old enough to be her father. It must be the wine, she thought. She had had two glasses before their meal arrived, another while she ate the shad roe.

"You want to become an actress?" Philips asked.

"Is—is that so foolish?" she asked defensively. "Is that so wrong?"

"There's nothing foolish about it, nothing wrong, either. If one has no ambitions, one never succeeds."

"I—I don't intend to vegetate in Ellsworth, Kansas, for the rest of my days."

"I doubt that you shall," he said. "Mrs. Epperson tells me you had your heart set on attending Claymore University in Indiana. They have a very fine drama department, I understand. I remember reading an article about Julian Compton in *Time* a few years ago—noted director gives up the bright lights of Broadway for the groves of academe."

"Claymore was a dream," Carol said quietly, gazing down at her dessert plate. "I should have known it—it would never come true. My Aunt Jessie says going to college is nonsense. She says I should meet a nice young man and get married as soon as possible. Uncle Edgar thinks I should go to work at his drugstore immediately. Good clerks are hard to come by. I've helped out there several times."

"You don't want to get married?" he asked.

"I—I want to *do* something with my life," she said, and there was a passionate tremor in her voice. "I want to *be* somebody, accomplish things. Most people—most people exist. I want to live."

Norman Philips heard that passionate tremor in her voice, that conviction found only in the very young before life has stripped away so many illusions. It saddened him, for those full of passion and conviction were invariably hurt by life, and he didn't want this girl to be hurt. She was so very beautiful, so radiant, and there was a touching vulnerability as well. How long would that last out in the cold, cruel world? Trapped in a loveless marriage all these years, blessed with all the material comforts and plagued with a sense of time gone by, opportunities lost, potentials unfulfilled, he longed to warm himself at the altar of her youth, longed for the temporary reassurance a girl like this could

give, but his decision was already made. Life might hurt her, but he didn't intend to.

"Finished?" he inquired.

Carol nodded. He signaled the waiter and paid the bill and helped her to her feet. "Some Enchanted Evening" was playing on the jukebox now. Norman Philips felt a tightness at the back of his throat. Fingers curled about her elbow, he led the girl toward the door. She was just a little unsteady on her stockinged feet. How easy it would be. How easy. There had been so many young women in his life—smooth, sleek, pretty creatures who accepted his expensive presents with greedy eyes and hinted for more while dispensing their favors—but there had never been one like this, one so innocent, so young. His manner became brusque as they stepped outside. The air was almost chilly. He was grateful for that. It helped.

"I'll take you home now," he said, guiding her toward the car.

"No," she said.

"What do you mean—'No'?"

"I told you earlier. I can't go home."

"That's nonsense. Your aunt and uncle—"

"I humiliated them today. Aunt Jessie will never live it down. Uncle Edgar couldn't care less what I do. They—they'll be glad to be rid of me at last."

"You're drunk, Carol."

"No. I may have been. I'm not now."

"What will you do?"

"I—I'll go to Wichita and get a job. I'll work at the Dairy Queen. I worked at the Dairy Queen in Ellsworth last summer. I—somehow I'll earn some money and—and if I can't go to Claymore I'll go to Kansas State, wait on tables, do anything I have to do to—to escape."

"And tonight?" he asked.

"I'll go home with you. You said your wife is in Europe."

"She is, but—"

Carol steadied herself against the side of the car and looked up at him with imploring eyes.

"You care," she said, and that tremor was in her voice again. "I sense that. You—you actually care what happens to me. You're kind. You're compassionate. I sense that, too. It—it's been so

long since anyone actually cared. Please let me go with you. I won't be any trouble, I promise."

"You don't know what you're doing, Carol."

"I think so. I think I do."

Philips hesitated, his throat so tight he could hardly speak. The girl looked up at him, fragile, lovely, hair spilling over her shoulders in the moonlight. Music drifted out through the windows. "As Time Goes By" now. Jesus! He fought with himself for several long moments, and then he opened the car door for her.

"I'll take you home with me, just for tonight, and you're to call your aunt as soon as we get there. You're to tell her you're spending the night with a girlfriend. Tomorrow—tomorrow we'll see what kind of arrangements we can make for you."

She was silent as they pulled out of the parking lot and back onto the road. He drove carefully, telling himself he was out of his mind, so tense he could barely contain himself. The girl was underage. He could go to jail for this. Thank God he'd given the servants the week off. Thank God he was currently batching it in that huge, secluded mansion outside Wichita. He'd never brought a girl there before, had always maintained a suite on the top floor of the Royalton Hotel for his girls, and . . . nothing was going to happen tonight. He'd give her a glass of milk and maybe a plate of cookies and put her to bed. Untouched. Hell, his son Cliff was older than she was, still at Yale, taking courses this summer to make up for those he had failed during the past two semesters. She was a child, a mere child, three years younger than Cliff. Nothing was going to happen tonight. He promised himself that as the Cadillac cruised down the dark, lonely road.

Ten minutes later he pulled into the drive, the lights of Wichita gleaming in the distance. He cut the motor off. His hands were shaking. He'd put the car in the garage tomorrow morning. Forty-six years old, bringing a seventeen-year-old girl home with him. Madness! Sheer madness. He got out of the car and took several deep breaths of the cool night air before walking around to open the door for her. She was wonderfully poised, and he had the feeling she was in complete control now while he was all thumbs. He dropped the keys twice before he got the front door unlocked.

He fumbled for the light switch. Lamps blossomed, softly illuminating the opulent foyer. Rich pastel carpeting, polished

wood surfaces, sumptuous fabrics. The girl was visibly impressed. He led her into the spacious den with its walls of books and large stone fireplace and sofa and chairs upholstered in soft leathers.

"You must be very rich," Carol said quietly.

"Filthy rich," he told her. "Inherited."

"What do you do?"

"I manage the Norman Philips Foundation. I sign checks. There's also a construction company and two department stores. They run themselves without any assistance from me. I suppose you'd call me one of the idle rich."

"All these books—you must read a lot."

"It helps pass the time," he said. "Look—uh—I'll show you to your room. You can shower and—uh—I'll find something for you to wear, a robe or something, and then maybe—maybe you'd like a glass of milk and some cookies before you go to bed."

He realized how ridiculous that sounded as soon as he'd spoken the words. What had happened to the experienced Norman Philips who was so smooth with the sleek, perfumed girls on the top floor of the Royalton Hotel? He felt as awkward and gawky as any adolescent, and she was as calm as could be, smiling an enigmatic smile at his offer of milk and cookies. Brusquely, he took her to one of the guest rooms, showed her the bath, brought her one of Cliff's dressing gowns that had never been worn. He pointed to the phone on the night table and reminded her to call her aunt and then left, walking briskly down the hall to his own bedroom.

Half an hour later he was back in the den, drinking a strong scotch and soda, wearing a glossy brown satin dressing gown over his shirt and trousers. He was calmer now. He intended to help this girl. Tomorrow he would see to it that she got a responsible job at Philips' Department Store here in Wichita. She was bright and personable, she should do very well. He would keep an eye on her throughout the summer, and come September . . . He looked up as she came into the room. Her feet were bare. The pale blue silk dressing gown was wrapped loosely around her slender body, belted at the waist, the sleeves turned up to accommodate her arms. He could tell she had nothing on under it. His good intentions seemed to melt. The tightness in his throat returned.

"Did you phone your aunt?" he asked.

She nodded. "I told her I was spending the night with a girl-friend and she told me she'd never be able to hold her head up in Ellsworth again after my disgraceful conduct. She didn't even ask my girlfriend's name."

"I'm sorry about that, Carol."

"It—it doesn't matter," she said.

She padded across the carpet toward him on her bare feet, pale blue silk rustling, clinging. He set his glass down. His cheeks paled. Carol smiled at him, aware of his discomfort, her eyes telling him it was all right, there was nothing to fear, telling him, too, of her loneliness, her hurt, her need to be loved.

"Carol—" he began. His voice was strained. "There—there's something I want to tell you. The Norman Philips Foundation is awarding three scholarships this year. You're going to Claymore, just as you dreamed, and on a full scholarship with a monthly stipend for expenses."

She looked at him, and tears brimmed over her lashes again. He had never seen anything as beautiful, as fragile as this young girl. It felt good to be able to help her, to use some of those Philips dollars for something genuinely worthwhile—a future.

"You're so kind," she whispered.

She touched his cheek. He blanched.

"No one has—has ever been so kind to me."

"The foundation has millions," he said tersely. "The money will be used for a good cause."

She curled her arms around his neck, resting her body against his, and he was only human.

"There—there is so much inside me," she murmured, "so much I want to share. Please let me share it with you."

"I could be arrested for this," he said weakly.

"We won't tell," she promised.

2

It sure ain't Brooklyn, kiddo, Nora Levin told herself as she walked down the main drag across the street from campus. The town itself was, well, charming, the kind of place Ozzie and Harriet would live, all clean and neat and freshly scrubbed. You could almost smell the apple pies baking. It was undeniably pretty, trees everywhere, flower beds, sidewalks, not a tenement building to be seen, not a deli in sight. Indiana, for God's sake! She might as well be in Timbuktu, but, here's the kicker, she liked it. She *loved* it. The air was so pure, the grass was so green, the people were so friendly. They liked Ike, every last one of 'em. Had to. Probably thought Mamie was a living doll with those silly bangs of hers. Little Nora Levin in Indiana, figure that one out, gang. And loving it!

The area here across from the campus was a bit jazzier, with trendy little shops that sold sweaters and sporting goods and collegiate clothes, a bookstore, a record store, a hair salon, an ice cream parlor, a pizza place, a drugstore, everything you'd expect. The movie theater was small and seedy and unquestionably arty, currently showing *The Bicycle Thief*. Yawn. You could buy yourself a hamburger, a milkshake, a Mexican meal, fried chicken and blueberry pie, but you were in real trouble if you happened to be looking for lox and bagels. Nora had never particularly cared for lox anyway. She paused in front of the record

store. A huge poster of Pat Boone dominated the front window. Pat was undoubtedly big in Indiana. So it wasn't exotic? So it held no surprises? She wasn't expecting Greenwich Village. It was pleasant and attractive and she adored those snazzy little ensembles in the window of the dress shop, cunningly displayed with sprays of fake autumn leaves. Sandra Dee would go into raptures. Nora strolled on, smiling at a couple of girls she'd seen at the dormitory earlier in the day. They smiled back, just like she was one of them.

The campus was gorgeous—mellow old brick buildings, cream and tan and brown, real ivy, shady lawns aswarm with tall, handsome boys and tall, beautiful girls, all of them confident, most of them blond. The boys wore slacks and short-sleeved sport shirts. The girls wore saddle oxfords and white socks and fluffy angora sweaters and full felt skirts with stiff cancan petticoats beneath. Most of the skirts had poodles on them. Some of the students wore clever little beanies with CLASS OF '59 stitched on the front, but she'd be damned if she'd wear one, freshman or no. Let some smart-assed sophomore ask her why she wasn't wearing her beanie and she'd tell him to take a flying fuck at the moon. Nora wasn't planning to take lip from anyone. She'd fought too hard to get here, and the battle had raged all summer long.

She'd been offered half a dozen scholarships—Columbia, NYU and Vassar among them—but they were all too bloody close to Brooklyn, too close to Sadie and Irving. Nora had her heart set on Claymore, its emphasis on fine arts, its English department one of the best in the country, with real writers on the staff, published writers, with people like Robert Penn Warren and James Street and Aldous Huxley dropping by for guest lectures. She had sent off her scholarship application on the sly, with all the proper records, the mandatory letters of recommendation, had waited anxiously for their answer. She was elated to learn it was affirmative and that she'd be attending Claymore on a full scholarship. Then she broke the news to her parents, and the battle began.

Sadie was a jewel, the best mother a girl could hope to have if you didn't mind someone breathing down your neck every minute and pumping you full of hot chicken soup every time you sneezed and pushing you forward and bragging on you every time she encountered a crony who happened to have a son of

marriageable age. Sadie's mission in life was to marry off her only daughter to a nice Jewish boy who was going to become a dentist, a doctor or an engineer. The fact that her only daughter wasn't at all interested was a constant source of anguish. Nora tactfully pointed out that she was still quite young, there was hardly a rush, and Sadie wailed that a girl couldn't get married too soon nowadays, the competition was fierce. Sadie had almost had heart failure when Nora announced that she was going to Claymore in September. It would be over her dead body, Sadie shrieked, and not one cent would she get from her father, not one red cent. Indiana, yet! It was on the other side of the world! They would never see her. What had she ever done, Sadie cried, to deserve such an ungrateful daughter? What had she ever done to deserve such grief? The child wanted to desert them, and they'd worked their fingers right down to the bone for her, giving her all the advantages and a brand-new mouton coat just last fall.

Irving, who was a darling, was a bit more sympathetic. He loved his little pumpkin dearly, worshipped the ground she walked on, in fact, and he could understand why she wanted to get away, but he lived in dread of Sadie's wrath and, when push came to shove, invariably sided with her. Irving was consumed with guilt. His brother Sid was in the garment district, had his own showroom and made money hand over fist. His brother Myron was a lawyer and lived with his wife and three sons in New Rochelle and bought a new Cadillac every year. His brother Aaron was a podiatrist with a thriving practice in Grosse Pointe, Michigan, and worth over a million. Irving was in the wholesale jewelry business, but his shop was in Brooklyn and business had never been exactly booming and Sadie could hardly look her sisters-in-law in the eye on the rare occasions they condescended to acknowledge her existence. She constantly reminded Irving of her humiliation, of his own ineptitude and lack of success, and he didn't dare defy her, not even for Nora's sake.

The scholarship would take care of tuition, dorm, lab fees and such, but she was going to need money to live on, quite a lot of it, and Irving reluctantly informed her it wouldn't be forthcoming. He couldn't let her go so far away. It would break her poor mother's heart. She'd just have to settle for Columbia or NYU. Then she could live right here at home, take the subway to and from the city just as she'd done when she was attending all those

fancy private schools they'd scrimped and scraped to send her to. He knew she'd had her heart set on Claymore, but . . . well, it just wasn't in the cards. Nora gave him a hug, knowing how much it hurt him to tell her this, loving him none the less because he had no spine, but she wasn't about to be defeated. She'd sling hash if necessary, but maybe she wouldn't have to. She was a writer, right? Now was the time to prove it. She was going to write as she had never written before.

Not those thoughtful, profound, beautifully wrought stories that impressed the hell out of her English teachers. They were terrific—almost as good as Katherine Anne Porter, far better than Faith Baldwin—but there was no market for them. Every last one she'd sent off to the slick magazines had been rejected. Not commercial enough. No punch. Not what our readers are looking for. So what were readers looking for? What kind of stories could a seventeen-year-old *wunderkind* write that would earn her some money? Nora went to the corner drugstore and took a good look at the racks. Old Mr. Abromowitz told her he could hardly keep the confession magazines in stock. The housewives and high school girls snatched them up as soon as they came in every month. He couldn't understand why anyone would want to read such trash. He was shocked when Nora bought copies of all of them, carting them away with a determined look in her eye. She didn't just read them. She studied them. Carefully.

So little Nora Levin became Queen of the Confessions. The first story she wrote was stilted and patronizing, full of big words, clearly written down, and the second wasn't much better. You're not writing 'em for your English teachers, kiddo, she told herself. You're writing 'em for the gum-chewing waitress at the Truck Stop Cafe. You're writing 'em for the high school girl who sells ribbons at Woolworth's after school is out. She began to get the hang of it with the third story, and with the fourth she'd definitely developed the knack. *Modern Romances* bought it immediately, bought four more in the weeks that followed. *True Confessions* bought three and said they'd be interested in seeing anything else she happened to have on hand. Both magazines paid peanuts, of course, but if you sold enough stories you could make a mint. Nora spent all summer long at her typewriter, pounding away, burning the midnight oil, Sadie wailing that she needed to get out, get some fresh air, meet some boys,

it wasn't healthy for a girl to stay shut up in her room, typing all the time.

By the end of summer Nora had earned well over two thousand dollars, and Irving was secretly proud, secretly delighted she had foiled her mother. Sadie was appalled. Sadie was apoplectic. "I Had a Sex Change Just Like Christine." "I Was a High School Call Girl." "My Months in Rio as a Love Slave." "Seduced by My Gynecologist." "His Love Sent Me to the Public Health Clinic." Seventeen years old, and she's writing about white slavery! A baby, and she's writing about venereal disease! What if someone found *out*? What would people *say*? Where did we go wrong, Irving? Where did we fail? Sadie had hysterics, said her life was over, said she'd never be able to step foot out of the apartment again, but when September came Nora boarded the train for Indiana, Sadie sobbing on the platform at Grand Central, begging her not to go, Irving smiling sadly and waving as the train pulled away.

Free at last. Free to be Nora, not Sadie and Irving's freak of a daughter who had an IQ of 198. Sadie hadn't exactly scrambled up onto the rooftop and yelled it through a megaphone, but there wasn't a friend or relative or neighbor who didn't know her daughter was a certified genius. Hell, there wasn't a soul in Brooklyn who wasn't familiar with the fact. Little Miss Mensa. Try and live that one down. Of course Sadie hadn't realized she was working against her own best interests, broadcasting it high and low. Nice Jewish boys weren't interested in nice Jewish girls who were brighter than they were. A girl who had read all of Proust and André Gide by the time she was sixteen? A girl who could solve any math problem in the blink of an eye? Great fun in the backseat of a car, right? Just the doll you wanted to take to the prom. Boys had always avoided her like the plague.

If she was going to be cursed, why did it have to be with a high IQ? Why couldn't she be cursed with beauty? Why couldn't she be tall and blond and have cheekbones to die for? No. Fat chance. She had to be cute. Cute as a bug. A Jewish June Allyson. Five foot two, eyes of brown. Naturally curly black hair, cut short now, though not in one of those godawful poodle cuts all the rage. She *did* have a turned-up nose. An adorable nose. It had cost Irving a fortune four years ago. Nora still remembered the pain. Cute as a bug and brilliant to boot. What chance did she have? Nora had realized a long time ago that she would

have to fight every step of the way if she was going to make the world sit up and take notice, and that was exactly what she planned to do.

Claymore was the first step. She was going to learn everything she could and write a novel that would shock the pants off people and send Sadie into a swift decline. She was going to be rich and famous, have movies made from her books, maybe even write a movie herself one day. She was going to hobnob with people like Noël Coward and the Lunts, trade quips with Mary Martin, call Laurence Olivier "Larry." Big dreams, sure, but you had to dream big if you wanted to make it big. You had to be ballsy. You had to believe. You had to be determined. Little Nora Levin was going to make it, and she wasn't going to drag her heels, either. If Françoise Sagan and Gabrielle Bernais could write best-sellers at eighteen, why couldn't she? Of course, they were both French, but an American girl could write a best-seller, too. She already had a crackerjack of an idea, so sexy it would make *Bonjour Tristesse* seem like *Elsie Dinsmore*. Fame. Fortune. So laugh. A girl should aspire to changing dirty diapers and making the perfect meat loaf? Not this kid.

Some students came spilling out of the ice cream shop, laughing together, belonging, the boys sturdily built, crew-cut, obviously athletes, the girls so pretty and flirty you could whip out a machine gun and blow 'em away. Nora had a hollow feeling in the pit of her stomach, felt insecure, an outsider, but she promptly banished the feeling. She was going to belong, too. She was going to be popular. Cute wasn't terrific, but it was better than being a dog. Some of the boys might actually prefer petite girls who had glossy black curls and shiny brown eyes and personality to spare. Nora intended to play down the brainy bit. She'd make good grades, sure, top the dean's list every time, but she'd keep quiet about it. No showing off in class. No waving your hand and answering all the questions and intimidating the boys. If you planned to write a sexy novel, you had to have some experience, and Nora was going to get that, too. Who'd believe she had never even been out on a real date? Cousins didn't count. She was as pure as the driven snow, but not for long, gang, not if she could help it. She'd bet her bottom dollar Gaby Bernais hadn't been a virgin when she wrote *Kisses for Breakfast*. Those French girls knew what it was all about, and Nora planned to do her homework as soon as possible.

A bell tolled somewhere on the campus, probably in the bell tower of the chapel. Four o'clock. Nora supposed she might as well get back to the dormitory. Perhaps her new roommate had arrived by this time. She hadn't shown up last time Nora checked the room, but she was bound to be here soon. Registration was first thing in the morning. Nora crossed the street and strolled over the grassy lawns toward Thurston Hall, passing the administration building, the library and the auditorium, all so mellow and serene, library windows open, long aisles of books visible. No soot and grime coating these hallowed walls, just pale blue-gray shadows from the trees. After the noise and congestion of the old neighborhood, it was like paradise.

A boy came jogging toward her in tennis shoes, blue sateen shorts and an old gray sweatshirt with the sleeves cut off. His golden-brown hair was worn in a crew cut, of course, and he had a deep tan. Six feet tall, if he was an inch. Muscles rippling. Great legs. She paused to watch him, and he grinned at her, waving as he passed. Big track star, no doubt, clearly used to having girls stare at him. He was absolutely gorgeous, she thought, if you happened to care for virile young Greek gods. Nothing like him in Brooklyn, that's for sure. Nora passed the boys' dormitory. A group of them were sitting out on the front steps, husky lads with roguish eyes. Lord, it was like being in a candy store. Research was going to be delightful. One of the boys whistled at her. He actually whistled at her! A first. She felt a wonderful glow as she walked on. Coming to Claymore was the smartest move she'd ever made, and no Sadie to keep tabs.

Thurston Hall was toward the rear of the campus. You could see the gym and the track and the tennis courts from the back windows. Grecian columns supported the portico in front. Tall, shady elms surrounded the cream stone building. Nora climbed the steps and went inside. Dozens of girls were chattering in the large downstairs lounge off the front hall. The place sounded like an aviary with all those bright, merry voices chirping away. Nora longed to go in and join them, be a part of it, but she was much too shy. Surprise. Who would have guessed it? Beneath that cocky facade she was as shy as a doe, painfully shy, particularly in groups. She'd never had a great many friends. The girls at the fancy private schools she had attended had all been rich and snooty and the girls in Brooklyn thought she was stuck-up

because she went to fancy private schools. It was a no-win situation. It was with some trepidation that Nora climbed the steps to the third floor now. What if her new roommate was like the girls at Dalton? What if she resented sharing the room with a Jewish girl? She walked down the hall to the corner room. The door stood open. Someone was moving around inside.

Nora forced a bright smile onto her lips and walked right in. The girl was taking clothes out of a suitcase. She was tall and slender and had long dark-gold hair the color of wheat and deep, pensive blue eyes. Rebecca of Sunnybrook Farm with cheekbones you wouldn't believe. What the hell was she doing in college? With looks like hers she should be modeling in Manhattan. She'd put Suzy Parker out of business in no time flat. Nora felt her heart sink. The smile froze on her lips. Just my luck, she thought. Of all the roommates I might have had, I have to wind up with a blond Debra Paget.

"Hi!" she said brightly.

The girl looked up. "Oh," she said. "I—I'm Carol Martin. I just arrived a few minutes ago. You must be my roommate."

"Nora Levin," Nora said.

She waited. The girl showed no reaction whatsoever to the name, didn't cringe, didn't shoot out her arm and yell, "Sieg Heil!" Instead, she smiled, a beautiful smile, warm and friendly. If I were lesbian, I'd be in love already, Nora thought.

"Welcome to Claymore," she said. "I just got here myself this morning. I've been out scouting the local terrain. Some neat shops across the street, a pizza parlor, that sort of thing. Real nifty."

"It—it's not at all like Kansas," Carol said.

"It's not like Brooklyn, either. Believe me."

"It's all so different and—well, intimidating. To tell you the truth, I—I'm a little scared."

You're scared? With those cheekbones? You should worry, kid. "Let me help you unpack," she suggested, moving over to the bed. "I've already hung my clothes up in the closet on the right. You can use the other one. We've each got our own chest of drawers, too. "Nifty."

She'd never used the word "nifty" in Brooklyn. Somehow it seemed to fit here at Claymore. Carol Martin smiled again. Nora felt like a dwarf beside this lovely creature, felt gawky and tacky in her straight, mid-calf-length plaid skirt and beige sweater with

short puffed sleeves. Carol wore a cool blue linen dress, simple
and exquisite. She exuded style, taste, poise, all the things Nora
lacked. Maybe some of it would rub off. Might as well look on
the bright side.

"What gorgeous clothes," she remarked, examining a pale
pink cashmere sweater.

"I worked in a department store this summer," Carol told
her. "I was able to buy everything at a good discount."

"The only way to buy. You were modeling?"

"Selling in Finer Dresses. It was a very good job. A—a friend
helped me get it. I received a very good salary and commissions
on all the dresses I sold, and—the ladies liked me. I made a lot
of sales. The money is going to come in handy. I'm here on a
scholarship."

"Really? So am I! Maybe that's why they put us together."

"I—I'm so glad they did." Could this ethereal goddess actually be insecure? "I was afraid I'd be rooming with—with one
of those rich, sophisticated girls who'd join a sorority and care
for nothing but social activities and making the proper connections."

"Sororities suck," Nora replied. "I came here to get an education, not to wear a little gold pin and trot around carrying
candles. I don't imagine I'll be rushed, but if I am I'll tell 'em
to fuck off."

"Me, too," Carol said.

"Not in those precise words, I'll bet. The boys are going to
go crazy over you," she predicted. "You're going to have to
fight them off with a big stick."

"I'm not interested in meeting boys."

"Please," Nora begged, "can I have your rejects?"

Carol laughed, and Nora saw that they were going to be friends
and felt a wave of relief. She couldn't believe her good luck.
Her new roommate was charming, demure, natural, intelligent
as well. You could forgive her those sculpted cheekbones, those
dreamy blue eyes, that tall, slender form. Carol seemed totally
unaware of her stunning good looks. Nora helped her hang up
her clothes and put away her things, and it was almost five-thirty
when they had finished. Neither of them had eaten lunch.

"Look," Nora said, "what do you say we skip eating downstairs in the communal dining hall tonight? It's bound to be a
zoo, and the food's bound to be dreadful—salmon croquettes,

green beans, tapioca pudding. Why don't we try one of the joints across the street? My treat.''

"I'd love to, but it'll be my treat."

"Mine," Nora insisted.

"Mine," Carol said firmly.

"Listen, sister, I'm the one who suggested—"

"Dutch?"

"You're on," Nora said.

They had hamburgers, fries and Cokes at the Silver Bell, a quaint little restaurant mobbed with noisy, merry students who all seemed to know each other. Nora kept her eye out for the dreamy track star she'd seen earlier, but he didn't show. She and Carol talked, and she learned that Carol came from a tiny town in Kansas, had lost her parents at an early age and had lived with her aunt and uncle, who had their own ideas about what she should do with her life. She said that a family friend had helped her get away from Ellsworth, had given her the job in Wichita and helped her find a room for the summer in a cheap but respectable boardinghouse. He had also been instrumental in getting her the scholarship. There was a wistful note in Carol's voice when she spoke about this "family friend," and Nora wondered if he might not have been something more.

Carol said that she hoped to become an actress, wasn't at all shy about confessing it, and she had come to Claymore because the drama department was recognized as one of the best in the country. Nora told her she was a cinch to succeed with her face and figure, and Carol said beauty wasn't important, look at Julie Harris, it was what was inside that counted. Nora took a deep breath and confided that *she* was going to become a famous writer, planned to write a sizzling best-seller as soon as possible. Carol didn't laugh at all. She said she thought it was wonderful to have high aspirations, you couldn't achieve if you didn't aspire, said she admired people who wanted to do great things. Nora took another deep breath and told her about the confession stories, and Carol was deeply impressed. The girls discovered that they had a great deal in common, despite their vastly different backgrounds.

Twilight was falling as they walked slowly back toward the dorm. They had talked for hours, felt they had known each other for years, and a strong feeling of kinship was already established.

"I guess you could call us a couple of Cinderellas," Nora said. "You think we'll make it? Think we'll get the glass slipper?"

"With your talent and determination, you're bound to."

"And you're a shoo-in," Nora told her. "We'll both get the slipper, kid, and it'll fit perfectly. Right?"

Carol nodded. "And we'll live happily ever after."

"Believe it," Nora said.

Freshman registration the next day was absolute chaos, with over two hundred confused, frustrated students dashing about the Student Union building, talking to faculty advisors, waving slips, standing in lines, trying desperately to get into the classes they wanted before they were filled. Nora was incensed when her faculty advisor, a smug, supercilious junior professor in the English department, informed her that she would have to complete freshman English before she could enroll in Stephen Bradley's creative writing course. Freshman English! Underline the subject once, the verb twice, pick out the adjectives and adverbs. Bullshit! She had no intention of wasting her time. You had to be ballsy, right? You had to be determined. She marched herself over to the ad building and demanded to see the dean and, surprisingly enough, was shown into his office. She told him in no uncertain terms she hadn't come to Claymore to waste a year with Mickey Mouse nonsense like freshman English. Look at her record, she demanded, look at her SAT scores, tell her she needed to rusticate with a bunch of fish who didn't know a dangling participle from a pain in the neck. Dean Hargrave assumed a very serious expression, trying his best to hide his amusement. He called for her file, consulted it, nodded gravely. He finally informed her that they would make a special dispensation in her case, permit her to skip freshman English and allow her to enroll in Dr. Bradley's class immediately.

"Thanks a bunch, Dean," she said cockily. "I had a feeling you'd understand. You're a real peach."

She signed up for world history, physics, girls' volleyball and music appreciation, just to have the requisite number of semester hours, and she felt as though she'd been through a battle before the day was done, the last class filled. She and Carol would have history and music appreciation together, but their other classes were separate. Carol was elated to have gotten into Julian Compton's advanced drama. He took only twenty students at a time

and was highly selective. He had studied her records and asked
her innumerable questions before finally signing her up. Nora
was delighted with Stephen Bradley. He was wry, cynical, burly,
a chain-smoker. He hadn't published a novel in a number of
years, true, but his *Summer of Decision* had not only won a
Pulitzer Prize but had been a blazing best-seller as well. What
he didn't know about writing wasn't worth knowing. He gave
her a stern look and asked if she was ready to work. Nora said
she was ready to work her adorable little ass off. Bradley roared
with laughter and lighted another cigarette. Both girls were
pleased with their successes but worn with exhaustion as they
trudged back to the dorm late that afternoon.

"We're on our way, kid," Nora said. "You got Compton. I
got Bradley. World, watch out. We're gonna knock you dead."

"I wish I had your confidence." Carol sighed.

"You call this confidence? This is just mouth, sweetheart. I'm
scared shitless."

"So am I."

"Whistle a happy tune," Nora suggested.

The next week was hectic as they attended classes, purchased
books, paid lab fees, acclimatized themselves to the campus.
Nora found history a bore, physics a drag, and girls' volleyball
was a joke. Music appreciation was fascinating. She didn't know
beans about classical music and was delighted when she was
able to tell Mozart and Vivaldi apart. Bradley was everything
she expected, with a no-nonsense attitude and the strong belief
that you wrote to be read, not to please a bunch of pseudointellectual critics. Nora was in love. Carol said Julian Compton was
the most stimulating man she'd ever met. He had directed several
smash hit plays in New York before coming to Claymore and
had worked with legendary names in the theater.

By the end of the second week, both Nora and Carol knew
their way around campus and were beginning to settle into the
routine of classes. By the end of the third week, they both felt
like veterans. Carol had a French lab and didn't get back to the
dorm until almost five on Friday. Nora was in their room, polishing off an essay about the Hittites on the manual typewriter
Irving had shipped to her from Brooklyn. After only three weeks
the room had that bright, messy clutter of personal possessions
that made it a home.

"This ought to knock old Beasley right off her rocker," Nora

said, whipping the final page out of the typewriter. "Homework all finished. How was French?"

"I've been doing advanced work in the lab—Dr. Clark said I might just as well. I have to take first-year French, of course, but I'm already a year ahead of the others. I had a very good teacher in high school."

"What's that book you have?"

"*Le Père Goriot.* I thought I might just as well read it."

"Balzac. I'm impressed, kid."

"You've read Proust."

"Not in the original," Nora said.

She got up from the desk and stretched, and then she looked around at the litter, finally gathering up a pile of books and lining them up neatly on the desk.

"Friday night," she complained, "and neither one of us asked to go to the sock hop at the gymnasium. What a blow to my fragile ego. Don't know if I'll survive it."

"You wouldn't go to the sock hop if they paid you, Nora."

"You're right, sweetie—Buddy Holly songs blaring on the P. A. system, enthusiastic sophomore boys stomping with giggling freshman girls. Hawaiian punch and cookies. Thrills galore for the true sophisticate. It would've been nice to have been *asked*, though."

"I was, actually," Carol said.

"Confession time. Was he dreamy?"

"Sweaty palms. He reminded me of the boys in Kansas."

"Hang in there, kid. Someday your prince will come. Listen, I don't think I can look another bowl of mashed potatoes in the face, not to mention the Jell-O. Why don't we skip mess call tonight and dash over to the Silver Bell again?"

"Sounds great," Carol said.

"We'll make an occasion of it, dress up. Okay?"

"Fine."

The dorm was abuzz with activity as they left an hour and a half later, dozens of girls rushing down the halls, popping in and out of rooms, hair in pink plastic curlers, bathrobes flapping. Big night. Big dates. Frenzied preparations. Nora was quiet and withdrawn as she and Carol started across the campus. She had changed into a navy blue dress with white polka dots, puffed sleeves with white cuffs and white Peter Pan collar. She wore high heels and hose, the seams carefully straightened, and she

had put on red lipstick and a suggestion of dusty blue eye shadow. All dressed up and no place to go. Carol was a great friend, the best, but she wasn't male. Cute apparently wasn't good enough, Nora thought bitterly. Not a single boy had asked her out since she arrived on campus three weeks ago. Hundreds of boys, and not a one of them interested in a perky little Jewish girl with personality to spare. That boy had whistled at her the first day, sure. Probably wanted her to fetch a stick.

"Something wrong?" Carol asked.

"Not really. I'm just in the pits tonight."

"Any particular reason?"

"It's my birthday, dammit."

"You should have told me!" Carol protested.

"I didn't want you to make a fuss. Irving sent me a new sweater. Sadie sent a hot-water bottle and a wool muffler and cap. I got a card from my cousin, Myron Jr. He's the one with the buck teeth."

"Dinner's on me tonight," Carol said. "I insist."

"All right, but if you order a cake and sing 'Happy Birthday' I'll break your arm."

The Silver Bell wasn't at all crowded tonight. Only a few of the tables were occupied. Carol and Nora took one near the back, and Nora stared glumly at the plastic bottles of mustard and ketchup. Carol smiled and told her to cheer up, it wasn't the end of the world.

"That's easy enough for you to say!" Nora snapped. "You look like some bloody high-fashion model. You could have any man on campus you wanted. Me, I couldn't even get arrested. Eighteen years old and never been kissed."

"Really? Never?"

"My cousin Myron laid one on me and tried to feel me up the night of his Bar Mitzvah party, but that doesn't count. I wanted to be kissed by his good-looking friend Eugene Cohen. Eugene was too busy making eyes at Renee Kuppenheimer to know I was alive."

"None of the boys at those schools you attended ever—"

"They were intimidated by me, called me Little Miss Mensa. I had braces on my teeth until I was fourteen," she confessed, "and before the nose job I frightened small children on the street. It wasn't until a couple of years ago that I blossomed into the ravishing creature you see before you now."

"You're as pretty as can be," Carol told her.

"So's Lassie. At least she has her own TV series."

Carol laughed, and Nora cheered up a bit as the waitress came shyly over to their table. Only a few inches taller than Nora, she had a fragile build and soft silver-brown hair worn long and enormous violet-blue eyes, light and clear. Her features were delicate and quite pretty in a childlike way, but her complexion was poor, pasty-looking, pitted with acne. Couldn't be a day over fourteen, Nora thought. Looked weak as a kitten. What kind of child labor laws did they have around here? A kid like this carrying heavy trays and lifting stacks of dishes. The girl smiled. There was something luminous and arresting about her, a curious presence despite the shy demeanor and bad complexion.

"Hello, Carol," the child said.

"Julie! I didn't know you worked here."

"I've been working here since the semester started. I was in the kitchen before, washing dishes. They promoted me to waitress last week. How are you doing?"

"Just fine. I didn't see you in class this afternoon."

"I—Doug wasn't feeling well and I—I thought I'd best stay home with him. How did the reading go? Did you do Portia's speech?"

Carol nodded. "Compton didn't make any comment. Jim Burke gave a terrific rendition of Hamlet's soliloquy. I was looking forward to hearing your Ophelia."

"It—it probably wouldn't have been very good." The child lowered her eyes. "I would have been terrified. May I take your orders?"

"Let me introduce you to my friend Nora Levin first. Nora, this is Julie Hammond. Julie's in advanced drama with me. Nora's my roommate," she told Julie. "Today's her birthday."

"You bitch," Nora said. "No one was supposed to know. Hello, Julie. I'm delighted to meet you."

Julie smiled again, as shyly as before. Her lashes were long and curling, her brows fine, delicately arched. What was it about her? You didn't pay any attention to the wretched complexion. You just looked at those incredibly lovely violet-blue eyes that were so innocent yet full of secrets. Your heart went out to her.

"We haven't had a chance to look at the menus yet," Carol said. "What do you recommend, Julie?"

"The shrimp basket's good. It comes with cole slaw and fries. I could bring some hot rolls, too."

"Sounds fine to me," Nora said.

"Two shrimp baskets, then," Carol said.

"What will you have to drink?" Julie asked.

"A double vodka martini for me," Nora told her. "A twist of lemon and go easy on the vermouth."

"Two Cokes, Julie," Carol said.

Julie took pad and pencil out of the pocket of her uniform, jotted down the order and left the table with another shy smile.

"They're taking infants at Claymore now?" Nora asked.

"She's our age," Carol replied. "She's just taking the one course—I believe Compton made some kind of special arrangement. She's married, working to help her husband get through law school. She's a sweet girl—really talented, too."

"Married? She looks like a child!"

"She's been married for over two years."

"Jesus!" Nora exclaimed.

Julie brought their order a short while later, deftly balancing the heavy tray on her palm. She put the shrimp baskets and Cokes in front of them, smiled that poignant smile of hers and left. Nora watched as the girl greeted a couple who had just come in and took their orders. There was something touching about her, a vulnerable quality you couldn't quite define. She returned to the table after a few minutes with a basket of rolls and a dish of butter, apologizing for the delay. When she left Nora shook her head. Hard to believe she was their age and already married. That brought her own lack of progress with the boys to mind again, and she frowned, squeezing dollops of ketchup onto her French fries.

"Happy birthday," Carol said, lifting her Coke in a mock toast. "How does it feel to be eighteen?"

"Shitty. I feel like a dismal failure. When Françoise Sagan was eighteen *Bonjour Tristesse* was published. Gaby Bernais had *Kisses for Breakfast* come out when *she* was eighteen. How can I ever write a sexy blockbuster if I don't meet some men, get some experience!"

"Your time will come," Carol assured her.

"Yeah, and the way it looks right now I'll be wearing orthopedic shoes and carrying a cane when it does. I want you to be

brutally honest with me, Carol. I want you to be frank—is it my breath?''

"The boys just haven't discovered you yet."

"Maybe I should wear a sandwich board with 'Available' printed on both sides, but that probably wouldn't cause any stampedes, either. 'Free Tail' might be more provocative.''

"You're incorrigible, Nora."

"No I'm not, sweetie. I'd just *like* to be."

They had almost finished their meal and were contemplating dessert when the silver bell over the door jingled and four boys walked in. Nora glanced up casually, then gasped and grabbed Carol's arm across the table.

"It's *him*!" she whispered excitedly.

"Who?"

"The track star, the boy I saw that first day jogging in those cute little blue sateen shorts. I told you about him."

"Oh. Which one is he?"

"The gorgeous one," Nora said under her breath.

It was him, all right. Tall and lean and mean. Muscular, but not too much so, not like one of those drippy weight lifters. He was wearing scuffed brown loafers and snug tan slacks and a soft pale lime-green V-necked sweater with white shirt beneath. His golden-brown crew cut was short and neat, accentuating the shape of his head, and his eyes were a mossy green, flecked with brown, witty eyes, wicked eyes. His features were rather foxlike, the cheekbones sharp, the nose long, the lips wide and thin, curling slightly at one corner. Not really handsome in a conventional sense, but talk about animal magnetism! The other boys were okay, too, obviously jocks like him, but they faded to invisibility with him around.

"Have you ever *seen* anything so delectable?" she whispered.

Carol glanced at him, unimpressed. "He's not my type," she said.

"Thank God for *that*!"

The boys took a table near the front window. Julie went over to take their orders, chatted briefly with the track star and then came back to ask if Carol and Nora wanted dessert.

"Cake?" Carol inquired.

Nora shook her head, trying not to stare.

"Ice cream?"

"I couldn't eat another bite. Who *is* he, Julie?"

Julie followed the direction of Nora's gaze. "Which one?" she asked.

"The sexy one. The one in the lime-green sweater."

"Oh, you mean Dick. Dick Sanders. He's a junior, twenty years old. He plays basketball and is on the track team, throws the discus, too, I believe. My husband gave him some private tutoring in geometry last year when Dick fell behind."

"Dick," Nora said. "What an auspicious name."

"Would you like me to introduce you to him?"

"Introduce me to him? Of course not! He'd think I was an idiot. He'd think I wanted to *meet* him!"

"We'll just have our check, please, Julie," Carol said. "I sure hope I see you in class Monday afternoon."

Julie smiled her shy smile, handed Carol the check and told Nora she had enjoyed meeting her. Nora said she hoped they'd meet again soon and, when Julie left, took a five-dollar bill out of her purse and slipped it under the edge of her bread plate. It was an outrageously big tip, sure, but the girl was enchanting and could probably use it. Her legs felt a little trembly as she and Carol started toward the cashier's stand. They were going to have to go right by Dick Sanders's table. Nora pretended an indifference she was far from feeling. As they passed the table Sanders looked up. He grinned.

"Hi," he said.

He was speaking to her. Nora was dumbfounded.

"Hi," she said, never at a loss for words.

"I'm Dick Sanders. I've seen you around campus."

If she couldn't win him with her fatal beauty, she'd hook him with her witty repartee. "You have?" she said.

"Couldn't miss a cute trick like you," he told her.

Nora smiled at him and they moved on and Carol paid the bill. Once outside she grabbed Carol's arm again and stumbled, feigning buckled knees. Her heart was actually palpitating. She'd never felt anything like this before. He had spoken to her! He thought she was a cute trick! Nora felt she might just die right here on the sidewalk.

"I can't believe it!" she exclaimed.

"I don't know what you're so excited about, Nora. He really wasn't all that impressive."

"So you have no taste, that's your problem. He's a dream, Carol. He's the sexiest thing I've ever seen. He thinks I'm a cute trick! Dick Sanders doesn't know it, sweetie, but from this day forward he's a marked man!"

3

*Julian Compton stood on the small stage with the dusty gold-*brown curtains and patiently explained to the three students with him that this was improvisation and you had to think, you had to feel, you had to react. The situation he had given them was simple enough: A boy and a girl are talking in the park and another boy comes up and asks for a dollar, which they refuse to give him. The second boy had to leave the stage with the dollar in his pocket. The students had gone through it three times already with unsatisfactory results. The girl, Carol Martin, had done well enough, looking surprised when the second boy came up to them, then worried, then frightened when the boys started arguing. Perhaps she reacted just a bit *too* much, Julie thought, watching from the back of the classroom. Carol was a lovely girl, warm and friendly, and Julie liked her a great deal, thought her very talented, but—well, if Julie were up there she wouldn't use quite so many gestures. She wouldn't define her feelings quite so broadly. Julie wouldn't dream of criticizing her friend—Carol was good, Julie knew she'd never have half her talent—but she couldn't help thinking how she would play the scene. If you were acting, people shouldn't *see* you acting. Not that I know anything about it, Julie reminded herself. I'm just here on a pass. I have no business being here at all.

The boys were bad. Bud Holdredge was a clean-cut blond

35

youth with a pronounced Bostonian accent, very Ivy League in neat slacks and cardigan sweater and shirt with buttoned-down collar. Jim Burke was a handsome, sturdily built boy with coal-black hair and intense brown eyes. He wore sneakers, faded blue jeans, an old T-shirt and a battered brown leather jacket, fancied himself the Brando type. They were two of Compton's best students, but he wasn't getting anything from them today. Bud was stiff and awkward, prissily refusing to hand over the dollar, and Jim slouched and mumbled and came up with lines like "Hey, man, I really need the bread." The rest of the class was visibly impressed by his antics—Jim was a favorite—but Julie could see that Compton was nearing the end of his patience.

Compton ran his fingers through his luxuriant silver-gray hair. With his craggy, battered features and moody blue eyes, he was an extremely attractive man, and most of the girls had crushes on him. Julie found him rather fatherly, sometimes stern, sometimes warm and teasing, almost always harried, exuding strong authority no matter what his mood. He was a wonderful man, and she still found it hard to believe he had taken such an interest in her. It didn't seem possible he could think she had a natural talent for acting. Maybe Doug was right. Maybe Compton just felt sorry for her.

"All right," he said wearily, "we'll try it one more time. I want you to *get* that dollar, Jim. Understand?"

"I've been tryin', man."

"You don't want to give it to him, Bud. You're not *going* to give it to him."

"But I'm gonna get it, right?" Jim mumbled.

Compton ignored him. He glanced at Carol and started to say something, then changed his mind. Carol looked disappointed, and Julie could see that she longed to question him. Compton rarely worked as hard with Carol as he did with the other students, rarely criticized her and almost never gave her directions. Perhaps it was because she didn't need them. Carol had remarkable stage presence, even if . . . even if she wasn't always totally convincing when she did a part.

"Let's go," Compton said. "Let's do it right this time."

"Why is it so important I get this dollar?" Jim asked. "I mean, am I hungry? Do I need to buy food? Am I a broken-down panhandler, begging for bread? Am I a hood, intimidating

an uptight, middle-class couple? It would help a lot, man, if I knew what my motivations were.''

"I don't *care* what your motivations are. Just get that goddamn dollar and get off the stage!''

Compton moved back, patience clearly wearing thin. Carol and Bud took their positions and began to talk. Bud asked her if she would like to go to the country club dance. Carol hesitated and looked pleased and then looked apprehensive and said she wasn't sure his parents would approve, she didn't belong to their set. Bud said that didn't matter at all. Neither of them noticed Jim approach. He crept nearer, looked all around and then grinned a sinister grin. He lunged forward and slung an arm around Bud's throat, rearing back, strangling him. Carol screamed and slammed a hand over her heart. Bud began to gurgle, his face turning bright pink. "Gimme your wallet!" Jim growled. Bud gurgled and hastily reached into his back pocket and pulled out his billfold. Jim took it and shoved Bud roughly aside. He peeled a dollar out of the billfold, thrust it into his pocket, threw the billfold down and sauntered away. Bud coughed and made croaking noises, his face still pink. Carol wrung her hands. The class applauded wildly.

"How was that, man?" Jim inquired. "Got the dollar, didn't I?"

"You got it, Jim," Compton said, shaking his head.

He glanced at the large clock hanging over the classroom door and, looking relieved, dismissed the class. Students got up from their seats and began to slip on coats and sweaters, ardently discussing the scene. Jim Burke swaggered, pleased with himself. He patted Bud on the shoulder and returned his dollar. Julie stood up and put on her old brown cloth coat. She was tying a brown-and-blue scarf over her head when Carol joined her. They always sat together in the back of the room. Julie smiled at her and told her she'd been very good. Carol smiled, too, but it was a hollow smile. Julie could tell she was still disappointed that Compton hadn't commented on her performance.

"Hey, you were somethin' else," Jim Burke said, joining them.

"Thank you," Carol replied.

Jim turned to Julie then and gave her a lovely smile. He really was a handsome boy, Julie thought, and she knew that beneath all that phony swagger he was a very nice boy as well.

"When am I goin' to do a scene with you, Julie?" he inquired.

"I—I'm just observing," she said shyly.

Jim gave her a friendly pat on the shoulder. "I've got a feelin' you'd be terrific to work with."

"You were very good today," Julie told him. "So much intensity. I was actually frightened."

"Yeah, I really got into it there for a minute. You ever decide to get up there and show your stuff, you can count on me to help. I'd be glad to rehearse with you beforehand."

Julie gave him a shy smile. Jim patted her shoulder again and swaggered away.

"You know him?" Carol asked.

"Not—not really. I was coming out of the library one evening last week with an armload of books Doug needed and I—I tripped on the steps and fell. I sprained my wrist. Jim happened to be walking by and he helped me to my feet and gathered up the books for me and insisted I let him take me to the infirmary to see about my wrist. I—I assured him it was only a light sprain. Jim said I was in no condition to carry all those heavy books, and he walked me back to the apartment, carrying them for me."

"That was very thoughtful of him," Carol said.

"He—he really is a very nice boy. He was warm and friendly and witty, not at all like he is in class. He didn't mumble, didn't swagger—he wasn't even wearing his leather jacket. He's actually quite sensitive and—extremely talented."

"He's a very good actor," Carol agreed. "If he'd stop trying to copy Marlon Brando and develop his own technique he'd be wonderful."

Carol put on her coat. It was a soft blue wool with belted waist and a full gray fur collar. Carol always dressed so beautifully. Most of the girls in drama class affected black leotards and wraparound plaid skirts and black turtleneck sweaters, very hip, very bohemian, their hair pulled back in pony tails tied with colored scarves. Not Carol. She had her own individual style. Julie always felt dowdy beside her, but there wasn't any money to spend on clothes. Even if there had been, she'd never have Carol's flair.

"You were excellent today, too," Julie said quietly. "That

part about not being sure his parents would approve—it was inspired. It gave the girl definition.''

Carol tied a blue silk scarf over her head. "Nora and I are planning to meet at the SUB for coffee and sandwiches," she said. "I wish you'd join us, Julie."

Julie shook her head as the other students noisily made their way out of the classroom. "I'd love to, Carol, but—I'd better get home to Doug. He's studying for an exam today and probably hasn't had any lunch. Besides, I—I have to report to work at three.''

"May I speak to you a moment, Mrs. Hammond?''

Both girls turned as Julian Compton approached. Carol squeezed Julie's hand and left. Compton and Julie were alone in the classroom. She felt ill at ease, even though she knew that he liked her, even though he was the kindest man she'd ever known.

"I'm disappointed you didn't feel like participating today, Julie," he said. "I wish you could bring yourself to take an active part. You're every bit as good as any of the others. Better than most of them.''

"You don't really know that," Julie replied.

"I know," Compton told her. "I have instincts about these things, and the one time I coaxed you up to read, you were magnificent. You *were* Hedda Gabler. You forgot all about Julie Hammond, forgot your shyness. Everyone in class was bowled over.''

"I—I was petrified.''

"But only for a few minutes. After you got into the role, you weren't nervous at all. How am I going to break you out of your shell, Julie? How am I going to teach you anything if you won't let me help?''

"I learn so much by just—by just observing, Mr. Compton. I'm not actually a student. The others would resent it if I—if I took up your time. Please—just let me watch.''

Compton frowned, his affection for this timid creature plainly visible in his eyes. She had a rotten complexion, her demeanor was painfully self-effacing, but Compton knew his business, and he knew she had a quality rare indeed. With training, with polish, with enough self-confidence, she could be another Laurette Taylor, another Maggie Sullavan. Compton had been teaching for eight years now, and in all that time he'd never had another student with this child's potential. Acting was mostly magic, he

knew. You could teach them technique. You could teach them how to project, how to use their bodies, but you couldn't give them the magic. It was a divine gift, and Julie Hammond had it in spades. He'd sensed it that evening last August when he had come upon her sitting on the bedroom floor, holding his two children absolutely spellbound. He'd been spellbound himself until she became aware of his presence and drew back into her shell.

"I want you to do something for me, Julie," he said firmly.

"What—what's that?"

"We're holding tryouts tomorrow night for the spring play. We're going to be doing *The Glass Menagerie*. You're familiar with it?"

Julie nodded.

"I want you to come to the tryouts. I want you to read the part of Laura. Will you do that for me, Julie?"

"I—" The girl looked pained.

"Do it," he said. "Come tomorrow night. Read for me. Okay?"

"We—we'll see," Julie replied.

It was with a heavy heart that Julie left the classroom and stepped outside. It was late November. The sky was gray with the promise of snow, and a cold wind swept across the campus, causing bare tree limbs to tremble. Julie loved *The Glass Menagerie*. She thought it was the most moving play ever written, and oh, what she could do with the part of Laura. How she could identify with that shy, frail creature who lived in a world of gentle fantasy, only to have it shattered by the intrusion of reality. Julie knew she could do the part, do it beautifully, with genuine feeling. Mr. Compton thought so, too. He believed in her. He believed she had the makings of a real actress. How she wished it were possible for her to try out for Laura, but she couldn't, of course. There was no way.

Julie walked past the Student Union building where Carol was meeting her friend for coffee and sandwiches. Nora, her name was, that bright, vivacious girl with the sparkling brown eyes and glossy black curls who had left a five-dollar tip that evening they'd come to the Silver Bell. How provident it had been, that money. Doug had had a tremendous outlay for tuition and law books and they'd had to pay the rent, and Julie wouldn't receive her salary until the end of the next week and all they had coming

in was the money she got in tips. The five dollars had gone for bread, bologna, mayonnaise, cans of soup. Julie had actually cried that evening when she found the bill folded under the edge of Nora's bread plate. That clever, pretty girl would never know what a blessing her tip had been. She had come into the Silver Bell several times since, sometimes with Carol, sometimes alone, always keeping an eye out for Dick Sanders. Julie enjoyed talking with her, however briefly. She secretly wondered how a girl so bright and witty could be interested in someone like Dick.

Before getting the job at the Silver Bell, Julie had done baby-sitting, Doug placing a hand-printed notice on the main bulletin board and in the faculty lounge, and that was how she had come to meet Julian Compton. One afternoon his wife called and questioned her carefully in her clipped English accent and, finally satisfied, asked her to come over to their house at seven o'clock. It was a lovely house, Tudor-style, quite a long way from Doug and Julie's flat, but she hadn't minded the walk. She made four dollars an hour for baby-sitting, and Mrs. Compton said they probably wouldn't get home until midnight. That meant a whole twenty dollars for just one evening. It was a lot of money, but then baby-sitting jobs weren't all that regular. A week might go by with only two or three jobs, and they might be for no more than a couple of hours while the parents went out to dine or to see a movie. Mrs. Compton almost turned her away from the door.

Andrea Compton had been an actress, Julie knew. She was a chic, glamorous creature in a red satin cocktail dress, her raven hair pulled back sleekly and worn in a French twist. Her cool gray eyes were filled with dismay as she stood in the doorway, staring at Julie.

"You can't possibly be the baby-sitter," she said. "Why, you're just a child yourself."

"I'm seventeen, ma'am. I'll be eighteen in December. My husband graduated with a B.A. two months ago, and he'll be starting to law school in September. I—I explained all that over the phone."

"Who is it, Andy?" Compton asked, stepping into the foyer. "Oh, it's the baby-sitter. Bring her on in. Hello there," he said, giving Julie a warm smile. "How are you with monsters? Bobbie wants to be a Mouseketeer, refuses to take off her Mickey Mouse ears—even sleeps in them, I believe. Brett thinks he's Davy

Crockett. I fear he carries a tomahawk for hand-to-hand combat with Indians. It's only rubber," he assured her.

Mrs. Compton still had reservations about leaving Julie in charge, but if they didn't leave immediately they'd be late to their dinner party. Her husband was confident she could handle the job, and they left a few minutes later, Mr. Compton very handsome in his dinner jacket and black tie. Bobbie was a precocious six, Brett a raucous seven, and they were indeed monsters. Bobbie stuck her tongue out at Julie and informed her she had yucky pimples on her face. Brett promptly attacked her with his rubber tomahawk. Julie wasn't a bit daunted. She told Bobbie she was every bit as cute as Annette and probably had a lot more talent, too. She told Brett she was frightened to death of Indians and had actually met one a couple of years ago when she was walking in some woods.

"Awww," he said disdainfully, "you didn't meet no Indian."

"I did so. He leaped out at me from behind a tree, yelling like a banshee. I almost had heart failure."

"He have a tomahawk?" Brett asked.

"A real sharp one, and—and it was stained with blood. I was sure I was a goner."

"What'd-ja do?"

"I took the tomahawk away from him. Then I scalped him. I'm an Indian fighter from way back. They know better than to mess with me."

"You made that up," he said, enchanted nonetheless.

Brett raced off to get his coonskin cap, and then he ardently recounted the plot of last week's episode of *The Adventures of Davy Crockett*. Julie gave him her rapt attention, asking several questions, and Brett decided she was the neatest baby-sitter they'd ever had. Not to be outdone, Bobbie put on her tap shoes and showed Julie the dance Annette had done on *The Mickey Mouse Club* Wednesday afternoon, then gave her a rather startling rendition of "The Mickey Mouse Mambo." Julie applauded vigorously and claimed she'd never *seen* such talent.

"You oughta be in show business, kid," she said.

"I'm gonna be. Mama used to be. She made a movie in England with Stewart Granger. We saw it on *Matinee at the Movies* last month. She wore lots of funny gowns with long skirts and big hats with feathers dripping on them. She got killed in the

end. A horse trampled her to death in the stables after she sneaked out to run off with the Gypsy.''

''I believe I saw that movie. Your mother is very beautiful.''

''She's old now. She gave up her career when she married Daddy. It was just as well. Margaret Lockwood was getting all the best parts. Daddy produced plays before he came to Claymore. He dudn't miss it at all. He says teachin's a lot easier on the nervous system.''

''I imagine it would be,'' Julie said thoughtfully.

At eight o'clock she took them into the kitchen and made peanut butter sandwiches and gave them glasses of milk. They watched the last half of a variety show on television in the living room, and then Julie tactfully suggested that it was nearing time for bed. Both children rebelled. She managed to get them upstairs and get them into their pajamas, and Bobbie started insulting her again and Brett was sulking dreadfully. In their toy box, she happened to find three hand puppets: a witch, a handsome prince, a princess with long yellow yarn hair, all three puppets sadly battered. She told the children she would put on a play for them if they'd be good and promise to go to bed afterwards. They reluctantly agreed, sitting down on the floor in Bobbie's bedroom to watch as Julie spread a blanket over a dressing stool and pulled it over to use as a stage, kneeling down behind it.

As a child, Julie had always loved putting on plays with her large collection of paper dolls, acting out all the parts, and she forgot herself now, forgot her audience, throwing herself into the impromptu drama with great enthusiasm. The prince was dashing and bold, the princess sad and tearful, the witch so wicked Brett actually cowered. Julie made up appropriate dialogue, performed each role with a different voice, and the children were enthralled. That was how Julian Compton found them when he came upstairs. The prince had rescued the princess and brought her safely back to his father's kingdom but, unbeknownst to him, the witch had put an evil curse on him and, in order to save his life, the princess had to return and sweep floors for the witch for the rest of her life. Julian Compton stood quietly in the doorway, watching, listening, as caught up as either of his children.

''But you can't go,'' the prince said in a deep, bewildered

voice. "You can't leave me after—after we've finally found each other."

"I—I must, Rudolpho. I don't want to—you must know that—but it's something I—I have to do." Her voice trembled with emotion as the princess turned away.

"There's another man, isn't there! That's got to be it! You're leaving me for another prince, that scoundrel Hal of Bulgaria. I saw him leering at you at the banquet."

"No—Rudolpho, please believe me—"

"I love you, Melisande. I *love* you, and you're leaving me!"

"It—it has to be. Please believe that."

"Go then! Leave! See if I care. I'll find someone else as quick as a wink. You're not the only princess on earth. One day you'll be sorry. One day when you're old and gray you'll remember Rudolpho and all that might have been—but it'll be too late!"

The prince stalked away and the princess stood there all alone for several moments, holding back the tears, and then she shook her head.

"I'll remember, Rudolpho," she whispered softly. "I—I'll never see you again, but—you'll always be there in my heart."

Bobbie sobbed woefully, tears pouring down her cheeks. Brett was making a manly effort not to do the same. Julian Compton couldn't believe it. The girl was incredible, absolutely incredible, so convincing in her magic that his own eyes were moist. His monsters, the one in Mickey Mouse ears, the other in coonskin cap, had been totally enraptured and couldn't contain their emotion now. The girl in the cheap pink cotton dress and shabby shoes sighed and sat up, the puppets still on her hands. When she saw him standing there in the doorway her cheeks turned pale.

"Mr. Compton, I—I didn't know you'd come home."

"The dinner was a bore. We left early. I see you've been entertaining my children."

"She's wonderful, Daddy!" Bobbie cried. "We want to have her every night!"

"Yeah!" Brett agreed. "She fights Indians, too!"

Julie put the puppets down and scrambled to her feet, horribly embarrassed. She'd rarely been so humiliated. Julian Compton smiled at her and ordered Brett and Bobbie to bed. They obeyed instantly, Brett dashing over to give Julie a hug before racing to his own room. Compton went downstairs with Julie and insisted

on giving her the whole twenty dollars, even though they had returned early. Discovering she had no transportation, he said he would drive her home.

"It—it isn't necessary, Mr. Compton. I'm used to walking."

"Come along, Mrs. Hammond," he said with mock severity. "I'll brook no nonsense from a chit like you."

Eyes downcast, cheeks flushed now, she followed him outside and got into the car. She gave him directions and sat there miserably as he drove toward the campus. Julian Compton was a glamorous figure at Claymore. He had made a brilliant career for himself in the theater, had worked with legendary names, and Julie knew that producers were still trying to lure him away from teaching and back into the fold. This man beside her had worked with Katharine Cornell, with Lynn Fontanne, and he had stood there in the doorway of Bobbie's room, watching her . . . watching her pretend that she could act, too. Still smarting from her humiliation, Julie wasn't aware that they had reached their destination, that Compton had stopped the car. He was staring at her, studying her profile in the pale summer moonlight.

"So you want to be an actress," he said quietly.

Julie looked up, startled. Her cheeks started burning again.

"I—I'm sorry I made such a fool of myself, Mr. Compton. I was just trying to—to amuse the children."

"But you *do* want to act, right?"

Julie swallowed, unable to speak. How had he known? How had he guessed that secret dream she had nurtured for years. Lots of little girls dream of becoming an actress, it was perfectly natural, a part of growing up, but she was grown up now and she still hadn't relinquished the dream. Julie clasped her hands together in her lap, swallowing again, consumed with guilt because he had found her out.

"Have you ever done any acting before?" he asked.

Julie shook her head, still unable to speak.

"None? Not even a high school play?"

"I—I didn't finish high school," she confessed. "I dropped out after I finished the tenth grade. I—it was—I got married, you see, and I couldn't—"

She cut herself short, in anguish. Julian Compton felt a rush of compassion for this overly sensitive, painfully shy child, but that had nothing to do with his next words. When it came to

spotting talent, he had an infallible eye, and he could be harsh, even brutal when his students showed a lack of it. He did not believe in wasting his time, or theirs.

"I would like for you to attend my advanced drama classes this fall, Julie," he said.

"Me?" Julie was dumbfounded. "But I—I couldn't—why would you want *me* to attend?"

"Because you have a rare and wonderful gift," he told her. "Because I feel that, with the proper training, you could be the most successful student I might ever have."

"Mr. Compton, I—I don't know what to say."

"Say you'll attend."

"But—I didn't even finish high school, I told you that. They wouldn't let me sign up for your class, and—and even if they would, I couldn't possibly pay the tuition."

"Let me make the arrangements, Julie. You won't have to register. You can audit the class—sit in," he explained. "As for your paying a tuition, we won't worry about that."

He had talked with her for a long time, trying to persuade her to attend the class, telling her that in all his years in the theater he had rarely witnessed magic like the magic he'd seen that evening. Working with her would be a joy for him. She would be doing him a favor. Julie had listened, unable to believe this was really happening to her, and in September, despite her reservations, despite Doug's vehement objections, she started coming to class, and now he wanted her to try out for *The Glass Menagerie*. He wanted her to play Laura.

Julie trudged across the campus in her old brown coat, a dull, insignificant sparrow compared to the swarm of merry, noisy students in brightly colored sweaters and bulky jackets and vivid woolen caps. No one spoke to her. No one really noticed her. Julian Compton had been wonderfully kind to her. She admired him with all her heart, worshipped him, in fact, although she was careful not to show it. Strange as it might be, he actually believed she had talent, believed she could become a real actress, and her playing Laura would be the first real test of his belief in her. He would be bitterly disappointed when she didn't show up for tryouts tomorrow night, but . . . How could she ever explain to him that it was out of the question?

She hadn't the time, to begin with. She had to go to work at the Silver Bell every afternoon at three except Sundays, and she

worked until ten. Even if she won the role, there was no way she could attend rehearsals, and even if she could attend, there . . . there was no way she could go out there in front of all those people and let them stare at her and see all her faults, all her deficiencies. She hadn't that kind of courage. She wasn't that brave. She could give a puppet show for children, yes, she loved children, children presented no threat, but . . . Julie sighed and left the campus, heading toward the row of shabby brick apartment buildings where she and Doug rented a basement flat. She could be Laura, a magnificent Laura, but only in the privacy of her own fantasy, not in front of the glare of spotlights, not in front of hundreds of hostile eyes. How could she explain these things to Mr. Compton, and how could she explain about Doug?

Doug would have a fit if she even mentioned trying out for the role. He had been livid when she told him about meeting Mr. Compton, about his wanting her to attend the drama class. It was a preposterous idea, he protested. It was senseless. It was stupid. It would be a complete waste of time, and she hadn't the time to spare. She'd make the time, Julie told him. It couldn't do any harm just . . . just to sit in on the classes, without paying any kind of tuition, without getting any credit. Doug had continued to object, and he had finally shrugged his shoulders and said if that was what she wanted to do, fine, she could do it, she could make a fool of herself, but he would have no part of it. For once Julie had gone against his wishes, and although he hadn't said anything else about it, she knew he resented her going to the classes. Whenever she tried to tell him about them, tell him about what she had learned, he just smiled that patient, superior smile and changed the subject. He didn't mean to hurt her feelings. He didn't mean to be cold. Julie realized that. He was working very, very hard and things hadn't been easy and he was under a lot of pressure and . . . and he hadn't wanted to get married in the first place.

Julie went down the short flight of steps and took out her key and let herself into their flat. It was rather chilly inside. The radiators were on the blink again. Although Julie had tried her best to make the place comfortable, make it pleasant, it still looked exactly like a basement that had been converted into a flat to bring in extra money. There was a living room, a bedroom, a bathroom, a small kitchen. Worn linoleum covered the concrete floors. The concrete walls were a dingy grayish brown,

a network of exposed pipes festooning one side of the living room. There were only two windows, set high up on ground level, and there was never enough light, but it was cheap and Julie consoled herself with the knowledge that one day, after Doug got his law degree, they'd have a much finer place.

Doug was stretched out on the faded salmon-pink sofa, a pile of cushions behind his back, a law book in his hand, a grave expression on his face as he studied by the light of the floor lamp. He was wearing tennis shoes and tan corduroy pants and an old chocolate-brown sweater, yet he still looked like a prince, just as he had that first time she saw him in the McCanns' pool house. He was tall and had a sturdy muscular physique and thick, wavy brown hair that was rich and glossy and always a bit unruly, errant locks invariably tumbling over his brow. His features were handsome, the cheekbones broad and flat, the jaw strong, the lips full and pink, generously curved. Behind the black horn-rimmed glasses his slate-blue eyes were stern and intelligent, but they could gleam with smoky passion, too, reflecting hunger and need. Julie still found it amazing that this glorious male was her husband now.

Doug looked up and saw her and put his book down. He sat up, stretching, throwing his shoulders back. Julie smiled. Despite his shrewd intellect and grave, serious demeanor, he had a healthy, animal quality and a lazy sensuality that filled her with delight. Doug liked his comfort. He liked his pleasure. Adjusting his horn-rims, he watched as she took off her coat and scarf and put them aside. He looked sleepy. He'd been studying since early in the morning, cramming for tomorrow's exam. Doug studied constantly, grimly determined to be the top man in his class.

"Hungry?" she asked.

"A little. It's cold in here. You'd better put on a sweater."

"I'm all right."

"The goddamn place is either boiling hot or freezing cold. I called the super about the radiators, but he hasn't done anything yet."

"I'll fix you a bowl of hot soup," she said.

Doug didn't answer. He yawned, shook his head and then reached for the heavy law book. Julie longed to go over and stroke his cheek and brush those errant brown locks from his brow, but he had his mind on the exam now and she knew it

would irritate him. Instead, she went into the kitchen and opened a can of vegetable beef soup and emptied it into a pan and put it on to heat on the ancient gas stove. She loved cooking for him, waiting on him, making him comfortable. Sometimes she wished she didn't have to work so hard and be away so much of the time, but she was doing that for him, too, and it made the long hours easier to bear. When Doug married her, Julie had vowed that he wouldn't have to drop out of school and that he would be able to go on and get his degree in law, even though her parents had disowned her and Doug's father withdrew all support.

But we've done it, she thought. Fortunately tuition for his senior year at Claymore had already been paid, and after . . . after the miscarriage, she had been able to find a job at Safeway and made enough money to pay expenses, though they'd eaten a lot of bologna, a lot of beans, and Doug graduated with top honors and won a partial scholarship to law school and that helped a lot. When she lost the job at Safeway she'd been able to do baby-sitting, and then she got her job at the Silver Bell and they were making it. Barely, but they were making it, without any help from his father or her parents. Julie took a box of saltines and two bowls from the pine cabinet, remembering that summer in Tulsa over two years ago when her prince had come, when her whole life had changed abruptly.

She was fifteen years old and had just finished the tenth grade, a pretty girl, her complexion clear then, not yet marred by acne. Shy, sensitive, she was always reading, usually a book of plays she'd taken from the library, her head full of fancy notions both her parents were quick to ridicule. They were good, honest, hardworking folk, the salt of the earth and damned proud of it, no time for nonsense, no patience with foolish adolescent dreams. Neither of them had finished high school, Okies, struggling to survive during the depression years, just like the Joads, both beaten down by life, toughened up, survivors. They couldn't understand how they'd spawned such a fey, dreamy child. "Artistic" she was, according to her teachers. Artistic wouldn't pay for the groceries. She'd find that out soon enough. Things were good for all of them that summer of her fifteenth year. They were living in the servants' quarters in the McCanns' palatial mansion. Her mother was the housekeeper, her father the gardener-chauffeur, and they were taking care of the place while

the oil-rich McCanns were in Europe seeing cathedrals and museums and buying a lot of vulgar, expensive junk to impress the folks back home in Tulsa.

Julie volunteered to help out in the house, but her mother was brusque, had her own staff, didn't need some clumsy, ineffectual chit of a girl underfoot mucking things up, getting in the way. Her father was harsh and uncommunicative, busy taking care of the grounds and keeping the cars shiny, rarely even noticed her existence anyway, certainly didn't have time for her now, and so Julie had the whole summer to while away. It was hot, hot, the fierce Oklahoma sun blazing down, sprinklers keeping the grass green, the flower beds blooming. Julie longed to swim in the enormous pool, the water so blue, cool and inviting, but her parents wouldn't let her, the McCanns wouldn't approve. She could spend time in the pool house, though, as long as she didn't bother anything. It was large, as big as a lot of houses were, with changing rooms, showers and a lounge with wet bar and comfortable, summery furniture. Julie spent almost all her time there.

During the day she would take her book out to the pool house and make a pitcher of lemonade and stretch out on one of the chaise lounges and read or just gaze out at the pool through the sliding glass doors and daydream. The McCanns had a portable television in the pool house, and in the evenings Julie would slip out and watch *Playhouse 90* and *Studio One* and *Philco Television Playhouse* and dream of one day starring in a drama by Sumner Locke Elliot or Paddy Chayefsky. She'd be every bit as good as Peggy Ann Garner or Pippa Scott or Erin O'Brian, she just knew she'd be. One day. People would laugh if they knew of her secret ambitions, but . . . it didn't hurt to dream about it.

And then one day in mid-June she looked out through the glass doors and saw the tall, sturdily built boy with the black horn-rimmed glasses and thick, unruly brown hair. He wore only a pair of brief red swim trunks and he looked like a prince, a young god, the horn-rims somehow accentuating his stern, handsome features. He took the horn-rims off, set them on the ledge and dived into the water. He swam strongly, briskly, one lap right after the other, with no splashing or playing about. Julie expected her father to come run him off at any minute, but it didn't happen. After the boy finished swimming exactly fifty

laps, he climbed out of the pool, retrieved his glasses and padded toward the pool house. He slid open the glass doors and
came inside and stood in the cool gray dimness, his body wet
and glistening, dripping on the tiled floor. He didn't see her at
first but seemed surprised to find the air conditioner running.
Julie knew that she probably shouldn't have it turned on, but she
figured the McCanns wouldn't mind too much.

The boy stretched, flexing his arms, arching his back, and she
was reminded of some vigorous, healthy animal. She felt strange
stirrings inside, and her heart was beating rapidly. The boy
sighed, sweeping wet locks from his brow, and then he spied
her there on the chaise lounge and scowled, looking hard and
intimidating. He asked who the hell she was and what the hell
she was doing there and Julie swallowed and tried to speak and
finally stammered that she was the McCanns' housekeeper's
daughter and had permission to use the pool house if she didn't
bother anything. He scrutinized her closely for several moments
and then he told her to relax, told her not to be so nervous, said
he wasn't going to rape her. At least not yet, he added. His
slate-blue eyes liked what he saw. Julie could tell that.

"Came in to get a towel," he said. "Forgot to bring one of
my own."

"There—there're some in the changing rooms," she said.

"I know. Be right back."

He returned a few minutes later, carrying a towel and wearing
one of the short terrycloth robes the McCanns kept on hand for
guests. He perched on a bar stool and toweled his hair dry and
smoothed it back with his hands, completely at home. Julie was
uneasy and knew she shouldn't be here alone with him, but she
hadn't been able to bring herself to leave. His name was Douglas
Hammond, she learned, and he was twenty years old and had
just finished his junior year at Claymore University in Indiana
and had come home to spend the summer with his father. Gus
Hammond owned the house next door, she knew. He was a
gruff, crusty oil man, as common as dirt, her parents said, worth
a fortune now after several successful strikes. His wife had
passed away nine years ago and he openly consorted with those
trashy women who hung around at the bars downtown and sometimes even brought them to the house. A crude and vulgar man,
drove a flashy Cadillac, spent a lot of time in the fields with his
men. Although his house was almost as large as the McCanns',

he didn't have a pool. The McCanns had told Doug he could use their pool whenever he liked.

Doug stayed for half an hour, talking, having a glass of lemonade with her, and that night Julie didn't dream of becoming the next Eva Marie Saint. She dreamed of Doug Hammond—disturbing dreams, unlike any she had ever had before. He came back over to swim the next day and the next one, too. They talked and he told her about college and about his problems with his father, and Julie could see that he liked her a lot. He was relaxed in her company, not tense and defensive like he was with his father, and he told her summer would be hell if he hadn't met her. On the third day he gently touched her face and told her she was a pretty little thing and Julie lowered her eyes, blushing faintly, already in love with him. He started coming over to the pool house in the evenings, too, to watch television with her, he said, but the set was rarely turned on. They sat in the shadows, moonlight streaming in through the glass doors, and he held her close and stroked her and Julie knew it was wrong, her parents would kill her if they found out, but he was wonderful, so gentle, so troubled, life as Gus Hammond's son a heavy weight to bear, and he made her feel wonderful, too, made her feel needed and wise beyond her years.

And one night, only a week after that first meeting, it happened, without either of them planning it, it just happened. They were together on the chaise lounge and he was holding her tightly and kissing her and then he was moaning, begging, saying he couldn't go on this way any longer, wanting her, wanting her so, and then he was on top of her, crushing her with his weight, and she was frightened but she loved him and didn't want to stop him and she felt his hands tugging, adjusting clothing and then felt something stiff and rigid and warm and he was parting her legs and plunging inside her and panic swept over her and she struggled and tried to get away from him but he kept right on thrusting inside her, pushing, straining, grunting loudly as he met the barrier within, and Julie felt a terrible pain as the barrier was ripped asunder. She cried out and he slammed a hand over her mouth and continued to grunt and thrust and the pain began to dissolve and melted into a tingling glow that grew and grew, filling her with unbelievable bliss. And later on, when he did it to her a second time, there was no pain at all, only the bliss bursting inside her, and she wept silently with joy.

He didn't come over to swim nearly so often, they didn't want to arouse suspicion, but every night he came to the pool house, sneaking over after it was dark, and her parents never knew, they thought she was watching television. It was an enchanted summer, swollen with passion, filled with delight she had never known possible, and she loved him with all her heart and soul. Doug loved her, too, she was sure he did. He proved it every night there in the pool house with his lips, his hands, his body. Someone cared about her. For the first time in her life someone really cared and she was wonderfully, gloriously happy. She belonged to him now and he belonged to her and somehow they would work things out. She was only fifteen, true, but that didn't matter, they were in love, Doug would figure out some way for them to be together for the rest of their lives.

Doug grew moody and remote as the summer wore on, but that was because of his father and the strain of being with him. They didn't get on well at all. His father was constantly on him, constantly lecturing him and telling him he had no idea what it was like to struggle and sweat and do without, to have neither pot to piss in nor window to throw it out, but he wasn't going to grow up a rich man's spoiled brat, no indeed, he was going to make something of himself. His father expected Doug to be perfect and make the best grades and excel at everything. He wasn't going to be crude and unlettered and vulgar like his old man, he was going to become a lawyer, the best damn lawyer in the country and maybe one day go into politics and, hell, why not, maybe even become President and show the whole goddamned world what kind of boy old Gus Hammond raised. His father didn't love him at all, Doug said. He loved nothing but his liquor, his whores and his oil wells, but he still expected his boy to become everything he wasn't. Just because he was a rich man's son didn't mean he didn't have to work his ass off. Julie understood, and she tried to comfort him, but that only irritated him, made him more remote. The only thing that soothed him was her body and those brutally passionate sessions in the pool house.

She began to feel puny as summer drew to a close, woke up in the morning with a nauseous sensation and felt dizzy during the day, but that was probably because it was so hot. The fierce Oklahoma heat hadn't abated at all, the sun beating down without mercy. Doug was due to go back to Indiana soon, the fol-

lowing week, in fact, and they still hadn't made any plans and she was beginning to worry. On Friday afternoon on her way to the pool house she fainted and woke up to find herself in bed with a damp cloth on her brow, her mother standing over her with a worried expression. They sent for the doctor despite Julie's protests and he examined her thoroughly and then asked her parents to step out into the hall. The door was slightly ajar. Julie heard the doctor inform them in a flat, emotionless voice that their daughter was pregnant. She remembered then, remembered she hadn't had her period for the last two months. How could she possibly not have noticed? Julie closed her eyes, trembling all over, wishing for death, feeling dead already.

The vegetable beef soup was boiling. Julie quickly took it off the burner. Her hands were shaking. She tried not to think about the terrible aftermath of the doctor's announcement, but as she poured the soup into the chipped blue bowls memories came rushing back in a torrent. Her mother's tight mouth, the disgust in her eyes, her father's wild rage, the slaps across her face until she finally broke down and told them about Doug and their nightly meetings in the pool house, Gus Hammond's outrage when her father dragged her next door and confronted him and demanded Doug be thrown into jail. She would never forget that nightmare scene in Hammond's study as an ashen-faced Doug was summoned to face the consequences of their love.

"She's fifteen years old!" her father yelled. "*Fifteen* years old! He's going to jail! I'm having him arrested immediately!"

"Is it true, son?" his father asked. "You the one who done it? You the one who knocked her up?"

"It's true," Doug said. "I'm the one."

Gus Hammond doubled up his fist and slammed it into his son's jaw. Doug went sprawling to the floor. Julie screamed and ran over to him and tried to help him up. He shook her hands away and rose slowly to his feet, his jaw already beginning to swell. Gus Hammond stared at him coldly, and when he spoke his harsh, gravelly voice was full of disgust.

"Couldn't keep it in your pants, could you? Couldn't go to a respectable whore and pay for it, could you? Had to have your nooky. Had to fuck a fifteen-year-old girl, had to rut like a dog in the neighbors' pool house. After all the money I've spent on you, all the advantages you've had, you can't keep your hands off a gardener's daughter. All my plans for you shot to hell, just

like that. You've made your bed, you little shit, and now you're gonna lie in it. You're gonna marry the slut, and then you're on your own, fellow. You'll never get another penny from me. You're gonna find out what it's like to face the world without a rich daddy indulgin' your every whim.''

"I—I don't want your filthy money!'' Doug's voice was trembling. "I've never wanted it!''

"Fine, fellow, 'cause you sure ain't gonna see no more of it.''

They were married three days later in a dusty, foul-smelling office downtown, her parents and Gus Hammond in grim attendance. Her parents had thrown her out. Suitcases in hand, she and Doug walked to the Greyhound bus station immediately after the ceremony and waited three hours until their bus arrived. Doug didn't say a word during the whole three hours, but as they boarded their bus he curled his arm around her shoulders. During the past year he had saved a couple of hundred dollars, and when they got to Claymore they'd been able to rent the basement flat. Doug began his senior year, and during the first few months he did private tutoring after his classes to make extra money, working with Dick Sanders and several others, and Julie was worried sick and her face broke out in bumps and no amount of lotion would clear them up, and then, two weeks before Christmas, awful pains wracked her body and Doug called a friend and borrowed a car and got her to the hospital, but she lost the baby anyway. Doug couldn't hide the relief on his face when he visited her in the hospital room the next afternoon. It was a blessing, she told herself. They couldn't possibly have made it with another mouth to feed. It . . . it was a blessing, but her heart was broken nevertheless.

She turned sixteen four days later.

Julie set the soup and the box of crackers on the worn wooden table and stepped to the doorway to call Doug. Immersed in his study, he didn't hear her at first, and then, after she called him a second time, he looked up and scowled and came on into the kitchen, book in hand. He read as he ate, ignoring her completely, but Julie understood. The exam was very important to him. He was determined to make the highest grade. He was determined to become a top-flight lawyer and show his detested father just what kind of man he was. Doug was cold and remote at times, yes, and at times he was sullen and irritable, but . . .

but that was because of the pressure he was under. Julie loved him with all her heart and soul, still, and even though she was often consumed with guilt for having caused their plight, she was making it up to him as best she knew how, working long, hard hours so he could remain in law school. One day, when he had his degree and their financial worries were over, Doug would be glad he had married her.

Julie fervently believed that. Sometimes it was all that kept her going.

She got up from the table and took their empty bowls over to the sink. Doug went back into the front room. She rinsed the dishes and thought about Mr. Compton and how disappointed he was going to be tomorrow night when she didn't show up to read for Laura. She was worried about that, but it couldn't be helped. Doug was right, she should never have started attending classes in the first place. It was a complete waste of time, but . . . but she enjoyed it so much. Maybe Mr. Compton would forgive her. Maybe he would let her keep on coming to class. Julie finished washing up and realized that it was almost time for her to leave for work. Doug looked up when she went in to put her coat and scarf back on. She smiled at him, the love in her heart so strong she could scarcely contain it. She would never become an actress, true, but Doug was going to become a brilliant lawyer.

Her own dreams didn't matter.

4

The dorm was strangely silent as Carol left her room with the shopping bag full of brightly wrapped presents. It was three o'clock in the afternoon, Christmas Eve, and all but a handful of girls had gone home for the holidays. Carol went down the stairs, her footsteps ringing loudly in the near-empty building. Last Christmas Eve she had been working in her uncle's drugstore. There had been an artificial green tree in the front window, garishly trimmed with tinsel icicles and cardboard gingerbread men and twinkling red lights, and the place had been mobbed with people frantically buying last-minute gifts. That bottle of cheap perfume for Aunt Martha. Those tortoise-shell hairbrushes for Grandfather. The box of chocolate-covered cherries for Sister LuAnne. Carol had been behind the cash register, ringing up sales until the store closed at eight, and she remembered that now and stoically refused to be depressed. I'm alone, yes, she told herself, but I'm a freshman at Claymore University, studying with Julian Compton. I could still be in Kansas, working for Uncle Edgar. Trapped. I will *not* be depressed just because I'm all alone on Christmas Eve.

Carol had dutifully mailed off presents to both Uncle Edgar and Aunt Jessie, but she had received none in return, nor had she received a Christmas card. When she had elected to remain in Wichita and work at Philips' Department Store last summer,

her aunt and uncle had made it quite clear that she was on her own now. They had fulfilled their duties. They wanted nothing more to do with her. Carol had written several letters to them during the past few months, all unanswered, and she had sent the Christmas presents as a final token of her willingness to remain on good terms, but she would write no more letters, make no further effort to stay in touch. It was just as well, she thought, moving down the final flight of stairs. They had never really wanted to take her in. They were undoubtedly relieved to have her off their hands. She was indeed on her own now, and her years in Ellsworth seemed like a hazy dream. It was as though her life had truly begun that evening when she had curled her arms around Norman Philips's neck and he had hesitated, nervous, and finally kissed her and gently initiated the innocent girl into the mysteries and wonders of womanhood.

He had been so kind, so tender. He had been so caring, and those few seconds of pain had been quickly eclipsed by the beautiful feelings that followed. In the morning, still wearing the pale blue silk dressing gown and nothing else, she had smiled a smile that expressed all her gratitude and all her newly born feelings for him. She was already fond of him, deeply fond, and she looked forward to letting those feelings grow into something even stronger. That was not to be. That very afternoon he made arrangements for her job and found the room for her at the boardinghouse and told her kindly, firmly, that it would not be wise for them to see each other again. Did he read what was in her heart? Did he suspect that she was already beginning to fall in love with him? Her disappointment was great, but her respect for him grew, for she realized that he was denying himself, thinking of her welfare.

He called frequently to check on her, but he broke his resolve only once, taking her out to dine in Wichita's finest restaurant. He wore a dark suit, a subdued red-and-blue striped tie, and he was the best-looking man in the room. He was kind, considerate, wryly humorous, treating her as he might treat one of his son's college friends. He told her that all arrangements had been made for her to attend Claymore, told her about the generous monthly stipend the foundation was granting. That night at his home might never have happened. She saw the unhappiness in his eyes and heard the loneliness in his voice. She longed to assuage it, and she wished he weren't quite so honorable a man.

Later that evening, when he walked her to the door of the board-inghouse, she stood up on tiptoes and kissed him lightly on the lips and he touched her cheek and looked at her for a long, sad moment and then left her there on the porch. She would never forget Norman Philips. She would be grateful to him for the rest of her life.

Mrs. Dillon, the dorm mother, was at the front desk as Carol stepped into the hall. Pattie, as all the girls called her, was plump, bustling, endearing, a widow with graying brown hair and bright black eyes, a pencil invariably behind her ear. She was confidante, counselor, watchdog and warden, as tolerant as the day was long but stern and unyielding if the need arose! A widow, she had her own apartment at the dorm, and her cat Mustard had free run of the entire building. He sat on the desk now, pretending to be a paperweight.

"Oh, Carol dear!" Mrs. Dillon exclaimed. "I'm so glad you've come down. I wanted to speak to you."

"What is it, Pattie? Have I been using too much hot water?"

Mrs. Dillon smiled. She wore a cream crepe blouse and wine-colored skirt and jacket, a festive sprig of holly on her lapel. Always a bit rumpled, she reminded one of a fussy, friendly pigeon. Carol adored her, as did every other girl at Thurston Hall.

"You probably *have* been, dear, but I'll withhold the infraction slip for the time being. Mustard, do move, dear—I need that report. The other girls are coming to my rooms tonight for a little party—nothing fancy. Actually, I just want to get rid of all that fruitcake. I'd love for you to come, if you have no other plans."

"I—I'm not sure, Pattie."

"Do drop by if you can—sevenish. We'll probably sing 'White Christmas' and grow all maudlin and make asses of ourselves, but what're the holidays for? Oh, and thank you for the present, dear."

"Another fruitcake," Carol said wryly.

"That makes twelve I've received now. You can see why I want to have the party. Delivering more presents?"

Carol nodded. "I'm taking these to my friend Julie. She lives off campus with her husband."

"Mind the walks, dear. They're slippery with ice. Hope to

see you later on this evening. Move it, Mustard. I *need* that report.''

Carol left the dormitory and started across the deserted campus, turning up the gray fur collar of her soft blue wool coat with its belted waist. The grounds were covered with a light frosting of snow and the sidewalks were indeed slippery, but she was wearing her pliant blue vinyl knee boots with rubber soles. It was thoughtful of Pattie to give a party for the girls remaining at the dorm, but Carol doubted she would go. She didn't really know any of the other girls, and somehow being with relative strangers would only make her loneliness worse. She missed Nora dreadfully.

Nora had reluctantly departed for Brooklyn a week ago. ''I'd much rather be trotted out and shot,'' she had confided, ''but if I don't go home for the holidays Sadie'll show up here driving a tank with half the National Guard in tow.'' She had blithely whipped off several new confession stories to finance the trip and pay for Christmas presents—''Bradley would shit if he knew I was writing this crap, but what's a girl to do?'' She and Carol had agreed not to get presents for each other, but they had gone in together to buy presents for Julie. Unbeknownst to Nora, Carol had purchased a beautiful leather portfolio and had it shipped to Brooklyn. Nora had admired it in the window of a department store and said it would be just the thing for her manuscripts.

Carol considered herself wonderfully lucky to have a friend like Nora, so bright and vivacious, so witty and irreverent, so very kind and tenderhearted beneath her tough, breezy facade. It was Nora who had suggested they buy presents for Julie.

''The kid needs a new coat—have you seen that mothy brown thing she's always wearing? Hell, let's play Santa Claus. That husband of hers isn't going to give her much, I can assure you. A scarf, if she's lucky. You can deliver the presents to her on Christmas Eve.''

During the past few weeks Julie had had coffee with them at the SUB after drama class a number of times, always a bit nervous amidst the noisy mob, never staying long, always careful to pay her share. She had started to participate in class a bit more, too, and Carol was amazed at the girl's natural talent. She confessed to Nora that Julie was already much, much better than she would ever be and Nora said that was a moot point, all three of them were going to be tremendously successful. Over coffee

at the SUB one afternoon Nora made Julie a member of their ultraexclusive Cinderella club and told her she was going to get the slipper too and become a great actress and knock 'em on their asses when she hit Broadway. Julie had smiled shyly at this nonsense, but Carol could tell that she was secretly thrilled to be included in Nora's grandiose vision of the future.

"We're a trio!" Nora exclaimed. "Right?"

"Right," Carol said.

"We're a triple threat. We're all gonna get the slipper."

"Right," Julie said.

"Let's drink to it. We oughta have champagne but this coffee'll have to do. Jesus! What-da they make it out of? Mud? You pay five cents for a cup of coffee and they bring you Mississippi silt—but what the hell! Here's to us, gang. All the way to the top and screw the rest of the world."

"Screw 'em," Julie said bashfully.

"You know what, kid? You're beginning to blossom."

"It—it's just nice to have friends."

"Sisters," Nora corrected her. "Who needs a fucking sorority?"

Carol remembered that afternoon as she shifted the shopping bag from one hand to the other and crossed the street, heading toward the row of red brick apartment buildings. The Silver Bell was closed today and Julie was bound to be home, her husband, too, probably. Carol had never met him, but he had come into the restaurant one night when Nora was there, and Nora said he was a cool number, smug and superior, treating Julie like dirt. Although Julie had never said anything about it, Carol suspected that her husband resented Julie's having friends or, indeed, any kind of life of her own. She was predisposed to dislike him, and when he opened the door of their basement flat a few moments later, she tried her best to smile a friendly smile.

"Yes?" he said.

"I'm Carol Martin," she told him. "I've come to see Julie."

He hesitated a moment, surprised, then moved back so that she could come in. It was much too warm inside. The radiators were crackling. Douglas Hammond wore a pair of snug brown gym shorts and a loose, ragged tan T-shirt with CLAYMORE across the chest. He was tall, extremely well built, extremely handsome in a stern, brooding way. An intellectual Heathcliff, Carol thought. He was barefooted. Behind the horn-rims, his

slate-blue eyes took in every detail of her dress and person, deliberately sizing her up, and he liked what he saw. Carol could tell that. He was visibly impressed by her clothes, her demeanor, probably thought she was a wealthy sorority type. Class, style, money—those things would matter to a man like this.

"Excuse my garb," he said. "The radiators are screwed up again and it's like a steam bath in here. Let me take your coat."

Carol set the shopping bag down and let Doug Hammond help her off with the coat. She was wearing her cool blue linen dress beneath it, and he appreciated its exquisite simplicity. He appreciated her looks as well. There could be no denying the smoky masculine interest in those slate-blue eyes. Julie's husband was highly sexed, Carol sensed that immediately, and she returned his gaze with one of frosty politeness. Hammond smiled and moved over to hang her coat up in a nearby closet. Carol glanced around the room, saw the worn linoleum, the dingy concrete walls, the exposed pipes. A pathetic, lopsided little Christmas tree stood on a coffee table, decorated with strings of popcorn and shiny dime store ornaments. Half a dozen clumsily wrapped presents were under it.

"Sorry about the heat," Hammond said, closing the closet door. "If I had known you were coming, I would have slipped on some pants."

He was deliberately drawing attention to his legs. They were nice legs indeed. Carol sensed that he was vain about his body, made it a point to stay in shape despite his intellectual pursuits. She was no more attracted to him than she was to Jim Burke or Dick Sanders or any of the other virile lads on campus. Compared to a man like Norman Philips, they were a pack of callow youths. Doug folded his arms across his chest, his legs spread wide, his head tilted to one side, all smoldering masculinity. It was entirely wasted on Carol. Rarely had she felt such aversion, though she was actress enough to conceal it.

"Is Julie not here?" she inquired.

"She should be back in a few minutes. She went to the grocery store for a few things—they're open until six."

"I—I really can't stay," she said. "I just wanted to bring Julie these."

She indicated the shopping bag. Doug took it and began to arrange the presents under the tree.

"Thoughtful of you to remember her."

"They're from my roommate as well. Wish Julie a Merry Christmas for me. I mustn't keep you."

Hammond placed the last present under the tree and set the empty bag aside, folding his arms across his chest again, biceps flexing.

"Relax," he said. "Julie would be crushed if she missed you. We get very few visitors in our humble abode. I won't bite," he added.

You'd like to, she thought. "Julie tells me you're going to be a lawyer," she said. "She says you're at the top of your class."

He nodded. "A man has to maintain his standards. It's rough, but I don't mind the hard work."

"You're on a scholarship, aren't you?"

"Just partial—tuition and fees, no stipend for living expenses. We've got to scrape for that."

Julie has to scrape for it, you mean. A key rattled in the lock. Hammond cocked his head. The front door opened and Julie stumbled in, clutching a huge brown paper bag full of groceries. She was wearing her old brown coat, a scarf over her hair. Her cheeks were flushed from the cold and the exertion of carrying so heavy a bag. She shifted it around in her arms and shoved the door shut with her foot. Hammond made no effort to assist her. Carol was incensed. Julie sighed and turned and saw Carol, and her violet-blue eyes filled with surprise.

"Carol! I—I didn't know—"

"I just came by to wish you a Merry Christmas," Carol said kindly. "Let me help you with those grocer—"

"I—I'll just put them in the kitchen—" Julie was flustered. "I had to work until ten last night and there's been no time to buy groceries until today and the store closes at—"

"You're babbling," Doug said. "Put the groceries away."

Julie nodded and scurried into the kitchen. Carol heard her moving around nervously, opening and closing the refrigerator door, and then she came back in and pulled off her coat and scarf and smiled her shy smile. She was wearing an old cotton print dress with puffed sleeves that made her look about twelve. Carol noticed that her brown shoes were badly worn, her thick white socks frayed, and she felt her heart might break. She wanted to fold this child in her arms, protect her, comfort her. Julie brushed a wisp of silver-brown hair from her temple and sighed, relaxing at last.

"It was so kind of you to stop by," she said. "I bought a little present for you, and—it's not much, but I thought of you when I found it and I intended to bring it over to the dorm later on this after—"

"Why don't you make our guest some coffee," Doug interrupted. "Iced tea might be more appropriate—it's so bloody hot in here."

"I ran into Mr. Jensen as I was leaving, Doug. He promised the radiators would be working properly by evening. We're always having trouble with them," she explained to Carol. "Would you like some coffee?"

"No. Please. I can't stay. I just wanted to bring your presents. They're from Nora, too."

Julie looked surprised, then confused, and when she spied the beautifully wrapped presents under the tree her eyes grew wide.

"You—you shouldn't have, Carol. You and Nora. I wasn't able to get you anything much, just—I sent a present to Nora in Brooklyn, she gave me her address, and—" Julie darted over to the tree and picked up one of the clumsily wrapped presents, handing it to Carol. "Here," she said. "I hope you aren't disappointed."

Carol could tell from the size and weight that it was a book. "Thank you, Julie," she said.

"Would—would you like to open it now?"

"Only if you'll open yours."

"I don't know—"

Julie glanced at her husband. Doug nodded his approval, and the girls sat down on the sofa. Doug plopped down on the old overstuffed green chair with a sprung bottom. He stretched his legs out, watching with a wry, superior expression as Julie pulled one of the presents into her lap, so excited her hands were shaking. She carefully loosened the glittery silver-and-red striped foil paper and set it aside to save, then took a pair of gray suede gloves out of the box, her eyes aglow with pleasure. Carol unwrapped her book. It was old, battered, green, still a bit dusty, obviously purchased from the used-book store. *Strange Interlude* by Eugene O'Neill. Julie had erased the price marked on the endpaper, but 50¢ was still visible in indentation. Examining the book, Carol was surprised to find it was a first edition.

"I think you would make a marvelous Nina, Carol," Julie said. "Lynn Fontanne did it on Broadway, I believe. Norma

Shearer did the movie. I saw it on television a couple of years ago.''

"I love it, Julie. It's a first edition, too."

"And I love my gloves. They're so beautiful—so soft."

"Open the other two packages."

"They're awfully big—"

Julie was as careful with the second present as she had been with the first one, painstakingly peeling away the Scotch tape and removing the expensive paper without tearing it. She gave an exclamation of delight when she discovered the gray suede knee boots. She had to try them on immediately. They fit perfectly. She gave Carol a hug, tears sparkling in her eyes. She'd never had anything so lovely, she exclaimed, and she really needed a pair of boots with so much snow and cold weather. She was stunned into silence when she opened the final present. It contained a soft pink wool coat with a heavy inner lining, made exactly like the coat Carol had worn, with a large gray fur collar. Julie stood up and put the coat on and belted the waist, the tears streaming down her cheeks now. She was absolutely radiant, despite the tears, and Carol found it difficult not to cry herself.

"I—I don't know what to say," Julie stammered. "Oh, Carol, it—it's the most beautiful coat I've ever seen. You shouldn't have—"

"Nora picked it out. She bought it at the shop across the street from the campus. The Sandra Dee Shoppe, she calls it. You look wonderful in it, Julie. It's very warm, too."

Julie brushed the tears from her cheeks and turned the collar up so that the soft gray fur framed her face. She turned to her husband for his approval and Doug nodded and said, "You look great, hon," and Julie smiled, those clear violet-blue eyes full of love almost painful to behold. She loves him, Carol thought. She loves him with a love that sees no flaws, finds no fault, knows no bounds. She doesn't mind living in this horrible flat or doing without or working like a slave to put him through law school because she loves him without reservation and she is doing it for him. Oh, God, please don't let her be hurt too badly and, please, never, never let me love like that.

"I must go," she said, standing up.

"Won't you stay a while?" Julie begged. "I have some fudge I made this morning, and I'll put some coffee on or—"

Carol shook her head. "I do have to get back. Pattie is giving a party for the girls still at the dorm, and I—I need to bathe and wash my hair and get ready."

Doug stepped to the closet to fetch her coat, helping her on with it and giving her another of those smoky looks. She ignored it and smiled at Julie. Doug padded to the door, opening it. Julie rushed over to give Carol another hug.

"This is the best Christmas I've ever had," she whispered. "Thank you so much. Please thank Nora for me, too."

"Merry Christmas, Julie. Thanks again for the book. I'll see you over at the Silver Bell tomorrow night. We all have kitchen privileges while the other girls are gone, but it's much easier to eat out."

"Come again," Doug said as he showed her out. "Next time I'll put some clothes on."

"Don't bother on my account," Carol said sweetly.

Slipping the O'Neill first edition into the large pocket in the skirt of her coat, she headed back toward campus. It was cooler than it had been earlier and the sky was that curiously opaque gray that promised more snow. The visit with Julie and her husband had depressed her. Julie was so in love with him and that love made her so blind and yet . . . and yet she's probably happier than Nora or I will ever be, Carol reflected. We're both consumed with a driving ambition, while Julie is content to live in the shadow of her husband, abandoning her own ambition in order to see his fulfilled. And she is probably more talented than either of us. Julie would have been the perfect choice for Laura in *The Glass Menagerie*. Carol knew that Compton had wanted her for the part, but Julie hadn't shown up at tryouts. Unfortunately I did, she reminded herself, and her cheeks burned anew as she remembered the humiliation she had felt when Compton waved her offstage without a single comment.

Carol crossed the street. The campus looked bleak beneath the darkening gray sky. She had been so full of hope that night last month when she arrived at the small tan brick theater near the administration building. She had been the fifth girl to read for Laura, and she had given her all, really getting into the part, she felt, and when she had finished Compton had waved his hand and called, "Next!" and that was it and Dee Patrick had been selected to play Laura. Dee was good, Carol had to admit that. A petite, soft-spoken brunette, she was physically right for the

part as well, but Carol had wanted it so badly. Later on she had read for Amanda, a better part, really, the one Laurette Taylor had done on Broadway. She became the aged southern belle, using a fluttery southern accent, giving her all again, and again Compton had waved her off without a word and Sharon Dimmock would be playing Amanda.

I don't have it, she thought. Compton knows it. That's why he ignores me all the time. He's tough, a professional, he knows his business, and he knows I'm just a starry-eyed girl from Kansas without a drop of genuine talent. Mrs. Epperson thought I was marvelous, yes, but she's never been out of Kansas. I'm wasting my time. I'm wasting Julian Compton's time, too. Both of us knew that after the first few classes, but . . . but I've tried so hard to deny it, stubbornly refusing to face the truth. I try. God knows I try. I give my all every time, but my all isn't enough. Not for someone like Julian Compton who has worked with *real* actors.

"Carol!" he called.

Carol looked up, scarcely able to believe her eyes. She had been thinking of him that very moment, and there he was, striding toward her, wearing a heavy gray tweed overcoat, a rakish red-and-green checked muffler wrapped carelessly around his neck, ends flapping. His luxuriant gray hair was windblown, and his craggy, attractive face wore an expression of pleasant surprise. Carol stopped, waiting for him to join her, and Julian Compton smiled, almost as though he was pleased to see her. The bulky tweed overcoat made him seem even larger, and his presence was almost overwhelming. How she admired him. How uneasy he made her. Those moody blue eyes of his seemed to look right into a person, seeing all the flaws, all the insecurities. At the moment they were full of friendly warmth, and that made her more uneasy than ever.

"What on earth are you doing here?" he inquired. "I thought everyone had gone home for the holidays."

I don't have a home to go to, Mr. Compton. "I decided to stay on campus," she said. "I—I had a lot of work to catch up on and thought this would be a perfect time for it."

"I see," he said. He didn't believe her. "I was just starting to unlock the side door of the theater when I happened to glance up and see you crossing the street."

"I've been delivering presents to Julie."

"Ah, yes—Julie," he said thoughtfully. "You two girls are good friends, aren't you?"

"I'm very fond of her. I—I think she's very gifted."

"That she is. The best student I've got."

As opposed to me, the worst. Compton seemed to read her mind, seemed about to make some comment, then apparently changed his mind. He shook his head and looked at her with amiable blue eyes and smiled. He seemed entirely different from the remote, authoritative figure she knew from class, but then she had never encountered him casually like this before. Carol kept her guard up nevertheless, remembering the snubs, remembering her humiliation at the tryouts. Compton sighed, thrusting his hands into the pockets of the bulky overcoat. He was an extremely magnetic man, she observed, not for the first time. His wife was a very lucky woman.

"Did you want something, Mr. Compton?" she inquired.

"Just thought I'd wish you a Merry Christmas. Thought you might give me a hand—not that I really need any help. I was on my way to my office. I've got a couple of dozen Christmas presents stashed away there—need to transfer them to the back end of my station wagon."

"I—I'd be glad to help," Carol said.

"You would? Come along then." He led the way back toward the small brick theater, the scene of her humiliation. "It's my monsters, you see. They snoop dreadfully, always find their Christmas presents no matter how well we hide them. Year before last Andy hid them in the attic—Brett and Bobbie found them, shook them, figured out what they were. Last year I stored them all away in the trunk of my Lincoln. Brett jimmied the lock. So this year everything's at my office, far from prying hands."

Compton led her down the short flight of steps and unlocked the side door of the theater. It led into the basement area where storage rooms, dressing rooms and such were located. He flipped a switch and a single light bulb dimly illuminated a long hallway. His office was located midway, directly beneath the stage. It was large, awash with books and theater journals, pleasantly littered, and the wall behind his desk was hung with posters of plays he had directed in New York and a collection of signed photographs—Shirley Booth, Fredric March and Florence Eldridge,

Lee J. Cobb, Tallulah Bankhead. Compton noticed her examining the latter and grinned.

"One of the reasons I left the theater—the incomparable, exhausting Tallulah. Before I worked with her this hair you see was a rich, dark chestnut. Turned silver almost overnight after I signed to direct her. She was brilliant, of course, wowed the critics and paying customers alike. I had a nervous breakdown."

"You've worked with so many wonderful people," Carol said.

"Indeed I have. Working with students is much less taxing. They've yet to develop what we call 'artistic temperament,' and you have the joy of discovering exciting new talents—like Jim Burke, for example. He's rough and raw and undisciplined at the moment, he's seen too many Brando movies, but once he discards his motorcycle boots and leather jacket and learns to enunciate he's going to go places in a hurry."

"You—you're very patient with him."

"That's what they pay me for," he told her.

Carol helped him carry the presents out to the station wagon parked behind the theater. It took three trips, and he regaled her with fascinating stories about his years on Broadway—the time Bea Lillie and Noël Coward came backstage after an opening, Bea in widow's weeds, Noël humming a dirge, the time Tallulah brought her pet lion cub to a rehearsal—and Carol was utterly enthralled. She so desperately wanted to be a part of that glamorous world. It meant everything to her. When they returned to his office to lock up, she summoned all her courage and brought up the subject that had been preying on her mind.

"Mr. Compton, you—you don't think I'm a very good student, do you?"

Compton was straightening some papers at his desk, and he hesitated. The question had taken him by surprise.

"On the contrary, Carol, you're an excellent student. You do all your work with enthusiasm. You're eager to learn. You're serious about it. Drama class isn't merely a lark for you as it is for some."

"Perhaps I didn't phrase that properly. I—I'm not very *good*, am I? You think I'm wasting your time."

Compton looked at this breathtakingly beautiful girl, and he felt a wrench inside. He had seen so many like her in the theater, and—yes, he had been rough on her. Perhaps he had even resented her, subconsciously at least. She was absolutely dedi-

cated, absolutely determined, a model student. A wretched actress. She tried. She took direction brilliantly. She had everything a person needed to make it in the theater except that one special ingredient—the magic. Carol Martin would never have that. Yet, because of her beauty, because of her striking presence, she was likely to go much further than those ten times more gifted than she. He had seen it happen over and over again during his years in the theater.

Talented, gifted, hardworking hopefuls living in cold-water flats and working in greasy spoons and attending all the auditions and turned down repeatedly, their talent going to waste, their dreams turning to dust, when all they needed was that one big break to become stars and make a valid contribution to the theater—Compton had seen them by the score, had been able to give a few of them a break. Most of them never had the chance to prove their merit. Most of them ended up as abject failures, scratching for a living on the fringes of the business, burned out by rejection. And the others—those bright, sleek, glittery ones blessed with magnetism and looks who, talented or not, were snapped up immediately, movie contracts waving, flashbulbs popping, success, riches and fame tumbling into their laps without the least effort on their parts. It was that aspect of the business he hated the most, and from the very first day in class he had put Carol into that category and, yes, resented her.

"I think that—uh—I think that with the proper training you might eventually develop into a competent actress," he told her.

"Competent," she said.

Julian Compton nodded. She was an extremely bright girl. She knew exactly what he meant. Compton could be brutally frank with his students, and he usually was, but he didn't want to hurt this girl. She was neither affected nor arrogant, like so many students, and she wasn't playing around with acting classes until she met the right boy. She was passionate about it, as was he. He wished he hadn't been quite so cool to her during the past months. When he had seen her crossing the street half an hour ago, all alone on Christmas Eve, looking so low, something had compelled him to go over and speak to her. He realized now it was because, subconscious resentment aside, he really liked the girl and admired her impeccable good manners, her intrinsic class. She couldn't help it if she happened to be ravishingly beautiful, if she happened to have a remarkable phys-

ical presence and precious little talent. She wanted to learn, and, by God, his job was to teach.

"You mean I have no future as an actress," she said.

"I didn't say that, Carol."

"You implied it."

"You might not have—quite what it takes to make it in the legitimate theater," he said carefully, and he saw the pain in her eyes, "but you're an extremely lovely girl and you have a great deal of presence. That should go quite a way toward compensating for your lack of—for any drawbacks you might have as an actress."

"But not in the theater."

"The theater isn't a visual medium—not essentially. I think you might be quite successful in television or in films. I could name scores of people without a smidgen of acting ability who've been phenomenally successful in those mediums. And—and you're not without potential," he added, hoping to soften the blow.

"Do you think I should drop out of class?"

"Of course not," he said.

"I don't want to waste my time—or yours."

"Carol, you—you're still quite young, and, as I said, you're not without potential. You're eager to learn, and I think there's a great deal I can teach you."

But you can't give me what Julie has. No one can. If I work, if I study, if I continue to give my all, I may one day be a competent actress. Competent. I'll never have Julie's magic. I'll never be great. I'll never be good. I'll be competent.

"Thank you for being so honest," she said quietly.

Compton straightened a few more papers and then, taking her elbow, led her out of the office. He closed the door behind him, locked it and, sighing heavily, led her down the dimly lit hallway. Carol was silent as they stepped outside. Compton turned off the light and locked the side door, fumbling with the keys. Carol put her hands into the pockets of her coat and touched the volume Julie had given her and smiled a wry smile. No chance of my ever playing in an O'Neill drama. If I'm lucky I may get a bit in an episode of *December Bride*.

"It's grown colder," Compton said, wrapping the vivid red-and-green muffler around his neck. "Bound to snow tonight."

"It looks that way."

"Thank you for helping me with the packages, Carol."

"It was my pleasure."

Compton looked at her, so elegant in the stylish pale blue coat, so classy and composed. This little girl from Kansas brought Grace Kelly to mind. She had the same serene beauty, the same cool poise. None of the talent, alas, but oh what studio lighting and a film camera could do with that bone structure and those lovely eyes. If only they wouldn't require her to speak and emote. *Am I being fair to her?* Compton wondered about that. *She's not yet eighteen, won't be until next month, if I remember correctly. She's got a lot of time to learn. In the meantime, it's Christmas Eve and she's all alone.*

"Listen, Carol," he said, "my wife's cooking her traditional English Christmas dinner tonight—stuffed goose, plum pudding, all that sort of thing. We always have it Christmas Eve. I'd love for you to join us—Andy would, too. There'll just be the two of us—and the monsters, of course."

Carol smiled. "Thank you for the invitation, Mr. Compton, but I'm afraid I can't make it."

"You've got other plans?"

"Pattie is giving a party in her rooms tonight," she said. "I told her I would be there, and I—I really couldn't disappoint her. Please wish your family a Merry Christmas for me."

"Merry Christmas to you, too, Carol."

He gave her a warm smile and walked around to the parking lot. Carol went back to the dorm, but she didn't go to the party. She couldn't face anyone tonight, couldn't force herself to be friendly and bright. She made a cup of tea on the hot plate she and Nora illegally kept in their room and turned the radio on low and sat at the window, gazing out at the deserted campus and listening to the Christmas carols. The sky grew darker. Shadows lengthened and twilight came and, just before nightfall, snow began to swirl softly in the air. Carol took her robe and soap and went down the hall to the showers, and at eight she was back in the room, ready for bed. She hadn't eaten anything, but she wasn't hungry. Maybe she'd have another cup of tea before she went to sleep. Pattie and the girls were undoubtedly having a festive time downstairs. Why did people always make such a big deal over the holidays? She was alone, yes, but it wasn't important. Carol turned off the radio and picked up a book and attempted to read.

At ten o'clock the telephone at the end of the hallway began to ring. It rang and rang, shrill and insistent. She expected someone to get it downstairs at the switchboard, but then she remembered that everyone was at the party and the switchboard was probably shut down. Someone was ringing the number directly from outside. Carol ignored the noise for a while and finally, impatiently, put her book aside and hurried down the hall and picked up the receiver.

"Yes?" she said.

"Jesus! You took your own sweet time answering. If you knew the trouble I had getting through in the first place."

"Nora? Is that *you*?"

"No, sweetie, it's Mary Pickford. You bitch, I thought we agreed we weren't going to exchange presents, and what do I find in the mail today? I find a package from you. I open it. Inside, a sumptuously wrapped box. I open *that*, too, and I find that gorgeous leather portfolio I admired a couple of weeks ago and I happen to *know* what it cost."

"Merry Christmas, Nora."

"What the hell do you think it makes *me* feel like? Like a schmuck, that's what. I got a package from Julie, too—*Lelia: The Life of George Sand*, by André Maurois. I've been meaning to read it all year long. She paid retail, the idiot. Did you deliver our presents to her? Did she like them?"

"She loved them. Everything fit perfectly."

"I wish I could have been there. I wish I could be *any*where but Brooklyn! We're Jewish, you know, we're not supposed to celebrate Christmas, but you think that stops Sadie? Any excuse for a gathering of the tribe. I've been up to my asshole in relatives ever since I arrived, and the food! I don't care if I never *see* another gefilte fish ball, not to mention the matzo. Turkey and dressing and cranberry sauce, too, Sadie is nothing if not open-minded."

"Are you having a good time?"

"Are you kidding? Cousin Myron was over this afternoon. He's still horny as ever, still has those unfortunate teeth. Eugene Cohen married Renee Kuppenheimer, by the way. I found that out yesterday. May they live happily ever after. Listen, sweetie, the reason I called—I think I left my physics notebook in the bottom drawer of my bureau and I need you to send it to me."

"Your *physics* notebook?"

"Call me crazy, I want to finish some problems while I'm here. What else is there to do? Run look and see if it's there, will you? I think it's under my sweaters. I'll hold on."

"This is long *distance*, Nora."

"And I'm the last of the big-time spenders. Go on, Carol. See if I left it in the drawer, then come back to the phone."

"It's your nickel."

"My nickel! My twenty bucks, you mean. Get a move on!"

Carol shook her head at her roommate's eccentricity and rushed back down the hall to their room. Nora's physics notebook was not in the bureau drawer under her sweaters, but a present was. It was relatively small and elegantly wrapped in silver paper and red velvet ribbon with a sprig of lovely artificial holly. Surprised, shaken, she frowned and carried it back down the hall to the telephone.

"Nora?" Her voice was trembling.

"You find my notebook, kid?"

"You know I didn't. I found—I think I'm going to cry."

"Don't you dare, you slut. Go ahead. Open it. I wanna hear that paper crackling. Are you opening it?"

Carol cradled the phone between shoulder and ear and hunched and carefully removed the lovely ribbon and began to loosen the tape, just as Julie had done earlier.

"Have you opened it yet? What's taking you so long?"

"The paper's so pretty. I don't want to tear—"

"Forget the fucking paper! Time is ticking away. Jesus! I'll probably have to whip off another story just to pay for this phone call! Have you got it open?"

"Al—almost."

Carol tore the paper aside to discover a flat black velvet box, and when she opened the lid she found a string of cultured pearls nestling on a bed of gray satin. They were perfectly shaped, perfectly matched, and the clasp was studded with tiny diamonds. Her hands shook. Tears filled her eyes, spilled down her cheeks.

"Well?"

Carol stared at the pearls, her lower lip trembling. "Nora—they're—I can't let you—they must have cost—"

"They cost three hundred and fifty bucks, plus tax. So what? So it's only money. It took me four and a half hours to write 'They Called Me Jailbait,' and that little epic paid for your pearls.

I couldn't resist them, kid. They're elegant and lovely, just like you. I'm not gonna get all sloppy and sentimental, but you don't know what it means to have a friend like you rooting for me. I wanted to get you something special.''

"I—I'll treasure them always.''

"At those prices, you'd damned well better!''

"I—I miss you so much.''

"I miss that ugly mug of yours, too. Merry Christmas, kiddo. I'd better hang up now or Sadie'll come in here with a butcher knife. I *told* her I'd pay for the call but she thinks I'm gonna stiff her with the bill. One more thing, I'm coming back a little early. I'll be there for New Year's Eve. We're gonna drink real booze and tear the place up, kid.''

"Oh, Nora, that will be so—so—''

"Are you *sob*bing? You'd think at your age a person'd show some self-control. I broke the news to the folks yesterday, told 'em I had to get back early to study for an exam. Sadie went into her number but I just let her shriek. I wouldn't dream of spending New Year's Eve with anyone else, kid. Nineteen fifty-six is gonna be our year!''

5

Nora felt like jumping for joy when, at the beginning of spring
semester, Dick Sanders transferred into her history class. Because of his athletic activity, it had been necessary for him to
change his schedule around, and on the first day of class in he
walked, wearing jeans and sweater, carrying his books, looking
absolutely devastating. He took a seat near the back of the room,
slouching sexily with his legs spread out. She and Carol were
sitting up front, dammit, and it would be much too obvious to
get up and move back. Nora dawdled a bit after class and Dick
sauntered right past her and grinned and said, "Oh, hi there,"
and then he slung his arm around the shoulders of Alice Hart
and asked her what she was doing that night and Alice said,
"What've you got in mind, big fellow?" Actually used those
words, the hussy. She was blonde and flashy and had big boobs
and wore tight sweaters and lots of lipstick. No chance for me
with tail like that swishing around, Nora thought bitterly, but
she didn't intend to give up, not even in the face of such formidable competition. She had been waiting much too long for a
chance like this.

"I'm going to get him," she told Carol.

"Why on earth would you want him?"

"Those sexy green eyes flecked with brown, that wicked grin,
those shoulders! All those bubbling male hormones! If I'm going

to get experience, it's important the man knows what he's doing, and I happen to know Dick Sanders has already qualified for a Ph.D. in screwing.''

"I hate to be blunt, dear, but Dick Sanders doesn't know you're alive. He goes for the obvious type like Alice Hart, pseudo-Marilyns who keep their eyelids at half-mast and lick their lips a lot.''

"Go ahead, bitch, rub it in!''

"You don't really want him, Nora.''

"Of course I don't!'' Nora snapped. "I've spent the past six months fantasizing about Boris Karloff! I may not have Alice Hart's equipment, but I've got other weapons. Brains, for one. Dick Sanders doesn't have a chance.''

"We'll see,'' Carol said.

"Hide and watch, sweetie.''

February went by and March arrived and spring came early. The tulips and hyacinths and daffodils began to bloom on campus. So did Nora. Some new outfits would undoubtedly help, she decided, so she knocked off "I Was Everyone's Girl'' and "My Brother, My Lover'' and hurried over to the Sandra Dee Shoppe and bought a new spring wardrobe, very fetching and feminine. It had no discernable effect on Dick Sanders. He continued to grin and say, "Hi there,'' when he happened to notice her, but his arm was invariably curled tightly around Alice Hart's shoulders. They might have been Siamese twins. His ardor for Alice apparently cooled and he took up with Helen Morrison, another blonde who went to a lot of Monroe movies and probably wore no panties. Although she hated to admit defeat, Nora saw that Dick Sanders wasn't about to pay attention to a zero like her, not when there were abundantly endowed babes like Alice and Helen on tap.

What is it with me? she wondered. The boys she met in her various classes were friendly enough, sure, a couple of them even teased her a little, but none of them ever asked her to hop over to the malt shop with them for a double chocolate shake. None of them asked her to go bowling or go to the movies or drive up to Inspiration Point for a quickie in the backseat of their Studebaker. It was frustrating as hell. Other girls had dates all the time. Half the girls at the dorm were going steady. More than a few of them had already been fitted for diaphragms. There was a whole lot of shakin' goin' on, yeah, but little Nora Levin

sure wasn't getting in on it. She was doomed to be cute, doomed
to be "nice," the kind of girl you patted on the head but wouldn't
dream of laying. In truth, she was quite shy and demure with
the boys, saving the wisecracks for Carol and Julie and a few of
her teachers.

At least things were going well with her classes. She was
making straight A's without half trying and had already determined to take more semester hours, go to summer school and
take a few night courses. No sense spending four years in college
when any dolt with half a brain cell could do it in three. She
was learning a lot in Stephen Bradley's class, too. He was positively brilliant, a marvelous teacher, witty, acerbic, gruff, totally irreverent when it came to the literary establishment. He
smoked in class, dripping ashes on his tweed jacket, drank coffee by the gallon and had a way of getting right to the core of
things. He taught his students to cut, to economize, to use clear,
simple sentences without an excess of adjectives and adverbs.
Style was all very good, he added, but without feeling the most
beautiful sentence had no punch. Write it from the gut or don't
write it at all, Make the reader *feel* it. Nora could see the im-
provement in her own prose. Bradley was merciless with his red
pencil, slashing her compositions to ribbons, but he was always
right and she appreciated the criticism.

He was quite fond of her, thought her a hoot. Nora made no
effort to curb the mouth when she was with Bradley. They had
coffee together at the SUB several times and discussed writers
and writing and good prose and bad. Both had a fondness for
F. Scott Fitzgerald, particularly *Tender Is the Night*, Nora's favorite, and Bradley agreed with her that Hemingway carried
economy to excess, although he did have emotional impact.
Bradley told her that if she wanted real writing she should go
back to Mark Twain, Twain was terrific, and he introduced her
to newer writers like Nelson Algren and William Styron and she
thought *Lie Down in Darkness* was a masterpiece. She told him
she was going to start writing her novel soon and he said, "Practice, kid, practice," and told her she had a great knack for dialogue, her dialogue was snappy, rang true. She said she had
learned a lot about dialogue from John O'Hara and Bradley admitted that no one did it better than O'Hara. Wreathed in cigarette smoke, gulping down coffee, speaking in that gruff, often
surly voice, Bradley was a fascinating man, a great inspiration.

Nora cherished those hours she spent with him. His was the only male companionship she had, and he *would* be forty-nine and overweight with four kids and a wife he adored.

In late March Gabrielle Bernais's second novel was published in America and *Look* did a long feature on her, with pictures. There was Gaby, the darling of Paris, sitting behind the wheel of her snazzy sports car, carousing in a smoky nightclub with a pack of youthful friends, sunning on the Riviera in a pair of shorts and a striped sailor's jersey, a tattered straw hat at her side. Gaby the gamine with her flat, boyish body and short, shaggy gold hair and the thin tan face of a young pirate. Nora read the article and studied the photographs with ill-disguised envy. Gaby was only nineteen now and they were calling her the natural successor to Colette. Gaby loved fast cars and jazz and American whiskey. She loved playing for high stakes at the gambling casinos and loved being in love although it was invariably sad and disillusioning. French critics adored her, and the American press hailed her as the most exciting literary celebrity since Kathleen Winsor. *A Woman Knows* was reviewed in all the major publications and shot to the top of the best-seller lists.

Nora bought it immediately, of course, and read it in one sitting. It was only 180 pages long, deceptively simple, very much like *Kisses for Breakfast*, in fact. All about love and lovemaking and the heartbreak it brings. Nora *knew* she could write as good a book, using an American setting, and, fired up, full of determination, she bought a new ream of paper and rolled the first sheet into her typewriter and worked like a demon for the next three weeks, oblivious to everything but the life she was creating there on paper. Oh, she attended classes, sat through them, but she was thinking about the novel all the while. She typed late, late into the night every night and bought Carol a pair of earplugs and an eye mask when she complained. She often forgot to eat, lived in another world, wildly exhilarated as the words tumbled onto paper, seemingly of their own volition.

Because You Care was about a sleek, sophisticated girl of eighteen named Sonia who wore bronze taffeta cocktail dresses and lived on Long Island with her handsome, worldly father and spent a lot of time at the country club being disillusioned with life. Sonia was having an affair with an athletic lad named Burt who bore a striking resemblance to Dick Sanders, and they made love under the pier and in the sand and in the backseat of Dad-

dy's Rolls but both were bored and seeking new sensations. Daddy fell in love with a lovely lady named Sally who wore red satin to the country club and used to be a model before she grew older. Sally was warm and giving and Sonia was insanely jealous, and she and Burt tricked Daddy into believing Sally was sleeping with a handsome South American who had a coffee plantation in Brazil. Heartbroken, Daddy blew his brains out in the trophy room and Burt and Sonia felt remorseful, decided to break up, and Sonia spent the rest of the summer drinking martinis and gazing out the window with sad eyes.

Finally finished, still exhilarated, Nora shyly handed the 210-page manuscript to Stephen Bradley after class and asked if he would mind giving her an honest opinion. Bradley looked at the manuscript, looked trapped and finally nodded curtly and said he'd get back to her. Nora waited anxiously, her head full of delicious fantasies. Bradley would read it and be bowled over and he would call his publishers and say, "Look, guys, I've just read a fabulous novel, blockbuster material, written by one of my students, you've gotta read it as soon as possible." They'd be bowled over, too, and snap it up immediately and she'd be hailed as the American Bernais and hit the best-seller lists, be rich and famous in the blink of an eye.

A full week passed, and Bradley made no mention of her book, gave no indication he had read even so much as the first chapter, and Nora began to have doubts for the first time. The delicious fantasies began to fade. She was a published writer, sure, she'd sold almost two dozen confession stories, but a novel was different. A novel required more than a facility with words and the ability to tap a market. A novel required *real* skill, depth, perception, insight. Nora read her carbon copy twice, and the prose seemed all right, free of grammatical errors. There was a good flow and a definite narrative thrust, and some of the dialogue was good, really good, but . . . was it perhaps just a little flat? Were these characters who had been so alive, so vivid in her mind alive and vivid there on the paper? Nora couldn't tell. Bradley still hadn't given any sign he'd read it, and the suspense was almost impossible to endure. Finally, on a Thursday, nine days after she had handed him the manuscript, he asked her to see him in his office at four that afternoon.

"I can't go," she told Carol.

"You have to, Nora."

"He's going to crucify me."

"Nonsense. It's a good book."

"You've read it?"

"I read the carbon while you were gone yesterday."

"You sneaky little bitch! What'd-ja think?"

"I—I thought it was very good."

"What the hell do *you* know?"

"It's almost four, Nora. Go see Bradley."

His office was in the administration building, on the third floor—the original attics had been converted into offices for various teachers. Nora's knees felt trembly as she climbed the stairs and she thought she might be ill at any moment. She wished she'd never given him the bloody manuscript in the first place, wished she'd never even mentioned it. Just who the hell was she to think she could write a novel? Bradley was probably laughing his head off. How would she ever be able to look him in the eye again after giving him that piece of shit, asking him to read it? Nora reached the third floor and moved down the long hall, a bank of windows on the right flooding it with sunlight, the roof slanting sharply. She stopped in front of his office door and swallowed and knew she couldn't face him. She'd rather face a firing squad and to hell with the blindfold. She raised her fist to knock, hesitated, closed her eyes tightly and finally tapped on the door.

"Come in," he called.

Nora opened the door. A cloud of smoke swept into the hall. The office was small, and it was literally filled with books, on shelves along the walls, stacked up on the floor, piled on the desk. Bradley sat behind the desk, pouring coffee from a thermos, a cigarette burning in the ashtray. He grunted at her and took a drag on the cigarette and a sip of coffee and then sighed wearily. There was her manuscript on the desk in front of him, the top page sprinkled with ashes. Nora closed the door and swallowed again and stood before him on wobbly knees. Bradley stubbed out his cigarette, lighted another and finally looked up at her. She smiled nervously.

"Ah," he said, "our budding novelist."

"It's shit, isn't it?"

"Please sit down, Nora."

"I'd rather stand."

"Suit yourself. Want some coffee? There's another cup around here somewhere."

"No coffee, thanks. Just pass the sentence. It *is* shit, isn't it?"

"Pretty much so," he admitted, "although there's some rather good writing here and there and some terrific dialogue. I'm impressed. The very fact that you actually sat down and wrote an entire novel at your age is impressive as hell. Most people just *talk* about writing a book. Few ever do."

"But it stinks."

"It stinks," he said frankly. "It's gauche and embarrassingly naive, a pathetic imitation of Gabrielle Bernais. Oh yes, I've read her new book, too. She knows whereof she writes."

"And I don't."

"Ever been to a country club?"

"My Uncle Myron took the whole tribe once. We had shrimp cocktail out on the patio and then went inside and watched the old ladies play Bingo."

"Ever wear bronze taffeta?"

"Hardly my style. You've gotta be tall and slim and striking."

"Like Sonia. Mind if I ask a personal question?"

"Fire away."

"Have you ever had sexual intercourse?"

"What do you think?"

"I think not, judging from the scenes in your novel."

"It shows?"

"It shows."

"Shit," she said.

Bradley couldn't resist a smile. She was such a clever child, so bright, far and away the best student he had, and she had the makings of a damned fine writer, too, once she grew up, once she learned a little of life. He lighted a fresh cigarette and inhaled deeply, studying her. The tough, brassy facade she often presented didn't fool him for an instant. She was basically shy and quite insecure, but then most real writers were. She sat there with her hands in her lap, utterly crestfallen and trying not to show it, her brown eyes full of brave defiance. Bradley remembered when he was eighteen years old, a farm boy from Ohio enamored of James Branch Cabell. *His* first novel, penned at the age of twenty, had been an outright imitation of Cabell—he shuddered at the memory—and it hadn't been nearly as prom-

ising, as stylistically polished as this child's book. James Branch Cabell had long since been forgotten by most of the country. Bradley suddenly felt very old.

"You're not a worldly young Frenchwoman, Nora," he said kindly.

"Tell me something I don't know."

"You shouldn't try to write like one. You should write about the things you know."

"Like Sadie and Irving and growing up bright in Brooklyn. That'd really wow the reading public. I want to write a best-seller."

"I imagine you will one day," he told her. "You have a remarkable talent already. Your work has energy and verve and a unique style—when you're not imitating Bernais, that is. Your dialogue is superb. All you lack is a little experience in life."

"Yeah," she said. "I've been trying to get some."

"Give yourself some time, Nora. Keep studying, keep learning, keep writing. You'll have that best-seller eventually."

So we're back to square one, Nora thought bitterly as she returned to the dorm. I can't write a best-seller until I get some experience and I can't get any experience because no male in his right mind will give me the time of day. I'm doomed to be a virgin for the rest of my life. Maybe in forty years or so I'll pen a trenchant novel about being an old maid and wow the critics with my sensitivity and sell four copies to relatives. Nora put *Because You Care* away and wondered what had ever possessed her to write it in the first place. Must have taken leave of my senses. She was depressed for days afterwards, resisting all Carol's efforts to cheer her up. Me get the slipper? Huh, fat chance of that. Screw writing. Screw Gaby Bernais, too. Someone obviously *has*, or she couldn't have written *A Woman Knows*. *I* sure as hell don't know. Haven't an inkling. Maybe I'll go into a nunnery. Do they *take* Jewish girls?

Despondent, defeated, uncharacteristically glum, Nora gave up any idea of winning Dick Sanders as well. I have about as big a chance of getting his attention as I do of receiving an invitation to Grace Kelly's wedding. He's delectable, sure, but I haven't a hope. He's only interested in bimbos with big bazooms and long blonde hair. Nora no longer lingered near the doorway before her history class, accidentally dropping a book just as he entered, no longer dawdled, timing her exit to correspond with

his. She paid no attention to him at all, although she was always conscious of his presence back there in class. Might as well try to hump Clark Gable, she told herself. The new wardrobe she had purchased remained in the closet, and the bottle of Chanel Number 5 wasn't going to be needed. T. S. Eliot was right, April *was* the cruelest month. She studied hard, had coffee at the SUB with Carol and Julie and still the depression hung on.

And then one day she stepped outside after her physics class and there he was, grinning at her, looking dreamy in old tennis shoes and faded, skin-tight jeans and a loose gray sweatshirt damp with perspiration. Gorgeous, sure, if you happened to like the type. Helen Morrison was nowhere in sight. His arm was curled around a basketball. Nora didn't bother smiling at him. Why waste her time? Seeing that she was going to walk right by him without speaking, he stepped in front of her, blocking her way.

"I've been waiting for you," he said huskily.

"Oh? What'd-ja have in mind, big fellow?"

It was a vicious imitation of Alice Hart, but there was no sense curbing the mouth. Nothing she said to him was going to matter anyway.

His grin widened. "You're a gas."

"Yeah. You oughta catch me when I'm in top form."

"I've been at the gym, practicing a few shots. Forgive the sweat."

"Sweat? I thought it was Aqua Velva."

"You ever see me in action, catch any of the games?"

"I'm too busy inventing games of my own."

"You *are* a gas."

"Look, Sanders, I'd love to stand here and chat with you, but I'm already late for my next class, so unless you want to screw I'd better hustle."

He chuckled heartily and shifted the basketball from one arm to the other and looked at her with brown-flecked green eyes aglow with amusement. She was a gas, all right, sure. The mere thought of the two of them screwing sent him into paroxysms of glee. Nora scowled.

"I've got a favor to ask," he said.

"Your place or mine?"

He chuckled again, clearly delighted. "I—uh—I've been having a little problem with history," he explained, "and Beasley

said if I wanted to pass, I better get some outside help, hire myself a tutor. I asked her if she had any suggestions on who I might get, and she told me you were her brightest student, said I might see if you were interested.''

I knew it wasn't my boobs. "You want me to tutor you in history?''

"Yeah. I'd—uh—I'd be willing to pay five bucks a session.''

I'd be willing to pay *you*, big fellow, but I don't want to seem too eager. Never hurt a girl to play hard to get.

"When do you want to start?'' she asked.

Sanders looked vastly relieved. "You mean you'll help me?''

"I'm a glutton for punishment.''

"How about tonight? We could meet at the library, say around seven, and work till nine or so. I'm pretty slow when it comes to remembering dates and stuff like that, but maybe you can help me remember 'em, help me sort out all those campaigns Napoleon was always making.''

You're no mental giant, sweetie, but with muscles like those who needs to be articulate?

"I guess we could give it a try,'' she told him. "If it doesn't work out we can always sneak into the stacks and screw.''

Sanders laughed loudly and gave her a quick hug and hurried on, dribbling the basketball on the walk. Nora was in a daze. Her spirits started to lift, and by the time she got back to the dorm that afternoon she could scarcely contain her elation. Carol was sitting on her bed with a pillow behind her back, reading *Marjorie Morningstar*, Herman Wouk's latest best-seller.

"I've just got one word to say,'' Nora announced.

"What's that?''

"Whoopee!''

"Good Lord! What happened?''

"A bloody *miracle*, that's what! I saw Dick Sanders today; he was waiting for me when I got out of physics class, and I mouthed off something awful and he thought I was a riot and he wants me to tutor him in history. Beasley recommended me for the job. I'm going to meet him tonight at the library at seven o'clock, just the two of us, we'll work at a secluded table. The game's on again, kiddo, and this time I'm gonna *win*.''

Carol gave her an exasperated look and shook her head.

"I've got one big problem though,'' Nora confessed.

"Oh?''

"What the hell am I going to *wear*? Be frank with me, Carol, I want your honest opinion—do you think the black velvet sheath would be pushing it?"

She arrived at the library shortly after seven in a simple brown skirt and a tan blouse, a vivid tan-and-daffodil-yellow scarf tied around her neck. Dick was waiting near the front desk, surrounded by friends, and when he saw her approaching he said something to them, waved farewell and sauntered out to meet her. He had an unusual walk, a kind of lazy, loose-kneed lope that was incredibly sexy. He was wearing jeans and a green-and-black striped nylon shirt with the tail hanging out, and his golden-brown crew cut looked freshly waxed. Girls gazed at him with longing, Nora observed, but then he was the Big Man on Campus, the star jock, a golden youth who, at forty, would probably be a washed-out insurance salesman, recalling these years of glory with a gnawing sense of loss. Nora was perceptive enough to realize that, but at the moment he was absolutely dazzling, and that was all that mattered.

"Ready to work?" she asked.

"Guess so," he said. "I put my books and stuff on a table in back."

"Great."

She was going to play it cool, take her time, let him slowly discover her charms and awaken to the possibilities. She didn't intend to throw herself at him, at least not right off the bat. She'd awaken his interest gradually, then reel him in. Tonight she was going to be all business. God knows I've got my work cut out for me, she thought half an hour later. Dick Sanders might knock 'em dead on the basketball court or on the discus-throwing field, but when it came to more cerebral pursuits he was almost hopeless. Not one of your bigger achievers. Sitting at a rather secluded table in back, surrounded by towering shelves of books, he frowned and gnawed the end of his pencil and tried desperately to follow her simple outline of the Napoleonic campaigns. Nora went over them again and again, even drew him a chart, but Dick couldn't grasp any of it. She kept repeating the information over and over again, one, two, three, and after an hour and a half a light bulb seemed to go on inside his head. He nodded and grinned and finally got it, mulled it over in his mind, trying to digest it. Nora sighed, exhausted.

"Hey," he said, "you're good. I got it. I understand now. That chart you drew helps a lot. Mind if I keep it?"

"Be my guest."

"Wanna take a break? Wanna go get a Coke or something?"

"We'd better keep on working. You've got the various campaigns. Now you've got to learn the dates of each one."

"Geez. Why do we have to learn junk like that?"

"You never know when it might come in handy. You'll be at a cocktail party one day and someone will bring up Napoleon's invasion of Russia and you can say, 'Oh yes, he entered Moscow on September fourteenth, eighteen twelve, but had to retreat because of lack of supplies and winter quarters.' You'll make a lot of points, impress all the guests."

"I've never thought of it that way," he told her.

"I'm sure you haven't, Sanders."

"Look, don't you think you could call me Dick? We're gonna be working together real close."

"I may not survive it." She sighed.

"Guess I'm kinda dense," he admitted.

"But gorgeous."

"You're kinda cute, Nora. Never known a girl quite like you."

"Back to the books, Buster. We've still got half an hour."

Shortly after nine Dick closed his textbook and yawned and threw his arms out, stretching lustily. He was so big and strong and muscular, bursting with virile energy, could probably go at it for hours on end. Nora lowered her eyes and primly gathered up her notebook and papers. Dick grinned and looked at her with green-brown eyes full of friendly affection. He might not want to jump my bones yet, but at least he *likes* me, Nora thought. That's progress. She fully expected him to walk her back to the dorm—it was late, it was dark, good manners required him to see her safely to the door—but Dick stood up and started to look around expectantly. Nora felt bitter disappointment when she saw Helen Morrison coming toward them. Shit. Helen was wearing a tight pink sweater and a wide gray cinch belt and a gray skirt so tight you could see the crack between her buttocks. Long gold hoop earrings dangled from her earlobes, and her mouth had been freshly painted with lush red lipstick.

"Hi, babe," Sanders said.

He slung his arm around her shoulders, pulling her close.

Helen wiggled a lot, butt twitching, boobs straining against the pink sweater. The subtle approach works every time, Nora thought ruefully. She got up, clutching notebook and papers to her less abundantly endowed bosom.

"Learn anything?" Helen inquired.

"Yeah. Nora's a treasure. She's been workin' me hard."

"How sweet," Helen said sweetly.

Fuck you, slut. The thought that Dick undoubtedly would was little consolation. Nora forced a tight, polite smile onto her lips. Helen looked at her as though she were some kind of amusing insect. Curling his arm loosely around Helen's throat, Dick handed her his books to hold and jammed his free hand into the pocket of his jeans, pulling out a crumpled five-dollar bill.

"I almost forgot," he said, handing it to Nora. "Tomorrow night suit you okay? Same time? Same place?"

"See you then," Nora told him.

"Great. Take care, kid."

Although it was one of her own favorite words, the "kid" hurt. Dick gave her a final grin and then steered Helen away, the two of them glued tightly together. If Dick was selling in- surance and mourning the golden years at forty, Helen would be overweight and frowsy, wearing sloppy houseshoes and a flow- ered wrapper as she cooked breakfast for her husband in a sub- urban tract house, eager to get him off to work so she could have her first drink of the day. Nora saw it clearly and tried to tell herself she was vastly superior to them both, but there was a hollow feeling in the pit of her stomach as she walked back to the dorm alone. Couples strolled across the dark campus, hand in hand, voices low, and laughter came from lighted windows. A terrible feeling of loneliness besieged her, so strong it was almost like physical pain.

"How did it go?" Carol asked.

"He likes me!" Nora said brightly, putting her notebook down on the desk. "I'm gonna get him, kid. Just you watch."

"You look a little—a little down, Nora."

"Down? *Me*? When I've got him on the hook at last? You must be imagining things. Look, the Silver Bell's open till ten and I skipped dinner tonight, as you know. Why don't we pop over and say hi to Julie and order a hamburger and fries. My treat."

"I'm not hungry," Carol protested.

"So be a friend. Come anyway."

"I guess I could order a cup of coffee," Carol sighed. "Let me get some clothes on."

"Shake it, kiddo. I'm ravenous."

Nora continued to meet Dick Sanders at the library several nights a week, and he confessed that he was showing definite progress in class, made an 82 on the last test, all thanks to her. He was friendly, relaxed, even started teasing her playfully. Nora maintained a brusque, all-business manner, knowing it was most likely to intrigue him. This guy had girls falling at his feet right and left, he was bound to wonder why *she* didn't. One night, as they headed toward their table at the library, he slung his arm around her shoulders and she felt her knees grow weak and felt sensations stirring inside and pretended not to notice the warmth and weight of that muscular arm pulling her close and the touch of that be-jeaned thigh bumping against hers. Jesus! A girl could lose complete control! This was the closest contact she'd ever had with a boy, her Cousin Myron excepted, and it was a heady experience. Nora was more businesslike than ever that night, drilling him on the American Civil War, and it wasn't easy keeping her mind on the subject at hand. Robert E. Lee was dead and buried, but Dick Sanders was alive and well and sitting right there across the table in all his virile glory.

Helen Morrison failed to show up to meet him when they finished work that evening. Maybe she tripped on those spike heels of hers and broke her pelvis, Nora thought cheerfully.

"Where's Helen?" she asked, ever so casual.

"Don't know. We broke up yesterday."

"Pity," Nora said. "You'll find a replacement soon enough."

"There are always a lotta girls around. Don't want to get too thick with just one of 'em. Helen expected me to give her my letter jacket. Next thing you know she'd be expecting me to give her an engagement ring. I'm havin' too much fun to be thinkin' about stuff like that yet."

"I see your point. I'm all for fun myself."

"Yeah?"

"Try me sometime, big fellow."

She was definitely getting frisky. Sanders laughed, slung his arm around her shoulders again and walked her to the front desk. Talk about bliss! Little Nora Levin crushed against the side of the great Dick Sanders, everyone in the library seeing them to-

gether. Maybe he'd walk her all the way back to the dorm to-night. Maybe tonight she wouldn't have to make the trip alone, feeling lonely and left out, feeling life was passing her by. No such luck. A couple of jocks were waiting for him at the front desk. Jack Palmer was built like a bull, with belligerent black eyes and a broken nose. Bud Knox had a short red crew cut and sexy brown eyes and a wide, amiable mouth. The three of them were apparently going out catting.

"Thanks a bunch, Nora," Sanders said, squeezing her shoulders. "See you tomorrow night."

He gave her another crumpled five-dollar bill. Bud Knox grinned. "What'd-ja do to earn that?" he inquired.

"You'd be surprised, cutie."

All three boys hooted with laughter and tromped out of the library, piling into a red Ford convertible parked in the lot outside. Nora watched the car roar away and walked back to the dorm alone.

Nora helped him with his written report on Ulysses S. Grant the next week and, chump that she was, said she'd type it up for him. Dick was thrilled and said she was a sweetheart, any favor he could ever do for her, just ask. Nora had a zinger on the tip of her tongue but decided not to blurt it out. Didn't want to scare the fellow. He hadn't found a replacement for Helen yet, and he was probably growing restless and, who knew, might even give her a second look if he got horny enough. Nora gathered up her notebook and papers and told him she would type up his report tomorrow afternoon and bring it to him when they met at their regular time. Dick frowned, looking pained.

"Geez, tomorrow's Thursday, isn't it? I can't make it tomorrow night. I promised the coach I'd watch some basketball film with him, check out the high school talent—and I've gotta have the report first thing Friday. What're we gonna do?"

"Slit our wrists?" she suggested.

"I've got practice tomorrow afternoon, one till four. I don't suppose it would be possible for you to bring it over to my place, would it? Around four-thirty? I hate to ask, but—"

"No problem," Nora said. "Where do you flop?"

"Hunh?"

"Where do you live?"

"Oh, me and Bud and Jack—you met 'em, remember?—we've got a place a couple of blocks off campus. On Chelsea. It's a

huge old Victorian house, painted gray, with lots of white gingerbread trim—it's located right behind the Safeway. The place
is a shambles. We just have the bottom floor. A married couple
rents upstairs.''

"I'll be there at four-thirty, report in hand.''

"Sure you don't mind? I feel like an utter heel, puttin' you
to all this trouble.''

"No trouble at all.''

"Tell you what, you bring the report over and I'll make you
one of my specialties.''

"You've got a specialty?''

"You're gonna love it,'' he promised.

Nora cut all her classes on Thursday. Who needed the hassle?
She wouldn't have been able to concentrate anyway. She lovingly
typed up Sanders's report and placed it in a neat manila folder,
and then she took a long, luxurious bath and washed her hair
and dried it and spent an hour and a half trying to do something
clever with it and finally said "Shit!" and let it curl naturally.
She carefully did her nails. Would Jungle Red nail polish be a
bit too flashy? Hell, why not go whole hog? Carol came back
from her classes and noticed the nail polish and arched one
eyebrow. Nora shot her the finger. She spent another hour doing
her face. Just a little eye shadow, soft brown with a suggestion
of violet, and lipstick, not much, just a touch to make her lips
look pinker. She spent thirty minutes trying to give herself provocative cheekbones with shadow and rouge, and the result was
comical. She scrubbed the gook off in disgust. Makeup wasn't
a big thing in her life. She rarely used it.

Panties. Bra. Garter belt. Hose. Beige silk slip. High-heeled
sandals, dark-yellow leather, with ankle straps. Carol watched
with a caustic expression as she donned this attire, and her eyebrow shot up again when Nora took out the new dress. It was
of thin, fine faille, pale lemon yellow with gold-and-orange
splotches. It had a halter top, a fitted waist, a gathered skirt that
ended in a multilevel handkerchief-point hemline. Seventy-eight
bucks at the swankiest department store in town. Nora put it on,
hooked it up in back and then looked at herself in the mirror
with critical eyes.

"Going to a party?" Carol inquired.

"Shut up. Jesus, I look exactly like Donna Reed in *From Here*

to Eternity, ready to take on all comers. I should never have put on the nail polish.''

''Actually, you look quite sweet.''

''One more crack out of you, bitch, and you'll be minus several teeth.''

Nora opened the bottle of Chanel Number 5 and dabbed it on lavishly at various strategic spots. She sighed then, put the bottle down, looked nervous and worried, looked frightened and, finally, looked resigned. She grimaced, picked up her small yellow leather purse and the manila folder and moved to the door, turning for one final shot.

''I'm off, sweetie. Wish me luck. If I come back here still a virgin it'll be over his dead body.''

Were people staring at her as she walked across campus? Were they snickering? Screw 'em all. Damn, how did women walk on these bloody high heels? Felt like she was on stilts. She crossed the street and headed toward Chelsea, self-conscious as hell, as nervous as she'd ever been in her life, her stomach flipping and flopping and her pulses racing like mad. You're out of your everlovin' mind, she told herself. She felt like a fool. She felt like a clown. She started to turn back several times but forged on ahead with grim determination. There was the Safeway on the corner of LaMarr. Special today. Roast Beef, 49¢ a pound. We Give Green Stamps. She moved past the side of the store and there stood the Victorian monstrosity on the corner of Chelsea and Blake. Jesus! It looked like something out of Charles Addams. The gray paint was flaking badly. The gingerbread trim was tattered. She half expected bats to swoop down and attack as she stepped onto the front porch.

Here goes, kid. Knockers up. Remember the Maine. Smile.

She rang the doorbell. She waited. She rang it again. There was a loud, banging noise inside and then the sound of footsteps. He opened the door. He was wearing tennis shoes without socks and the blue sateen shorts and old gray sweatshirt with sleeves cut out he had been wearing her first day on campus, when she saw him jogging. The sweatshirt was eight months older and much the worse for wear. The blue sateen shorts had a shiny sheen. He smelled potently of sweat. Nora smiled brightly. Dick looked at her with some dismay.

''You goin' to a party later on?'' he asked.

"I thought we were gonna have a party of our own," she replied.

He grinned. I know. Don't say it. You're a gas.

"Come on in," he said. "Got the report?"

"It's right here in my hot little hands."

"I sure appreciate this, kid."

"Kid" again. Couldn't he see she was a provocative, alluring woman? Nora followed him into a large, airy foyer littered with cardboard boxes, abandoned sports equipment and a disconnected jukebox covered with dust, and then he led her into a spacious, high-ceilinged room that, at one time, had obviously been the parlor. The floor was bare. Faded beige shades hung at the windows. Barbells and a contraption that looked like some kind of rack stood in one corner. A bench press? Something like that. There was a narrow bed with crisp sheets, no spread, a couple of wooden chairs, a desk, a shelf crowded with bronze sport trophies, a stolen STOP sign, a pair of boxing gloves. An untidy stack of *Fitness and Health* magazines sat on the desk. Charming. The place had a real ambience.

"This is my room," Dick explained. "Jack and Bud live in back. They're out this afternoon."

"How convenient," Nora said.

"It's not much, but it beats stayin' at the dorm."

Dick took the report from her and put it on the desk and picked up a green plastic dish filled with something that looked like brown pellets.

"Want some soybeans?" he asked.

"No, thanks. I'm on a diet."

"They're real good for you, fulla protein and stuff. Give you lots of energy."

"You have some." Nora indicated the barbells. "You lift weights?"

"Yeah. Every day. I was workin' out when you rang the doorbell. If he's gonna be any good, a fellow has to keep in shape."

"I hear you're real good, big fellow."

Mae West couldn't have delivered the line better. Dick seemed a bit puzzled, and then he decided she was being a gas again and grinned broadly. Nora sighed. Maybe she should do card tricks. In truth, she was scared out of her wits and wasn't at all sure her knees weren't knocking together. She couldn't keep her eyes off those legs, those broad shoulders, and that sweaty smell

was like some heady aphrodisiac. Sitting across the table from him at the library was one thing. Being here in his room with him, he half naked, the bed only a few feet away, was something else altogether. How many girls had he banged on that bed?

"Sure you don't want any soybeans?" he said.

"Positive."

Dick set the bowl down. He looked slightly ill at ease, as though he expected her to leave, and then he slapped his thigh and began to nod his head, realization dawning.

"Oh, yeah. I almost forgot. I promised to give you one of my specialties, didn't I?"

"I thought you'd never get around to it."

"Hold on. I'll be right back."

He left the room and Nora took a deep breath. *Here's your chance to make a quick getaway, kid. Run for your life. So you're still a virgin? So what? No need rushing things. Hate to break it to you this way, kid, but you're not cut out to be a femme fatale. Get your ass* out *of here while you still have a chance.* Her feet seemed rooted to the floor. She couldn't move. She heard a strange, whirring noise coming from a kitchen in back of the house. *He's making me a drink. He's going to bring me a Hurricane or a Grasshopper or something lethal like that. Maybe it'll help.* Dick came padding down the hallway and came into the room looking very pleased with himself and carrying two vanilla milkshakes. At least that's what they looked like. Nora smiled a bright smile.

"Here we go," he said.

"It looks delicious."

He handed her one of the drinks. She accepted it with trembling hand.

"Bottoms up," he said.

"What a lovely idea."

It went right over his head. He turned his glass up and drank with great relish. Nora took a tentative sip of hers and gagged. *Jesus! It tasted just like chalk dust!* Dick finished his and told her it was liquid protein, filled with wheat germ and lots of good stuff like that. Nora said it sounded fascinating but she really was on a diet and suggested he drink hers too, as he obviously needed a lot of protein to keep that body looking so fit and gorgeous. Dick accepted with alacrity and drank it down and set the glasses aside, looking at her with bemused green-brown eyes

and a furrowed brow, as though trying to solve some particularly difficult problem.

"You're a funny girl," he said.

"I know. A regular riot."

"That dress you're wearin'—you put it on for me, didn't-ja?"

"Of course not. I just grabbed the first thing I saw in the closet."

"You *do* look kinda nifty."

"I love your choice of words."

"All those cracks you're always makin'—if I didn't know better, I'd almost believe you wanted to get laid."

"Believe. Believe."

"Geez—are you serious?"

Nora didn't say anything. She couldn't. Her knees were really beginning to shake now. She swallowed. She just wanted out of here. His eyes seemed to darken, gleaming with an entirely new interest, and his lips slowly curled into another grin, a different kind of grin this time, not warm and friendly but wicked, definitely wicked, and—Jesus!—something was stirring in his shorts. He padded slowly toward her and Nora thought she would scream as his big hands reached out and took hold of her shoulders and began to knead her flesh. This was what she wanted, sure, she'd fantasized about it, but now that it was actually happening it was frightening as hell.

"You really are a cute little thing," he murmured. "I guess I was so involved with Helen I never really noticed just how cute you are. You wanna get laid, I'm just the guy you're lookin' for."

He was backing her toward the bed. Nora giggled nervously.

"We—uh—we needn't be in such a big hurry," she protested.

"No time like the present, babe."

He gave her a shove. She tumbled onto the bed. It was as hard as a rock. She fell back, banging her head on a pillow as hard as the mattress. She knew a girl was supposed to smile provocatively at this point and writhe around a lot, just like Rita Hayworth, but she could only stare in stunned horror as he pulled down his shorts. So *that* was what it looked like? Not a pretty sight! It was all swollen, pointing right at her, throbbing. Dick leaned over and whipped up her skirt and slip and caught hold of her panties and jerked them down and then he lunged, falling on top of her, knocking the breath right out of her. Jesus! He

must weigh at least a ton! He was crushing her to death. Her skirt was up over her face, and Nora struggled blindly and finally managed to get it down to her chin and he slammed his mouth over hers, smothering her cry of protest, and she felt it touching her stomach and then he arched his buttocks up and reached his hand down to adjust things and then he crammed it right in.

Holy shit! She struggled furiously but that only spurred him on, made him more excited. It was hot and hard, thrusting deeper and deeper, tearing her apart. Nora tried to catch hold of his hair and pull his head back but his crew cut was too short so she caught hold of his ears and tugged and he thought that was some kind of game so he thrust even harder, his weight squashing her against the hard mattress, the springs beneath creaking loudly with a crazy rhythm, and then she felt it tearing, ripping apart. The agony! She thought she was going to die right there under him. The pain seared and scalded and then, crazy, crazy, it began to melt into pleasure and she felt a tingling glow begin to spread, making her toes curl, making her wild, and she lifted her hips, really beginning to feel it now, and then he gave a mighty grunt and moaned and fell limp, crushing her flat with his full weight and leaving her suspended up there on a ledge. He moaned again and finally rolled off her, his chest heaving. He sighed deeply and after a few moments got up and padded to the bathroom.

Nora had managed to adjust her clothing and gain some semblance of control by the time he came back into the room.

"Geez," he said, "I didn't know you were still a virgin."

"A virgin? Me? That was all an act. It drives the boys wild. I carry a little pellet of red ink around just to give it verisimilitude."

"Yeah?" He actually believed her.

"Sure," she said frostily.

"Well—uh—it was great. Look, I gotta hustle or I'll be late and Coach will have a fit. I'll just get my clothes and stuff out of the closet and take everything to Bud's room, shower and dress there."

"Peachy."

"You go on and use this bathroom in here, clean up, whatever, take all the time you need. I'll see you around. Really don't think we need to keep studying at the library anymore, do you?"

"You seem to be doing fine now."

Dick took his clothes out of the closet and started toward the door. Nora was sitting on the edge of the bed.

"One more thing," she said.

He turned, his mind on his appointment now, the quick, energetic workout almost forgotten.

"You *did* use something, didn't you?"

"Oh—that. Yeah. I slipped it on while you were getting your skirts out of your eyes. I always keep a spare package under the edge of the mattress."

"Real thoughtful of you," she said.

"Catch you later, babe."

Don't hold your breath, Buster.

Nora put on a bright, cocky facade for Carol, but acting wasn't Nora's forte and Carol could see something had gone wrong, and she was much too tactful to ask questions. Nora's visit to Dick Sanders's place that afternoon was never mentioned, might never have happened. A few days later Dick took up with a tittering blonde freshman with wet red lips and wide blue eyes, and the next afternoon as Nora was on her way back to the dorm Bud Knox moved onto the walk in front of her, blocking her passage. He smiled a sly, knowing smile and told her they had a great flick at the Eastside Drive-In, just outside of town, and he'd be pleased as punch if she'd consider going to see it with him that night. Nora studied him in silence for several long moments, taking in the short red crew cut and the sexy brown eyes, the wide, amiable mouth and lean, well-muscled body. If at first you don't succeed, try, try again. You no longer have anything to lose.

"Pick me up at eight," she said.

Nora was going to be very, very popular.

Can I do it? Do I have enough courage? Julie nervously prepared lunch, mincing boiled eggs and sweet pickles for the tuna salad, and her hand was shaking as she opened the refrigerator to take out the mayonnaise. *Whatever possessed me to have that photograph taken, fill out that form and send them in? Just as though I thought I had a chance. Mr. Compton asked me to, yes, said he thought I would make a marvelous Charlotte Corday, but . . . I can't do it. I can't go there this afternoon and read for Eric Berne, the great Eric Berne. This isn't a school play. This is a movie, a real movie!* Julie dumped the eggs and pickles into the bowl of tuna fish, added mayonnaise, mixed it all together with a fork. Her hand was still shaking. *I'm too timid and frightened to try out for Laura in* The Glass Menagerie, *but at three-thirty this afternoon I'm scheduled to read for the legendary Eric Berne for the leading role in his multi-million-dollar production of* Daughter of France.

The play, by Terrence Ogilvy, had been a modest success in his native England and, on Broadway, had been the critical success of 1952, if hardly a box office smash. Fionella Reed, the noted British actress, had received the Tony for her portrayal of Charlotte Corday, the convent-bred French girl who, during the height of the Revolution, gained admission to the tyrant Marat's room under false pretenses, stabbed him to death in his bath and

was subsequently guillotined. Twentieth Century-Fox had purchased the film rights amidst a veritable blitz of publicity. Ogilvy was flown over to write the screenplay and the studio bosses deemed it too stagey and gave it to Nunnally Johnson to "open up" and Johnson's script was unsatisfactory, too, and it was given to a writer who specialized in war films and, with the collaboration of a writer who had worked on an early version of *The Robe*, a "filmable" script was finally produced, the intimate stage drama transformed into a sweeping historical epic to be filmed in Technicolor and Cinemascope. Jean Simmons was announced for the part of Charlotte Corday, then Leslie Caron, then some young French actress named Brigitte Bardot who had made only a few minor films, none of which had been released in America. Like so many before it, the project languished, was repeatedly taken up and put aside, and then Eric Berne took it over and vowed it was going to be the ultimate film of his career, his *Gone With the Wind*.

Julie had read all about it in the columns. Though she would blush to admit it, she never missed Louella Parsons's column, Hedda's either, and sometimes she went to the college library and surreptitiously read *Variety*. All of America knew about Berne's Search For Corday. It had received a phenomenal amount of publicity, almost as much as the search for Scarlett two decades before. He didn't want Simmons for the part, didn't want Caron, didn't want a young French actress who couldn't speak a word of English. He wanted an American girl, someone fresh, someone new, a total unknown who would be identified forever after as Berne's Corday. Berne had been traveling all over the country for the past six months, searching for his Corday with great fanfare, accompanied by a fleet of reporters and photographers. *Life* had done a feature on the search. Movietone had done a news segment. Louella and Hedda gushed about it. Berne had gone on the Jack Paar show, talking about his ideal Charlotte, promising to present her on the show ere long. It was the Big News in the entertainment world until the announcement that Grace Kelly would marry Prince Rainier.

Cynics said in print that the whole thing was a gigantic publicity hoax, a gimmick to bolster an ill-conceived project that, if it ever *was* filmed, would undoubtedly be the biggest bomb since Hiroshima. The public wanted Marilyn in a tight fuchsia dress, wanted Brando in T-shirt and jeans, wanted Cooper riding

the range with stoic expression, six-shooter at his side. A movie about an obscure French girl who stabs a guy to death in his bathtub? Ticket-buyers would stay away in droves. The same cynics were quick to point out that the temperamental and surly Berne was hardly the consummate film artist. Sure, he had directed that classic mystery film in the forties, but its success was due to its haunting, melodic theme song and the ethereal beauty of its leading lady. Most of his films were glossy garbage, many of them box office duds, and he had never repeated the success of *Megan*. Now he was going to make a huge Cinemascope epic about an eighteenth-century French chick who murders a tyrant and gets her head lopped off for the trouble, starring an unknown, a ribbon clerk from Chicago, a farm girl from Nebraska. Good luck, Eric. The search had been going on for far too long, he was milking it now, and the Kelly-Rainier wedding had easily eclipsed it. The public was beginning to lose interest, was beginning to be as cynical as his critics. When all was said and done Jean Simmons would probably play the part. They were going to invest all that money in an unknown?

Despite his critics, despite the growing lack of interest by both the public and the news media, German-born Berne continued to trudge across the country, and now he was right here at Claymore. Over seventy girls had applied to read for him, girls from all over Indiana, not just students, and Berne had set up a tight schedule in order to accommodate them in two days. Berne was a personal friend of Compton's, staying with Compton and his wife rather than stopping at a hotel, and the readings were being held at the little theater on campus where, two months ago, Dee Patrick had given a superb performance as Laura in *The Glass Menagerie*. Dee had read for Berne yesterday, and Julie was scheduled to read at three-thirty this afternoon, Carol at four. I can't go through with it, Julie told herself, adding a few spices to the tuna salad. It's absolute madness. I'll get up there and . . . and I won't even be able to open my mouth. Madness. Why would they even consider me for Corday when there are so many beautiful girls like Carol and so many genuinely talented girls like Dee to choose from?

Julie had read the original play and had been moved to tears, particularly by Charlotte's final speech to her fellow Frenchmen before she steps up onto the scaffold to be guillotined. She *felt* the part, felt the young woman's strength, compassion and no-

bility, her love for her country and her willingness to sacrifice her own life in order to save that country more grief. When she was reading the play, Julie had become Corday, and she knew— yes, deep down inside, she *knew*—she could play it. Compton thought so, too. He had asked her to send in her application to read for Berne, had sent her to a photographer he knew to have a flattering picture taken. The photographer was a genius. He had carefully applied makeup to her face first, covering the blemishes, and then he had spent almost an hour arranging lights. The results were incredible. Julie could hardly believe that soulful, sensitive, attractive girl in the photograph was actually her. And he hadn't charged her a penny, said he was doing it as a favor to Compton. That remarkable photograph had been sent off along with her application and this afternoon she was supposed to show up at the theater and read for Eric Berne.

She hadn't told Doug anything about it, of course. There was no need to antagonize him. There were only three days of classes left now and final exams were upon them. Doug had taken two, had three left, and he was literally studying night and day. There was no need for him to know about it. Bobbie, who worked at the Silver Bell on Sundays, had agreed to work for her today— Julie would work for Bobbie next Sunday—so she had the entire day off. It wasn't like trying out for the spring play, she told herself. That had been impossible. There had been a strong chance she would actually get the part of Laura, and she couldn't have taken off work for rehearsals. She hadn't a prayer to win the role of Corday, but . . . but if by some amazing fluke she did, there would be a great deal of money and she could put Doug through the next two years of law school with ease, and they could move to a nicer place. She'd come back here after the movie was completed, of course, and Doug would be so very proud of her and . . . Dream on, Julie, she thought wryly. You've been spending too much time with Nora, listening to all that nonsensical talk about getting the slipper. Things like that happen only in the movies. They don't happen to girls like me.

Doug liked his sandwich bread lightly toasted. She put two slices into the toaster and pushed the lever down. Doug was upstairs on the rooftop now, wearing bathing suit and T-shirt, stretched out on a rubber pad, reading his text. May had been unusually warm, and now, in its last week, it was summertime and the flat was almost unbearable, like an oven. Julie didn't

mind it so much, she had learned to ignore the heat, but Doug couldn't stand it. He complained constantly, was touchy and irritable, lashed out at her sometimes without the least cause. He was studying so very hard, of course, and he *was* sensitive to the heat. Perhaps, if her tips were generous enough, she would be able to buy a small window unit air conditioner before it got much hotter. Maybe Mr. Graffa would allow her to work longer hours this summer. There was no reason why she couldn't as Mr. Compton wouldn't be conducting classes during the summer. Julie wished he were. She hated to think of going for three long months without that glorious stimulation, that joy.

Little by little, under Compton's careful guidance, she had lost much of her shyness in class, had begun to participate far more than she had earlier. Only last week she had done a scene with Jim Burke, he playing a hoodlum, she playing a gum-chewing streetwalker, and when it was over the whole class had burst into wildly enthusiastic applause and Carol had hugged her tightly and Jim had scratched the side of his head and peered into the distance and mumbled, "Hey, Chick, you're somethin' else, ya know, outta sight." It was still painful, she was still petrified with fear at first, but it was so stimulating, so exciting that she didn't mind nearly as much as she had. Far from resenting her, the other students seemed actually to be rooting for her, seemed to be proud of her progress. She had promised Compton that she would try out for the next play—they were doing *Summer and Smoke* in the fall—and if she got a part she would simply make some kind of arrangements with Mr. Graffa or whoever she happened to be working for then. Doug wouldn't like her doing it, he'd raise holy hell, in fact, but she'd worry about that when and if the time came. Acting was . . . it was the only thing she had that was *hers*. Everything else she did for him.

Julie took the toast out of the toaster and made his sandwich and put it on a blue plate and sliced it into two neat triangular halves. She took down the potato chips and poured them into a bowl and put the bowl onto the table along with the sandwich. Doug liked things neat when he ate, and she tried to make each meal, however humble, a small ceremony. One day they'd have lovely china and real silverware and she'd be able to serve something besides bologna and tuna fish sandwiches and canned soup. Folding a paper napkin, placing it beside the plate, Julie left the

flat and entered the main building and started up the flights of stairs leading to the rooftop. She hoped Doug had remembered to take his suntan lotion. She'd hate for him to get sunburned. Opening the door, she stepped out onto the rooftop, momentarily blinded by rays of brilliant sunlight.

"—might be fun," a low feminine voice said.

"Yeah, it might at that."

Julie heard laughter then, tinkling, feminine laughter, then Doug's husky chuckle. Shielding her eyes against the sun, she peered across the roof, and there was Doug in his old red swim trunks and a white T-shirt, sitting up, arms curled around his knees, grinning at a girl in short white shorts and a yellow halter top. She had long, lovely auburn hair and deep-blue eyes and a beautiful body. Julie recognized her immediately. She was Anne Hendricks, a twenty-two-year-old student who was divorced but still living in the third-floor apartment she had shared with her husband. Anne said something to Doug and he chuckled again and then looked up and saw Julie and frowned. Julie moved closer, her step hesitant.

"You want something?" he asked gruffly.

"I—"

Her throat was tight. Why should she be embarrassed? Why should she be ill at ease? She tried to speak, but the words remained frozen in her throat as Doug glared up at her, his eyes sullen behind the horn-rims. Anne Hendricks smiled an enigmatic smile, amused, and, in one lithe, graceful movement, rose to her feet, her sleek auburn hair swaying. "See you later," she told Doug, and then she moved past Julie with that enigmatic smile still playing on her lips. Her body glistened with a light film of perspiration, and Julie could smell her perfume. Anne Hendricks was a glorious female animal, glowing with health and sensual allure so potent it was almost tangible. How long had she been up here with Doug? What had they been talking about? The door closed as Anne left the roof, and Julie still couldn't find her voice. Doug scowled and picked up the law book he had abandoned beside the rubber mat.

"Well?" he demanded.

"I—I just came up to tell you lunch is ready," Julie said.

She turned then and left the rooftop and went back down the long flights of stairs and back to the flat, and she stood in the kitchen, staring at the refrigerator without seeing it. She had a

strange, hollow feeling inside, in the pit of her stomach, and her throat felt tight. Was this jealousy? Julie had never experienced anything like it before, but there had never been a reason before. Doug spent a great deal of time alone while she was working, yes, and many, many nights he stayed late at the law library, studying, but she had never . . . never given it a thought. He was a handsome man and on the few occasions when they were out together she noticed girls looking at him, but Doug wasn't . . . he wasn't interested in that. He wasn't interested in anything but making the best grades, being the top man in his class. Of late he hadn't even made love to her that often, and when he did it was almost like an afterthought. Immersed in his studies, he ignored her much of the time, moody and irritable, lashing out at her when she did something wrong or something failed to suit him.

She heard him entering the flat. He came into the kitchen, his bare feet slapping on the worn linoleum. He pulled out his chair, sat down, gave an exasperated sigh. Julie turned around, trying to put the mutinous thoughts out of her mind. His T-shirt was damp with sweat, and his hair was damp, too, a spray of errant locks tumbling across his brow.

"Where's my milk?" he asked sullenly.

"I—Doug, I'm sorry, I forgot to buy any yesterday."

"Goddammit! Can't you remember anything?"

"I could make some iced tea," she said.

"I don't want tea. You know I like a glass of milk with my sandwich. Is that too goddamned much to ask? I bust my buns studying night and day, trying to make the grade, and you can't even remember to buy groceries!"

"I work, too," she reminded him. "It isn't always convenient to buy groceries before work, and the stores are closed when I get off. If—if you're not satisfied, I—I suggest you do the grocery shopping yourself. You have as much time as I do."

Doug looked up at her, his dark eyes full of anger. Julie could hardly believe she had been so bold.

"What is this?" he asked slowly.

"I—I'm not a slave, Doug. I'm a wife."

"Yeah? And what's that supposed to mean?"

"I—I do everything I can to make it easy for you, to make you comfortable and keep things running smoothly, but—but—"

"But?" he prodded.

"I have feelings, too," she said.

"Yeah, sure, you have all kinds of feelings and you express them freely in that fucking drama class. You're so goddamned busy wasting your time with that crap you can't buy groceries, can't get the laundry done on time. You may be a sensitive soul in drama class, but don't try any of that shit with me. I'm liable to slap you silly."

Julie didn't answer. She could feel the tears welling, but she refused to shed them. She loved him so much, and sometimes . . . sometimes he was so very unlovable. He had slapped her in the past, on more than one occasion, but he was always remorseful afterwards, always apologized. Doug was brilliant and he was under a great deal of pressure and he was moody by nature. She tried to understand, tried to make excuses for him, but sometimes it was difficult. Sometimes she felt . . . Julie closed her eyes, refusing to look too deeply, afraid of what she might see.

"You've changed, Julie," he told her.

"I'm no longer fifteen years old," she said.

"That goddamned drama class, it's changed you, given you ideas. Those two girls—that Carol and that little Jew—they're not a good influence."

"I have a right to friends, Doug."

"You've got a husband. That should be enough."

I have a husband who rarely speaks to me in a civil voice, who rarely even acknowledges my existence. She longed to say these words aloud, but there wasn't any point in arguing with him, not when he was in one of these moods. When exams were over, when he was able to relax a little, things would be better and they would be close again. She believed that. She had to believe it. The alternative was altogether too frightening. Doug finished his sandwich and stood up, brushing the errant locks from his brow.

"Look," he said, "about Anne Hendricks—nothing was going on."

"No?"

"I was up on the roof, studying, and Anne came out and sat down beside me, started talking. What was I supposed to do, shove her off the roof? I'm fully aware of her reputation—think

I don't know why her husband divorced her? You have nothing to worry about on that score."

"I'm not worried, Doug."

"I'm going back up now," he said. "Some iced tea might be nice after all. You can bring me up a glass before you leave for work."

"Take your suntan lotion. I don't want you to get burned."

"Always thinking of me," he said, his good humor restored. "What would I do without you, hon?"

"I really don't know, Doug."

She didn't take the tea up to him. She took a bath and dressed carefully in her best brown skirt and a neat white cotton blouse, fastening a narrow red leather belt around her slender waist. She brushed her silvery-brown hair until it gleamed and, feeling bold, applied a light coat of pink lipstick to her lips. Julie studied herself critically in the mirror. If only her complexion weren't so bad. If only she were tall and blonde and stunning, like Carol, or bright and witty and vivacious, like Nora. She had no illusions about herself, none whatsoever. She knew she was drab, knew she was meek and unassertive as well, but . . . but there was so much beauty inside, longing for release. She wasn't ready to give up her dream, not just yet. It might be a complete waste of time, but she was going to read for Eric Berne, and she was going to give it everything she had.

Determined, Julie left the flat and started toward campus, thinking about Charlotte's last speech and how she would interpret it. Charlotte wouldn't be defiant, wouldn't declaim. She wouldn't be resigned, wouldn't cry. She would be calm, and she would speak in a quiet, level voice, addressing the assembled crowd as she might address a single friend. Her voice might tremble a bit toward the end of the speech and she might smile a faint, sad smile, but her nobility must be *felt*, not stressed by gesture or inflection. Julie crossed the street and strolled across the lawn toward the theater, completely immersed in thought.

"Thank God!" Carol exclaimed, hurrying over to join her.

"Oh—oh, Carol. I didn't see you."

"I'm so glad I saw *you*. I couldn't possibly walk into the theater alone. I'm a nervous wreck."

"I guess all of us are nervous."

"At least you have a chance. You're a superlative actress. I

don't know why I even signed up to read. Compton didn't give me any encouragement, I can assure you.''

"You'll be wonderful, Carol.''

"I'll be wretched. I've gone over the speech again and again, trying out various interpretations. Eric Berne is going to die laughing when I march out there and start ranting.''

"Nonsense.''

"They—they say he's very testy, say he's got a terrible temper, yelling at actors, bullying them dreadfully. He'll probably come after me brandishing a butcher knife. Do—do I look all right?''

"You look lovely, Carol.''

That was an understatement, Julie thought. Carol was wearing a pink linen shift, simple and exquisite, with matching pink high heels. Her dark-gold hair was neatly brushed, falling in a gleaming cascade. She looked absolutely breathtaking, tall and elegant, exuding a cool poise she was apparently far from feeling. Julie glanced down at her own scuffed brown shoes and felt shabby in comparison, but she felt no resentment. Carol was her friend, was as insecure as Julie herself in many ways and really had no idea just how beautiful she was. Carol took her hand now, squeezing it tightly as they approached the theater.

"Berne has his assistant and his secretary with him,'' Carol said, "and a whole fleet of reporters—there's someone from *Life*, someone from *Coronet*, half a dozen photographers. I talked to Dee last night and, Julie, they have a *movie* camera, like the ones they use for newsreels.''

Julie could feel her nerves grow taut, felt that fluttering sensation in her stomach. Her throat felt tight. Her mouth felt dry. Had Carol not been holding her hand so tightly, she would have turned and fled. That strong resolve she had felt earlier had completely evaporated now, and she experienced something very like stark terror. She didn't show it, of course. On the surface she was as calm as could be.

"There are all sorts of rumors afloat,'' Carol continued. "Dee heard one of the girls who read yesterday say *she* had heard Berne's assistant talking to some official from New York. The girl had stepped out into the lobby to get a drink of water and the two men were standing nearby, she couldn't help hearing them. Anyway, Berne's assistant was telling this other man that word had come down from the studio that Berne was to find his

Corday im*med*iately or they intended to abandon the whole project. That's why he brought so many reporters and photographers to Claymore with him, Dee said.''

They were in front of the theater now. Carol squeezed her hand so tightly that Julie winced. They stood there for a moment, both petrified, and then Carol sighed and let go of Julie's hand.

"I—I guess we might as well go in," she said.

"We might as well," Julie replied.

"I'm terrified."

"So am I," Julie admitted.

"I know just how the early Christians felt when they went out to face the lions. Shall—shall we go in?"

Carol looked pale. Julie managed a reassuring smile, and they went on into the lobby. A group of bored-looking reporters were milling around restlessly, all of them a bit unkempt, most of them smoking furiously, several with cameras slung around their necks. They weren't local newspeople, Julie sensed that immediately. All had the hard, cynical appearance of big-city veterans, like extras from *The Front Page*. None of them paid the slightest attention as she and Carol came in. A tall, thin woman in a brown suit approached them, looking every bit as bored as the reporters. Her sleek black hair was pulled back into a tight bun. Her thin lips were painted red. Her manner was crisp and officious, dark eyes glittering as she stared at them. Julie recognized her from a newspaper photograph. She was Lelia Standish, Eric Berne's private secretary and, according to all reports, a strong power behind the throne.

"You've come to read for Mr. Berne?" she snapped.

Julie nodded. Carol turned a shade paler.

"Names?" the woman demanded.

"I'm Julie Hammond. This is Carol Martin."

The woman gave them a sharp, suspicious look and then marched briskly over to a desk and picked up a clipboard and consulted it.

"Julie Hammond," she said, "three-thirty. Carol Martin, four. You know the procedure? You'll wait in the designated room until Ron comes to fetch you and then you will go onstage and read for Mr. Berne and answer any questions he might have and then you will *leave the theater* at once. We can't have all

you girls cluttering up the place, distracting Mr. Berne. Have you got that?''

Julie nodded again. Lelia Standish strongly resembled Gale Sondergaard and acted as though she were playing a scene from *The Spider Woman*. She glowered at them for a moment or so more, and then she signaled to a young man who was leaning against the wall, shoulders hunched, arms folded across his chest. He wore a sleeveless brown-and-white striped jersey and snug tan denims and a wide leather belt. He sauntered over to them, affable, relaxed, as though he found this all a rather amusing lark. Julie had seen his picture in the *Life* article. He was Ron Majors, Berne's assistant and right-hand man. As he came nearer, she saw that he wasn't nearly as young as he had seemed at first. His tan, attractive face was a bit weathered, tiny lines etched about his mouth and eyes. The eyes were a clear blue, his light-brown hair sun-streaked and tousled. He must be at least thirty-five and, though still lean and muscular, looked rather like a Beach Boy going to seed.

"Two more aspiring stars?" he asked.

"Two more," Standish said wearily.

"Relax, girls," Majors told them, "it'll all be over with before you know what hit you."

Carol smiled nervously, still in a state of shock, but Julie felt a curious calm come over her. These were real Hollywood people. They had actually worked with Eric Berne on film locations all over the world. Lelia Standish helped him with budgeting, had a strong voice in casting, was his irreplaceable aide according to the papers, and the same was true of Ron Majors. Julie remembered seeing in Louella's column that Majors had been a stunt double for Tab Hunter before he went to work for Berne. They were awesome figures, both of them, and this was a dream, a nightmare. It wasn't really happening at all. It was a dream, and she would wake up any minute now and be in her own bed and the panic would evaporate and she wouldn't have to go out onto an empty stage and read for the great Hollywood director. She wasn't calm. Julie realized that. She was totally numb instead.

Carol seemed to be in even worse shape—cool self-confident Carol who never showed the least sign of nerves in class. She took Julie's hand again, and Julie managed another reassuring smile as Ron Majors led them out of the lobby and down a long,

dark hallway to the backstage area. She could hear voices on-stage as he led them past stacks of painted flats and into a large, windowless room that had been cleared and converted into a waiting room for the occasion. A chubby brunette in a lime-green frock sat on one of the metal folding chairs, nervously tugging at the handkerchief in her lap. She had lovely brown eyes and a plump pink mouth and seemed on the verge of tears, looking up in terror as they entered the room. A coffee table was littered with magazines and overflowing ashtrays and a col-lection of half-empty coffee cups.

"This is Myrtle," Ron told them. "Myrtle came all the way from Marysville on a bus to be with us today."

"Is—is it time yet?" Myrtle asked nervously.

"Just a few more minutes, sweetheart."

He smiled his affable smile and left, and Myrtle tried valiantly to control her trembling. Poor darling, Julie thought, forgetting her own fear. She tried her best to draw the girl out, chatting pleasantly, asking her questions, but it was wasted effort. Ron returned fifteen minutes later and took Myrtle away, and Carol said she would kill for a cigarette even though she didn't smoke. After a few more minutes Ron came back again and asked if either of them would like some coffee. They both declined. He lingered, leaning against the wall, arms folded across his chest again the better to display his bronzed biceps. His clear blue eyes studied them amiably.

"There's nothing to be worried about," he assured them. "Eric's a sweetheart. Don't believe any of that nonsense you read in the papers. He's one of the kindest men you'll ever meet, gentle as a lamb. He's been wonderful to the girls, coaxing them patiently, drawing them out. You see his last movie?"

Carol nodded, distracted.

"Remember that scene where Linda Darnell was out in the garden waiting for her lover to return from the war? Eric couldn't get anything out of her, Darnell had a hangover, just stood there like a block of wood through a good twenty takes. Did Eric scream? Did Eric bully her? No. Know what he did? He had a violinist brought in. The guy starts playing this sad, sad love song, and the next thing you know Darnell's looking all wistful and forlorn and she's fighting back the tears. Man's a genius."

Neither girl spoke. Majors was determined to put them at ease.

"Remember the scene where she left her car out in front of the restaurant? Remember the guy who comes and parks it for her? That was me. I filled in at the last minute. Used to do bit parts and stunt work myself before I started working for Eric, and I can tell you from my own personal experience—the man's the greatest."

"I—I think I will take a cup of coffee," Carol said.

"Sure. How about you, Julie?"

Julie shook her head. Ron brought Carol her coffee and then glanced at his watch.

"Well—you girls hang in there. I'll be back as soon as the Master's finished with Myrtle."

"He's nice," Julie said after Ron had left.

"I suppose. I was too nervous to notice."

"Poor Myrtle. She was terrified."

Carol nodded, looking thoughtful. "All that way on a bus, nursing a dream, and—I fear she hasn't a hope."

"I guess we all need our dreams," Julie said quietly, "even if they never come true. Without them life—life would be bleak indeed."

"Hundreds and hundreds of girls all over America reading for Eric Berne and dreaming of the slipper—only to discover it doesn't fit. It—it's sad. What do you do then? What do you do when—when you finally realize it's all a myth, it's never going to happen?"

"You keep dreaming," Julie said.

"You keep deluding yourself, you mean."

"Dreams do come true, Carol. Sometimes they do."

Carol was silent for several moments, gazing into space, examining her own dream, and then she sighed and took a sip of her coffee and set the cup down on the littered table. Julie sat quietly, clasping her hands together in her lap, looking so very young, looking so vulnerable and frightened. Carol felt a rush of affection for her friend. She hoped Eric Berne had the sense to realize how good Julie was, what a superlative actress. It would be so wonderful if one of them, at least, really did get the slipper.

"Good luck, darling," she said. "I'll be rooting for you."

"I'll be rooting for you, too."

They sat in silence then, each immersed in thought as the huge clock on the wall ticked loudly. Half an hour passed. Ron came

to fetch Julie and she had a moment of sheer panic and stood up on trembling legs and followed him out of the room. Was she going to faint? No, no such luck. Ron held her elbow in a loose grip and guided her around a pile of boxes and over a coil of rope and then they were on the stage and Ron left her. Stage center was brightly lighted, the rest in gloom, the area beyond the stage dark as night. Julie could sense people out there in the first two rows and saw soft blurs that might be faces. Two men approached her from the shadows.

Julian Compton moved into the lighted area, wearing his old tweed sport coat and a dull red tie. He smiled warmly. Julie felt a wave of relief.

"Hello, Julie," he said softly. "I'm glad you made it. Julie, I want you to meet Eric Berne. I've told him quite a lot about you."

The famous director joined them, and Julie was startled. He didn't look at all like his photographs. They showed a harsh, sullen man with brutal, Germanic features and a bulky body. Her first impression was one of great gentility. He was a large man, yes, stout, with broad shoulders and a thick, bullish neck, but there was a softness about him. His face was soft, too, rather jowly, the mouth thick, the nose blunt, the large, dark eyes woeful, half shrouded by heavy lids, bags beneath them. His thin brown hair was plastered flat to his skull in an attempt to conceal incipient baldness, and his ears seemed oversized. The director was undeniably homely, but he had incredible presence and personal magnetism that was absolutely mesmerizing. Julie could understand now why all those famous actresses had fallen in love with him.

"Ah, she is frightened," he said. "This is foolish, Julie. Me, I am not a monster. You do not believe those stories they write about me? I do not torture the young actresses. I am the—what do you call it?—I am the pussycat."

His voice was deep and guttural and strangely seductive, and even though he had been living in America for the past twenty years he had a pronounced German accent. Those dark, woeful eyes seemed to bathe her in warmth. He took both of her hands in his, squeezing them gently.

"Eric does not bite you. You are not afraid now, right?"

"I—I'm still a little nervous," she confessed.

"This is natural. This is always the case. Eleanora Duse—I

meet her when I am a young man in Germany, she comes to perform in Berlin—every night, she is terrified before she goes on stage. She trembles. Her knees shake. Duse is the greatest actress of her day, and she is pale and wishes to die each time she must go out and face an audience."

"You—you actually knew Eleanora Duse?"

Berne grinned, and there was a mischievous twinkle in his dark eyes. "I am the handsome young man then. She takes a fancy to me. This is her custom. She pines for D'Annunzio, he breaks her heart, and she seeks consolation in the arms of the handsome young men. I am one of them. Seeing this ugly brute before you now, this is hard for you to believe, no?"

"I can—I can easily believe it, Mr. Berne."

"Ah, Julian, this one—she is after my heart. Maybe we do not bother with the reading. Maybe I just take her home with me now."

He was still holding her hands. He squeezed them again, tightly this time, looking into her eyes, smiling. He released them and patted her shoulder affectionately. The man was indeed mesmerizing, exuding a magic spell that seemed to work miracles. Her fear was completely gone. The nervous tremors had vanished. She wanted only to please him, to give him her very best.

"We are ready now?" he inquired.

Julie nodded and Berne asked if she wanted a script and she shook her head. The men left the stage and Julie could see the two dark forms moving in the darkness, heard a seat squeak as Berne sat down. She closed her eyes, summoning all her strength, and the transformation occurred and Julie Hammond disappeared, reality receded, and she was a young French girl in a drab gray prison dress, hair clipped off, face smeared with dirt, standing before the awesome guillotine with her hands tied behind her back. Maybe they wouldn't be tied, but it felt right. There was a vast crowd watching her, those who had come to jeer and throw rotten vegetables, those who had come to weep, and she knew she had only a few moments, knew she must somehow explain her action to these people and give them something to think about or else her sacrifice would be in vain.

"All right, Julie," a guttural voice growled.

She didn't hear the voice. She heard only the voices of the crowd, and she stood quietly, waiting for them to subside. Fi-

nally there was silence and everyone was waiting, watching her. She spoke in a quiet, level voice that could yet be heard at the furthermost reaches of the crowd. She told them of her years in the convent and all the treacherous things that had been happening to her beloved country while she was saying her prayers, unaware. She told them of leaving, of seeing blood flowing in the streets, heads carried on pikes, terror reigning. She told them of her childhood, the France she had known then, the love and compassion that had prevailed even amidst the hardship. She was only one insignificant girl, it was true, but she knew she had to do something, anything, to prevent this horror from growing even more.

"My friends," she said, and there came the faint tremor in her voice. "I did what I did not because there was hatred in my heart, I did it because there was love there, love for my country, for you, its people. It was not an act of retribution, there was no vengeance involved. It was an act of love."

The smile came then, trembling on her lips, barely visible, and a tear was slipping slowly down her cheek. She looked up at the glittering blade awaiting its victim. She would not let them see the fear that swept over her, would not give in to it. She raised her eyes to heaven and then she looked at her fellow Frenchmen for a final time.

"I leave you now," she whispered. "I leave you with my love and the fervent prayer that you will—will spread it throughout our troubled land."

She bowed her head. The theater was so silent you really could have heard a pin drop. Several moments passed. Julie raised her head, Corday gone now, a timid, apprehensive girl in her place. She peered out into the darkness, waiting, and after another moment there were low voices and a seat squeaked noisily as someone shifted position.

"This is good, Julie," Berne called. "Thank you so much."

Ron came back onstage then and took her elbow and led her into the shadowy wings. He guided her to the long, dark hallway that would take her back to the outer lobby and told her she had been marvelous, told her they all appreciated her auditioning for them. It was over. Ron left her, and Julie started toward the lobby, feeling drained now, grateful that it was behind her. She felt sure Berne hadn't liked her or else he would have questioned her after she finished. She had almost reached the lobby when

she spotted the side door that, she knew, led into the small inner lobby behind the rows of seats. She hesitated, remembering Lelia Standish's cautioning them to leave the theater at once as soon as they finished reading. She would dearly love to slip back in and watch Carol's reading. Why not? What would they do, shoot her? Feeling quite daring, Julie opened the door noiselessly and slipped into the darkened inner lobby and crept across it, taking an aisle seat on the very last row, a shoulder-high curtained partition separating it from the lobby.

The brilliant light bathed the worn floorboards stage center. As her eyes grew accustomed to the darkness, Julie could see the people down front, Compton and Berne and half a dozen others. Berne and Compton were standing, talking in lowered voices. This went on for some time—Julie wished she could hear their words—and then Compton shook his head and the two men turned as Ron led Carol into the light. She looked positively dazzling, tall and slender and serene in her tasteful pink dress, her hair like dark, molten gold. The light emphasized those perfect features, the wide mouth, the glorious cheekbones, the sad, lovely eyes. Eric Berne stood there, staring, and it was several moments before he and Compton went up onstage. She might have been a nervous wreck earlier, but Carol seemed completely composed now, cool and poised as Compton introduced her to the director.

"Ah, she is frightened," Berne said, taking her hands. "This is foolish, Carol. Me, I am not a monster."

He was no longer speaking in a lowered voice and Julie could hear each and every word and she was startled to find they were the identical words he'd used with her. He even told her about Eleanora Duse. He . . . he wasn't sincere at all. Julie had felt an instant rapport with him, had felt he was genuinely interested in her, and she realized now that it had all been an act. He was mesmerizing, yes, and he had pervasive, seductive charm, but it could be turned on and off at will. Maybe it was true what they said about Hollywood people. Maybe they *were* all phony. Eric Berne might well be the monster they said he was, and as she watched him plying Carol with that potent charm, Julie couldn't help but be reminded of the story of the spider and the fly. Won't you step into my parlor, he seemed to be saying, and Carol was every bit as overwhelmed as Julie herself had been.

The men left the stage and took their seats in the front row.

Carol waited patiently for Berne's signal, and when he gave it she took a deep breath and began, and although it wasn't at all the way Julie had done it, it wasn't really bad. Carol declaimed, and there was passion in her voice, and she used many gestures, and, yes, they were rather broad, but Julie was caught up, and she believed. Compton had worked with Carol during these past months, and she had improved a great deal, Julie thought. She might not be the greatest actress ever to step onstage, but . . . she was so radiant, had such an incredible presence that it didn't seem to matter. Carol looked up at the invisible guillotine and trembled, fighting the fear, controlling it, and when she launched into the final part of the speech, her voice was strong and her eyes seemed to glow with a shining nobility. Back ramrod-straight, shoulders back, she faced her countrymen with courage and extended her arms as though to embrace them all.

"I leave you now!" she announced passionately. "I leave you with my love and the fervent prayer that you will spread it throughout our troubled land!"

Berne and two other men began talking in low voices down front while Carol stood there in the light, waiting, frightened now. Several minutes passed, and Julie could see that Carol's hands were trembling. Eric Berne finally stood up and said something to Compton, who also got to his feet.

"This is beautiful, Carol," Berne called. "Ron will take you down to the office your Professor Compton has graciously let me borrow."

"You—you want me to wait?" Carol asked in a pained voice.

"This is so. We have much to talk about."

Carol looked as though she might faint. Ron sauntered out and took her by the elbow, and Carol shook her head, clearly in a state of shock as Ron led her away. Sitting in the darkness in the back row, Julie was horrified to see Compton and Eric Berne heading up the aisle. They would have to pass right by her. She sank down into the seat, terrified they would see her even though it was so dark. The men were talking and, intent on their conversation, moved past without even glancing in her direction. They stopped in the lobby, standing only a few feet away from where Julie was sitting.

"You do not tell me about this one, Julian," Berne said in his thickly accented voice. "All the time I am with you you do not even mention her. She is something, this one. She has the

look. She has the presence. She has much to learn, this is true, but this is no problem.''

"I think you're making a big mistake, Eric. Carol is a beautiful girl, but Julie Hammond is brilliant. She's the best student I've ever had, and she's already a more accomplished actress than dozens I've worked with. She has all the magic of a young Maggie Sullavan. You saw her. You heard her. She was magnificent and you bloody well know it.''

"She is good," Berne said, "but she has no color, she has no spirit. Her face is pitted with the acne, this is not appealing, and she is married as well. This would not go over with the public. This other girl, this Carol Martin, she is perfect.''

"She can't act, Eric.''

"As I say earlier, this is no problem. Half the bitches in Hollywood, they cannot act either, but I get the performance from them. Give Eric Berne a block of wood, he gets the performance from it. The studio wires me, they inform me I must select my Corday immediately and so I bring the press, I bring the cameras, determined to find her here, perhaps this student you tell me about when we talk over the telephone. I see her. I am impressed, yes, this I will admit. She is an actress. I do not want an actress. I want a star.''

"So Carol gets the part," Compton said dryly.

"This girl, she will be my greatest discovery," Berne said. "We do a newsreel this afternoon. Next week she is on the cover of *Life*. I introduce her on the Jack Paar show. Come, Julian, we go out now. I tell the press I have found my Corday.''

Julie heard a door open, close. Moments later there was a furor in the outer lobby.

Julie left the theater, unnoticed.

7

It was November now, and the huge, drafty old movie studio outside of Paris was cold, despite all their efforts to heat it. One more day, God willing. As she moved toward her dressing trailer, Carol sent up a silent prayer that all would go well today and this nightmare would end. High overhead, lighting technicians busily set up lights on the catwalks while, below, the set swarmed with dozens of people busily doing their jobs, the rest of the studio like a vast dark cave. Carefully stepping over an electrical cord, Carol smiled at one of the workers. He grinned, giving her the victory signal. All the crew adored her, particularly the French, for she was invariably kind and she spoke the language. They had rallied round her magnificently these past months, and she was grateful to each and every one of them. Without their support and encouragement she would probably be in a padded cell somewhere, gibbering incoherently.

"We have the lights ready in forty-five minutes," Jacques told her. "We make you look very beautiful."

"Bless you, Jacques."

"The close-ups yesterday, ah, you are Helen of Troy. I slip into the projection room. I watch. Even The Demon agrees they are perfection."

"They should be. It took him five and a half hours to shoot them."

"He is the bad man, that one. Maybe we murder him for you after the shooting is finished today."

"It's an idea," Carol said.

Jacques grinned again and went back to work. Carol moved on. Hammers were banging as carpenters did some last-minute reinforcement on the set. One of the walls had almost collapsed yesterday when she opened the door. Berne had loved that. It had afforded him another opportunity to castigate her in front of everyone. She had stood there quite calmly as he ranted and raved and called her a clumsy idiot, a silly bitch, a rank amateur deliberately sabotaging his film, and when he finally wound down she extended a stiff middle finger and there was a round of applause. The fact that ninety percent of the people involved with the filming stood behind Carol incensed Eric all the more.

The Demon was nowhere in sight. He was undoubtedly huddled in his office with Lelia and Ron, talking to California on the telephone, firing off cables. He'd appear soon enough, wearing his knee boots and gray jodhpurs and herringbone tweed jacket, looking for all the world like a caricature of Cecil B. deMille with his megaphone and green felt golf cap. Maybe the crew *would* murder him. There wasn't a court in the world that wouldn't call it justifiable homicide. Carol smiled at the thought. She smiled rarely these days.

It was nine o'clock in the morning. Carol had been at the studio since six, a limousine whisking her through the wet gray streets of Paris. She was already in costume, a charming pink cotton eighteenth-century gown with white organdy fichu and a draped overskirt. She hadn't donned her wig yet, and her short-clipped gold hair looked incongruous with the period costume. She had spent an hour in makeup, but her face still looked too thin, her blue eyes haunted. It had taken Perc quite a while to conceal the shadows beneath them. In two months she would be twenty years old, and this morning she felt a good seventy-four.

"Morning, luv," Sir Robert said.

"Oh—you startled me. I—I'm a little jumpy this morning."

Sir Robert Reynolds grinned. The celebrated English actor hired to play Marat was in his late fifties now, still a very attractive man with his tall, lean body and rather effete, chiseled features. He wore a gray peruke and a quantity of makeup, a navy blue brocade dressing gown over his flesh-colored body stocking. Personable, warm, professional to the core, he had

been one of Carol's strongest supporters, working with her privately when it became apparent that she would get no direction from Berne. Those long sessions in her suite at the Hotel Meurice had been invaluable to her, and she had learned far more than she could have learned at any drama school.

"I must say, you look quite ravishing this a.m.," Sir Robert said. "If I must be stabbed in my bath, I'm glad it shall be done by you. I shall die a happy man."

"You died three weeks ago," she reminded him.

"Six hours thrashing around in that bleeding tub, clutching my chest, rolling my eyes. Death agonies duly filmed—a magnificent performance, if I do say so myself. Today we film the actual stabbing, and then—it's a wrap."

"Six and a half months," Carol said wearily. "Not the happiest experience of my life."

"You've done a valiant job, luv. You deserve a Purple Heart. I, on the other hand, deserve an Oscar. Think there's a chance?"

"I wouldn't count on it," she told him. "I seriously doubt sixteen people will ever see this epic. They, undoubtedly, will be forced into the theater at gunpoint."

"It's not that bad, luv. With all the publicity we've received, the studio might even make a small profit. You've done a very good job under the circumstances, and there'll be other films."

"For you, yes. I'll be lucky to get a job selling nylons."

Sir Robert grinned again and, blue-green eyes twinkling, patted her on the arm.

"Must dash off and write a letter to Larry, tell him how sensible he was to turn down this role. See you on the set, luv. And Carol—"

"Yes?"

"When you stab me, do, please, be gentle."

"I shall," she promised.

Carol stepped into her trailer a few moments later and shut the door behind her. It was cold here, too, although one of the crew had brought her an electric heater. It glowed bright orange but gave off very little heat. She sighed and sat down on the sofa and reached for a cigarette from the box on the table. She had taken up smoking several months ago. It's a wonder I haven't taken up hard drugs, she thought bitterly, reaching for the box of matches. Over a year and a half as Eric Berne's "discovery" and pet protégée had definitely taken its toll.

While lighting the cigarette, she caught a glimpse of herself in the mirror over the dressing table. The girl in the glass seemed a stranger to her. Carol Martin was already an international celebrity, her first film yet to be released, but who the hell was Carol Martin? That fresh, wholesome, enthusiastic girl they wrote reams about might have been entirely fictional. She was nothing at all like the young woman with a nervous stomach and trembling hands who now sat in the trailer. What had happened to the kind, sensitive college girl with a heart full of dreams? Claymore seemed an eternity ago. Lord, it was November. Nora was starting her third year of college, a senior now, for she had indeed taken night courses and gone to summer school. Julie's husband was starting his final year of law school, with Julie still working to put him through. If only Julie or Nora could be here now to hold her hand. She wrote to them both regularly, frequently phoned Nora long distance, but she had seen neither of them since she left Indiana.

Carol smoked nervously, rapidly, filling the trailer with soft blue-gray clouds. What had happened? Eric Berne, that's what had happened. Berne had signed her to an exclusive seven-year contract, and he considered her his personal property, as indeed she was, at least professionally. The contract was not with the studio, it was with Berne, and it stipulated that Carol couldn't make films with anyone else except on loan-out arranged through him. Eighteen months ago that contract had seemed like a dream come true, but now it seemed like a prison sentence. Lincoln freed the slaves, she thought, but he forgot all about Hollywood.

Oh, it had been thrilling at first. Carol had been completely bedazzled and totally in awe, unable to believe this was happening to her. Berne swept her away from Claymore before she could even finish her last two exams, there had hardly been time to say good-bye to Julie and Nora, and then she was being photographed and interviewed in New York City, hundreds of reporters and photographers swarming into the suite at the Plaza. Then, frozen with fear, she found herself on the Jack Paar show, all those lights blazing, those gigantic black cameras churning, millions of people watching her. Dody Goodman hugged her exuberantly. Jack Paar wept real tears as Berne told him how this little girl from Kansas was going to become a major star. The next day they flew to Kansas in a private plane and, confused, disoriented, she found herself standing in front of the

cornfields while a photographer from *Life* took dozens of pictures. He shot her sitting out on the front porch with Aunt Jessie and Uncle Edgar, that had been a real thrill, and he snapped her at the Dairy Queen where she had worked one summer, insisting she wear one of the paper hats and hold up a tray with a banana split. Limos swept them back to the airport before she could even say hello to Mrs. Epperson.

It was back to New York for two more weeks of interviews and photographs and three more national television shows, Eric always at her side, Eric holding her hand, Eric parading her about as though she were a trained seal. The *Life* article appeared. Carol was on the cover, standing in front of the cornfields with windblown hair and a bemused expression, looking very young, very fresh and wholesome and bewildered. Berne decided that the hair must go. It was too long, too conventional. He took her to the most exclusive hair salon in New York and the long gold waves were clipped off and she was given an extreme Peter Pan cut, very chic, very striking. More photographs were taken, and her haircut made national news. An extensive shopping spree followed and she acquired a complete new wardrobe, each and every garment personally selected by Eric Berne, right down to the underwear. The price tags were unbelievable. Two thousand dollars for one evening gown. Three thousand dollars for a white satin evening wrap beaded with jet and lined with black satin. Carol was astounded, and she was weary, bone weary, longing, praying for a few minutes of her own without Eric or Lelia or Ron in attendance.

A full month was to pass before they finally left for California. Berne found her a "suitable" apartment in Beverly Hills and early every morning one of the limousines picked her up and drove her to the studio, where she learned to walk, learned to speak without a Kansas accent, learned to fence, had costume fittings, posed for publicity photos, all under the close supervision of Eric Berne. She had lunch at the commissary and caught glimpses of Gene Tierney and Clifton Webb and Susan Hayward and Jeanne Crain and the younger stars like Mitzi Gaynor and Dale Robertson and Jeffrey Hunter. *They* were all working on pictures, but she was still being "groomed." *Daughter of France* would commence filming soon, Berne assured her, it was still in preproduction, she must be patient. She was interviewed by Louella, who gushed and informed her readers that Carol was

fresh and unspoiled and a sweet, sweet girl, America's Favorite Cinderella. She was interviewed by Hedda, who wore an utterly preposterous hat and fired questions at her in a crisp voice and scared the shit out of her.

And Eric was always there, seeing that she had the best teachers and the best photographers, introducing her to the studio bosses and telling them they had a new star on their hands. With the aid of the publicity department, Eric carefully orchestrated her "romance" with a handsome young actor who was under contract to the studio. Brence was charming and polite and good-natured, duly took her to Ciro's and Mocambo and splashy movie premieres at Grauman's Chinese Theater and then went home to the costume designer with whom he lived. The fan magazines wrote countless articles about Carol Martin and Brence LaSalle. They were almost as popular as Debbie and Eddie. The boy in the windbreaker was the perfect prince for America's Favorite Cinderella, and the public approved. Everyone in Hollywood assumed she was sleeping with Eric Berne. She wasn't. She was very, very fond of him, and he was quite affectionate with her, but he hadn't made a single attempt to seduce her.

Carol crushed out her cigarette and poured a cup of coffee from the silver thermos. She seemed to live on caffeine and nicotine these days, but at least she wasn't drinking. An occasional glass of white wine was her limit, and Gaby and her fast pals were always amused when she ordered ginger ale or a Coca-Cola at the noisy dives they frequented in Saint-Germain. She sipped her coffee, recalling those early days, while outside the trailer men still scurried about on the catwalks setting up lights and calling instructions and making a great racket.

Eric had been so different in the beginning. Bossy and possessive, true, frequently stern, but kind, too, so very considerate, seeing to her every need. Carol supposed it was inevitable she fall a little in love with him. He was no Adonis, but oh what charm he had, what overwhelming magnetism. She could easily see why Linda Darnell and Ann Sheridan and Paulette Goddard and a dozen others had been so taken with him. Eric was a very powerful man in Hollywood, and he had given her a feeling of security in a crazy, glamorous, bewildering world that sometimes left her feeling she had tumbled down a rabbit hole. Carol didn't really belong, she knew. She was there on a pass, and Eric had always been on hand to calm her and comfort her and

give her the assurance she so desperately needed. He treated her like a beloved daughter, indulging her and pampering her and scolding her, too, at times. Her feelings for him deepened, and Carol clung to him as a drowning man might cling to a spar.

All that changed abruptly when, finally, they flew to France and the filming actually began. Eric was very unhappy with the revised script. He was unhappy with the sets, the costumes, the casting. He had wanted Olivier for Marat, got Sir Robert instead. He spoke very little French but, because of regulations, half the work crew and technicians had to be French, and he was constantly having to deal with French government officials in order to get permission to use actual historical sites for exterior scenes. Nothing satisfied him, and he secretly feared his *Gone With the Wind* was going to be the disaster his enemies predicted it would be. He was in a foul mood from day one and, fearing failure as he did, badly needed a scapegoat. He found one in the raw and inexperienced young actress who had never been in front of a camera before and didn't know the first thing about film acting.

He turned on her. Viciously. Carol was confused. She was bewildered and hurt and completely at a loss, unable to understand his radical change in attitude. The man who represented security, the man who had guided her and protected her and treated her like a daughter now shouted at her, raged at her, mocked her. He took a perverse delight in humiliating her in front of cast and crew, gloating when her nerves snapped, when she burst into tears. Carol tried. She tried valiantly. She wanted to learn. She wanted to do a good job. She wanted to make him proud of her. She wanted direction, but Eric didn't direct her. He shouted. He bullied. He demeaned her and called her a stupid bitch. Carol felt as though the floor had dropped from beneath her and was well on the way to a complete nervous collapse. After four weeks, after a particularly humiliating episode, she fled the set in tears and knew it was over, knew she couldn't go on any longer. It was then that Sir Robert came to her trailer.

The renowned English actor had just recently arrived in Paris, and they had yet to film any of his scenes. He had been visiting the set that day, watching the proceedings with a jaundiced eye. Fifty-six years old, a professional actor since the age of seventeen, Sir Robert saw immediately what was going on and knew

the reasons why. He had a strong sense of justice and it went against the grain to see Berne abusing this child and setting her up to take the blame for what was clearly an ill-fated project. Larry had turned the film down, wisely, of course, but Sir Robert had very little strength of character when it came to money, and the salary he was being paid would enable him to make the much-needed repairs on his estate in Kent. *Daughter of France* wouldn't hurt his career, wouldn't matter one way or the other, but it could easily destroy this charming girl who so clearly wanted to do a good job. He knocked lightly on the trailer door and, receiving no answer, stepped inside. Carol was sobbing, her eyes wet with tears, a wad of Kleenex in her hand.

"Tough, luv, isn't it?" he said.

Carol looked up in anguish, and she was startled to see Sir Robert standing there before her. She had been introduced to him only that morning, and she had been very much in awe. He was one of the greats, his *Lear* a legend, and a flood of embarrassment swept over her as she realized he had witnessed her humiliation on the set. She wiped her eyes and sat up, and Sir Robert grinned that engaging grin that had helped make him a matinee idol during the late 1920s and throughout the '30s. Suave, distinguished, dapper in his trim Savile Row suit and a pale blue ascot, he took out an exquisite platinum case and offered her a cigarette. Carol shook her head, and Sir Robert lighted one for himself with a matching platinum lighter.

"I—I'm sorry," she said miserably.

"Oh, no, luv, you mustn't apologize. You were perfectly right to leave the set like that. I would have too, I fear, at your age. I hadn't much confidence back then. I didn't have the sense to stand and fight. I let everyone walk all over me."

"He—I don't understand why he—"

"It's plain to see, luv. He's got a bomb on his hands, and he has to cover his tracks. You've been elected to take the blame for what will almost certainly be—uh—something less than a triumph for Eric Berne."

Carol was still shaken, still embarrassed, and at first she didn't comprehend what he was saying. Sir Robert perched elegantly on the arm of a chair and exhaled a plume of smoke.

"He's out to ruin you, you know. He can't *fire* you, not after all that publicity about the search and his marvelous 'discovery'—the public would turn on him. If you walk out, he's guilt-

free in the eyes of the public, and *you*'re the quitter, the girl who couldn't make it.''

"My God, I can't believe he—"

"Oh, it's a diabolical little scheme, and apparently it's working just as he planned. You're ready to give in, give up, and Eric Berne has his scapegoat. Pity.''

"That son of a bitch.''

"An opinion shared by everyone who's ever worked with Berne, I understand. I suppose you'll go back to Kansas and marry the boy next door. This is a tough business, luv, and only the tough survive. There's no room for whiners, no room for quitters. You have to fight.''

"That rotten son of a bitch!''

"You're a very sweet girl. It's probably just as well you leave this business.''

"I'm not *go*ing to leave!''

"No?''

"He—I can't believe he—I—I'm not going to let him get away with it! I know I'm not—not very good, but I *can* be. I know I can be, if only I have the chance to learn—to grow.''

"That's the spirit, luv. You photograph divinely—the cameraman told me you have a luminous quality the camera loves—and with a little help you could give a very creditable performance.''

"That's the problem. He won't *give* me any help.''

"It's not in his best interest. I'd be delighted to work with you, Carol. I've done a little directing in the past, and I have a vested interest in this epic. It's going to receive no plaudits, but *I* intend to be brilliant, as usual. If you don't look good, I don't look good.''

Carol was stunned. She stood up and paced back and forth, fuming, unable to believe anyone could be as . . . as Machiavellian as Eric Berne. He was deliberately sabotaging her career, hurling her to the wolves so that he wouldn't be blamed for a film clearly doomed from the beginning. Well, it wasn't going to work. He wasn't going to drive her away. Carol felt something harden within her, a tight core of strength she didn't know she had, and a steely determination filled her. She intended to stand up to the son of a bitch. She intended to fight back. It wouldn't be easy and it wouldn't be pleasant—she wasn't a fighter by nature—but, by God, she'd show the bastard what she was made

of, and it wasn't sugar and spice and everything nice. She paused in her pacing to take one of her cigarettes and light it. She smoked furiously, momentarily forgetting the presence of Sir Robert Reynolds.

He coughed discreetly. She turned to him, and he saw the determination in those lovely blue eyes. The little girl from Kansas had spunk after all. From the looks of her, she had a formidable amount of spunk.

"You—you'd actually work with me?" she asked.

"On the side. In private. I'd dearly love to see the mighty Berne foiled in his nefarious plans. Alas, I can't stand injustice, and what he's trying to do is dastardly indeed."

Carol looked at the still-handsome, world-famous actor who was so willing to come to her rescue. Why? After all she had been through, all she had seen, she couldn't help but be a bit suspicious of his motives. Sir Robert seemed to read her mind, and again he grinned.

"You're learning, luv. Never take anyone at face value, not in this business. I assure you my intentions are quite honorable. I hope to keep my youth, and I fear he'd desert me in no time flat if I started seducing attractive young costars."

"I—" Her cheeks flushed a delicate pink.

"Are you game, luv? Shall we put one over on Berne?"

Carol hesitated a moment, and then she nodded decisively. "Let's," she replied.

"Sure you've got the stamina?"

"If—if I have to be a bitch, I'll *be* a bitch."

"Bully for you, luv."

"You—Sir Robert, I—I can't tell you how much—what it means to me for an actor like—of your stature to—oh, shit, I'm going to start crying again, I can feel it."

"I reread the script last night. I may cry myself."

Sir Robert put out his cigarette and stood up, taking Carol's hand and giving it a reassuring squeeze. "Come on, luv. We'll get some lunch and plan our strategy. Eric Berne just may have met his match."

Carol reported to work the next day with grim determination, and when Berne began his shouting, his bullying, she stood her ground firmly and refused to let him shake her. She read her lines as Sir Robert had instructed her to read them and refused to waver. Berne was livid, but he was unable to break her down,

and a battle royal began that caused everyone involved with the movie to take sides. The studio people, the money people, naturally took Eric's side and commiserated with him for having to work with such a highly strung, untrained and temperamental young actress. Almost everyone else—the technicians, the grips, the cameraman, all her fellow actors—took Carol's side and spread horrifying tales of Berne's shouting, his maniacal tantrums, his sadistic bullying of the sweet, unspoiled girl who couldn't satisfy him no matter how she tried. Explosions on the set made news on two continents, and there were those who wagered the film would never be finished. Others, more cynical, claimed it was all publicity carefully generated to keep *Daughter of France* in the public eye.

Two months ago, the "near mishap" on the set had made blazing headlines all over the world, and there were photographs of the gigantic guillotine and a shaken young star having hysterics in the arms of the wardrobe woman. A full-scale replica of the original guillotine had been built at enormous expense and set up on the original site. Hundreds of extras were hired and put into period costume and the execution of Charlotte Corday had been filmed at a cost only a few thousand higher than the cost of a relatively modest feature film. There had been a number of problems with the weather, problems with the lights, problems with the leading lady. She kept blowing her lines and couldn't do anything to please her volatile director. Corday's lengthy final speech finally filmed, she was led up the steps of the scaffold, forced to her knees, her head fastened into the wooden stocks beneath the blade.

There was a delay while lights were rearranged. They were to shoot several close-ups before a dummy was substituted for the actress and the blade descended to sever an amazingly lifelike replica of her head that had been planted with a plastic pouch that would burst on contact and spew blood in all directions. The stocks were very uncomfortable and Carol's knees were beginning to cramp and she insisted she be set free until the lights were ready. Berne told her to shut up and be professional. Fifteen more minutes passed. She was in agony and pleaded with him. Berne ignored her. A crew member finally took it upon himself to defy the monster. He leaped up onto the scaffold and loosened the wooden stocks and helped Carol to her feet only seconds before a rope broke and the blade came

crashing down. The actress had hysterics. The director turned gray. The crowd roared. Photographers scrambled to capture it all for posterity.

BERNE ALMOST BEHEADS STAR, *Variety* announced in letters four inches high, a statement that surprised few who had worked with Berne before. Carol was sedated and briefly hospitalized and was so shaken she had to recoup for four days at the St. Tropez home of her friend Gaby Bernais. The mishap cost them two more days—all those hundreds of extras earning full pay—and Carol's stand-in was used for the remaining shots. If it was a hoax, as many believed it was, it was certainly the most spectacular hoax in recent memory and garnered a gigantic amount of publicity for the film. Berne welcomed his star back from St. Tropez with huge bouquets of pink roses and a large pear-shaped star sapphire suspended on a chain of fine platinum, a jewel so expensive Elizabeth Taylor had passed on it when it was shown to her at the exclusive shop on the Champs Elysées. The photographers were on hand for the return, too, and in their PEOPLE column *Time* ran a picture of the thin, pale-looking actress with cropped hair holding up the gem and smiling tearfully at the bulky director.

"You're not getting it back, you bastard," Carol informed him.

"But, Carol, my precious, it is the gift. It is my apology."

"You're not deducting it from my salary, either."

"But of course not. The studio pays for it."

"I didn't think the money came out of your pocket, you miserly son of a bitch."

"This is not nice, talking to your Eric this way. I am very concerned over this accident. I feel very bad about it, am horrified it happens. Come now and give us a hug. The photographers are waiting."

"Go fuck yourself," she said succinctly.

Remembering the incident now in her dressing trailer, Carol shuddered anew. She wouldn't put it past the son of a bitch to have arranged the whole thing himself, as a lot of people believed he had. It was certainly his style. The fact remained that if Jean-Claude hadn't released her when he did, she would literally have shared the fate of Charlotte Corday. Carol was prepared to give her all for this movie, but there were limits. The studio couldn't have bought the publicity for a million bucks.

They could bloody well pay for the sapphire. Carol had placed it in a safe deposit box for possible future resale. At five hundred dollars a week, plus expenses, she was hardly making a fortune. Prior to coming to France, her weekly salary had been half that amount. Wisely, she was putting most of it in the bank.

Carol lighted another cigarette and glanced at the clock. Making films was mostly a matter of waiting around for hours on end. They were lucky to get five minutes of film in the can on any given day, and when Eric was having one of his tantrums they usually got less. Thank God it was almost over with now.

Sighing, she picked up the latest issue of *Paris Match*. There was a photograph of her dancing with one of Gaby's pals in a smoky Left Bank dive. The boy was a tall, handsome French youth with wavy black hair and sad brown eyes, wearing the standard uniform of snug black slacks, black turtleneck and a boxy black leather jacket. She wore a black satin cocktail dress by Hubert de Givenchy and a long rope of pearls. The pearls were real, a gift from Berne in happier days. It was a rare issue of *Paris Match* that didn't have at least one picture of her. Paris had gone mad over her. She was young and fresh and enthusiastic and loved everything French, and she spoke the language, too, if not exactly like a native at least with relative ease. When she became friends with Gabrielle Bernais and began to pal around with her set, the French people as a whole embraced her with open arms and the nation unofficially adopted her. Carol was the darling of the French press, and on the few occasions when she had time to prowl around the fascinating city, she was greeted with broad smiles and friendly waves. *Chère Carol* was almost as beloved as Gaby herself.

She had met the dashing young French novelist during her second week in Paris. Filming hadn't started yet and Eric was still being civil and *Vogue* was doing a photographic essay— Fresh Young American Girl in Paris Wearing the Latest French Creations—and the studio considered it a tremendous coup. They were on the Place de la Bastille from which streets radiated in every direction like the spokes of a wheel. Carol was wearing a flowered, full-skirted frock by Balmain, holding the strings of four dozen balloons and trying to look spontaneous and exuberant while the photographer changed his lens. They had been shooting all day all over the city, Carol changing clothes in the back of a van and longing for a little respite. People had been

fussing over her and pulling at her and barking orders and she was absolutely exhausted. The photographer raised his camera and yelled that he was ready and Carol smiled and looked up at the balloons with delight and let go of the strings and the camera clicked, clicked, clicked, capturing it all.

A snazzy red sports car convertible whizzed past, circled back, slammed to a halt with much screeching of brakes. A gamine with a tanned pirate's face and a windblown mop of short, tawny gold curls got out and approached them with an amiable smile. She wore black chino pants and a black-and-white striped sailor's jersey and a loose, floppy red nylon raincoat. "Gaby!" the French in the crowd shouted. "Here's Gaby!" Gaby Bernais ignored the furor and moved directly over to Carol, introduced herself, told her she had been reading about her and, grinning, welcomed her to Paris.

"Fantastic!" the photographer roared. "I've got to get some shots of this for the magazine. Carol Martin and Gaby Bernais together! Fantastic! Vreeland will go wild!"

Gaby amiably consented to pose and the photographer shot two rolls of film, the two girls chatting all the while. Carol had been enchanted with the wry and worldly pixie. She told her how much she had enjoyed all her books—the latest had just recently appeared—and told her about Nora's admiration as well. Gaby had been enchanted with the beautiful, naive American girl with her engaging manner and guileless charm. The two of them felt an immediate rapport and when the photographer was finished, they fled to Gaby's car and raced off with screeching tires despite the fact that there was one more location left to shoot. Eric had been livid and Carol admitted that it was very irresponsible of her, but she had enjoyed herself immensely, tooling through the streets of Paris with Gaby in the red convertible, going out to dinner at a cheap but marvelous restaurant and afterwards to a basement dive full of smoke and jazz and sinister-looking hoodlums who were actually students from the Sorbonne. Gaby introduced her to a peculiar little man with shaggy hair and thick glasses who looked very depressed. He was Jean-Paul Sartre. The self-conscious, uptight-looking matron beside him was Simone de Beauvoir. Later on, Jean Cocteau and Jean Marais arrived, and they were much more fun.

There had been many more evenings since, and Gaby had become a good friend, showing her the city, introducing her to

celebrity pals, advising her to take a lover when her nerves got out of hand. If she were in love, Gaby insisted, she wouldn't let Berne rile her so much. There were dozens of candidates, handsome and engaging young French actors, painters, poets and philosophers who were delighted with Gaby's American pal and eager to console her, but Carol was a product of the American Midwest and not yet ready for casual coupling for the sake of her nerves. Thank God for Gaby, though. She had been a great support these past months, as had Sir Robert and most of the crew. I suppose I've been quite lucky, really, she thought, putting *Paris Match* aside. She lighted another cigarette, and a few minutes later her hairdresser came in with her wig and helped her put it on and a man came in to touch up her makeup and then it was time to go out and face The Demon.

He was there beside the camera with megaphone in hand, wearing his outlandish deMille garb and looking glum today, not at all fierce. Brilliant banks of lights bathed the set, Marat's private chambers with dark mahogany wainscotting and pale rose wallpaper and authentic period furniture, a huge porcelain tub in the center of the room. Still wearing his robe, Sir Robert was chatting with a grip. Ron Majors rushed over to Carol, looking a bit anxious but grinning nevertheless. He was wearing tennis shoes, tight blue jeans and his usual sleeveless jersey, today's deep purple. The former stuntman and bit actor seemed to live in perpetual fear that someone might fail to notice his muscular bronze biceps. Carol had come to detest him heartily. He was invariably cheery and his sun-streaked brown hair was invariably tousled. His amiable facade deceived no one. Ron was as tough as nails and always had his own best interests at heart. His own best interests meant catering to Berne's every whim, bolstering his ego and carrying out his commands with brisk efficiency, no matter whose body he had to step over in the process. He patted Carol on the arm now, his grin broadening.

"You look lovely, sweetheart. We're all ready. Know your lines?"

"No, Ron, I do not know my lines. I've had the fucking script for a good half year and I've rehearsed the scene with Sir Robert a dozen times, but I do not know my lines."

Ron raised his hands as though to defend himself. "Okay, okay, I was out of line. I shouldn't have asked such a stupid question. Promise me one thing, sweetheart. Promise me you

won't agitate Eric today. He's really down, always is the last day of shooting."

"I won't agitate Eric," she promised.

"Good girl. I knew I could count on you. You're a real peach."

"Ron, dear," she said sweetly, "do both of us a favor. Go sit on something sharp."

Ron looked hurt and then shook his head and departed. Lelia Standish came over to Berne with a clipboard and they conferred in low voices for several minutes and then the Spider Woman left and Berne said something to the cameraman. Carol felt her stomach tightening as it always did. She braced herself for the onslaught. "Places!" Berne shouted through his megaphone. Sir Robert removed his robe and gave it to an assistant, his torso bare, a snug flesh-colored body stocking covering his privates and lower limbs. One of the crew members gave a low, appreciative whistle. Sir Robert grinned and climbed into the tub full of water. Carol took her position several feet away. They had already filmed her entrance, filmed her close-ups and reaction shots, filmed Sir Robert's dramatic death and several shots of a shiny blade plunging into a fake torso with a profusion of blood spurting. All that remained was the murder itself, a relatively simple scene with only four lines of dialogue. With luck they should get it in the can in five or six hours.

"Ready?" Berne purred.

"Ready," Sir Robert said pleasantly. "Jesus, this water's as cold as ice today."

"Miss Martin?" Berne said.

"Ready," Carol said. "Oh, shit, the knife. I haven't got the knife."

"Wonderful," Berne said acidly.

The prop man rushed onto the set with knife in hand, apologizing profusely to Carol. She thanked him politely. Berne scowled. He thundered orders. The filming began. Sir Robert picked up a large sponge and squeezed it and, suddenly aware of her presence, looked over his shoulder at Carol. She stood quietly, clutching the knife concealed behind the folds of her skirt.

"Who are you?" he asked angrily.

"I am Charlotte Corday," she said calmly.

"Why have you come here?"

"I have come for France."

"Cut!" Berne yelled. "Miss Martin, you have come here to murder him. You are nervous, apprehensive, distraught. I realize that it is asking the impossible, but do you think you might register a little emotion?"

Carol nodded. Berne cursed. The boy with the clapper rushed out with TAKE TWO chalked on the board beneath the title and scene number and they began again and Carol gave an identical reading. Berne wanted arm-waving melodrama, but she and Sir Robert had determined that Corday would be calm, deliberate, saddened by what she must do yet determined to carry it out. The two of them had worked for hours analyzing, perfecting, working on inflection, and she didn't intend to alter her delivery one jot. They did thirty-four takes. Berne shouted, threw his arms in the air, called her names, and she continued to deliver the lines as she had delivered them in the beginning. One of the lights went out and they had to wait while it was replaced. The sound man started picking up an ominous buzzing on the boom and they had to wait until he discovered its source and an electrical short was repaired. Sir Robert demanded fresh, warmer water. His body makeup had to be touched up repeatedly, for it melted and streaked under the blazing lights. Carol's makeup had to be repaired, too.

It was like working in hell, working under those lights, and if it was hell Berne was Satan himself, doing his best to break her down, make her cry and rush off the set, but these tactics hadn't worked in quite some time. She stood her ground. She suffered. She endured. He stomped over to her with fists clenched and called her a stupid bitch, a hopeless amateur, shouting in her face, and she didn't so much as blink. He called her a cow, an idiot, a wooden dummy, and she finally sighed and calmly suggested he take a running jump at a flying doughnut. Berne's face turned scarlet. He seemed to have a seizure. Sir Robert snickered in the tub, unable to help himself. Berne whirled on him. Sir Robert shook his head slowly, daring the director to light into him. Berne retreated, calmed himself down as best he could, and they began all over again. After the first twenty takes Carol was drenched with perspiration and she had to bathe and have Perc apply fresh makeup and then change into a duplicate costume and wig. That held them up for another hour and fifteen minutes, Berne ranting to Lelia and Ron all the while, Sir Robert

wearing his robe and cheerfully playing a game of gin rummy with pals on the crew.

It was four-fifteen before an enraged, frustrated Berne finally conceded defeat and let them finish the scene. "I have come for France," Carol said quietly, sadly, and then she pulled the knife from behind the folds of pink cotton and stepped over to the tub and plunged it into his breast, the shiny blade telescoping into the hilt while seeming to drive into flesh. Berne wasn't satisfied, and she had to stab Sir Robert seven more times before he yelled "Cut and print!" It was over. Carol couldn't believe it. The last shot had been filmed. There were cheers all around as Berne stalked off the set, followed by an anxious Ron Majors. Sir Robert climbed out of the tub and threw his arms around Carol and got her all wet and she felt tears spilling over her lashes as he hugged her tightly.

"We did it, luv!" he exclaimed. "Berne has final cut and God knows what he will do to us in the editing room, but we did it! We gave our best. I intend to phone Louella long distance this very evening and tell her Carol Martin is my all-time favorite costar. Viv and Lillie and Wendy will probably come after me with *real* knives, but I've always loved danger."

"I—I'll never be able to repay you for what you've done, Sir Robert. Working with you has—I've learned so much, and—"

Sir Robert hugged her again, touched, the look in her eyes all the reward he wanted for those hundreds of hours he'd devoted to working with her. She had delivered a better-than-competent performance, and in some of the scenes she'd been good, bloody good indeed. He released her now, slipping on the robe an assistant handed him. Tying the sash, he grinned and said he'd better go dry off before he caught pneumonia, said he'd catch her later.

Carol spent the next hour saying good-bye to all the crew, distributing carefully chosen gifts to each and every one of them, thanking them for their support. Makeup removed, gown and wig returned to wardrobe, she was wearing street clothes when Sir Robert tapped on her trailer door and strolled in with a grin, a handsome tan camel's hair overcoat draped elegantly over his shoulders and a brightly wrapped package in his hand. He presented it to her with a melodramatic flourish, and she opened it to discover a silver cigarette case with art deco designs etched

onto the lid in gold. It was absolutely gorgeous, with the smooth, mellow patina of age far more beautiful than shiny newness.

"It—Sir Robert, it's one of the loveliest things I've ever seen."

"Open it," he said.

Carol snapped it open. Inside the lid, in tiny diamonds, was "To Robbie from Noël" and, below that, "And from Robbie to Carol" in tiny garnets, her birthstone. Tears sprang to her eyes again. Never had she been so touched. This man, this legend, second only to Olivier in professional stature, was the kindest, most generous she had ever known and he had literally saved her career. She loved him dearly and, had his predilections been different, would have been deeply in love. She examined the exquisite case, so moved she was unable to speak.

"Noël gave it to me in nineteen thirty-three," he told her. "I'd been doing one of his plays on the West End—took the role over after he'd grown bored with it. He taught me everything I know about timing and delivery. 'Young man,' he said, 'do you want to spend the rest of your life swashbuckling about in a pair of tights, making the ladies swoon, or do you want to *act*?' He drove me quite mercilessly and was brutal in his criticism, but I learned. In all honesty I must add that he was extremely miffed when the play ran for another eight months and the critics claimed I was even better in the part than Noël had been. That case has been a sort of talisman to me for almost a quarter of a century. I want you to have it now."

"I—I don't know what to say."

"I hope it will remind you of our sessions together. I hope it will inspire you to keep on learning and keep on growing as an actress. I expect great things from you, my dear. If you fail me, I fully intend to track you down and take that case back."

"I won't fail you," she said quietly.

He gave her a robust hug and Carol brushed the tears from her eyes and handed him a small box wrapped in gold paper. The platinum cuff links, each set with a small, perfect gray pearl, had cost a small fortune, far more than she could afford, but she would gladly have paid twice as much. Sir Robert declared them the finest cuff links he had ever owned and said he would wear them with great pride. He hugged her again. Carol put on her coat and scarf, and they left the trailer, strolling slowly through the vast, chilly studio, calling final good-byes to those still milling about. Although Carol was relieved that the hell was finally

over, she felt a certain sadness as well. All these friends she had made would no longer be a part of her life. Most of them she would never see again. It was rather like a family breaking up, all of them going their separate ways now that filming was completed.

Two limousines awaited them outside, for she and Sir Robert were staying at different hotels. There was to be no wrap party tonight. Sir Robert was flying back to London first thing in the morning, she knew, and their paths might never cross again. She wasn't going to cry again. She wasn't. Sir Robert smiled and said, "Cheerio, luv," and they promised to write and she kissed him and smiled brightly, sadly as he climbed into his limousine and it drove off. Carol got into her own car and was silent throughout the long, tedious drive back to the Hotel Meurice. Paris was still gray and damp, spangled with bright, multicolored lights now in the early evening, and the traffic was horrendous, particularly as they neared the Arc de Triomphe. It was well after seven when Carol stepped into her suite. She would have to hurry. Gaby was going to pick her up at eight-thirty.

An hour later, wearing black high heels, hose and the stunning black Givenchy cocktail dress with elbow-length sleeves, scooped neckline and full, flaring skirt, she stood in front of the mirror, brushing her sleek golden cap. The severe short haircut made her dark-blue eyes seem larger, made her cheekbones seem higher, and it had started a vogue, particularly among fashion models here in Paris. Sighing, she put the hairbrush down and applied just a touch of pink lipstick to her lips, a hint of gray shadow to her lids. The elegant, sophisticated woman in the mirror bore little resemblance to the dewy-eyed, wholesome girl who had left Indiana eighteen months ago.

There was a knock on the sitting room door. Carol glanced up at the clock. Gaby was fifteen minutes early, which wasn't at all like her. Perhaps it was because of the occasion. They weren't going to one of the clubs with the gang tonight. Gaby was taking her to a very formal, very elegant diplomatic reception. It would be rather stuffy and pompous, Gaby claimed, but there would be a number of literary and artistic figures Carol really should meet, and the food would be divine. The food sounded particularly attractive at the moment. She hadn't had a bite since her morning croissant. She opened the door to greet her friend and was dumbfounded to see Eric Berne standing

was a foolish, dramatic gesture quite unworthy of her, but it made her feel much better. When Gaby arrived five minutes later she was furiously smoking a cigarette, far more upset by the scene than she cared to admit.

"I passed Eric Berne downstairs in the lobby," Gaby said. "He looked absolutely furious. Pink roses are scattered all over the hall outside. Did I miss a drama?"

Carol nodded and took another long drag on her cigarette and crushed it out in a crystal ashtray.

"I think I *have* become a bitch," she said.

"Oh?"

"I told Eric to fuck off. I threw him out."

"High time, too," Gaby said.

"I used to be so nice. I never used language like that. I had no temperament at all. I was kind and thoughtful, and I—I was *nice*."

"You're still nice, darling."

Carol lighted another cigarette and told Gaby what had happened. Gaby listened with visible sympathy, shaking her head at the director's villainy. Tawny gold curls attractively tumbled, roguish brown eyes aglow, she wore a brown satin Dior with tiny bronze bugle beads adorning the bodice, a matching cape lined with bronze silk draped across her shoulders. Usually attired in casual student garb and not tall enough for haute couture, she looked rather like a little girl playing dress-up.

"So that's it," Carol said miserably. "I've just burned all my bridges behind me."

"And opened new avenues," Gaby added. "Half the filmmakers in France are dying to work with you. You've enchanted the whole country. Claude Bouchet for one will be delighted to know you're available."

"Bouchet?"

"He's a brilliant young director—only thirty-three years old and terribly attractive. He makes stylish, moody suspense films à la Hitchcock, full of symbolism and subtle eroticism. The critics revere him already, and he's only made four films. You met him, remember? The one who said he would cheerfully murder to have you in his next film. Bouchet is going to be one of the greats ere long, I assure you."

"Do you think he really wants to work with me?"

"Bouchet never says anything he doesn't mean, darling. To-

morrow we'll tell him you're now at liberty. Tonight we must go to this reception. You'll meet a lot of important people.''

''I really don't feel like going now, Gaby.''

''Nonsense. Fetch your wrap.''

Carol obeyed reluctantly. They took the elevator down to the elegant lobby. Half a dozen attractive men were milling about, and all of them turned to gaze as the two celebrated young women passed.

''You know,'' Gaby said, ''now that you plan to remain in France for a while, you really must take a lover.''

''I'm not interested, Gaby.''

''You're not interested because you haven't met the right man yet,'' Gaby informed her. ''I've been introducing you to sexy youths with beautiful bodies and dangerous eyes. Not your type at all, I've decided. All of the men you've been attracted to have been quite a bit older. You're not looking for a virile youth who will demolish you with passionate embraces. You're looking for a father figure who will take care of you.''

''You think so?''

''I understand these things. Maybe tonight at the reception you will meet a handsome older man who will sweep you off your feet.''

''Jesus, I hope not.''

''It would do you a world of good,'' Gaby said wisely.

Brian Gregory was absolutely perfect and it scared the shit out
of her. He was twenty-six years old and tall and blond, with
clear blue eyes and a wry grin and a lean, muscular body he
carried with athletic grace and he was brilliant, too, smart as a
whip. He was a graduate student, had done military service in
Korea after leaving a fancy military school, had gone to Princeton afterwards and had come to Claymore for his advanced degree in engineering. If that wasn't enough, his family was loaded,
lived in New Rochelle, and as soon as *he* got his degree, two
weeks from now, he was stepping into a cushy job with a prestigious firm in New York. He was witty, good-natured, sexy as
all get-out, the living incarnation of every girl's dream in this
year of 1958. Mr. Right was alive and well, and he wanted to
marry her, for Christ's sake, little Nora Levin, the kid voted The
Girl Most Likely To by half the jocks on campus only a couple
of years ago. Who was gonna believe it?

Nora had met Brian on campus last year and he had found her
cute as a button and loved her smart mouth and soon they were
going steady and there were no other boys. Bye-bye, track team.
She had all the experience she needed and he was a *man*, not a
boy, mature and level-headed and purposeful and terribly serious
about the future and his career in engineering. Fun, too. Playful.
White teeth and blue-blue eyes and blond-blond hair and clean-

cut, virile good looks, that sexy wry grin, that soft, husky voice.
Jesus! Half the girls at Claymore panting for him, chasing after
him, and he chooses *her*! He was absolutely fantastic in the sack,
too, but he hadn't made a move on her until after they were
going steady and, get this, he actually respected her afterwards.
Brian Gregory was in love with her, gave her roses and a heart-
shaped box of chocolates on Valentine's Day, took her to the
senior prom, Brian a dream in his white jacket and black bow
tie and maroon cummerbund, she feeling silly as hell in her
peach organdy-over-taffeta gown and white magnolia corsage. It
was enough to cause a girl to lose all her perspective.

"I'm telling you, Julie, I don't know what to *do*," she said.

"You love him, don't you?"

"I don't know. I'm overwhelmed. I'm bedazzled. I've been
in a daze ever since the first time he asked me out last September, but—love? I don't know. He makes me feel like—like there's
music inside me. I know that sounds corny as hell."

"I understand," Julie said. I used to feel that way myself,
she added silently.

"He's everything a girl could want—and more," Nora said.
"I guess maybe I *do* love him, but—Jesus, can you see me in
New Rochelle? Brian would commute to the city five days a
week and we'd live in a fancy house in a fancy neighborhood
and belong to the country club and wouldn't they just love me?
His parents almost had coronaries when he told them I'm Jewish
but they rose nobly to the occasion and said if he really loved
me that was all that mattered and they would give their blessing.
Awfully white of them."

They were in the library, in the labyrinth of stacks in the rear,
and Julie was taking books from a cart and putting them on the
shelves. When she had been selected to play the lead in *Summer
and Smoke* in the spring production last year she had given up
her job at the Silver Bell. Julian Compton had gotten her this
job at the library, with flexible hours, and he had also made her
his student assistant. She was bringing home fifty dollars more
a month than she had waitressing, and the work was far more
pleasant. Julie had also played the leading role in *The Philadel-
phia Story* last fall and in *Picnic* two months ago, her versatility
nothing short of amazing, Nora thought. Some accused Compton of playing favorites, giving her all the leads, but no one
could deny she was a brilliant actress. She really should have

won the lead in *Daughter of France*, but, considering what had happened to Carol, it was a blessing she hadn't.

Julie picked up a heavy red-bound tome, checked the numbered tab glued onto the bottom of its spine and, standing up on tiptoes, placed it on a shelf.

"I don't see what being Jewish has to do with it," she said.

"You wouldn't, sweetie, that's one of the reasons I love you."

"I thought everything went well when he took you to meet them over the Easter holidays."

"Oh, everything went swimmingly. He fetched me in Brooklyn and drove me to New Rochelle and we turned into this driveway and I saw this gigantic white mansion with white pillars in front and a pool in back and gorgeously groomed lawns and I almost wet my pants. A butler opened the front door—a *butler*, I kid you not—and I felt exactly like Kitty Foyle, only Jewish. His mother gave me this warm smile and a polite peck on the cheek and his father pumped my hand vigorously and asked me how I was at least four times and his kid sister stared at me as though I'd just landed from Mars."

"You told me they were very gracious."

"They were so goddamned gracious I wanted to die. Dinner was formal, Spode china and Waterford crystal and silver flatware, linen napkins, the works, every course served by a maid in uniform. Mr. Gregory wore a five-hundred-dollar suit and a fifty-dollar tie and talked about the business—he's retired now but still keeps his finger in. Mrs. Gregory, Adele, you must call me Adele, my dear, wore a little purple chiffon number she'd picked up in Paris and her second-best diamonds. Her hair is lavender, did I tell you? She was so fucking hospitable and broadminded I wanted to shove a pie in her face only we didn't have pie, we had lemon mousse."

Julie smiled and took another book from the cart and placed it on its proper shelf. Nora ran a hand through her short black curls and made a face.

"His little sister asked me if it was true I couldn't eat ham. She's fourteen and wears braces and looks exactly like a munchkin. I was so well bred you wouldn't believe it, didn't say 'shit' once. Next morning we all had breakfast by the pool and the men went to play tennis at the club and me and Mom and Kid Sister made polite noises till they got back, Adele ever so dis-

creetly asking about my background and visibly wincing at the word 'Brooklyn.' ''

Nora sighed, following as Julie pushed the cart over to another shelf. Although Nora had made other friends during the past two years Julie was still her closest friend, and they spent far more time together than they had been able to do when Carol was still at Claymore. Julie's jobs as a library aide and student assistant to Julian Compton kept her on campus five days a week, and she was not as reluctant to spend time away from Doug as she had been. Although still overly shy and sensitive, Julie had matured a great deal, Nora thought. The theater work had given her more confidence in herself and an identity other than that as Douglas Hammond's wife.

"What happened then?" Julie asked.

"The men came back, and Brian looked so gorgeous in his white tennis shorts and white sweater with blue-and-red stripes I wanted to jump his bones that very minute but I managed to restrain myself. After a light lunch of chilled asparagus consommé and lobster salad Daddy Gregory took Brian and me to see the property he'd bought and plans to build a house on as soon as Brian settles down. The house will be a wedding gift. Kid Sister tagged along and kept staring up at my nose. 'I had it done, dear,' I finally told her. She seemed quite relieved. I longed to slug the slut."

"How do *your* parents feel about Brian?"

"When I first told Sadie about him she shrieked, 'My God! A goy! He's never had lox in his life!' When I added that his father was worth several million dollars she turned six somersaults, yelled 'Yippee!' and told me mixed marriages were all the rage today. When he came to pick me up and she finally met him she fell all over him and started sobbing like he was a long-lost son and got him to promise to stay for dinner when he brought me back from New Rochelle. It was an evening to remember, believe me, Sadie pulling out the family album and bragging about how cute, how sweet, how smart I am and what a catch I'd be for some lucky man—and the crazy thing is, he *still* wants to marry me."

"What about your father?"

"Irving thinks Brian's very nice. 'Are you serious about him, pumpkin?' he asked, and I said, 'Yeah, Pops, I guess I am.' He looked kinda bothered and began to scratch his head. 'What

about your writing?' he asked. 'I thought that was the most important thing in the world to you. You going to give up all of those dreams?' It made me stop and *think*, Julie.''

"I imagine it did."

"What *about* my writing? *Am* I going to give up all those dreams?"

Julie looked at her with disillusioned eyes and then placed another book on the shelf. "You still believe in the slipper, don't you?" she asked quietly.

"Carol got it. We're gonna get it, too. Maybe not as *soon* as she did, but it—it's gonna happen, Julie."

Julie didn't answer. She pushed the cart over to yet another shelf, removing a book, putting it in its place. Nora didn't follow her at once. She stood where she was, looking doubtful, looking frightened and very young, and then she snapped back to herself and sighed, trotting over to where Julie was working.

"I do love Brian," she said, "I'm almost certain I do, but it's scary, Julie. He's perfect and I'm a neurotic mess. He's white bread and I'm rye. He's cool and confident and I'm always fretting, always worrying. If I married Brian *he*'d be my life and the next thing you know I'd be driving the kiddies to school in my very own station wagon and picking Brian up at the train depot and cooking pot roasts and reading *Ladies' Home Journal* every month."

"It's the American dream," Julie said.

"Not for me. Not for *us*."

"You—you're lucky to have someone who loves you so much, Nora."

"I suppose I am," Nora said thoughtfully. "I—I still can't believe it's happened. All those boys—and then someone like Brian comes along and he wants to marry me and make me a respectable woman. I *do* love him, and I know he loves me, but—Jesus, I can just see myself at forty, sitting by the pool at the country club, working on my third martini and eying the lifeguard and—and telling myself I coulda made it, I coulda written that best-seller, I coulda been a contender if only I hadn't copped out and given up my dream. It's a tough decision to make."

"Is he pressing you?"

"He popped the question before the Easter break, as you know, and I refused to accept the ring. I told him I'd think about

it, told him I'd give him my answer as soon as he gets his degree
and I get my diploma, and that's just two and a half weeks away.
He's not pressing me, no, he's being wonderfully patient and
understanding, but he fully expects to slip that diamond ring
onto my finger the minute I get my diploma.''

Julie started to say something and hesitated, frowning, looking strange indeed, and then she dropped the book she was holding and pressed her hand against her brow, leaning against the
bookshelf.

"Jesus!" Nora exclaimed. "What is it? What's the matter?"

"I—" Julie straightened up and shook her head. "I—I just
felt a little dizzy. All that reaching and stretching, the—the dust—
I—I'm all right now, Nora.''

"You scared the hell out of me!"

"Everyone gets a little dizzy now and then. Don't look so
concerned.''

"Sure you don't want to sit down for a few minutes? Sure
you don't want me to get you some water or something?''

"I'm fine. I really have to get the rest of these books shelved,
Nora, and then I have to straighten the card catalogue. It's after
six. Don't you have a date with Brian tonight?''

"Yeah, he's taking me to the Cellar tonight. Big deal. Kerouac
and Cassady are supposed to be passing through, are supposed
to stop by and listen to the bongos, but I'm not holding my
breath. I'd as soon skip it, but Brian has never been before and
he's curious. I've got a nifty beatnik outfit to spring on him, and
I told him to be sure and dress down and skip the deodorant.
Julie, are you sure you're all right?''

"Positive.''

"Let's go to lunch tomorrow, okay? Unless Compton needs
you you'll be free until two, right? I only have one class in the
morning, and it's over at eleven o'clock. We might even go to
the Silver Bell for old times' sake.''

"That'll be fine, Nora.''

"And it's my treat, too, kid. I just sold another epic to *True
Confessions* last week. You'd think they'd be sick of my stuff by
this time, but they're always clamoring for more and a girl always needs a few extra bucks. I'll see you tomorrow, sweetheart.''

"See you," Julie said.

Nora left the library and hurried back across campus to Thurs-

ton Hall. She had a choice room all to herself now, and she was rather fond of the place, even if she didn't spend a hell of a lot of time there. Seniors had special privileges, and if sometimes they didn't come back to the dorm in the evening Pattie Dillon tactfully failed to notice. The place was full of chattering girls in curlers and bathrobes, as usual, and someone was banging on the piano in the lounge. Nora waved at Pattie, stopped to chat for a minute with a couple of girlfriends and then went to her room. Only six-thirty, she had worlds of time. Brian wasn't going to pick her up until nine. No sense getting to the Cellar early. The place didn't really start grooving until ten at the earliest.

The mail had arrived while she was out this afternoon, and one of the girls had slipped Nora's under the door. She picked it up, going through it with that eager anticipation she'd felt for the last three weeks. Two bills. A circular. Pay the bills, dump the circular. A letter from Sadie. Read it later when you're ready for a load of guilt. A postcard from Carol. Sandy white beach, indigo sky, quaint old buildings in faded multihued pastels. She had completed the Claude Bouchet film and was spending a few days in St. Tropez with Gaby Bernais. Long letter to follow soon. A catalogue from Brentano's. Look through it later. A brief note from the editor at *True Confessions*. Check enclosed. Send us more stories like the last one. Nothing from Ross Sheridan. Not a word. Shit. Maybe he lost the fucking manuscript. Maybe he *burned* it. A postcard acknowledging receipt of manuscript six weeks ago and then dead silence.

Nora put the mail on her desk, disappointed, feeling that familiar letdown. Why do you keep building your hopes up? You know it's shit. Bradley *told* you it was shit. It's shit, Nora, he said, but it's damned readable shit. Couldn't put it down. You might just have something here, kid. Yeah, sure, she thought glumly. I might just have something. Four hundred and seventy-eight pages of unmitigated crap. Nine months I spend on that book. Nine bloody months, so the people at Julian Messner could laugh their heads off. So Bennett Cerf could mail me a poison-pen letter. So some asshole at Doubleday could send me a form rejection letter that wasn't even *signed*, for Christ sake. So Mr. Ross Sheridan, the hotshot New York literary agent, could stuff my manuscript away in a desk drawer and forget its existence. Who the hell needs any of 'em? There's not a girl in this dormitory who wouldn't give both eyeteeth for just one eve-

ning with Brian Gregory and he wants to *marry* me, and me, I still believe I'm gonna be a big best-selling writer. Fuck *you*, Grace Metalious.

Peyton Place was responsible for it all. It had caused a great hue and cry when it came out, shocked the pants off the entire nation, was banned in Canada, soared to the top of every best-seller list, sold to the movies immediately, became the most controversial novel in decades, and its author, a drab, overweight housewife from a small New England mill town, became a celebrity overnight. Countless articles were written about her and her shocking exposé of sub rosa affairs in a postcard-pretty town much like the one she lived in. Nora had read it immediately, of course, and she admired the hell out of it. Actually *Peyton Place* was little more than a sexed-up, updated version of *King's Row*, but it was quite well done, with a good structure, decent writing and characters who were as real as the people next door. Nora preferred *King's Row*, which was even steamier, if a bit more subtle, but Grace Metalious vastly intrigued her. The plump "Pandora in Blue Jeans," as the journalists called her, was living proof that the slipper was real. If a plain, self-educated housewife in her thirties could get it, why not a crackerjack *wunderkind* in her junior year at Claymore?

Fired with inspiration, Nora bought two new reams of paper and started *This Heaven, This Hell*, writing, rewriting, giving it everything she had, neglecting her studies, totally immersed in the intense, overheated world she was creating on paper. Her book wasn't set in a small New England town, it was set in an affluent suburb, and while her characters were more sophisticated than Mrs. Metalious's, they were even more active in the bedroom, under the rosebushes, in the broom closet and, on one memorable occasion, in the shallow end of the municipal swimming pool. Lack of experience was no hindrance this time round, but with Julie's help she smuggled a copy of Krafft-Ebing out of the library to research a few of the more esoteric variations. She frequently worked all night long, with no roommate to complain about the typing, and when she finally finished it early in January, she was sure she had a huge best-seller on her hands.

Stephen Bradley thought it had possibilities, too. He read it promptly and admitted he hadn't been able to put the damned thing down. It was shit, yes, he couldn't deny that, but the characters were vibrantly alive, you genuinely cared about them, the

story was fast-moving and the writing wasn't half bad. *This Heaven, This Hell* was several cuts above *Because You Care*, the book she had written during her freshman year, and, well, it just might have a chance. *His* publisher wouldn't be interested, but he said it wouldn't hurt to send it around, see what happened. Nora sent it to Messner first, because they had published the Metalious novel. They weren't interested, nor were Random House or Doubleday. In the library one afternoon Nora read an article about Ross Sheridan, wonder-boy agent who claimed he could sell anything. She wrote to him, telling him about herself and the novel she had written, and a week later she received a reply from one of his aides, requesting she send the manuscript to their offices. She did. There was a postcard acknowledging receipt and then zilch. Six weeks without a word. Ross Sheridan was probably too busy giving cocktail parties for Jason Pollen and hustling deals for all those mystery writers to remember she'd even sent him the bloody book.

Depressed, Nora showered and started getting ready for her date with Brian. Black ballet slippers, black leotard, black turtleneck sweater and a black wraparound skirt. Dead-white make-up base and powder, pink-white lipstick and smoke-gray eye shadow. Halloween time, but that's the way you dressed to go to the Cellar. There wasn't anything she could do about her hair, no way she could have a pony tail or long, limp locks hanging down to her shoulders. The beatnik chicks were cool, real cool, smoked pot, read Allen Ginsberg, were obedient little slavies to macho men like Kerouac and Cassady who, privately, preferred each other. What a crock, Nora thought, but playing being Beat was the fad and probably wasn't any more harmful than swallowing goldfish or stuffing yourself into a phone booth with twenty other guys.

"Hey, Nora!" a girl called, pounding on her door. "Your dreamboat's waiting in the lounge."

Brian stood up when she entered the room. Seeing him for the first time always took her breath away. It was as though she had forgotten just how gorgeous he was, how stunning, how perfect. That thick blond hair, always neatly brushed and gleaming, no crew cut for this guy, those blue blue eyes, those virile, chiseled features, that dazzling smile. Nora felt the rush, the glow, the music inside, and she still couldn't believe *she* was responsible for that smile and that wry, loving look in his

eyes. So what is he? Out of his mind? Dozens of beautiful girls all over the place, hundreds, and he chooses a loser like me. Gotta be something wrong with him, she told herself, trying to look cool as Brian came over to her and took her hands in his.

"Hi," he said.

"Hi yourself."

"What's that gook on your face? What's that garb you're wearing?"

"I'm Beat, man. Dig? Thought I told you to dress down."

"I *did*," he protested.

"White buck shoes, white cord jeans, short-sleeved powder-blue sport shirt, buttoned-down collar, no tie, no jacket, yeah, I guess you dressed down. Guess you'll have to do."

"You want me to take it all off?"

"Not yet, sweetie," she said.

Brian grinned and pulled her into his arms and gave her a light kiss. Nora pulled away, indicating the other girls waiting for their dates.

"We've got an audience," she told him. "Let's not give 'em a show. They'll think you're after my body."

"They'll think right."

He curled one arm around her waist and led her out of the room. "Eat your hearts out, girls," she called over her shoulder.

Brian drove a battered blue Ford convertible. Nothing pretentious or self-consciously patrician about him, he was a regular fellow, one of the guys, fancy background and big bucks notwithstanding. His mother had flipped when he decided to come to Claymore for his engineering degree—Claymore? *Indiana*? How declassé, particularly after four years at Princeton—but Claymore's school of engineering was perhaps the best in the country and Brian couldn't care less about its social status. God knows his blood was blue, but he hadn't an ounce of snobbery in his makeup. Brian laughed at his mother's affectations and shrugged at his father's obsession with wealth. He was completely at ease with himself, and he was at ease with the world as well. If I could just find one teeny-tiny flaw I'd feel a helluva lot better, Nora thought.

"Do you squeeze your toothpaste from the bottom up?" she asked.

"Of course."

"Ever eat crackers in bed?"

"Never."

"I'll bet you crack your knuckles in private."

"Well—" he drew the word out, then hesitated.

"*Do* you?"

"I could," he said, "if it would make you happy."

"You're an excellent driver, too. *I* would have run that yellow light, if I drove, that is."

"You don't drive?"

"Are you kidding? I grew up in Brooklyn."

"I'll have to give you lessons," he said. "Why all the questions?"

"I'm trying to convince myself you're for real."

"I've got lots of faults," he assured her.

"Yeah, sure. I've never heard you say 'shit.' When you were a little boy, I'll bet you helped old ladies cross the street. You're sexy and virile and fun to be with and intelligent and level-headed and hardworking and wealthy, not to mention gorgeous. Did I mention gorgeous? You're too good to be true, Gregory. I'm gonna wake up and find this was all some kind of crazy wish-fulfillment fantasy and you never existed at all."

"If I have my way, you're gonna wake up in my arms."

"I suppose you think you're gonna take me back to your apartment tonight."

"Had it in the back of my mind," he admitted.

"Think you're gonna jump my bones, don't you?"

Brian nodded.

"Hold that thought," she said.

Like dozens of other "coffee houses" that had sprung up all across the country since the media explosion over Kerouac and *On The Road*, the Cellar was dingy and dimly lighted and pretentiously bohemian, fishnets hanging on the bare gray walls, sawdust scattered over the bare floor, candles leaving waxy trails on the wine bottles setting on every table. The place was packed with world-weary somnambulists in uniform attire who smoked filter-tipped Kools and drank wretched espresso and gazed at each other as though staring into an open grave, all of them having the time of their lives. Someone was invariably beating the bongos, and, suddenly inspired, some bearded youth in a dingy gray sweater, usually a sophomore, would leap up and recite his newest poem, "i am the eye of the universe and i've

gone blind, baby,'' something along those lines, and the chicks would nod wearily, the hipsters would say, "Cool, man, cool," and everyone would feel wonderfully unconventional. Real Beats might prowl North Beach in San Francisco and huddle in filthy pads in Greenwich Village, but here it was strictly improvisation and God forbid Dad should be late with next month's allowance.

"Some scene," Brian said.

"Look bored," Nora warned him, "and for Christ sake don't smile. They'll think we're tourists."

"Gotcha," he said.

A black-attired waitress with limp, stringy hair and dead-white makeup led them to a table and took their espresso orders and Brian looked terribly out of place in his neat white cords and freshly ironed powder-blue shirt, his gleaming blond hair carefully combed. "Hey, man, get a load-a th' square," someone said, and Brian seemed pleased. Nora kicked him under the table, and he dutifully assumed the bored, burned-out look. Someone put a jazz record on and some cats decided to groove on the dance floor. There was much lethargic shuffling and finger snapping and cries of "Dig it, man." Their espresso came and Brian grimaced as soon as he sipped it and said he'd a helluva lot rather have a Coke. Nora informed him that he simply wasn't with it. All the chicks and quite a few of the hipsters eyed him appreciatively, and Nora felt inordinately proud.

"Like the music?" she inquired.

"Actually, I prefer the McGuire sisters."

"Bite your tongue!"

"What's wrong with the McGuire sisters?"

Nora sketched a cube in the air. He looked at her in mock exasperation and behaved himself admirably for the next hour or so, not even smiling when the inevitable bearded youth got up and recited the inevitable poem, "i howl alone and the wind eats my words." All around them people discussed William Burroughs and Djuna Barnes and existentialism and Happenings and nobody mentioned the Phi Delta party or tomorrow's trigonometry exam. Nora was vastly amused. She had read Kerouac and crowd and found them almost as tedious as England's Angry Young Men. Aimless, drifting, asocial, apolitical and amoral, they seemed to her a group of self-obsessed, self-indulgent dropouts who needed a good hot bath and steady employment. With

his craggy, movie-star good looks, Kerouac was undeniably a glamorous figure, extravagantly exploited by all the media, but the philosophy he espoused was strictly for mental retards. He and Cassady were a no-show that evening—what the hell would they be doing in Indiana, for God's sake—but around eleven another interesting couple did appear.

"Hey cats," a hipster at the next table said, "dig the straights."

Nora turned to stare. The girl was tall and slender, with sleek auburn hair worn in a chic French twist. She had haughty green eyes, high, patrician cheekbones and a sullen mouth, and she was wearing a simple emerald-green sheath that had cost somebody a bundle. The man with her wore brown slacks, a brown-and-tan checked sport coat and a tobacco-brown tie. He had dark, unruly hair, slate-blue eyes and handsome, moody features. He wore black horn-rims. His arm was wrapped around the girl's waist, his manner quite proprietary as he led her to the table the waitress chose for them. Nora watched as they ordered espresso, as Doug Hammond took the girl's hand and gazed deeply into her eyes and talked to her in a low, sincere voice.

Nora recognized the girl immediately. She was Cynthia Lawrence, a nineteen-year-old junior, very big in the sorority set. Her father was Matthew Lawrence, the celebrated corporate lawyer. He had his own law firm, had his own skyscraper, for that matter. He was one of the wealthiest men in Chicago, had inherited millions from his first wife, the South American Doris Duke, coffee plantations, opal mines, you name it. Cynthia was the issue of his second marriage, to Cissy Vandercamp. The Vandercamps were Chicago's first family. Cynthia was a living, breathing heiress, minor league, to be sure, but due to come into a sizable fortune one of these years. So that's the way the wind blows, Nora thought bitterly. She wondered how long it had been going on. Quite some time from the looks of them. The son of a bitch!

"Something wrong?" Brian inquired.

"Let's get out of here, okay?"

"Sure."

"Look, sweetie," she said as they left, "I'm in a rotten mood. I'd rather you took me straight back to the dorm tonight."

"Something I've done?"

"No, Brian, it isn't you. You're super. God knows I don't deserve you. I just don't feel like going to your apartment. Is that all right? No hurt feelings? No wounded ego?"

"No hurt feelings. No wounded ego."

"You're a peach. I'll make it up to you."

"Promise?"

"Cross my heart."

"You've gotta deal," he said.

Nora had lunch with Julie at the Silver Bell the next day, and Julie looked rather pale, merely picked at her food, seemed unusually subdued. Nora wondered if she knew the bastard was cheating on her. She chattered vivaciously, telling Julie about the Cellar, telling her about ordering her cap and gown that morning and how Bradley was grousing because she had selected him to robe her at the robing ceremony, which meant *he* had to rent one, too. Cheapskate hated to fork out the twenty bucks. Julie pretended to listen, even smiled now and then, but Nora could tell her mind was on something else. Life was downright shitty sometimes. Julie was one of the good guys of this earth, genuinely good through and through. She deserved nothing but the best, and she got an arrogant, deceitful, opportunistic asshole like Doug Hammond. Me, I'm the town pump for almost two years and I get someone like Brian. Tell me it's fair.

"I can't believe graduation's so close," she said. "Can't believe this is all coming to an end."

"Have you decided what you're going to do?" Julie asked.

"Not yet. I'd be an idiot to turn him down."

"I suppose you would be."

"I should have my head examined for even hesitating. Men like Brian Gregory are few and far between. It's just that—well, I have this crazy idea there should be more to life than settling down with a good man, raising kids, trading recipes with the girls. It's a good life, sure, but I'm not sure it's the life for me, even though I love him."

"You'll make the right choice," Julie told her.

"That's what scares me. What about you and Doug? He'll be getting his degree the same time I get my diploma. You two made any plans yet?"

"We—we haven't discussed it," Julie replied. "Doug's the top man in his class, and—and I know he's received offers from

various law firms, but he hasn't—he hasn't decided yet just exactly what he's going to do. He doesn't want to rush into anything."

"That's perfectly understandable. It's a big step."

"I—whatever happens, I'm going to miss you," Julie said as they left the restaurant a few minutes later.

"Oh, we're gonna keep in close touch," Nora informed her. "We're sisters, remember? An exclusive sorority of three. I'll walk you to the library, sweetie, and then I've got to hit the books. Three finals next week."

Sunday morning at ten Brian picked her up in his battered blue convertible, a picnic hamper in the backseat. They drove thirty-five miles out of town to a small state park with trees and a lake. It was a glorious day, the sky a towering canopy of pale, pale blue, brilliant sunshine bathing grassy green lawns and making shimmery silver reflections on the water. Brian followed a twisting road through the trees until they finally came to a remote, secluded spot far removed from the area where families gathered and students swam. He spread two blankets on the grass near the water's edge while Nora looked around her with a skeptical eye. They were on a small crescent of land, completely surrounded by trees. It was as private as private could be and she suspected that Brian had something in mind besides just a picnic. He took the hamper out of the car. He wore scuffed loafers without socks, black Bermuda shorts and a light-blue nylon pullover.

"I'm not so sure about this," she said doubtfully. "Sure there aren't any bears in those woods?"

"Quite sure," he said.

"Snakes?"

"Only a few."

"I've never *been* on a picnic. I'm not so sure I'm gonna like it."

"You're gonna love it."

"Yeah?"

"Yeah," he said.

"I'm not really the outdoorsy type, you know."

"I'll break you in gently."

"Jesus, you're not one of those rugged males always trooping off on camping trips, are you? Hunting, fishing, crap like that?"

"Just an occasional picnic," he assured her.

She watched with some fascination as he kicked off his loafers, whipped off his pullover and unzipped the Bermuda shorts. He was wearing a dark-blue swimming suit beneath them. He looked at Nora in her white sandals and flowered sundress and grinned.

"Come on, let's go swimming."

"I don't swim, and I don't have a suit."

"I'll teach you to swim, and you don't need a suit."

"No?"

"No. The one you were born with will do."

"Smart-ass."

"Come on. I'll teach you a few strokes."

"Sounds tempting. But it isn't fair. *You* have a suit, and—"

"That's remedied easily enough."

He pulled off his swimming suit and grabbed Nora's wrist and pulled her toward the water and she shrieked and he laughed and she finally took off sandals, sundress and undies and they went into the water and Nora shrieked again because it was so cold. They frolicked for over an hour, splashing, ducking each other, carrying on like two carefree children. Brian attempted to give her lessons but she was hopeless, totally inept, always sinking the moment he let go of her. He finally gave up and gave her a big kiss. Exhausted, elated, Nora got out of the water and dried herself off with one of the towels he'd brought and Brian didn't bother with a towel. He stretched out in the sun and let its bright rays do the job for him. He fell asleep and after a while she tickled his nose with a blade of grass and he groaned and opened his eyes and grabbed her wrist and pulled her into his arms and they made love for quite some time there on the grass as birds called and leaves rustled lightly in the breeze.

They went back into the water afterwards and then dried off and dressed and sat down on the blankets to enjoy the repast he'd provided, and what a repast it was. There were pastrami sandwiches on rye and turkey sandwiches on whole wheat and potato salad and deviled eggs and olives and delicious chocolate fudge cake and a thermos of milk and a thermos of cold lemonade. Nora asked Brian where on earth he'd gotten the food, surely he hadn't prepared it himself, and he grinned sheepishly and confessed that Mrs. Giliberto from the mom-and-pop store near his apartment had fixed everything up for him for an exorbitant fee and let him borrow the hamper as well. He *could* cook

though, he confessed, and she said it was just as well as she couldn't open a can of beans without performing a sudden appendectomy. Brian chuckled.

"You think I'm kidding? When I was twelve years old I went into the kitchen and started to open a can and the opener slipped and Irving had to rush me to the emergency ward. They took fourteen stitches. To this day Sadie throws herself in front of the door if I even *look* like I'm going into the kitchen."

"Poor baby," he murmured.

"I can't cook, I can't sew, I can't iron, I'm a lousy housekeeper and can't balance a checkbook or do any of the things a good little wife is supposed to be able to do with ease. Let's face it, I'm a fantastic lay, but I'd make a rotten helpmate."

"That's a matter of opinion."

"You want a wife who'd scorch your shirts, give you indigestion and let all your socks get full of holes?"

"I want you," he said simply.

Nora folded her napkin and looked at him. He had finished eating, too, and was placing things neatly back into the hamper. Sunlight burnished his hair and a heavy wave tilted across his brow. You're a bloody fool, Nora Levin, she told herself. Grab him. Grab him while you've got the chance. If you don't, you'll regret it for the rest of your life.

"Why, Brian?" she asked, and her voice was serious. "Why me?"

"Because I love you," he said.

"Why? I'm not beautiful. I'm not well bred. I'm foul-mouthed and flashy, pushy, neurotic, consumed with ambition, and God knows I'm not pure. There were a lot of boys before you. A lot. It's not something I'm particularly proud of, but it happens to be a fact."

"I know about the other boys, Nora. I understand. You were insecure. You were trying to find yourself."

"That's one way of putting it. You could have any girl you wanted, someone fabulous."

"I want you, and I happen to think you're fabulous as hell."

"Yeah?"

"You talk tough, but you've got the kindest heart of anyone I know. You're not a raving beauty, no, but you're real and you make all the beauties look like so much plastic. You're warm

and funny and vulnerable and I'd like to spend the rest of my life taking care of you.''

"I don't want someone to take care of me, Brian. I want to write.''

"You can still write.''

"When? After the laundry is done? After the kids are old enough to attend school?''

"Lots of wives do things like that in their spare time—write, paint, make pottery. I *want* you to be creative.''

"Sure you do. In my spare time.''

"I want you to have outside interests.''

But you'll never understand that writing is as important to me as engineering is to you. Maybe even more so. It's a consuming need, something I've got to do, as necessary as breathing. It could never be an "outside interest." Jesus, how easy it would be if I were conventional and only had to make the conventional choices. Big church wedding or small affair. This china pattern or another one. Why do I have to be so goddamned driven? Why can't I revel in the miracle of this man and forget those crazy dreams? Who the hell needs the slipper when you've got Prince Charming in the palm of your hand?

"I love you,'' he said.

"I know.''

"You love me, too.''

"I suppose I do.''

"Then—''

"We're from two different worlds, Brian. I know that sounds trite as hell, but it happens to be true. I'm not New Rochelle, I never could be. I'll always be Brooklyn.''

"That doesn't matter to me.''

"It matters to your parents.''

"They don't know you. When they do, they'll love you just as I do.''

"Sure,'' she said.

"I want to make you happy, Nora. I think I can.''

"Maybe you could, but—I'm not what you need, Brian. I'm not sure *I* could make *you* happy.''

"It's a risk I'm willing to take.''

"That's mighty big of you, pal.''

"You know what I mean.''

"Of course I do.''

"I want to marry you."

"So you've implied."

"I won't press. I promised I'd wait till graduation for your answer, and I will, but I'm getting itchy."

"Are you?"

Brian nodded and smiled and pulled her into his arms. He kissed her for a long, long time, and she ran her palms up his back and over his shoulders, feeling smooth musculature beneath the nylon. His kiss was tender and firm and loving, yes, loving. She knew now the true meaning of that euphemism "make love," for Brian made love to her, masterful yet tender, hungry yet caring. She loved his taste, his smell, his strength, his warmth, and a wonderful abandon possessed her as his arms crushed her close, as his lips continued to press and probe. How glorious to contemplate having him every day and every night, to wake up in his arms every morning.

Brian lifted his lips, his eyes full of mischief.

"I'm also getting horny again," he said.

"I noticed that."

"You look so fetching in that sundress."

"So fetching you want to rip it off me, right?"

"Something like that."

"It's what—three o'clock? We've got plenty of time. Rip away, big fellow."

Nora felt gloriously replete as they drove back to Claymore. She sat very close to him, his right arm curled around her shoulders as he cruised leisurely down the highway. The sun went down and the darkening gray sky was blurry with fading pink-and-amethyst banners. It had been a wonderful day, and she doubted if she would ever in her life be happier than she was at this moment. One day, she knew, she would look back on this moment—the two of them side by side and silent, content, the motor purring, the wind ruffling her hair, colors blurring against the gray—and it would be as beautiful in memory as it was in reality. Yet she was still no closer to her decision. She was still torn, uncertain and uneasy. She would think about it later. Now she was content to savor the ashes of aftermath and the beauty still glowing inside.

Night had fallen when they reached Claymore. He took her directly back to the dorm. Both of them had exams the next day, and both needed to study. Nora found it extremely difficult to

concentrate on the books, but she passed the exam with flying colors and was feeling quite chipper as she returned to the dorm at two o'clock in the afternoon. The mail had arrived. She carried hers up to her room.

Another letter from Sadie. More guilt. Four more bills. Thank God she'd sold the story to *True Confessions*. A copy of *The Atlantic Monthly*. A flyer from the Sandra Dee Shoppe. Terrific sale on summer duds, come see us soon. A letter from New York City. From New York City! At last! She stared at the return address, dazed. He had written at last! Nora sat down on the edge of her bed to catch her breath, nervous as hell now. What if he didn't like the book? Her hands trembled as she ripped open the envelope.

ROSS SHERIDAN LITERARY AGENCY
44 East 41st Street
New York, New York

May 19, 1958

Miss Nora Levin
Thurston Hall
Claymore University
Claymore, Indiana

Dear Miss Levin:

It is with a great deal of interest that we have read your manuscript, *This Heaven, This Hell*. It reveals an astute understanding of human nature and has a compelling narrative flow. Although it needs revision and is perhaps a bit too sexually graphic for today's market, it nevertheless shows a fresh and exciting new talent.

In your cover letter, you mentioned you would be in New York early next month. If it is convenient, I would very much like to talk with you about your writing and your future with the Ross Sheridan agency. I look forward to hearing from you soon.

Sincerely,

Ross Sheridan

Ross Sheridan

rs/mb

Nora read the letter several more times before finally folding it and putting it back into the mangled envelope. Excitement swept over her and she wanted to shout, she wanted to sing, she wanted to break into a dance. The excitement soon waned, eclipsed by sorrow and a sense of loss, dread, too. It wasn't going to be easy to break the news to Brian.

9

*It was a beautiful suit, dark navy blue, elegant and classy, ex-*actly the suit a new young lawyer would wear. It had cost far more than she could afford to pay, but she had put it on layaway four months ago and had finally been able to make the final payment today. Julie left the clothing store with the long white box under her arm and decided to walk back to the apartment rather than wait for the bus. It was two and a half miles, but the exercise would do her good. Doctor Grayson had told her she needed all the exercise she could get, although, of course, she mustn't overdo it. She was young and healthy and he expected no problems, but she needed to build up her strength. Actually, now that the morning sickness had abated, Julie had never felt better or stronger in her life. Her whole body seemed to tingle with health, and she felt a radiant glow inside.

Her skin seemed to glow as well. Doctor Grayson had given her a tube of ointment to use on her face, and after all this time her complexion had begun to clear up. She suspected her pregnancy had something to do with that, too, as all the other lotions and ointments she had used had been ineffective. It seemed miraculous. Only a few tiny pit marks remained, and those were barely visible. Julie walked briskly, feeling the play of muscles in her legs, feeling the strength and the glow. She hadn't felt this way with the first baby. She had felt worn and weary, constantly

distraught, but the circumstances had been responsible for that. Doctor Grayson had assured her there was absolutely no reason why she shouldn't carry this baby to full term and have a relatively easy delivery.

Doug didn't know yet. He . . . he had a great deal on his mind, so many decisions to make. With his grades, his record, he had naturally had a great many job offers. It seemed important law firms did scouting, just like football coaches, and Doug had gone out to lunch with several representatives who wanted him on the team. He didn't discuss it with her—he never discussed anything with her nowadays—but Julie knew he would soon accept one of those offers and they would leave Claymore and begin a whole new life together. He had attended his last class this morning, and in just two days he would graduate at the head of his class. He would wear this handsome new suit, and she would be so proud of him, so proud. When . . . when it was all over with and he had his degree, she'd tell him about the baby. They'd be able to afford a baby now, as soon as he signed on with one of those important firms.

Things were going to be all right between them. She believed that. She had to believe it. She had worked so long, so hard toward this goal, and now that they had almost reached it nothing . . . nothing would go wrong. He was unhappy with her, true, bitterly resented her acting and the time it consumed, but she hadn't been able to disappoint Mr. Compton, not after all he had done for her. She had played the leads in the last three plays, and it had been a wonderful, elating experience, but she was prepared to give up acting entirely for Doug's sake. A home, a family—those were the important things. She loved the magic of the theater, loved being a part of it, but she didn't have that obsessive hunger for success that had motivated Carol and motivated Nora as well. Carol wanted to be an actress more than anything else in the world, just as Nora wanted to be a successful writer, and both were willing to sacrifice everything to realize that dream. It . . . it would be lovely to have a successful career in the theater, but not if it meant giving up home and husband and children. That dream came first.

This had been brought home to her two months ago after the opening night of *Picnic*. She had played Madge, and during that time onstage she had actually *been* a beautiful, discontented young woman from a small town prepared to give up the safe

for the excitement of life with a virile stranger, brilliantly played by Jim Burke without leather jacket and Brando mannerisms. In flowing blonde wig and thin melon-pink dress, she had sighed at the heat and boredom, filled with longings easily incited by the dashing, ne'er-do-well Hal. A transformation occurred, as it always did, and afterwards in her dressing room she felt plain and shy, Julie again, wondering why all these people were coming in, beaming, lavishing her with compliments. Julian Compton entered with a short, dumpy, brusque-looking woman with short-cropped gray hair and fierce blue eyes. She wore a drab gray dress and smoked incessantly, fitting cigarettes into a long black holder. Julie judged her to be in her mid-fifties at least, and she felt uneasy as the woman stood at the edge of the crowd, smoking, frowning, tapping her foot impatiently and staring at her with an alarming intensity. When the crowd thinned out Compton shooed the others away and only the three of them remained.

"Julie," he said, bringing the woman forward, "I want you to meet Sonia Lezenski."

Julie felt the hair on the back of her neck prickle, felt the color vanish from her cheeks. Madame Lezenski was perhaps the most famous drama coach in America, a legendary figure in theatrical circles. Born in Russia, forced to flee with her family during the revolution, she had had a brilliant career in the theater in Paris before immigrating to America. She had done a number of films during the thirties, character parts mainly, and had eventually given up acting to teach. Her students had included some of the most celebrated names in theater and films, and many of them still claimed they couldn't make a move without Sonia's help. She was tough, feisty, opinionated, autocratic, a tyrant, a genius, and she never took on a student unless she was thoroughly convinced that student had the seeds of greatness. As Julie stared, completely tongue-tied, Compton explained that his friend Madame Lezenski had come to Claymore at his request, just to see Julie's performance. Sonia Lezenski fitted another cigarette into the end of her holder, lighted it, inhaled deeply, than gave a curt nod. With her square, jowly face, much creased and wrinkled, she looked rather like a bulldog eager to snap up a bone.

"You are right, Julian," she barked in a harsh, guttural voice, "she's got the magic, this one, just like you told me. Janice

Rule, she does *Picnic* on Broadway. She is good, but she is not as good as this one is, not half as good. I take her back to New York with me, we work, she will become an enormous success. You!'' she snapped at Julie, blue eyes flashing. ''You are prepared to work as you have never worked before? You are prepared to put yourself in my hands? You are prepared to obey my every order, to live for nothing but your art?''

''I—Madame Lezenski, I am very flattered, but—''

''It will not be easy! This I promise you! I am very difficult, hard to get along with. I am stubborn, testy, a dictator. I am a demon, this everyone says and it is true, but I am the best. What I see tonight on the stage, it moves me to the core. Me, Lezenski, I cry real tears when I see such talent, such rare, rare talent. You will be my prize student. Together you and I will create a new legend on Broadway.''

Julie saw the woman and heard the words, but it was difficult to believe any of it was real. She was sitting here at her dressing table in front of a murky mirror in this shabby, dusty dressing room backstage in the college theater, still wearing the long blonde wig and thin melon-pink dress, and Madame Sonia Lezenski was telling these things to her. Sonia Lezenski! It was happening just as Nora claimed it would. This dumpy, ugly woman who looked like a bulldog was her fairy godmother and she was holding out the slipper. Julie felt numb.

''You will come with me to New York,'' Lezenski announced. ''I will help you find a place to live, you will find some menial job to pay for your food, your rent. We will start to work immediately.''

''Madame Lezenski, I—I *am* flattered, like I said, but I—I have a husband.''

Sonia Lezenski made a face and waved her hand, dismissing such unimportant details. Husbands! Who needed them? The butt of her cigarette crackled violently as she drew on the long black holder.

''I couldn't leave him, and even if it were possible, I—I couldn't possibly afford to take lessons with—''

''Money! This is not important! Money I have coming to me in rivers. I take this blonde sex symbol on as student, against my will, as a favor to one of my dear friends, she is not bad, she has potentials, but she is tormented. She cannot make a decision, cannot function, she is a sleepwalker who must be

prodded. She makes me her guru, this I do not like but it happens. Now when she makes a film I must go with her and sit on the set and watch and tell her she is wonderful and for this I am paid a fortune, more money than I ever believe it is possible to make. I work with you and we do not worry about money. Later, when you are the huge success, *then* you can pay me."

"I—"

"You will not give me an answer yet. You will think about it. Tomorrow we will have lunch and discuss all the details. I will meet you at twelve in Julian's office. He will drive us to a quiet restaurant."

"I—I'll be happy to lunch with you, Madame Lezenski, but—"

"Fine! It is settled. Come, Julian, now we go talk to this boy. He is a magnificent Hal. If only Bill could have been here to see this production. He would have wept, too. Perhaps I will persuade him to write a new play for these two young people I discover in Indiana."

They left the dressing room and Julie removed wig, dress and makeup and brushed out her hair. Twenty minutes later she joined the others onstage for the opening night party—bright lights, spiked punch, sandwiches, loud, pretentious chatter, clouds of cigarette smoke—and the quiet girl with her shy smile and poor complexion, in her simple white blouse and brown skirt, looked nothing at all like the beautiful, sensuous Madge who had enraptured the audience an hour earlier. Julie saw Sonia Lezenski standing with Jim Burke, her cigarette holder waving as she subjected him to a barrage of words. In jeans and leather jacket, Jim looked dazed, unable to believe the great Sonia Lezenski had seen his performance and approved it. Julie wandered about, deeply disappointed because Doug had not come to see the play and accompanied her to the party. She had asked him and he had said he would try to make it, but apparently he had been too busy with the books. Tonight's triumph seemed curiously hollow without Doug here to share it with her.

An elated Jim Burke drove her home on his motorcycle, telling her of his decision to leave for New York immediately— Sonia Lezenski was going to take him on—and begging her to come, too. Just think, William Inge really *might* write a play for them one day. Jim was going to be a big, big star, he promised her. He was going to take Broadway by storm. It'd

be terrific if Julie came, too. Hell, they could be the new Lunts, just buddies off stage but behind the spotlights a sensational team.

Working so closely together, she and Jim had become very good friends. He was one of the nicest boys she knew, always thoughtful and helpful, always bringing out the best in her. For some reason he didn't feel he had to put on a front with her, and, with Julie, he was relaxed and engaging, exuding a boyish charm quite different from his Brando-inspired swagger. Although he was extremely virile and sexy—all the girls were mad for him, of course—theirs was a purely platonic friendship. Jim respected her and knew she loved her husband and had never made a pass, although there had been any number of exuberant hugs. He was very fond of her, she knew, and Julie treasured their friendship. Jim *was* going to be a huge success in New York—she felt it in her bones—and she was going to be very proud of him.

It was quite late when Julie got back home and Doug was already asleep, sprawled out on the bed with his bare legs all tangled up in the sheets.

Julie didn't go to bed. She sat on a chair near the bed in the darkened room and watched the play of moonlight and shadow on floor and walls and listened to her husband's breathing and thought about Sonia Lezenski's offer and the slipper. In her heart, in her soul, she knew that she could become a successful actress, perhaps even a great actress. She knew what was inside her, knew now that she could express it on stage, and Lezenski wouldn't have wanted to take her on if she hadn't known it, too. It would be hard and it would be risky, so much depended on chance, on luck, on the right break, but with a powerful person like Lezenski behind her half the battle would be won. Julie thought about it and Doug groaned in his sleep and turned over, clutching the pillow in a fierce grip as, in his sleep, he usually clutched her. No longer fifteen years old, a grown woman now and far more perceptive than many people would believe, given her shy demeanor, she was fully aware of all his faults, but she loved him, she loved him with every fiber of her being, and she still believed things would be right between them and they would be happy once Doug got his degree and they were able to make a new start. They would have children, a nice home, and Doug would be a tremendously successful lawyer and she

his proud, contented wife. She couldn't give that up, not . . . not even for the slipper. Fame and fortune would mean nothing without Doug.

Julie paused for a red light and shifted the long white box from one arm to the other. She had lunched with Lezenski the next day and regretfully informed her of her decision to remain with her husband. The celebrated dramatic coach calmly fitted another cigarette into her holder and lighted it with care. She exhaled plumes of smoke and nodded curtly. "This is a large decision to make. You are not impulsive, you are level-headed, this is good. If you change your mind, Sonia will welcome you with open arms." Julie wondered if she had made a grave mistake—Nora would think her mad for passing up an opportunity like this, Carol would, too—but five weeks later she started to feel queasy and realized she had missed her last period. Yes, she thought as the light changed, I made the right decision. Crossing the street, she headed toward the campus, passing the shabby second-run theater where *Daughter of France* was playing.

It was probably the only theater in the country where the film was still showing, and it was held over here only because of Carol's having been a student at Claymore. When it opened, the movie had been savaged by the critics, and, as predicted, the public stayed away in droves. It had a short, limited run and was quickly yanked from the theaters. Cynical Hollywood insiders declared that the only reason it had ever been completed in the first place was so that the studio would have a good tax loss. Eric Berne held a press conference and placed the blame for the debacle entirely on Carol's head, citing her temperament, her arrogance, her complete lack of professionalism or even a modicum of talent. He had released her from her contract and he apologized to the American public for foisting such a hopeless, undisciplined amateur on them. Carol's name became synonymous with lack of talent and she provided material for many a comedian's monologue. "If a bomb were to drop on this theater tonight," emcee Bob Hope quipped during the nationally televised Academy Awards ceremony, "Carol Martin just might have a career." One lone critic in Berkeley, California, a young woman named Pauline Kael, carefully pointed out that the film was horribly written, ineptly directed and garishly produced, that Carol Martin had a luminous screen presence and, under

the circumstances, had given a more than adequate performance. Unfortunately her voice was lost in the general condemnation.

Poor Carol, Julie thought, moving on down the street. She got the slipper, all right, but it hadn't worked out the way it was supposed to. The public who had taken her to their hearts in the beginning had turned on her with vicious glee, and America's Favorite Cinderella was now a laughingstock, the butt of show biz jokes. Julie knew that she herself would have been completely demolished by the experience, but Carol hadn't let it defeat her. She was a fighter, determined to prove them all wrong. She had just completed a film in France and, according to a letter Nora had received a couple of weeks ago, was about to begin another next month. Julie admired her spirit and believed in her ability. Carol *had* been good in the film, even if the film itself was an abomination, and she was convinced Carol would ultimately succeed, despite her disastrous debut.

Julie was tired by the time she finally reached the apartment. The walk had been longer than she thought. Wearily, she put the box down on the coffee table and went into the kitchen to make herself a cup of herbal tea. She leaned against the counter as the tea steeped, looking at the dingy walls and worn linoleum, the ancient pine cabinets. Soon they would leave this hideous apartment behind, and she would have a bright, shining kitchen with modern appliances. Julie wondered what it would be like to have their own house and a lawn, perhaps even a small garden. She wondered what it would be like not to have to work such long, hard hours to make ends meet. The bad times were behind them now. It had been tough and there had been times when it had seemed hopeless, when she had despaired, but they had made it, they had finally come through. She wished Gus Hammond and her parents could be here to see Doug receive his degree, but her parents had disowned her and Doug hadn't heard from his father in all this time.

Julie stirred a spoonful of honey into her tea and took it into the living room with its exposed pipes and shabby old pink sofa. She wondered where Doug was. His class had been over at eleven, and it was after four now. Had he had a luncheon engagement with a representative from one of the law firms? She didn't think so. Perhaps he was with one of his friends. Now that classes were over they were . . . they were probably having a final get-together. He was probably drinking beer in one of the

pubs with a group of his buddies. She wasn't going to think about the other. She wasn't. It had meant nothing at all. They had just been strolling across campus together that evening she was leaving the library after working late, and if Doug had had his arm slung around the girl's shoulders as they passed under the lamp and she spied them, it . . . it didn't mean anything. Julie remembered the sharp, stabbing pain, the doubts that besieged her when he didn't come home until after one o'clock in the morning. He claimed he had been with friends, and the lovely red-headed girl probably *was* just a friend, and he would forget all about her as soon as they left Claymore. She wasn't going to let the doubts besiege her again. She wasn't going to subject herself to that agony.

It was six-thirty when Doug finally came in. Julie had put the suit box away in the closet. She had prepared dinner. She was setting the table when she heard his key in the door. Removing the apron tied around her waist, she stepped into the living room. Doug wore the brown-and-tan checked sport coat she had given him last year and a brown tie, and he carried a briefcase, looking very much the lawyer already. His thick brown hair was tousled and, behind the heavy black horn-rims, his slate-blue eyes were unusually sober. How handsome he was, even handsomer now than he had been when she had first spied him there by the McCanns' pool back in Tulsa. That seemed so long ago, Julie thought. They had been through so much together since then. She felt a rush of love for this man who was far from perfect, true, but her reason for being nevertheless.

"You look tired," she said quietly.

"I've been busy."

His voice was curt. He put the briefcase down and loosened his tie, and Julie could see that something was bothering him. He was agitated, uneasy, a deep furrow above the bridge of his nose.

"Dinner's ready," she told him. "I—I made pork chops and applesauce, your favorites."

"I'm not hungry," he said.

"But—"

"I said I'm not hungry, Julie. I stopped by the library this afternoon. You weren't there."

"Today was my day off. I thought you knew that. I—I had an

errand to run downtown. Did—was there something you wanted to talk to me about? You don't usually stop by the library unless—''

"Yes," he interrupted, "there's something I want to talk to you about, but—" He hesitated, frowning, very uncomfortable. "I suppose it can wait a little longer. What were you doing downtown?"

"I—I intended it to be a surprise but—" Julie went over to the closet and took out the box. "I put this on layaway four months ago and took it out today. I wanted you to look extra nice when you get your degree. It's a very important occasion for both of us."

Doug took the box from her and sat down on the sofa and opened it. Pushing back the layers of tissue paper, he looked at the handsome navy blue suit without expression and then set it aside. Julie watched, both hurt and surprised by his lack of response. She had worked so hard to pay for that suit, had herself done without in order to get it for him, and he gazed at it without the least interest.

"Don't you like it?" she asked.

"It's a nice suit, Julie."

"You can wear it with your blue-and-silver-gray striped tie. I had your black shoes resoled and polished, and they look almost like new. You're going to be ever so—"

"I don't want to discuss clothes," he said.

He stood up, his mouth set in a determined line.

"What *do* you want to discuss, Doug? Something's wrong. I sensed it the minute you came in. What is it?"

"Us," he said.

"Us?"

"That's what I want to discuss."

"I don't see—"

"It's all wrong, Julie. Both of us have known it for a long, long time. I never wanted to get married in the first place—you know that—but I hadn't much choice in the matter. I—we've made the best of things these past four years, but—"

He cut himself short, looking pained. This wasn't pleasant for him, she could see that, but then it was hardly a picnic for her. Why didn't she feel anything? Her whole world was falling to pieces all around her, and she felt nothing at all.

"You want to leave me," she said.

"I'm going to Chicago, Julie. As soon as I pick up my degree I'm flying to Chicago in a private plane. I'm going to work for a law firm there."

"I see."

"The salary, the benefits—it's a wonderful opportunity for me."

"And you don't need me anymore."

"It isn't—"

"Now that I've worked like a slave for four years to put you through the last year of college and through law school, you don't need me anymore. You never intended to—I never meant anything to you but—you used me and I let you because—because I love you."

Doug scowled. Nothing was more discomfiting than the truth, and it *was* the truth. Julie knew that. Deep down, on some level of consciousness, she had known it for quite some time, but she had refused to acknowledge it, even to herself. Foolishly, she held to the dream, deliberately deluding herself. She saw that now, but it didn't help one bit. Oh, Jesus, the shock was wearing off now and the numbness was gone and the feeling came in waves, threatening to rend her asunder, yet when she spoke her voice was perfectly level.

"I assume Cynthia Lawrence will be flying to Chicago on the same private plane," she said. "I assume it is her father's law firm you will be working for."

He looked surprised at that. He looked guilty, too.

"I saw the two of you together one evening as I was leaving the library," she explained. "The next day I pointed her out to a friend and asked her name and—and he told me all about her."

"So you know," he said.

"I know. I understand. I suppose she's in love with you. I suppose you will use her too. She'll be very, very helpful. Af—after you get rid of me I suppose you intend to marry her. You'll go far, Doug. Oh, Jesus, you'll go very, very far."

I'm not going to cry. I'm not. I refuse to cry. I refuse to break down in front of him.

"You've figured it all out, haven't you?" he said.

"I think I have."

"Look, Julie, I'm sorry about this, but—yes, Cynthia and I

are going to get married just as soon as the divorce goes through. I've been to see a lawyer. I've already filed.''

"You don't believe in wasting time, do you?"

"I'm beginning a whole new life, Julie, and—you wouldn't—it's not the kind of—"

"I wouldn't fit in," she said, "that's what you mean. I'm not wealthy. I'm not a socialite. I'm not educated. I wouldn't make the right impression. I wouldn't be an asset. I—I'm just a dumb little nobody from Oklahoma, good enough to wait on tables and put you through school but certainly not the sort you'd care to be seen with at an executive cocktail party."

Doug made no reply. He had no defense. What she said was the truth, and both of them knew it. He tugged at his tie again and averted his eyes, glancing at the exposed pipes, feeling wretched. Julie smiled a tight little smile and shook her head at her own foolhardiness. But I did it because I love him, she told herself. I love him still. God help me. So this is how it feels to have your heart break.

"I'm pregnant, Doug," she said.

He looked at her in disgust. "What kind of a fool do you think I am? Do you actually believe I'm going to buy that crap? Do you actually believe it's going to work a *second* time?"

"I'm pregnant," she repeated. "I've been to the doctor. You'll become a father in early January. I didn't want to tell you until after—after you got your degree. I was saving it for a surprise. I actually thought you'd be pleased because—because we could afford a child now."

"Jesus! It's true, isn't it?"

"It's true."

"I guess you'll have to get rid of it," he said. "I guess I'll have to find an abortionist, make the arrangements."

Her eyes held his. She shook her head.

"No, Doug, I'm not going to get rid of it."

"I'm not going to be trapped a second time, Julie. No way. If you don't want to have an abortion, you'll just have to go it alone."

"I have no intentions of 'trapping' you. I won't fight your divorce. Go ahead with your plans."

"I'm not a complete heel, Julie, despite what you believe. I—I'll make sure you're taken care of. I'll pay alimony—I'll be able to afford it easily enough. If you have a child, I'll pay child

support, too. I'm going to be making a very good salary, and once Cynthia and I are married there'll be even more money. I want to be fair."

That tight little smile played on her lips again, and she shook her head. Her husband frowned. He expected tears. He expected anger. He didn't expect this quiet dignity, this unnerving composure. He could deal with tears and he could deal with anger, but he didn't know how to deal with her calm expression and those level violet-blue eyes that looked at him unflinchingly and saw into his soul.

"What is it you want, Julie?" he asked irritably.

"I don't want anything," she said. "I don't want alimony. I don't want child support. I've managed to support the two of us for the past four years. I imagine I can support myself and my child without any help from you."

"If you're trying to make me feel bad, you're doing a damned good job. I feel like the world's greatest shit."

"Is your conscience actually bothering you? I don't imagine that'll last too long, Doug. I imagine you'll recover in record time. When were you planning to leave the apartment?"

"As soon as I get my degree. We'll be flying out that night."

"I suggest you leave now," she said.

He looked startled. "Now?"

"Right now. As soon as you can pack your things. I don't want you staying here another night."

"You don't have to be so unreasonable about this, Julie. I don't have a place to go. I don't have the money for a hotel room. You can't just expect me to—Jesus! Can't we be civilized about this?"

"I don't feel very civilized at the moment," she told him.

"You're actually going to throw me out?"

Julie picked up her purse and took out her wallet. She had been paid two days ago and had thirty-five dollars in cash. She pulled it out and handed it to him.

"This should pay for a room tonight and the taxi to get you there. If it isn't enough, I suggest you call Cynthia."

His cheeks flushed a dark red, and he looked at her with his mouth set in a tight, ugly line. Julie gazed back at him without flinching, without betraying a single emotion, and, clutching the bills in his hand, he finally stormed into the bedroom and began to pack his clothes. Julie stood there for a long time without

moving, afraid to move, afraid she would break into little pieces if she so much as breathed too hard, but it didn't happen. She went into the kitchen and put the food away and washed the dishes and the calm contained her like a tight, invisible shell. She finished in the kitchen and went back into the living room and heard him on the telephone, ordering a taxi.

Doug came into the room with two old suitcases, a tennis racket under his arm. He moved past her and opened the door and set suitcases and tennis racket outside, and then he came back and placed the top back on the white box and picked it up. He would look very handsome in the navy blue suit, yes, but she would never see him wear it. The irony of it brought yet another smile to her lips. Doug thrust the box under his arm and angrily shoved a thick brown wave from his brow and adjusted his horn-rims.

"My lawyer will be in touch with you," he told her.

"Fine," she said.

"Good-bye, Julie. Been nice knowing you."

He stepped outside and slammed the door behind him and she heard him carrying his things up the steps and, a few minutes later, heard the taxi honk in front. She did not break down. There were no sobs, no tears. The tight, invisible shell protected her still, and a curious numbness inside held the pain at bay. She stepped into the bedroom and looked around at the disarray he had left, drawers open, contents either scattered, the closet door standing wide, her own clothes either pushed aside or hurled to the floor, and, calmly, she straightened things up, put clothes away. She found a worn old tan T-Shirt with CLAYMORE printed across the chest in brown—he had overlooked it or deliberately left it behind—and she remembered the times he had worn it and she almost broke down then. Almost. Julie folded the T-shirt up and put it in the bottom of a drawer and finished straightening the room and looked at the bed and knew that she wouldn't be able to sleep on it tonight.

Julie went into the living room and sat down on the shabby pink sofa, and she was still sitting there as the light turned pale gold and faded to a misty gray. Darkness came and filled the room with blackness and eventually silvery beams of moonlight streamed in through the window and made shimmering patterns on the floor, but she did not get up to turn on a light. She sat there, holding a cushion against her breast, and the tears

brimmed at last and she sobbed and clutched the cushion tightly. She cried for a very long time and then she wiped her eyes and, mercifully, slept, curled up on the sofa. Bright sunlight brushed her lids and awakened her in the morning, and she got up and felt grief and loss and emptiness, and it was overwhelming, but there were no more tears. There was no time for them now. She had to get on with the business of surviving.

She was in a cluttered office in back of the library at five o'clock that afternoon, sitting at a long wooden table piled high with new books. They had come in earlier, and Julie's job was to stamp them with the library stamp, declaring them Property of Claymore University Library, and to paste a small library label inside each front cover. It was tedious, time-consuming work, but Julie was grateful for it today. It helped. Rub the stamp on the ink-soaked pad, stamp the book, neatly and carefully so that the ink doesn't smear, place the label on the sponge, gummed side down, moisten it thoroughly, place the label on the inside front cover, smooth it down, close the book and set it aside and move on to the next one. The very monotony was somehow soothing. She had been at it for four hours, working steadily, like an automaton, and there were still at least three dozen more books to stamp and label.

She didn't look up when the door opened, assuming it was one of the other aides come to take a break or have a quick cigarette. She reached for another book and opened it and stamped it and looked up when Nora sighed. Her friend was wearing a tan skirt and a pale yellow sweater. Her customary vivacity was missing today. Her face looked slightly pale, and those lovely brown eyes had a sad expression, faint gray shadows beneath them, as though she, too, had had a very bad night. Nora sighed again, smiled a brave smile and sat down across the table.

"Hi," she said listlessly.

"Hi. You—you look **awful,** Nora."

"Thanks, kid. I needed that. I really needed that today. I'm ready to jump off a high building and my best friend tells me I look like shit. I *know* I look like shit. You shoulda seen me before I bathed my eyes. I didn't get much sleep last night. In fact, I don't think I slept at all."

"You talked to Brian. You—you told him."

Nora nodded. "Last night. He took me out to dinner. I told

him I couldn't marry him. I told him that I had to write, that it was the most important thing in the world to me. I told him I wasn't right for him, that both of us knew that, that I was doing him a favor—and I *am*, Julie. If we got married, it—it would be disastrous. I know that. Brian knows it too, deep down, but he—he loves me and he still believes love conquers all obstacles.''

Julie applied the gummed label to the book and smoothed it down, then set it aside and reached for another. Nora fell silent, remembering, more subdued than Julie had ever seen her.

"How did he take it?" she asked.

"He was very polite. He was hurt—God, the pain in his eyes—but Brian is a gentleman and a thoroughbred and he nodded gravely and smiled a sad smile and said I had apparently given it quite a lot of thought, and I nodded and he said, 'I guess that's it, then.' He drove me back to the dorm and walked me to the door. He took both my hands in his and held them tightly and looked at me and—and told me I would always have a special place in his heart. He kissed me lightly on the lips, and then he let me go. I watched him walk back to his car and I thought—I didn't think I could take it. I longed to call him back and tell him it was all a mistake, I couldn't possibly live without him.''

"But you didn't."

"I didn't. I went inside and went to my room and—and I cried most of the night. Me, the cynical sophisticate with a smart, snappy answer to everything. Can you believe it?"

"You're not as tough as you think you are."

"I'm tough as nails and you bloody well know it. He—he'll get over it, Julie, and one day he'll thank me. He'll meet the right girl, a poised, perfect Vassar graduate with blood as blue as his—someone named Tracey or Wanda or Gwen—and his parents will approve and the munchkin will adore her and all his friends'll welcome her into the fold with open arms. She'll fit right in, and—and he'll remember the kooky Jewish girl back in college and give thanks every night for his narrow escape.''

"You do yourself an injustice."

"I'm right. I *know* I'm right, but—it doesn't help at all. Oh, Julie, I—I really do feel like jumping off a high building. I've never been so miserable in my life.''

"I'm sorry, Nora."

"It—I feel better just talking about it."

"That always helps."

"I'm going to get over it. I'm going to be strong."

"Of course you will be."

"I'm going to New York and I'm going to *make* it. I'm going to write that blockbuster if it kills me. I've got to now. I'd never be able to forgive myself if I gave him up and then fell flat on my ass."

Julie didn't say anything. She stamped and labeled another book and then set it aside. How ironic it was. Nora had just given up what she herself had wanted more than anything else—a husband who loved her, as Brian loved Nora, a home in the suburbs, a peaceful, domestic life with children. Acting, no matter how satisfying, could never take the place of that. Nora sighed again and glanced at the clock.

"It's almost your quitting time. Know what I'd like to do? I'd like to get drunk."

"You don't drink," Julie reminded her.

"I know. I—I don't suppose you'd like to keep me company tonight?"

"I'd love to."

"Doug won't mind?"

"Doug isn't in the picture anymore."

"What do you mean?"

"He left me yesterday. He has filed for divorce. He's flying to Chicago with Cynthia Lawrence."

"Jesus! Oh, Julie—I'm so sorry. I come storming in here and bellyache about my own problems like the selfish bitch I am, and all the while—forgive me, darling."

"There's nothing to forgive."

Julie stood up, brushing a speck of lint from her brown skirt and pushing a lock of hair from her cheek. "I can finish this in the morning," she said. "I just have to speak to the head librarian and then we can leave."

Five minutes later they were strolling across campus, late afternoon sunlight spreading shadows over the lawns. There were few other students around at this hour. Many had already left for the summer. Julie knew the pain was there inside, waiting to savage her, but calm still possessed her, holding the pain at

bay. Quietly, she told Nora what had happened. They paused by one of the fountains.

"Oh, darling," Nora said, taking her hand. "It must have been terrible for you—and you were all alone last night. You should have called me. You should have—what are you going to do now?"

"I don't know. I—I talked to Mr. Compton this morning. He wants me to apprentice at a summer theater in Cape Cod, said he would make all the arrangements for me, but I—I don't think I should do that. There's something else, Nora. I'm pregnant."

"Holy shit," Nora whispered. "You told him?"

Julie nodded. "He wanted me to have an abortion."

"The son of a bitch! I hope you told him to go fuck himself."

"Not in those precise words. I—I'm not going to fight him. I'm going to let him have his divorce, Nora. I'm going to have my baby and—I'll make it somehow. I don't have anyone to turn to, but—"

"What the hell do you mean, you don't have anyone to turn to?" Nora let go of her hand and gave her an angry look. "What am *I*, chopped liver? We're sisters, you silly bitch, and sisters stick together. I'll tell you what you're going to do. You're going to go to New York with me. We'll get an apartment and you'll take care of yourself and have your baby and I'll be an aunt. After the baby comes we'll find a nurse for it and you can go study with that Russian woman you told me about and become a famous actress."

"Nora, I appreciate your offer, but I—I don't have any—"

"If you mention money I'll slap your face, I swear it. I can make plenty of money for both of us. Even if Sheridan doesn't sell my book right away I can whip off enough confessions to keep us in crackers and keep a roof over our heads. It'll be an adventure, Julie."

"Nora—"

"I'm not taking any lip—it's settled. Come on, we're going to go back to your apartment and I'll help you pack. You're not going to spend another night by yourself. We'll stay at the dorm tonight, and tomorrow we'll settle everything here and then it's off to the train station."

"Graduation. Your diploma—"

"They can send it to me. Stop dawdling, kiddo. We've got things to do, places to go. Right?"

Julie had vowed she wouldn't cry again, but the tears came nevertheless, brimming over her lashes, trailing down her cheeks. Nora took her hand again and squeezed it tightly.

"Right?" she repeated.

"Right," Julie said.

10

It was April and the sky was slate gray and Paris seemed to be etched in shades of mauve and pewter and dingy brown. The chestnuts might be in blossom and the trees in the *bois* might be green, but who would notice on a day like this, with puddles everywhere and a fine mist still falling? Carol didn't mind the weather at all. After three grueling months on location in Morocco with Roger Hanin and Françoise Arnoul, it was wonderful to be back, to be able to shop and relax or do nothing at all unless the spirit moved her. There wasn't another film on her agenda at the moment, but that didn't bother her in the least. She was in strong demand and another script would come along and, in the meantime, how delicious to stroll along the Champs Élysées this gray afternoon, a belted transparent plastic raincoat over her green-and-black checked skirt and long-sleeved black jersey, the plastic hood pulled up over her short-clipped hair.

Filming in Morocco had been exhausting, yet it had been exhilarating, too. A Hitchcock-inspired thriller—Hitchcock was a God over here, everyone seemed to be imitating him—it featured a remorseful criminal, Hanin, in love with a disillusioned nightclub singer, Arnoul, and indifferent to the waif downstairs, Carol, who is in love with him. After a plethora of fights, stabbings and chases through the twisting alleyways of the Casbah, waif turns in nightclub singer who is actually a spy and, for her

trouble, is strangled to death by Hanin, who then gives himself up to the police. It was her second film with Claude Bouchet, a stylish, suspenseful romp filmed in murky Technicolor that would do great business over here and have a limited run in select art theaters in the States. Hanin was ruggedly handsome and great fun to work with, Arnoul was pleasant, if a bit reserved, and Claude was a charmer, driving them all mercilessly but with Gallic good humor.

After the first Bouchet film, Carol had gone immediately into a frothy comedy with Daniel Gélin and Dany Robin, playing a madcap, high-heeled heiress who attempts to take Gélin from wholesome Robin. After a brief rest she had done a drama with Maurice Ronet, her performance as Ronet's neglected and love-starved wife winning plaudits from the French critics. The film she had just completed was unlikely to wow the critics, but it had been an interesting role and fun to do. Without exorbitant, inflated budgets and Machiavellian studio intrigue behind the scenes, filmmaking in France was far more relaxed than it was in America. Carol had done four films over here now, and on the set of each there had been a casual intimacy and a feeling of jaunty camaraderie that was wonderfully refreshing after the ordeal with Berne.

Although she was not yet a full-fledged star—she had yet to receive top billing—Carol was vastly popular with French film audiences, and she was making a living, if not a fortune. More importantly, she was learning her craft, and she knew she was getting better with each film. All three of the films she had done earlier had played in America, in art houses only, but none had generated any particular interest. Her name was still mud over there. Over there she was still a joke, but they'd sit up and take notice one of these days. Foreign films were becoming more and more popular and were receiving more and more attention in America, and Carol vowed she'd soon have Hollywood begging for her services. The next film she made would do it for her or, if not, the one after that, but Carol Martin would come home in triumph, and she could hardly wait to see Eric Berne's face when she picked up her Oscar.

The unlikelihood of that happening brought a smile to her lips. Carol had learned to take herself less seriously, but if you were going to fantasize, you might as well go all the way. She might not win an Oscar, but she *would* prove herself to her

countrymen. In the meantime, she was enjoying herself immensely. She loved Paris. She loved her work and her stimulating new friends and her charming eighth-floor apartment on the Avenue Ingres with its balcony overlooking the Bois de Boulogne. She missed Nora and Julie, with whom she kept in very close touch, and she missed hearing English spoken, but life had been good to her these past two years. She was completely on her own, and she was making it, gradually building up a respectable body of work, and if there were periods of loneliness, that was a small price to pay.

Gaby still insisted she would be much happier with a lover. Gaby was never without some bronzed youth with thin lips and cruel, seductive eyes, was always breaking up, suffering nobly, falling in love all over again with the next handsome scoundrel. That was fine for Gaby, she seemed to thrive on it, but it was hardly Carol's style. She had had a brief affair with one of her costars, a devastatingly attractive man considerably older than she, but she had refused to let him break her heart and ended the affair herself. There had been a couple of other short affairs, light and pleasant and harmless, but she had yet to meet the man she was ready to suffer over. She wasn't averse to a bonbon now and then, but the main course had no appeal. The sweet torments of love might delight Gaby and inspire yet another wry, trenchant novel, but Carol could live without it. She never intended to be hurt as Julie had been hurt when her husband walked out on her. The pain was half the pleasure, Gaby claimed, a uniquely French viewpoint incomprehensible to a girl from the American Midwest.

A stout matron in a hooded red raincoat approached, walking her black poodle. The poodle wore a red raincoat too, prancing along as though it owned the pavement. Carol smiled. The woman recognized her and nodded warmly. Although Carol was American, a race secretly despised, the French accepted her as one of their own. She didn't receive nearly the press she had received when she first arrived—no one seemed to receive any press today except Brigitte Bardot, who had exploded upon the scene like a Roman candle—but she was still a favorite with both press and public and was still featured regularly in *Paris Match*. It was nice to be liked, to be accepted, particularly after all of the abuse she'd received from her countrymen after the release of *Daughter of France*. That had hurt. It had cut to the bone,

but she had survived it, and she would make them eat their words ere long.

The light drizzle turned into rain, and Carol quickened her step, grateful that Le Drugstore was just up ahead. It was one of her favorite places to shop in Paris. A chic version of the American institution, it had a pharmacy, a tobacco shop, a large book department, a stylish notions counter and a restaurant that served divine pastries. Dodging a puddle, she hurried inside, immediately at home. Le Drugstore wasn't at all crowded at this hour. It stayed open until two in the morning and did a thriving business late at night. Carol wanted to buy the new Françoise Mallet-Joris novel. Mallet-Joris was Gaby's contemporary and every bit as good, although she hadn't received the attention Gaby and Sagan had. Carol browsed for half an hour, picking up the new Simone de Beauvoir, Romain Gary's latest and the Mallet-Joris.

Leaving the book department with her parcel, she happened to spy a whimsical stuffed monkey, pink and gray, with large, soulful eyes. Unable to resist, she purchased it immediately for her godson, Danny, who was now four months old. She had sent Julie an exquisite French bassinet and a silver cup for the baby, but Danny would probably appreciate the monkey more in months to come. She had seen pictures of him, of course—Nora had turned into an inveterate camera nut after the baby's arrival—and he was a chubby, healthy-looking infant with Julie's eyes and an endearing double chin. The clerk said she would be delighted to ship the monkey for her. Carol signed a gift card, gave her Julie's address and tipped her generously. It was as she started out of the store that she saw the tall American boy with brick-red hair and a bewildered expression. He was standing at the counter in the pharmacy, desperately trying to make himself understood to the stony-faced, indifferent pharmacist.

"I—uh—jay mal ah le—tete? No, that's head. Jay mal ah la gorge and I—uh—jay need une medicine pour mah mal gorge. Comprendez-vous? Damn, I wish I'd paid more attention in French class!"

The boy was in his mid-twenties, quite attractive, wearing brown slacks, a beautifully tailored brown-and-rust checked sport coat and a deep-rust silk tie. Clearly affluent, he had that clean-cut, charmingly naive look of many American youths in a world-weary Paris. His dark-brown eyes were rather watery, she

observed, and his handsome nose was undeniably red. Pulling a crisp white handkerchief from his pocket, he let out a monumental sneeze and then gave the pharmacist a woeful look.

"Pour mal ah la gorge—gorge, that's throat, isn't it? Une medicine pour mal ah la gorge, si vous play?"

The pharmacist shook his head, deliberately obtuse. Although France would be in dire straits without the money American tourists poured into its coffers, many Parisians resented their presence and some, like this pharmacist, who Carol suspected spoke perfect English, were rude and difficult. Stepping over to the counter, she asked the boy if she could be of service.

"You speak English? Thank God. I've got this wretched sore throat, a bad cold, too, and I wanted to get something for it. My high school French is terrible, and I didn't take it at Yale. I never thought I'd find myself in France but Dad and I came over here on business and—ah—ah—" He whipped his handkerchief out again, just in time to catch another monumental sneeze.

In now flawless French Carol told the pharmacist to bring her some medicated throat lozenges and a bottle of aspirin. He complied speedily, and she told the boy the price and helped him sort out the franc notes. He was quite large, tall and muscular, and he somehow reminded her of a great, engaging puppy. She smiled at the look of relief in his eyes.

"Don't know how to thank you," he said. He had a charming midwestern accent. "Dad speaks perfect French, but I didn't want him to come out in weather like this. If you hadn't come along, I don't know—"

He cut himself short, really looking at her for the first time. Carol saw recognition fill his eyes, then disbelief. He stared at her for a long moment, clearly in shock.

"It—it *is* you," he exclaimed. "Carol Martin. *High Heels at Breakfast.* I saw that film back home—they were showing it at a little art theater. That scene where you get tipsy and start disrobing in front of the guests and Daniel Gélin jerks off the tablecloth to cover you up—funniest thing I ever saw, deliciously risqué. You were fabulous."

"Why—thank you," Carol said.

"I know you've made other movies, but that's the only one I've seen. You're my father's favorite actress! Geez, he's never going to believe this, never in a million years."

The handsome youth squinted his eyes and scrunched his nose

up and quickly retrieved his handkerchief, sneezing quite violently. He apologized profusely, then shook his head.

"Dad's going to think I made this up. He—" He hesitated, and she could see an idea dawning. "I don't suppose—no, of course you wouldn't—couldn't even ask you."

"Couldn't ask me what?" she inquired.

"I'm meeting Dad at four at the bar in the Plaza Athénée, that's where we're staying. Dad didn't want to make this trip, said I could handle everything myself, but I insisted he come, too. My mom just recently died, you see, and I thought a change of scene—Geez, you're not interested in all this."

"On the contrary. You were going to suggest something."

The boy lowered his eyes, looking suddenly shy and about twelve years old. "I was going to ask if—if you'd like to join us for a drink at the hotel, but a famous actress like you—of course not. You don't know me from Adam, and I could be a dope-crazed sex maniac or something."

"I'll take that risk," Carol told him.

"You—you mean you'll *come*?"

"Only if you'll swear you're not a dope-crazed sex maniac."

"I'm not!" he protested. "Really, I'm the nicest guy you'd ever hope to meet, besides my dad, that is. He's the greatest guy in the world. He's going to fall right out of his chair when he sees me walking in with you. I can hardly wait to see the look on his face. Are you sure you don't mind? I'm not trying to pick you up, I swear it."

"I'd be delighted to have a drink with you and your father. We'll have to walk, I fear—we'll never find a taxi with this rain. The Plaza Athénée isn't far."

"Here, let me take your package."

"Did you come out without an umbrella?"

He gave her a sheepish nod. Carol insisted he buy one, and a few minutes later they were walking in the rain, umbrella overhead. The rain fell noisily, splattering all around, and they didn't attempt to talk. Carol felt very young and strangely carefree. The boy was charming and very American and clearly not on the make. Taxis hissed past, splattering water, and other pedestrians scurried along under their umbrellas. Rain pelted down on top of their own, but it was quite large and protected them adequately. The boy stumbled, almost losing his balance. Carol seized his arm. They both began to laugh. The doorman was

appalled when, a few minutes later, they dashed into the sumptuous lobby of the Plaza-Athénée like two riotous schoolchildren. The boy folded up the umbrella and Carol removed her raincoat and they checked both, along with her package of books. She smoothed her hair down and smiled as her new friend sneezed again. His nose was even redder than before, his eyes still watering, and after he had his drink she was going to insist he take his medicine and go right to bed. It dawned on her that she didn't even know his name yet.

"It's five after four," he said, his voice beginning to grow hoarse. "My dad will already be waiting. I can't tell you what this means to me, Miss Martin. I never for a minute believed you'd—"

"Let's not keep Dad waiting any longer," she said.

The bar of the Plaza-Athénée was filled with sleek, soignée women in expensive designer clothes and distinguished, handsomely attired men, the atmosphere exclusive and redolent of wealth. Carol felt underdressed in her simple skirt and jersey, but her poise and cool elegance made them seem chic. Heads turned as they made their way toward a table near the back. The man seated there rose slowly to his feet, and his face turned pale. Carol saw him and felt the shock sweep over her, but she lost none of her composure. The boy introduced her to his father and Carol smiled politely, as though he were a stranger, and he managed to control his own shock and carry it off with quiet aplomb. His son suspected nothing.

"Can you *believe* this, Dad?"

"It's—quite a surprise."

"I told her she was your favorite actress and asked if she'd join us for a drink but I never thought she'd come, never in a million years. First I had to convince her I wasn't a dope-crazed sex maniac."

"I imagine that took some doing," his father said.

Norman Philips helped her into her chair and asked her what she would have to drink and signaled the waiter and ordered a glass of white wine for her and a scotch for his son and another bourbon for himself. The boy's name was Cliff and she remembered now seeing a photograph of him that night in the mansion outside of Wichita. He was like a younger, heartier version of his father, muscular and vigorous instead of lean and trim, exuberant instead of suave. He told his father about their meeting

at Le Drugstore and how knocked out he had been when she agreed to join them for a drink, and their drinks came and young Cliff continued to chatter merrily, pausing now and then to sneeze, his voice growing hoarser by the minute.

"I think you've about had it, son," his father said. "I think you'd better go upstairs and go to bed. Ask them to send up a couple of hot-water bottles."

"And be sure to take your medicine," Carol added. "Those throat lozenges have codeine in them. They'll help immediately."

"I can't believe this," Cliff protested. "I'm sitting at a table with a famous movie star, and my father sends me up to bed. I *am* beginning to feel a bit woozy and feverish. I—ah—ah—" He sneezed yet again and gave Carol an apologetic look.

"Thank you again for coming," he said. "I—uh—I guess it'd be gauche to ask for your autograph?"

"It would be gauche indeed," his father informed him. "Go on, get out of here. Miss Martin and I will finish our drinks."

Cliff grinned, stood up, told Carol good-bye and left the table, pausing on his way to the door for another mighty sneeze. Carol and Norman Philips looked at each other, silent, both a little ill at ease now that they were alone. She toyed with her wineglass, finding it hard to believe she was really sitting at a table with him. How many times had she thought of him over these past years? He had changed very little. His dark auburn hair was still sleek, a few silver strands above the temples now, and his deep brown eyes seemed a bit sadder, but he was still wonderfully handsome, still made her feel warm and secure and content.

"You have a charming son," she told him.

"Cliff's a good boy. I'm very proud of him."

"I—he didn't tell me his name. I didn't know you were going to be here. He just said you were a big fan of mine and asked me to join the two of you for a drink and—on impulse, I agreed to come."

"I'm glad you did."

"This kind of coincidence—Gaby would never use it in one of her novels. It would seem much too farfetched."

"Real life is full of such coincidences."

"What are you doing in Paris?" she inquired.

"We've opening a French boutique in both our department stores—perfumes, gloves, scarves, handbags and such—and Cliff

wanted to come over and speak to the manufacturers directly. He's a brilliant businessman. He's taken over everything in Wichita, the business, the foundation, runs it all much more efficiently than I ever did.''

"He seems so young.''

"Cliffs twenty-seven. Don't let that exuberant exterior fool you. He's got a mind like a steel trap when it comes to business.''

"Married?''

"Engaged. A lovely girl. They'll be taking over the big house after they marry. I—it's a little large for me. I'll move into an apartment in town, I imagine. Would you care for another glass of wine?''

She shook her head. "Your son told me your wife died recently.''

"It was inevitable," Philips said. "Her doctor told her she'd die within a year if she didn't stop drinking. Clarisse continued to drink.''

"I—I'm sorry," she said, lowering her eyes.

"Oh, Clarisse was a well-behaved drunk, and if you're going to be an alcoholic, it's best to have several million dollars. You can go to the most luxurious sanatoriums to dry out before your next toot, and somehow your friends are much more tolerant if you're wearing diamonds and a Dior original when you pass out in their pantry. I resigned myself to her drinking years ago.''

He's suffered, she thought. He's suffered far more than I ever suspected. With a marriage like that, no . . . no wonder he needed someone to love when he took me home with him. She had sensed his strength immediately, but there had been a curious vulnerability as well. It was a combination most women found irresistible, particularly when the man was so attractive. He's lonely, and he's unattached now, and that's a dangerous combination, she told herself. He has a beautiful mouth, perfectly shaped, and those fine, dark brows . . . You'd best watch yourself. Carol looked up. Their eyes met.

"I've thought of you often," he said.

"And I've thought of you.''

"I've been following your career. You got a bum rap on the Eric Berne movie. The movie was awful, but you were good.''

"Thank you.''

"*And the Sea Is Blue* was a superb film. You did a wonderful job. Maurice Ronet was excellent, too. I saw it three times."

"They showed it in Wichita?"

"At a drive-in," he confessed, "on a double bill with *Mam'zelle Pigalle*, a Bardot movie. Two sizzling French flicks, adults only. I felt silly as hell sitting there alone in my Cadillac surrounded by hot rods full of amorous teenagers."

"You went three times?"

He nodded, smiling. It was a lovely smile.

"I'm very flattered," she said.

Their eyes met again, and there was a long silence as both remembered that night four years ago. There had been a magical chemistry between them from the beginning, and the chemistry was stirring anew. Carol felt it with every fiber of her being. She was twenty-one years old now, a grown woman, and she had met some of the most attractive, most exciting men in the world. None of them had awakened the taut, tender feelings she felt swelling inside her now. He wasn't a famous actor, a notorious womanizer, no, but he had a special appeal that was overwhelming. Every instinct warned her to draw back, to resist, to thank him for the drink and politely withdraw. She didn't want the main course, her career was much too important to her, and this man could never be just a pleasant diversion.

"Are you involved?" he asked.

Carol shook her head. "Not at the moment."

"But there have been men?"

"None like the first," she said.

She hadn't meant to say that. It just came out.

"I want to see you again, Carol. There is an important dinner appointment tonight with one of Madame Chanel's representatives. As Cliff won't be able to make it I'll have to fill in for him, but tomorrow night—" He hesitated, looking into her eyes again.

"I'm afraid I'll be busy tomorrow night," she told him.

"I see. I—I suppose it was a rotten idea."

"My friend Gabrielle Bernais has a play opening tomorrow night. I have to attend—Gaby would never forgive me if I missed it. I have an extra ticket," she added. To hell with her instincts. Danger be damned. "If you'd like, we could go together."

"I'd like that very much," he said.

"I live at Number Ten Avenue Ingres, on the eighth floor. I'll

leave your name with the concierge. Most of the men will be in black tie, but you needn't bother. We should leave around seven, the theater's on a small back street and quite difficult to find.''

"I'll be there on the dot.''

Norman Philips walked her to the lobby and helped her on with her raincoat and held her package of books while the doorman whistled for a taxi. He helped her into the backseat of the taxi and held her hand a moment longer than necessary, and as the taxi pulled away she looked through the rain-streaked rear window and saw him standing there on the wet pavement in front of the grand hotel, a tall, strikingly handsome older man watching the taxi depart and oblivious to the rain that spotted his dark suit and wet his auburn hair. You're a fool, a fool, a fool, she told herself. You should never have agreed to see him again. But as horns blared and tires hissed and the taxi hurtled her through congested streets there was a smile on her lips she wasn't even aware of, and a delicious anticipation glowed inside.

Although Carol had acquired a cool patina of sophistication these past two years in France, the next evening, as she was dressing, she felt exactly like a girl getting ready for her first prom. What to wear? The scarlet chiffon was stunning, but, well, perhaps a bit too dramatic. The blue Chanel suit was nice but not quite dressy enough. She finally settled upon a sleeveless black Dior, simple and clean-lined, with a black cord sash at the waist and a straight skirt that fell just below the knees. The matching black cloak was lined with gleaming white silk. She used perfume sparingly, applied just a suggestion of rouge and gray eye shadow and brushed her hair until it clung to her head like a short, tight dark-gold cap.

The doorbell rang at six-fifty-seven. Her nerves were in shambles, but he hadn't the least inkling when she opened the door. Beautifully composed on the surface, she greeted him with a polite smile and graciously accepted the lovely bouquet of pink roses. He was wearing a superbly cut tuxedo with black tie and gleaming white shirtfront and black satin cummerbund and looked so handsome she felt her heart leap. Norman Philips was fifty years old and looked a good ten years younger, like one of those mature, distinguished male models one found in *Gentleman's Quarterly*.

"The roses are lovely," she said. "I'll just take a minute and put them in water.''

"Nice apartment," he remarked.

"I was lucky to get it."

"Did you decorate it yourself?"

"One of Gaby's friends helped. I wanted something elegant yet warm and inviting. Pale blues and grays and whites. Lots of plants, books, carefully selected paintings."

"It suits you," he said.

Carol placed the roses in a tall crystal vase and added water. He stepped over to the balcony. It was a pleasant evening and the French doors were open. Below and beyond he could see the treetops of the *bois*, shadowy now at twilight. The multilevel rooftops of Paris with their tilted angles and chimney pots and skylights caught the last fading rays of sunlight. Seeing him standing there, Carol felt a tightness in her throat. She had dreamed of him last night—she had dreamed of him countless times during the past four years—and now he was actually here. He turned, smiled, and she smiled back, polite, rather reserved, in perfect control. She had no intention of becoming involved. A pleasant evening together, that was all. There was no place in her life at the moment for the kind of relationship involvement with this man would mean.

"Ready?" he inquired.

Carol nodded. He helped her into her wrap. She picked up her small black satin purse, and they left the apartment, silent on the way down in the elevator. She wondered if he was as ill at ease as she was and if, like her, he was concealing it behind a polite, careful facade. She noticed his hands, lean and brown, strong. Beautiful hands. He curled one of them lightly around her elbow as they left the elevator and passed through the foyer. He had hired a car for the evening, long and black and sleek, terribly expensive. She remembered that he was a very wealthy man. He might be from Kansas, but he had a relaxed, cosmopolitan air rare in any American male.

"How is Cliff?" she asked as he helped her into the backseat.

"Better. I insisted he stay in his room all day. When he found out I was taking you to the theater he felt very left out. Envious, too."

"The two of you seem to have a wonderful relationship."

"Cliff and I spent a lot of time together when he was growing up. If his mother wasn't traveling, she was at some swank san-

atorium, drying out. I tried to compensate. We've always been close."

Traffic was heavy, and their progress was slow, and they chatted politely, both ill at ease and pretending not to be. Carol longed to question him about his life, his marriage, his women, for surely there had been other women. She asked instead if he was enjoying his stay in Paris, if their business was going well. The luxurious car moved grandly and at a snail's pace through a twisting labyrinth of streets, finally arriving at the Theatre Edouard VII, trickily located in a blind alley between the Bar du Cyros and a Russian restaurant. Norman took the tickets from her and escorted her into the lobby crowded with glittering people. Carol saw Jeanne Moreau and Serge and Christian Marquand, Irwin Shaw, Ann and Art Buchwald, Roger Vadim and Annette Stroyberg, the breathtakingly beautiful Swede who had taken Bardot's place in his bedroom. There were reporters and photographers galore, for a Bernais opening was always an occasion. While America knew Gaby only as the author of short, affably cynical novels, in Paris she was also celebrated for her work in the theater. Her first two plays had been extremely successful, her third had a modest run and this, her fourth, raised great expectations.

"Here you are!" Gaby cried, rushing over to them. "And this is your gentleman friend. Introduce me later, darling. I'm a wreck at the moment. We're having a get-together at the Russian restaurant after the play—I have a feeling everyone is going to need a lot of vodka. Do bring him over."

She hurried away, looking like a nervous little girl playing dressup in a moss-green velvet Balenciaga. Gaby had reason to be nervous, for, as it turned out, the play was a big disappointment. Abandoning her usual chic milieu, Gaby had set it in turn-of-the-century Paris, with two brothers, one a roué, the other a scholar, vying for the favors of a capricious courtesan. Jean-Claude Brialy and Jean-Louis Trintignant were excellent as the brothers and Michèle Morgan made a sumptuous courtesan, but the story was trite, the pace leaden and the entire production suffered from an excess of red plush. The audience was polite, but Carol felt sorry for Gaby as she and Norman moved up the aisle, just behind Vadim and his beauteous Swede.

"Bernais as Bernais is unique," Norman remarked. "But Bernais as Jean Anouilh doesn't work."

Carol was surprised by his insight—and his knowledge. The play *had* been like a poor imitation of Anouilh, who, she knew, was one of Gaby's idols. That Norman was conversant enough with French drama to perceive this underscored the fact that, Kansas or no, he was a literate, sophisticated man second to none in cosmopolitan savoir faire. She was quite impressed, and she was very proud to be seen with him.

"Shall we go to the get-together next door?" he inquired.

"Gaby would be crushed if we didn't."

"It's bound to be a wake."

Carol smiled. "You don't know Gaby!"

And, indeed, when they entered the restaurant Mlle. Bernais was perched on the edge of a table, downing a vodka, surrounded by friends and chatting vivaciously with Christian Marquand. Her latest youth, blond, muscular, thin-lipped, stood nearby looking both hostile and impatient. Gaby waved to them, and Roger Hanin came over and gave Carol a gigantic hug and a sultry Jeanne Moreau tapped Norman on the arm and asked if he had a light. He lighted her cigarette with a platinum lighter and Moreau smiled the sulky-provocative smile of hers and inquired if he was in the theater. Hanin swept Carol away, dragging her over to meet some of his buddies and reminisce about Morocco. The restaurant grew more and more crowded. Vodka flowed profusely. Piroshki, caviar and blinis were in abundance on the buffet tables. The atmosphere grew heated and riotous, no one enjoying it more than the playwright herself.

"They call it the New Wave," a journalist was saying. "A group of young, inventive, revolutionary new filmmakers who couldn't care less about traditional values. They want to experiment, to astound. Truffaut, Godard, Guy Masson, they're the lads to watch. They're going to make a great noise, mark my words. Film as we know it in France will be changed forever."

"Guy Masson?" Hanin said. "Never heard of him."

"He hasn't made a full-length film yet, he's spent most of his youth writing film criticism, but he's a genius—the most exciting of the lot. Some of his ideas are startling. He's an intellectual, a radical, looks like an emaciated Apache, but he can hold you spellbound when he talks about film. He's trying to get financing for his first film now, and if it's made, it's going to be a landmark, I assure you."

Carol was intrigued. She had heard about the New Wave, of

course, but she had considered them a bunch of rowdy, ragtail, undisciplined children—most of them were still in their mid-twenties—flying in the face of conventional values. Suddenly realizing that half an hour must have passed since Hanin dragged her away, she felt a pang of guilt and looked around for Norman. He was probably miserable in this crowd. She spotted him across the room, talking with Irwin Shaw and Peter Viertel. Moreau was still with him, looking magnificent in crushed red velvet and pearls, laughing at one of his remarks and devouring him with those wide, moody eyes. Mature, experienced, one of the most exciting women in the world and one of its greatest actresses, she obviously found the man from Kansas most interesting. Someone tugged on Carol's arm, pulling her away from the crowd around Hanin.

"It was dreadful, darling, wasn't it?" Gaby said brightly. "Frankly, I'm surprised the critics didn't rise en masse and come after me with machetes."

"It was pretty awful," Carol admitted.

"But such fun to do. I never really care what happens to the play—I can always write another novel. I just love being in the theater, working with the actors, soaking up the atmosphere."

Gaby smiled her pixie smile, cheerful as could be, a little high on vodka, blithely celebrating in the face of disaster. Jean-Claude Brialy looked upset. Trintignant looked stoic. Michèle Morgan hadn't bothered to come to the party. Shaking her short, tawny-gold curls, Gaby seized another vodka from the tray of a passing waiter and took a healthy swig.

"Jeanne seems quite intrigued with your gentleman," she said. "He must be something if he can keep her captivated."

"He's something," Carol told her.

"Is he the one, darling?"

"He—he could be, if I allowed it to happen."

"Let it happen. Life without love—" Gaby paused, as though such a thing were unthinkable. "You need to be in love, darling. It gives one a reason for getting up in the morning."

"It also hurts."

"Love is like champagne. It lifts your spirits, it makes you sparkle, and you feel gloriously alive. If you have too much there is often a hangover, but that is a small price to pay."

"That sounds like one of your books."

"My books are me," Gaby said blithely. "Here comes Alain,

looking particularly sullen. We shall probably fight tonight—he has a violent temper—but in the early hours of the morning it will be such fun to make up.''

Gaby's youth came over and took her arm roughly, demanding they leave. He was dangerously attractive, if you cared for the type. Gaby rested her hand on his lean cheek and ignored the fiery look in his eyes. She smiled coquettishly, told him he would have to be patient and, pulling her arm free, waved him away. Her brown eyes sparkled as she turned back to Carol.

"Forget Coca-Cola, darling," she advised. "Try the champagne."

She gave Carol a hug and hurried away to greet Eddie Constantine and Edith Piaf, who, having skipped the play, were just arriving. The American-born actor was having a great vogue in French gangster films, his Lenny Caution series extremely popular. With his battered, Bogart face and flashy silk suit he looked like a hoodlum but was the most genial of souls. Piaf, all in black, appeared shaky and disoriented, her huge dark eyes full of pain. Carol moved across the room toward Norman but was intercepted by Gerard Philipe, who was currently making Vadim's *Les Liaisons Dangereuses* with Moreau and Stroyberg. They were already having censorship problems, he informed her. He said several nice things about Carol's performance in *And the Sea Is Blue* and added that he hoped they'd have an opportunity to work together soon.

Norman and Moreau were discussing the theater when Carol joined them. His French was almost perfect, she observed. Moreau took Carol's hand and smiled a radiant smile and told her she was fortunate indeed to have so charming and intelligent a companion. She apologized for monopolizing him and told Norman he was fortunate, too. Giving Carol's hand a friendly squeeze, she moved away to speak to Vadim and Stroyberg. Carol looked up at Norman, and there was no one else in the room. She sensed that he felt the same way. The noise, the glittering crowd were a mere background. Their eyes met and held and a long moment passed before Norman finally grinned and asked if she was ready to leave. Carol nodded. He tucked her arm in his and led her toward the exit.

Their car was parked down the street. Both were silent on the way back to the Avenue Ingres. It was a comfortable silence. There was no need to talk. Paris at night was festooned with

dazzling, multicolored lights, like an aging beauty who has decided to wear all her jewels at once. Carol had been here for over two years, and this was the first time she had felt the full magic of Paris. The city seemed somehow different tonight, warm, welcoming, enfolding them both in its spell. Perhaps what they said was true. Perhaps Paris really was for lovers. But he isn't my lover, she reminded herself, and he's not going to be. Norman reached for her hand in the semidarkness of the backseat, holding it firmly in his own. He isn't. I'm not.

The limousine glided to a stop in front of her apartment building. Norman helped her out and they stood there on the pavement. A streetlamp nearby made a warm yellow pool, intensifying the shadows. She could smell flowers and damp soil from the *bois* across the way, and she could smell him and feel his warmth. Her knees felt curiously weak. Her throat felt tight again. There was an ache inside, an emptiness that yearned to be filled.

"Shall I ask the driver to wait?" he asked quietly.

"I—I'm tired of Coca-Cola," Carol said.

Norman arched one fine, dark brow, puzzled.

"I want champagne," she added. "Why don't you tell the driver you won't need him anymore tonight."

Norman pulled her to him and kissed her lightly on the lips. Carol waited in front of the building while he stepped over to dismiss the driver, and a moment later the car pulled smoothly away. Norman took her hand and led her into the building. There might be a hangover, a very bad hangover, but she already felt her spirits soaring, felt wondrously, gloriously alive. Gaby was going to be very proud of her.

There was a balcony in her bedroom too, and sunlight streamed over the marble bannister the next morning and gilded the hardwood floor with a misty gold. He was still asleep, completely nude, the sheets twisted around his thighs, his bare chest and one leg exposed. He had the lean, solid body of an athlete, his skin a soft tan, and he had the strength and energy of a man many years his junior. He had proved that last night. Carol stood near the open French windows, nude herself beneath the thin blue robe that was belted at the waist and fell to mid-thigh. Birds were singing in the *bois*. She had never paid that much attention to them before. Again she felt the magic of the city. It seemed to smile, to welcome her into the ranks. Norman stirred, a lock

of dark auburn hair tumbling over his brow. He opened his eyes. He saw her standing in the misty gold light. A lovely, boyish smile formed on his lips, and her heart seemed to swell until she thought it might burst.

"What's that I smell?" he asked.

"Bacon, eggs, warm croissants, coffee."

"Delicious smells. I'd better get up."

Carol shook her head and left and returned a few moments later with a tray. There were strawberry preserves and a crock of butter for the croissants, a pitcher of rich cream for the strong coffee. Norman was sitting up, his back propped against the headboard, the sheet pulled modestly up to his waist. Carol smiled and sat down beside him, carefully balancing the tray on his knees.

"I've never had breakfast in bed before," she confessed.

"Never?"

"Never. Help yourself."

Norman grinned. His hand moved up her bare thigh.

"I meant help yourself to the food."

"You're far more appetizing."

"You need your strength," she said.

"There's that," he agreed.

They both ate heartily. Food had never tasted so good before, she thought. His white dress shirt and tuxedo jacket were draped over the back of a chair and his pants folded neatly over its arm. Carol's high heels were in the middle of the floor, one upright, one on its side, her black Dior, her underclothes shamelessly abandoned beside them. The morning sunlight grew brighter, silvery now, dazzling rays streaming inside. She felt a wonderful languor in her bones. The bedsheets smelled of perspiration and love. She finished eating, set her dishes on the floor and watched him, her eyes glowing, a soft smile on her lips. Norman took a sip of coffee and a bite of croissant. Unable to resist, she touched his arm and ran her palm over the strong, muscular bicep and along his shoulder, resting her fingers against the nape of his neck. His skin was smooth like silk and warm to the touch. She ran her fingers through the thick auburn hair on the back of his head and he took a final sip of coffee and a final bite of croissant and then set his own dishes on the floor, along with the tray. He wrapped both arms around her and covered her mouth with his own and soon they were lost again in last night's rapture.

It was noon before both had bathed and dressed. Carol looked fresh and appealing in sandals and a simple lime-green cotton dress. His tuxedo was slightly wrinkled and incongruous at this hour, his tie a little crooked, but he looked deliciously handsome nevertheless. Carol stood up on tiptoes and gave him a light kiss, singing inside, flooded with radiance. Was it really possible for a person to feel this happy, or was she still inebriated? Gaby was right. It was exactly like champagne, and she wanted more and more and more.

"Cliff will probably think you've been kidnapped by Gypsies," she said.

"I doubt it. Cliff's a big boy. He knows I am too, which, all things considered, is quite generous of him. Most sons think their fathers are doddering incompetents."

"Is—is your business in Paris almost finished?"

He nodded. "We're scheduled to fly home day after tomorrow."

Carol didn't say anything. He saw the look in her eyes and smiled.

"Cliff's raring to get back. We've been here for two weeks now, and he has a lovely fiancée waiting in Wichita. I, on the other hand, do not have a fiancée, and there's no reason on earth why I should fly back just now."

"Oh?"

"I can think of a number of reasons to stay."

They had dinner at Maxim's with Cliff the following evening. The decor was opulent. The food was incredible. The service was perfection. Cliff had fully recovered from his cold and sore throat and was so genial and engaging it was almost indecent. He told Carol about his plans for the boutiques and the shopping mall he hoped to build in a year or so and he told her all about Stephanie, whom he could hardly wait to see again and whom he was marrying in June. Neither Carol nor Norman could get a word in edgewise, but over dessert Norman was finally able to inform his son that he would be staying on in Paris for a while. Cliff looked surprised and then he looked at the two of them in something like wonderment. Then he grinned. Had they not been sitting at a table in one of the most elegant restaurants in the world he would undoubtedly have pounded his father on the back.

"Just be sure you get back in time for the wedding," he said.

"I'll try," Norman promised.

Cliff left for home the next morning and his father checked out of the Plaza-Athénée and moved into Carol's apartment. The concierge was quite perturbed, scowling, making ugly noises, but Carol gave her a lavish tip that squelched all qualms and brought a beaming smile to her lips.

"She can scarcely draw breath without expecting a tip for it," Carol confided as they went up in the elevator. "She invariably looks the other way, but it's frightfully expensive."

"For you?"

"For the other tenants. You happen to be the first man who's ever brought his luggage up to my apartment."

"Oh?"

"The others had their own rooms," she teased.

They entered the apartment and Norman put his bags down and pulled her into his arms and they skipped lunch. The afternoon was divine, both greedily savoring its splendors, and pale pink-gold sunlight was fading on the floor when they finally got out of bed. Norman smiled lazily, looking at her with sheepish dark-brown eyes, feeling young, feeling strong, feeling proud. Carol stretched languorously, wonderfully replete, limbs slightly sore, the ashes of aftermath glowing deliciously inside. They stood there in the fading sunlight, gazing at each other, and Norman reached across and took her hand and squeezed it gently, a tender affirmation of the beauty and the bliss they had just shared. She had never experienced such joy.

They dined at the Tour d'Argent that evening, Carol in her scarlet chiffon, Norman in a dark suit and silk tie, and Carol toyed with her wineglass, looking into his eyes with a half smile on her lips. He reached for her hand across the table and played with her fingers. People smiled, for they were so obviously in love, the beautiful, beloved young actress and the handsome stranger with gleaming auburn hair. They had oysters and duck and a brie that was wonderfully ripe and runny. Through the windows they could see Notre-Dame and the Seine and the Île Saint-Louis, softly spangled with lights. It was like something from one of those gloriously romantic forties movies, Carol thought, yet it was really happening and she felt every bit as sublime as Ingrid Bergman, and Norman was much better-looking than Charles Boyer.

The following morning Carol's agent sent her a script young

Louis Malle was going to direct. She read it after breakfast. Malle wanted her for the leading role, a bored, unhappily married woman who has an intense affair with one of her lawyer husband's young colleagues. It was the sort of role Moreau played to perfection and it would be quite a challenge, a far cry from her wholesome American image. The script was sexually explicit—Malle would handle it with great artistry, she knew—and there was a nude bathing scene that would probably run into censorship problems. She was tempted, sorely tempted, but they wanted to begin filming almost immediately on location in Saumur. She turned the film down, even though she longed to do it.

"Are you sure that's wise?" Norman asked quietly.

"There'll be other movies," she said.

"Malle is a fine young director."

"He's going to be one of the greatest."

"You didn't have to turn the movie down, Carol."

"I'm enjoying my champagne."

Paris seemed to put on her finest face for them in the weeks that followed. The air was soft and hazy, the skies a pale violet-blue, the old stone buildings and monuments bathed in a pale silvery light, and how they enjoyed it, strolling hand in hand, savoring the awesome beauty and the fragrant perfumes of the city. They eschewed the weighty splendors of the Louvre for the Jeu de Paume, admiring the Degas, the Cézannes, the Monets and Gauguins. Carol had never been there before, and Norman was pleased to introduce her to his favorite museum. Carol had never been to the Eiffel Tower either—only tourists went there—and Norman insisted they go. They rode all the way to the top and she was as thrilled and delighted as any child, the breeze billowing her skirts, tourists chattering noisily, eating junk food and pointing out landmarks.

They wandered along the quais and browsed among the rickety, tattered bookstalls, discovering treasures. Carol was elated with a portfolio of eighteenth-century prints, exquisitely done, covered with dust and picked up for a mere pittance. Norman found a battered first edition of Proust and a French edition of *Mrs. Wiggs and Her Cabbage Patch* which brought a smile to his lips. They ate in small, noisy restaurants with sawdust on the floor and copper pans on the walls, sharing benches and tables with workmen, passing huge baskets of bread and plates

of sausage and tureens of marvelous soup. They explored narrow twisting streets with ancient old buildings jammed together like so many petrified wedding cakes, and Carol discovered that the Paris of Balzac was still very much in evidence if one searched hard enough. They wandered into dusty, crowded antique shops hidden away on back streets, and in one of them Norman found an exquisite white-and-pink Sèvres vase etched with gold, something Madame Du Barry might have owned at one time, and he bought it for her, paying practically nothing. The wizened old crone who ran the shop thought it was a piece of junk.

One afternoon they went to the Palais-Royale and wandered through the shady arcades while children romped among the flower beds. They located the plaque beneath the apartment where Colette had lived for so many years, her blue lamp always visible from the moonlit gardens, and they stood quietly, looking up at the window. Carol told Norman how she had discovered Colette at the age of thirteen, taking a copy of *Chéri* from the Ellsworth library, discovering a whole new world through the eyes of that greatest of French novelists. Norman suggested they go to Père-Lachaise and visit her grave. It was late afternoon and drizzling lightly when they arrived. All the flower stalls were closed and Carol had so wanted to place a bouquet on Colette's grave. Someone had recently left a large bunch of pale pink roses on Chopin's tombstone. Carol hesitated for a moment and then took a single rose for Colette. Norman agreed that Chopin would not have minded at all.

They rarely went out at night, preferring to stay home and watch moonbeams stream over the bannister and silver the floor, but Gaby insisted they celebrate with the gang one night. The rowdy group went to Sexy's on the Champs Élysées, and Norman was amused by the strippers. They shared a bottle of champagne with a couple of pimps in a bar in Pigalle, had onion soup at L'Escargot in the early morning hours, watching the market porters of Les Halles slinging enormous sides of beef over their shoulders and shambling along in bloodstained white overalls. Gaby was sad and weary by this time, her great brown eyes woeful as she confided that Alain had deserted her for a dancer from the Folies-Bergère, stealing several of her paintings before he left.

"You'll have to write a novel about it," Norman told her.

"I intend to," she confessed, brightening considerably. "It's going to be my best—straight from the heart."

April melted into May and May was marvelous, flowers abloom on every street corner, it seemed, Paris at her magical best. Carol felt like a completely different person. She felt young for the first time—she had never felt young before, not like this— and she felt gloriously carefree, no grueling hours inside a drafty studio, no schedule to meet, no script changes to learn. Every morning she woke up in Norman's arms, and every day seemed like Christmas, sure to bring wonderful presents—a brioche shared at an outdoor cafe, a stroll through shady paths in the *bois*, a silk scarf bought at one of the swanky shops, a tender kiss exchanged as they crossed one of the old stone bridges spanning the Seine. Norman was almost like a youth as they explored the city, playful, teasing, so very handsome in the casual clothes he had purchased—white slacks, striped jerseys, leather sandals, very French. He was warm and protective and made her feel cherished, and he was a magnificent lover, masterful yet tender, tireless and strong and caring, so caring. The champagne was heady indeed, and she was deliciously inebriated.

June came and with it the heat and the hordes of tourists. No one remained in Paris in June, not if they could possibly escape. Gaby invited them to come to St. Tropez for three weeks, as Cliff was not to be married until the last of the month. They gratefully accepted. Norman rented a car and they took Highway 7 from Paris and they arrived in the late afternoon. Gaby had bought a rambling old villa near the beach, surrounded by cork oaks, after the huge success of her first novel. St. Tropez was a quaint, quiet fishing village then, rarely visited by the chic and successful, and it appealed to Gaby primarily because Colette had kept a house there for several years. Vadim filmed *And God Created Woman* in the town, and suddenly its sun-drenched beaches and the multicolored old houses climbing up the hillside became a mecca for pleasure-lovers who equated the town with sun, sin and sensuality. Hotels, shops and bistros sprang up like so many glossy mushrooms, prices soared, but even progress and the invasion of cafe society couldn't destroy the charm of the old port.

Gaby's villa was just outside of town, relatively isolated and with its own private stretch of beach, within easy walking distance through the pines and oak trees to all the shops and the

marvelous old restaurants like L'Auberge des Maures, where Colette used to dine on crayfish and herb salad. The air smelled of pine and salt and iodine, wonderfully invigorating, and despite the trendy shops and new hotels and nightclubs, St. Tropez was incredibly, spectacularly beautiful, the sea gray-green, spangled with sunlight, the beaches blazing white sand, the sky a deep indigo canopy overhead.

Gaby was a perfect hostess, extremely casual, leaving her guests to do whatever they pleased, to swim, to sun, to shop, to join in the sorties to the nearby casinos in the evening or stay home. Her new lover, Jacques, was blond, bronzed and far more amiable than Alain, a handsome, charming brute who did stunt work in films and hoped to graduate to acting. His roving eye and his fondness for variety would inevitably lead to more heartbreak, Carol knew, but for the moment Gaby basked in the glory of his strength and virile beauty. The wooden floors of the huge, sprawling old house were sprinkled with sand, damp towels and bathing suits scattered about, the place aflood with books, magazines and unexpected guests who dropped by for a few hours or a few days, plenty of room always available for the chums from Paris.

Carol and Norman bought unbleached cotton pants and rope espadrilles and explored the twisting streets and alleyways and the old port with its fishing boats and tar pots and nets hung out to dry, its smell of rotting wood and moss and barnacles. They wandered through the woods and fields surrounding the town, climbed the cliffs and enjoyed the magnificent vistas. They sunned on the beach and went to the restaurants alone or with the gang, went dancing in the clubs and wandered home late at night under the starlight, strolling leisurely along deserted beaches as waves washed the sand and le jazz hot spilled into the night from the clubs nearby. In their sparsely furnished room in back of the house, the windows open to the night, they made love in the old brass bed with its mosquito net while the crickets chirped beneath the flagstones outside and an owl hooted in the surrounding woods.

Carol was delighted when Cecil Saint-Laurent stopped by for a visit one day. His *Caroline Chérie* had been phenomenally successful a few years back, spawning a number of sequels and a film version starring Martine Carol. Still in his thirties, Saint-Laurent was an eminent historian, an authority on the theater

and one of the most prolific writers in France, holding a record for noms de plume before his breakthrough with the Caroline series. His most recent heroine, Clothilde, a charmingly amoral lass who worked for the underground during the days of occupied France, was almost as popular as Caroline. Saint-Laurent had written the screenplay for *High Heels at Breakfast*, the comedy Carol had done with Daniel Gélin and Dany Robin, and he was one of her favorite people, astonishingly erudite, marvelously witty, with a wry, wicked humor quintessentially French.

"I loved the latest Clothilde," Carol told him.

"The wench is wildly popular," Saint-Laurent confessed. "I suppose it's all her love affairs. Many readers, alas, skip over my painstakingly researched historical passages to see who Clothilde will pop into bed with next."

"She does it with such flair, Cecil. As did Caroline. Did I ever tell you *Caroline Chérie* was banned from the Ellsworth library? It was far too French for Kansas, I fear. I managed to get a copy and read it anyway. I was in the tenth grade at the time."

"Most unsuitable reading matter for a girl that age, I must confess. Did it corrupt you?"

Carol smiled. "Judge for yourself. Have you written a new film for me?"

"I'm afraid not. Clothilde keeps me far too busy. Speaking of films, word is that the new Louis Malle is going to be a masterpiece. They're filming in Saumur, and several American companies are already fighting for distribution rights. It's going to clean up."

Carol was silent a moment. Norman, who was sitting out on the terrace with them, gave her a peculiar look. Saint-Laurent had no idea she had turned the movie down.

"Who—who's playing the lead?" Carol finally asked.

"Moreau. She completed the Vadim film on a Tuesday, began the Malle on Wednesday. It's quite a role, I understand. Jeanne is already a star in France, of course, but this one is going to make her an international celebrity. It's that kind of film."

Gaby insisted Saint-Laurent spend the night, and that evening the group went to the Hotel de la Ponche for a festive meal, wine flowing freely. Carol was unusually quiet, smiling her sphinx smile and not joining in the general merriment. Paris and his typewriter called, and Saint-Laurent left the next morning,

promising to write Carol another comedy as soon as Clothilde permitted. That afternoon Carol and Norman went for a long walk on the beach, passing La Madrague, the villa Brigitte Bardot had purchased. Both were barefooted, Norman's thin white cotton pants turned up to mid-calf, Carol wearing a blue-green dress of handkerchief cotton with a cord sash at the waist, sea spray dampening the billowy skirt. Two gulls circled overhead shrieking noisily. A boat with an orange-and-gold striped sail bobbed against the misty violet-blue line of the horizon.

"I'm sorry about the film, Carol," he said. "I should have insisted you go ahead and do it."

"There—there'll be another film," she replied.

"This one was the one you'd been waiting for. It would have brought you to the attention of the Hollywood moguls."

"Jeanne will have the success. She deserves it far more than I do. I'm happy for her."

"You wanted the part."

"I wanted you more," she told him.

"You've been struggling so long. I—" He hesitated, shoving a shell out of his path with his toe. "I'd like for you to give up the struggle, Carol."

"What do you mean?"

"I have to fly back home at the end of next week for Cliff's wedding, as you know. I'd like you to come with me."

"Norman, I—"

"I'd like to make it a double wedding," he continued. "I want to marry you, Carol. It's no secret that I'm in love with you, and I think you're in love with me, too."

"I am, you know that, but—"

"I know your career means a great deal to you, but—you could still continue to make films, and you wouldn't have to worry about money. I have no responsibilities whatsoever—Cliff has taken over all the business—and we could live anywhere in the world, wherever your work might take you."

And what would you do while I was making films? How happy would you be with me getting up at four-thirty in the morning to be at the studio by six and coming home at seven or later with several pages of dialogue to memorize before the next day's shooting? How long before you would begin to resent my work, resent me for not giving you enough attention? How long before you would insist I give up making films altogether? I would be

a rich man's wife. I wouldn't need to work. I might not even want to. It's a dream, Norman, a beautiful dream, and how I wish I could buy it, but . . . my career means too much to me. I wish it didn't, but I've worked too hard, too long, to give it up for . . . for a steady diet of champagne, no matter how glorious that might be.

Carol wanted to say these things aloud, but she didn't, yet Norman seemed to read her mind, seemed to understand her reservations. They walked on in the damp sand in silence, and after a few moments he reached over and took her hand.

"I love you, Carol."

"And I love you. These—these past weeks have been the most wonderful I've ever had."

"It could always be like this," he said. "I—I won't pressure you about it, Carol. I—I'd just like you to consider it."

"I will," she promised.

Gaby, an inveterate gambler, was taking Jacques and a few glittery pals to a casino that evening. Norman and Carol were staying home. Carol stepped into Gaby's room at eight o'clock and closed the door. Wearing a pair of tight black satin toreador pants and a short, sleeveless tunic covered with shiny black-and-silver spangles, Gaby was scurrying about, searching for her shoes. She glanced up, surprised to see Carol.

"Have you changed your mind, darling? Decided to come along after all?"

Carol shook her head. The worried look in her eyes gave Gaby pause, and she promptly sat down on the edge of the bed, concerned.

"Is something wrong?"

"Not—not really. I just wanted to—something has happened, and I wanted to talk about it. If—this is probably an inconvenient time. We can talk about it later."

"Nonsense. The casino doesn't really come alive until after ten. Jacques and the others can wait. What is it, darling?"

Carol told her about Norman's proposal and her own reservations about such a marriage. Gaby understood immediately and nodded gravely as Carol listed all the reasons why she feared it wouldn't work. Short, tawny-gold curls clinging to her head like a shaggy cap, enormous brown eyes solemn, Gaby sighed when Carol finally fell silent. Neither of them spoke for several moments.

"I love him, Gaby. I—Oh God, I don't want to hurt him."

"Of course you don't."

"He says I can go on making films, but—that wouldn't work, Gaby. You know it wouldn't."

"Men, even the most generous, even the most loving, want us to devote all of our attention to them," Gaby said quietly. "They pretend to be broad-minded and understanding but anything that takes us away from them is ultimately a source of contention. Despite what they may say to the contrary, they want us exclusively to themselves."

Carol nodded. She knew it was true.

"On the other hand, he's a marvelous man, darling. You may never meet another like him. What wouldn't I give to have someone like your Norman in my life."

"Would you give up your writing?" Carol asked.

Gaby didn't answer. She didn't need to. The answer was in her eyes. Give up her writing? She might as well give up breathing. Carol felt the same about her own work. Champagne was glorious, but one couldn't live on a steady diet of it. No one knew that better than Gaby. When she was working on a book or play, lovers, friends, fun and fast living were all put on hold, and she lived the life of a recluse until the work was done. Her men invariably resented it, and it invariably caused violent arguments and tumultuous partings. But . . . but Norman wasn't like Alain and Jacques and the other men in Gaby's life, Perhaps he would be supportive and stand behind her. Perhaps he wouldn't mind taking a backseat and sitting idly by while she pursued her film career. Perhaps . . . but it wasn't likely. Carol realized that.

"You must do what you think best, darling," Gaby said gravely.

"I know. And what is best—what is best in the long run— might be extremely painful for both of us."

Talking with Gaby had helped but it had solved nothing. Carol left the room and joined Norman on the terrace. It was a gorgeous night. Crickets were chirping. A gentle breeze rustled the leaves and the fragrant smell of summer flowers scented the air. The others left a short while later, Jacques unusually handsome in his dinner jacket, Gaby eager to get to the tables, all of them chattering merrily as they piled into Gaby's sleek, frightfully expensive new sports car. Carol poured herself a glass of white

wine from the decanter on the glass-topped table, settling back down into her white wicker chair with its dusty cushion. He asked if she would like to wander down to the wharf and have some crayfish. She shook her head and said she just wanted to enjoy the evening. Norman was content to do the same. In white pants and loose striped jersey, his hair rather tousled, he was beautiful in the moonlight, and her heart swelled with love. Why must it be this way? Why must she have to make a choice? Carol prayed she would have the strength to make the right one.

True to his word, Norman didn't press her in the days that followed. He was relaxed, amiable, charming and wildly passionate when they were alone together in their room at night. Perhaps it might work. Perhaps it just might. She needed more time to think, more time to consider. She really would like to go to Kansas for Cliff's wedding, even . . . even if she didn't stay. She could stop in New York on the way back to see Nora and Julie and the baby. Norman would understand if she asked him to wait a few more months. Surely he would. It might be a mistake to go to Kansas with him, though. He might interpret that as a tacit agreement to marry him later on. He was scheduled to fly back in just three days now. Carol knew she would have to reach a decision soon.

The decision was made for her the following afternoon. She and Norman were having lunch on the terrace of a quaint old restaurant in St. Tropez proper, eating shrimp and artichoke salad under the striped umbrella awning as skimpily clad sunbathers passed on their way to and from the shops. Having stayed out until after five this morning, the others were still home in bed, Gaby considerably poorer after her losing streak at the tables. As the waiter brought them another carafe of white wine, a gleaming beige Rolls-Royce came tearing down the narrow old street, slamming to a halt in front of the restaurant. Carol was stunned to see a tall, slender man in his late fifties bound out of the car with the vitality of a youth. He was wearing narrow white slacks, a pale blue silk shirt and a dapper white silk ascot. His hair was longer than she remembered, and the lean, slightly effete face was handsomely tan.

"Sir Robert!" she cried, leaping to her feet.

The distinguished British actor cleared the distance between them in no time flat and caught her up in a vigorous hug, almost cracking her ribs. Tears of joy and delight sprang to her eyes.

Sir Robert hugged her again and then held her at arms' length, examining her with a merry grin on his lips.

"Still as lovely as ever, lass, but—what's this? Has my Corday got tears in her eyes? Are you that upset to see old Marat again? Are you going to seize a knife and stab me in the chest like you did last time we met?"

"My God! What—what on earth are you *do*ing here?"

"I've come for you, my lovely. I searched for you all over Paris and finally discovered you had come to St. Tropez. I had a perfectly hideous drive down here and when I arrived at Chez Bernais a short while ago a totally nude young Adonis with blond hair informed me that Mademoiselle Bernais was still sleeping it off and that you were probably having lunch here with your friend."

"Oh, I—forgive me—"

Norman had risen to his feet earlier. Carol had completely forgotten him in her joy at seeing Sir Robert Reynolds again. She introduced them and the two men shook hands. Norman asked Sir Robert to join them and asked the waiter to bring another glass. Carol was still stunned as they all sat down, Sir Robert beaming, his blue-green eyes full of boyish glee.

"Still have your talisman?" he inquired.

Carol picked up her white straw purse and took out the beautiful silver cigarette case with its gold art deco designs and mellow patina of age. "I keep it with me always," she told him. "It's brought me a great deal of luck."

"I should say so. I saw the Ronet film, luv. You were magnificent, and you were even more magnificent in *High Heels at Breakfast. Exactly* the type we need. We're in a wretched bind, Carol, and you've got to bail us out."

"What—what are you talking about?"

"I'm starting a new film, luv, four weeks on location in Paris. The company arrived three days ago, location shooting to begin next Tuesday, the interiors to be filmed back home at Pinewood. It's about a roguish English aristocrat and his family stranded in Paris without a cent and desperately trying to stay afloat and find the fare home. Terrence Rattigan wrote the script—it's one of his finest pieces, frothy, droll and deliciously wicked. Margaret Rutherford plays my dotty old mother who shoplifts and fences the loot in order to pay our hotel bill. Lilli Palmer plays my bitchy, brittle, but delightful wife. Alas, the young actress signed

up to play my daughter was rushed to the hospital with a burst appendix as soon as we arrived, and the producers were in a panic. Shooting begins next Tuesday, as I said, and it's imperative we find a replacement pronto. No problem at all, I told them. I'll fetch my Corday. She'll be perfect. They ran a print of *High Heels at Breakfast* and practically fell all over themselves hurrying to your agent's office to sign you up. I took it upon myself to fetch you back to Paris. Tried to reach you by phone first, couldn't get through.''

"Gaby's phone is out of order."

"So I gather. You'll love the part. Muriel is pert, perky and very modern, fending off the advances of two husky soccer players while attempting to seduce a French nobleman whom she and her father hope to fleece. Louis Jourdan is playing the nobleman. You have some wonderfully funny scenes and one that's very risqué, if comedically so. Your agent's a bandit, by the way. They're going to pay you the moon. Say you'll do it, luv. There'll be several nervous breakdowns and a possible suicide if you don't.''

"I—"

"I brought a script. It's in the car. Read it today. I'm whizzing over to Cannes to visit a couple of friends, and I'll be back tomorrow afternoon for your answer. You can't fail me, luv. You're driving back to Paris with me if I have to *kid*nap you!''

The script was every bit as wonderful as Sir Robert had promised. She spent the afternoon on Gaby's terrace, reading it. Muriel was flip, sexy and had tremendously funny lines. She was as much a rogue as her father, both of them irreverent and lighthearted and in cahoots. She couldn't turn it down. She simply couldn't. Sir Robert was depending on her, and it was a showcase part in an all-star production. Hazy blue shadows were beginning to spread over the uneven gray flagstones when she finally put the script aside. A plump white cat was snoozing beside one of the old stone pots full of red geraniums. The pitcher of lemonade she had brought out was warm, the ice long since melted. Bees droned in the purple bougainvillea spilling over the low stone wall. Norman stepped outside, gave her a smile and then stepped over to gaze at the darkening blue sea.

"It's almost six," he said.

"Norman, I—my word, I had no idea it was so late."

"I've been playing gin rummy with young Jacques. Is the script good?"

"It's marvelous," she said, feeling awful.

"Maybe it will help compensate for the Louis Malle film you gave up in order to be with me. You'll do it, of course."

"I—"

"I insist, my love. I've been very, very selfish, keeping you to myself all this time. I saw the look on your face when Sir Robert was telling you about the film—the exultant glow, the anticipation, the joy—and I realized just what I had been keeping you from. I realized I—I couldn't compete with your work, nor would it be fair to you if I tried."

"Norman—"

"I'm thirty years older than you, Carol—neither of us has bothered to consider that. I've had my time in the sun, and I'm not selfish enough to keep you from yours. I would, my love. Without wanting to, without meaning to, I would hold you back."

Carol stood up. Tears glistened in her eyes again, spilling down her cheeks in tiny trails. Norman stepped over to her and curled one arm around her waist, drawing her to him, brushing the tears away with his free hand.

"You mustn't cry," he said. "This is best. We both know that."

"I—I love you," she whispered.

"I know, and I'll cherish that knowledge for the rest of my life."

"Norman, I—I don't have to do the movie. I don't *want* to do it! We'll go back to Kansas together and—and I'll marry you, and—"

He placed his fingers over her mouth and shook his head, drawing her nearer, holding her close.

"The phone was repaired while we were out this afternoon. I called the nearest airport and made my reservations. I fly out tomorrow morning at ten, land in Paris and change planes there."

"No!" she cried. "Norman—"

"This shall be our last evening together, my darling. Let's make it special and festive. We'll put on our finest attire and go to the best restaurant in St. Tropez and then walk home along

the beach and then—I imagine we can find something else to do.''

"I—Oh God, I don't want it to end!"

Norman tightened his arms around her and after a while he led her inside and they had their evening, but Carol didn't feel festive, she felt as though her life were ending, and she knew she couldn't possibly endure this pain, couldn't possibly survive the loss of him. She borrowed Gaby's car the next morning and drove Norman along the coast to the airport, lovely vistas of sea and hillside greeting them at every turn, and he checked his bags and they waited in the lounge, Norman holding her hand, Carol silent, consumed with grief, fighting back the tears that threatened to fall anew. His flight was announced. There were very few passengers. She stepped outside with him. The plane was very small, a flight of metal steps rolled up to the open door. The other passengers moved toward it, shoulder bags and cameras swinging jauntily. Norman took both her hands and squeezed them and looked into her eyes. He smiled a tender smile and kissed her lightly on the lips for the final time.

"I love you," he said.

"I love you," she whispered.

"See you in the movies, my darling."

He left then and boarded the plane, and in a few minutes it took off and soon became a tiny silver speck against the azureblue sky and part of her soul seemed to be torn out of her, seemed to fly away with the plane. Carol stood there outside the glass doors for several minutes, surviving, and then she returned to the car and drove back along the spectacularly beautiful coastline to St. Tropez and Sir Robert and a future without champagne.

11

If I have to read one more sweet nurse romance, I'm going to jump right out of this chair and *scream*, Nora promised herself as she stared at the pile of manuscripts Charlie, the office boy, had just dumped unceremoniously on her desk. I could do without lesbian novels, too. Baritone babes in heavy fur coats and dark glasses, mournfully prowling the bars. Will the paperback audience ever get tired of this crap? And when the hell is Mr. Ross Sheridan ever gonna let me handle real writers instead of his paperback hacks? Two fucking years I've worked here and I'm still shoveling shit over to Ace and Manor and Popular Library and I've yet to handle a hardback. Count your blessings, sweetheart, at least you're not handling the shoot-'em-ups and the epics about bug-eyed green men from Mars. Wearily she reached for the manuscript on top of the new pile. *Nurse Dalton's Chance* by Elsie Prentice. Jesus! Give me a break. No need to read it. Stuff it in a manila envelope and send it over to Manor. They published all the Elsie Prentice sagas. Include a cover letter saying this one's special and we want five hundred bucks more and a two percent increase in royalties.

Nora typed up the letter—the first paragraph oozing with enthusiasm for Elsie's latest, the second paragraph demanding more money and strongly hinting that another publisher was champing at the bit for this writer's output—then placed it in a huge en-

velope along with the manuscript and gave it to Charlie, telling him to send it out immediately to Manor, giving him the editor's name. The next gem on the pile was a number entitled *Too Hot for Hell* by Burt Stone. Hard-boiled stuff, voluptuous blondes, tough detective who mows 'em down with a mean right and a sawed-off shotgun, sex and violence in machine gun prose. No need to read this one either. Signet was making a bundle with the Burt Stone originals. A poor man's Mickey Spillane, Burt Stone was actually a sweet little lady from South Carolina in her sixties, but who the hell is gonna buy *Too Hot for Hell* by Bessie Mae Rawlins? Off to Signet with the usual demands for more money this time. Ten o'clock now. Time for a coffee break. Nora stood up and stretched.

The salt mines were humming, as usual. Twenty desks crammed into a large airless room with dreary tan walls and a corrugated white ceiling stained yellow from all the cigarette smoke. Manuscripts heaped on desktops and stacked untidily on the floor, more arriving by the minute. A water fountain. A coffee machine and two stacks of cardboard cups on a battered wooden table, along with a green glass kitty for nickels. The cheap son of a bitch made them pay five cents for every cup of coffee they drank and woe unto anyone who tried to sneak one without paying. At least cream and sugar were free. Phones ringing shrilly. Typewriters banging away. All the little slaveys hard at work while Mr. Ross Sheridan was ensconced in splendor in his private office, busily making big deals for big-name writers.

I come to New York because I think he's gonna sell *This Heaven, This Hell* and make me a star, and every publisher in New York turns it down and the bastard likes me, thinks I'm cute, cons me into coming to work for him. I visualize glamor—chic lunches at the Four Seasons, tête-à-têtes with top editors, squiring glamorous authors around in limos—and what do I get? I get his paperback hacks. I get to meet Bessie Mae and take her to Patricia Murphy's for shrimp salad. The job did have its perks, though. Occasionally there was a fancy party for one of the big authors, like the one for Jason Pollen tonight, and Ross expected all his bright young women to attend wearing their brightest smiles and their fanciest attire. Free booze. Caviar. Smoked salmon. Doggie bags after the shindig. *Ross* carried home the doggie bags, but the girls always managed to smuggle

out a bottle of scotch or some fancy canapés wrapped up in a paper napkin.

Ross Sheridan was a rogue, a charlatan and the scourge of the industry according to his competitors and a number of editors in publishing, while to his writers he was the Boy Wonder. The boy was bald now and in his late fifties, but he was as flashy, as flamboyant, as volatile as when he first stormed onto the publishing scene like some rapacious carpetbagger and cornered the markets on mysteries and paperback originals. Sheridan was one of the few agents who advertised, running showy, tantalizing ads in the trades and many of the pulps that promised YOU TOO CAN BE A PUBLISHED WRITER! While he did represent a few top-selling authors and cooked up fabulous, highly publicized deals for ghost-written celebrity autobiographies—he was still hoping to bag Sonia Henie and Vera Hruba Ralston—the bulk of his business was in paperback originals doled out to efficient, ambitious young assistants like Nora and Sage Conway. However, most of his fortune had been made from books that never saw print at all. This was what his competitors resented most of all, what they considered unethical, unprofessional, fraudulent and downright foul. Sheridan just considered it good business and kept trotting off to the bank.

Nora shook her head, thinking of his racket, scam or, as he liked to call it, "service." Very few people believe they can automatically paint a masterpiece, compose a symphony, perform brain surgery or step onto a stage and sing grand opera. Every kid on the block believes he can write a best-selling novel, despite lack of education, experience, or even the most basic comprehension of English grammar and syntax. Shell-shocked clerks in tobacco shops in Kentucky and stout, gum-smacking housewives in Missouri scribble on yellow pads or type away on decrepit Remingtons convinced they're going to be the new James Jones, the next Kathleen Winsor. These were the people who saw his ads and leaped at the chance to become rich and famous overnight. Hundreds of manuscripts came flooding into the office every month, and Sheridan charged a hefty reading fee for each one. They were turned over to a group of poorly paid employees—the peons—who glanced at them, kept them for a few weeks and then sent them back with one of half a dozen form letters stating that while the book showed great promise it needed considerable work on plot, structure, character, dialogue or

220   *Jennifer Wilde*

"I'll try. We Sheridan girls have got to stick together. We're going to take over this town one of these years."

"You'd better believe it," Nora said.

Both of them were startled as the door to Sheridan's office flew open and the man himself charged toward them. "My God!" Nora whispered. "He's found out about the slugs!" Of medium height, quite rotund, his bald head gleaming, Sheridan wore gray slacks, an expensive pale blue silk shirt, a gaudy blue-and-red tie and, on the pinky of his left hand, a signet ring with a gigantic diamond. His usual checked sport coat was missing. Somehow, for all the money he spent on clothes, Ross always managed to look like a race track tout with pretensions of grandeur. His blue eyes were flashing now. His cheeks were a vivid pink. He seemed to charge the air with nervous energy as he slammed to a halt in front of them and seized Nora's arm.

"You!" he roared.

"I did it!" she cried. "I did it and I'm glad! I'll wear sackcloth and ashes, I'll crawl to work on my knees, but please, please don't fire me, Boss. I've got a gray-haired, paraplegic mother to support, and my baby brother needs an operation. You can't fire me. You just *can't!*"

"What the hell are you talking about?"

"Just getting into the spirit of things."

"If there's one thing I don't need today, I don't need a smart-mouth giving me lip! An emergency's come up, and you've gotta help me out—you're the only one I trust not to screw it up."

"Who do I have to kill?"

"Lip! That's all I get around here, lip! James Hennesey's in town. I'm supposed to meet him at Copenhagen at one, go over the new contracts with him, get him to sign 'em. There's a crisis with Jason—he's been on a binge, got into a drunken brawl in the village in the *wee* hours, socked a cop, got tossed into the slammer. I've gotta bail him out and sober him up and see he gets to the party tonight."

"Bless your heart," Nora said.

"Look, it's what—ten-fifteen? I want you to pick up the contracts from Meg at eleven and go home and change into something sexy—Hennesey has an eye for the ladies—and then take a taxi to Copenhagen and meet him and charm him into signing the contracts, then bring 'em back to the office."

"I don't look sexy in this?" she demanded.

"I'm in no mood, Nora. No mood. Don't agitate me! It's gonna cost me a bundle to bail that bastard out, and sobering him up isn't gonna be a picnic either."

"I'm to take a taxi? A real *taxi?* Who's gonna pay for it?"

"I'll pay for the fucking taxi! I don't want you arriving at Copenhagen all hot and mussed up, but you'll bloody well *walk* back to the office when you finish with Hennesey."

"You're all heart, Ross. I expect a raise for this."

Sheridan made an exasperated noise and turned to glare at Sage. "You traitor!" he hissed.

"If you'd given me that raise I asked for a couple of months ago I wouldn't be leaving," she said sweetly.

"Raises! Day in, day out, that's all I hear! You all wanna bankrupt me! At least now I'll have a spy at Dell. Still coming to the party tonight?"

"Wouldn't miss it," Sage replied.

"My best girl deserting me—no loyalty at all in this fucking business! No wonder I've got bleeding ulcers."

He gave them both a belligerent look and charged back to his office, flying back out in a minute or so in a green-and-brown checked sport coat that had to be seen to be believed. He rushed out of the office, knocking over a stack of manuscripts as he did so, off to the pokey to bail out his alcoholic superstar.

"I'm crushed," Nora said. "I thought *I* was his best girl."

"Those are the breaks," Sage told her. "I envy you your lunch with Hennesey. He's quiet, reserved and absolutely gorgeous, looks like a scholarly Heathcliff—the kind of guy you'd love to leap your bones."

"Charming," Nora said. "No one's leaped my bones in so long I've forgotten what it feels like. You don't meet that many available men in publishing. They're either happily married or happily living with each other."

"Tell me about it," Sage said.

At eleven o'clock Nora fetched the contracts from Meg, Ross's private secretary, left the office, walked to the nearest subway station and, fifteen minutes later, was unlocking the door to the apartment she and Julie had taken on West 72nd Street, near the Hudson River. The neighborhood wasn't all that enchanting, but the West Side had its own special color and raffish ambience and the apartment was large and relatively cheap. She thought about dashing up to Hannah Lichtenstein's apartment and giving Danny

a hug but decided it might upset his routine. Hannah was a godsend, taking care of Danny all day while Julie worked at the studio and took her classes with Sonia Lezenski. At eleven months old he was a handful: willful, spoiled and utterly enchanting. Locking the door behind her—one did in New York—Nora sighed, undressed and took a quick shower, then settled in front of the television set in an old robe. She had to bang the side of the set to clear the picture.

This Life of Ours came on at eleven-thirty, one of the most popular soaps on the small screen, and if she was lucky she'd catch one of Julie's scenes before it went off at twelve. Sonia had gotten her the job two months after Danny was born, and in the past nine Julie had been raped by her evil brother-in-law, was committed to an insane asylum, escaped, suffered amnesia and had a touching romance with a handsome truck driver who found her wandering along the side of the highway. She was back in River City now, fully cured, fending off the advances of the resident suave rake and trying to convince her sister to get a divorce. It wasn't art, but it was work, it was good experience, and the pay wasn't bad. Something better would come along soon. Julie was a magnificent actress and she was going to be a star. Nora was sure of it.

She sat through a commercial for Oxydol and a commercial for Gerber's baby food and then watched a fluffy lamb frolic while someone sang, "Pamper, Pamper, new shampoo, gentle as a lamb, so good for you," and then the screen flickered and there was Julie in closeup, looking distraught, looking noble, tears streaming down her cheeks as she explained to her sister how Bill had left the party with Roger and dropped Phyllis off and stopped by Ann's and had an argument with her over the inheritance and then . . . then came home and raped her while she, Jane, was in California. Jane recoiled in horror and refused to believe it and Julie told her she must divorce him, she must, he didn't love her at all but was only after the inheritance which Ann and Mark were going to get anyway. Nora couldn't keep track of all the names and relationships, but she was mesmerized by Julie's performance. Artistry. Sheer artistry. She made the rest of them look like amateurs. Jane ordered Julie out of her house and Julie bit her lower lip and fought the tears and shook her head in sad resignation and left and Jane began to shriek in anguish as the credits rolled.

Jesus! Twelve. She'd have to hurry. Something sexy, he said. Sexy was hardly her style, but maybe the dark-red sheath would qualify. Carol had sent it over from Paris last Christmas, a perfect fit, perfect lines, deep deep red linen, sleeveless, with form-fitting bodice and waist and a straight, mid-calf-length skirt. Not that there was that much form to fit, Nora thought bitterly, slipping it on. Petite and thin and considerably less than well endowed. The dress was decidedly smart, though, striking if not sexy. She applied red lipstick sparingly and brushed her hair. The short black curls were gone now, replaced by a sleek, shiny pageboy cut that was extremely flattering and made her face look thinner and more interesting. What the hell, she thought, might as well use some eye shadow too, give the guy a real thrill. She smoothed pale blue-gray shadow on her lids, used a little mascara and then moved back to study the effect. A femme fatale I'm not, she decided, but I'm not so bad either. If James Hennesey likes thin, petite Jewish girls it's in the bag.

She had to walk all the way up to Broadway to flag down a taxi, hell with her black high heels. A couple of guys whistled! That made her feel better. In the taxi, black purse with contracts and necessities in her lap, Nora tried to remember all she knew about James Hennesey. Born and raised in North Carolina, he had graduated from Chapel Hill, had been a Marine commando during the Korean War and afterwards took his doctorate at Berkeley on the veteran's program. He had then taught American literature at Clemson and, like every other lit. professor in captivity, dreamed the novel he was working on would liberate him from the politics and poltroonery of the academic world. A trenchant yet sensitive novel about the Korean War and its demolishing effects on three boys from a small southern town, *All Glory Gone* had been hailed by the critics, yet it had only a modest sale. The movie version, with Aldo Ray, John Saxon and a young television actor named Robert Redford, had fared dismally at the box office. Hennesey's second novel, *Together We Fall*, was about a sensitive southern boy's disillusionment when he discovers his idolized older brother is actually a womanizing heel. It got the full first page of *The New York Times* book section, was deemed a masterpiece by most of the reviewers across the country, sold barely enough copies to make back its advance. It, too, was filmed, with a screenplay by Hennesey himself. The film was a huge hit, Angela Lansbury receiving an

Academy Award nomination as best supporting actress for her portrayal of the boy's fluttery, possessive mother.

Nora sighed, shifting uncomfortably on the taxi seat. While Hennesey was unquestionably a powerful writer, while his was a very prestigious name in literary circles, his books did not sell strongly. Sheridan had just placed his third novel with Prentice-Hall, and Hennesey was going to be less than enchanted when he saw the contracts and the small size of the advance. Ross had done well to get the fifteen thousand he had finally squeezed out of Prentice-Hall. Doubleday and Little, Brown had offered considerably less. Nora was not looking forward to this particular luncheon, even though it was a first for her.

The taxi let her off in front of Copenhagen. Nora gave the cabbie a generous tip—Ross was paying, after all—and started toward the door. She was under the striped awning and reaching for the door handle when she heard someone calling her name. She turned. She felt her blood freeze when she saw him strolling toward her, looking wonderful in his neat gray flannel suit and blue silk tie, looking gorgeous. His blond hair was a bit longer and stylishly cut, and when Brian Gregory smiled that familiar smile, it made her heart melt just as it had two years ago. He took both her hands in his and squeezed them, and Nora tried to smile, tried to act casual when all she wanted to do was run.

"This is wonderful!" he exclaimed.

"Wonderful," she agreed listlessly.

"Imagine running into you like this—I didn't even know you were here in New York. I've been watching all the best-seller lists, haven't happened upon your name yet."

Rub it in, you bastard. "I'm working for a literary agency, I'm meeting a client here for lunch, as a matter of fact. You—you're looking wonderfully fit, Brian."

"You're looking pretty wonderful yourself. I like the new hair style, it makes you look all grown up."

"I *am* all grown up."

"It's been a while, hasn't it?"

"Almost two years," she said.

He smiled again. Jesus, she thought, how did I ever let him get away?

"How are you, Brian?" she asked.

"Things are going great," he admitted. "I love my work, and I'm married now. Maybe you read about it in the papers?"

"I must have missed it."

"Her name's Stacey. She's a marvelous girl."

She would be. "I—I'm happy for you, Brian."

It was true. She was indeed happy for him. Things had worked out exactly as she had known they would for him. He had gotten over her and he had met a marvelous girl named Stacey who was obviously as blue-blooded as he and would be the perfect wife, the perfect helpmate, an asset to him professionally and socially, but it still hurt, it hurt like hell to realize all she had given up. Nora had never realized just how much she loved him until it was all over, and seeing him now was more painful than she would ever have believed.

"Stacey," she said. "Vassar?"

"Smith."

"Westchester county?"

"Boston, actually. Beacon Hill."

"I'm pleased. Do give her my best."

"I will," he said, and his eyes grew serious. He was still holding her hands. "You know—you were right about things, Nora. It—at the time I was ready to kill myself, thought my life was over, but now I realize you had both our best interests at heart when you broke it off."

He let go of her hands and moved back, smiling that smile again. She was smiling, too. It seemed to be frozen on her lips.

"We had some great times, didn't we?" he said thoughtfully. "I'll remember them always with special fondness in my heart. Hey—why don't we get together for lunch sometime? I'm just on my way back to the office now. Let me give you one of my cards. Call me anytime. We'll make an appointment. It's been swell seeing you again, Nora."

She took his card and put it into her purse and Brian gave her a friendly hug and, shaken, Nora went inside and went immediately to the ladies' room, to pull herself together. You're a smart, tough New York career girl now, kiddo, she reminded herself, and you made a lucky escape two years ago and you bloody well know it. The tears spilled over her lashes and she was furious with herself and wiped them away and, wouldn't you know it, her mascara was all smeary and she looked like both her eyes had been blacked. You're in an elegant restaurant to meet a famous writer, she scolded, making repairs at one of the mirrors. You'd rather be in New Rochelle darning socks?

Baking apple popovers? Waiting for hubby to come home from the city so you can discuss crabgrass and the price of sirloin? You've got an exciting, stimulating life and you're going to be a famous writer so straighten up this minute!

Fifteen minutes later, makeup repaired, looking every inch the efficient, self-assured career girl, Nora followed the maître d' to a table near the corner where James Hennesey had already been seated. Copenhagen was the current favorite with publishing people, and Nora spotted Ayn Rand at a table with her new editor from Random House. Rona Jaffe was at another table, looking like a radiant pixie and exchanging gossip with Aubrey Goodman, the twenty-three-year-old author of *The Golden Youth of Lee Prince* whom the critics were calling the Scott Fitzgerald of his generation. Nora was thrilled, envious, too. One day soon she'd have *her* table at Copenhagen and people would stare at her and envy her success. Hennesey rose slowly to his feet when she reached the table, and Nora felt something very like a shock wave.

He was tall and lean, a bit too lean, perhaps, with broad, bony shoulders and narrow waist and hips. He wore gray slacks, a handsome dark-gray corduroy jacket, a light-blue cotton shirt, a deeper-blue knit tie. His hair was black as coal and naturally wavy, and his face was lean, faint hollows beneath those high, sharp cheekbones. His nose was thin, his mouth wide and pink and undeniably sensual, the lower lip full and curving, but it was those incredible eyes that fascinated her. They were a deep, smoke-gray, sensitive, intelligent and stern, too, eyes that could glow with compassion or flash with hostility. He was not at all handsome in any traditional way, but he was one of the most attractive men she had ever seen.

"Miss Levin?" he said.

"That's right. How did you know my name?"

"Ross called me earlier and said you would be meeting me."

"I—I hope you're not disappointed, Mr. Hennesey."

"You're much prettier than Sheridan," he said.

It was a cool statement of fact, not a compliment at all. His voice was softly husky, each word pronounced slowly, lazily and with a pronounced southern drawl she found wildly appealing. He helped her into her chair, which was just as well, for her knees felt suddenly very weak. He sat down across from her and studied her with those cool, smoke-gray eyes and she dropped

her purse and retrieved it, feeling nervous and disoriented, feeling like an idiot. She noticed his hands. They were large, with wide palms and long, blunt fingers, strong hands, beautiful, very masculine. She could imagine them gripping her thighs. The image alarmed her and she quickly banished it, striving to assume a crisp, businesslike manner.

"Are you feeling better?" he inquired.

"Hunh?"

"I saw you come in fifteen minutes ago. You looked very upset. You went directly to the ladies' room."

"Oh—yeah."

She was making a great impression. She could see that. Hunh. Yeah. He probably thought she was some kind of mental retard. She was still upset over the encounter with Brian and . . . and in no condition to cope with this intimidating stranger. Jesus, he was attractive. Beneath that icy, reserved exterior, one could sense wiry strength and potent sexuality, made all the more intriguing because of his tight control. Those eyes studied her with cool objectivity, as though she were some unusual specimen he was attempting to classify and file away mentally. Nora had the feeling he could look straight into her soul and see all the scars.

"Would you like something to drink?" he asked quietly.

"I—uh—maybe a glass of white wine."

Hennesey signaled the waiter and ordered a glass of white wine and another bourbon for himself. Nora managed to compose herself. He was still looking at her. His eyes were kind now and full of interest. His mouth was perfectly chiseled, that lower lip so full, so pink. She longed to rub her thumb over its wide curve. Let's face it, kiddo, you're horny. It's nothing to be ashamed of. He's a vastly intriguing man, and you haven't slept with a single male since coming to New York. Little Miss Prim and Proper, trying to compensate for all those jocks back at Claymore. Their drinks came. She sipped her wine slowly. It helped. He made no attempt at light chatter. A cool one, he was. Terribly self-possessed, terribly confident. Probably superior as well. A college professor. A literary writer. Probably looked down his long, aquiline nose at anyone who didn't write like James Joyce or William Faulkner.

"I've brought the contracts," she said crisply.

"So I assumed."

"I'm sure Ross spoke to you about them. It—this sale isn't

quite what we hoped to get for you, but, frankly, the market is tight right now and we're not getting as much for any of our top authors at the moment.''

"That right?''

"On the plus side, Prentice-Hall is one of the best houses. Ross is convinced they'll do very well by your book. You should make good royalties even if the advance isn't what—what we may have hoped for.''

"You're extremely diplomatic, Miss Levin,'' he said quietly. "I can see why Sheridan sent you to do his dirty work. What did he think? Did he think I was going to grab him by the throat because he couldn't get the kind of money for me he gets for Jason Pollen?''

"I—we were disappointed. We had hoped—''

"I am a realist, Miss Levin. I have published two novels which have been extremely well received by the critics. The second one won a Southern Fiction award which was quite gratifying to my ego but meant absolutely nothing to the book-buying public. I have been fortunate enough to have two film sales, but my books have sold dismally. How much did he get?''

"Fifteen thousand,'' she said.

"Under the circumstances, I find that more than generous. Prentice-Hall is taking a big risk. May I see the contracts?''

Nora took them out of her purse and handed them to him. There were five copies, the bottom four onion skin. Hennesey quickly scanned the top copy and frowned once or twice, nodded, then gave a resigned sigh. He took a pen from his breast pocket and signed all five copies. She asked him to initial clauses seven and twelve, where indicated. He did so, then gave the contracts back to her. Nora put them into her purse, vastly relieved.

"Shall we order?'' he inquired.

She nodded. He signaled the waiter again and ordered for both of them. It was rather presumptuous of him, she thought, but his selection was perfect, and she wouldn't have dared order anything so expensive herself. She finished her wine. All around them voices chirped brightly and ice tinkled in glasses and cutlery rattled against china, but the two of them might have been utterly alone. He was studying her again, the interest in his eyes quite apparent. A slight frown made a furrow above the bridge of his nose.

"Over it now?" he asked.

"I think so. I—you must have thought me some kind of idiot."

"A man?"

"Someone I used to know. I ran into him just outside."

"You must have loved him."

"I did. I—I didn't realize how much until—until it was over."

"All the sad young women," he said thoughtfully. "They come to New York hoping for fame and fortune, hoping to find Mr. Right and a fairy tale ending, finding instead disillusionment and pain. Rona Jaffe captured the milieu perfectly in her novel—" He indicated the table where the vivacious young author was now enjoying a dish of chocolate mousse.

"Do you know her?" Nora asked.

"I met her at a party in Beverly Hills."

"I think she's wonderful. I loved *The Best of Everything*."

"It was a remarkable book."

"You think I'm one of the sad young women?"

"Aren't you?"

"Not at all. I—I'm very positive. I'm one of the ones who is going to make it."

"You're not looking for Mr. Right?"

"I don't even date," she informed him. "Oh, occasionally I go out with my roommate, her friend Jim Burke and one of his actor pals, but it's strictly buddy-buddy time. Actors have only the one subject, you know—themselves. If the subject begins to stray from their looks, their talent, their achievements and prospects, their eyes begin to glaze over."

"And the man who upset you?"

"Past history," she said.

Their food arrived, and Nora concentrated on her salad. James Hennesey seemed to be musing over what she had told him, his gray eyes thoughtful. He asked no more questions, might have been alone at the table. So much for being a femme fatale, she thought, spearing a shrimp. As she was leaving, Rona Jaffe happened to spy Hennesey, waved and came over to their table. Hennesey stood up, greeted the young author politely and introduced Nora as his agent. Nora told her how much she had enjoyed her book. Rona looked pleased, thanking her warmly. It didn't seem fair for anyone to be so young, so attractive and so successful. I could learn to hate her, Nora thought.

"Have you read any of *my* books?" Hennesey asked after the charming Miss Jaffe departed.

Nora nodded. "I thought *Together We Fall* was marvelous, very touching, very sad, beautifully written."

"And *All Glory Gone*?"

"It was a—a little brutal for my taste."

"It was a brutal war," he told her.

"Did you—did you actually do things like that?"

"Like Clark Davis, you mean? I was a Marine commando. I went out on a number of night missions when silence and secrecy were imperative. I learned to use a piano wire, just like Clark."

"It must have been dreadful."

"It was necessary."

"And you went from that to teaching American literature. It seems so incongruous."

"I frequently longed to garrote my students, too," he confessed. "Trying to teach the niceties of Robert Frost to a pack of yawning football players and tittering cheerleaders isn't the most gratifying work I can think of, nor is exchanging pleasantries with empty-headed faculty wives and their neurotic, brownnosing husbands, each and every one of them working on the great American novel and scared shitless they won't get tenure."

"So you went to Hollywood," she said.

"I have a place in Malibu. I write screenplays, most of which never get produced. The work is mindless and undemanding, the pay is good, and I have plenty of time left over to do some real writing."

"You sound quite cynical about it."

"I told you before, Miss Levin, I'm a realist. I could starve in a garret to produce my masterpieces, but I'd much prefer to be well fed in Malibu, the ocean washing the sand outside my back door, Vivaldi playing on the hi-fi and my two golden labs curled up beside the hearth."

"You like dogs, then?"

"I like dogs."

"Maybe you're not so bad after all."

His eyes met hers, held them. Nora felt another shock wave. James Hennesey was the sexiest man she had ever met, not in any obvious, macho way but exuding pure virility all the more exciting because of his cool restraint and detachment. She low-

ered her eyes, quickly finished her food and refused dessert. The waiter brought their bill, and Nora handed him the credit card Meg had given her to use. Hennesey continued to watch her as she nervously took out her compact and checked her face in the small round mirror. Her cheeks looked a bit flushed. Thank God this was almost over with. The waiter came back again and she added a generous tip to the bill, added the total up, then signed it and put the card back into her purse.

"I'm going to be in New York for the rest of the week," he said as they moved toward the door. "I'd like to see you again."

"I don't think—"

"I'd like to see you tonight."

"I'm afraid I have other plans for tonight, Mr. Hennesey."

"Tomorrow night?"

"I—"

"Afraid?"

"Extremely cautious."

"I'm really quite a nice guy, once you get to know me. I rarely garrote the women I take out."

"Considerate of you," she said.

He opened the door for her. They stepped outside under the awning.

"Tomorrow night?" he repeated.

Nora didn't answer. His lips curled into a faint half smile.

"I'll get your number from Sheridan. I'll give you a call."

He turned then and left, stepping out to the curb halfway down the block and hailing a cab. Nora stood there under the awning, watching him. She had rarely been so frightened. She had never met anyone like James Hennesey, and every instinct told her any kind of involvement with him could only mean emotional disaster. She didn't have time for anything like that right now. She had a best-seller to write, a world to conquer. If he *did* call, she vowed she would be too busy to see him. Only fools went around asking for trouble.

Julie was in the kitchen with Danny when Nora got back to the apartment. It was after five and she was exhausted and there was still the party she had to attend. Julie looked up and smiled and hoisted another spoonful of mashed potatoes into Danny's yawning mouth. He gurgled, rolled his eyes at Nora and banged his fists on the plastic tray of his high chair. Nora grinned, melting with adoration when he yelled, "No-No!" and lifted his

arms to be rescued from his mother's ministrations. He was a plump, stockily built creature with his father's slate-blue eyes and dark-brown hair.

"No-No!" he yelled again.

"Finish your potatoes, kiddo. Jesus, you're a messy eater. Look at the gook on your face. Yuck! That's spelled with a Y, Buster. Almost finished, Julie?"

"Almost. He's already had his carrots."

Julie was wearing old white sandals and a simple blue cotton dress. Her face, without makeup, looked rather pale. Her violet-blue eyes looked enormous. She was exhausted, too. Nora could see that. Julie worked very, very hard at the studio and at her classes, giving her all at all times. When she wasn't toiling in front of the cameras or in Lezenski's class, she was studying lines and working on interpretation. Wiping Danny's face with a dampened cloth, she lifted him out of the high chair and set him on his feet. He waddled over and plopped down amidst a pile of wooden blocks Nora had bought for him a few days earlier.

"See, No-No," he said, holding up a red-and-blue block.

"I see, pumpkin. You play with your blocks like a good boy and let your mother and Auntie No-No visit for a while. Okay?"

"'Kay, No-No."

Nora sat down at the kitchen table, and Julie began to clean up the mess feeding had created. For some reason strained orange carrots were splattered all over the front of the old refrigerator.

"I saw some of the show today," Nora said. "Your last scene. I had to come back here and change for a luncheon engagement, managed to check out the last fifteen minutes. You were marvelous, love."

"Thank you."

"Jane gonna divorce Bill?"

Julie shook her head. "Bill's going to murder Ann and blame it on Jane. I have an affair with the randy young attorney who defends her when Jane goes on trial."

"Randy young attorney. Hmmm. About time you found happiness."

"He's involved with the mob," Julie told her.

"Figures," Nora said.

"Want a cup of coffee?"

Nora shook her head. "I'm just gonna sit for a few minutes then go take a long soak in the tub—I've got this fucking party tonight. Ross sold the film rights to Jason Pollen's new novel and some Hollywood people are coming. Big deal. I'll try to sneak some snacks home."

"Interesting luncheon?"

"I had lunch with James Hennesey. Gave me the willies. He's frightfully attractive and he'd like to see me again and it scares the shit out of me. I—I have the feeling I could easily lose my senses where Mr. James Hennesey is concerned, and I'm not about to risk it."

Julie finished cleaning up, poured herself a cup of black coffee and sat down, promptly lighting a cigarette. She had taken up smoking shortly after the divorce, it soothed her nerves, she said, and she smoked incessantly now. Julie was under a great deal of strain, raising a baby, making a living, pursuing her career in the theater, and the strain was beginning to show in that lovely face. Although the pit marks were gone, the hot lights and the heavy makeup she had to wear for the cameras had given her complexion a pasty look and the skin seemed to be stretched tightly across those delicate cheekbones. She still looked like a child, but a child who has been battered and betrayed by life. The glorious violet-blue eyes were full of lost illusions.

"What are your plans for the evening?" Nora asked.

"Jim's coming over. We're going to order Chinese, and I'm going to help him with his lines. He got the part, you know. The play opens at the Schubert in two months. They leave for New Haven in five weeks."

"Is it a good part?"

"It's the second lead, a showcase part. He plays a psychopathic college student who murders his girlfriend and tries to pin it on Sean Garrison. He has a couple of wonderful scenes. I—I really think this is the one that's going to make him a star."

"Maybe so."

"He's a marvelous actor," Julie assured her.

"I agree wholeheartedly, love."

Jim had already appeared in three plays, one modest success off Broadway and two flops on Broadway, and he was getting quite a lot of attention, Walter Kerr deeming him an exciting

new personality and a star of the future. He and Julie were very close, and she was pleased for him, feeling not the least resentment that Jim was getting the breaks sooner than she. They spent most of their spare time together, taking Danny to the zoo, eating in cheap cafes, taking in the film festivals at the Thalia. It was close friendship, not romance, although Nora suspected that Jim was in love with Julie, afraid to declare himself lest she send him away.

"Soon you'll get a play, too," Nora told her. "It's inevitable."

"And in the meantime, I'm working," Julie said, lighting another cigarette. "We should be able to afford a new sofa next month."

"God knows we need one. This place is a dump."

"But it's ours," Julie said.

"And it has character. I'd better go start my bath, love. I'd give anything if I didn't have this shitty party, but Ross insists we attend 'em all, add a little class. You and Jim have a good time. Save me some moo goo gai pan."

At eight-fifteen Nora was stepping out of the elevator into the foyer of the spacious penthouse apartment of Jason Pollen's publisher. Soft music was tinkling. The caterers were setting up the tables. Smoked salmon. Caviar. Sliced beef and turkey. Wonderful hors d'oeuvres. A dazzling array of bottles crowded the surface of the white marble bar. No expense spared tonight, but then Hollywood people were coming, press, too. Kilgallen would probably appear, looking like a startled chipmunk in a tight satin sheath. Nora gave herself a quick examination in the mirror: pageboy long and sleek, face made up for party time, simple black brocade cocktail dress with spaghetti straps, black velvet waistband, narrow skirt. Chic. Sophisticated. The black high-heeled pumps were already killing her.

"Here you are," Sage said. "Right on the dot. The onslaught's due to begin any minute now. Ross's in the kitchen pouring black coffee down Jason's throat. You look divine."

"So do you."

Sage was wearing a strapless leaf-brown linen sheath and a fake Aztec necklace of gold, green and blue, looking like something from *Vogue*.

"Why is it I always feel like a call girl at these shindigs?" Nora inquired.

"We serve the same function, only we don't put out."

"Some of us don't," Nora replied, glancing at another girl from the office neither of them liked.

"You mustn't be unkind, Nora. Celia's just a girl who knows how to get a head."

"So they tell me."

Shortly thereafter the guests began to arrive, and Nora and Sage went into their number. Their function was to greet the guests, smile, charm, empty the ashtrays, make pleasant chatter, keep things perking, see that everyone had plenty to eat, plenty to drink. Nora made like an airline stewardess and scintillated and the place was soon packed with authors, editors, boisterous Hollywood types with loud voices and smelly cigars. Kilgallen did appear sheathed in pink satin, and Jack Paar came, too, Jason being a frequent guest on his show. Ross darted about looking very nervous, his bald pate gleaming with perspiration, his maroon velvet dinner jacket extremely ill advised. He slapped backs and pumped hands and negotiated deals, filling the air with his own electricity. The guest of honor still hadn't made an appearance at nine-thirty, but no one seemed to notice. Everyone was too busy trying to make an impression on everyone else. Eyebrows were elevated when a beaming Truman Capote appeared at ten, looking like a wicked elf in black velvet suit and pink bow tie. Jason and Capote had recently blasted each other's prose in print, their "feud" avidly chronicled by the lightweight press.

"Christ!" Ross roared. "What the hell is *he* doing here?"

"Don't ask me," Nora said. "*I* didn't invite him."

"Jason is going to shit!"

"Where *is* Jason?"

"He's still in the kitchen. Dick's working him over with cold wet rags, feeding him more coffee."

"With all that coffee, I doubt seriously he'll shit."

"Lip! There's Bennett, he looks glum; Rand must be acting up. Go fetch him a drink, make a pun, cheer him up. If I get through this evening alive, it'll be a miracle."

"If I get through this evening alive, I expect a hefty raise."

"Go!" he thundered.

Nora smiled and chatted with Bennett Cerf and cheered him up and endured his atrocious puns and then she casually sauntered past the buffet table, spying two unopened tins of caviar

on a box behind it. She had already spirited a bottle of Chivas Regal out onto the terrace, hiding it behind a potted rubber tree plant. She sauntered on, awaiting the right opportunity. The noise level was deafening. The air was dense with smoke. Capote was holding court in one corner. Kilgallen was taking notes. Sage was fending off the advances of a tipsy Pulitzer Prize-winning historian. The kitchen door banged open and there was a mighty roar and Jason Pollen finally made his appearance, charging upon the party like some crazed, wounded lion.

Pollen was the darling of the literary establishment, deified by *The New York Review of Books*, given a cover by *Time*, hailed by most of the critics as Hemingway's successor and the Great Hope of American Literature. Nora found his prose turgid and self-indulgent, his macho posturing sophomoric, but with the exception of Capote and one or two others, hers was a voice in the wilderness. Bursting upon the scene with a gigantic novel about boxing, Pollen had captivated critics and public alike with his crude, bullish shenanigans, many marriages, drinking bouts and drunken brawls. A self-proclaimed genius, Pollen declared himself the best goddamned writer in this whole goddamned country and continued to churn out turgid epics that, because they were dense, because they were wordy and frequently incoherent, most felt must be brilliant. A former boxer himself, Pollen was a Man's Man with a vengeance, outdoing Hemingway himself in ostentatious virility.

Forty-six now, he was stockily built, not overly tall and running to fat, with a battered, jowly face, a broken nose, squinty black eyes and blond hair that roiled atop his head in short Harpo Marx curls. Roaring mightily, grabbing a drink, he wore soiled gray slacks, white shirt, a brown tie torn loose at the throat and a deplorably rumpled brown tweed jacket. He hailed guests with gusto, reeling dangerously and putting on a dandy act as the middle-aged enfant terrible of American letters. He bragged loudly about the brawl last night, laughed about his time in the slammer, grabbed another drink, kissed a startled young editor, stopped dead still when he spotted Truman Capote grinning at his performance.

A dead hush fell over the crowd. Pollen turned pale, and then he turned pink and began to stamp the floor with one foot, exactly like a bull. With a mighty yell he slammed his fist down onto a glass-topped coffee table, smashing it to smithereens.

He took several deep breaths, snorting, getting ready to charge. Breaths were held. Sheridan looked as though he might faint.

"Oh, come *on*, Jason," Capote chirped. "No one has to work *that* hard to prove he's got a pair of balls."

Pollen reeled backward as though sustaining a blow and then he threw his head back and roared with laughter, reeling toward Capote and slinging an arm around his shoulders.

"I *like* this little bastard!" he yelled. "He may write affected, prissy stories, but he's got *guts*! Where's the bartender? I wanna buy my little buddy a drink!"

There was a round of applause and sighs of relief and the incident would undoubtedly be written up in a dozen columns, garnering tons of publicity for both of them. Seizing her opportunity, Nora deftly snatched the two tins of caviar and, unnoticed, carried them out to the terrace and placed them behind the rubber tree plant, to be retrieved later and carried home in the shoulder bag she always brought to these parties. It was pleasantly cool on the terrace. Nora rested her elbows on the smooth marble bannister and gazed at the misty black sky, starless, streaked with moonlight. Below, the city was shadowy black blocks spangled with light, and Nora remembered those corny scenes in countless B movies where hero or heroine stood on bridge or balcony gazing at the New York skyline and raised a fist and vowed, "New York, I'm gonna conquer you yet!" And, corny as it was, that's exactly how she felt, her heart filled with longing, with need, with determination.

Someone pinched her ass.

Nora whirled around. A short, rotund man with beaming moon-shaped face, horn-rimmed glasses and thinning brown hair grinned at her in the light streaming out through the French windows. In natty black suit and flashy blue silk tie, he reminded her of the Pillsbury Dough Boy, plump, amiable, full of mischief. Her ass still smarted. He had quite a pinch.

"How 'bout it, chick? Why don't we ditch this dump and have ourselves a *real* party at my suite at the Pierre."

"Fuck off, creep."

"Whatsa matter? My money not good enough for you?"

"How'd you like a knee in the groin?"

The plump little man looked puzzled, the huge brown eyes behind his horn-rims suddenly bewildered. "You mean you're not a bimbo?" he asked.

238 Jennifer Wilde

"I'm not a bimbo. I happen to be a literary agent."

"A literary agent, hunh? Jesus, my mistake." He looked properly apologetic, and then he grinned a wide grin. "You're still a knockout broad, best looker in the whole joint."

"You need a new pair of glasses, Buster."

His grin grew even wider. He exuded boyish amiability, and you couldn't help but like him, even if he was an ass-pincher. Nora sighed, pretending to be disgusted. The man took out an enormous brown cigar, unwrapped it and bit the end off, then lighted it with a solid gold lighter. Hollywood. Had to be. Nora squinted, examining his face more closely, and she remembered seeing his picture then and realized who he was. Terry Wood, born Irving Goldstein, former story editor at Twentieth Century Fox and, for the past decade, hotshot film producer, celebrated for his all-star epics based on best-selling novels, his brazen rip-offs of others' story ideas and his phenomenal exploits at the gambling tables. Because he could spell "cat" without a "k," because he had been chummy with Fannie Hurst during the thirties, Hollywood considered him "literary." Rumor had it that Schulberg had based his Sammy Glick on this same Terry Wood, né Goldstein.

"A literary agent, hunh?" he said, puffing on the cigar. "So what da ya handle?"

"Shit."

"What kinda shit?"

"Sweet nurse romances. Hard-boiled detective tales. Lesbian novels."

"Afraid there's not much demand for any of them in my line of work. I'm Terry Wood, maybe you've heard-a me. I make movies."

"I've heard of you," she said dryly.

"Yeah? What'd ya hear?"

"I heard you were an unprincipled rogue, a charlatan, a thief, a plagiarist and the most brilliant producer in Hollywood."

"The last part's true," he admitted candidly. "Ever see any of my movies?"

"Several of them. They're sleek, glossy, grabby, terrific entertainment. You know what the public wants."

"And I deliver every time. You're a gutsy little broad, aren't ya? Not a bit intimidated by me. I like that. Most people tremble

in their boots because I'm so powerful and important. Gets kinda tiresome. Actually, I'm very lovable.''

"And your wife doesn't understand you," she said.

"The last one understood me well enough, took me for a couple of million, a house on Rexford Drive, a chalet in Gstaad and a fortune in diamond baubles. She also took my chef, damn the bitch, good chefs are hard to come by.''

"You producing Jason's latest epic?''

"Naw, I just flew in with the guys, hoping to find me another hot property. I'm lookin' for another blockbuster, something along the lines of *Peyton Place* and *The Best of Everything*, something with a lotta attractive young people and a whole lotta humpin'.''

Nora looked at his amiable, moon-shaped face and took a deep breath, mind racing a mile a minute. Why the hell not? What did she have to lose? Couldn't hurt anything. Although she didn't drink that much, she longed for a slug of whiskey to give herself courage. She took another deep breath, then plunged right in.

"I just happen to know about a book you might be interested in. It's not finished yet, won't be ready to show for at least a couple of months, but it's a doozy, has everything.''

Terry Wood took another puff of his cigar. The butt glowed bright orange in the semidarkness. The noise of the party roared behind the French doors, a frenzied, muted background. Nora's throat felt tight. Her heart was beating much too rapidly. The producer was suddenly all business, his eyes shrewd behind the thick horn-rims, all amiability gone. Poppin' Fresh had been transformed into a shark. No one survived on top in Hollywood for over twenty-five years without being a tough son of a bitch, and Nora suspected Wood was one of the toughest.

"So what's it called? What's it about?''

"It—it's called *The Slipper*,'' Nora said nervously, improvising. "It's about—about these three young girls who meet in college, all of 'em dreaming of fame and glory. One of them, Anne, she wants to be a—uh—a dress designer and she's wonderfully talented, always making gorgeous sketches of clothes, but she—she's very shy and timid and she's only eighteen and she's married to a cold, handsome son of a bitch and working as a waitress in a greasy spoon to put him through med school. He meets a

rich debutante who can do more for him and divorces Anne and leaves her penniless and pregnant.''

"So?"

"So she comes to New York with her friend—uh—her friend Susan, determined to make it as a designer. Susan is a beauty, cool and lovely, she looks like Grace Kelly, and *she* dreams of becoming a top fashion model. All the men are after her, but she—uh—Susan's in love with a man old enough to be her father. He's spoiled her for all the gorgeous young studs who flock around in droves. Unfortunately, he's very married, and his wife refuses to give him a divorce. All the fame and riches she acquires as a model can't compensate for her broken heart.''

"And the third girl?"

"Her name's Billie. She's bright and cute and cocky, and she's very insecure. Billie desperately wants to be popular in college but boys don't like girls who're smarter than they are, so she's a wallflower, all alone on Saturday night. Billie wants to be a journalist, works on the college paper, hopes to get a job with *The New York Times*, and she's good, damned good, but lonely. She decides to do something about it, goes out with a jock who needs help with his term paper in English and puts out for him. She starts going out with his buddies on the track team and soon becomes the town pump, the most popular kid on campus with the horny set.''

Terry Wood puffed on his cigar, the butt crackling brightly. He took it out of his mouth, flicking ashes onto the terrace floor.

"And then?" he asked.

"Billie goes to New York with Anne and Carol—I mean Susan—and after a lot of hardship and a lot of heartbreak, all three of them make it. All three of them get the glass slipper. That's where the title comes in, you see. Every girl dreams she's gonna be the next Cinderella, dreams she's gonna get the slipper and live happily ever after, but only a few of them do.''

Nora leaned back against the bannister, exhausted, amazed at her own gumption. Terry Wood smoked his cigar, silent. So he didn't buy it? So what the hell? It was a long shot anyway, but at least she'd gained something. As she was hastily improvising, rearranging facts, her mind click-click-clicking with ideas, Nora realized that it *was* a great premise, realized that this was exactly

the brainstorm she had been waiting for. Susannah Hart was going to retire as of right now. No more mysterious mansions and brooding heroes and cries in the night. Nora Levin was going to write *The Slipper* whether Terry Wood liked the premise or not.

"And who's the author of this masterpiece?" he inquired.

"I am," she said defiantly.

"You got something to show?"

"Not yet. I—I will have soon, though."

"The town pump, hunh?" he mused. "Sure you don't wanna come to my suite at the Pierre?"

"I'm positive."

She marched over to the French doors and opened them and the noise of the party blasted them in waves.

"Hey—"

"Up yours!"

"Hey! Wait a minute! What's your name?"

"My name's Nora Levin," she called over her shoulder. "I work for Ross Sheridan."

The party was going full blast. Jason was having a noisy set-to with the Pulitzer Prize-winning historian. Capote was gossiping merrily with a trio of overdressed society matrons. Sheridan was still bounding about making deals, making points. Nora resumed her duties and the evening wore on and toward midnight she saw Ross talking with Terry Wood. She'd probably lose her job. Who cared? She had some money in the bank, the Susannah Harts were bringing in a modest amount of royalties, and all she wanted to do now was start *The Slipper* while the ideas were still sizzling. The party finally broke up at one in the morning. The last guest tottered out. Jason was sprawled out in an armchair, dead drunk, snoring loudly. Ross was busily filling up doggie bags to take to his apartment, and he thoughtfully gave each of his girls five dollars for cab fare, not wanting them to take bus or subway at this hour. Tins of caviar and bottle of Chivas Regal stored safely in her large shoulder bag, bag slung over her arm, Nora left, idly wondering if Terry Wood had found himself a bimbo for the night.

She felt like shit the next morning. She had hardly slept at all, thinking about the encounter with Terry Wood, thinking about *The Slipper*, the ideas coming fast and thick as she pounded her pillow and tried to sleep. Julie was already gone

when she got up, had already taken Danny upstairs to Hannah Lichtenstein's apartment. Nora bathed, dressed, had two cups of strong black coffee while staring listlessly at *The Today Show*, then left for the office. She sat at her desk and gazed glumly at the new stack of manuscripts, envying Sage, who had fled the salt mines and would start work at Dell Monday. It wasn't going to be the same without her. Nora pulled the top manuscript from the pile and made a face. I can't do it, she told herself. I can't possibly read another trenchant epic about lesbian love in Greenwich Village.

At ten-thirty the door to Ross's private office flew open with a bang and he loomed in the doorway, crackling with nervous energy.

"Levin!" he yelled. "Get your ass in here, pronto!"

This is it. He's gonna fire me. Well, at least I won't have to read *Sisters in Sin*. Ross glared at her and showed her into the office and closed the door, his expression grave. She gazed at the rich mahogany paneling, the maroon carpeting, the silver-framed photographs of celebrity authors, the expensive crystal decanters of liquor on the portable bar. The vast desk was littered with books, papers, contracts, three telephones, one of them red. Quite a layout. Sheridan sat down behind the desk and indicated she sit in a chair in front of it, and Nora obeyed dutifully without a single smart remark. Wasn't up to it this morning.

"I talked to Terry Wood last night," Ross said grimly.

"You did, huh?"

"I talked to him again this morning—two times. You're fired!"

Nora didn't say anything. She should have cared. She didn't. He handed her a slip of paper. It was a check. For two thousand dollars? Two thousand? Talk about your severance pay! He must be out of his bloody mind.

"I've also talked with Simon and Schuster, they want to do the hardback, and I've had calls from Fawcett, Dell, Signet, Pocket Books and Avon, pleading to have first crack at paperback reprint. Word gets around fast in this business! It's not even noon!"

"What are you talking about?"

"I'm talking about *The Slipper*! Terry Wood is crazy over the idea and he called a pal of his at Simon and Schuster first thing this morning and they're hot to trot, want to see something as

soon as possible, and word leaked out to the paperback houses immediately. We're talking a huge package deal here, movie, hardback, paperback, one hundred percent of each, no sharing of subsidiary rights. Twentieth Century Fox is going to subsidize the hardback promotional campaign, they're willing to spend a fortune putting it on the best-seller list and keeping it there as long as possible.''

"Jesus," she whispered.

"We're talking big bucks, too, sweetheart. We're talking half a million, maybe more—book clubs, foreign rights, God knows what else. *The Slipper* is already a best-seller, and not a goddamn word's been written. I *assume* not a word's been written.''

Nora shook her head. Her face was pale.

"I—I was just improvising, making it up as I went along, just—''

"The check you're holding is for your living expenses. You're gonna get your ass out of here and park it in front of your typewriter and you're gonna *sit* there until I have a synopsis and sample chapters to show. Wood's flying back in three weeks to have a look.''

"But—''

"No buts! Get outta here! Get to work! I told Wood I'd seen the first six chapters, told him they were brilliant. Told Simon and Schuster it was a cinch, told 'em it was gonna be the biggest thing since *Forever Amber*. You'd better not fail me, kid!''

"I—I'll have to clean out my desk, and—''

"I'll have someone do it for you, send everything over to your apartment later on. This is it, Nora baby. This is the big time. If you come through like I think you're gonna, it's gonna be roses the rest of the way!''

"Ross, I—''

"We're in, sweetheart. We're gonna make publishing history!''

Stunned, Nora stepped outside twenty minutes later. The sidewalks were packed with pedestrians, as always, businessmen with briefcases, matrons with shopping bags, a bustling, colorful swarm of humanity. Taxis and vans roared down the street with much blasting of horns and slamming of brakes. A street vendor was loudly hawking the virtues of his hot pretzels beneath the red-and-white umbrella of his cart. Gripping her purse, Nora started trudging toward Broadway and the nearest subway station

and then, as the full realization hit her, she stopped dead still right there in the middle of the sidewalk. People shoved past her with angry, impatient looks, but Nora beamed. She felt a burst of elation so glorious she could hardly contain it. My God! It's happened! It's really happened! After all those years and all those dreams and all that work! She stood there smiling, another New York crazy, and then she darted between two parked cars and started waving her arm wildly to flag down a taxi. No more filthy subways for this girl. It's finally happened! Little Nora Levin's got the slipper at last!

12

Poor Meg was certainly having her share of problems. Blake,
the randy young lawyer, had successfully defended her sister
Jane and Jane was cleared and Bill, her husband, who had raped
Meg, had run off with a nightclub singer and Blake wanted to
marry Meg and Meg finally agreed and they had a glorious honeymoon and it was only then that she discovered his mob connections. In the ensuing months, Blake had tried to sever his
connections with the mob and go straight and Meg had been
kidnapped by the mob and held captive in a basement and Blake
had had to cooperate with the mob and get the information they
demanded or else Meg would be murdered. Meg wasn't murdered, she was rescued by a handsome police detective, and
Blake spilled all he knew about the mob and was gunned down
and died in her arms and now Meg was deeply involved with
Steve, the blond detective, who was investigating a series of
mysterious killings in River City's Chinatown district. *This Life
of Ours* was the number one soap on television, Julie its most
popular actress, and the pace was horrendously taxing.

Blazing hot lights made the set an inferno. Microphones dangled overhead. The cameras were rolling. Robert Shippley, playing Steve, gave her a sober look and slipped his revolver into
his shoulder holster. Julie, as Meg, looked upset and tried valiantly to hide it, tried to be brave. The phone rang and Steve

answered it and told his partner that yeah, this was it, this was the big one, ten o'clock tonight, the old warehouse where they stored firecrackers. Still in her diaphanous blue nightgown, boldly revealing for television, Julie looked determined now, viewers fully aware of her plan to follow him to the warehouse, Steve still in the dark.

"Take care, Meg," he said. "When I leave, I want you to lock the door behind me. Don't open it for anyone, you understand? Unless you hear my voice on the other side, don't open the door for *any*one."

"I won't," she promised. "Oh, Steve—be—be careful. If anything happened to me I don't know what you would—shit! Sorry, John. I wasn't concentrating. These goddamned lights."

"No sweat, Julie baby. Relax. Take ten, everyone. We'll start at the top after the break."

"Sorry, Bob," Julie told Shippley. "I don't know what's wrong with me today. You were doing a wonderful job. I'm the one who fucked it up."

The handsome young actor smiled and gave her a hug. The least temperamental of actresses, always prepared and always professional, Julie was the favorite of cast and crew. She rarely blew her lines, and incidents like today's were extremely rare where Julie was concerned. Leaving the set, stepping into the coolness of shadows, she lighted a cigarette and smoked rapidly, fighting back a sudden rush of tears. She was utterly exhausted and it was imperative they get the episode in the can today and now they'd have to tape the whole bloody scene over again. Tape wasn't nearly as flexible as film. You couldn't start and stop and splice together. Unless there was a "freeze point," a close-up, say, where the frame was absolutely still and could be matched in editing, you had to start the scene all over again, which was one of the reasons minor flubs and mishaps often remained in the televised episodes. They were always on a tight schedule and it was too expensive and too time-consuming to tape a scene over unless it was absolutely necessary. Julie finished her cigarette and lighted another, glancing at the clock, praying they'd be finished by four.

"Okay, gang," the director shouted. "Let's do it again. Take it easy, Julie. It's only a soap, for God's sake. Millie, better powder Bob's face a bit, I see perspiration. You okay, sweetheart?" he asked Julie.

"I'm fine, John. Please forgive me. Today's my son's birthday, he's two years old, and we're giving him a party this afternoon and I—I guess I was concerned about that."

"This is the last scene, love. We'll have it in the can in no time. *Soap Opera Digest* wants to interview you again this afternoon—they'll be waiting in—"

"John, I—"

"No problem, sweetheart. I'll see 'em myself, give 'em some handouts and a new glossy, tell 'em what a great little trouper you are, tell 'em you've got to attend your kid's birthday party, ply 'em with liquor and get them to reschedule the interview for next week."

"You're a marvel."

"I'm the best goddamned director working on soaps, and you happen to be the best actress I've ever worked with. I gotta feeling you're not going to be with us much longer. Gotta feeling you're gonna be whisked away to star on Broadway or make feature films. It's inevitable, baby."

Millie freshened up her makeup, too, and Julie and Shippley took their positions. The hot lights blasted them again. Julie took a deep breath, preparing herself, and then she became Meg. The cameras started rolling. The scene went relatively well. Shippley had trouble getting the revolver into his holster, but he covered nicely, and there was a faint mike shadow on his final close-up, but the director decided to let it remain. Fifteen minutes later, Julie was in her dressing room, makeup removed, face creamed, having another cigarette as she summoned the strength to dress.

It seemed she was always tired these days. Work here at the studio was extremely grueling, the pace never letting up, and there were her classes with Sonia and the occasional reading as well. A number of soap actors moonlighted off Broadway and on, carrying a double load, and Sonia was determined that Julie get that big break and leave television. Julie had been up for a role in the Albee play, had been called back three times, had finally lost out to another actress, and she had won a supporting role in the revival of Coward's *Hay Fever* which unfortunately folded after three weeks of dismal box office. Sonia continued sending her out, certain that big break was just around the corner, and in the meantime Julie had to keep up on her lines and try to provide some kind of home life for Danny, who was old

enough now to resent his mother's constant absence and who clung to her when she was at home, a sweet, loving child who was gradually becoming whiny and unruly. This wasn't *fair* to him. It wasn't fair to either one of them. He needed a home. He needed stability, and he needed a father, too, not just a rowdy pal like Jim who spoiled him outrageously and then failed to appear for several days running.

Danny no longer had a father. CHICAGO HEIRESS AND HUSBAND KILLED IN CRASH, the headlines blared two months ago. Douglas and Cynthia Hammond had been flying back from Barbados in a small private plane, there had been a storm, the pilot lost control, all three of them had been killed instantly. When she saw the picture of Doug and Cynthia in the paper, Julie had studied her emotions closely, trying to gauge them, but the grief, the sorrow did not come. The man in the photograph had his arm slung around his wife's shoulder and there was a broad smile on his lips, and he was like a stranger. She felt nothing. The handsome, affluent man with his stylishly cut hair and three-hundred-dollar dinner jacket might indeed have been someone she had never known. Julie had never laid eyes on him again after he left the basement apartment that night before graduation. The divorce had all been handled smoothly and efficiently through lawyers, Julie refusing both alimony and child support. She had not contacted Doug when his son was born, and Doug had made no inquiries. For all he knew she might have aborted it after all, might have had a miscarriage like before. He simply hadn't been interested enough to inquire. One day Danny would ask questions about his father, and she would make up some pleasant, plausible story for him, but now she wanted merely to forget. She was sorry about the plane crash, of course, it was terrible and tragic, but she felt no grief, felt no loss. She had gone through that over two years ago, and she never wanted to suffer that way again.

Sighing, Julie removed her robe and dressed in her street clothes, a simple white cotton blouse, a full brown skirt a little too short, a pair of worn brown loafers. Smoothing her hair back from her face, she tied it in back with a faded pink scarf. It wasn't quite four o'clock. There would still be time to stop by for the cake and hang up the balloons and crepe paper streamers before Hannah brought Danny down. Bless Hannah. Julie knew she could never have made it without her. Hannah was paid well,

but no amount of money could pay for the tenderness, the loving care and concern she lavished on her charge. Danny was closer to Hannah than he was to his own mother, and that worried Julie a lot. She didn't want it to be this way. She dreamed of a home in the country, a dog, a garden, a husband who would love her and Danny and give them a simple, uncomplicated life so her Danny could grow up strong and healthy and normal. Danny was the most important thing in the world to her, far more important than acting, becoming a star. She had realized that some time ago, but acting was the only thing she knew, the only way she could make a decent living for them.

Julie left her dressing room and started down the dingy hall toward the reception area with its phalanx of secretaries and security guards. Those dreams she had so tenderly nourished during her teens seemed foolish now. Julie loved acting, but she hated all that went along with it, hated the stress, the tension, the rivalry, the frustrations, and personal celebrity meant nothing to her. She hated the interviews, the attention, and although she was always charming and accessible, she hated the crowds of teenaged girls who waited outside the studio, swarming around her when she stepped out the door. I thought I wanted the slipper, she told herself, but . . . but now all I want is a simple life for me and my son. I'll never find it in this business. Oh God, if only Doug had loved me as I loved him. If only . . . Julie put on a pleasant smile for the secretaries and waved to her favorite security guard and, pausing to slip on her brown cloth coat, stepped outside into the icy January cold.

The cold didn't deter them a bit. They were all out there, at least twenty of them, most of them with familiar faces. "Meg!" they shouted and "Julie!" they cried, and they swarmed around her with autograph books and glossy studio photographs and she smiled and made pleasant talk and signed the pictures, signed the books, patiently answering their silly questions, gracious even when they lunged at her like salmon going upstream. What possessed them to stand out here in the cold for hours on end, waiting for a chance to see her? What mysterious glamor did they believe she was imbued with? The glamor was all an illusion in the eye of the beholder. This huge tan building that dominated a grimy corner on the West Side, the dusty hallways within, the hot lights, the coils of electrical cables, the gimcrackery sets that photographed far better than they looked.

There was no glamor in these, no glamor in the hours and hours of backbreaking labor. A plump blonde teenager chewing a wad of gum told Julie she thought she was wonderful, and Julie smiled, thanking her. Another girl asked her if she and Steve were ever gonna get married, or were they just gonna keep sleeping together like they'd been doing the past three months. Julie told her that that was up to the producers and scriptwriters but, as far as she was concerned, she *enjoyed* sleeping with a man as handsome as Steve. The girls all giggled, adoring her, and it was then that Julie happened to look up and see the man again.

He was standing beside a mailbox a few yards away, wearing the same nondescript blue suit, watching her with that same bland expression. His hair was a grayish brown, his face utterly unremarkable, everything about him insignificant and forgettable, but Julie recognized him at once. She had first seen him loitering on the corner outside the apartment when she left for work early one morning two weeks ago. He had pretended to be reading a newspaper, but she was conscious of his eyes on her as she hurried toward the bus stop. She had seen him again a few days later as she was leaving the Carnegie Hall building where Sonia conducted her classes in one of the studios. He was loitering on the steps that time, again with a newspaper, and again she had been conscious of his eyes watching her intently. He had no newspaper this afternoon. He stared at her openly, with a curious bland indifference, and Julie felt a chill that had nothing to do with the cold. It . . . it was no coincidence. He was definitely keeping track of her. He knew where she lived, where she worked and where she attended class. New York was a city of crazies, and even though there was nothing at all frightening about the man, no menace in his manner, she couldn't help feeling a twinge of alarm.

As the girls continued to bombard her with questions, Julie tried to retain her composure, tried to smile. She gradually edged her way toward the curb and felt a wave of relief when she saw the motorcycle roaring down the street, biker in jeans, brown leather jacket, sun shades and a flamboyant gray-and-yellow muffler wound casually around his throat, ends flying. He slammed to a stop at the curb, and the girls had hysterics, identifying him immediately. That windblown, coal-black hair, those handsome,

chiseled features, that jaunty, carefree manner could only belong to the hottest young actor on Broadway.

"It's Jim Burke!" one of the girls yelled. "Jim! Jim! We love you, too! Are you and Julie going steady?"

Jim gave the girls a cocky grin as Julie climbed onto the back of the motorcycle, wrapping her arms tightly around his waist, and then he revved the motor, roaring away. Julie clung to him, resting her cheek against his broad shoulder as they darted through the congestion of West Side traffic. Jim zipped between grimy yellow taxis, soared around delivery vans, breezily passed a crowded city bus, in complete command. *Life* had featured a picture of Jim on his motorcycle after he won last year's Tony Award as best supporting actor for his performance as the psychopathic college student in *An Easy Murder*. The press had made much of his unconventional attitudes, his bike, his shabby loft apartment in the village, his cocky charm, his consummate professionalism onstage. A gigantic hit, *An Easy Murder* was still running, and Jim was being deluged with fabulous offers to do television and films. He was a star now, the most exciting new personality since Brando, and Julie was very, very proud of him.

Slowing down, Jim gently eased the bike onto the curb in front of the apartment, braked and, after Julie had dismounted, took out his chain and locked the bike to a lamppost near the front steps. Julie brushed an errant lock of hair from her brow, watching him. Success invariably changes a person, she knew, and success had certainly changed Jim Burke. He was less intense, more relaxed, at ease with himself and with the world. Despite the bike, the jeans, the leather jacket, he had abandoned all Brando mannerisms and developed his own style, easygoing, jaunty, engaging. Success, somehow, had brought all his best qualities to the fore, and she considered herself fortunate indeed to have such a friend. She smiled as he casually slung his arm around her shoulder and asked her what was on the agenda.

"I've got to put up the balloons and crepe paper streamers, pick up the cake from the bakery on Amsterdam, stop by Gristede's and buy the ice cream. Hannah's bringing him down at five-thirty. I want everything to be ready by then."

"Tell you what, doll, you go on up and start with the streamers and balloons and I'll go get the cake and buy the ice cream. What flavors?"

"Danny loves chocolate. You might get some vanilla, too."

"Consider it done. See you in a little while."

He gave her shoulders a squeeze and started on foot for Amsterdam, and Julie went inside and up to the apartment. Although they could easily afford something better now, a nice place on Central Park West or a nice address on the East Side, neither she nor Nora had considered moving. Hannah was here, for one thing, and since the gigantic success of *The Slipper* Nora spent a great deal of time in California, working on the screenplay with Terry Wood and Nunnally Johnson. Hanging in the foyer was an enormous poster featuring a radiant, beaming Nora in black-and-white and, in color, a copy of the book and three words, THE SLIPPER SIZZLES, below, in smaller print, Simon & Schuster, $3.95. Beside the poster was a framed blowup of *The New York Times* best-seller list with *The Slipper* in the number one slot. Beneath this, also framed, was a cover of *Publishers Weekly* featuring *The Slipper* and another photograph of a grinning Nora. Rarely had a book received so much promotion, rarely had one leaped onto the lists and stayed there so long a time. It had been number one for twelve consecutive weeks, in the top five for eighteen more, and although the book had been published early last spring, it was still hanging in there, number nine this past Sunday. Nora had received reams of personal publicity, the most talked-about young writer since Françoise Sagan, and she thrived on her celebrity, loving every minute of it.

Locking the door, removing her coat and hanging it up in the hall closet, Julie stepped into the living room and was startled to see the Hottest Young Writer of the Decade standing on a kitchen chair, taping the end of a crepe paper streamer onto the light fixture. Nora was wearing a summery yellow dress printed with gold-and-beige flowers, her sleek black pageboy falling across her cheeks as she secured the tape. Her suitcases and a large package from the post office were in one corner.

"Nora! I thought you were in California."

"Jesus!" Nora exclaimed. "You scared the shit out of me!"

"You didn't hear me come in?"

"I've been concentrating on these bloody streamers, love," Nora said, climbing down from the chair. "I got in around two-thirty—did you think I was gonna miss my Danny's birthday

party? Terry said they wouldn't need me again till next Monday, so I hopped the first plane.''

"How's the screenplay going?"

"We finished the bible a couple of weeks ago, Nunnally's working on the actual script now. He's a love, not only brilliant and literate but charming as hell to boot. I'm working very closely with him as 'technical advisor,' informing him of salient little items such as the fact that girls living together in a New York apartment never have enough closet space and that while they might frequently borrow each other's clothes, they'd never use each other's perfume and makeup.''

"It sounds like you're having a marvelous time.''

"I am, love.''

Nora smoothed back her pageboy, surveying her handiwork. Bright crepe paper streamers were looped across the ceiling, along with clusters of colored balloons. Everything was done. She must have been working ever since she arrived.

"What do you think?" she asked.

"It looks lovely," Julie said.

"It was a thrill blowing up all those balloons, I can tell you. Where's Claymore's gift to Broadway?"

"He's gone after the cake and ice cream.''

"Thoughtful of him. Want a drink?''

Julie nodded. Nora went over to the portable bar and poured them both glasses of white wine. Although they hadn't moved, they had dressed the place up considerably with new drapes, new furniture. The bar was black lacquer, vaguely Chinese, and the couch Julie sat down on was smoke-gray velour, very plush. A bright red leather hassock made a striking contrast. Nora handed Julie her wine and then curled up on the other end of the couch, folding one leg under her.

"I needed this," Nora confessed, sipping her wine.

"So did I.''

"Rough day?''

"I blew my lines. We had to retape an entire scene.''

"I've been watching the show almost every day. There's a portable set in the office. You and Steve going to get married?''

"He's going to be seduced by a rich matron who wants to put him into politics and I'm going to be wooed by a handsome, sinister Chinese warlord who wants to use me to get back at Steve, who wrecked his smuggling operations.''

"Jesus. What will they think of next?"

"There's not much telling."

Success had changed Nora, too, Julie thought. There was a new glow, an indefinable aura of glamor and sophistication that hadn't been there before. Like Jim, Nora was more at ease with herself now, the insecurity and driving need to succeed replaced by a confident air she wore well indeed. There was a new maturity, too. The girl had become a woman, poised, self-assured, lovely, too, in her way. Little of the awkward college student remained in the chic, polished, highly successful young novelist.

"I love your dress," Julie said. "Hardly suitable for January, though."

"Perfect for California. You wouldn't believe the weather. Snow? Out there they don't know what it is. I—I'm halfway thinking of getting a permanent place in L.A."

"Oh?"

"Remember James Hennesy? Remember me telling you about meeting him at Copenhagen the day before I left the agency?"

"If I recall, you found him very attractive."

"I'm seeing him. I met him at a party in Beverly Hills. *With These Regrets* bombed, you know. Prentice-Hall gave it a big send-off, and the reviews were terrific, but it barely sold three thousand copies and there wasn't a paperback sale. He's working on a screenplay for the studio, a vehicle for Patricia Owens and Jeffrey Hunter, romance and industrial espionage in the pharmaceutical business. He drove me back to the hotel after the party and, well, I've spent a couple of weekends with him in Malibu."

"Serious?"

"It could be."

"Are you in love with him?"

"I'm not sure. He's the most exciting man I've ever met, brilliant, mercurial, magnificent in bed, but there's a lot going on beneath the surface. I—I'm never quite sure where I stand with him."

"Be careful, darling."

"Caution's my middle name," Nora told her, finishing her wine. "By the way, I brought that package up—they were holding it downstairs. It's from Paris, addressed to Danny. Carol sent it. It weighs a ton."

They removed twine and heavy brown paper to discover a

large oblong box handsomely wrapped in birthday paper. Julie set the present with the others on a card table she had moved in earlier.

"*Knaves Like Us* was playing at the Thalia last weekend," she said. "Jim and I went to see it again. Carol was absolutely marvelous, so was Sir Robert. It's a pity it didn't have wide release over here."

"Too British for the general public," Nora said. "She *was* marvelous. Carol has developed into a superb actress. Hollywood's going to wake up one day and see what they're missing. They still think of her as the amateur who wrecked *Daughter of France*."

Nora had flown to Paris last September and spent three weeks with Carol, meeting her early idol Gaby Bernais and enjoying the glamorous Parisian nightlife. Although her French was wretched she had enchanted the Frenchmen with her vitality, her wit, her flashy American chic. They were loath to let her go, but she had returned to New York with a plethora of gifts for Julie and Danny and a stunning new Parisian wardrobe.

"I wonder if she's started the new film yet," Julie said.

"That madman was still trying to find financing, the last I heard. I met him in Paris—did I tell you? Guy Masson. He's supposed to be some kind of genius, but he looked like a hoodlum to me. Thin as a rail, pockmarked face, dark glasses, moth-eaten T-shirt and a shabby black suit that looked vintage 1945. He hasn't ever made a film before, but Carol says the script is brilliant and wildly innovative. If they ever get it off the ground, her costar's going to be a former wrestler making *his* first film. What can I tell you?"

"Is—is she still pining over Norman Philips?" Julie asked.

"She hasn't gotten over him yet," Nora said. "I doubt she'll ever completely get over him. She blames herself for not coming back to America with him, not marrying him. She feels he needed her, feels she let him down. She's kept very, very busy, socially and professionally, but the sadness is still there inside."

"Poor Carol."

"She's strong. She'll survive. She'll come out on top, too, just you wait."

"I've no doubt she will," Julie said quietly. "I just wonder if it will all have been worth it."

Jim rapped noisily on the door then, and Julie got up to let

him in. He gave her the ice cream, gave Nora a grin and handed her the box from the bakery, unwinding the muffler from his throat.

"How's the Hottest Young Writer of the Decade?" he inquired.

"Cool," she said.

"Been gettin' any in California?"

"You've been spying, you son of a bitch."

"You look fabulous, babe."

"You look every bit as obnoxious as you looked back at Claymore when you were giving Julian Compton such headaches. That leather jacket's definitely passé, darling, and so are those boots."

"They're part of my image."

Nora took the cake out of the box and set it on the table in the small dining nook adjacent to the living room. It was set for five with festive paper hats and napkins, Danny's high chair at the head of the table. Julie put away the ice cream and returned to the living room to find Jim mixing himself a scotch and soda. She longed for a second glass of wine or something even stronger but knew both Jim and Nora would look askance. She rearranged the presents on the card table. Nora had added two to the collection, both huge and handsomely wrapped, and Julie was still curious about the gift a grinning Jim had brought earlier. The three of them sat down and chatted, close friends, comfortable, utterly at ease with each other. Julie wished she felt less weary, more in a party mood.

"So how's Hollywood?" Jim inquired.

"Glorious. Sunshine. Palm trees. Jewelry stores. Paradise."

"You really *like* it out there? I hear the place is full of phonies."

"That's New York provincialism speaking. Some of the most brilliant, inventive and stimulating people I've ever met are living in L.A. They have style and sophistication New Yorkers can only dream about."

"Sounds to me like you've been brainwashed, babe."

"Come on out. See for yourself."

"I just might do that one of these days."

Hannah let herself in with her key at five-thirty, Danny toddling behind her, plump and sturdy in a pale blue jumper with a fading Howdy Doody across his chest. Spying Nora, he let out

a lusty "No-No!" and charged, wrapping his arms around her legs.

"Mind the dress, sweetheart. It set me back three hundred bucks in the swankiest shop in Beverly Hills."

Hannah sighed wearily. A large, amiable soul with silvering black hair, woeful brown eyes and a generous nose, she exuded comfort and compassion, rather like an oversized Molly Goldberg. A shapeless purple wool tent dress failed to minimize her considerable girth. She carried an enormous brown bag as shapeless as her dress. Nora felt sure it contained any number of home remedies and a quart jar of chicken soup just waiting to be heated up. Jewish mother she might be, but Hannah was remarkably unlike Sadie, who, to Nora's eternal relief, had moved to Miami with Irving several months ago. A hunk of Nora's movie sale money had gone toward the purchase of their condo and a mink stole for Sadie.

"Bah-woons!" Danny exclaimed, noticing them for the first time.

"You betcha," Nora said.

"And pwe-sents! For me?"

"A couple of them might be," Nora confessed.

" 'Cause it's my birthday! Wight?"

"Right," Jim said.

"That's whutta said."

Releasing Nora's legs, Danny grinned at Jim and Jim made a fist and feigned a blow and Danny put up his dukes and Hannah's eyebrows shot upward in exasperation. Jim leaped up, grabbed Danny around the waist and heaved him up over his shoulder, Danny squealing with rapturous delight. Jim was really quite marvelous with Danny, Julie thought. In many ways he was still a child himself. They delighted in each other's company, romping and roughhousing together, and many a time a sleepy Danny had crawled into Jim's lap to be tenderly held and crooned to until he dozed off to sleep.

"How 'bout it, buddy?" Jim cried, swinging a squealing Danny around. "Wanna party? Wanna have some cake and ice cream?"

"Yeeeess!"

"Jesus," Nora said, "this is disgusting."

"Does he *need* this stimulation?" Hannah inquired. "Was he a good boy today? Did he eat his spinach? No! Did he throw it

across the room? Yes. Did he take his nap? No. He wants to watch his mommy on the television and I tell him she's already off and he says he wants to watch cartoons and I tell him there aren't any on and he says he'll settle for Captain Kangaroo and I pick up a pillow and I tell myself if I smother him to death any judge in the country will call it justifiable homicide."

"I hope you spanked him," Julie said.

"Lay a hand on that precious child? I should say not!"

A rambunctious Danny was finally settled into his high chair by an equally rambunctious Jim, paper hats were donned, then Julie lighted the two candles atop the cake. "Happy Birthday" was sung and Danny blew out the candles and then scooped a fingerload of icing off the cake and popped it into his mouth. Hannah's eyes flew heavenward, as though for support, and Julie lighted a cigarette, smoking it nervously while the others had their cake and ice cream, much of Danny's winding up on cheeks and chin. He was so like his father, she thought, the same eyes, the same dark-brown hair, the same handsome features clearly discernible beneath the chubby flesh. For a second time that day she fought back an impulse to burst into tears. Instead she cleaned Danny's face with a dampened napkin and lighted another cigarette.

"Now!" Danny cried. "Pwe-sents!"

Jim and Danny sat on the living room floor and Hannah sat on the couch and Julie poured herself another glass of white wine and watched as Nora handed presents to Danny, one by one. Ribbons were ripped aside. Colored paper was torn off with glee. Carol had sent him a beautiful set of tin soldiers, exquisitely hand-painted, each one with its own resting place in the hinged, triple-layered velvet-lined box. Auntie Carol was the lady on the phone, Julie reminded Danny. He had talked to her a number of times. Danny nodded and grabbed the next package, a huge stuffed Mickey Mouse almost as large as he, from Nora. She told him that she had gone all the way to Disneyland to get it for him and he'd bloody well better appreciate it. Danny said he bloody well would. There was a stuffed Goofy, too, also from Disneyland. Hannah gave him coloring books and Crayolas, and Julie had bought him several new shirts, pants, a new coat and winter boots, all of which Danny sullenly disdained. "I wanted a toy!" he informed her. Jim's gift was the last, and Danny

yelled with delight when he discovered four battery-run race cars with their own plastic track ready to be assembled.

"Wowweee!" he shouted. "Let's race 'em, Jim!"

"Bet I beatja!" Jim challenged.

"Betja don't!"

Julie fetched a trash bag, and Hannah and Nora helped her clear up the litter of ribbon and paper while Jim, on hands and knees, patiently assembled the plastic tracks, frowning as he consulted the directions. An exhausted Hannah gave Danny a hug, squeezed Julie's hand and went upstairs to her own apartment. Nora and Julie cleared the dining room table and washed the dishes, squeals sounding from the living room as the races began. Putting the last dish away, Julie dried her hands and lighted yet another cigarette.

"You're smoking too much," Nora said.

"I know."

"You really should try to cut down."

"I will."

"I noticed that second glass of wine, too. You never used to drink anything at all. Is something wrong, Julie? Is there something we should talk about?"

Julie shook her head. "I—it's just the strain, Nora. I never seem to have any time for the things that matter. I'm always working, always memorizing lines, always going to classes, going to auditions. Danny's getting out of control, and I—it's nothing. I just need some rest. I'll be all right."

"We'll talk tonight, love, after I get back."

"You're going out tonight?"

"I talked to Ross earlier. The Literary Guild is having a party tonight and he thinks I should make an appearance. He's sending a limo for me at seven. We're having drinks at the Plaza beforehand with Rona and her beau."

Julie looked at her friend and she felt a great rush of affection, gratitude as well. Nora had stood by her from the beginning, through the divorce, through the pregnancy, Danny's birth and the difficult months that followed until she finally got a job and could pay her share of expenses. They had indeed been closer than sisters, and Julie knew she could never have made it without Nora.

"I—thank you for being concerned, Nora," she said.

"What are sisters for?"

"I—I'm so happy for you. Have I ever told you that? You've struggled so hard for so many years and—and now you have everything you always wanted."

"Not everything. Not yet—but I'm working on it."

"I'm so glad you're my friend."

"You'll do yourself in a pinch, love."

"Have a good time at the party."

"I intend to, and when I get back I've got a couple of things to show you, a couple of frocks. I couldn't resist 'em. They're you, darling. You're gonna be gorgeous in 'em."

The races were still progressing noisily when Nora left, looking stunning in a patterned red-and-black velvet Dior with a matching black velvet cloak. Danny cheered lustily as his car zipped ahead of Jim's, and Jim wore a chagrined expression, brow furrowed, mouth turned down, very intent, cursing his car. Danny won and Jim accused him of cheating and they had a hearty, amiable squabble. Jim insisted they have one more race, determined to win this time, and Danny was elated at this opportunity to beat him again. Jim suggested they trade cars, Danny said "No way!" and Julie tactfully reminded Jim that he had a performance tonight. He sighed and stood up, looking disgruntled.

"We'll have a rematch later," he promised Danny, "and if I *catch* you cheating you're gonna get a fat lip."

"Yeah?"

"Yeah! You all right, babe? You look a little tired."

"It's been a long day. Thanks for all the help, Jim. I don't know what I'd have done without you."

"Bye, Jim! Thanks for the racers."

"Bye, tiger. I'll call you later, Julie."

After Jim left, Julie helped Danny put away his new toys, and then she sat in the large gray velour chair that matched the sofa and looked at the liquor cabinet and decided no, she wouldn't have another glass of wine. She hadn't eaten a bite since lunch— Hannah had fed Danny before she brought him down—but she was much too weary to go back into the kitchen and cook something. How she used to love to cook for Doug. How she had dreamed of lavish meals on fine china while she warmed a can of soup or prepared tuna salad. Doug was dead now, his life snuffed out in an instant. She remembered that virile young prince who had stepped into the McCanns' bathhouse wearing

only a brief red swimsuit and his black horn-rims. Something seemed to snap inside, something that had been there like a tight, hard knot ever since she saw the article and the picture in the newspaper. Julie started as Danny caught hold of her legs and pulled himself into her lap. She held him very close, very tight.

"I love you, Mommy," he said sleepily.

"I love you, too."

"I *like* the clothes."

"I'm glad you do, precious."

"You gotta go to the television tomorrow?"

"I'm afraid so."

"I thought maybe you could stay home and we could play with them tin soldiers Auntie Carol sent me."

"I wish I could."

"Hannah's no fun. Guess I'll have to play with 'em by myself."

He yawned and, nestling his head against her bosom, was soon fast asleep. Julie held him close, her lower lip trembling. The crepe paper streamers and clusters of balloons bobbed gently overhead. There was a muted rumble as the elevator doors opened, closed, laughter and footsteps in the hall. The tears Julie had been fighting all day long finally fell now, sliding down her cheeks in glistening trails. It was a long, long time before she finally carried her son to his bedroom and put him to bed.

Nora left Sunday night, taking the red-eye to Los Angeles, and the following Saturday Jim and Julie took Danny to a puppet show in the village, then had a festive hot dog lunch on a bench in Washington Square, undeterred by the cold. Jim took them back to the apartment and left for his matinee performance, and a weary, fretting Danny protested noisily when Julie told him it was time for his nap. She finally subdued him and a few minutes later he was sleeping peacefully, cheek on pillow, knees drawn up, derriere elevated, a soft blue blanket covering him. Julie settled down on the couch with the script of a new play Sonia had sent her. It was to be produced off Broadway, Sonia knew the director and he happened to be a fan of *This Life of Ours* and thought Julie would be perfect for the part of Cassie. She was to read for him, the writer and the producers next Tuesday.

A dark comedy, *At the Robert E. Lee* was set in a sleazy, decrepit hotel on the Lower East Side run by a dotty old southern

gentlewoman who is very fond of her pink gin fizzes and has no idea the young ladies renting her rooms walk the streets for a living. Her nephew, a shy, awkward, straitlaced youth from Virginia, comes to put his aged, certifiable aunt into the funny farm and sell the hotel to a firm that wants to tear it down and build a parking lot. The ladies of the evening are determined to prevent this, and Cassie, a raucous blonde, is their ringleader. Jake is smitten with her, wants to reform her, and antic complications ensue before the inevitable happy ending. The play was biting, witty, full of satire and social commentary, and Cassie was a dream part. She was tough, tart and, of course, had a heart of gold, with a tender and moving scene toward the end of the play when a drunken Lavinia is about to be carted off and the girls evicted. Though it owed much to Albee and Joe Orton, *At the Robert E. Lee* had brassy energy and a wonderfully gritty good humor. Julie fell in love with it immediately. What a joy it would be to play something besides the long-suffering Meg, she thought, putting the script aside.

She could play Cassie, she knew she could, and if she got the part and the play was successful she might even be able to leave *This Life of Ours*. Her contract was up for renewal on April 1, and there was already talk about a considerable raise in salary. How glorious it would be to bid them adieu and let the writers have Meg mowed down by Chinese gangsters or run over by a beer truck or something equally preposterous. Pouring a glass of white wine, lighting a fresh cigarette, Julie thought about how nice it would be to work in front of a live audience instead of a mute camera. And if she was in a successful play, if she could give up the soap, there would be plenty of time during the day for Danny. He would only have to stay with Hannah during the evenings when she was at the theater and Hannah would probably be willing to keep him down here so he could go to sleep in his own bed.

Loud knocking on the door startled Julie out of her revery, and she got up and crushed out her cigarette, wondering who it could possibly be. They had a buzzer, a doorman below, and, with the exception of Jim, who was always allowed to come right on up, all visitors were announced. It was barely four. Jim was still at the theater. Perhaps it was a delivery boy. Julie opened the door. She stared at Gus Hammond in stunned amazement.

He looked smaller, as though he had shrunk with age, a griz-

zled little man with squint lines around icy slate-blue eyes and a face weathered by the fierce Oklahoma sun. His hair was completely gray now. He must be in his mid-sixties, she thought, and he looked it. He wore tooled leather boots and a beautifully tailored tan suit and a black string tie with a silver-and-turquoise tie holder at the throat, Oklahoma attire, strangely incongruous here in New York. The expensive clothes somehow only emphasized the wizened face and the nut-hard quality of the man who wore them. Julie remembered that terrible scene in his study when he had slammed his fist into Doug's jaw and knocked him down and called her a little slut and told Doug he was going to have to marry her. It was like a nightmare still, in memory.

"How did you find me?" she asked.

"It took weeks. I hired a private detective. He finally tracked you down for me."

The man with the newspaper. She understood now.

"Aren't you going to ask me in?"

His voice was as harsh and gravelly as she remembered, a voice acquired in the oil fields, shouting orders at roughnecks. She moved aside and he stepped into the foyer and she closed the door and led him into the living room. There was a framed photograph of Danny, taken three months ago, standing on top of the liquor cabinet. Hammond spotted it at once and went over to examine it. Julie picked up her glass of wine and finished it. Although she knew he had no power over her, no possible means of harming her, Julie was still apprehensive. What could he possibly want with her after all these years? Why had he hired a private detective to track her down? Hammond finally turned away from the photograph. His eyes were misty. She realized that he was a lonely, miserable old man, and all his millions were little solace to him now.

"How did you get up here without the doorman announcing you?" she asked.

"I told him I was your father-in-law. I said I wanted to surprise you. I gave him a very generous tip."

"I see."

"I was afraid you wouldn't let me come up."

"I probably wouldn't have."

"I wonder if I could have something to drink?"

"Certainly. Scotch?"

He nodded. Julie poured the drink and handed it to him. He

drank it down in three rapid gulps. She lighted another cigarette. She could see the disapproval in his eyes. Nice girls didn't smoke. Nice girls didn't keep liquor in their living rooms. To hell with his judgments. She was no longer a pathetic little fifteen-year-old girl. What could it possibly matter what he thought about her now?

"He looks exactly like Doug," he said, indicating the photograph.

"He does indeed," she said coldly.

"I didn't know—I wasn't sure—" His voice seemed to crack and he took a moment to compose himself. "Af—after my son died I found out through his divorce lawyer that you were pregnant when Doug left you. He told me you'd moved to New York. I—I had to find you. I had to see if—if it was true, if my son had indeed had a child."

"I had a child," she said. "Your son didn't. Your son wanted nothing to do with it. Your son never even inquired to see if I had given birth. He died without knowing, or caring, whether or not he was a father."

"You have a right to be bitter, Julie."

"I suppose I do."

"I'm sorry."

"I'm extremely busy, Mr. Hammond. I have several things I need to do this afternoon. What do you want?"

"I want to—" Again his voice seemed to crack. He looked very uncomfortable. "I—I'm a harsh man, Julie. I fully realize that. I'm crude and uneducated, a tough son of a bitch who just happened to hit it lucky and make a fortune. I never had any illusions about myself, but—I wanted something better for my boy. When he let me down, I—because of my disappointment and in the heat of anger I did him a grave injustice. I did you an injustice, too. I had second thoughts later on, but I had too goddamned much pride to—to make amends for my action. I let my boy walk out of my life and now he's gone, and I have to— I have to live with what I did."

Julie said nothing. She remembered, and she refused to feel sorry for him now.

"I can never make it up to Doug," he said. "It's too late for that. If you'll let me, perhaps I can make it up to you—and to my grandson."

"You want to give us money?"

"I—yes. I've got millions, Julie. Millions and millions, and I have no one. I'm all alone. I'm sixty-six years old and the second richest man in the whole goddamned state and I live in a huge monster of a house with thirty rooms and no one to talk to except servants. I—I'm lonely," he confessed, and she knew that confession cost a great deal to a man with his thorny pride.

"I'm sorry about that," she said.

"Let me—"

"Danny and I want nothing from you, Mr. Hammond. Some of your money might have been welcome when Doug was struggling to get his law degree and I was working eight hours a day as a waitress to help him through, when we were living in a dingy basement with exposed pipes in the living room and not enough money for decent clothes or—or sometimes not even enough food, but—no, thank you, Mr. Hammond. I managed to support your son until he no longer had need of me, and I'm making a very good living for my own son now. We don't need you. We don't need your millions."

"You're very hard," he said harshly.

"Perhaps I am. Perhaps I've had to become that way in order to survive."

"This place, this neighborhood—" Hammond made a sweeping gesture, taking in the whole West Side. "This is no place for my grandson to grow up in. When the limousine stopped in front of this building I saw niggers and Puerto Ricans and I happen to know you share this apartment with a Jew."

Julie made no reply. She lighted another cigarette.

"The kind of work you do, the people you associate with—" His face hardened, the lonely old man supplanted by the harsh, angry Hammond she recalled so vividly. "It's not a decent atmosphere for a child. This actor you're sleeping with, he's little better than a hoodlum. I don't intend to see my grandson grow up in—"

"I think you'd better leave, Mr. Hammond."

"I intend to see my grandson."

"Danny's taking a nap. I have no intention of disturbing him. Will you leave quietly, or shall I buzz the lobby and have them send up a security guard to escort you out?"

Gus Hammond glared at her, his blue eyes blazing with hostility, his hands balled into fists, fists planted on his thighs, his stance that of a cocky bantam pugilist. Julie emitted a plume of

smoke, took another drag on her cigarette, gazing at him with level violet-blue eyes that belied the nervous turmoil within. She wasn't intimidated by him, she told herself. She wasn't going to let him bully her as he had bullied everyone else for most of his life. He had no legal rights whatsoever, and when it came to her son's welfare she was ready to fight like a veritable tiger.

"I intend to see my grandson," he repeated.

"You wrecked your son's life, Mr. Hammond," she told him, and even as the words left her lips she realized their cruelty. "I'm not going to allow you to wreck Danny's. I'm not going to allow you anywhere near him."

"You fucking little tramp. You're not *fit* to bring up my grandson!"

Julie stepped over to the buzzer, her finger poised over the button. "Are you going to leave, Mr. Hammond?"

"You're going to regret this," he promised.

Hammond stormed out then, slamming the door so savagely that Nora's framed *Publishers Weekly* cover tumbled to the floor. Shaken, her legs trembling, Julie collapsed into the large gray chair. Danny came toddling sleepily into the room, awakened by the noise. He rubbed his eyes and looked around in alarm and Julie smiled at him and held her arms out. He climbed up into her lap, and she told him there was nothing to be alarmed about and told him a story to distract him. Later on, after she had calmed down, she took him into the kitchen and he helped her make cookies, stirring the batter himself, slopping only a fourth of it onto the counter. No one's ever going to take you away from me, my darling, she promised silently. I'd kill before I'd let that happen.

On Tuesday afternoon, after she left the studio, Julie read for Hank Stevens, the director, and Aaron Vinton, the author of *At the Robert E. Lee*, and the three men and one woman who were to produce it. Standing on the bare, darkened stage, only one light making a hazy pool stage center, she did the scene toward the end of the second act where the raucous, tough-as-nails Cassie tearfully informs Jake that the Robert E. Lee is Lavinia's life, that she will die if taken away, that the Robert E. Lee is the only home she and the other girls have ever known and begs him to reconsider. She gave a good reading, she knew that, and she wasn't really surprised when Sonia, who was also her agent,

phoned two days later to tell her they had unanimously decided to give her the part.

With April and her contract renewal looming, the producers of *This Life of Ours*, fearful of losing her, were willing to do everything possible to keep her contented. Let her have her little fling off Broadway, they reasoned, keep her happy, make things easy for her. The play will probably open and close before it's time to sign her name on the dotted line. Consequently, Meg was grazed by a bullet when gunfire erupted at the old Chinese warehouse, was rushed to River City Hospital and went into a deep coma. Julie only had to report to the studio three mornings a week, working only till noon then, lying comatose in a hospital bed with bandaged head while Steve or Jane wrung their hands or talked to the doctor about her chances of recovery. Rehearsals for *At the Robert E. Lee* went wonderfully well, and Julie was thrilled to discover that Larry Blyden was cast as Jake, Eileen Herlie as Lavinia. The play was to open at the Theater de Lys on March 10th, and it had all the makings of a huge success.

One Tuesday in mid-February Jim picked Julie up outside the television studio and whisked her down to the Village on his bike for lunch. She didn't have to report for rehearsals until one-thirty, so they had ample time for a leisurely meal at one of his favorite restaurants. There was sawdust on the floor and red-and-white checked cloths on the tables and a hand-printed menu taped to the front window. For roughly a third of the price they would have paid at one of the chic restaurants uptown they had a meal twice as tasty: London broil steak, baked potatoes, green salad, homemade rolls. Working as hard as they did, both believed in eating a hearty lunch. The place was filled with a raffish village crowd who recognized both Julie and Jim and politely ignored them. Jim sighed deeply, pushing his plate back.

"What time'd you say you have to report to rehearsal?"

"One-thirty."

He glanced at the clock hanging over the door. "Better hurry up and finish your steak. I'll walk you to the theater and come back for my bike later. You're finished? Want some apple pie?"

Julie shook her head and they left a few minutes later and began to stroll toward the theater which was only a few blocks away. It was a lovely day, warm for February, Julie in a gray-and-violet plaid wool skirt and a violet sweater, Jim in his brown leather jacket and a black wool turtleneck. He took her hand,

and she smiled, so comfortable with him, as comfortable as she would be with an affectionate older brother, she reflected. They strolled past a used-book shop and a leather goods shop featuring handmade purses and belts and gloves. Julie loved the Village. Despite the influx of tourists and its self-conscious artiness, it had a relaxed, friendly ambience found no place else in the city.

"Got some news," Jim said.

"Oh?"

"David has posted the closing notice. *An Easy Murder* bites the dust after Saturday night's performance."

"Jim, I—I'm so sorry."

"I'm not." He grinned, squeezing her hand. "We've had a nice long run, and, if you wanna know the truth, I was getting kinda tired of playing a psychopathic killer. I'm ready to play something else—like a dashing young private eye, for example."

"A private eye?"

"With a sexy, slightly daffy blonde secretary named Bingo and a streetwise teenaged sidekick who talks tough, knows judo and helps me out of a lot of jams every week."

"That sounds like—"

"Sounds like *77 Sunset Strip, Hawaiian Eye, Bourbon Street Beat* and a host of other Warner Brothers' series. Mine'll be a bit jazzier, a bit less staid, more sex, more violence, a sure-fire smash, they tell me. I signed the contract yesterday. You won't believe the salary, I couldn't believe it myself. I also get a shot at feature films—they've already lined me up to costar with Natalie Wood during my summer hiatus."

They paused for a red light. Julie felt a sharp pang inside.

"That—that means you'll be leaving for California," she said.

"End of the month, babe."

The light changed. They crossed the street. "I—I'm very happy for you, Jim," she said.

"I'm pretty excited about it. It's a dream of a deal and a steppingstone to better things out there. There's just one hitch."

"What's that?"

"You and Danny won't be with me," he said.

Julie didn't say anything. They passed a handmade-jewelry shop, a gay bar, a paper company, an antique store, a shop featuring East Indian artifacts and a boisterous Irish tavern. Jim was still holding her hand, and he pulled her to a stop in front

of another used-book store, remaindered André Gide novels piled behind the dusty glass windows. His handsome face was grave. He looked terribly uneasy, as though afraid to speak.

"I—uh—look, I got something to say. We've been best buddies for—for a long time now, babe, and I—uh—well, to tell you the truth I guess you and Danny mean the world to me. Danny's like—I couldn't love my own kid any more than I love him."

"He loves you, too," Julie said quietly.

"I never thought I'd want a kid, not until Danny came along, and—I never thought I'd wanna get married until—Damn! I wish I had some brilliant scriptwriter right now. He'd provide the perfect words, and I'd provide the feeling. What I'm trying to say, babe, is—I guess I'm in love with you, I guess I have been for quite a while."

"Jim—"

"I never said anything. I didn't want to frighten you. I didn't want to risk spoiling our friendship. I knew you'd had a rotten time with your husband and I knew you must be pretty well turned off men after what you'd been through and I figured—well, with time you might decide we weren't all bastards, might even—might even grow to care for me a little."

"I—Jim, I—don't know what to—"

"I guess this isn't very romantic standing here in front of a hundred copies of *Lafcadio's Adventure* and *Strait Is the Gate*, but—I'd like to marry you, Julie. I'd like you and Danny to come to California with me."

There were tears in Julie's eyes. She had rarely been so touched, and she had rarely been so torn. She did care for him. She loved him in a very special way. She dreamed of a man who would love her and Danny and give them a secure, settled life, but Jim wasn't that man. He did love her, Julie had known that for months, and he loved Danny, too, but Jim was dedicated to his art, and she knew instinctively that acting and his career would always come first. The life Jim could give them would be heady and exciting and full of ups and downs, full of love, too, but it would not be settled. While she did love him, it was in no way sexual, and—and Jim deserved far more.

"You could go ahead with the play," he said, and there was an edge of desperation in his voice. "You and Danny could fly out and join me after the run. I love you, Julie."

"And I love you."

Jim saw the sadness in her eyes, and he knew, and the pain and disappointment in his own eyes was terrible to behold. Nevertheless, he managed a jaunty grin. He shook his head.

"But not in that way," he said.

"Not in that way," she told him. "I—I hope you will always be my dear friend, Jim."

"You know I will, babe. If you ever want anyone killed, just let me know. I'll always be there for you, come what may."

He pulled her into his arms then and kissed her gently on the lips, and he held her close for several long moments there in front of the bookshop. Julie touched the back of his neck, so sad, wishing things could have been different. She was so grateful this wonderful man was a part of her life, so sorry he wasn't the right one. Jim released her and stepped back and grinned another jaunty grin and they walked on, hand in hand, finally stopping in front of the Theater de Lys. Larry Blyden was just arriving. He waved. A taxi rumbled down the street. New York noises made a jangling background to the emotions both of them were feeling.

"Knock 'em dead this afternoon, babe," he said.

"I will."

"How 'bout a late dinner tonight, after I finish wowin' 'em? I'll stop by the Gingko Tree and pick up a couple of their specials."

Julie shook her head. "I'll make your favorite pasta instead. I have all the ingredients."

"Sure you wanna go to all that trouble?"

"Quite sure."

He gave her another quick hug and then turned and walked briskly back down the street, his leather jacket flapping, the bright afternoon sunlight burnishing his dark hair. Another tear trailed slowly down her cheek as Julie watched him leave. It glistened there for a long moment before she finally brushed it away and went inside to work.

Jim left the first of March, and Julie missed him dreadfully. She hadn't realized before just how much his friendship meant to her or just how much she had come to depend on him. Nothing seemed the same without Jim. The city was bleaker, and there was a great void. It was even harder on Danny. Julie had her rehearsals, the play was opening in less than two weeks, she was frantically busy, but Danny couldn't understand why his

rowdy chum, his buddy, his playmate since infancy was no longer there. Julie explained that he was in California with Auntie No-No and Danny asked if he would be back and she hesitated and told him he would be gone for some time and great tears welled in Danny's eyes, spilling over his lashes.

The play demanded every minute of her time, and she was able to spend even less time with Danny than before. Julie felt guilty about that. She knew Danny needed her now, needed reassurance, needed to know she wasn't going to disappear from his life, too, like Jim, but there was nothing she could do about it, not until the play opened. If it was a success, as she had every reason to believe it would be, she'd make it up to him. She'd be able to give up the soap and spend every day with him. That was some consolation as she took the subway down to the Village early every morning and returned late in the evening, totally depleted, weary through and through.

Julie was a nervous wreck the afternoon before the opening. Hank had told them all to stay home, rest, relax, unwind, store up their energy, but she wasn't able to relax. Danny was with Hannah—she couldn't possibly cope with him this afternoon, not in the state she was in—and Julie paced the living room, smoking one cigarette after another, desperately wanting a drink but not daring to pour one. If only Nora were here to hold her hand, but Nora was in California with Terry Wood, the script finished now, casting begun. Julie crushed out her thirtieth cigarette and lighted yet another and when the telephone rang she actually cried out. Taking a deep breath, brushing a silvery-brown strand from her brow, she picked up the receiver with trembling hand.

"Hello," she said.

"One moment please." A nasal voice. Static. "Julie?" another voice inquired. The static rose like a wave, crested, vanished, and suddenly the line was clear. "Julie, is that you?"

"Carol?"

"It's me, darling. I just wanted to call and wish you well tonight. You must be terribly nervous—I know I would be—but I know you're going to be a smash."

"Carol, it—it's so good to hear your voice."

"The play sounds marvelous, darling. I do so wish I could be there with you tonight, but I've just started a new film, started it day before yesterday actually, and everything's wildly disor-

ganized here. I think I must be out of my mind agreeing to work on a film with a director who's never made a film before and a costar who's never been in front of a camera in his life."

"You're doing the Guy Masson film?"

"The man's insane, darling. We're shooting in the park and he's using a hand-held camera. You'd think we were making a home movie, and the salary is nonexistent. I furnish my own wardrobe—jeans and a tight jersey—and I'm supposed to symbolize innocence or something, the whole film's full of symbolism."

"It—it sounds exciting nevertheless."

"It is," Carol confessed. "We're having a ball. We may not have a *movie* when we're finished, but we'll have had a riotous good time."

"You'll be marvelous."

"And so will you, Julie. I want you to know I'll be rooting for you tonight. I'll be there in spirit if not in the flesh. I'll write you a letter and tell you all about *Le Bois*, and you must write back and tell me all about the opening."

"I will," Julie promised.

"Give Danny a hug for me. I miss you."

"I miss you, too."

Julie felt better after Carol's call. She had one small glass of white wine and calmed herself down and finally left the apartment and took the subway down to Christopher Street. Larry gave her a hug and wished her well and Hank grinned and told her they were going to kill 'em tonight and she went to her dressing room to discover a plethora of telegrams and half a dozen lovely bouquets of flowers, from Nora, from Jim, from Carol, from Bob Shippley, from her producers and a small, touching bouquet from Hannah and Danny. Julie sat down at the dressing table and applied Cassie's garish makeup and put on the short, curly blond wig and then donned the sleazy red-and-purple nylon dress Cassie wore in the first act. Her nerves were frayed. She was terrified and knew she wouldn't remember a single line, knew she was going to disgrace herself the minute she stepped onstage. She made her way into the wings. Larry squeezed her hand. He was trembling himself. Eileen took her position behind the desk onstage, a battered ledger before her, wooden pigeon holes behind. She looked like someone about to face a firing squad. They could hear a muffled rumble beyond

the closed curtains as the audience settled down. Julie longed to flee the theater.

The lights went out. The curtain came up. The shabby lobby of the Robert E. Lee was bathed in a bright glow as Eileen turned a page of the ledger, humming to herself, reaching for her glass of pink gin. Two of the ladies of the evening sauntered in, bickering about a john, and Eileen gave them a fond look and Julie felt nauseous, knew she was going to throw up, knew she couldn't possibly go on, and she closed her eyes and her cue came and Julie disappeared and Cassie swaggered boisterously into the lobby and looked around and put her hands on her hips and sighed with disgust and said, "It ain't much but it's home!" and the laughter came. She was safe. She was home free. It was going to be all right.

The audience loved it. They hooted with laughter throughout. They gave noisy cheers when the reprieve came and Lavinia and the girls were allowed to stay. Applause thundered when the curtain came down. There were seven curtain calls. The audience gave them a standing ovation. They had a great big rollicking hit on their hands, or at least it seemed so until the critics had their say. The reviews were scorching. Walter Kerr confessed that the play was amusing, the cast quite good, but the story was hackneyed, the characters mere caricatures and the laughs cheap and obvious. Clive Barnes found it deplorably old-fashioned and totally devoid of wit or the least relevance. In his inimitable style and with his customary compassion, John Simon savaged it mercilessly and added that, in her garish makeup and blonde wig, "Soap Opera Diva Julie Hammond looks and acts like a shrill drag queen having a bad night at the Baths." While allegedly literate, sophisticated New York theatergoers might possibly be able to go to the bathroom on their own, they certainly couldn't purchase a ticket without being told what to see by a small group of critics with their own personal axes to grind. The play was doomed.

Eight nights later a despondent Julie sat in her dressing room, removing her makeup after the evening's performance. They were already playing to a half-empty house, and they'd be lucky if they stayed open till the end of the month. All that work, all that energy, all that effort, gone down the drain because a few men found the play unworthy of their superior approval. It was like the Christians and the lions. Thumbs up, you live. Thumbs

down, you're eaten alive. Julie wiped the cold cream off and then washed her face with a cloth dipped in water. She was wearing a shabby cotton robe. Her hair was pinned up and covered with the net she wore under her wig. Now she would be forced to sign the new contract with ABC. She had no choice. Two more years of suffering nobly on *This Life of Ours*. Meg would come out of her coma, and God only knew what would happen to her next.

The dressing room door flew open and Julie was startled to see a radiant Nora, marvelously chic in a red satin de Givenchy with trapeze skirt. Satin rustled noisily as Nora rushed to throw her arms around Julie.

"You were brilliant, love! Positively brilliant! I've always known you were a magnificent actress, but until tonight I didn't know just how magnificent you were!"

"Nora! You—I thought you—"

"I got in this afternoon. I've got a tremendous surprise for you, love. Terry's with me. I've *forced* him to watch the soap for the past two months, and—"

"He's here? At the theater?" Julie was appalled.

"He's gone to get our things from the cloakroom. He'll join us in a few minutes. Julie, he's been watching the soap every day and tonight he was absolutely mesmerized by your performance. He couldn't believe he was watching the same woman. I insisted he come to New York with me. I knew if he could see you in this play, see your range, he'd be—"

"Terry Wood's coming backstage? With me looking like this! I love you, Nora, but sometimes—"

Julie tore the net off her head and unpinned her hair and started brushing it vigorously. The door opened again, and a rotund, moon-faced man came in carrying a gray vicuna overcoat and a gorgeous full-length black sable Julie had never seen before. He tossed the sable to Nora and dumped the vicuna across a chair and, eyes twinkling behind his horn-rims, gave Julie a tremendous smile.

"So we meet at last!" he exclaimed jovially. "I've been hearing a lot about you, little girl, and I've been seeing a lot of you, too. This one has insisted I watch your soap. Thirty minutes a day, it costs me a fortune, but I watch, I let everything go, I sit in front of the television set, and I say to myself, this girl, she

has something. Tonight, I am astounded! She's the one, I tell myself.''

Julie was standing now, gazing at him with puzzled eyes. Nora was grinning like the Cheshire Cat. Julie longed to slap her.

''Everything's set on *The Slipper*,'' Wood informed her. ''Nunnally's written a great script. Negulesco is directing. Hope Lange is playing the model and Susan Strasberg is gonna play Billie—remember how great she was in *Picnic*? Lana Turner is doing a cameo as head of the modeling agency, and we've signed Greg Peck to play the older man. The only part we haven't cast yet is Anne.''

Nora dumped the sable on top of the vicuna and gave Julie another vigorous hug. Terry Wood was beaming now.

''We were looking for someone with that special quality, a young Margaret Sullavan, luminous, sensitive, vulnerable—My God!'' he interrupted himself. ''Those eyes! They're gonna photograph like a million bucks. The complexion isn't so hot, make-up'll take care of that, but the bone structure is perfection!''

''I—I don't understand,'' Julie said.

''I've found our Anne!'' Wood announced.

Nora took hold of both Julie's hands and squeezed them, her lovely brown eyes sparkling with excitement.

''You and Danny're coming back to Hollywood with me, Julie. You're going to play Anne. You're going to take the town by storm. Terry's gonna arrange a fabulous contract for you at the studio. Carol and I both got the slipper, love, and now it's your turn! You're gonna be a star!''

13

A French starlet who fancied herself the new Bardot cavorted on the beach with a lethargic lion cub as a crowd of photographers snapped hundreds of pictures. When her bikini strap "accidentally" popped and her breasts were exposed, more photographers appeared, shouting lustily, snapping away as the starlet pretended to blush. She made an effort to cover her major assets with her arms, but somehow they kept bobbing into view. The lion cub yawned and curled up on the sand and was soon asleep. The sky was a clear blue-white, the Mediterranean a deep azure. Sumptuous yachts were anchored in the harbor like so many floating white palaces, while up and down the Croisette flags of every nation added festive color as they flapped in the breeze. Horns blared noisily as hundreds of Rolls-Royces and limousines and battered taxis inched along in the perpetual traffic jam that plagued Cannes at this time of year. The annual film festival was in full swing. Some 10,000 outsiders had converged on the elegant, ordinarily serene seaside town, many of them in the business of making movies, most of them making deals, a vast number of them simply on the make.

Hundreds of new films were shown here every year, the official entries at the huge, ornate *palais*, Festival Hall, while countless others were on view at small, dingy theaters on various side streets behind the Carlton Hotel. While everyone breathlessly

awaited announcement of the awards, art had precious little to do with it. A Cannes Film Festival award meant big money at the box office, and money was the name of the game. Hollywood moguls and European independents and oil-rich Arabs and Greek tycoons came to talk deals, percentages, grosses, rentals, to brag, barter and bribe, to form new partnerships and dissolve old ones. The press came like a swarm of locusts. Prostitutes of both sexes arrived in droves, international film stars and jet set darlings lending a bright glitter to the motley, perspiring throng. There were round-the-clock parties, in private villas, aboard yachts, in hotel suites and on the beaches, fireworks exploding every night as the madness progressed. The atmosphere was a combination of Mardi Gras, the Fourth of July and a major civil disturbance. The only thing lacking was tear gas. Carol wouldn't be surprised if that was forthcoming. After four days of this insanity, she would gladly have hurled a few cannisters herself.

If Guy and Jean-Claude and I survive this with all of our limbs intact it will be a bloody miracle, she told herself as she made her way along the beach toward the Carlton Hotel. It was a huge, grotesquely ornate white monstrosity gleaming brightly in the late afternoon sunlight, the official headquarters of the festival, and they were damned lucky to have suites. It was packed to the rafters. Several members of the press corps were actually camping out in the lobby, and getting past them every day was like running a gauntlet. Carol had a shapeless blue-and-purple cotton beach robe over her bathing suit and a purple scarf over her head. She wore dark glasses. Thus far, no one had recognized her this afternoon. They were too busy pursuing Romy Schneider and Curt Jurgens and Anouk Aimée. There had been no press conferences this afternoon, thank God, and she had actually been able to get away from the hotel and get a little sun. Four hours of wandering along the beach by herself seemed like a great luxury amidst all this insane brouhaha.

They had been besieged ever since they arrived. *Le Bois* was the official French entry this year, and word was out that it was an unquestionable masterpiece, Masson the greatest, most innovative director since D. W. Griffith, Jean-Claude the most exciting film personality since the young Gable, Carol a cinch to win Best Actress. Revolutionary camera angles and zoom shots notwithstanding, *Le Bois* was actually a simple love story filmed in grainy black-and-white about a naive American girl, Carol,

who inadvertently causes the downfall of a breezy, engaging small-time French hood, ex-wrestler Jean-Claude Bresson. The film was poorly lighted, jumpy, technically an inept, amateurish disaster that really did resemble a home movie, yet the French film critics had shouted themselves hoarse lauding its virtues—for reasons that took Carol completely by surprise.

Guy Masson was a Communist. She had known that from the first, had given it not a thought. Half of France was, if not Communist, at least far left, it seemed, and Carol paid no attention to anyone's politics. During the filming of *Le Bois* neither Carol nor Jean-Claude had detected the least political content. It was a loosely structured love story with cops-and-robbers overtones, a *nouvelle vague* version of a Hollywood forties *film noir*. She was amazed to discover in *Cahiers du Cinéma* that the film was a vehement denouncement of American capitalism. The girl, wide-eyed, naive, was supposed to represent America and through ignorance and indifference she callously destroys the world-weary, street-wise petty thief, who was supposed to represent Europe. Carol couldn't see it that way, but the critics cheered and lauded its brave, potent political statement. Anti-Americanism was definitely in now at Cannes, the Far Left holding sway. Glossy, vulgar American films with their garish Technicolor and inane content were invariably dismissed with a sneer. Of late the awards usually went to some dreary Russian epic about a boy and his tractor or a depressing Brazilian tract about disfigured transvestites working as migrant farmers. All this taken into consideration, *Le Bois* stood a very good chance of winning Best Picture, but Carol knew she hadn't a prayer of winning Best Actress. She was American, for one thing, and she hadn't acted at all in the film. She had simply been herself.

Leaving the beach with its starlets, lion cubs, photographers and bronzed hustlers, Carol crossed the terrace of the Hotel Carlton. Every table was occupied. She noticed a grizzled, aged Darryl F. Zanuck sitting with a pompous, pontificating Orson Welles and a bored-looking Juliette Greco. Greco was the latest of Zanuck's bony European Galateas. After his dismal failure to transform mistress Bella Darvi into a film star—her acting was said to make the perennial starlet Terry Moore look like Sarah Bernhardt—the former head of Twentieth Century Fox had attempted to do the same with Greco. Her films had been as di-

sastrous as Darvi's. He had recently teamed her with Orson in something called *Crack in the Mirror*, which he had written himself under a pseudonym. A few of their relatives might have seen it. Everyone else treated it as though it were a contagious disease. Eric Berne had introduced her to Zanuck when he was still head of the studio, but Carol doubted seriously he would remember her. Passing their table, she heard Welles praising his own genius, as he was wont to do. Juliette wearily downed another Pernod. Zanuck stared into space, looking suicidal.

The noise level inside the lobby was even higher than it had been outside on the terrace. Telephones rang. Bellboys scurried around in frantic haste. Voices rose in shrill determination to be heard above the hubbub. Carol spotted handsome actor Stephen Boyd chatting with—yes, it *was* Hedda Hopper under that preposterous flowered hat. Rumor had it he was sleeping with her. Hedda certainly mentioned him in her column often enough, which would explain Boyd's attentiveness. With the gradual breakdown of the old studio system in Hollywood, Hedda and Louella no longer wielded the power they had during the golden days, but, like dinosaurs from another era, both still tromped around attempting to terrorize their prey. Most merely laughed at them nowadays.

Carol moved through the luxurious, congested lobby, feeling secure behind her dark glasses. "There's Carol Martin!" someone shouted, and suddenly she was surrounded by reporters and photographers who seemed to spring at her from every direction, all of them pushing and shoving to get closer. Blazing flashbulbs blinded her. Someone grabbed her arm, whirling her around. Questions were fired at her in French, in English. She felt she was in the middle of a maelstrom, felt faint, felt a panic attack building as faces pink with excitement pushed nearer, as voices rose shrilly, as more questions were fired, more flashbulbs popped.

"Are you and Bresson sleeping with each other!"

"Are you a Communist!"

"Think you're gonna win Best Actress!"

"Eric Berne's here! You run into him yet!"

Carol tried to keep her composure but it was impossible as someone yanked her arm again, as a photographer grabbed her dark glasses and ripped the scarf from her head. Because of *Le Bois*, she was the most popular and sought-after actress at Cannes

this year and she had given dozens of interviews and attended countless press conferences already, but this was insanity. These weren't newspeople, these were vultures, working for the scandal sheets and scurrilous tabloids. Out of the corner of her eye she saw a frenzied Hedda Hopper shoving her way through the melee, flowered hat shoved over one eye, face set in a fiercely determined scowl. Hedda slammed her purse into a reporter's face and viciously shoved a photographer out of her way.

"You!" she shrieked. "Carol Martin! How could a decent American girl appear in such a filthy piece of Commie propaganda!" Hedda had recently elected herself the guardian of American democracy. "It's a scandal! It's an outrage! How can you—"

And suddenly, from out of nowhere, Jean-Claude Bresson was there in front of her, wearing tight gray pants and wide black belt and loosely fitting white silk shirt with full-gathered sleeves, looking exactly like some jaunty buccaneer with his battered face and wavy black hair. Carol couldn't swear he had swung from a chandelier and leaped into the middle of the crowd, but it seemed he had. Enormous brown eyes flashing with excitement, wide mouth curling in a devilish grin, he pushed a photographer away, knocked a reporter to the floor, swept Carol up into his arms. With debonair aplomb he cradled her close with one strong arm and pushed his way through the crowd, socking a reporter in the jaw, kicking a photographer in the groin, dozens of flashbulbs blazing silver-blue as he carried her to the elevators, the press in hot pursuit. She caught a quick glimpse of Hedda clutching the arm of a sofa, dragging herself up from the floor, flowered hat hopelessly crushed, and then the elevator doors opened and Jean-Claude shoved her inside and slugged a couple more reporters and then darted in himself just as the doors were closing.

"You're absolutely insane, you know," she said dryly.

"I was marvelous!" he protested.

"We'll be on the front pages of every scandal sheet in the world."

"It will be good for the movie, no? Guy will be delighted. We are a hot item."

Jean-Claude spoke no English and his French was heavily accented. He was half Sicilian and, though born in France, had spent half his life in Italy and spoke in a raspy twang that com-

bined the worst features of both languages. It was a unique sound and wildly sexy.

"Did you actually swing from a chandelier?" she asked.

"Is easy. I leap up on a table, grab the chandelier, give myself a send-off and—voilà! I swing over their heads and drop down in front of you. It is the snap for me to do. Before I take up wrestling, I am an acrobat in circus in Milan."

"Lord!"

"They love it! They get a few bruises but they get a marvelous story and some fantastic photos, no?"

"I can't believe you're for real."

"Me, I am going to be a big movie star now, no? I don't have the pretty face like Alain Delon, but I have the panache, the personality, the rugged sex appeal. I read what they say about me in the papers. It is a blast, no?"

Carol couldn't help smiling as the elevator doors opened and they stepped out. Jean-Claude was full of innocent arrogance and boyish braggadocio, an utterly charming lad of thirty-six who was a disarming combination of both Peter Pan and Captain Hook. Long, lean, loose-limbed, he had wildly unruly hair and a thin, pockmarked face with hollows beneath those huge, guileless brown eyes. His nose had been broken a number of times, and if his mouth wasn't actually a mile wide, it seemed that way. Virile, athletic, breezily confident, he was a primitive, unspoiled, and there had never been anyone quite like him in movies before. He was going to be a huge star.

He followed her into her suite and promptly went over to the liquor cabinet and poured himself a strong whiskey, grinning happily as Carol ran fingers through her hair and checked herself in the mirror for bruises. She and Jean-Claude had been lovers ever since the second day of shooting. He was an amusing playmate, incredibly sexy and absolutely phenomenal in bed, but his boyish antics had begun to pall after all these months. She adored him and he adored her, but, for both, the relationship was merely a lighthearted diversion, very French, not at all serious.

"This American film producer, he waylays me this morning," he confided. "He wants me to come to Hollywood, wants to make me a big cowboy star like Gary Cooper. I tell him no, I think not. I do not speak the English, and it is too hard for me to learn. I think I become huge superstar in France first and *then* go to Hollywood and become a cowboy."

"You'd look great in chaps and a ten-gallon hat," she told him.

"You think so? With this ugly mug of mine?"

"That ugly mug of yours is arguably the sexiest mug I've ever seen," Carol said. "The women are going to go crazy over you and men are going to love your carefree independence and *joie de vivre*."

"This is so," he admitted. "Me, I am determined I will become the champion wrestler in Europe, and this I do. Once I get them in my headlock, they are at my mercy. I tell myself I will become the big movie star, too, and already it is happening. I knock them off their socks."

Carol smiled again and started toward the bedroom. "We're due at Festival Hall at seven," she said. "We're supposed to look very glamorous for the screening, and that's going to take me at least a couple of hours. Run along to your own suite, pet."

"But I am horny!" he protested.

"It'll keep," she assured him.

"You are throwing me out? I rescue you from the clutches of the bad guys and this is the thanks I get? You are a heartless bitch."

"Guilty as charged," she replied.

He scowled a mock scowl. "I make you pay for this later."

Jean-Claude finished his whiskey in two gulps, grinned amiably, waved his fingers at her and left. Carol sighed, relieved. She was in a blue mood and not at all up to amorous dalliance, however pleasant it might be. She removed robe and bathing suit, slipped on a thin white silk wrapper and poured herself a whiskey, wandering over to the window to gaze out over the Croisette and the Mediterranean beyond. She was worried about Gaby and tempted to call, but she knew Gaby would think she was checking up on her and probably resent it. Gaby would get over her depression. She would find another lover, and there would be another film. The one she had written had been shown last night, a typical Bernais love story set in the twenties, elegantly costumed, gorgeously shot in muted Technicolor, full of wit, sighs, sadness, with a glorious Michel Legrand score. It had been viciously booed by the hypercritical, politically oriented festival audience and Gaby herself had been hissed as they left the *palais*. Ordinarily she would have shrugged it off with a

...........u over the breakup with
........blond tough. She had left Cannes early
......ing, heading for Paris in her Aston-Martin.

Poor Gaby. The muscular blonds were getting tougher, more venal, and the hedonistic life-style—the jazz, the whiskey, the nightclubs, the fast cars—was beginning to take its toll. Her work had suffered. The short, sad novels of bittersweet love were all very well, but it was time for the artist to grow now, to reach, to develop new themes. Gaby had it in her to become a genuinely great novelist, but this would never happen if she continued to repeat herself. Gaby knew this. She felt guilty about it. Of late she had driven herself to even greater excesses with liquor, jazz, men, speed. It was no longer charming and piquant. The artist within her demanded a settled life and time for reflection, the very things Gaby denied herself. Her last two novels had sold well enough, but the critics had called them shallow and repetitive, and, indeed, they had been. Gaby had pinned all her hopes on the film she had written, hoping it would re-establish her credit with the critics. While sumptuously produced and superbly directed and acted, it was as empty and insubstantial as the last two novels. Unless something happened soon, Gaby's career was in serious trouble.

Finishing her whiskey, Carol set the empty glass on the windowsill, gazing out with sad eyes. The sun was almost gone now, the sky deepening to purple, a violet-gray haze settling, and lights had begun to come on aboard those elegant yachts, flickering like pale golden fireflies in the dusk. Carol felt the pain and loss inside, as she always did when she was alone, when there was no distraction. She missed him still, after all this time, missed him as much as she had that first day after she had driven him along the coast to the airport. He had not written. There had not been so much as a postcard from him, and she understood. She knew that it was probably better this way. She had sent a lovely wedding present to Cliff and Stephanie and had received a charming thank-you note and, months later, a witty letter from Cliff describing the honeymoon in Acapulco and the ground-breaking ceremonies for the big shopping mall he was building. He sent his love. He did not mention his father.

Those first weeks after Norman's departure had been sheer hell, and Carol could never have survived them without Sir Rob-

pixie smile, but Gaby was already s̶
Edouard, her mo̶st recen̶t̶
this mornin̶
THE SLIPPER

ert and the other marvelous̶
own personal support group. Lilli Palm̶
ping, her husband, Argentine-born German actor Carlos̶
son, patiently squiring them around and keeping them amused
with his witty stories of his Hollywood years costarring in movies with Lana Turner and Yvonne DeCarlo as a fiery Latin lover.
Margaret Rutherford watched over her on the set like a fussy
mother hen, giving her tea and teaching her to knit and smothering her with affectionate attentions. In the evenings Sir Robert
took her out to dinner and to clubs and tried his best to keep
her smiling. Her heart was breaking over the loss of Norman
and she often went on crying jags and she felt she had made a
dreadful mistake and not a day passed that she didn't want to
abandon the movie and fly to him.

She was playing a giddy, lighthearted, carefree British girl.
Comedy was much more difficult to do than heavy drama, required perfect timing and a sure deft touch, but, because of the
wonderful support and assistance of her fellow workers, she gave
one of the best performances of her career. *Knaves Like Us* was
the finest movie she had ever made, and she fully expected it to
bring her to the attention of those in Hollywood who had spurned
her after the Berne disaster. That wasn't to be. Kitchen-sink
realism was in vogue in England, Angry Young Men and L-
Shaped Rooms and Lonely Long-Distance Runners. *Knaves Like
Us* was considered old-fashioned, bombed in Britain and had a
very limited distribution in America. She had given up so much
in order to make this particular film—and for what? She had lost
Norman. She had gained nothing whatsoever.

She had done two more French films in quick succession, one
with Marc Allegret, one with Louis Malle, both fine, neither
released in America. She had deliberately kept as busy as possible—work was a kind of anesthesia, holding the pain at bay,
work was her salvation—and she found herself drinking more,
smoking more, taking more lovers. While never promiscuous,
she had had three brief, unsatisfying affairs before *Le Bois* and
Jean-Claude, and that concerned her. Carol wasn't pleased with
herself and didn't like what she was becoming. Despite five years
in France working in an ultrasophisticated milieu, she was still
the clean-scrubbed American girl from the Midwest, and . . .
and she was terribly homesick. She didn't want to be a glamorous expatriate. She wanted to go home.

Abandoning the window, Carol took a long, hot bath, did her hair, applied her makeup. She missed Julie and Nora. They were sisters in spirit, sisters in heart, and she hadn't seen Julie in five years, had only seen Nora when she came for her brief visit several months ago. Nora was a best-selling novelist now, a glamorous celebrity in her own right, and Julie was in Hollywood with a fabulous seven-year contract, doing her first movie. Contracts like hers were a rarity nowadays, but the studio believed in Julie, believed she was going to become a great, great star. Carol felt cut off, felt left out. She wanted to share her friends' successes, revel in them, be there for them. That was difficult to do with only telephone calls and letters. She missed them both, and she missed America, missed hot dogs and pizzas and trashy television shows and foolish fads and that glorious, generous American spirit that made her country so great. Ike and Mamie were out and John and Jackie were in, inaugurating a whole new era, shorter skirts, bouffant hairdos, go-go music, and she felt she was missing out on it all. She loved Paris, and the French had been very good to her these past years, but . . . oh how she longed to speak her own language and be with her own kind.

Finally dressed, Carol stepped over to the full-length mirror for a quick inspection. The sleeveless, glossy black satin gown had a long, narrow skirt, a very high neck and no back at all. It was simple, understated and extremely elegant. Her short-clipped hair was like a gleaming, closely fitted dark-gold cap, feathery edges framing a face that seemed thinner now, the eyelids etched with soft gray shadows, high cheekbones more pronounced. Her mouth was a dark pink, sad, and the deep-blue eyes were much too worldly, much too wise. There was nothing of the college girl about her now. She was a sophisticated woman, sleek, glamorous, with her own special style, but inside she felt as young, as frightened, as vulnerable as she had the day she fled her high school commencement exercises and ran into the cornfields.

There was a merry knock on her sitting room door and a moment later Jean-Claude strolled jauntily into her bedroom, where she was still standing before the mirror. He looked marvelously dashing in his tuxedo, his black tie a bit crooked, his jacket unfastened and swinging as he moved, a black satin cummerbund at his waist. The elegant attire accentuated that

ugly-fascinating hoodlum face with its enormous brown eyes and incredibly large, incredibly sensual mouth. He came up behind her and grinned at her in the mirror and gripped her shoulders with huge, strong hands. He nuzzled the nape of her neck. His lips moved down her spinal cord, and Carol arched her back.

"I love this gown," he told her. "It leaves your back bare."

"Don't be naughty, pet. We're due downstairs in ten minutes."

"Ten minutes? That's plenty of time. I shall ravish you thoroughly, and you will not look so sad. You are not wearing the bra," he said, discovering it with his hands.

"Not with this gown."

"This gown—I could go crazy."

"You're already crazy. I don't know why I put up with you."

"Because I am the lovable clown," he told her, "and I make love to you with wild abandon."

"Maybe that's it," she agreed.

Jean-Claude grinned and whirled her around to face him and kissed her for a long time, his hands exploring all the while. He was so expert, so engaging and completely without inhibitions. Carol pulled back and touched that lean, pockmarked cheek and ran her thumb along the full curve of that sensual lower lip. Jean-Claude caught the ball of her thumb between his teeth. She smiled, pushing him away.

"We'd better go downstairs," she said.

"I'd rather go down."

"You're shameless."

"This is so. Who wants to attend a lousy screening and a lousy party afterwards? I would rather make love to you."

"I'd enjoy that more myself," she confessed, "but duty is duty, my pet, and Guy would kill us both if we didn't show. Besides, you look much too appetizing in your tuxedo to let it go to waste. The ladies will be weak in the knees when they see you tonight."

"You think?"

"I know."

"The ladies always go for me," he said cockily, "even when I am merely the acrobat and the wrestler in purple trunks. Now that I will be the big movie star, I will have to fight them off with a stick, no?"

"With a stick."

"Alain Delon will be green with envy."

He helped her with her long black stole lined with white satin and handed her the small black evening bag, and they went downstairs. Most of the press had already departed for Festival Hall, stationing themselves outside in order to waylay celebrities as they entered, and the lobby wasn't nearly as crowded. Guy Masson was waiting for them, looking extremely nervous, looking tense. He wore black jeans, a black turtleneck sweater and, as usual, his perpetual dark glasses. Carol couldn't remember ever seeing him without them. The director was not very tall, skinny to the point of emaciation and full of nervous energy. He heaved a sigh of relief when he saw his stars step out of the elevator and, crushing out his cigarette, rushed them outside to the waiting limousine. Traffic was congested, their progress little more than a snail's pace. Masson nervously gnawed his nails and smoked four more cigarettes before they finally arrived. They could have walked in a third of the time, but the limousine was mandatory.

Although she had seen the film a number of times, Carol had never seen it inside a theater, with an audience, and she was apprehensive now. There was a roar from the press as they climbed out of the limousine, more questions, more blinding flashes. Masson met the press with a sullen glare. Jean-Claude gave them a jaunty grin, keeping his arm tightly around Carol's shoulders. As they entered the auditorium and took their seats, there was a stirring round of applause from the far left, pro-Masson faction. Carol saw Hedda Hopper sitting a few rows ahead of them, unmistakable in pink-and-green beribboned hat, Boyd beside her. The lights went down. Carol reached for Jean-Claude's hand. The huge white screen filled with jumping, jumbled black-and-white lines, and then *Le Bois, un film de Guy Masson*, and there was another hearty round of applause and several cheers and a number of noisy "Boos!" as well, one of them from the gossip columnist in the pink-and-green hat. Jean-Claude gave her hand a tight squeeze and told her it was going to be all right.

And suddenly there she was, in tight jeans and striped jersey, walking in the park, pausing to sniff a flower, tossing a stick to a dog, the personification of fresh, wholesome innocence. The camera lingered over her face as sunlight spilled through the

trees. She smiled pensively. She turned, startled, and Jean-Claude came hurrying toward her in a sleazy checked sport coat, and he grabbed her and clamped a hand over her mouth and dragged her over to a bench, wrapping his arms around her, kissing her passionately as two gendarmes passed by, obviously searching for someone, paying no mind to the two lovers entwined on the bench. Carol shifted in her seat, terribly uncomfortable. Jean-Claude had a dynamic screen presence, but she thought she looked bland and unattractive and awkward. She was even more uncomfortable when, having frolicked with him in the park, she agreed to let him hide out in her apartment, which had an American flag and a photograph of Eisenhower on the wall. Shyly, she disrobed and climbed into the unmade bed with its rumpled sheets and Jean-Claude leered and tore his own clothes off and leaped into the bed with her and they started wrestling and he finally pinned her and they made love under the sheets.

The lighting was dreadful, the film grainy, the camera angles bizarre and confusing, but the scene was still potently erotic and seemed to go on forever and Carol was embarrassed. As Jean-Claude finally fell limp atop her and she wrapped her arms around his naked back, the camera zoomed in for a close-up of her face, a triumphant smile on her lips, then zoomed over for a tight shot of the American flag and a grinning Eisenhower. My God, Carol thought, it really *is* political. Later on, after they have quarrelled, after he refuses to give up his way of life in order to accommodate her own, the girl tearfully confides in a jaded newspaper friend who in turn calls the gendarmes and they burst into the bedroom and the petty thief is led away in handcuffs, a close-up of his shackled wrists, a close-up of the girl with a sad smile on her lips, a close-up of the American flag and then *FIN* in huge block letters.

Hedda Hopper leaped to her feet. "It's a scandal!" she shrieked. "Communist filth! The film should be burned!" Her outcries were drowned by thundering applause. Pandemonium prevailed. They had to fight their way out of the theater and to the waiting limousine, people swarming over to pound Masson on the back and pump his hand or jeer at him and wave their fists. Carol kept her head lowered, sheltered against Jean-Claude's shoulder, his arm protecting her. She felt dreadful. She felt sick. She felt she had betrayed her country. *Le Bois* was

indeed anti-American, vehemently so, and she had never realized it until tonight. Her spirits had hit rock bottom by the time the limousine reached the private villa above Cannes where the reception was being held tonight. Spotlights bathed the red-white-and-blue French flags draped across the white marble portico. There was more applause, and a band started playing the French national anthem as they entered.

The party was very festive, very elegant, by invitation only. Anouk Aimée looked stunning in a flame-colored Balmain sheath. Jean-Pierre Aumont was handsome in his tailored tuxedo, wife Marisa Pavan demure in silver-gray silk. At least three hundred people were here, and while there were dozens with famous faces, the majority were important executives and distributors, the wheeler-dealers who kept the international film industry awhirl. Carol was amazed to learn that a score of the most important and powerful distributors in America were already fighting for distribution of *Le Bois*. With that curious masochism that seemed a national trait, Americans ardently embraced anything that criticized them, perhaps in order to show their open minds and tolerance. *Le Bois* was clearly destined to be a great success in the country it so zealously denounced. Carol smiled and downed champagne and accepted compliments on her performance, wishing she had never heard of Masson or his film. Federico Fellini made his way over to her, beaming, exuberant, Giulietta Masina beside him in gold-spangled yellow silk. The Italian director was one of Carol's idols, *La Dolce Vita* her favorite film. After her bravura performances in *La Strada* and *Le Notte di Cabiria*, the petite, dumpy, waiflike Masina was considered by many the world's greatest actress.

"Bravo!" Fellini roared, seizing her hand, lifting it to his lips. "You forget these wearisome Frenchmen with their dreary politics. You come to Rome with Fellini! He will make you a great star!"

"I would love to work with you," she said.

"These French! No color, no imagination, no showmanship, no verve. Just tedium. Me, I put you in a splashy fantasy with stupendous sets. I star you with Mastroianni. I make the whole world sit up and take notice!"

Carol smiled. It was cocktail-party talk, she knew, but it was flattering nevertheless. Giulietta Masina grinned her waif grin, shook Carol's hand and told her she had enjoyed the film al-

though she wasn't sure what it was all about. The Fellinis moved on and Carol talked to a Hungarian director who had just made a movie about falcons and had her photograph taken with the Aumonts. She received more compliments, had another glass of champagne, smiled politely and pretended to be enjoying herself and longed to escape. Guy was surrounded by moneymen eager to exploit him. Jean-Claude was dazzling the ladies and delighting select members of the press with outrageous stories of his adventures as a wrestler. Carol moved into the spacious foyer and sat down on the stairs with her glass of champagne, and it was there that Jean-Claude found her twenty minutes later. His hair was tousled, his brown eyes asparkle, a wide grin on his lips.

"This is something, no? They all think Jean-Claude is a riot. That lady in red satin, the director's wife, she tries to feel me up and begs me to take her out to the parking area for a quick bang in the backseat of her husband's Bentley. This lady is in her fifties."

"Charming," Carol said.

"I tell her I am not that kind of boy. The lady in red satin says a very ugly word and gives me the finger. Is this nice? I smack her bottom. She is outraged. Everyone laughs."

Carol downed the rest of her champagne. She was more than a little tipsy and felt wretched. Jean-Claude's eyes filled with concern.

"You do not feel well?"

"Get me out of here," she pleaded.

"This I will do."

He fetched her wrap and led her outside. The night air was cool. Below, the Côte d'Azur was like a string of gold and silver spangles tossed against a velvety backdrop. Moonlight spilled down in milky rays. Dozens of cars and limousines were parked on the broad expanse beside the villa, the drivers in a huddle, smoking, talking, passing a bottle around. Jean-Claude looked at all the limousines, bewildered, and then, choosing one at random, opened the front door on the passenger's side and helped Carol in. A liveried driver came running over, shaking his fist violently.

"This is my car!" he yelled. "You cannot do this!"

Jean-Claude gave him an amiable shove. The driver reeled backward, crashing to the ground twenty feet away. Jean-Claude

climbed into the limo, closed the door, discovered keys in the ignition, and they were soon on their way down the hill, ten drivers on foot in hot pursuit. They were left behind after the first curve. Jean-Claude was laughing, delighted with himself. Carol stared moodily through the windshield. He asked if she wanted to go back to the hotel and she shook her head and suggested they just drive around for a while. Jean-Claude was enjoying handling the huge car and pleased by her suggestion. They drove around the hills, through sleepy villages, past luxurious private villas. It was well after midnight when they finally reached the hotel, Jean-Claude casually leaving the limousine out front for the doorman or someone to attend to. Carol felt somewhat better, although she was still deeply depressed. The early edition of tomorrow morning's papers had just come out, and as they walked past the newsstand a blazing headline caught Carol's eye: GABY ALMOST KILLED IN CAR CRASH.

"My God!" she cried, clutching Jean-Claude's arm.

Jean-Claude snatched a paper, tossed the vendor a bill and quickly scanned the front-page article. Carol was much too upset to read it. She was wringing her hands, utterly distraught.

"It happened this afternoon," he told her. "She was on the outskirts of Paris. It was raining hard. She was driving ninety-five miles an hour and the car leaped over the curb and overturned and crashed into a tree. They took her to the hospital immediately. Several bones are broken and she is still unconscious and there may be brain damage, may be internal—"

"I've got to go to her!" Carol cried.

"Of course," he said calmly.

"There—My God, there's not a flight out until eight o'clock in the morning, and—"

"This is no problem," Jean-Claude told her, all traces of the merry clown gone now. "Come, I take you up to your room. You change, pack a few things in a small bag. I will take care of everything."

He was as good as his word. He was marvelous. An hour later he returned, wearing tan trousers, a rust-colored turtleneck, a brown leather jacket, and he drove her to a small private airport where a plane was waiting. Carol was wearing a beige Chanel suit and a white silk blouse and carrying only her purse and a small tan overnight case. She was startled to learn that Jean-Claude was going to fly them to Paris himself. It shouldn't have

surprised her that he had his pilot's license. For all his cocky
bravado and boyish shenanigans, he was a highly accomplished,
extremely competent man who knew precisely what he wanted
and went after it with cool aplomb. Sitting beside him in the
tiny cockpit, Carol felt a lurch in her stomach as the small plane
lifted, but the flight itself was as smooth as it could be, Jean-
Claude handling the controls with practiced ease. Carol smoked
half a pack of cigarettes, trying to maintain some semblance of
calm. The velvety black sky turned to ashy gray and faint pink-
ish stains had begun to glow in the east as they landed in Paris.
A car was waiting for them, another example of Jean-Claude's
efficiency, and forty minutes later they were in the hospital waiting room.

Gaby was in intensive care. They were not allowed to see her.
Carol met Gaby's parents for the first time, a respectable middle-
class couple from Rouen who, while supportive and loving, had
always been somewhat bewildered by the exotic creature they
had brought into the world. Her brother Georges, whom Carol
had met before, was a husky blond with Gaby's brown eyes who
looked like a soccer player. He was a lawyer in Rouen. He informed them that Gaby's skull had been split open but there was
no apparent brain damage. Her left leg was broken, her right
arm and three ribs, one of them almost puncturing her lung.
They had performed surgery twice. She was still in a coma, and
they were monitoring her vital signs. At this point it was touch
and go, although the doctors were optimistic about a complete
recovery, barring any unforeseen complications. It was futile for
them to remain at the hospital, but Carol insisted. By late afternoon her Chanel suit was rumpled, her white blouse limp. She
had drunk innumerable cups of coffee and, at Jean-Claude's insistence, had had an indigestible lunch at the hospital cafeteria.
Gaby's parents were numb. Georges had kept busy fending off
the press, begging for a little privacy.

Gaby came out of her coma at nine that evening. Her vital
signs were good and she was moved to a private room. Her
mother was going to stay with her and Jean-Claude drove Georges
and his father to Gaby's flat and took Carol home and stayed the
night. Guy called from Cannes, furious that his stars had departed. Jean-Claude promised him that they would be back in
time for the awards ceremony the following Friday night. They
spent the next day at the hospital and the next as well. Gaby had

been given great doses of morphine for the pain and was incoherent. She barely recognized Carol when she was allowed to see her for a few minutes on the second day. Gaby continued to improve, and although she was still on morphine, the dosage was reduced.

Four days after the accident, Jean-Claude drove Gaby's parents to her flat for a much-needed rest. Georges was busy dealing with the press, who were trying to label the accident a suicide attempt, and Carol came in to sit with Gaby for a few hours. The room was aflood with flowers and cards and a huge stuffed aardvark perched on a shelf. Gaby looked dreadful, her left leg and her right arm in casts and her chest encased in plaster, her head bandaged, gauze beneath her chin and across her brow and her face discolored with bruises. Her enormous brown eyes were alert, though, and a faint, sad smile flickered on her lips as Carol came in with yet another huge arrangement of flowers.

"You're awake," Carol said brightly.

"Please," Gaby said weakly, "don't be cheerful. The nurses are cheerful and so are the doctors. They bubble with good humor. I long to slaughter each and every one of them."

"Thank God. You're yourself again."

"And you're supposed to be in Cannes."

"Jean-Claude and I came as soon as we heard."

"Jean-Claude is here, too?"

"We've been here for four days. You don't remember Jean-Claude coming to see you yesterday? He brought you that stuffed aardvark over there. You told him it looked exactly like him."

"I—I don't remember too much until this morning. Everything before that is—rather hazy. I—it's so good to see you, Carol. There's so much I want to say. I've been doing a lot of thinking."

"Gaby, I—"

"It *was* an accident, Carol, despite what people might believe. I know the press implied it was deliberate, that I was upset over Edouard and disappointed over the reception of the film, but—I simply lost control of the car. I was driving too fast. I always drive too fast."

"I know, darling."

"No more. I—this accident has suddenly made me realize that—that I am not invulnerable. I was carefree, heedless, he-

donistic and enjoying every minute of it. The world was my oyster, and I loved it. I loved being rich, loved being famous, loved living in a rarefied world beholden to no one, not even beholden to myself.''

"I really don't think you should talk about—you're still very weak, darling, and you mustn't tire yourself out with all this—"

Gaby raised her left hand, silencing her friend.

"I need to say it all. I need to—to crystallize it all by putting it into words. Remember when Nora was here and we all three sat on the floor in my apartment and passed a bottle of wine around and talked about the slipper? It made a deep impression on me. I got the slipper at a very early age; a middle-class girl from Rouen writes a novel at seventeen, and suddenly she becomes one of the most famous young women in the world. I took to it like—how do you say it in America? I took to it like a duck to water—yes, that's it—and I took it all as my due, and I took my gift for granted and ignored the fact that it was this gift that made it all happen to begin with.''

Gaby paused, her brown eyes thoughtful. She reached for the glass of water on the bedside table and sipped some through the bent glass straw, and then Carol took it from her and set it back down.

"You got the slipper, too, Carol, and so did Nora eventually, but—it wasn't because we were merely lucky, because someone just happened to wave a magic wand. We got it because we were gifted, because we were unique, because all of us had worked very hard. I, for one, was too busy living the good life to accept the responsibilities that come with success. I realize now that it isn't the life that is important, it's the work. That's all that lasts. That's all we can leave behind.''

Carol nodded, silent.

"In the beginning, they compared me to Colette. They said I was destined to step into her shoes. Perhaps I could have—I *will*—but I was too busy having a good time to take my work that seriously. It came so early, you see. It happened so quickly. The critics were right. I was having a ball, but my novels had become shallow and repetitious. The jazz, the whiskey, the fast cars, the beautiful men—they were all exciting, but—they're all ephemeral, Carol. When all is said and done, there's nothing left except the memory of sensation. What I put down on paper,

that lasts. That's what gives me real satisfaction, and—and I am going to devote the rest of my life to being the best writer I can possibly be.''

Her voice had grown gradually weaker until it was little more than a whisper. She paused again, weary. Carol sat down beside the bed and took her left hand and squeezed it, and Gaby managed another faint smile. She was in a great deal of pain. It was almost time for her next shot.

"The work—it is the work that counts," Gaby said. "It was terrible for you when Norman left. You feared you had made the wrong decision, but the work is what counts for you, too, Carol. You loved him, but love is not enough for people like us. If you had gone with him, your career would have suffered, and ultimately you would have been even unhappier. Do you under— am I making any kind of sense?''

Carol nodded, squeezing her hand again.

"Perhaps we're not meant to have it all," Gaby whispered weakly. "But we are the lucky ones, just the same. We have so much inside us, so much to give. If—if we don't give it, we die inside. I was dying inside because—because I wasn't giving enough, and you—your acting—''

"That's enough, darling," Carol said. "I understand. And you're right, of course.''

"Love—love is ephemeral, too," Gaby said. "It comes and goes, but the work is there forever, in print, on film. It—what it gives us no man could ever match.''

It was true. Carol realized that. Norman had realized it, too, and that was why he had left her, why he hadn't written. Silent tears spilled down her cheeks. She brushed them away as a nurse came in to give Gaby her shot of morphine. Gaby gasped and winced when the needle entered and then she drifted off to sleep. Carol sat with her until Georges came to relieve her two hours later. She and Jean-Claude came to see Gaby Thursday morning. Her condition was much the same but she recognized Jean-Claude this time and told him the aardvark was actually *prettier* than he was. He grinned and kissed her bruised cheek and informed her that she'd pay for that remark later, when she was back on her feet. Gaby smiled weakly. Carol told her they were flying back to Cannes that afternoon, and Gaby nodded, looking at her with huge sad eyes.

"Remember what I said, Carol," she whispered.

"I will," Carol promised. "Take care, darling. We'll be back in two or three days."

Cannes seemed even more unreal than it had before. With the awards ceremony scheduled for Friday night, excitement was at fever pitch, and there was a frenzied air to the festivity. Voices were shriller, laughter sharper. Movement seemed speeded up. Carol was reminded of some glittering *Walpurgisnacht*. She and Jean-Claude were bombarded with questions when they returned. They refused to discuss Gaby. Carol kept to her rooms at the Carlton as much as possible, and Friday night, as she dressed for the ceremony, it was with grim resignation. *Le Bois* was certain to win, that was already a foregone conclusion, but she would have to sit there with a fake smile on her lips as they announced someone else as best actress. She wore a simple floor-length shift of midnight-blue velvet, sleeveless, backless, a chic, glamorous style Dior had created especially for her. The matching wrap was appliquéd with glittery silver and ice-blue lamé flowers and lined with ice-blue silk. Jean-Claude gave her the ultimate compliment when he came to fetch her. Carol couldn't help but smile as he stood there with hands on hips, steadily rising.

"I take it that's *not* a pistol in your pocket," she said.

"I can't help it. You look ravishing."

"Since there's no time for a cold shower, I suggest you think of something very neutral."

Jean-Claude grinned, adjusting his trousers. He looked ravishing himself in his tuxedo. Carol was very, very fond of him, and she was going to miss him when this was all over. He would be involved with another film, as would she, and they would drift apart and there would be—how had Gaby put it?—nothing left but the memory of sensations. Carol linked her arm in his as they stepped into the elevator. It had been impermanent from the first, no strings, an amiable arrangement that suited them both, but those memories would be happy ones. She would always be fond of him, and they would always be friends.

Traffic was more congested than ever before, with mounted police directing the onslaught. Guy, again in black turtleneck, gnawed his nails to the quick. The *palais* was bathed in gold-and-silver light, the press going wild as the incredibly glamorous crowd moved into the building. Monica Vitti blew kisses and

Yves Montand looked surly. Gina Lollobrigida, in strapless pink satin spangled with silver, had her own camera and snapped pictures herself as the photographers snapped her. Franco Zeffirelli and Luchino Visconti arrived at the door at the same time, each studiedly ignoring the other. A roar arose from the assembled crowd as Guy, Carol and Jean-Claude got out of their limo. Policemen held the hoi polloi at bay but the press swarmed forward. Guy told them to fuck off. Carol tried to smile as thirty flashbulbs went off. Jean-Claude tripped a reporter and grinned merrily as he crashed to the ground. It seemed an eternity before they finally reached the lobby, and there stood Eric Berne, talking with Genevieve Page.

Oh God, Carol thought, clutching Jean-Claude's arm. Just what I needed tonight. Eric was wearing a tuxedo and a black satin cummerbund and his face was pink and fleshy and his thick lips were smiling and his bald pate was gleaming. He saw her. He nodded. Carol acknowledged the nod with a polite smile, moving on into the auditorium with Guy and Jean-Claude. Eric's career hadn't fared so well since *Daughter of France*. He was no longer affiliated with any studio and was working independently now. He had done a dismal, overblown black-and-white World War II epic not even John Wayne could salvage at the box office, followed by a gritty, down-home, corn-pone story of modern-day southerners that featured an all-star cast and managed to insult the intelligence of every man, woman and child in America. He had recently purchased film rights to a gargantuan best-seller about Israel, and critics were already shuddering at the thought of what he'd do with *that* story.

Jean-Claude helped her into her seat, aglow with excitement. "This is fantastic, no?"

"Fantastic," Carol said dryly.

"Jacques Démy, I meet him in the bar this afternoon. He buys me a drink. He asks me to do a picture for him all about a flashy gangster who wears a Borsalino hat and mows his rivals down with a machine gun. It is a comedy, set in the thirties, huge budget, Technicolor, and he hopes to get Brigitte Bardot for the gangster's moll."

"It sounds marvelous."

"Bresson and Bardot! Just imagine!"

He was already leaving her, but Carol had no regrets. She

was very happy for him. He was going right to the top, and it couldn't happen to a nicer fellow. He squeezed her hand as the lights were lowered and the seemingly interminable ceremonies began. There would be another film for her too, and one day, perhaps one day soon, she would go back to America in triumph. She thought of Wichita and Norman and the life they could have had together, and she felt sad, felt empty inside, but, in her heart, she knew that Gaby was right. It was the work that counted, the work that gave her true satisfaction. She had wanted so desperately to become an actress, and she had succeeded, against all odds. She knew she had not been that good in the beginning—Julian Compton had seen it at once—and she knew she had had that first lucky break because of her looks. Eric Berne had taken a raw amateur and tried to transform her into a film star, and it hadn't worked. The movie had been a disaster, and . . . and I probably deserved all the vicious criticism I received at the time, Carol reflected, but I worked, I learned and I gradually mastered my craft. I'll never have Julie's magic, that's something you're born with, but I have a respectable body of work behind me now and I have actually been nominated for best actress at Cannes. I can hold my head high now. I no longer need apologize to anyone.

There was a blast of bugles and thunderous applause filled the auditorium. Guy and Jean-Claude were on their feet. Jean-Claude was cheering. Completely lost in thought for over an hour, paying no attention whatsoever to the tedious proceedings onstage, Carol had no idea what was happening. Jean-Claude seized her by the arms and pulled her to her feet and gave her a hug that almost broke her ribs and kissed her soundly. Everyone was watching. People were still applauding vigorously. "Go on!" Jean-Claude exclaimed, giving her a rough shove toward the aisle. "Go up there and receive your award!" And Carol found herself in the aisle in a state of shock, unable to believe this was actually happening. Photographers were snapping her picture. They were waiting for her up onstage. Filled with disbelief, Carol moved down the aisle in her high heels and the backless midnight-blue velvet Dior. Her poise, her serene composure belied the confusion inside. Somehow she manipulated the steps and moved across the stage without falling, and she smiled a radiant smile at the handsome movie actor who handed her the award. He kissed her cheek and led her to the microphone. The ap-

plause died down. People were waiting. What was she supposed to say? She was in the middle of a dream. None of this was real. She looked at the award cradled in her arms.

"I—I don't know how I'm going to get this into my suitcase," she said, and they loved it. "There are so many people to thank. I want to thank each of the judges and I want to thank Guy and Jean-Claude and—and there's someone else in the audience I want to thank as well."

She didn't know she was going to say it. The words seemed to come unbidden to her lips. He was sitting near the front of the auditorium, and his bald pate gleamed. Carol knew she should feel triumph and a sweet revenge, but she didn't feel that way at all.

"Years ago, when I was a—a very young girl from a little town in Kansas, Eric Berne gave me an opportunity every girl dreams about. I was raw and inexperienced and—and pretty poor material indeed, but Eric believed I had talent and he put me into a movie. It—the movie wasn't a success, it was a terrible bomb, in fact, but if Eric hadn't believed in me, if he hadn't given me that opportunity, I wouldn't be here today. Thank you, Eric," she said quietly, and she held up the award. "Thank you for making this possible."

The applause and cheers were deafening. There wasn't a person sitting out there who didn't know about the *Daughter of France* fiasco and Berne's treatment of her and the vicious statements he had made about her afterwards. Her generosity to the man who had so maligned her was something unheard of in this business, and it won them all over, even her detractors. Eric's face turned pinker than ever, and tears streamed unabashedly down his cheeks. A photographer from *Time* was kneeling in the aisle, immortalizing this remarkable spectacle for his magazine. Carol listened to the cheering and tears came to her eyes, too, but she managed to blink them back.

"There—there's one other thing I would like to say," she continued when the cheering died down, and again the words seemed to come unbidden to her lips. "I—I am so glad you have given this award to an American. I love my country. I'm proud to be an American. I accept this award as a citizen of the greatest, most compassionate country on earth."

Pandemonium broke out in the auditorium. The "Boos!" were vehement. They were drowned out by the cheers. A fistfight

actually broke out between a hard-core Communist French scriptwriter and a grizzled sixty-year-old American director who had four Academy Awards to his credit. Everyone was standing. Guy was as white as a sheet. Jean-Claude had a headlock on a lout who had yelled something derogatory about his Carol. Hedda Hopper was leaping up and down, waving her wide-brimmed flamingo-pink hat in the air and cheering herself hoarse. The girl from that little town in Kansas had just set the entire Cannes Film Festival right on its ear. It was an evening none of them would ever forget.

14

The Pacific was a bleak slate-gray at this hour, achurn with foamy whitecaps, and waves washed vigorously over the sand, leaving lacy white trails. It was barely seven. The sky was overcast, as gray as the water, but the sun was up there behind the clouds, desperately trying to shine through. Sturm and Drang galloped ahead in the damp sand, barking at the waves, cavorting outrageously, and Nora sauntered along, weary after her brisk two-mile walk, heading back to the beach house now at a leisurely pace. She loved Malibu at this hour of the morning. The bronzed musclemen, the girls in bikinis, the teenagers in black rubber wet suits were nowhere to be seen, and the people who lived in the expensive houses that had begun to spring up were still sleeping off the revelry of the night before. James groused that they were spoiling the place. It was getting to be a goddamned suburb of Beverly Hills, he complained. Soon they'd be surrounded by film stars and studio executives and millionaire accountants. His own beach house, humble and rustic as it was, all redwood planks and glass windows, was already worth many times what he had paid for it a few years ago, and he was constantly being badgered to sell. Malibu, alas, was becoming chic and that spelled doom as far as James was concerned.

Thinking of his complaints, Nora smiled to herself. James was so thornily determined to scorn the seductive blandishments

of Southern California. He lived on the beach but he didn't own a single bathing suit. He worked for the studios, and they paid him well, his script-writing assignments enabling him to live well and write his novels, but he despised the film industry and everyone connected with it. Staunchly independent, he refused to play the game, rarely attended the parties, was sullen and unsociable when he did. Consequently, he was being offered fewer and fewer assignments. That suited him fine. Let the whores have 'em, he said. He had real work to do. Nora shook her head. With all the guys in this town, I've gotta fall in love with the one who has integrity, or what he *thinks* is integrity. A glutton for punishment, that's me. I oughta have my head examined. Not that it'd do any good. My head's been in the clouds ever since our first evening together.

Sturm and Drang, the golden retrievers, began to bark with gleeful excitement, bounding toward the man who approached and jogging along beside him. He wore tennis shoes, a worn, sleeveless gray sweatshirt and short cut-off jeans. He was tanned, muscular, gorgeous, thick black hair in tumbling disarray. The dogs barked, leaping all around as the man reached Nora and stopped, his chest heaving. His sweatshirt was damp with perspiration. His hair was damp, too. He wiped his brow, gasping. Sturm and Drang continued to caper about, licking his sturdy legs.

"Down boys," Nora said.

"That include me?" the man asked.

"Particularly you."

"You don't wanna fuck?"

"It's a bit early in the morning, love."

"How 'bout a cuppa coffee, then?"

"I'd love one."

He wiped his brow again and then gave her the breezy smile that captivated millions of viewers each week. *TV Guide* had dubbed him the Sexiest Male on Television only last week, his picture on the cover with a grin on his lips and a gun in hand, an adoring Bingo clinging to his arm. Duke Henry, the hero of *Market Street West*, was the most popular private eye since Peter Gunn. The series was a smashing success, and Warner's was already renegotiating his contract with a hefty raise in salary. Jim Burke had become a gigantic star. He couldn't appear in public without being mobbed by hordes of squealing fans who

waved autograph books and tried to tear his clothes off. Fortunately, none of them were around this morning. Seizing her hand, Jim led Nora past the grassy sand dunes toward the sumptuous beach house with a terrace overlooking the water. Nora was wearing a vivid yellow blouse and white cotton slacks with the cuffs turned up. Her feet were bare. She let out a yowl as she stepped on a piece of broken shell. Jim grinned.

"You'll live," he said.

"Up yours! It's Hollywood scum like you who're ruining the area. Jesus! This place musta set you back a bundle."

"It did," he confessed, "but my agent assures me it's a terrific investment. A guy as popular as I am needs a retreat, a place to get away from his worshipful public."

Jim sat her down at the glass-topped table on the terrace and went inside to fetch the coffee. Nora rubbed her foot. The dogs began to nose around the plants and flowers that grew in glazed white pots. Sunlight finally began to seep through the clouds, streaming down in bright silvery-yellow rays, gilding the water with a million dancing reflections. The brisk salt air was wonderfully invigorating. How could anyone stay inside on a morning like this? Jim came back out a few minutes later, wearing a short beige terrycloth robe, carrying a tray with coffeepot, cups, freshly baked cinnamon rolls and two glasses of orange juice. Nora gave him a suspicious look.

"*You* didn't bake those cinnamon rolls?"

"I've got a Japanese houseboy," he confessed sheepishly.

"Figures," she said.

"He takes marvelous care of me. Cooks like a dream."

"So when'dja get back? I thought you were still in South Carolina, filming the Erskine Caldwell thing."

"*Roughshod*. Based on one of his early stories. Got back three days ago. Film's in the can. I've got two weeks' free time, then we leave for San Francisco to shoot exteriors for the series."

"How'd the movie go?"

"I think it's gonna be great. I play a moonshiner outracing the feds and trying to save his still and making life miserable for the girl who loves him. Natalie had other commitments. Diane McBain took over the role."

"Diane McBain? All that lipstick, all that shiny blonde hair?"

"The girl's a great actress. The studio's kept her busy playing glamorous hussies in Troy Donahue films, and she's never really

had a chance to show her stuff till now. She plays a fugitive from Tobacco Road in a cheap cotton print dress, no makeup, hair a mess, gives a performance that'll surprise the hell out of you. Hope Warner's has the sense to utilize her talent—knowing the studio, they'll probably put her in another glossy Technicolor soap as the bitchy debutante who snubs Connie Stevens."

Nora took a sip of coffee. "So you like making movies," she said.

"This one was originally written for Paul Newman. He's gonna be sorry he passed it by. I'm a mean son of a bitch who outfoxes the feds, roughs up the ladies and nobly lets himself get shot in the end so his kid brother can flee. I die in Diane's arms. I've smacked her around all through the film, but she can't resist my manly charms."

"Sounds like a winner," Nora said wryly.

"It's a good flick. Not the sort of thing I'd wanna play too often, but it's not Duke Henry. I'm gettin' kinda tired of that guy."

"And you want to play Hamlet."

"Eventually," he said.

His voice was serious. Nora gave him a look. They both burst into laughter. Sturm tried to jump into Jim's lap. Jim pushed him away. Nora broke a cinnamon roll in two and gave half to each dog. Drang curled up at her feet, tail thumping the tiles.

"So you're still with Hennesey?" Jim said.

Nora nodded, stroking Drang's golden fur. "I've got my apartment in Beverly Hills, but—I've been spending most of my time out here."

"I never thought a chick like you'd flip so hard over a guy. Figured you were too cool, too smart."

"So did I."

Jim shook his head. "I can't understand why you'd go for a guy like Hennesey when you could've had me."

"I could've had you?"

"At any given time."

"Jesus," she said, "I'll never be able to forgive myself."

Jim grinned again and poured himself another cup of coffee. The cinnamon rolls were delicious, with raisins and gooey white icing. Nora took a second. After that long walk she could afford it. Sea gulls squawked in the distance. The waves washing the sand made a swishing, soothing sound. James would be up and

about by now. He'd be wondering where she was. She really shouldn't linger too much longer.

"He finish that book he was writing?" Jim asked.

"Three months ago. Ross has been trying to place it with just the right publisher. I'm keeping my fingers crossed he gets a good advance. It's very important. James has invested so much in this book, and—"

"And the last two bombed, right? Look, if he ever needs a job, we could use another good writer on *Market Street West*. I've read a couple of Hennesey's scripts. He's got a great sense of structure, writes terrific dialogue. Just say the word and I'll see he gets put on the series."

Writing screenplays was demeaning enough. James would probably turn pale at the thought of writing for television, but it was very sweet of Jim to make the offer. Nora was touched.

"You're a nice guy," she said quietly.

"Hey, what're friends for? What's the point of being rich and successful if you can't lend a hand to people you care about?"

"And you were such an asshole in college," she said.

"Actually, I was a sweetheart back then too. You just never took time to find out. I—uh—I've been kinda outta touch in the backwoods of South Carolina, no *Hollywood Reporter*, no Hedda, no Louella. Has Julie finished filming *Impulse* yet?"

"They're behind schedule, have three or four more weeks of filming, I understand. She hates the part. It's emotionally taxing, playing a woman just recovering from a nervous breakdown who discovers her husband is sleeping with her big sister and plotting to send her back to the funny farm."

"I read the novel. The role's bound to be demanding, and Julie gives her all, throws herself completely into any part she plays. It's hard to just cut it off when the cameras stop rolling. You tend to take the part home with you when you're as into it as Julie always is."

"Word is it's got a built-in Academy Award. If she doesn't get an Oscar for best supporting actress for *The Slipper*, she's certain to get best actress for *Impulse*. The studio's building her up as the greatest actress to hit Hollywood since Luise Rainer."

"She is," Jim said.

"The bastards put her into *Impulse* three days after she finished *The Slipper*, no break whatsoever, and they've got a third

one lined up just as soon as she finishes this one. They're bloody well gonna get their investment back on her.''

Jim stared out at the water. He was still in love with her. He had gone out with dozens of shapely Hollywood starlets and a couple of famous actresses many years his senior and had a reputation rivaling that of young Warren Beatty, but Nora knew he'd gladly abandon the glitzy nightlife in a minute for the chance to stay home with Julie and Danny.

"If you talk to her, tell her I said hi," he said. "It's kinda hard to keep in touch with both of us being so busy. I sent Danny a stuffed alligator from South Carolina. Guess he got it."

"I'm sure he did." Nora rose to her feet. "I've got to run," she said. "Carol's arriving at one. I'm meeting her at the airport. If you're gonna be free, we'll all get together for lunch sometime next week."

"Great. I'd love to see Carol. Give her all my best, and give me a call about lunch. Number here's the same as the old one."

Jim gave Nora a hug and insisted she take the rest of the cinnamon rolls, which he wrapped in a napkin. Nora hugged him back and then made her way down to the beach. The sun was shining brightly now, burnishing the dogs' gold fur as they frolicked on ahead, making tracks in the wet sand. James's house was a half mile on up the beach, perched on a small bluff with redwood steps leading down to the water. Sturm and Drang bounded up them, barking merrily, and Nora sighed. They were worse than a couple of kids.

The house, though small, was wonderfully built, with huge windows giving a view of the ocean from every room. James had built it himself with help from two of his marine buddies in the construction business. It was pure California rustic with redwood deck, hemp door handles, varnished hardwood floors that always seemed to be gritty with sand. There was one large central room with a rough-hewn stone fireplace and step-down kitchen area, two bedrooms and a bath adjoining. One of the bedrooms had been converted into James's workroom. The whole house was flooded with books, magazines and records, a complicated hi-fi system rigged up in the main room. Vivaldi was playing softly as Nora stepped inside. The dogs came in, too, Sturm leaping onto the battered couch covered in oatmeal-colored corduroy, Drang curling up in front of the fireplace.

"James?" Nora called.

"I'm shaving. Be out in a minute."

Nora stepped down into the kitchen area. He hadn't had breakfast yet and she put on a pot of coffee, something she could safely do without burning down the house or imperiling life and limb. Gleaming pots and pans hung suspended from a ceiling rack and one drawer was filled with lethal-looking cutlery, but Nora wouldn't dream of touching them. James did all the cooking. Even making coffee was a risky venture for her. She'd scalded her hand a number of times until she got the hang of it. So I can't cook, she told herself. Big fucking deal. Not that many cooks can write a blockbuster best-seller.

James stepped into the room, wearing tennis shoes, faded jeans and a worn navy blue T-shirt. Nora felt that wonderful lift inside she always felt when she saw him again after a brief separation. He was tall, lean, rangy, not at all handsome with those hollows beneath his sharp cheekbones, those wide lips, that thin nose, but the sexual magnetism was almost palpable. His coal-black hair was neatly brushed, but the thick waves still looked unruly, one slipping over his brow. His moody smoke-gray eyes examined her closely, as though trying to ascertain some area of vulnerability.

"Where have you been?" he asked.

"I went for a long walk on the beach. I needed some time— I needed to be alone for a couple of hours."

"I see. Because of last night."

"Last night doesn't matter, James."

"I was in a rotten mood. I shouldn't have said what I did. I shouldn't have taken my frustration out on you. You know I love you."

"I know."

"You know I'm hard to live with."

"I've no illusions on that score."

"You ought to find yourself a tame, domesticated lover who would appreciate your good points instead of a sullen lout who puts you down because of his own insecurities."

"Call me crazy, but I've always preferred Heathcliff to Edgar Linton. Besides, you're a terrific lay."

He arched one eyebrow. "Yeah?"

"Care to prove it?"

"Later, perhaps."

"Things have come to a pretty pass when a girl can't even get

laid," she complained. "You gotta headache, or is it that time of month?"

James Hennesey smiled and padded over to wrap his arms around her, gazing down into her eyes from his superior height.

"I don't deserve you," he said.

"Tell me something I don't know."

James spotted the cinnamon rolls setting on the counter. He moved back, frowning.

"Where did those come from?"

"Jim Burke gave them to me. I ran into him this morning on the beach and he asked me up for a cup of coffee. He owns that new house, you know, the one that looks like a glass-and-chrome Taj Mahal."

"Burke," he sneered. "Duke Henry."

"You needn't sound so disdainful."

"A television actor. A mechanical pretty boy with a tooth-paste smile."

"He happens to be a very good actor," Nora said defensively. "He also happens to be a very good friend."

"Coffee all he asked you up for?"

"No," she said. "He took me into his bedroom and slowly disrobed me and we fucked like minks for the next two hours. That's why I look so bruised and haggard."

"We're doing it again," he said.

"I notice that."

"I'm an ungrateful shit."

"At times, yes, you certainly are."

"So why don't you leave me?"

"I happen to love you, you bastard."

James went over to the counter and poured himself a cup of coffee and examined the rolls, finally selecting one. He lounged against the counter, sipping the coffee, looking at her with low-ered brows, smoke-gray eyes moody, remote. Something had happened. There was something he hadn't told her. Nora wished she smoked. She could have used a cigarette just then.

"Ross called," he said after a while. "The phone woke me up. He keeps forgetting it's three hours earlier out here."

Nora held her breath. She had been dreading this call. She had read his new novel, and while it was beautifully written, extremely literate and filled with insightful observations about the human condition, it was difficult going for the average reader.

Masterpieces were all very well for required reading in college classrooms, but those ladies responsible for purchasing eighty-five percent of all fiction wanted something a bit more entertaining.

"So what did he say? Has he sold the book?"

"The call was for you," James said. "The paperback edition of *The Slipper* has just gone into its nineteenth printing. They expect it to sell another million with the release of the movie."

Jesus. Just what his ego needed right now.

"You're going to make out like a bandit when royalties come in at the end of the month. He says he'll need a U-haul truck to deliver all the money you've got coming."

"Ross always had a way with words."

"Congratulations."

"What did he say about your book, James?"

"It's still out. He expects a solid offer in a day or so. It won't make anything like *The Slipper*, of course, but perhaps a couple of readers will appreciate it."

"It's a marvelous book."

"Sure it is."

"What you write is—it's very special. You write for the discriminating reader. If you wanted to write a big commercial novel, you could."

"Sure, and if not I can always write another screenplay based on a trashy British thriller that may or may not get produced sometime within the next ten years. Look, hon," he said, setting down his coffee cup, "I've got to drive to Long Beach. There're a couple of research books I need, and Acres of Books is the only place I'm likely to find them. I don't know when I'll be back."

"I'm picking Carol up at the airport this afternoon. I don't know when *I* will be back, either."

"Catch you later, then."

If you're lucky, you son of a bitch, she said to herself as he walked out of the room. She heard him revving up the motor of his old Chevrolet a minute or so later. The dogs perked up, looking surprised, then looking dejected and upset. Nora angrily opened a can of dog food and broke a fingernail and said "Shit!" and scooped the dog food into two brown plastic bowls and then set the bowls on the hearth. The dogs ignored them. Sturm began to whine. Nora told him to shut up in no uncertain terms.

"I will *not* feel guilty for writing a huge best-seller and making a lot of money," she added. "If he thinks I'm going to apologize for my success, he's got another think coming. In fact, he can go *fuck* himself!"

The dogs barked, in total agreement.

Nora bathed, put on her makeup, brushed her long pageboy until it shone with blue-black highlights and then put on a pair of gold sandals and a simple gold-and-brown striped cotton sundress with halter top, fitted waist and short full skirt that had set her back a hundred and fifty bucks at a shop in Beverly Hills. She checked the dogs' water bowl, told them she'd be back and left, clutching her yellow straw purse. She climbed behind the wheel of her metallic bronze Thunderbird and, five minutes later, was speeding along the freeway with several thousand other cars that seemed to be driven by suicidal kamikaze pilots.

She loved it. She drove every bit as fast as the others, switching lanes with the greatest of ease. To a girl born and bred in Brooklyn who had known nothing but subways and buses and the occasional taxi, it was a thrill driving your own car, being in control. It made her feel grown up and independent and carefree. Those first lessons had been a bitch and her driving instructor had almost had a nervous breakdown and she'd dented more than a few fenders before she got everything down pat, but now she was a demon on wheels and loving every minute of it. Pressing her foot down on the accelerator, she passed a van and cut in front of a green Cadillac. The driver honked viciously. Nora put her arm out the window and extended a stiff middle finger, feeling better than she had felt all day, her good humor restored, eager to see Carol again. What a joy it was going to be having her here in Los Angeles, the three Cinderellas from Claymore together again at long last.

There wasn't a bigger name in the business than Carol Martin at this particular moment in history. Forget Monroe and her tardiness and her tormented love affairs. Forget Taylor and her tricky health and that multi-billion-dollar Egyptian disaster they were trying to salvage in Rome. Carol's acceptance speech at Cannes and the furor it had caused had made headlines throughout the world, and suddenly she was a saint, suddenly she was an all-American heroine, suddenly she was the hottest thing going. *Le Bois* had not only broken all existing box office records for an art film, it was a dead cert for best foreign film come next

March and the Academy Awards. Carol had been deluged with offers from her native land, every studio in town wanted her, and she had finally accepted a two-film contract with Universal at an astronomical salary, with script approval, cast approval, director approval and sundry clauses and guarantees unheard of in the old days.

She was coming home in triumph. All those years of self-imposed exile in France, all that bad press, all those jokes about her acting ability, all that humiliation, and they were rolling out the red carpet now. Sometimes the good guys did come out on top. Nora was positively elated. *The Slipper* was having its world premiere at Grauman's Chinese Theater tomorrow night and Carol would be able to go with them. Who could ask for anything more? There're a couple of things I could ask for, Nora thought, taking the exit, heading for the airport parking lot. But I'm not going to think about James. I'm not going to let him spoil my day. I hope that moody son of a bitch gets lost in Acres of Books and never finds his way out.

Nora had difficulty finding a parking place—didn't you always?—and it was almost time for the plane to land as she raced toward the terminal. There it was, pulling up right now, a huge silver bird inching along behind the rank of observation windows, and, shit, wouldn't you know it, there were the reporters and the photographers and the studio representative. Screw 'em. Pushing her way to the front of the assembled crowd, Nora watched anxiously as the passengers began to come in, clutching their hand luggage, looking a little dazed after the long flight from New York. Nora stood on her tiptoes and craned her neck, looking for Carol.

And there she was, as cool and regal as Princess Grace any day of the week and every bit as lovely. The short-clipped Joan of Arc haircut was gone. Her hair was longer, pulled back sleekly from her face and fastened in a neat bun, and it was lighter now, a pale white-gold, extremely flattering. She was wearing a pale pink-orange Chanel suit and a white silk blouse with a large bow at the neck and carrying a white handbag many women would kill for. Carol smiled at a fellow passenger, said good-bye to him and looked up and saw Nora and Nora let out a whoop and raced toward her and suddenly they were holding each other and both sobbing with joy and the photographers were snapping pic-

tures and the reporters were yelling questions and the studio representative was urging them to follow him to the VIP lounge.

It took them a good hour and twenty minutes to get away. A limousine was waiting to take Carol to the Beverly Hills Hotel. Carol dismissed it, dismissed the studio representative, thanked him for the roses, said she would be in touch and followed Nora out to the parking lot. She had posed for hundreds of photographs, it seemed, answered hundreds of questions, handling it all with a serene poise that was positively awesome. Her luggage was being sent ahead to the hotel by the studio rep. They were alone at last. The remote movie queen vanished, and they both began to chatter at once, as close as ever. Carol removed her shoes as soon as they were in the car.

"You've no idea what a strain that all is," she complained. "I've had to learn to deal with it these past months. Polite reserve is the only way to survive the barrage of questions, the popping flashbulbs. I wanted to yell at them to leave us alone. Oh, Nora, it's so good to see you!"

"It's kinda nice seeing you, too."

"You're actually going to drive this car yourself?"

"Just you watch."

"You haven't changed a bit."

"Thanks a lot. I'll put a bag over my head."

Carol smiled. Nora whisked onto the freeway with breezy abandon, causing a cacophony of blaring horns.

"So how does it feel to be an international superstar?" she asked.

"Scary," Carol said. "Everyone pays much more attention to me now, but inside—" She paused, reflecting. "Inside I feel exactly the same. I wonder why everyone is making such a fuss."

"You're a certified heroine, kid, turning the other cheek to Berne, standing up for your country. You made the cover of *Time*. You made the cover of *Newsweek*. You can do no wrong."

"And it can all vanish in no time flat. How well I know. I was on top once before, remember? America's Favorite Cinderella. It's taken five years for me to live that down. What if I bomb again?"

"You're gonna be a smash, love. Universal's handing you the moon. They've got a big investment to protect."

"I—I'm not too sure about this first film," Carol confessed. "It's a remake of an old Fannie Hurst novel, pure soap, but

they're updating it. Ross Hunter is producing. That means jewels, furs, haute couture, elaborate interior decoration, someone like John Gavin as costar.''

"And that means socko box office, love. *Imitation of Life* had 'em standing in lines for hours, made buckets of money. *Back Street* with Susan Hayward didn't do so bad, either. Hunter knows exactly what he's doing. He's single-handedly trying to bring glamor back into movies, and the public's starved for glamor.''

"I'm banking on that," Carol said. "I need a big box office success. I debated about signing with Universal. Fellini has a new project and he wanted me to do it, something about an unhappy married woman who lives in a Technicolor fantasy world. It sounded fascinating, but—I don't want to become Queen of the Art Houses. I want to work in America, so Giulietta Masina is going to play the part and I'm going to star in *Mannequin*.''

"You made the right choice," Nora assured her.

"I hope so. I can't afford to flop a second time."

Nora whipped around a florist's delivery truck and into the next lane and speeded up even more, keeping an eye out for the Highway Patrol.

"Julie wanted to be here to meet you, too," she said, "but she's in the middle of another film."

"How is she, Nora?"

"Not too well. They're working her to death, and she's under tremendous strain. Her life's not her own, she claims. The studio is giving her a huge buildup. If she's not working in front of the camera she's giving interviews or posing for stills or 'being seen' at all the right places with carefully selected male starlets.''

"I remember that scene well," Carol said.

"Julie hates it. The studio runs her life completely. They rented her house and hired her servants. They furnish her car and select her clothes and supervise her social life—all in her own best interests, of course. They don't want her to 'worry' about anything. They also don't want the public to know she's been married and has a child, not good for her image, so Danny is a deep, dark secret.''

"You don't mean it?"

"She'll adjust to it all eventually, I suppose, but sometimes— sometimes I feel almost guilty for getting her into this. We spend

as much time together as possible, which isn't much with her schedule. Hannah came to California with them, so Danny's well taken care of. Julie asked me to give you her love and tell you she's looking forward to seeing you.''

Nora took an off ramp and they were soon cruising through the swank environs of Beverly Hills, sumptuous mansions, dazzlingly neat lawns, glitzy shops and boutiques. Palm trees stood sentinel in majestic rows. Flowers bloomed in lush profusion. Nora drove more slowly, savoring the luxury of it all, and Carol took a cigarette from the silver cigarette case with art deco designs in gold. She lighted it with a matching silver-and-gold lighter.

"What a beautiful lighter," Nora remarked. "Did Sir Robert give that to you, too?"

"Jean-Claude gave it to me. He swiped my cigarette case and took it to a jeweler and ordered him to design a lighter to match. He gave it to me at the airport in Paris, just before I left. He was supposed to be filming that afternoon, but he played hookey to see me off."

"Miss him?"

Carol nodded. "He was a delightful interlude, nothing more, but I'll always be fond of him. Our parting was jolly and lighthearted but sad nevertheless. I'm afraid I cried. Jean-Claude's eyes were moist, too. We both have our careers to think of, and I doubt we'll even write, but—it was nice while it lasted."

"I guess you've gotta be philosophical about these things."

"You do if you want to survive," Carol said quietly.

Nora stopped for a red light on Sunset Boulevard and then drove even more slowly as they neared the hotel.

"How is Gaby, Carol?" she asked. "Has she fully recovered yet?"

"She'll walk with a slight limp for the rest of her life, but she's doing marvelously well. She's still in a nursing home for the morphine—she became addicted to it—a purely medical thing. She was in so much pain and they had to give her so much—she simply couldn't withdraw from it all at once. It's almost under control now. She'll be leaving in a couple of weeks, and she hasn't been idle. She's been writing a magnificent book. It's called *A Journal to Myself*, about her treatments at the nursing home and her reflections on her work, on life, on love, on the perils of early success."

"It sounds wonderful."

"It's unlike anything she's ever done before, as good as anything Colette ever wrote, and it's going to put her right up there with the greats. The *enfant terrible* of French letters has grown up. I suppose it's something we all have to do eventually."

Surrounded by palm trees, emerald-green lawns and beautifully tended flower beds, the Beverly Hills Hotel stood in all its gaudy pink splendor, site of many a juicy scandal, birthplace of many a recordbreaking deal. Carol was expected. A car jockey whisked Nora's car away. A doorman opened the door with a dramatic flourish. Inured as they were to celebrity, the staff was nevertheless extra attentive and obsequious as Carol entered. It was as though royalty had arrived. Warren Beatty and Joan Collins were just stepping out of the Polo Lounge. The hot young actor and the English beauty paused for a moment, watching. Beatty seemed to be watching with a bit too much interest. Collins tugged his arm and urged him on. The desk clerk looked a bit apprehensive as an unsteady Laurence Harvey staggered toward the men's room a young blond athlete had just entered.

The studio had made all the arrangements, and Carol and Nora were escorted out to the bungalow that had been reserved for her. Four of the bungalows, Nora knew, were still kept by Howard Hughes. One was for Hughes, one, a quarter of a mile away, was for wife Jean Peters, and one was for his eight Mormon bodyguards. The fourth bungalow was left empty and no one was allowed inside, not even maintenance men. Nearby was the bungalow where Yves Montand and Marilyn Monroe had conducted their noisy affair after Simone Signoret departed for Paris. Each bungalow was a compact little mansion, and Carol's was choice, in the back, away from the street noises.

"Jesus," Nora said, surveying the splendor. "The studio's certainly giving you first-class treatment."

A bottle of Dom Perignon was chilling in a silver bucket. There were baskets of fruit and a tray of fancy hors d'oeuvres. The spacious, elegantly appointed sitting room seemed to be aflood with white and salmon-pink roses. It impressed the hell out of Nora. Carol accepted it all with her customary composure, idly picking up the room-service menu.

"Had lunch?" she inquired.

Nora shook her head.

"Hungry?"

"Famished."

Carol placed a call, and a short while later a waiter arrived with lunch, baked potatoes smothered in sour cream and caviar à la Maxim's in Paris, Elizabeth Taylor's favorite meal, the waiter confided. He uncorked the champagne for them, filled two crystal flutes and made his departure, pocketing a generous tip.

"And to think we used to slop around the dorm, munching on Fritos," Nora observed.

"Those were the days," Carol said. "We've talked about everyone else," she added. "Now I want to hear all about you and James Hennesey. I read the books you sent me. He's a brilliant writer."

"That's the problem," Nora told her. "He's so bloody brilliant the average reader feels intimidated. They pick up one of his novels, say, 'Hmmm, this looks interesting,' and then take a copy of *The Carpetbaggers* over to the cash register."

"He's very attractive," Carol said.

Nora nodded. "And you've only seen pictures of him. He's the most magnetic man I've ever met, positively crackling with sex appeal. He's moody and often sullen and sometimes very tender and always thoughtful and quite jealous and—Jesus! I love him, Carol. I don't feel like I'm my own person anymore. My whole life seems to revolve around James and his moods. I'm either walking on eggshells, trying not to wound his fragile ego, or walking on clouds, full of amazement that a man like James could possibly be interested in me."

"He must be very special."

"He is. He's no knight in shining armor, and he's not Mr. Right, either, not unless you happen to be a dyed-in-the-wool masochist. He's thorny and infuriating and complex and—I must be out of my fucking mind."

"You've got it bad."

"And that's not good. I know. I've never been in love before, and I'm not at all sure I like it. Oh, I was fond of Brian, but I wasn't in love with him—not like this. He represented all that I wasn't, all I could never be, and that was the chief attraction. With James it—it seems he's a part of my very soul. We've had some terrific rows. I've moved back to my apartment here in Beverly Hills half a dozen times, but he always comes after me, always persuades me to come back to Malibu with him."

"When am I going to meet him?"

"Tomorrow night. He's taking us both to the premiere. I—I hope I haven't painted too black a picture. James is a wonderful man, and he can be very charming, he usually is, but he's so concerned about the new book and I'm making so much money and—oh, shit! Let's have some more champagne."

"I'll order another bottle," Carol said.

Nora was in a very good mood as she sped back to the beach house the next day. It had been very late when she returned yesterday. After all that champagne, it had seemed unwise to get behind the wheel of a car, so she and Carol relaxed and talked and then it was time for dinner and Carol insisted she stay and time seemed to evaporate and it was after nine when she got back to Malibu and James was frantic. He'd been phoning her apartment for hours, phoning all her friends, had been on the verge of phoning the police when she finally came in. He seized her, glared at her furiously, then crushed her to him and held her tightly and told her he'd almost gone out of his mind. He hadn't bothered to find out where Carol would be staying, had, in fact, forgotten that she was picking Carol up at the airport. Nora was extremely flattered by his concern. He might be a moody son of a bitch, but he cared. He genuinely cared. It was a cool evening. He lighted a fire in the fireplace and piled rugs in front of it. What followed was sheer enchantment.

In jersey and jeans, he had walked along the beach with her this morning, his arm curled tightly around her shoulders, and he had cooked a big breakfast and told her about the idea for a new book that had come to him as he was driving back from Long Beach. He was jotting down notes as Nora left to drive into town to fetch his old tuxedo which she had exhumed from moth balls and carried to the cleaners the week before. It hung in the backseat now, enshrouded in a black plastic bag. Turning off the freeway, she headed for the beach, excited about the premiere. The studio was sending a limousine, and they were to pick Carol up at seven. It was going to be a glorious evening.

She knew something was wrong the minute she stepped inside, tuxedo bag in hand. Notes abandoned, James was sitting at the window and gazing moodily out at the water, still wearing the faded jeans and gray-and-black striped fisherman's jersey, sleeves shoved up to his elbows. He didn't look up as she came in. Both dogs were very quiet, as though sensing his mood and afraid to agitate him. Sturm thumped his tail. Drang whined

softly. Nora could hear the waves washing the sand on the beach down below and the distant shriek of a sea gull.

"I'm back," she said brightly. "The cleaners did a marvelous job on the tux. It might be a shade old-fashioned with those wide black satin lapels but I'm gonna be so gorgeous no one'll pay any attention to you."

He looked up. He didn't reply. Nora went into the bedroom, hung the tuxedo up in the closet and returned to the main room, ready for battle. She was not going to let anything spoil this evening. She'd been looking forward to it for weeks. In a sense she'd been looking forward to it all her life.

"Ross called," she said.

"Ross called," he told her.

"So?"

"He sold the book."

"Terrific."

"Putnam's bought it. They paid the generous advance of thirty-five hundred dollars. That's three thousand five hundred. According to Ross, I was damned lucky to get that. Seems every other publisher in New York turned the book down flat as a poor risk."

"Putnam's is a fine house. They'll—"

"Goddammit, Nora, didn't you hear what I said? I got peanuts for a book I put my heart and soul into. They'll print it up, slip it into the stores in the dead of night and it'll die, just like the last one, just like the one before that. Three thousand five hundred! You'd think I was a first novelist. You'd think I didn't have a reputation, think I hadn't sold two books to Hollywood and won awards and—goddammit, what's the point!"

"The point is you wrote the book you wanted to write," she said quietly. "You refused to compromise. You refused to make concessions to public tastes. You were true to yourself, true to your art—and you're to be admired for it. It's a wonderful book, and I'm sure—"

"Don't patronize me, Nora."

"Patronize you?"

He was on his feet now, arms folded across his chest, brows lowered, gray eyes smoldering.

"I spend fifteen months writing, polishing, sweating, *bleeding* over every word, honing every phrase, trying to write something worthwhile that will have *meaning* and what do I get? I get

zilch. You knock off a piece of crap in two and a half months and make a million bucks.''

"A piece of crap?"

"You're not going to stand there and tell me it's *literature*?"

"I wouldn't dream of it," she said coldly. "I wrote a book a lot of people happened to enjoy. I didn't try to educate them or reform them or elevate them or change their lives, I tried to entertain them, and, on the face of it, I'd say I did a pretty damned good job of it."

"You think I'm a fool because I don't write crap? You think I should become a whore like you and—"

"Oh, I'm a whore? I'm glad that's out in the open."

"I have integrity. I have self-respect. I have to live with myself, and I have to write the best I can, and if the public doesn't like it, if the publishers don't want to publish it, that's just too fucking—"

Nora turned and went into the bedroom and shut the door. She called the studio and told them to cancel the limousine and then she called Jim Burke and asked him how he'd like to take a couple of nifty glamor girls to the premiere tonight and told him to pick her up at her apartment around six-forty-five and then she packed her bag. The majority of her things were still at the apartment, and it didn't take her long. James was waiting for her when she stepped out of the bedroom with bag in hand.

"There are a few books and records that belong to me," she said, "but I haven't time to gather them up now. You keep them."

"Goddammit! You can't walk out on me now. I need you. I need you now more than ever. You know I didn't mean what I said. You know I was just upset. I'm *still* upset. I need you, Nora. I love you. You're not walking out on me."

"Think not?"

"Nora—"

"Good-bye, James," she said.

She was trembling as she climbed into the Thunderbird. She backed out of the sandy drive and turned the car around and didn't look back even though she heard him calling her name. The hefty, silver-haired doorman in his neat gray uniform greeted her effusively when she reached the elegant apartment building only a few blocks from the Beverly Hills Hotel. She was one of his favorites, and he insisted on carrying her bag up for her while

an assistant took over at the door. Nora thanked him, tipped him, went inside and burst into tears, but there were no signs of tears when Jim arrived at six-forty-five, stunning in a two-thousand-dollar tuxedo that was quite a change from the brown leather jacket and jeans he had worn in New York. Nora was wearing a gown of tea-colored satin, by Balmain, and looked rather stunning herself, as Jim was quick to inform her.

"Gorgeous might be a more appropriate word," he said.

"You know—there's something about you, Burke."

"Yeah?"

"Under the right circumstances I could go for you in a big way."

"Wanna fuck?"

"We've gotta pick Carol up in fifteen minutes."

"Just my luck."

"Thanks for doing this, Jim. I know it was awfully short notice, and you probably had another date arranged. It—it means a lot."

"You okay? Anything you wanna discuss?"

"I'm peachy, and there's nothing *to* discuss."

"Want me to beat him up for you?"

"Let's go. Carol's a big star now, and stars don't like to be kept waiting."

Nora was pleased with the way she looked until she saw Carol. Carol was wearing a Dior with a high-necked, sleeveless, tight tunic top completely covered with glittery pale apricot sequins, the long skirt in alternate folds of soft, swirling beige and pale apricot chiffon. Lana Turner in her heyday had never exuded more glamor.

I'm gonna kill the bitch, Nora thought.

She explained that James had been unable to make it and Jim had agreed to fill in. Carol lifted one brow but was too tactful to ask any questions. She settled into the limo with her small beige satin evening bag and smiled at Jim, whom she hadn't seen since their days in Julian Compton's class. They chatted about Claymore, about the skits they had done together, about their careers in the intervening years, and Nora sat back, silent, promising herself she wasn't going to be miserable, vowing she would enjoy herself. The terrible hurt inside would go away eventually. She was a tough, shrewd cookie from New York, not some sappy, dewy-eyed yokel, and she wasn't going to start

bawling again. She was one of the best-selling writers in the country and they'd made a movie of her book and this was her night, goddammit. This was what she had dreamed of all her adult life and she wasn't going to mope and be miserable. She wasn't.

Klieg lights turned, criss-crossing the sky with silver spears outside of Grauman's Chinese Theater with its gaudy pagodas and celebrated courtyard with footprints of the stars. Barricades had been set up to hold back the mob, and there was a red carpet leading up to the entrance. Shrill screams filled the air as limousines pulled up one by one, unloading their precious cargo, and it was hokey and old-fashioned and wildly exhilarating, a throwback to the golden days of Hollywood. The crowd went wild when Jim Burke stepped breezily out of their limousine and reached in to help Carol Martin out. Dozens of teenaged girls shrieked with mad abandon and shoved forward, almost overturning the barricades. Uniformed policemen had to link arms to hold them back. The din was deafening. Flashbulbs exploded with the fury of a lightning storm as the mob yelled "Jimmy!" and "Carol!" I might just as well be invisible, Nora thought as Jim helped her out of the limo. Who's that other broad? What's *she* doin' with 'em? Jim took her arm with his left, Carol's with his right and led them toward the entrance as the girls continued to shout and the policemen strained to hold them back. A local radio station was broadcasting tonight's festivities, a jolly emcee in a flashy blue satin tuxedo standing in front of a microphone and urging Jim and Carol to step over and say a few words to our listeners. Just like *Singin' in the Rain*, Nora thought. Jesus, this is really happening, and my book is responsible for it all.

"Jim, Jim Burke! Come on over! Tell our audience how it feels to be one of the lucky folks here tonight. Jim, I needn't remind our listeners, is the star of *Market Street West*, one of the top ten shows on NBC, and he's with the glamorous Carol Martin. Come on over, you two!"

Nora tried to withdraw, but Jim pulled her forward.

"Hello, Burt!" he cried. "It's *great* to be here. *The Slipper* is going to knock 'em dead, and this little lady is the reason why. Nora Levin, author of the best-selling novel it's based upon. If it weren't for her, none of us would be here tonight."

"Uh—Nora Levin!" Burt enthused, looking pissed. This wasn't television, after all. Who th' hell cares about chopped

liver when we're surrounded by caviar. "Nora! Tell us, how does it feel to see your book up there on the giant screen?"

"I haven't seen it yet," Nora said.

"Wonderful! And Carol! Carol Martin! We're all so glad to see you back where you belong. Carol recently won Best Actress at Cannes, and we all know about *that*! Looking forward to seeing the film, Carol?"

"I certainly am, Burt," Carol said. "Nora and I were roommates in college, and I'm very proud for her. Even back then I knew she was going to be a successful writer. *The Slipper* is a wonderful novel, and I know they've made a wonderful movie from it."

I'm gonna bawl, goddammit. I can feel it. I'm the luckiest girl alive to have friends like these. Fuck James Hennesey. Who *needs* him?

"Julie Hammond, who is one of the stars of the movie, was also in college with us," Carol continued, "as was Jim. Tonight is like an old college reunion for the four of us. I hear Julie gives a magnificent performance."

"And here she comes!" Burt cried. "Julie Hammond, the brilliant young actress! With Terry Wood, celebrated Hollywood producer who discovered her in New York and brought her here for her first film!"

Wood and Julie had just alighted from their limousine and were walking up the red carpet. The crowd was cheering. Although they had yet to see her on the screen, they'd all read about the sensitive, superlative young actress, in fan magazines, in the Sunday supplements, in the columns, in countless newspaper articles. No actress in recent memory had received such a strong buildup from a major studio. Moon-faced, bespectacled, looking more rotund than ever in his satin-lapelled tuxedo, Terry Wood proudly escorted her up to the microphone. Julie was wearing a yellow-gold silk gown with full puffed sleeves and a modest, heart-shaped neckline, the Edith Head creation bespangled with thousands of gold sequins. Her hair was a light golden-brown now, almost blonde, and her face was exquisitely made-up. She was smiling, but her enormous violet-blue eyes looked spacey and she was a bit unsteady on her feet. Nora wondered just how many tranquilizers she had gulped down in order to get through the evening.

"Terry! Julie! Step right up! It looks like *The Slipper*'s going to be another box office bonanza for you, Terry."

"We're all very proud of the film," Wood said smoothly, "and we're all very proud of this little girl here—" He patted Julie's hand. "She's going to be a major star. We're talking Stanwyck. We're talking Shearer. She's got that special magic Hollywood hasn't seen in years."

"How do you feel about all this, Julie?" Burt gushed.

"I'm very happy to be here tonight," Julie said. Jesus, she sounds like a marionette, Nora thought. "*The Slipper* is a lovely film, and I'm very proud to be a part of it."

"Great! I understand you're—Hey, listen to that crowd roar!" Burt interrupted himself. "Guess who I see coming toward us now? It's Robert Wagner and Natalie Wood, Hollywood's Happiest Couple!"

Inside the lobby, Julie and Carol embraced each other, and Nora could see that Julie was definitely out of it, so heavily tranquilized she scarcely knew where she was. Ushers in fancy uniforms led them to their reserved seats, and Nora sat down beside Carol, watching Julie smile brightly as she and Wood took their seats a few rows ahead of them. I'm going to have to speak to her again about those bloody pills, Nora thought. She's taking altogether too many, and not just the tranquilizers. I don't care if the studio doctor does prescribe them, they're turning her into a basket case. Vitamins, my ass. Jim was concerned, too, frowning as the lights were slowly lowered and the glamorous audience grew still.

Nora forgot everything else as drums rolled and the Twentieth Century Fox arc lights crossed the screen. The screen turned a misty blue, and as Johnny Mathis began to sing the hauntingly lovely theme song, a glass slipper floated through the mist, gleaming like crystal, three female hands trying to grasp it as the credits rolled. When she saw BASED ON THE NOVEL BY NORA LEVIN she felt the tears brim over her lashes, and she cried silently through most of the movie. That was her baby up there. Those were her characters. Nunnally Johnson had written a marvelous screenplay, true to the spirit of her novel, and Negulesco had done a brilliant job of directing. The cast was wonderful, and, as Anne, Julie was absolutely magical, completely dominating the film even though her part was no larger than the others. Sensing what she must be feeling, Carol reached for her

hand in the darkness, squeezing it tightly, and there were tears in her eyes as well. Deafening applause and enthusiastic cheers filled the auditorium as the music swelled and Mathis began to sing again and the final credits began to roll.

"Thank God I didn't wear mascara tonight," Nora said. "Do I look okay? Am I a complete mess?"

"You look radiant, darling," Carol assured her.

"Jesus—it was—it was wonderful."

"Pure schmaltz," Jim said.

"Get stuffed, Burke," Nora snapped.

By the time they arrived at Romanoff's, Nora had repaired her makeup and was perfectly composed and ready to party. Hollywood's favorite watering hole for over two decades, Romanoff's was as gaudy and outlandish as its proprietor, Prince Michael Romanoff. Born Harry Gerguson, son of a Brooklyn tailor, Romanoff claimed vague kinship with "the late Czar," was called a prince among fellows and known as "Hollywood's only honest phony." An engaging, beloved eccentric who claimed he air-expressed his pongee shirts to Sulka in Manhattan every week to be laundered, he was a solemn, dignified figure with close-cropped, graying hair and a bulbous nose, always impeccably tailored. He greeted them with regal aplomb, although he sniffed disdainfully at Jim. A self-proclaimed snob, he considered television actors below the salt and beneath his notice.

Romanoff also disdained the press, ordinarily barring them from his exclusive eatery, but as the studio had rented the place for the evening and invited quite a number of them, he tolerated their presence. Hedda Hopper was resplendent in a long-sleeved black silk frock with shoulder pads, cinched waist and full mid-calf-length skirt, her wide-brimmed black silk hat festooned with pink velvet roses. Stephen Boyd, who had played the evil Messala in Ben-Hur, was at her side, even handsomer in tux than he had been in Roman tunic. Radie Harris of The Hollywood Reporter bounced about beaming at everyone and spreading good cheer. If one was to believe her columns, Radie had never met a major star who wasn't absolutely crazy about her and became a dear friend. Mike Connelly, from the same publication, was also on hand. Nora knew that one of the leading male columnists in town was rumored to have been a major source of information for the now-defunct Confidential, feeding them scandalous tid-

bits about the stars in exchange for their not publishing a story about his own peccadilloes.

Hopper and Connelly both made a beeline for Carol as they entered. Connelly reached her first.

"Carol! I'm Mike Connelly. I interviewed you five years ago when Berne brought you to my office. Remember? How do you feel about being back in—"

"I wanna talk to you, Martin!" Hopper cried, seizing her arm. "Let's go over there in the corner where we can talk privately."

"I believe I was here first, Hedda," Connelly protested.

"Don't mess with me, Connelly!" Hedda snarled. "I'm the one who taught you how to make up your eyes."

"Jesus," Nora said. "I could use a drink."

"So could I," Jim confided. "Come on, let's get smashed."

The place was packed with glamorous celebrities and important executives, as well as press and photographers, but a hush fell over the assemblage as Terry Wood came in with Julie Hammond, and it was followed by a burst of spontaneous applause. This was Julie's evening. *The Slipper* was Julie's film. Everyone who had seen it knew that. Holding onto Terry's arm, looking beautiful in her bespangled yellow-gold silk gown, Julie was stunned by the applause and smiled nervously. Inside, she was the same shy, vulnerable girl she had been when she was working at the Silver Bell, Nora knew, and all this attention and hoopla was hard for her to take. Her eyes no longer had that spacey look, but she seemed extremely edgy. The tranquilizers must have worn off. Jim sipped his drink, gazing at her with eyes that betrayed his deepest emotions.

"Is she gonna be all right?" he asked as press and photographers swarmed around Julie.

"She's tougher than she looks," Nora told him. "She's had to be in order to survive."

The party was festive indeed. The film was a surefire hit, and Nora was hugged and congratulated by dozens of people, several of whom she didn't know. Jim finally managed to secure them a booth and bring plates of food. Nora saw Carol talking with a lean, handsome older man with silver hair, warm blue eyes and a pleasant smile. He was quite tall, over six feet, very distinguished in his superbly tailored tuxedo, and he seemed fascinated by Carol. Nora recognized him at once. He was Blake

Dougherty, screenwriter-turned-producer, with a number of prestigious movies to his credit and his own production company. He had been around for a long time and was one of the most admired men in the industry. Catching Nora's eye, Carol waved, said something to Blake Dougherty and then joined them at the booth.

"Anything going on there?" Nora inquired.

"Mr. Dougherty was just telling me how much he admired some of the movies I did in France."

"He seemed to be admiring *you* a great deal, too."

"Don't be silly, Nora. Blake Dougherty is a happily married man."

"And I hear his wife is very ill. He ask you for a date?"

"Of course not. Stop playing Cupid, darling. Is this my drink, Jim? Do let me have it."

"Feel free," Jim said.

"What did Hedda want?" Nora asked.

"Blood. Not mine, fortunately. She wants to do a feature article on me, and I agreed to give her an interview next Thursday. She promised me that if Louella got to me first I'd regret it till the day I died."

"Someone ought to poison them both," Nora observed.

"I had hoped to get a chance to visit with Julie," Carol said. "It doesn't look like that's going to be possible tonight."

"No one's had a chance to visit with her," Jim said sullenly. "The goddamned press hasn't given her a moment's peace since she got here."

"Nora, baby!" Terry Wood exclaimed, coming over to their booth. "Well, it looks like we did it, doesn't it? Looks like we've come up with one great big lollipop of a hit. When're you gonna get off your keister and start writing me another blockbuster? When're you gonna stop mooning around over Larry Loser and get on with your own career? You need an office, you need a secretary, you need an expense account—anything you need, you just let me know. I want another Nora Levin novel to put on the big screen."

"I'm flattered, Terry, but I haven't got another idea yet."

"Idea? You need ideas? I got files fulla ideas. Look, doll, let's you and me get together for lunch next week, okay? I'll have my secretary set it up and give you a call. We can't have a

tremendous talent like yours goin' to waste. Ah, here comes our little star!''

Smiling at well-wishers, looking a bit desperate, Julie made her way over to the booth, an eager photographer in hot pursuit. As she reached the booth, he snapped another picture, the flash-bulb blinding them all.

"Please," Julie begged. "No more. You've taken dozens already. Please just let me visit with my friends for a while in peace."

"Just one more, Miss Hammond! Just one more!"

The photographer aimed the camera directly into her face and pressed down on the button. Julie winced as the silver-blue flash exploded. Jim leaped to his feet, grabbed the camera, hurled it to the floor and gave the photographer a brutal shove that sent him reeling. There was shocked silence all around as the photographer regained his balance, saw his wrecked camera and moved toward Jim with blazing cheeks and fists at the ready.

"You son of a bitch! That camera cost me—"

"No problem! No problem!" Terry Wood cried cheerily, throwing his plump arms around the photographer, holding him back. "Just a little accident, nothing serious. We'll buy you another camera. We'll buy you two! Go get yourself another drink, fellow, okay? I gotta girl I'm gonna introduce you to at the studio tomorrow. One of our shapeliest starlets. She'll let you take her picture any way you want it. Know what I mean? You come see me tomorrow, and we'll set it all up and get you your new cameras. Okay?"

The photographer nodded a surly agreement and stalked away, glaring angrily at Jim over his shoulder.

"Nice going, Burke!" Wood snapped. "Just a little accident, folks!" he merrily assured everyone nearby. "No big deal. Nothing to write home about. Everybody enjoy themselves!"

Tears were streaming down Julie's cheeks. "Please take me home, Terry," she pleaded.

"Sure, baby. Sure. It's been a big evening, and you've had a little too much excitement. Come on, we'll leave right now. Smile for the people, baby. Let 'em see how happy you are."

The producer led Julie away. Nora finished her drink in two swallows.

"I think I've had just about enough festivity for one eve-

ning," she announced. "I'd like to leave, too. Is that all right with you, Carol?"

Carol nodded and, as one of Romanoff's minions hastily cleared up the debris of the broken camera, Jim escorted them out of the restaurant and gallantly handed them into the limousine. They drove to the Beverly Hills Hotel, and Nora remained in the limousine while Jim walked Carol to her bungalow. A few minutes later they were on their way to her apartment building. Beverly Hills at night was like a glittering jewel box ashimmer with lights. The pain began to gnaw at her again, and Nora sat silently in the backseat as the sleek limo cruised the short distance with silken ease.

"Sorry I was such rotten company tonight," Jim said as he walked her to the heavy glass doors.

"I couldn't have made it without you, love."

"Is there any hope for me, Nora?"

"I don't know, Jim. She's very fond of you. She's going through a rough time at the moment, and I—I just don't know."

"In the meantime, I've got one terrific friend in you," Jim said, striving for a light touch. "Sure you don't want me to come up with you? Sure you don't wanna fuck?"

"Will you give me a rain check?"

"Most reluctantly," he said.

"Good night, love. Thanks a million."

"Night," he said.

He pulled her into his arms and kissed her lightly, affectionately on the lips as the doorman pulled open one of the huge glass doors. Nora watched Jim walk back to the waiting limousine and then she shook her head and moved on inside. James was sitting on one of the beige sofas across the lobby, beneath the gold-and-bronze macramé wall hanging. He stood up. He was wearing snug black pants and white shirt and dark-blue tie and a gray corduroy jacket. He looked terribly upset. He also looked repentant. Nora moved toward the elevator and he intercepted her, his smoke-gray eyes full of anguish.

"I've been waiting down here for over an hour," he told her. "The doorman wouldn't let me go up to your apartment."

"I must remember to tip him for that," she said.

"Look, Nora, I don't know what to say."

"Then maybe it would be best if you didn't say anything at all."

Her voice was crisp. He was distraught. Nora could see that. He loved her. She could see that, too. He was afraid, for she had never been cool and remote before. She'd been hot-tempered and venomous and once she'd even broken a plate over his head, but she had never been composed like this, as though he were a stranger. She stood there in her tea-colored satin gown, looking at him with icy indifference and that scared him. If only he knew how she longed to throw herself into his arms and tell him it would be all right. Julie and Carol weren't the only ones who could act. She had picked up a pointer or two herself along the way, and they stood her in good stead now.

"I didn't mean to say what I said, Nora."

"I'm sure you didn't," she replied. "I'm sure it all just slipped out in the heat of emotion."

"That's right. I was upset. I didn't mean to say any of it."

"You didn't mean to say it, but that's how you feel, James. If you didn't feel that way the words would never have come to your lips."

"Okay. Okay. I don't care for your writing. Is that a crime? I think you write crap. I resent your success. Does that make me a monster? I'm human, and human beings have flaws. I suppose I have more than my fair share of them, I've never pretended to be perfect, but—you're the grandest thing that ever happened to me. I *love* you."

"I know you do."

"You love me, too."

She nodded, still cool, still composed.

"So come back to Malibu with me. I—I'll make it up to you. I know I'm hell to live with, but I'll try, Nora. I'll try to do better and show my appreciation and not be such a bastard and—come back, Nora."

"Not this time, James."

He looked as though someone had just handed him a death sentence.

"It isn't going to work," she said, and her voice was kinder now. "Both of us know that, James."

"We'll *make* it work," he protested.

Nora shook her head. She remembered the good times, the tender moments, the laughter and exhilaration when James was in a good mood, and she remembered the magnificent sex, but it wasn't enough. It wasn't enough. She hadn't written a single

word since she'd been with him. Her entire life had revolved around James, around his moods, and she knew this couldn't continue if she was to survive as an individual and as a writer.

"No," she said. "For the past year I've been living your life, James. It's time I got back to living my own."

"You *love* me."

"That's what makes it so goddamned hard," she told him.

She stepped over to the elevator and pushed the button. He followed her, desperate now.

"You're *ending* it? Just like that?"

"It'll be okay, James. Eventually you'll find yourself some sweet, submissive young thing who will be content to sit at your feet and gaze at you in awe and pour oil on the flames of your genius. She'll probably enjoy it. I'm not cut out for it. It's altogether too taxing."

"That's unfair. You know I don't ask you to—"

"I'm very tired, James. It's been a rough day. Why don't you just go on home and leave me be."

"I'm not leaving without you."

"I'm afraid you'll have to."

"Nora—"

There was desperation in his voice and anguish in his eyes and she almost broke down then. She almost gave in and listened to her heart instead of her head, but the elevator doors opened with a soft swoosh then and saved her from herself. She stepped inside the elevator and looked at him with sad eyes and then she pushed the up button and left him standing alone as the doors closed. It was the most difficult thing she had ever done in her life.

15

South Medford, New Hampshire, was a beautiful little town near the Maine border, peaceful, serene, quaint, the perfect location for filming *Jerico's Castle*, and Meadows Inn was undeniably charming and comfortable, but Julie loathed the town and loathed the inn and loathed the script based on the sensational best-seller about adultery, incest and lesbianism in a small New England village. She didn't want to play Valerie Novack, even if it was a plum role every young actress in Hollywood had campaigned for. The role was very intense and very dramatic, with another surefire Academy Award nomination, and Julie knew it was going to be even more emotionally draining than her role in *Impulse*, just completed four weeks ago. She had fought against the role and the studio had informed her she would take it or take suspension without pay, so here she was in New Hampshire, in the downstairs lounge of the inn, and the bartender was a doll, a real sweetheart, patiently listening to her tale of woe even if it *was* after midnight and all his other customers had long since departed.

"—didn't want to play another heavy role, I told them, give the part to Yvette Mimieux, she'd be marvelous and she's dying to do it, let me play something lighter, let me do a comedy, let me, please, please let me have a couple of months off, I'm exhausted, but I'm not a human being, you see, not any longer,

I'm a commodity, a moneymaking machine. I'm the hottest young actress in Hollywood right now, did you know that? You don't believe me. Read Louella. Read Hedda. Read *Life*. I was on their cover last month, and mine is the most stunning screen debut since Ingrid Bergman made *Intermezzo* and I'm sure to win the Oscar for *The Slipper*. Read *Life*. There's bound to be a copy around here somewhere. I'm luminous and magical, but I'm also very modest and unassuming, no temperament and no pretensions, as sweet and natural as the girl next door. One more. Pour me just one more, Joe. That's your name, isn't it? Joe? All bartenders are named Joe."

"It's late, Miss Hammond, and I think perhaps—"

"Set 'em up, Joe. I have an innocent, virginal quality like young Jennifer Jones in *Song of Bernadette* and it shines through no matter what role I may be playing, and that's why the studio doesn't want the public to know about my son. I have a son, his name is Danny, he'll be four years old in January, and it'd blow my image if the public found out about that, found out their virginal, luminous Julie had been married for over five years and fucked by her husband for four and a half of those five years and gave birth to a son. We have to keep it hush-hush, and that's why Danny isn't here with me, too many people from the press snooping around film locations. Hedda knows, of course, and so does Louella, but Hedda and Louella are well paid by the studios to keep their mouths shut about certain things. I miss him, Joe. We've only been here for two days, and I miss him dreadfully and he can't understand why Mommy's in New Hampshire and he's still in Hollywood with Hannah. Just one more. Don't be a bastard. I know I'm a little tipsy, but I'm not disturbing anyone, am I? Am I making a spectacle of myself? Am I driving away your paying customers with my obnoxious behavior and foul language?"

"Of course you're not, Miss Hammond, but—"

"You're supposed to be open until one o'clock and it isn't one yet so set 'em up, Joe. I need some rest, I told them, I need a couple of months off before I start another film and they said you gotta contract, sweetheart, you're gonna play Valerie No-vack or you're gonna go on suspension startin' right now. Look at all we've done for you. You're a fucking star. One movie in release and you're already a fucking star. Thousands of girls'd give their left boob to be where you are so stop bitching and

show a little gratitude. Pour me my drink and make it snappy, big boy. I love that line. I used it in a play I did in New York, off Broadway. I played a raucous hooker. Nobody was worried about my image back then. Nobody cared whether I'd been married or was living in sin or selling it on the street corner. My performance was all that counted. I hate Hollywood. I don't want to be a fucking star. I want to be with my son. I want to rest. I need some rest, Joe. I need another drink, too, so be a sweetheart and pour me just one more.''

"Please, Miss Hammond—''

"Problem, Steve?'' someone asked.

"She's had a little too much, Mr. Jensen. I don't think she needs another one. She hasn't made any ruckus or caused any problems but she's been drinking steadily since eight o'clock. All those other Hollywood folks went up to their rooms over a couple-a hours ago, but I can't persuade Miss Hammond to call it a night.''

Julie whirled around on her stool to see who Joe was talking to and looked up into the bluest pair of eyes she'd ever seen. The man was very tall and had a lean, muscular physique and thick dark-blond hair and looked like some Viking warrior incongruously dressed in gray corduroy slacks and a powder-blue sweater with white-and-gray patterns across the chest.

"When'd they hire you?'' she asked. "You're not playing Anson Wentworth, you're not playing the high school principal, and, don't take offense, but you're a bit too old to be playing one of the football players who rape me. Oh, I bet you're one of the stuntmen. There's that big fight scene in the gymnasium, they're going to shoot it next week, and—''

"Why don't you let me take you up to your room, Miss Hammond?''

"Jesus, you're just like all the rest of them, aren't you? You think just because a girl works in the movies she's got the morals of a mink. You're gorgeous, Mr. Stuntman, but I don't fuck strangers. I don't fuck anyone. Haven't you read *Life* magazine? I'm an old-fashioned girl. If you want to get laid, I suggest you go knock on Loni Danton's door. She may be a bit long in the tooth but she's still a glamorous star and I understand she'll fuck anything that isn't nailed down. I'm surprised she hasn't appropriated you already.''

The man smiled. Those blue, blue eyes were full of amusement. He wasn't as young as she had first assumed him to be. That ruggedly handsome face had a battered, lived-in look. He must be pushing forty, but he was in superb condition. He'd have to be to be working in stunts.

"Tell you what," she said, "I won't fuck, but I will buy you a drink. I could use a little company. Joe's all right, but, well, to be perfectly frank, he's a crashing bore. No fun at all. Stingy with the drinks, too. He thinks I don't know he's been watering them down."

"You'd better let me take you up to your room."

"You don't give up, do you? I might be a little tipsy, but don't think I don't know what you're after. Shove off, sweetcakes. If you keep bothering me I intend to call the manager of this dump."

"I *am* the manager of this dump," he told her. "Lund Jensen, at your service."

"Lund Jensen? What kinda name is that?"

"Norwegian," he said.

"You're Norwegian?"

"My grandparents were. I'm one hundred percent American, Yale graduate, served my country valiantly in Korea, found I wasn't cut out to be an engineer, went back to school, took a course in hotel management, came back home to South Medford and became manager of this dump. The former owners decided they couldn't take another New Hampshire winter and retired to Florida and made me a good offer and I now *own* this dump as well."

"You expect me to remember all that?"

"I don't expect you to remember any of this, Miss Hammond."

"I'm not that drunk, Mr. Lund."

"Jensen," he corrected her. "Lund's my first name."

"It's a very silly name," Julie told him. "So you're throwing me out of the joint?"

"I'm graciously escorting you to your room, as befits mine host. Are you going to come peacefully, or do I have to sling you across my shoulder and carry you?"

Julie drew herself up with great dignity. She climbed down off the stool, stumbling quite badly. Lund Jensen caught hold of her arm, holding her up. He had very large hands. He was a very large man, very muscular, but he was lean, and he looked wonderful in his sweater. He looked kind, too. She decided to be friendly and let him help her up the stairs. Nothing so modern as an elevator at Meadows Inn. The stairs were very old and there was a tricky turn halfway up and she didn't want to fall flat on her ass.

"I'm not really a lush," she confided as he led her out of the lounge.

"I'm sure you're not, Miss Hammond."

"I'm just so unhappy, you see. My little boy's back home in Hollywood and I—I miss him dreadfully. I don't get smashed like this very often, I promise you."

"I'm sure you don't."

They started up the stairs and her legs suddenly felt like water and everything began to blur. Edges and outlines seemed to grow fuzzy and colors seemed to melt together and grow hazy. He held her arm firmly and curled a strong arm around her shoulders, holding her, and she grew dizzy and knew she wasn't going to make it. They neared the tricky turn and Julie closed her eyes and felt his arm tightening and the haze turned black and the next thing she knew she was in her bedroom, sitting on the bed, and he was standing there in front of her holding her shoulders.

"We made it," she said.

Her voice seemed to come from a long distance. He was standing there beside the bed, yes, and he was holding her shoulders, she could feel his fingers digging into her flesh, but he looked all fuzzy, a blur of blue sweater, a blur of dark-blond hair, a face with fuzzy features and blue, blue eyes peering down at her with grim intensity.

"I guess I'm out of it," she said.

"I guess you are."

"You must think I'm awful, an awful person. I'm not. I'm not, not really. I miss my son, I miss my Danny, and I didn't want to do this movie. I get very involved with every role I play, you see, that's the way I work, I have to identify very closely, it has to come up from within me, and Valerie's going to be very demanding. She has an affair with her illegitimate half brother without either of them knowing they're related and she gets pregnant and her mother makes her get an abortion and then she's raped by two football players, and—I have to *feel* all those emotions, I have to experience all that—"

"I don't think you'd better talk anymore, Miss Hammond. You'd better try to get some sleep."

"Sleep. Yes. Bathroom."

He helped her to her feet. She stumbled into the bathroom and pulled open the mirrored door of the medicine cabinet over the sink and groped for the bottle of pills and the pills rattled as she tried to pry off the lid and suddenly he was there beside her, so big, filling the room it seemed, and he grabbed the bottle out of her hand and cursed and shook his head and then saw the other bottles on the shelf and cursed again and took them, too, and Julie began to pound on his chest with her fists.

"I've got to have my pills! I can't sleep without them! You've no right to take them!"

"I don't intend to have a corpse on my hands in the morning," he informed her.

"I've got to sleep!"

She was sobbing now, and he wrapped his arms around her and held her close and tight and rocked her and she rested her cheek against his broad chest, feeling the soft nap of the sweater, feeling his warmth, feeling secure as his arms tightened even more and he murmured words that were very gentle and came from a long, long distance. He took her back into the bedroom and sat down on the bed with her, holding her still, and she tried to talk, tried to tell him how sorry she was for causing so much trouble, but the words were trapped in a black void and she couldn't make them float to the surface. He continued to murmur soothing words she couldn't understand. He was so warm, so strong, so gentle, a wonderful man, not a stuntman, no, he wasn't with the picture. He was . . . Julie couldn't remember who he was but he was there and she was safe and that was all that mattered.

Julie woke up the next morning feeling like death. She knew now just what the expression meant. She had never drunk so much in all her life and, oh God, she never would again. She promised herself that as she struggled into a sitting position. She was under the covers. She was wearing her thin blue nightgown and nothing else at all. How had that come about? There had been a man. He . . . he had brought her up to her room, and . . . Julie frowned, trying to remember, and then she groaned as someone knocked loudly on the door. The door opened and a plump, cheery maid came bustling in with a tray

holding coffeepot and cup, cream and sugar, a rack of buttered toast and a slim crystal vase with a single pink rose.

"Who—" Julie moaned. "I didn't—what time is—"

"It's seven-thirty," the maid said brightly.

"Seven-thirty? Oh Jesus," Julie said. "I was supposed to be downstairs an hour ago."

The maid nodded briskly. "That director fellow, Mr. Stevens, he was downstairs in the lobby with Loni Danton and them other Hollywood folks. They were waiting for you. Mr. Jensen told Mr. Stevens you were feeling a bit under the weather this morning and would be a little late."

"Jensen?"

"Lund Jensen, the manager. Mr. Stevens wanted to send a doctor up here to your room but Mr. Jensen said he'd already attended to that, said you'd be fine in a couple of hours and would join them then."

"Lund Jensen," Julie said.

She began to remember, and she felt even worse.

"He's the one sent me up with the coffee. The rose was his idea, too. We all of us love working for him. Couldn't ask for a better boss, though he can be stern when he has to be. I remember the time that new bellboy stole a watch from one of the guests' rooms, and—"

"Thank you," Julie said. "You may go now."

"My pleasure, Miss Hammond."

The maid departed and Julie drank the whole pot of coffee, remembering everything, and the humiliation was almost as bad as the throbbing headache. He must think she was one of those stereotype Hollywood basket cases living on alcohol and pills. He had sent a rose. The rose was his idea, the maid had told her. Julie set the tray aside and went into the bathroom. All the bottles of pills were gone. He had taken them with him, the bastard. No problem. They'd be easy enough to replace. But what was she going to do this morning? She had to have something to get her started. Didn't she? Did she? There was a time not so long ago when she never even took an aspirin unless it was absolutely necessary. She could use an aspirin right now. She could use several. She took a long hot bath and somehow, God only knew how, she was able to report for work by nine-fifteen.

Although it was only four short blocks away, a studio car

drove her to the location. They were shooting in front of the lovely old white clapboard church with its tall gray steeple and narrow windows. Four huge aluminum studio vans were parked nearby and there was a crowd of onlookers. Everything was set up, the area around the church a veritable jungle of cables and cranes and cameras. The extras were in costume. Loni Danton was wearing her yellow linen dress and smoking impatiently, her blonde hair carefully coiffed and lacquered with spray. She shot Julie an angry look. Loni Danton had been a big, big star throughout the forties and early fifties, a rotten actress but the personification of Hollywood glamor, as celebrated for her scandalous love life as for the glossy MGM epics in which she appeared. There had been too many scandals, too many innocuous Technicolor bombs, and her star had long since begun to tarnish. Loni was bitter about playing a mother role, bitter about her billing—"And Loni Danton as Martha Novack"—and bitterly resented the young actress who was getting all the attention *she* used to command.

"Here the little slut is!" she snapped. "Glad you could make it! We've been waiting for over two hours."

"Lay off, Loni," the director warned.

John Stevens was a grizzled veteran in his mid-sixties, though he looked a decade younger. Tall and rangy, with cynical gray eyes and floppy sand-colored hair generously streaked with gray, he'd been around since the silents and he'd seen them come, seen them go. He had no illusions whatsoever about this crazy, fucked-up business or the people in it, but he felt a special fondness for this little girl who clearly had no business being in pictures. She was already on the pills, already hitting the booze. A real pity.

"You feeling all right now, Julie?" he asked. "You look a little pale. Think you can make it?"

Julie nodded. She was rushed into the makeup van and makeup was applied and her hair combed and styled, color heightened with fine gold dust. She was dressed in the peach organdy dress with puffed sleeves and eyelet lace inset at the neckline and when they were finished with her she looked like a demure seventeen-year-old high school student. She felt fifty, her head still throbbing painfully when she left the van. The director patted her arm. Loni gave her a nasty look. Lights and microphone were tested, and shooting eventually began. It was a very simple

scene. Valerie and her mother came out of the church and stopped to speak to the minister and Phil Sherman stood nearby, hands thrust into his jeans, looking at Val. She smiled at him and Martha, her mother, pulled her aside and said, "Stay away from that boy, Valerie. Do you hear me? Stay away from him!"

It took them four hours to get it on film.

They broke for lunch, and that afternoon they shot the scene where Valerie and Phil wandered into the woods, hand in hand, exchanging shy looks and clearly very much in love, both unaware that they are half brother and sister—Phil being the bastard son of Valerie's long-dead father. They were shooting a mile outside of town, the trees in glorious autumn splendor, gold and yellow, bronze and brown and blazing orange. It seemed to take the crew forever to get everything set up, and Julie smoked half a pack of cigarettes, lighting one right after the other. Biff Norris, who played Phil, was twenty-nine years old, made up to look a convincing nineteen. He was a good-looking, personable youth who had been at the studio for years, never graduating to leading roles but dependable, competent and steadily employed in secondary roles like this one. He and Julie made a very attractive couple as they walked into the woods. Shot after shot was ruined because of an airplane flying overhead, a shadow falling across their faces, a microphone buzzing, a generator failing. Julie still felt like death and it was hard to look innocent and dewy-eyed, but they finally got the scene in the can before the sun went down.

She didn't see Lund Jensen that evening. She had dinner in her room. She didn't go down to the lounge. She hadn't remembered to speak to John about replacing the pills, she had been too busy, and she didn't know how she was going to get any sleep without them. She studied her script, restless, edgy, and she finally undressed and climbed into bed, damning Lund Jensen for his high-handedness and yet . . . she remembered his strength, his warmth, and she knew he had taken the pills for her own sake. Had he not been there, she might indeed have taken too many, drunk as she was, might indeed have died. That thought frightened her badly. Lund Jensen may well have saved her life last night. She remembered his face, that battered, lived-in look, those blue, blue eyes. He was a stranger and she didn't ever want to see him again, she was much too ashamed, but he had cared what happened to her. He had held her close and

rocked her in his arms until she finally went to sleep . . . Julie slept, without the aid of alcohol or pills, and when she woke up at six the next morning she felt remarkably rested.

Loni Danton was a total bitch during the next three days, trying to determine just how far she could go, just how much she could get by with. She hated her wardrobe. It made her look much too old. She had no intention of wearing that hideous blue print, even if Edith Head had designed it. Stevens explained that she was playing a prim shopkeeper with only a modest income and she wouldn't wear velvet, wouldn't wear pearls, this wasn't MGM, goddammit. She didn't like her lines. There weren't enough of them. Loni wanted to dominate every scene she was in and she bloody well tried to do just that, fussing with a handkerchief, brushing her skirt, patting her lacquered blonde tresses, doing everything she could to distract attention away from Julie. Stevens called her hand time after time.

"I'm an actress," she snapped. "I happen to be giving a performance."

"One that could mercifully be called inadequate," he retorted. "Lay off the cheap tricks, Loni. They're costin' us money."

She gave him an icy look and stalked off to her dressing trailer. Stevens wearily called for a break.

"Check this broad out," he advised Julie. "Learn how not to conduct yourself on a film set. Her problem is she's not getting fucked enough. Loni Danton without a young stud on tap is a very unhappy lady."

On the afternoon of the third day Loni threw a royal tantrum and icily informed everyone that she was a star, she didn't need this shit, she was walking off the picture. John smiled a beatific smile and told her that Eleanor Parker was waiting in the wings, ready to fly out at a moment's notice, she'd been his first choice for the part to begin with. Loni burst into tears and sobbed that no one understood her, giving a much better performance than she had ever given on the screen. After that she was as meek as could be, taking direction like a dream. A handsome young lighting technician in tan windbreaker and tight jeans caught her eye and she invited him into her trailer during the next setup.

"Problem solved," Stevens said. "Guy's a hustler from L.A. I had him flown in yesterday. It'll add a few thou to the budget, but it'll be worth it if it keeps that bitch in line."

"I—I hope I'm never like that," Julie said.

Stevens looked at her for a long moment and then shook his head. "It happens to the best of 'em eventually, sweetheart," he said bitterly. "Give yourself a few more years."

Two days later Julie had her first opportunity to really explore the town. They were filming the fight scene in the gymnasium that afternoon, and her presence wasn't required. She left Meadows Inn after lunch and strolled leisurely down tree-lined streets with lovely old-fashioned houses, golden leaves drifting down as she walked along the sidewalks, past the green with its old cannon, past the red-brick library and the post office and newspaper office. The shops on South Medford's main street were all fascinating, very up-to-date but retaining an old world charm. She bought postcards in the drugstore and had a chocolate soda in the ice cream parlor. The people here were friendly and warm and didn't make a big deal over her. They all recognized her, she could tell that, but they were much too polite to intrude on her privacy. She had never seen so many friendly smiles.

It was after three when she started back to the inn, and as she passed the hardware store a tall blond man in tan denims, tan turtleneck sweater and brown nylon windbreaker stepped out, carrying a bag of nails. Julie stopped, and she felt a blush tinting her cheeks. He nodded and gave her a warm smile. She was seeing him clearly for the first time, without an alcoholic haze, and he was as good-looking as she remembered, rugged and real. She didn't know what to say. She finally decided it would be better to say nothing at all, and she walked on past him. Lund Jensen fell into step beside her.

"Going back to the inn?" he inquired.

Julie nodded, keeping her eyes averted.

"Mind if I walk partway with you?"

"It's a free country, Mr. Jensen."

"You remember my name," he said.

"I remember everything," she retorted. "I suppose I should thank you for what you did."

"It's not necessary. That wasn't the first time I've helped a tipsy guest up to her room. I seriously doubt it'll be the last. By the way, just in case you've been worrying, I had Mrs. Gibbons come up and get you into bed. Mrs. G. was working night shift."

"I haven't been worrying," she said coldly.

"Look, Miss Hammond, if I'm bothering you, just say the word and I'll fall back and leave you alone."

"You—you're not bothering me. I'm just—I'm just horribly embarrassed. I made a terrible spectacle of myself, and you must think—"

"I think you were very unhappy because you were missing your little boy so you drank a bit too much. I took your pills because I didn't want you to croak on us. Things like that give the inn a bad name."

"I'm sorry to have caused you so much trouble. You were—very kind."

"I try to make all my guests feel secure. So, tell me, what happens after you have your abortion and get raped by the two football players? Do you commit suicide?"

Julie shook her head. "I let myself be seduced by the exotic and attractive female art teacher who's been casting soulful glances at me throughout the movie. As the final credits roll we leave together for an uncertain future in New York."

"I really must read that book," he said. "I understand the people living in the author's hometown raised quite a ruckus when it came out, wanted to run her out of town on a rail for depicting them in such lurid colors. What do you think of *our* little New England town?"

"I think it's enchanting," she told him.

"Very few rapes," he said sadly. "Not much incest or lesbianism, either, but it'll do in a pinch. We've got excellent schools, several churches, a fine community theater, our own symphony orchestra. If things get too dull, Boston and New York are only a few hours away by train."

"It—it must be wonderful living in a place like this," Julie said wistfully.

"It is. That's why I came back. It gets pretty lively around here during the skiing season. Our slopes are among the best in the country, and there's a great influx of colorful, fun-loving types—a real winter carnival atmosphere. That explains all the inns and lodges you see nestled among the hills."

Leaving the main street, they turned onto one of the tree-lined streets Julie had strolled down earlier. There was a gentle breeze, and gold and yellow leaves whirled in the air like scraps of bright confetti and then drifted slowly to the ground. It was one of the most beautiful sights Julie had ever seen. Jensen saw the look

of awe in her eyes, and he was silent, pleased that she was moved by the beauty, rather surprised as well. The sensitive young woman walking beside him this afternoon bore little resemblance to the drunken, babbling woman he had taken upstairs last week. He felt very protective toward her. He felt emotions he never thought he would feel again after Nicole died. That had been ten years ago, a long, long time, and he had assumed those particular emotions were long since beyond him.

"It's so beautiful here," Julie said.

He nodded, a dark-blond wave spilling over his brow.

"And peaceful," she added.

"Most of the time," he agreed.

"These houses—"

She stopped to look at one in particular. Beyond a white picket fence and spacious lawn stood a large two-story Victorian house, pale yellow with white shutters and white gingerbread trim around the front verandah. It had the mellow patina of age and recalled a more gracious era when there were close families and time to savor life and serenity in which to do so. How lovely it would be to live in a house like this, she thought.

"It was built in eighteen eighty," Lund told her, "by an immigrant who came here to establish a textile mill. The mill was closed almost thirty years ago, but the house still stands. I'm rather fond of the place."

"It's my favorite," Julie said.

Lund opened the white picket fence. "Want to see inside?"

"I—" She hesitated, looking doubtful.

"It's all right." He smiled. "I grew up in this house. It belongs to me now."

"I—I thought you lived at the inn."

"I keep rooms there, but I spend as much time as possible here at home. A place this big, this old, keeps me pretty busy—" He held up the bag of nails. "I'm always having to do repair work. I'm currently putting down new flooring on the back porch. Put in new electrical wiring only a few months ago."

"You did it yourself?"

"Working on the house is great therapy, and I suppose I'm what people call handy. There's some lovely antique furniture inside, a nice collection of porcelain. Want to have a look round?"

Julie still hesitated. She looked into those blue, blue eyes and

she knew the invitation was perfectly innocent. He was an honest man, an admirable man, and unlike those people who surrounded her in Hollywood, he had no ulterior motives. She longed to see the house, and she longed to spend more time with him as well, but instinct told her it would be unwise.

"I'm sorry," she said. "I have a very important phone call to make. I'd better get back to the inn."

"I see."

He covered his disappointment with a friendly smile.

"I wonder if you'd let me take you out to dinner tonight?" he asked, and until that moment he had had no idea he was going to say those words. "There's a marvelous restaurant up in the hills, best cuisine in the county."

"I—I really don't—" She paused, looking pained.

"I understand," he said quickly, covering. "An important Hollywood actress like you, a hayseed like me—I shouldn't have asked. Forgive me for being so presumptuous."

Lund Jensen was a Yale graduate, a veteran of Korea. He was virile, good-looking, an intelligent and capable man who lived in this small town by choice. He was hardly a hayseed. He made the men of Hollywood seem like so many glossy automatons.

"What time would you like to leave?" she asked.

"Seven all right?"

"Seven is fine. I'll be waiting for you in the lobby."

"Fine."

"Formal?" she inquired.

"Semi. I'll be wearing a suit."

"Till seven," she said.

There was absolutely no reason for Julie to be nervous, but she was as she came downstairs that evening. She had spent an inordinate amount of time dressing, finally selecting a black silk frock completely overlaid with cobweb-fine black lace, the narrow sleeves off the shoulder, the skirt full, a black velvet band at the waist. Carol and Nora wore haute couture with great flair, but Julie always felt insecure, as though she were pretending to be something she wasn't. Would he think she looked ridiculous? Would he think she was trying to put on airs? The desk clerk gave her an admiring look as she passed. Loni Danton and her handsome young stud were on their way up to her room. He paused on the stairs to glance back at Julie, his look admiring,

too. Loni gave his arm a savage jerk, leading him on up the stairs.

It wasn't quite seven. Julie put her black velvet wrap over the back of a chair and took cigarettes and lighter out of her small black satin evening bag. She felt like a fool. She had no business being here. She had an early call in the morning. She should be upstairs studying her lines. She smoked rapidly, nervously, panic rising. She wouldn't know how to act. She wouldn't know what to say. She should never have agreed to go out with him. She crushed out her cigarette, and there he was, looking quite impressive in a beautifully tailored black suit, white shirt and dark-blue tie, a black overcoat draped casually over his broad shoulders. His thick dark-blond hair was neatly brushed. He smiled warmly and handed her a single long-stemmed red rose.

"You look very beautiful," he told her.

"So do you," she said.

Lund Jensen chuckled. Julie blushed.

"I shouldn't have said that," she confessed. "I—I'm afraid this is all very new for me."

"In what way?"

"I've never dated before. I—there was a friend in New York, we went out together a lot, but—it was as friends. The studio has arranged several evenings with carefully selected escorts who took me out to parties or clubs so we could be seen together and photographed, but—this is new."

"What about your husband?"

Julie lowered her eyes. "We—we never dated," she said, and then she sighed. "I'm talking too much, making a fool of myself already. I'm terribly shy, you see, and—are you sure you want to go through with this?"

"Quite sure," he said gently.

He helped her with her wrap and, holding her elbow lightly, led her out to the old black Cadillac waiting at the cub. He opened the door for her, helped her inside and then climbed behind the wheel, starting the motor. It gave several ominous coughs before catching, and Lund shook his head.

"I hope it runs. I usually drive a station wagon. This one is usually in my garage, gathering dust. I had it cleaned and polished this afternoon."

"I'm honored."

"Couldn't expect a Hollywood star to ride in a battered station wagon with a dented fender."

"I'm not a Hollywood star—that's all studio hype. Loni Danton is a Hollywood star. I—I'm just a working mother, and I happen to work in films."

They drove slowly out of town. Julie was at a loss for words. She lighted another cigarette. They wound their way up one of the hills and by the time she finished her cigarette he was pulling up in front of a sprawling lodge with red and blue neon lights making hazy reflections on the blacktop in front. She put out her cigarette and he helped her out of the car. The night air was cool and crisp and laced with woodsy smells. There were very few other cars, and although she could see dim lights inside, the place looked almost deserted. Lund led her inside. Jukebox music was playing softly.

"The place is quite lively during the season," he told her. "I prefer it like this. Ah—here comes André."

"Lund!" the maître d' exclaimed. "It's been a long time."

"Sure has," Lund said. "This is Miss Hammond, André. We want your very best table."

The maître d' smiled and led them into a huge, dimly lighted room, candles burning in red glass bowls. There was a dance floor, several dozen tables and a bank of plate glass windows that looked out over the hills and the sky beyond them. Only four of the tables were occupied. The jukebox was an old-fashioned one, soft colors glowing and changing in the semidarkness as the music played. André led them to a table near the windows.

"Drinks?" he inquired.

"A scotch for me," Lund told him. "Julie?"

"A glass of white wine, please," she said.

André left, and Julie felt very ill at ease until a personable young waiter in white jacket brought their drinks. She longed to gulp the wine down and order another immediately, but she didn't, of course. She sipped it slowly and pretended to be attentive as Lund talked about running the inn. When the waiter returned to see if they wanted another drink, she shook her head, indicating her half-full glass. He handed them menus, and Julie scanned hers in the light of the candle and finally asked Lund if he would order for her, as he knew what was good. He nodded, placed the order and then looked at Julie as she nervously lighted a cigarette.

"Make your phone call?" he inquired.

"I made several. The studio is going to have a fit when they see my phone bill. I called my agent, and then I called the head of the studio. I told him that I was sending for my son and if they didn't like it, they could find someone else to do this picture. My—I'm afraid my voice was shaking, and he was very concerned, very amenable. He said they only wanted me to be happy and if having Danny here would make things easier, by all means send for him, the studio would pay all expenses."

"Bravo," Lund said.

"He wasn't thinking of me, he was thinking of the picture. They'd be in a terrible bind if I walked, particularly after all the advance publicity they've generated about my winning this much-coveted role. He gave in to me about Danny because he had no choice, but I've no doubt he'll find a suitable punishment for me later on."

"Jesus. Are they really that bad?"

"They think they own me, you see," Julie told him. "I'm a piece of property, not a human being. They tell me where to live, what to wear, what to say and who to see, and—it's as if I no longer have any free will. When I signed the contract, I agreed to give them my services, not my soul. They pay me extremely well, and I give them the best of my ability as an actress, but I don't intend to give them my soul as well—not any longer."

"They can only push you as far as you let them," Lund said.

"I—I realize that. That's why I defied them about Danny. After I spoke to the head of the studio I called Hedda and told her Danny was coming here and the press was sure to find out about it and if she wanted an exclusive, I would give it to her. So Hedda's going to write an article about Julie Hammond's marriage and divorce and child. I'm sure it'll be a hokey sob story full of maudlin sentiment and pathos, but at least the truth will be out and I'll no longer be forced to hide my son's existence."

"When is he arriving?"

"Day after tomorrow. Hannah's bringing him out, and of course she'll stay to watch after him while I'm filming. I hope you'll have room for them."

"No problem," Lund said. "I'll move you into our family

suite. It has three bedrooms, a large sitting room, even a small kitchen. There'll be plenty of room for all three of you."

"You're very kind," Julie said.

Lund smiled. "Not necessarily," he said. "The studio's paying the bill, and I intend to charge them an arm and a leg."

"Do that," she urged.

"Hey, you actually smiled. You have a lovely smile. Ah, here comes our food. Wait until you taste the lobster thermidor. You're going to love it, I promise."

His voice was rich and husky and gentle, a reassuring voice. She felt secure with him, felt safe, and much to her surprise she found herself talking to him about her marriage over dinner. She told him everything, and it seemed so natural to be talking to him this way, so right. Both refused dessert and over coffee Lund told her about his own marriage. Her name was Nicole, and they had married during his last year at Yale. Two years in Korea had followed, and Nicole had waited for him in their apartment in Boston. On his return, he tried to establish himself in engineering, but competition was tough and jobs weren't easy to come by. Nicole stood by him, encouraging him. She even took a secretarial job herself in order to help make ends meet. One rainy afternoon Nicole left her office early and was standing on a corner waiting for the red light to change when a speeding driver braked violently and lost control of the car. It skidded and leaped the curb and Nicole was killed instantly.

"How—how dreadful for you," Julie said quietly.

"It was pretty hard for a while," he confessed. "I gave up on engineering, it had never really interested me that much to begin with. I took courses in hotel management and then I left Boston for good. I came back home to South Medford and moved into the old house with my father—my mother had passed away some years before. I was lucky enough to get on at Meadows Inn, assistant manager at first, then full manager. My father died a couple of years later, leaving me the house and a substantial amount of money. When the Mabes decided to sell out and move to Florida, I was able to buy the place."

"You like running the inn, don't you?"

He nodded. "It's interesting work, and there's a lot of variety, a lot of people around. You—" He hesitated a moment and then he looked into her eyes. "You don't have much time to feel lonely."

But you are lonely nevertheless, she thought. She wanted to reach across the table and take his hand. Lund gave her an apologetic smile and said he was sorry, he hadn't meant to bore her with his life story. Julie told him she was flattered he felt he could talk to her. They looked at each other in the flickering light of the candle, the rest of the room hazy with shadows, romantic music playing softly on the jukebox, and both of them felt it happening. Both of them were reluctant to acknowledge it for what it was.

"Hey," he said lightly, "everyone else's gone. It must be getting late, and I imagine you have to get up early in the morning."

"I do indeed," she confessed.

Both of them were quiet during the ride back to the inn, and Lund escorted her up to the door of her room. Julie took her key out of her purse and handed it to him and Lund unlocked the door. They looked at each other without speaking, both knowing now, both afraid to examine the feeling too closely or put it into words. Julie still had the rose. She smelled it and smiled and he put his hands into his trouser pockets, feeling suddenly gauche. It had been so long, so very long. He had forgotten what to do. Should he kiss her? He wanted to. Would she be offended? She seemed to be waiting, too.

"Thank you for a lovely evening," she said finally.

"It was my pleasure. I hope we can do it again."

Julie didn't say anything. She looked into his eyes for a moment and then she stepped inside and quietly closed the door. Lund Jensen stared at the door and called himself every kind of fool for thinking there could ever be anything between them. She was a Hollywood actress, he ran an inn in a small New England town, he would probably only see her in passing until the film company departed for good. Tonight had been an evening out of time, one of those rare evenings that had nothing to do with reality, that could never happen again. They would probably both be embarrassed in the morning.

Jensen arranged to have all her things moved into the family suite the following day, but Julie didn't see him. Nor did she see him the day after. She assumed he had been too busy to get in touch with her. She had been very busy herself. Maybe he didn't care to see her again. She had talked too much, and he undoubtedly thought she was an imbecile, opening up like that to a

stranger, revealing so much about herself. She'd never even talked to Jim so openly, so intimately. Their evening together already seemed like a dream, something that had never happened at all, and it was probably just as well. Danny and Hannah were arriving this afternoon, and that was all that mattered.

Stevens rearranged the shooting schedule so that she could have the afternoon off and be on hand to meet them when they arrived. She was waiting in the lobby when they came in, Danny bustling about and bursting with excitement, Hannah exhausted, exasperated and ready to commit murder. Danny babbled on about the plane ride, the lady in uniform had given him a toy, they'd eaten ice cream and cake and he'd thrown up. A great big black car met them when they landed, and they'd driven forever and seen lots and lots of colored trees and he didn't think they'd ever get here, it was so far, and could he have a puppy? He wanted a puppy more'n anything and Hannah said he'd have to talk about it with her. Hannah was an old meanie, no fun at all, wouldn't let him go up and see the pilot and help him fly the plane, made him keep his seat belt fastened and said a very naughty word when he threw up on her.

"I'm gonna kill him," Hannah said firmly. "They'll give me the chair for it, I know, but I'll fry *glad*ly."

"Yah-yah-yah," Danny taunted.

"Danny!" Julie scolded. "Come on, let's go see our rooms, and then we'll order dinner. It's almost six o'clock."

"I want more cake!"

"I'm gonna do it," Hannah promised. "I swear it. One of these days he's gonna push me too far and I'm gonna do it. Those stairs look tricky. Give me your hand, lamb. It's a hot bath and bed for you right after dinner."

Danny may have been a trial to Hannah during the trip from California, but he was a joy to the staff of Meadows Inn. The desk clerk, the switchboard operator, the bellboys, the maids were all enchanted by him and within two or three days he had them all eating out of his hand. The switchboard operator let him sit in her lap and "help" her with the calls, and the cashier let him count the pennies. The bellboys played games with him during the slack hours. The maids let him ride down the halls on their pushcarts. The Plaza might have its Eloise, but Meadows Inn had its Danny and even Hannah had to admit that he wreaked very little damage. He did slide down the bannister

once or twice, busted his little buns good and proper, served him right, and it was true he'd been caught tossing his red rubber ball against the wall in a back corridor, but never once did he pour water down the mail chutes. He was astonishingly angelic, captivating one and all, particularly the owner-manager.

Julie was working extremely hard. There was quite a lot of tension on the set and she was under a great deal of strain, and when she came in after shooting it was Lund said, Lund this, Lund that from her son and that marvelous Mr. Jensen from Hannah. Mr. Jensen took us for a ride in his station wagon, I didn't see anything wrong with it and Danny was growing awfully restless being cooped up here all day. Lund bought me an ice cream. Lund took me to the rock shop and I got this pink rock, see, it's called quartz. I hope you don't mind, but I let that marvelous Mr. Jensen take Danny fishing this morning, he assured me it would be perfectly safe in the boat and Danny would wear a safety jacket. Mommy, Mommy, I caught a *fish*, a *big* one, well, at least I helped Lund pull it in. He's gonna have it gutted and cleaned and I'm havin' it for dinner. He's really quite thoughtful, Julie, took me to Stitch 'N Sew so I could get some new purple yarn and flew kites with Danny this afternoon.

Julie fully intended to search Jensen out and thank him for being so attentive and kind, also to make sure that Danny wasn't making a nuisance of himself, but she left so early in the morning, and when she came back in the late afternoon, she was exhausted, thoroughly depleted. They were filming the rape scene and it had taken three days already. It was extremely complicated, with close-ups, reaction shots, a great deal of action and dialogue, all shot in tiny bits that would be pieced together in the editing room. They were shooting it seven miles from town, in the woods and by a small lake, and everything that could go wrong did. Steve Murdock, who played Bill, was twenty-one years old, a former child star on television and a thorough pro, but Todd Burton, who played Eddie, was a husky, handsome youth of nineteen who had never made a movie before, winning this role only because he was the special protégé of an important producer at the studio. He meant well and he tried hard to follow directions, but getting a believable performance from him seemed almost impossible.

The crew was on the edge of the lake, lights, cameras, microphones all set up, half a dozen trailers and huge vans parked

all around. The trees were blazing with color. The water was still. During the past three days they had done all Julie's scenes with both boys, the scene where Steve Murdock roughed her up and tore her dress, her flight through the woods with Todd in hot pursuit, just one scene remaining now, plus close-ups and reaction shots. They had been trying to get this last scene in the can for hours now. Try though he might, Todd couldn't seem to do anything right. John Stevens was at the end of his rope as they waited for Todd to have his makeup repaired.

"Anyone else would've been replaced days ago, when he kept blowing all his lines in that scene with Steve," he grumbled, "but you don't replace the producer's boyfriend. Kid has good intentions, but he can't act for shit."

"He's very good-looking and George says he photographs like a dream," Julie said. "Be patient with him, John. Everyone has to start somewhere."

"Not in a four-million-dollar Cinemascope production, they don't. Christ! Okay, sweetheart, I'll keep my cool. We'll shoot it again. Are you all right? He hurt you?"

Julie shook her head. Although they had carefully choreographed this particular bit, Todd, like most amateurs, was over-enthusiastic, and he invariably got carried away and was much too rough. It wasn't intentional. She knew that. He was a very nice boy, and with his thick brown hair and dark-blue eyes he did indeed photograph like a dream. She smiled at him as he returned from makeup, wearing tennis shoes, a white football jersey with purple number and very tight jeans. The bodice of Julie's blue dotted swiss frock was torn and her face was smeared with dirt and her hair was tangled. Todd gave her an apologetic smile as he approached. There was a long wait as one of the lights was replaced and a technician fiddled with the microphone dangling overhead.

"Sorry I keep blowing it, Miss Hammond," he said politely. "I'll try to get it right this time."

"You're doing fine, Todd. It—it's a very difficult scene. Just forget you're acting. Just—just pretend you're really going to rape me."

A blush tinted the boy's cheek. Although built like a quarter-back and extremely virile, he was as shy as she was.

"All right!" Stevens yelled. "Microphone working okay? The light ready? Look, Todd, Steve's already mauled her and torn

her dress and she got away from him and has been running through the woods and you've been chasing her, getting angrier by the minute, hornier, too. She pauses for breath by the edge of the water and you come tearing out of the trees and you seize her and drag her away from the water and throw her down on the ground. 'You're not getting away this time, baby,' you say and then you fall on top of her. That's all. You got it? Think you can do it?''

Todd nodded nervously. They took their places, Julie standing at the edge of the water, looking anguished, looking terrified. There was a shadow across her chin. They had to readjust the lights. Thirty minutes later they started filming. Todd came tearing out of the trees, looking angry, looking horny, and he stumbled and fell and John yelled "Shit!" and then yelled "Cut!" There was mud on Todd's jeans. He had to change into another, identical pair. Julie had a cigarette, a nervous wreck by this time, trying not to show it. They started again and Todd seized her arm brutally and jerked her away from the water, leering, eyes full of lust, and then he hurled her roughly to the ground and placed his hands on his thighs and looked down at her and leered some more and shouted, "You're gettin' away from me this time, baby," and John Stevens threw his hands up and said "Cut" and said "Let's try it again" in a sepulchral voice.

The scene was traumatic enough in itself. Julie had to psych herself into it, had to become a terrified young girl about to be raped, and the constant retakes and long waits made it much worse. As the afternoon wore on, she felt her nerves snapping, felt the tears coming on, and while that was very good for the scene, while it suited her character's state of mind, it was emotionally demolishing. God, she needed something. She needed something badly. Why hadn't she replaced the pills? What was she trying to prove to herself, doing without them all this time? They did the scene again, and, really getting into it now, Todd almost pulled her arm out of its socket when he grabbed it and knocked the breath out of her when he shoved her to the ground. Tears sprang to her eyes. She started to sob hysterically and it was great, it was marvelous, she was giving a fantastic performance and Todd yelled "You're not gettin' away this time, baby" very convincingly and then he leaped on her, forgetting the choreography, forgetting the head stuntman's careful instructions and demonstration on how to fake it, how to fall without hurting her.

Julie screamed as the full weight of his body landed on top of her.

"Cut!" Stevens yelled. "Great! It's a take! Good job, Todd. You finally came through and you did it with flying colors. Julie, sweetheart, you were nothing short of sensational!"

Todd climbed off of her and scrambled to his feet and reached down to take Julie's hand. She shook her head violently and covered her face with her hands and continued to sob. Stevens yelled for the doctor and then she felt his long arms wrapping around her, pulling her up, holding her tight. "I'm sorry," she sobbed. "I—I'm all right. I'm—" And she continued to sob and he was leading her away, leading her to her trailer, helping her inside, and she looked up through her tears and saw his face, white and frightened, and she knew she must get hold of herself but she couldn't seem to stop sobbing. The doctor came and she flatly refused to let him examine her. She was all right, she was just upset. Please, please go away, she begged. He asked if she was still taking the tranquilizers and she shook her head and he said he'd get another bottle immediately, stronger this time. He left and Julie finally managed to control the sobbing. John was still very white, still very frightened.

"I'm all right now," she said in a trembling voice. "It was just—the scene was so intense, and—"

"I'm revising the shooting schedule," John told her. "We'll shoot the reaction shots later, back home in the studio if we have to, but you're not doing any more work on the rape scene now. We've got enough footage already and the rest of it's in the can except for the shot of Steve pulling his jeans up—we don't need you for that."

"You don't have to—"

"I'm going to shoot Loni's meeting on the green with the high school principal tomorrow, she'll raise holy hell but that's just too bad, she's been loafing for four days now. After that I'll shoot Carolyn's scene out on the school lawn where she's examining her students' sketchpads and glances up and sees you going past in your gym shorts—we'll shoot your bit later on. You're taking a week off, sweetheart."

"That isn't neces—"

"I'll shoot around you. We won't lose a single day. You've been working your ass off, giving one hundred percent. You need some time off. Can't have you cracking up on us."

Julie gave him a grateful look. Stevens gave her a hug. The tears still spilled slowly down her cheeks, but the awful trembling inside had stopped now. John left and the wardrobe woman came in to help her out of the tattered dotted swiss and into her street clothes. Bathed in light, looking replete and satisfied, Steve Murdock was pulling his jeans up in front of the camera as the studio car drove Julie away.

Hannah was appalled by the sight of her when she got back to the inn. She put her to bed immediately.

Julie stayed in bed for the next two days, getting out only to take scalding hot baths. Her body was stiff and sore and there were several bad bruises. The baths helped. So did the tranquilizers and the sleeping pills the doctor had sent up to her room. Hannah watched over her like a mother hen, seeing to her every need, and Danny was an angel, behaving himself splendidly, sitting on the edge of the bed, gazing at her with woeful eyes and stroking her hand. She smiled and told him she would be fine, she just needed to rest. Reassured, he ran off for a ride down the hall on Nettie's cart and a game of Fish with Mike. On the third day Julie felt much better and decided she would lunch downstairs. Hannah fretted, said she still looked weak to her, said she'd better not overdo it. Julie ignored her and continued to dress. Room service was sending up hamburgers and french fries for Hannah and Danny, but she wanted to get out of the suite for a while.

She felt remarkably fit as she went downstairs. Her body was still a bit sore, but the stiffness had gone and the bruises had already begun to fade. It was rather early, barely eleven-thirty, and the restaurant was almost deserted. Like the lounge, it was charmingly rustic in decor. A waiter showed her to one of the tables and Julie explained that she hadn't had breakfast and asked if it would be possible for her to have an herb omelet. He said, "Of course," and inquired if she'd like a drink while she waited. Julie hesitated a moment, longing for a glass of cool white wine, but strength of character prevailed and she told him she'd love coffee. She lighted a cigarette and was gazing at the old-fashioned prints hanging nearby when Lund Jensen came over to her table.

"Hello there," he said.

She looked up, startled by the sound of his voice. He was wearing a soft wheat-colored turtleneck sweater and tan slacks

and looked like a rugged Viking god with that thick blond hair and those vivid blue eyes. He smiled, extremely casual, as though their evening together had never taken place.

"I hear you've been ill," he said. "Feeling better?"

"I wasn't really ill, I—I was just exhausted and—yes, I'm feeling much better now."

"Overwork?"

"In a manner of speaking. We filmed the rape scene. One of the boys got carried away, forgot we were acting and roughed me up a bit—not intentionally. He was very perturbed, sent flowers and candy and a charming note thanking me for helping him with our scenes together."

"You get it all filmed?"

"There are some reaction shots and we were supposed to shoot a brief scene of my crying and pulling my dress back up after the boys have left, but I think John plans to cut to the forest ranger bringing me into the house. We're shooting all the interiors back in the studio, except for those in the gym."

"Making movies must be a very complicated business," he said.

"It is."

The waiter came with a pot of coffee. He brought two cups. Lund hesitated and then asked if he could join her for a few minutes. She nodded, her manner cool. She remembered how close she had felt to him that evening, how much she had talked, how intimately. He probably thought she was a fool. He hadn't made an effort to see her again in all this time. Julie felt very ill at ease, but she was glad to see him nevertheless.

"I want to thank you for being so kind to Danny," she said. "He and Hannah have been telling me about—about all the things you've done for them. I hope Danny hasn't been a nuisance."

"Not at all. He's been a delight."

"He's extremely fond of you."

"At least I've made points with one member of the family," he said.

Julie looked up at that. She saw his eyes and all that was in them. Lund lowered his eyes, pouring coffee for both of them. Could . . . could she have been wrong? Could their evening together possibly have meant as much to him as it had to her? Julie was confused.

"So when do you go back to work?" he inquired.

"Not for three more days. They're shooting around me fo
the rest of the week."

"I—uh—I don't suppose you'd like to go to a fair tomorrow?'

"A fair?"

"A county fair, over in Maine. They have rides, harness races,
junk food, interesting booths, handicrafts for sale—I thought
Danny might enjoy it. You might find it amusing yourself."

"I'd love to go," she said.

"You would?"

"I've never been to a fair."

They left at ten o'clock the next morning in Lund's battered
station wagon and drove over a mountain and were in Maine and
at the fairgrounds before eleven. Hundreds of people were already milling about, simple, unsophisticated people for whom
the fair was an annual event, and, in her yellow sweater and
brown-and-yellow checked skirt, Julie felt wonderfully carefree
and at ease. No one recognized her. No one stared. Danny went
into ecstasy when he saw the merry-go-round and the ferris
wheel, and they rode on both, Julie enjoying herself almost as
much as he did. Lund smiled at her as they went around on their
painted horses, he on a dappled gray with Danny in front of
him, Julie on a chestnut with orange ribbons. They had chili-
burgers for lunch and then ice cream sandwiches, and, as they
strolled leisurely among the booths, it seemed natural for Lund
to curl his arm around her shoulders.

Julie bought a beautiful handmade patchwork quilt, she
couldn't resist it, and she also bought homemade apricot preserves for Hannah and some lovely lace-edged handkerchiefs to
send to Nora and Carol. Danny spotted a giant panda sitting on
a shelf at the shooting gallery and fell in love with it and Julie
told him it wasn't for sale, you had to win it. Lund grinned and
paid his dollar to the man behind the counter and took the gun
and began to fire at the pink ducks parading on a platform in
back of the booth. He was wearing jeans and a loose soft brown
suede jacket over a tan jersey, and with the sun burnishing his
dark-blond hair he looked about twenty, Julie thought. Lund
held the gun steady and squinted his eye and fired and a loud
ping accompanied each shot. He hit every duck, handed the gun
back to the man and, grinning, gave Danny the panda he had
won. Danny was thrilled and felt they should all have some
cotton candy to celebrate.

Julie was fascinated by the harness races. Lund encouraged her to select a horse and place a bet. She hesitated, studying the animals carefully, finally finding one she liked and betting ten dollars on him. She lost, but it didn't matter. The horses were beautiful, the races were exciting and it was nice to be sitting in the shady grandstand after walking all over the grounds. They spent almost two hours watching the races, and then Danny had to have a candied apple and ride the dodge-em cars. Julie begged off but stood watching as Danny and Lund tried their best to commit mayhem in the tiny cars, banging each other with demonic glee. She was smiling the whole while, and it suddenly dawned on her that she was having fun. She couldn't remember ever having enjoyed herself more, and the man in the flapping suede jacket was responsible for it. She and Doug had never done anything like this. She and Doug had never had fun. There had been no time for anything so frivolous.

It was after four when they abandoned the cars and joined her. Danny was exhausted and beginning to grow fretful, and Julie suggested they leave. Danny protested vehemently, but Lund swung him up onto his shoulders and let him ride piggyback to the parking lot. Lund unlocked the station wagon, having stored the panda and Julie's purchases in back earlier on. Danny curled up in Julie's lap as they drove away and was sound asleep by the time they started going back over the mountain.

"Would you like to go out to dinner tonight?" Lund asked.

"I—it's been a wonderful day, Lund, but I'm really too tired to dress up and—"

"How 'bout a home-cooked meal then? At my house."

She was surprised. "You cook?"

"Not well," he admitted, "but I do have a lot of groceries. I don't suppose *you* cook?"

"I'm a marvelous cook."

"Really? I don't believe it."

"I guess I'll just have to prove it to you," Julie said.

They left a still-sleeping Danny at the inn with Hannah, and Lund drove to the grocery store to pick up a few extra items. Julie went in with him, helping him select ingredients for the salad, and then he stopped by a liquor store and bought a very expensive bottle of wine. The St. Moritz Bakery was the last stop. Lund paid a small fortune for a Black Forest cake and carried the white cardboard box out to the station wagon very

carefully, as though he were afraid it might explode. Julie smiled. In many ways he was still like a little boy, and she found that very engaging.

The kitchen in the gracious old yellow-and-white Victorian house was large and old-fashioned, with a glazed red-brick floor and a huge butcher block table. Copper pots and pans hung on one beige wall, and Julie was relieved to see that the kitchen had all the modern conveniences, right down to an electric can opener. Everything was sparkling clean. Mrs. Henderson was responsible for that, Lund explained. She came in four times a week, kept the house in order and him in line. Julie let him chat while they put away the groceries and then shooed him out of the kitchen. She cleaned the lettuce and put it in the crisper and took two chickens out of the freezer. Was there cooking wine? Yes, she found a bottle in the cabinet. Herbs? A whole rack of them on the counter, next to the cookie jar.

For the next two hours she was in heaven. Lund changed into a pair of old khaki pants and a sweatshirt with YALE emblazoned across the chest. He lighted a fire in the living room and, while delicious smells wafted out of the kitchen, set the dining room table with the good silverware and the Spode china that had been his mother's most cherished possession. Julie stepped to the doorway in a wraparound apron and announced that everything was ready just as he was lighting candles in the porcelain candelabra. He helped her bring the food in, then helped her remove the apron, his hands lingering on her waist for a few seconds as she brushed a wisp of hair from her cheek. The meal was superb, the best he ever had, Lund declared. He suggested they take the rest of the wine into the living room. Julie cleared the table and put the food away, but Lund wouldn't let her do the dishes. Mrs. Henderson would take care of them in the morning, he informed her, leading her into the living room where the fire burned cozily, spreading flickering yellow-orange reflections over the polished hearth. Julie took her glass of wine and curled up in the comfortable wingback chair, and he perched on a footstool nearby.

"It's been a wonderful evening," she said wistfully.

Lund nodded in agreement, gazing at her in the firelight. She was beautiful, he thought, fragile and vulnerable yet full of hidden strengths. He wanted to hold her, to protect her, to love her for the rest of his life. He said none of these things, of course.

"Even better than our first evening together," she added.

"That was special, too," he said.

"It—it was for me," she told him. "I was afraid—I thought—when you didn't try to see me again, I thought you must think me a fool because I talked so much, told you so much about myself."

"And I thought you must think me a rube because I live in a small town, because I'm not famous, because I run an inn instead of doing something glamorous and exciting like most of the men you must know."

"I don't know all that many men," Julie said quietly. "The one I'm with at the moment suits me fine."

She looked up. Their eyes met.

"Something has happened," he said.

"I know."

"So—what are we going to do about it?"

Julie looked away from him, staring into the fire for a long moment before answering.

"I suppose we'll be sensible," she said.

"I suppose we must be," he agreed tersely.

"I'm sorry, Lund."

"You're right, of course. We must be sensible. We're not moony adolescents. We're intelligent adults. You have a seven-year contract and a career. I have the inn and my life here."

There was bitterness in his voice, sadness, too. He stood up and took the iron poker and jabbed at the fire and then he put it down and sighed and jammed his hands into the pockets of his khaki pants, the loose sweatshirt bunching up.

"I guess I'd better take you back to the inn," he said.

Neither of them spoke during the short drive back to the inn. Lund parked in front and came around to open her door. He took her hand, helping her out, and Julie looked at him and wanted to feel his arms holding her, wanted to rest her cheek against his chest and feel his warmth and his strength and forget reality, if only for a few precious moments. She thanked him politely for a beautiful day and a lovely evening and asked him not to see her up to her room.

"Very well," he said. "We'll be sensible, Julie, but—I want to see you again."

"Of course," she agreed.

"As often as possible. Until you leave."

She nodded. "I—I'd like that."

He took hold of her shoulders and looked into her eyes and started to kiss her and then controlled himself and let go of her and jammed his hands back into his pockets. He stepped back, his blue eyes full of anger, though she knew it wasn't directed at her. It was directed at life, at fate, at circumstances. She told him good-night in a very quiet voice and hurried into the inn. Neither of them slept much that night.

Lund took Julie and Danny for a picnic in the hills the next afternoon and it was relaxing and they were very careful to keep things light. The next day was Halloween and Julie and Lund went to a shop in town and bought Danny an oilcloth goblin costume and a mask and a large cardboard jack-o'-lantern with wire handle and that night they took him trick-or-treating, sauntering from house to house in Lund's neighborhood. Danny was beside himself with excitement, racing up to front doors, banging loudly, yelling "Boo!" and "Trick or treat, money or eats!" and beaming behind his mask as his jack-o'-lantern was filled with delicious goodies Hannah would be carefully doling out to him in days to come. As the three of them strolled along beside a low picket fence, Lund on one side of Danny, Julie on the other, it occurred to her that anyone not knowing them would undoubtedly take them to be a family. Julie put the thought out of her mind as quickly as possible, letting go of Danny's hand so that he could rush up to yet another old Victorian house with porch light burning.

Julie went back to work, and she was kept frantically busy. They shot the scene where she was walking around the side of the schoolhouse in her blue dotted swiss dress, books held to her bosom, when Steve Murdock intercepts her and asks if she'd like a ride home. They shot her climbing into the car beside him and Todd leaping in and slamming the door, trapping her between them. It took two days to get all the bits right. Julie did a complicated scene in front of the dress shop with Loni, the two of them arguing, Loni finally slapping her in the face. Loni slapped her quite hard, and she did it several times throughout the afternoon as take after take was spoiled for one reason or another. Julie rubbed cold cream on her cheek that evening and begged off when Lund arrived to take her out to dinner.

They saw each other three or four times a week, and Lund continued to take an active interest in Danny during the day,

aking him fishing again and buying him treats. The leaves were
beginning to fall fast now, and John Stevens drove them all even
harder as they had several more scenes to complete. A large
contingent of press people arrived to interview the stars and
watch location filming for a couple of days, this all arranged by
the studio and driving John into a frenzy. Julie had Thursday
off, as they were shooting scenes with Phil Sherman and Carolyn
Jones and wouldn't need her. Lund had planned an outing, but
at the last moment she had to cancel and spend the day being
interviewed by *Parade* magazine and posing for a cover photograph. Lund said he understood, but she could see the bitter
disappointment in his eyes. The man from *Parade* asked her
pointed questions about her early marriage and divorce, and Julie patiently repeated the sudsy, bittersweet story of thwarted
young love Hedda had concocted when she "broke" the story.
She refused to let them take pictures of Danny.

Loni chose that particular evening to have a very public
knockdown, drag-out brawl with her young stud in South Medford's most exclusive restaurant. He socked her brutally in the
eye. She stabbed him in the arm with a fork, and he seized her
by the throat and choked her almost into insensibility before a
waiter pulled him off her. A writer from *Newsweek* happened to
be in the restaurant and learned that Loni's lover was actually a
"paid companion" over twenty years her junior. The stud was
shipped back to L.A. on the next available plane and a distraught
Loni, in dark glasses, a colored scarf wound around her neck,
told the press it was all a wretched misunderstanding. The ensuing scandal quickly assumed front-page proportions, and the
studio was thrilled as it meant tons of free publicity for *Jerico's
Castle*. For cast and crew it meant even more hard work as they
had to double up and shoot around Loni until her hideously
swollen black eye healed sufficiently to be concealed by makeup.

As the end of filming drew near, the tension increased. Julie
was under a great deal of strain, but she forged ahead and managed to avoid another nervous crisis like the one she'd had filming the scene with Todd. Lund was largely responsible for that.
After a frantic, exhausting day of filming, he would take her to
some quiet, out-of-the-way diner and they would sit in a booth
and talk, sharing a wonderful closeness, and that helped her
come down and relax and shed the tensions of the day. Lund
was very much in love with her, Julie knew that, but he was

tactful and circumspect and careful never to step over the invisible line they had drawn. Yet that something unspoken was there between them at all times, and neither could deny it.

"You look low tonight," he said one evening. "Anything wrong?"

Julie shook her head. "Just—strain. They shot Phil's suicide last week while I was being interviewed, and today we did the scene where I find his body in the woodshed. It—it wasn't easy."

"He's your half brother in the film, right?"

"And Loni breaks up our affair and makes me get an abortion and the people in Jerico find out about it and I get a bad reputation and—and that's why the football players take me out to the woods. Phil beats the bejesus out of them in the school gym when he finds out about it and then goes out to the woodshed behind his house and—and today I found the body."

"It's a crazy way to make a living," Lund said.

Julie nodded and Lund ordered another glass of wine for her and then began to tell her about an amusing incident in the kitchen at Meadows Inn and she forgot the emotional stress of the scene and began to relax. This was so much better than taking pills and sinking into oblivion. What was she going to do when she no longer had him to help her through the strain? She didn't want to think about that. It would be over all too soon.

And on a morning in the second week of November she was in makeup and costume by eight and it was a brilliant sun-spangled day and they were in front of the castle perched on a hillside overlooking the town. A huge gray stone edifice with several turrets, it had been the home of an eccentric Hungarian countess for almost sixty years and had recently been purchased by two interior decorators from New York who planned to turn it into a hotel. It made the perfect Jerico's castle of the title. Julie smiled as Carolyn Jones joined her, looking very exotic and attractive in her severe black shift and multicolored costume jewelry. A brilliant, vibrant young actress many critics had compared to a young Bette Davis, Carolyn was playing the art teacher and doing it with consummate skill. This was the last scene to be shot on location and everyone was eager to get it over with as quickly as possible.

By nine-fifteen everything was ready. Julie crushed out her cigarette and she and Carolyn took their places. John gave them a few final instructions and moved away and they began filming

a few minutes later and everything went beautifully. The two young women strolled up the slope and paused at the appointed spot and gazed up at the castle and Carolyn explained to Julie that it had been built by a famous nineteenth-century sculptress who had lived here with her female companion, the strong castle walls protecting their love from the eyes and the condemnation of those who might pry. Some love had to be protected by castle walls, she added. They exchanged a look and Julie nodded sadly and Carolyn took her hand and John yelled "Cut!" and it was over, they had done it in a single take and everyone was jubilant.

Hannah had already started packing when Julie got back to the inn at twelve o'clock. Lund picked her up at one and they had lunch at his house, neither of them wanting to be around other people on this, their last afternoon. Lund had prepared a salad and sliced cold turkey and ham and bought a bottle of fine white wine, but Julie merely toyed with her food and Lund gazed at her with sad resignation. There was to be a gala party at one of the restaurants that evening. Julie had to attend and she had asked him to come with her, but Lund had refused, knowing he would feel awkward and out of place. She was leaving early the next morning. This was the last time they would be together, and it wasn't working. Both of them were miserable and pretending not to be and it was a terrible strain. Julie finally said she really should get back to the inn to help Hannah with the packing and Lund nodded, actually relieved. He suggested they walk as it was only a short distance and such a lovely day.

The last leaves of autumn were falling as they moved slowly down the sidewalk. Lund told her that the first snow would be here soon and the skiing season would begin and South Medford would be transformed into a merry winter playground. Julie said she wished she could be here to see it. Lund said he would love to teach her how to ski. Julie said that would be great fun, and then she fell silent, afraid to say any more, afraid her voice would tremble and all the things she really wanted to say would come rushing out. They turned the corner and started up another street, gold and yellow leaves scuttling along the sidewalk before them.

"I suppose you'll be very busy once you get back," he said.

"I will be. We'll be filming all the interiors. John hopes to finish by the tenth of December, but—you never can tell. It may take longer."

"I'm going to miss you, Julie," he said.

"I—I know. I'll miss you, too."

"I love you," he said.

"Lund—"

"I love you, and I want to marry you. I know I can't. I know it's out of the question, but—I'll always be here, Julie. I'll always love you. If ever you should need me, if ever—"

He broke off before he made a complete ass of himself. He didn't say anything else until they reached the inn. They stopped in front of the steps, and Lund thrust his hands into his pockets, rocked back on his heels and affected a casual air he was far from feeling. He was wearing his soft brown suede jacket and a dark-blond wave had tumbled over his brow.

"Look," he said, "I—uh—I have a few errands to run in town. I'm not coming in with you. I guess this is it. No point in my seeing you off in the morning, things will be frantic enough as it is. Give Danny a hug for me, will you? I'm going to miss him, too. Take care, Julie. Please take care of yourself."

"I will," she promised. "Good-bye, Lund."

"Good-bye," he said.

"And—thank you," she added. "Thank you so much for everything."

Julie turned then and hurried on into the inn. She went to the party with John that night and forced herself to smile, forced herself to act festive, and the grief inside was like a living thing eating away at her. She drank far too much champagne and when she woke up at dawn she had a wretched hangover and the bustle and confusion of leaving was even worse than she had anticipated. Danny was impossible, he didn't want to leave, and Hannah was frantic over a suitcase she was convinced one of the bellboys had misplaced. At seven-thirty they were climbing into the car that would take them to the airport and she hoped against hope that he had changed his mind, that he would show up at the last moment and see them off. He didn't. Danny was crying as they drove out of town and Julie held him in her arms, held him tightly, fighting to hold back tears of her own. It was over now. She would never see him again. She would just have to forget Lund Jensen, put him out of her mind completely. It was the sensible thing to do.

16

Accustomed to the damp, drizzle and cold of Paris in winter, Carol was amazed that it could be so lovely here in California in mid-January. Silvery-blond hair pulled back in a neat bun, dark glasses hiding her eyes, she was wearing a pale apricot wool shift and a matching apricot coat belted at the waist, an elegant ensemble created for her by Chanel, and it was really a bit too warm. Brilliant sunlight spilled down from a clear blue-white sky this Saturday afternoon. Most of the people strolling on Hollywood Boulevard wore no coats at all. Several of them recognized her. Carol could see their reactions, first surprise, then doubt, then certainty followed by staring. A plump matron in stretch pants and a flowered overblouse nudged her even plumper companion and pointed.

"It *is* her! I told-ja, Mabel."

"She's gorgeous!" Mabel exclaimed.

"And walkin' down Hollywood Boulevard just like a normal person. People back in Sioux City aren't gonna believe it when I tell 'em."

Carol repressed a smile. She was walking down Hollywood Boulevard just like a normal person because there were no parking places anywhere near Pickwick's and she had had to park in a lot four blocks away. There were several nice bookstores in Beverly Hills, but Pickwick's, here in *the* heart of Hollywood

proper, had the best and largest selection. Carol walked inside and removed her dark glasses pausing to examine the new releases stacked up on one of the front tables. *Assembly*, a collection of short stories by John O'Hara. She would have to buy that one, and *The Prize*, a new novel by Irving Wallace. She had met Wallace and his lovely wife, Sylvia, at a party last month and both had exuded genial charm. She and Sylvia had had a fascinating conversation, Mrs. Wallace holding her spellbound with tales about her days as the youngest fan magazine editor in Hollywood.

Carol picked up three more new books and carried them to the counter and asked the clerk if he would hold them while she browsed some more. The clerk did a double take when he recognized her, said he'd be glad to and watched as she went over to the children's section to select some picture books for Danny. That was the reason she had come, but Carol could never go into a bookstore without buying half a dozen things for herself. She picked out several colorful, amusing books she thought Danny would like and carried them back to the counter.

"Shall I ship these for you, Miss Martin?" the clerk asked as she handed him a check.

"I'll take them with me," she replied.

"You'll enjoy the new Wallace. It's his best yet. We can hardly keep it in the store."

"I enjoy all his books. His first, *The Fabulous Originals*, is one of my all-time favorites."

"Miss Martin?"

The voice was soft and husky. Carol turned, surprised. The man had silver hair and warm blue eyes and a pleasant smile. He was quite distinguished-looking and impeccably groomed in a gray suit and a subdued wine-colored tie. He was lean and extremely tall, so tall she had to tilt her head back slightly to look into his eyes.

"I thought it was you," he said.

"Mr. Dougherty. How nice to see you again."

The clerk handed Carol her package of books. Blake Dougherty handed him a copy of *Flowering Judas* by Katherine Anne Porter, and the clerk rang it up on the cash register.

"Do you read a great deal?" Dougherty inquired.

"As much as I can," Carol said. "I love Katherine Anne Porter, by the way."

He smiled, handing the clerk a bill. "You have exquisite taste. I wanted to reread these stories. It's been ages, and I couldn't find my copy. I fear it's been boxed up and stored away along with thousands of other books I no longer have room for in the house. I hope it isn't lost. It's a signed first edition. Katherine Anne wrote a special inscription."

"You knew her?"

"Many, many years ago, when both of us were considerably younger, when I fancied myself a writer, too."

Dougherty took his change and the book from the clerk, and the two of them walked out of the store together.

"I didn't know you wrote," Carol said.

"It's a deep, dark secret," he told her, "and it was a long time ago. Katherine Anne was the worldly, experienced older woman every young man should be fortunate enough to know. She gave me a lot of encouragement, but the results were hardly earth-shaking. One small book of short stories, published, I daresay, before you were born."

"I would love to read them one day."

"Perhaps I'll send you a copy. Are you in a hurry, Miss Martin?"

"Not particularly."

"I wonder if you'd like a cup of coffee. C. C. Brown's is just down the street."

"I'd love a cup of coffee."

"Let me carry that package for you. It looks heavy."

C. C. Brown's had the best ice cream in town and their hot fudge sundaes were famous, each served with a separate pitcher of hot fudge on the side, to pour on yourself. Although temptation was immense, Dougherty and Carol settled for coffee. Carol watched with envy as a waitress carried a tray of sundaes over to a group of young people in one of the booths.

"Sure you don't want one?" Dougherty asked.

"I'd love one but, unfortunately, I'm working right now and, as I'm sure you know, the cameras add a good ten to fifteen pounds. If someone wanted to do something really worthwhile they would invent a lens that made us actresses look *thinner*. We're all starving to death."

Blake Dougherty smiled and stirred sugar into his coffee. Carol had been impressed with him when she met him at the party at Romanoff's after the premiere of *The Slipper*, but she

hadn't realized just how good-looking he really was. He had lean patrician features and a deeply tanned complexion that made his thick silver hair all the more striking in contrast. His mouth was full and firm and beautifully shaped, and his blue eyes were warm and intelligent, sad as well. Carol knew his wife was suffering from an extremely rare blood disease and was now being cared for in a private clinic. She wondered if she should inquire about her condition but finally decided against it. Lolly and Blake Dougherty had been one of Hollywood's most admired couples for over twenty years, he a dynamic and innovative producer, she a renowned hostess. They were at the top of the "A" list in Hollywood society, their annual parties rivaling those of Basil and Ouida Rathbone in elegance. He was a gentleman in a town where gentlemen were scarce, but there was nothing soft about him. He exuded power and confidence and that, of course, made him all the more attractive.

"So how are they treating you at Universal?" he asked.

"They're treating me like royalty," she confessed. "I have my own bungalow, complete with kitchen, bath and sitting room—I think it belonged to Yvonne DeCarlo when she was queen of the lot. They completely redecorated it for me in my favorite colors and fabrics, and I also have a luxurious trailer on the set itself. It's a far cry from making films in France, I can assure you."

"How is the filming going?"

"Marvelously well. Edith Head has designed a fabulous wardrobe, I drip furs in every scene, it seems, and Ross is letting me keep the clothes. David Miller is directing—he's a dream to work with—and Sean Garrison is my leading man. He's wonderfully handsome and a very good actor. Faye Holden plays his mother and—and that worries me a little."

"Is Faye giving you a hard time?"

"I haven't even met her yet. She only has three scenes, but they're extremely powerful. Just one of them is with me, and we start filming it Monday. I—I'm a little intimidated by the thought of working with her. Faye Holden is a legend."

"That she is," he agreed.

"The term 'movie star' might have been invented for her. If Clark Gable was King, Faye Holden was unquestionably Queen. She started in the silents, and she's still here."

"She has tenacity, all right."

"I'm afraid she'll have me for breakfast," Carol said.

He smiled again. "Faye has done a lot of things in her day, but to the best of my knowledge she's never seriously wounded another actress—although I believe she did once stab Norma Shearer with her knitting needles. Shearer undoubtedly provoked the attack. She and Faye were archrivals at MGM back in the thirties."

"Is Miss Holden really the monster they say she is?"

"Faye's tough as nails. She's had to be. She came up the hard way, and she was never really accepted. To millions of fans she might have been queen of the movies, but to the Hollywood establishment she was always the waitress trying to pass herself off as a lady. She took a lot of snubbing back in the old days, but she's survived all her detractors and is still a star."

"Is she difficult to work with?"

"Faye's a professional right down to her lacquered blood-red fingertips. As long as you scrape and bow and indulge her every whim and acknowledge that she's the only one who knows anything about making pictures—it's a piece of cake."

"You haven't made me feel one bit better," Carol informed him.

"I'll tell you something—and it's one of the best-kept secrets in Hollywood. Faye Holden comes on like Godzilla, for whom she's frequently mistaken, but underneath that formidable exterior she's terribly insecure and has a heart of pure marshmallow."

"I'll keep that in mind," Carol said.

The smile flickered once more on those beautifully shaped lips. He finished his coffee and looked down at the empty cup, toying with it idly. His wife had been in the clinic for some months, Carol knew, in a hospital before that. It must be terribly hard on him, she thought. He was lonely, at odds, in need of sympathetic companionship, and that was undoubtedly why he'd asked her for coffee. He was interested in her as a woman, she could see that, but Blake Dougherty was a gentleman and a man of integrity, and he would never make an overt pass at another woman while his wife was living. Carol admired him for that. Friendship, yes, he might ask for that, but he would never ask for anything more under the present circumstances. He looked up at last, setting the cup aside.

"Any idea what your next film will be?" he asked.

"It's to be a comedy, as yet untitled, and the script is delight-

ful. I play Sandra Dee's prim, extremely straitlaced older sister. I take her under my wing after our parents die and am horrified by her boy-crazy shenanigans. She keeps telling me I should loosen up and enjoy life and, under her guidance, I do just that during a vacation in Palm Springs. I get drunk, do a striptease in a bar, captivate John Gavin, the family lawyer, whom I've rebuffed repeatedly during the first reel. It's witty and charmingly risqué, a soufflé that should be a lot of fun to film."

"When do they start filming?"

"In March, I believe. I'll have a few weeks off between films."

"And after the second one, you're free, right?"

Carol nodded. "I refused a long-term contract. I signed to do only two films for Universal. I'm pretty sure they're going to offer me another contract and I may well sign, but—I didn't want to be tied down, in case something more interesting comes along."

"Very wise of you," Dougherty said.

He started toying with his coffee cup again, and Carol could see that he had something on his mind. She finished her own coffee and watched his long, elegant fingers curling and uncurling around the thick white cup.

"You say you like to read, Miss Martin. Tell me, have you ever heard of a book called *Remember Dennie Lane*? It came out a number of years ago, got a few glowing reviews, promptly sank into oblivion. It's about a young girl in Texas during the depression. Her family was very wealthy, lost everything in the crash, and after their father's suicide Dennie and her older brother have to try and salvage the wreckage. Dennie's an intelligent, compassionate, extremely sympathetic character who happens to have one fatal weakness."

"Men," Carol said. "She's a nymphomaniac, driven by compulsive desires she can't control. I read the novel when I was in high school. It was beautifully written and terribly sad."

"You've actually *read* it?" Dougherty was amazed. "It couldn't have sold more than a couple of thousand copies."

"One of them was purchased by the Ellsworth Public Library. I believe I was in the eleventh grade when I checked it out. I found it very moving, and the ending was heartbreaking. I cried when she strolled across that deserted oil field and tossed her cigarette aside and the field caught fire and flames sprang up all

around her. I'm sure there was a lot of symbolism I didn't understand at the time, but—I remember Dennie Lane. The book
is still vivid in my mind after all these years.''

"It would make a wonderful film," he said.

"It certainly would," Carol agreed.

"I own the film rights," he confessed.

"Oh?"

"I bought them outright when the book came out. I've been
trying to get a workable screenplay for quite some time. I finally
turned it over to Mary Loos and Richard Sale and they've written
a magnificent script. It captures the essence of the book yet
works beautifully in cinematic terms. I'm hoping to start production in late summer."

"How exciting," she said.

"I'd like for you to read the script, Carol."

"I—I'd love to read it."

"I've been searching for the right actress to play Dennie for
quite some time, too. A couple of years ago I happened to go
to an art theater to see a movie called *And the Sea Is Blue*,
primarily because I'm an admirer of Maurice Ronet's work.
When I saw your performance as his restless, love-starved wife
I said to myself, 'There's my Dennie.' "

"I'm very flattered."

"At that point I still didn't have a working script, and then a
new project came up and I was deeply involved with it, but—I
hadn't forgotten you. When I met you at Romanoff's, I knew my
initial reactions were right. You've got all the qualities the part
requires."

The waitress came over to see if they wanted anything else,
and he shook his head. Carol said nothing more about the part.
She would indeed love to play Dennie Lane, it could be the role
of a lifetime. If Blake Dougherty still wanted her when she had
finished her commitments at Universal, he would contact her
agent. In the meantime, it wouldn't hurt for her to read the
script. Mary Loos and Richard Sale were two of the best in the
business, and if Dougherty was pleased with it, it was bound to
be superb.

He gripped her elbow lightly as he guided her through the
door. He was so tall, so elegant in his gray suit and wine-colored
tie. His thick silver hair was handsomely styled, kept that way,

no doubt, by the best barber in L.A. Carol smiled up at him as they stepped outside.

"Thank you for the coffee, Mr. Dougherty."

"Can I give you a lift?" he inquired.

"My car's in a lot just a few blocks away."

"I see. I—" He hesitated a moment, looking into her eyes. "I wonder if you might like to come to brunch tomorrow. My wife is ill and I no longer give parties, but for several years friends have come to the house for brunch every Sunday. It's a casual thing and I've kept it up even though Lolly is—even though she is no longer able to serve as hostess. Christopher Isherwood and Don Bacardy will be there, Dick and Mary, three or four others. I'd like it very much if you could join us."

"I'd love to," Carol told him, "but unfortunately I have a date."

The disappointment was clearly visible in his eyes.

"Of course," he said. "I should have realized that a young woman as attractive as you would naturally be booked up for weeks in advance."

Carol had to smile at that. Not a single male had asked her for a date since she arrived in Hollywood. She had gone to a couple of parties with Jim Burke and Nora, but that didn't count. Contrary to popular belief, men didn't hotly pursue single young actresses. They were either intimidated by the fame or, like Dougherty, assumed she would already be booked up. Many a lovely and world-famous star spent Saturday night alone, sitting beside a phone that never rang. It was not something that caused Carol much concern.

"My date is with my four-year-old godson," she confessed. "My friend Julie Hammond is in Arizona, filming a western, and because of the rugged conditions she couldn't take Danny with her. I promised her I'd stop by and see him now and then and help keep him amused. Tomorrow I'm taking him to Disneyland."

"I see."

Was she imagining it, or did he look relieved?

"Perhaps you'll come some other Sunday," Dougherty said. "It's been very pleasant talking with you, Miss Martin. If you'll permit me, I'll send you a copy of the script and maybe we can discuss it later on."

"That would be lovely."

Carol gave him her new address, and Blake Dougherty handed her her package of books. He took her hand for a moment, gripping it firmly. You've a very lovely man, Carol thought, and you're a very lonely man, too. She smiled and thanked him again, and Dougherty released her hand. He seemed reluctant to let her go. They stood there in front of the ice cream parlor for another moment and he finally smiled a sad smile and said good-bye. Carol walked on down the boulevard toward the side street where her car was parked.

She thought about the encounter as she drove home. Blake Dougherty was an important and powerful man in Hollywood, and he was undeniably attractive and appealing, but Blake Dougherty was married and he was over thirty years her senior. She would love to work with him, but she didn't intend to see him again unless it was in a professional capacity. She had worked too hard, too long to get where she was to risk it all by getting involved with an older married man, however platonic their relationship might be. Blake Dougherty wanted sympathetic companionship at this point, but Hollywood gossip would interpret it otherwise, and she couldn't afford that. Carol had sacrificed Norman for her career, and she wasn't about to jeopardize it now for a charming stranger who needed someone to help him through a difficult time.

Carol left her car in the underground parking garage and took the elevator up to the lobby. Although the studio had volunteered to help her find a house, she had rented the penthouse apartment here in the building where Nora lived. It was completely, luxuriously furnished, and when her things had arrived from storage she was able to add homey, personal touches. Carol picked up her mail and rode on up to the penthouse. She wished Nora was here now, a long, lively chat would be a great boost, but Nora had left four days ago for a month in Mexico City, where she would be gathering information for an article for *Cosmopolitan* magazine.

Putting books and mail on the coffee table, Carol removed her soft apricot coat and hung it in a closet, surprised to see that it was after five already. The sun would be going down soon, the myriad lights of L.A. springing up like multicolored jewels flashing in the night, and Carol would spend another Saturday night all alone. With Nora in Mexico City, with Julie filming a "psychological" western under strenuous physical conditions in

Arizona, with Jim busily squiring half the shapely starlets in town, there wasn't even anyone to pal around with. You're on top of the world, she reminded herself. You've finally made it, starring in a multi-million-dollar production for one of the major studios. Carol changed into a loose, comfortable lounging gown and went into the kitchen to pour herself a glass of tomato juice. Returning to the living room, she phoned Hannah and asked to speak to Danny.

"Ready for Disneyland tomorrow, sweetheart?" she inquired.

"Oh, I am, Auntie Carol. Can we ride all the rides? Can we go see the haunted house?"

"I'm game if you are. I'll pick you up at nine-thirty. We'll spend all day. What have you been doing with yourself today?"

"Nothing much," he said glumly. "I watched television for a while, but Hannah made me turn it off, said it was gonna ruin my eyes. I wanted to put on my suit and go swimming, but she won't let me go near the pool unless I've got an adult with me who can swim. She can't," he added.

"Poor baby. Maybe we'll go swimming when we get back from Disneyland tomorrow. I bought you a surprise today!"

"What is it?"

"If I told you, it wouldn't be a surprise."

"I miss Mommy," he said in a plaintive voice.

"Of course you do, darling. I miss her, too. She'll be back in just a few weeks, and in the meantime you and I will do lots of fun things."

"I wanted to see the cowboys and horses," he whined. "*I* wouldn't mind living in a crummy motel in a tacky little town and driving twenty miles in a jeep to location every day. Mommy hates it. She cries every time I talk to her. She didn't want to go to Arizona. Those meanies made her, and she only got to fly home for three days for Christmas."

"I know, darling, but—you go to bed early tonight," she said, changing the subject. "I'll buy you a pair of Mickey Mouse ears tomorrow, and you can wear them all day."

"Okay," he said, still glum. "Bye, Auntie Carol."

"Good-bye, darling."

Carol sipped her tomato juice, thinking about Julie. She had defied the studio by having Danny join her in New Hampshire and telling the press of her early marriage, thus destroying the studio's carefully constructed "image" of her as a virginal young

girl. As punishment, they had put her into the western three weeks after she returned in the role originally scheduled for Diane Baker. Carol had read the script and knew it was a grueling role indeed. Julie was playing the wife of stern, sanctimonious lawman Jeffrey Hunter, who is also the preacher in a small Arizona community. When he hangs their partner, outlaws Neville Brand and Ray Danton burn his ranch and abduct Julie. After being brutalized and abused by both men, she manages to escape, only to be rejected by her husband, who considers her sullied. In the climax of the film, Julie is trapped in a mountain cabin with her severely wounded husband. When the outlaws advance, seeking final revenge, she takes her husband's rifle and kills Danton and, when he breaks into the cabin, stabs Brand with a knife. A poor man's *High Noon*, with overtones of *Duel in the Sun*, it was violent trash that would undoubtedly fare well at the box office, but Carol knew the harsh, demanding role must be totally demoralizing to someone with Julie's sensitive nature.

Something had happened to her in New Hampshire. Carol didn't know what it was—Julie hadn't discussed it with her or with Nora either—but she had returned with a stoic resignation her friends found alarming. She was drinking more, taking more pills and, according to reports, her conduct on the set had become erratic and unprofessional. She had had a bitter fight with Ralph Carpenter, the director, did not get along with her costar and had failed to show up for work several times, claiming "nervous exhaustion." The press had learned of it, of course, and several stories had appeared, the most damaging by Miss Louella Parsons, who informed her readers that success had gone to Julie's head, that she was entirely too fond of her liquor and that her temperamental outbursts were causing serious and expensive delays in the filming of *Fury in Leather*. Louella was taking her revenge on Julie for giving the story of her marriage to Hedda, but the piece had appeared nationwide in syndication and had done considerable harm to Julie's reputation.

It was all the studio's fault, Carol knew. They should have given Julie time off after *Jerico's Castle*, but as soon as interiors were completed, they had shipped her off to Arizona to do this new film. Julie had not had a decent rest period since arriving in Hollywood, had been put into one demanding role right after another, and very few young actresses today could stand that kind of pressure. The studio had spent a fortune launching Julie

as the new Maggie Sullavan, and they didn't seem to know or care that they were destroying the very qualities they should most protect. Several of the older Hollywood greats were publicly lambasting the old studio system that had held them in bondage, Bette Davis and Olivia De Havilland among the most vocal, Kathryn Grayson and Esther Williams bad-mouthing MGM now that they were working independently. While to some this might seem like gross ingratitude to the studios that had made them famous, Carol realized that they had valid reasons to complain about their years of servitude.

A seven-year contract meant that one was completely at the studio's beck and call, a chattel, a commodity to be utilized as the studio saw fit. While it had definite advantages, it had even more drawbacks. A vital young talent like Piper Laurie could be held back, publicized as the starlet who ate flowers and put into a series of outlandish costume swashbucklers, totally wasted until she broke away from her studio and electrified Hollywood with her brilliant performance in *Until They Sail* and, most recently, in *The Hustler*. The old studio system was breaking down now, Julie's one of the last of the seven-year contracts. Carol privately wondered if she would be able to last it out without cracking up completely.

Sighing, she finished her tomato juice and picked up her mail, delighted to see a thick letter from Gaby. At least someone was doing well. Gaby had completely recovered from her morphine addiction and was leading a much quieter life, working as she had never worked before. *A Journal to Myself* had already been published in France to much acclaim and was a strong contender for the Prix Goncourt. Opening the letter, Carol discovered two thin pages and a smaller, sealed envelope. Gaby breezily informed her that the new novel was coming along wonderfully, that she had purchased an elegant town house in Paris and had met a marvelous man, a magazine publisher forty years old who absolutely adored her and was keeping her in line. He made the gorgeous youths of her past seem trivial indeed, Gaby confessed and added that a wedding just might be forthcoming in the near future. In closing, she wrote that she had discovered the enclosed photographs this past week when she had been cleaning out her desk and thought Carol might like to have them.

Carol put down the letter and slit open the thick envelope. The photographs spilled onto the coffee table in scattered dis-

array, a few of them color, the majority black-and-white. Oh God, she thought. Oh God, no. I don't need this now. I don't need to be reminded of those golden days. I've tried so hard, so long to forget, and now . . . Damn you, Gaby. You didn't do it deliberately, you thought you were being kind, but . . . Carol picked up one of the pictures and gazed at it. There she was, sitting at the table on the terrace in St. Tropez with Cecil Saint-Laurent, he looking like a chic pixie in his white linen suit, she so thin and tan, her hair clipped so short, cork trees visible in the background. Norman had been playing cards with Jacques that afternoon while she and Cecil chatted about novels, and, yes, here was a snapshot of the two of them, Jacques blond, bronzed, wearing only a minuscule swimsuit, gazing down at his cards in consternation, Norman in striped jersey and white chinos, looking so very relaxed, with the wind ruffling his rich auburn hair, eyes half shrouded as he placed a card on the table.

Here a picture of Gaby, looking bright and insouciant and very French in sandals, shorts and halter top, watering the plants on the terrace. Jacques must have snapped this picture. Here Gaby and Jacques together, he still in the brief swimsuit, his arm around her shoulders, Gaby still holding the pitcher and looking up at him with sparkling eyes. Norman had snapped that one. Carol clearly remembered him crossing the terrace with camera in hand, remembered Gaby's merry laughter and Jacques's cries of protest when she poured the pitcher of water over his bare shoulders. The memories came flooding back as she picked up yet another photograph, she and Norman walking along the beach, Norman in his white chinos and a loose, light-blue cotton shirt with the tail hanging out, she in a billowy dress of thin white handkerchief linen, both of them barefooted, waves washing the sand at their feet. The sun had been like a golden ball that day, its rays bathing them with warmth, and he had smelled of salt and sand and sweat and they had made love as soon as they returned to their room at the villa.

His body, the silken smoothness of his skin as she rubbed her palms over the musculature of his back, his weight, the warmth of him, his hands tenderly stroking her cheek, her hair, her breasts, his mouth covering hers and the blissful abandon as late afternoon turned to evening and the crickets chirped in the night as they lay entwined. Carol put down the snapshot and picked up another, Norman alone, incredibly handsome in black tie and

white dinner jacket, hair dark and glossy and neatly brushed, a faint smile lifting one corner of his mouth as he gazed into the camera. They had gone to the casino and he had admired her red chiffon gown and Gaby had lost a small fortune at the tables and Jacques had gotten into a heated argument with one of the croupiers. They had watched dawn breaking over the water, the sky gray and then pink and gold and the water suddenly ashimmer with millions of spangles, Norman's left arm curled around her shoulder, her red chiffon skirt billowing in the breeze as they strolled to one of the open-air restaurants and had strong coffee and croissants and watched the fishermen taking their boats out.

Carol put the photographs aside and the memories continued to sweep over her: their first meeting there on the road in front of the cornfields, their first evening together, Norman so tender, so concerned when he discovered she was a virgin. Paris and Cliff and Le Drugstore and seeing Norman in the bar of the Plaza-Athénée. Together in Paris, the wonderment of it, the happiness they shared, the champagne feeling that filled her with blissful inebriation. St. Tropez, lunch on the terrace of the quaint old restaurant in town proper and Sir Robert arriving in his gleaming beige Rolls-Royce and her decision to make *Knaves Like Us* and that heart-wrenching drive along the coast to the airport. Their final moments together, the look in his eyes, his hands squeezing hers. His last words to her.

Night had fallen and the apartment was dark, shafts of moonlight streaming in through the balcony windows. Carol did not turn on the lamp. She sat on the sofa, holding a cushion to her bosom, and the grief was as real and as strong as it had been that day. "See you in the movies, my darling," he had said, and then he boarded the plane and she had not heard from him since, not a single word. She had kept in touch with Cliff. She sent cards to him and Stephanie every Christmas and on their wedding anniversary and she had sent a lovely baby gift when she received an announcement of the birth of their son. She heard from Cliff on occasion, brief, chatty letters that rarely mentioned his father. He was opening a new mall. Stephanie was pregnant again. Carol had given him her new address and telephone number and also a number he could use to reach her at the studio. He hadn't called, of course. There was no reason for him to call. It was foolish to keep on exchanging cards and notes, but he

was her one link with Norman, and if Cliff had her number perhaps Norman would ask for it one day and . . . Foolish thought, foolish fantasy.

Carol strolled out onto the balcony and stood there gazing at the multicolored lights that shimmered in the night. They were misty, all blurred together, but that was because of her tears. Here I am, she thought, on top of the world, yes, and all alone, and I love him still. I will always love him. I've made it. Against all odds, I've made it. I've achieved my goals, and I am here where I've always wanted to be and Norman is in Wichita and I haven't heard from him once in all this time. How is he? Is he happy? Does he remember, too? Her lounging gown was thin silk and the night air was cool and she folded her arms around her waist, ignoring the cold. Why did I decide to make that movie? Why didn't I fly back with him? We could be together this very moment. I have it all now, Hedda said in her article, but I had to give up so much. So much. Is it worth it? Carol rubbed her arms, shivering as a cool breeze swept across the balcony, causing the curtains behind her to billow. Why can't I forget? Why must I miss him so after so long?

Carol went inside, and she slept very little that night. She spent the next day with Danny at Disneyland, and that was a blessing. He was delightful and they had fun and it helped a great deal. They rode the rides and saw the haunted house and the wild west show and ate corny dogs and tacos and saw the grand parade and Snow White gave Danny a kiss on the brow. Carol was exhausted Sunday night, but she felt much better. She put the photographs away in a bottom drawer and vowed she wouldn't look at them again. At five-thirty the next morning she was driving to Universal on still-dark streets and assuring herself she had made the right choice.

During the fifties, Universal had been the undisputed home of the B movie. With their stable of attractive and talented young contract players, the studio churned out splashy, hokey Technicolor entertainments that delighted a nondiscriminating public and caused cash registers to ring. Rock Hudson was *Taza, Son of Cochise* and Tony Curtis played *The Prince Who Was a Thief* with a pronounced Bronx accent. Julie Adams fought off the advances of *The Creature from the Black Lagoon* and young Lori Nelson captured his fancy in the sequel. There was a plethora of sex and sand dramas with Yvonne DeCarlo and countless

westerns with a wooden Audie Murphy back in the saddle again and again. However, with their spectacular successes with *Pillow Talk* and *Imitation of Life* two years ago, the emphasis had now shifted to bouncy, mildly risqué comedies and elaborately mounted women's pictures like *Mannequin*.

Carol drove through the gates and parked in her allotted space. The sun was just beginning to come up, the enormous gray sound stages still nested in shadow as she trudged wearily over to makeup. A buxom and very bleached Mamie Van Doren was gossiping happily with her makeup man as he did her cheekbones. She gave Carol a friendly wave and crossed a pair of extremely shapely legs. Carol climbed up into her chair. A sleepy Suzanne Pleshette was in the next one, having her face done for *Forty Pounds of Trouble*. An exuberant and freckled Doris Day breezed in, radiating high spirits and carrying a huge bag of doughnuts which she cheerfully distributed.

"How can you be so perky at this hour of the morning?" Carol demanded, accepting a doughnut.

"I don't know. I just wake up that way."

"I'd wake up that way, too, if I were going to spend the day making love to Cary Grant," Mamie quipped.

Doris grinned. She and Grant were currently filming *That Touch of Mink*, another bright comedy which should help insure her position as the number one box office attraction in movies.

"I hear you're going to work with Faye Holden today," she said, bouncing up into her chair. "Are you nervous?"

"I'm petrified," Carol confessed.

"I met Faye at a party once," Mamie informed them. "She scared me silly."

"Faye's all right," Suzanne said sleepily. "Just treat her like royalty and watch your back."

Carol was full of nervous apprehension as, at eight-thirty, she stood by her trailer, watching the technicians finish lighting the set. She was wearing a simple, exquisite white satin gown with long, narrow sleeves and padded shoulders. It had a modestly low sweetheart neckline, fitted waist and long, narrow skirt. An opulent cascade of white fox furs went with the outfit, but she hadn't donned them yet. The lighting director yelled final instructions to the crew and asked Faye Holden's stand-in to move a little to the right so they could get a proper fix. Carol's stand-in had already been lighted. The drawing room set was sump-

tuous, all pale yellow and off-white and muted gold, a huge white dish of bronze and golden orchids on the low white coffee table. No expense was spared in a Ross Hunter production. The public wanted luxurious sets and glamorous people in elegant clothes, he knew, and that's exactly what he gave them—with resounding success.

Carol lighted another cigarette. Everything was ready. Faye Holden had yet to appear. David Miller strolled over and gave Carol a reassuring smile. Faye would be here in a couple of minutes, he told her. She was far too professional to be really tardy, but she always had to make the grand movie star entrance. He was right. Two and a half minutes later Miss Faye Holden did indeed appear, and her entrance was unquestionably grand. Accompanied by her secretary, her own hairdresser, her own makeup woman and a winsome young man whose duties were unclear, she moved with majestic hauteur, smiling that famous glazed-eye smile and nodding graciously to one and all.

On the screen, Faye Holden looked six feet tall, but that was because of her regal presence. In reality she was much shorter, but everything else was the same: the very broad shoulders that had inspired shoulder pads during the thirties, the slender waist and narrow hips. She was wearing gold shoes and narrow bronze slacks and an elaborate bronze hostess coat embroidered in gold and silver and amethyst. Her hair was bronze, too, cut short and sprayed to helmet stiffness. The eyebrows were thick and dark, the enormous, wide-open eyes giving her a startled look, the famous "Faye Holden" mouth painted a vivid red. Holden had never been a beauty, even in her youth, but her oversized features were a cameraman's dream, superbly photogenic, and at fifty-nine she was magnificently preserved, exuding grandeur.

Carol put out her cigarette. David led her over to Holden and performed introductions. Carol wondered if she should curtsy. Instead she smiled politely and said she was very honored to be working with her. Holden gave her a drop-dead look.

"We'll see what you can do," she snapped. "Let's get this show on the road."

David explained the scene briefly, and they went over their marks. Holden managed to be both patient and patronizing. She took her place and immediately informed the lighting technician that he hadn't done his job properly, and sure enough there was a faint shadow on her cheekbone and they had to readjust one

of the lights. Carol wondered how on earth she had known. Holden tartly informed her that when you'd been in this business as long as she had, you could *feel* it if the lights weren't right. Ten minutes later they started shooting. Carol, draped in furs, entered the drawing room and Holden icily informed her that John wouldn't be taking her to the opening tonight, that John was on his way to Boston and wouldn't be seeing her again.

"You thought you had him in your clutches, didn't you? You thought you were going to trap him into marriage. I had your number from the first, and I wasn't about to let my son marry a pushy little trollop from the wrong side of the tracks."

"You should know about the wrong side of the tracks, Mrs. Marlow. I believe your father was a railroad switchman from Biloxi, Mississippi, and your mother ran a boardinghouse. Of course, you married well—after your stint in the chorus at Minsky's."

"You little tramp!"

"No, Mrs. Marlow, I'm not a tramp. I was selling perfume behind a counter at Saks when he met me, yes, but that doesn't make me a tramp. I happen to love your son, and he loves me."

"Love! You think I don't know what's been going on? You think I don't know who paid for those furs, that gown? You think I don't know who's paying the rent on this town house? Jack—I mean, John—shit! Sorry, David. Amateur hour. Let's do it again."

They did it again and yet again. Holden was nervous. She hadn't been in a major picture in two years. Her last had been a B horror flick in which she played an ax murderess. This was her "comeback." Holden had been making comebacks and hanging on tenaciously for the past decade. A dinosaur from another era, she adamantly refused to sink into the tar pits along with most of the rest of her contemporaries. The lady had guts, and you had to admire her for that, Carol thought. Holden blew her lines twice more, but she eventually got it right and gave an electrifying performance no other actress in Hollywood could have approached. No one played a tough bitch like Faye Holden. She had patented the role thirty years ago and had been playing it in varying degrees ever since.

They finished the long shot at two o'clock in the afternoon and began to set up to shoot the same scene in close-up, first with Faye, then with Carol. The film editor would splice various

close-ups in with the long shot to avoid a static effect and give the scene variety and movement. Her makeup refurbished, her bronze hair sporting a new coat of spray, Faye returned to the set and sat down in the canvasback chair next to Carol as her stand-in patiently endured the tedium of having the lights set up to best show off her features. Carol smiled. Faye gave her another drop-dead look and accepted the glass of water the winsome young man brought over. Carol soon discovered that it wasn't water. Hundred-proof vodka, from the smell of it.

"You're good, Martin," Faye said abruptly. "Damned good, and I don't say that about many of these young upstarts in pictures today. They've got a pair of tits and a shapely ass and they think they're a star. You've got the real stuff, the stuff we had back in the old days."

"Why—thank you, Miss Holden."

"Call me Faye. I kept blowing my lines this morning, I was scared shitless, and you were wonderful. You did your best to help me, make it easier. Most of these young bitches would've thrown a tantrum or made disparaging remarks. You *wanted* me to be good, I could see it in your eyes."

"You *were* good. No one could have done it better."

"You've paid your dues, Martin. You fell flat on your ass in your first picture and got back up and refused to let 'em defeat you. I admire that. I love a fighter. I've always been a fighter myself. I saw a couple of your foreign films. You learned your craft over there. You're a pro. You know what you're doing and you do it damned well."

"I wish I were better," Carol confessed.

"So you're not a natural, so you're not 'inspired.' Neither was I. You rely on techinque instead of instinct, but the audience out there isn't aware of it. Strong technique and tough professionalism will carry you a hell of a lot further than soulful introspection. You wanna endure? You wanna stay up here on top?"

"It—it's the most important thing in the world to me."

"Get yourself a man," Faye told her. "Get yourself someone rich, someone powerful, someone important in the business. A producer or a director or a studio executive. Someone who'll have your best interests at heart and can further your career. This is a man's town, sweetheart. It always was and it always will be. It's the men who run things, make all the decisions. If

you wanna have a real career, get yourself a man who can guide your career and be there to see you get the best parts.''

"That sounds—terribly cynical, Miss Holden.''

"Faye. Sure it's cynical. It happens to be a fact. Look at Shearer. That bitch couldn't act her way out of a wet paper bag—she gave new meaning to the word affected—but she had Thalberg behind her and she got all of the plums. I got all of the leftovers. No way I could compete with her when she was balling the boss every night. Look at Jennifer Jones. She's got talent, yes, but that's not why she gets all those fabulous roles. She gets them because she's Mrs. David O. Selznick.''

Faye took another generous slug of vodka. It really might have been water for all the effect it had on her.

"Without a powerful man behind her in this town, a woman is at the mercy of the winds of chance. You're young, you're beautiful, you're talented. I could name five dozen who had just as much goin' for them and have long since been forgotten. Why? There was no man behind them. Back in the old days, a few of us fought and clawed our way to the top without a sponsor, but the studios had real power then, and, believe me, we all had to service our share of executives in order to keep a foothold. I like you, Martin. I'd like to see you make a real mark in this business, and you could. You could have one of the really big careers. Take my advice. Get yourself a powerful man.''

Faye finished her vodka, took up her knitting and gave it her full attention, ignoring Carol completely. Their conversation might never have occurred at all. Carol returned to her luxurious trailer, thinking about what Holden had said. She meant well, Carol was certain of that, but . . . Faye Holden was a relic from another era, and her views would naturally be colored by her own experience. This was 1962. Things were different. A powerful man like . . . like Blake Dougherty, for instance, could help a girl's career, certainly, but one could have a career without that kind of sponsorship. Carol herself was the living proof of that. She had made a career for herself through hard work and determination, and she didn't need some man to insure she maintained it.

It took them the rest of the day and most of the next morning to get all of Holden's close-ups. Although it was neither required nor expected of her, Carol stood out of camera range and fed

lead-in lines to Faye, making it easier for her to react more naturally and give a better reading. Holden didn't respond accordingly. When her closeups and reaction shots were finally completed, she departed with entourage in tow, leaving Carol to do her own without assistance. Faye Holden was a star. A star didn't feed lines for someone else's close-ups. They broke for lunch and, still in her street clothes, Carol ate in the commissary. Gregory Peck was sharing a table with Mary Badham, his young costar in *To Kill a Mockingbird*, and a rather grim Audie Murphy was sitting with Dan Duryea and Joan O'Brien, who were in *Six Black Horses* with him. A vivacious Sandra Dee, working on *If a Man Answers* with Bobby Darin, rushed over to give Carol a hug and say she was looking foward to playing her bratty little sister.

After lunch, Carol spent an hour and a half in makeup and, resplendent, was helped into the white satin gown again. They were having problems with a boom mike when she arrived on the set, ready for her close-up, and there was a half hour's wait before shooting began. She was wearing the white fox furs now, and it was very hot under the lights. She gazed at a nonpresent Holden and calmly, with emotions restrained, informed her that she should know about the wrong side of the tracks. She had filmed her first lines satisfactorily when one of the lights blew, casting half of her face in shadow. David Miller yelled "Cut!" and told Carol it would be at least another forty-five minutes before they would be ready for her again. Relinquishing the furs to the wardrobe assistant, Carol started to her trailer, and a flustered-looking secretary hurried toward her.

"Miss Martin!" she exclaimed breathlessly. "I'm so glad you're free. We have a phone call for you. Ordinarily we wouldn't bother you, of course, but—well, it's long distance and they had your private number and they said it's very important—"

"Long distance? Who is it?"

"I don't know, Miss Martin. They just sent me over to see if you would take the call. The party is still on hold."

"I'll take it," Carol said. "Can you have it transferred to the phone in my trailer?"

"No problem at all. It'll take a few minutes, but we'll ring you."

The girl scurried off, and Carol entered her trailer with a worried furrow between her brows. Long distance. It had to be

either Nora or Julie and it had to be something serious for them to call her at the studio. Had something happened to Nora in Mexico City? Had Julie finally reached the breaking point on the set in Arizona? Carol lighted a cigarette and smoked it rapidly, seizing the phone the moment it rang.

"Hello?"

"One moment, Miss Martin," a cool, officious voice said.

There was a clicking noise, and then another voice came on, a male voice she didn't recognize.

"Carol?" The voice sounded strained, far away.

"Yes, this is Carol Martin. Who—"

"I didn't think I was going to be able to reach you. Didn't think they were going to put me through."

"Who—Cliff? Is—is that you?"

"I'm calling from Wichita. I—I hate to bother you like this when you are working, but I felt you should—I—I felt you'd want to know."

Carol was standing, holding the phone in one hand, cradling the receiver between shoulder and ear, and she didn't say anything. She couldn't. A terrible premonition swept over her, and she knew, she knew, and she knew it was something she couldn't face, something she couldn't endure. She sat down and took a deep breath. No, she cried silently. No, no. Please, please, dear God, no.

"Carol? Are you there?"

"I'm here," she said. Her voice was perfectly calm.

"It's Dad. He—he was on the golf course, he's been playing a lot of golf lately, said it gave him something to do, and—he was on the third hole and it happened all at once, Carol. His heart. It—the doctor said it just gave out."

"No," Carol whispered.

"We—we're all shook up about it, of course, but the doctor said there was no pain. Cardiac arrest. He died instantly. I—the funeral is tomorrow morning and I know you can't come but—I thought you would want to know. I felt I had to call you."

"Of course."

"He loved you, Carol. He never said anything about it, never mentioned those weeks you spent together in France, but—he loved you. I know he did. He went to see your last two pictures several times and—when I was cleaning out his desk this morning I—I found a collection of clippings about you and several

photographs. I could tell he—I could tell he looked at them often. The clippings were worn, and the photographs—"

His voice broke. He repressed a sob.

"Thank you for calling, Cliff," she said quietly.

"He loved you," Cliff repeated.

"And I loved him," she whispered.

Carol replaced the receiver and waited for the emotion to sweep over her in a tidal wave, but it didn't. It was locked inside. She took another cigarette out of the case Sir Robert had presented to her so long ago and lighted it with the matching lighter from Jean-Claude. How can I be so calm? Why don't I cry? Why don't I sob? I can't endure this. I can't. I can't possibly go on. We could have been together. I could have made his last years so happy. Oh, Norman. Norman. I loved you. I loved you with all my heart and soul. Why, why why did I let you leave without me? I loved you, and I wanted you so badly. So badly. And now it's too late. you're gone, and you never knew how . . . how much I loved you.

Carol finished her cigarette, and still the tears didn't come. She was perfectly calm on the surface, impossibly calm, sitting here in her luxurious trailer in a sumptuous white satin gown. Norman was dead. He died without knowing how she longed for him, how she loved him. She didn't sob. No. She couldn't let those emotions free. She had to keep them contained inside her. Some things are too dreadful and too painful to endure and a numbness sets in and we can't feel and it is nature protecting us and that's what is happening to me. The clock is ticking. I've been sitting here for twenty-five minutes and I'm dying inside and I don't feel a thing.

There was a knock on the trailer door.

"We're ready, Miss Martin," an assistant called.

Carol stepped outside. A makeup man rushed over to add a bit of powder and rouge and freshened up her lipstick, and she patiently endured it, feeling nothing. The hairdresser fussed with her hair and finally stepped back, satisfied. The wardrobe woman arranged the billowy cascade of white fox furs on her shoulders. Carol thanked her politely, thanked them all. She stepped into the blazing flood of lights and took her spot and felt the heat brushing her cheekbones, her brow, and yes, she was dying inside, but she had a job to do. Norman was gone. Oh God. Oh, dear God.

"Ready, Carol?" David inquired.

Carol nodded and the boy with the clapper stepped in front of the camera and clapped it and Carol gazed into the camera and the camera was John's mother and she wasn't going to let her break them up, no, she loved John, she was going to fight for him.

"No, Mrs. Marlow," she said, "I'm not a tramp. I was selling perfume behind a counter at Saks when he met me, yes, but—"

She stood under the sweltering lights in the white satin and white furs, and she did her job. This is what you have always wanted, she told herself. This is what you have worked for all these years. Carol did her job, and no one knew her heart was breaking.

17

Luis Montoya was tall and dark and handsome and determined to prove to her that what they said about Latin Lovers was really true. Señor Montoya was a diplomat, very wealthy, very distinguished, horny as hell, too. He had been trying all evening to get her out into the gardens, and once out in those gardens with all the secret nooks and crannies and hidden bowers a girl was as good as gone. Nora smiled sweetly and said no, she didn't care to see the moonlight and roses and mosaic tiles. Luis looked crestfallen. He looked absolutely gorgeous too in his black tie and tailored tuxedo with that big red-and-silver sash slanting across his chest. Nora didn't know what the sash signified but it was bound to mean something important, just like those decorations he was wearing. Luis was a big cheese, no question about it, as handsome as Fernando Lamas and even sexier with those enormous brown eyes and that pencil-thin mustache.

Nora took another sip of her champagne, glancing around the spacious room. It was packed with a posh crowd, diplomats from half a dozen embassies, Mexican socialites and American millionaires, the men in elegant formal attire, the women dressed to the hilt and with a chic that would put Paris to shame. Mexico City was extremely cosmopolitan and ultrasophisticated, at least on this level. Tonight's affair was being thrown by an American oilman and his wife, and their home was a veritable palace in

Mexican motif, white stucco, red tile roof, colored mosaic tile everywhere. Real Renoirs and Utrillos hung on the walls along with exquisite Mexican rugs. The food was superb. The champagne was the best. A typical night on the diplomatic circuit. Nora wasn't certain whom this party was being given for—a German count? a Swedish explorer? an Argentinian textile tycoon?—but everyone was busy making points or making each other. Señor Montoya was still trying his damnedest to make her.

"Look, sweetie," she said, "I love your looks and your shaving lotion is divine, but no sale."

"I do not understand," he said plaintively. "You do not like me?"

"I think you're a living doll, Señor Montoya. I just don't happen to feel like being banged on some cold marble bench behind a clump of rosebushes while guitars are strumming in the distance. Call it perverse. I like to know a guy a couple of days before I let him screw me."

Some of that oozing Latin charm disappeared. The huge, soulful brown eyes turned cool.

"You American girls like to shock with your frank language and your breezy freedom. You have emasculated your American men and turned them into a race of overgrown boys whom you rule with ease, but when you meet a real man you become frigid and afraid."

"Nice try, love," Nora retorted. "Now I'm supposed to show you I'm not frigid and afraid, right?"

"It's worked before," he confessed.

"It's not gonna work this time. There must be at least fifty gorgeous women here at the party tonight and I'm sure at least half of them would cheerfully trot out into the gardens with you. Why don't you give one of them a thrill and let me drink my champagne in peace."

"Half of them I have slept with already," he said. "They do not have for me the—how is it you say?—the challenge. The thrill of the chase, this is what excites a man. What he can have without effort, he does not want."

"Great point. I'll be sure to use it in my article. *Cosmo* readers will love it. I'm writing an article about American girls away from home. How they react to a new culture and how they adapt, how they change, what happens to the old attitudes and standards

when their family and friends aren't around to look over their shoulders."

"And what does happen?" he inquired.

"A lot. You'll have to read my article. In the meantime, do me a great big favor and fuck off."

Señor Montoya's handsome face tightened angrily, his flat cheekbones burning a bright pink. He was Mexican aristocracy, from one of the oldest, wealthiest families, an esteemed diplomat to boot, and he wasn't used to being turned down. He muttered a very uncomplimentary word under his breath and marched off to seek new prey. Nora smiled to herself and raised her champagne glass. She must have attended over a dozen of these piss-elegant diplomatic affairs during the past three and a half weeks, and at each one of them there had been a suave handsome Latin male who tried his best to get into her pants. She was American and she was a new face and therefore she was up for grabs. Screwing the naive American girls seemed to be the favorite sport of these arrogant Latin men with their smooth manners and worldly charm. A number of girls fell for it, she had discovered, but not all of them were that wide-eyed and naive. Nora had interviewed over a hundred girls for her article, and she had learned that the majority of them were more than capable of coping with that particular menace. Her readers would be delighted to learn that American girls living and working away from home were holding their own.

Actually, she had finished her article over a week ago, but she didn't intend to send it to New York until after she flew home, two days from now. *Cosmopolitan* had put her up in one of the city's grandest old hotels, had provided introductions to the crème de la crème of the diplomatic and business community and were paying all her expenses as well. Nora was having a ball, and she didn't intend to leave until it was absolutely necessary. It had been marvelously stimulating, interviewing all those girls, older women as well, and it had been a joy to get back to her typewriter in the afternoon when everyone else was taking a siesta, great to pound the keys again, to write something besides a laundry list for a sullen would-be genius. This trip had been a blessing. She was well rid of James Hennesey, the sod, and it was wonderful to be free and on her own again.

Seeing her standing alone, Ted Andrews hurried over. Ted was twenty-seven years old and had clear blue eyes and light-

brown hair and the handsome, clean-cut features of a grown-up Boy Scout. Ted was a diplomatic aide at the American Embassy, her official escort tonight, and Ted took his duties very seriously.

"Can I get you something, Miss Levin? Would you like another drink?"

"I'm doing fine, Ted."

"Would you care to see the gardens?"

"Jesus, not you, too!"

Ted looked puzzled. Nora grinned.

"Sorry, love. It appears the gardens hold a particular allure for most of the gents here tonight, but I should have known that's not what you had on your mind. You'd probably actually show me the mosaic fountain."

"It's quite impressive," he told her. "I'd be glad to—"

"You run on back to Andrea and enjoy yourself, pet. I'll just finish this champagne and nibble some more canapés."

"I feel dreadful, neglecting you this way."

"You haven't been neglecting me. I've been circulating. I promise not to send in a bad report to your boss. Just make sure you get me back to the hotel when it's all over with. I plan to have several more glasses of this delicious champagne."

Ted was clearly relieved. "If you're sure you don't mind—"

"Scram, sweetie."

Ted was very much in love with Andrea Johnson, one of the secretaries Nora had interviewed, a lovely, vulnerable blonde whose heart had been broken earlier on by a wealthy Latin much like Luis Montoya. Ted had broken into her apartment when he smelled gas, had hurled a chair through the window and cut off the gas and rushed Andrea to the hospital, consoling her in the weeks that followed her attempted suicide. He joined her now, dancing attendance on her. She tolerated his attentions, but it was clear she still pined for the handsome rogue. Would Ted win her over? Would he make her forget the heartbreaker? Nora was quite intrigued.

She was intrigued with Lilian, too.

Lilian, currently holding court across the room in crushed gray velvet and a fortune in amethysts, was a sleek, tanned brunette with violet eyes from Waxahachie, Texas, who had come to work as a secretary for an oil company based in Mexico City, married the boss a year later and was now one of the American community's grandes dames. Lilian was throwing tonight's bash.

She was celebrated for her parties. She was also, she had confessed to Nora during a lengthy interview, bored out of her mind. Her husband devoted twenty-four hours a day to the business, and Lilian was left with nothing but time and money, far too much of both. She had had a score of lovers in the past twelve years, the latest, a virile blond tennis pro, currently occupying the guest house beyond the gardens. Lilian was thirty-nine. The pro was twenty-seven. He gave her private lessons on the tennis court out back and was well paid for his services both on and off the court.

Sven, the pro, resplendent in white dinner jacket and black tie, was chatting amiably to a trio of adoring young women, one of them a seventeen-year-old nymphet with glossy brown hair, pouty red lips, determined blue eyes and a figure that might easily stop traffic. It was admirably displayed in a strapless white satin gown much too bold for a girl her age. Teresa was the spoiled and pampered daughter of one of the embassy's head honchos, and she clung to Sven's arm tenaciously. Would the little slut snare him away? Would the restless and amoral but sympathetic Lilian lose yet another lover?

"Bored?" Ellen McCann asked.

Nora snapped out of her revery. "What—I—I'm sorry. Did you say something, Ellen?"

"I was just wondering if you were bored. You've been standing in the same spot for the past seven minutes, staring into space."

"I was thinking," Nora said.

"About a man?"

"About—I *think* I was thinking about a new novel."

"Really?"

"I—I'm not sure yet."

Ellen smiled. Ellen was the private secretary of a prominent American diplomat stationed here in Mexico City. After their interview, Ellen had become a chum, taking Nora to the National Museum to see the Aztec Calendar Stone and to Chapultepec Castle and driving her out to San Juan Teotihuacán to see the Pyramid of the Sun. Ellen's story was just as intriguing as Andrea's and Lilian's. A plain, painfully shy girl from Boise, Idaho, Ellen had come to Mexico City a few years ago to work as a typist at the American Embassy. Away from the stultifying, repressive influence of her overbearing parents, she had bloomed.

Rigorous dieting had melted away superfluous poundage. Contact lenses had taken the place of her thick glasses. Her drab brown hair had been tinted to a rich chestnut, loose flowing waves replacing the tight braids worn in a coronet atop her head.

Her shyness vanished, too, and Ellen had quickly lost her virginity. She had fallen in love with the married forty-three-year-old American diplomat for whom she was now working, and he had fallen in love with her. Unable to get a divorce, he had set her up in a small, comfortably furnished apartment, and Ellen was blissfully content as a Back Street wife. Or was she? She spent every workday in the office with him and he visited her several evenings a week, but was that really enough? Was Ellen as happy as she claimed to be? Was any woman—particularly one as charming and attractive as Ellen—really content to settle for only half?

"You're off again," Ellen said.

"Hunh?"

"Staring into space. That novel must really be taking shape."

"I think it is. I think I've got all my major characters, and I've got their stories, too."

"Just be sure you change the names," Ellen said wryly.

"I will," Nora promised.

Nora finished her champagne, ate a couple of fancy canapés and forced herself to circulate. Most of the people here tonight she had met earlier at other parties. George Michaels, Ellen's boss, was talking to a colleague and kept glancing up discreetly to keep track of Ellen, watching as she moved from group to group. His gray-green eyes were sad as he looked at her. He paid no attention at all to his wife, a tall, sullen redhead in black satin and diamonds who had already had too many Scotches. Jesus, Nora thought, I wish I had my notebook with me. I *will* have to change the names, of course, and rearrange some of the facts, but it's a natural. Ross will flip over the idea—he'll want me to knock out an outline right away—and Terry Wood will be mad for it.

Nora talked with a genial Swedish explorer with blond beard and discovered that yes, tonight's affair was in his honor, Lilian's husband's company was financing his next expedition. He had lean cheeks, piercing blue eyes and thick, unruly blond hair to match his beard. He said that he'd heard the mosaic fountain out in the gardens was something to behold and asked Nora if she'd

like to see it. She politely refused. I should never have worn this black lace dress, she thought. I shouldn't have worn the red rose in my hair, either. Every man at the party is horny tonight. It must have something to do with the climate. Good for a girl's morale, though, even if she's not in the mood to play.

A discouraged Ted Andrews took Nora back to the hotel at midnight. Andrea had left earlier with one of her girlfriends. The handsome young man dutifully escorted Nora to the door of her room and told her it had been an honor for him to be her official date for the evening. Nora smiled and touched his cheek and then, impulsively, she asked him in for a drink. Over a Scotch and soda in the sitting room, Ted woefully poured out his side of the story. Andrea liked him, sure, but she treated him like a big brother. She kept pining for that cad who had led her on with promises of marriage and then dropped her when he'd had his fill. She couldn't seem to forget him.

"Make her forget him," Nora said. "Stop treating her like an invalid and start treating her like a desirable woman. Get tough with her. Get romantic. If you don't want her to treat you like a big brother, stop acting like one."

"Is—" Ted paused, thinking. "Is that how I've been acting?"

"Looks that way, pet."

"You think I should make a pass?"

"I think you should do more than that. You're a very attractive guy, Ted. Pack up your merit badges and take out the Aqua Velva. If you want to win her, you've gotta woo her."

"Gee, Miss Levin, I—thank you," he said, standing. "Thank you for the Scotch and thank you for being so understanding. I guess you famous novelists know all about love and stuff like that."

"You betcha," she said.

Nora showed Ted out and changed into a white terrycloth robe. She wouldn't be around long enough to see how it all turned out, but she'd put her money on Ted. *Peter* would win *Heather*, but only after shaking her silly, tossing her into the sack and proving to her he was twice the man Ricardo had been. Ideas were coming fast and furiously now. Nora whipped out her notebook and sat down on the sofa, curled her legs under her and began to scribble away. The stories of Andrea, Lilian and Ellen were quickly transferred to paper in a hurried outline, but the facts were only a starting point. Her imagination took

over, one idea suggesting another. Janice loses her lifeguard to the young sexpot, yes, but she is consoled by the handsome Swedish explorer—better make that Norwegian—and, abandoning her indifferent husband and the luxurious life in Mexico City, she takes off to the Amazon with her new lover. The Amazon? We'll have to think about that. By three-thirty she had fifteen pages of notes and a very rough outline for her next novel.

Jesus, I hope I can read this in the morning, she thought wearily, staggering into the bedroom. The whole bloody book had come to her almost full-blown, and she couldn't wait to get started on it. She had missed writing. She hadn't realized just how much until now. I loved the son of a bitch and I suppose I learned something from the affair, I suppose I grew up a little, but I damned near let him sabotage my career. *He* was the writer. I was a hack who happened to hit it lucky. Fuck that. Fuck him, too. I may not be literary and pretentious and I may never pen a masterpiece but I'm a better writer than James Hennesey will *ever* be. Jesus, can I pick 'em. Nora wrapped her arms around the extra pillow in the darkness, trying to forget. She was better off without the moody bastard, wouldn't take him back for a million bucks, didn't *want* him back, but it still hurt nevertheless.

Noisy, persistent pounding on the door penetrated her brain. It wouldn't go away, no matter how she tossed, no matter how she turned, and finally she gave an anguished moan and opened her eyes and the room was flooded with bright sunlight and someone was still pounding noisily on the door. "Jesus Christ!" she exclaimed, struggling into a sitting position. She was still wearing the white terrycloth robe. It was horribly wrinkled. Her eyelids felt like they weighed about forty pounds each, and her head might have been stuffed with damp cotton. She swung her legs over the side of the bed and moaned again and somehow managed to stand up, weaving precariously. The pounding continued. It sounded like someone was using a battering ram.

"Will you please the fuck hold on a minute!" she shrieked.

The pounding ceased immediately.

She staggered out of the bedroom and into the sitting room, tightening the sash of the short, wrinkled robe. She ran her fingers through her hair, finding a dozen tangles. She hadn't bothered to remove her makeup before she went to sleep. Her face must be a hideous mess. She must make the Bride of Franken-

stein look like a beauty queen. Fuck it. Whoever the hell woke
her up at this ungodly hour deserved a good fright. Blinking her
eyes, feeling like hammered shit, Nora unlocked the door and
flung it open, glaring defiantly at the cretin who had dared disturb her beauty sleep. He'd bloody well have a good reason or
there'd be hell to pay.

He was wearing fancy tooled black leather boots and tight,
faded jeans and a loose shirt of thin white handkerchief linen
with the full, billowing sleeves gathered at the wrist. Over it he
wore a brightly colored serape, red and gold and yellow and
orange and blue, gaudy as hell, and a huge sombrero perched
atop his head, the enormous brim slanted forward, hiding his
eyes. The wide, perfectly chiseled mouth was grinning an idiot
grin. He tilted his head back and Nora saw his eyes. They were
full of mischief.

"You son of a bitch!" she cried.

"Is that any way to greet an old and treasured friend?" he
protested.

"What the hell are *you* doing here? And what the hell makes
you think you can come battering my door down at six o'clock
in the morning?"

"It's almost noon," he informed her.

"Who *gives* a shit!"

"My, my, this isn't the Nora Levin I know and love. I don't
mean to hurt your feelings, my love, but you look a fright.
There're black streaks running down your cheeks, mascara, I
presume, and your makeup is all caked and cracking and your
lipstick is—"

"Go to hell!"

"Hung?" he inquired kindly.

"I am not hung! I stay up half the night, making notes, and
then someone pounds on my door with a medieval battering ram
and wakes me out of a perfectly sound sleep and—Jesus! I need
coffee. Lots of it."

Jim Burke grinned, moved to one side and then pushed a
heavily laden room service cart through the door, almost running her down. Nora staggered to one side, glaring at him as he
whipped out a white linen cloth, spread it over the round table
near the window and began to remove the dishes from the cart,
making a hideous din as he did so. There was a rack of toast, a
pot of jam, four plump sausage links, a heavenly-looking omelet

covered with orange sauce and a huge silver pot of coffee. She hadn't eaten any dinner the night before and had had nothing but a few canapés at the party. She realized she was ravenously hungry. Jim poured a cup of coffee and handed it to her.

"Thank you," she said sullenly.

"I've already eaten, several hours ago. I checked at the desk downstairs and found you hadn't ordered anything yet so I arranged to surprise you myself like the thoughtful friend I am."

"Thoughtful my ass. Pounding on the door like that. I thought I was being besieged by Saxon warriors. You never answered my question. What are you doing here?"

"Promotion. The top Mexican network is picking up *Market Street West* and the studio sent me down to shake hands and spread goodwill and make appreciative noises. Ran me ragged all day yesterday. Today I'm on my own. Knew you were here—tried to get you last night, you weren't in—and decided I'd show you the town."

"I've seen the town," she snapped. "I feel like shit. I'm spending the day in bed."

"Splendid. I'll join you."

"Fuck off, Burke."

"Drink your coffee. Eat your breakfast. You'll feel much better."

"I really should shower and clean up first, but—to hell with it. I'll clean up later. That omelet looks fabulous. Are you staying here at the hotel?"

He nodded, sombrero brim flapping. "I fly back tomorrow morning."

"I fly back tomorrow afternoon."

"I'll change my flight. We'll go back together, and you can hold my hand during takeoff. I usually get airsick. So what have you been doing?"

"Busting my buns. I've interviewed over a hundred American women living and working in Mexico City and gathered reams of fascinating material and have written a positively brilliant article that's gonna knock their socks off, and I've also gotten a tremendous premise for a new novel. That's why I was up so late, I was jotting down ideas, sketching out an outline."

Jim perched on the arm of the sofa, watching her eat. That garish Technicolor serape was too bloody much. So was the sombrero. He must have picked them up at one of those tacky tourist stalls.

"Had any good sex?" he inquired.

"That's none of your bloody business."

"Bet you have," he teased.

"As a matter of fact, I've had none at all, but not for lack of opportunity. All the men down here are horny as hell. Last night I was propositioned by an arrogant Latin diplomat, a bearded Swedish explorer and, just before the party broke up, a glass-blower from Venezuela on a mission for the South American Trade Commission."

"It's that incredible body of yours and those come-hither eyes," he told her. "I'd like to jump you right now, even if your hair does look like it exploded during the night."

"Thanks, Burke. You're great for a girl's ego."

"What're friends for? Hurry up and finish your breakfast, babe. We've got places to go, things to do. You've been hob-nobbing with the aristocracy and doing the diplomatic circuit. Today you're gonna have fun."

"Yeah?"

"I promise."

It took Nora one solid hour to pull herself together. She showered. She styled her hair. She did her face. She put on white sandals and a fetching yellow sundress appliquéd with white daisies and was stuffing necessities into a square white straw purse with a yellow scarf tied around the handle when Jim returned to fetch her. He was still wearing the sombrero and serape. They received several shocked stares as they made their way through the elegant lobby downstairs, but Jim carried it off with grand aplomb, nodding regally at a horrified British matron in a purple silk suit who peered at him through her lorgnette. A long, sleek black limousine was waiting for them outside.

"How do we rate this?" Nora inquired.

"I'm a big television star, remember? Think I'm gonna travel around in a dusty old taxi held together with chicken wire?"

"The studio's paying?"

"The studio's paying," he said, helping her into the backseat. "By the way, you look almost human now. I love that yellow dress. You ever made it in the backseat of a limo?"

"Lay off, Burke. I'm still not awake yet."

Jim grinned and gave her a hug.

"So how are you?" he asked as the limo pulled away. "Really, I mean."

"Really? I'm fine, Jim."

"Over it yet?"

"I think. Almost. I still—once in a while I still think of him, and I kick myself for wasting a full year with the son of a bitch, but—I've got my act back together. I guess I needed someone like him to keep me from getting too cocky and full of myself. I guess—oh, hell. It's over now and I'm older and wiser."

"Poor baby."

"Fuck you, Burke, and take your hand off my knee. Where are we going?"

"We're going shopping."

"I've already been shopping. My friend Ellen took me to the most exquisite shops—I thought I was in Paris again. I bought a cocktail dress that'll knock your eyes out. It's patterned on a flamenco costume, cleverly modified for evening wear. Cost me a mint, but—"

"You haven't been to the Market?"

"Why would I want to go to the Market? That's for tourists. Mexico City has some of the most elegant shops in—"

"Today you're gonna be a tourist," he informed her.

"Jesus," Nora groaned.

When they arrived and alighted from the limousine, the Market was already aswarm with dozens of shoppers who couldn't possibly be anything but tourists: women in stretch pants and overblouses, men in print shirts and Bermuda shorts with cameras slung around their necks, many of them, alas, with noisy children in tow. Jim's sombrero and serape caused no stir whatsoever, although one man from Pittsburgh did come over and ask, "Hey, buddy, where'd-ja get that? I gotta have one." There were hundreds of stalls, it seemed, where one could haggle for baskets, leather goods, shawls, linen, jewelry, bright pottery, alabaster bookends, wooden chests, picture frames and, of course, every kind of junk food, Mexican variety. It was gaudy and noisy and congested, yes, but it was also exciting, and Nora found herself enjoying it all immensely. Jim bought a set of colorful wooden puppets for Danny—señor, señorita and piebald horse—and Nora found some beautiful lace mantillas, as fine as anything she had seen in the shops. She bought two, pale violet-blue for Julie, creamy beige for Carol, and haggled ardently with the vendor. Haggling was a great sport at the Market, for the

vendors normally asked at least twenty-five percent more than they expected to get.

Two hours later, both of them laden with purchases, they tumbled into the limousine.

"Having fun?" Jim inquired.

"I love all my bargains. I had no idea you could buy so many really wonderful things. Julie and Carol are going to adore their mantillas, and those carved ivory combs are exquisite. I really shouldn't have bought the pottery, but it was so pretty, so inexpensive."

"And so heavy," Jim groaned. "I had to drag both boxes full back here to the limo and stash them in the trunk."

"I'll have them shipped home. I promise to ask you over for a wonderful meal so you can eat off them."

"You gonna cook it?"

"Are you kidding? I'll have it catered."

"In that case, you're on."

"Where are we going now?"

"To the Plaza Monumental."

"But that's a bullring!" she protested.

"I know. I have two fabulous seats in the *barrera* on the *sombra* side. I believe we're in the first row."

"I don't want to go to a bullfight!"

"You can't visit Mexico without seeing a bullfight. They won't allow you out of the country unless you can prove you've seen at least one. It's colorful and exciting, and this is the height of the season. All the best matadors will be in the ring."

"Jim!"

"You're gonna love it," he told her.

Nora sulked all the way to the Avenida Insurgentes Sur but she had to admit that the 50,000-seat Plaza Monumental was impressive, already packed solid with eager spectators when they arrived. They were indeed in the first row on the shady side of the ring, and it was altogether too close for Nora. Jim explained that bullfighting was a noble tradition, an artistic pageant celebrated for its stylish rituals. The bulls used here in Mexico City were carefully bred for the ring, the strongest, bravest creatures, a real match for the matador. Nora felt queasy already, but she relaxed a little when the music rang out and the pageant began. The richly dressed matadors strutted into the ring with embroidered capes swinging from their left shoulders, followed by the

banderilleros and picadors. Making their way to the official box, right next to where Nora and Jim were sitting, the matadors removed their hats and bowed and Nora marveled at their costumes close up.

One matador in particular caught her attention. His costume was all gold spangled with silver and bronze. He was lean and lithe and graceful, with dark flashing eyes and a beautiful smile. He was smiling directly at her! She was startled a few minutes later when he removed his gorgeous cape and flung it at her. One moment she was sitting there admiring his thighs and the next moment she was being smothered in gold lamé and bronze satin.

"What'd he do *that* for?" she exclaimed, removing the rich folds from her face.

"He's honoring you," Jim said, grinning. "You're supposed to drape the cape over the railing. He's probably going to dedicate a bull to you. If you play your cards right he might toss you an ear."

"Tell him not to bother!"

The first bullfight began and the crowd roared when the enormous muscular bull came charging into the ring, a magnificent beast with a glossy black hide gleaming like satin in the sunlight. Nora held her breath as the picadors began their work, pricking the poor confused animal. The banderilleros followed and soon the bull was bleeding and festooned with short lances gaily decorated with colored paper, angry and charging wildly, the lances wobbling on his back as he wheeled this way and that, trying to elude his tormentors. It was horrible! It was inhuman! Nora covered her eyes. The crowd loved it, cheering with lusty glee. Peering cautiously through her fingers, Nora saw the bull in the center of the ring, snorting and stamping the ground. He wheeled suddenly and charged one of the horses. When she heard the horse's shriek and saw what happened Nora let out an impassioned cry and leaped to her feet.

"Get me the fuck out of here!" she screamed.

Jim yanked her back down into her seat. "We haven't even seen the matador yet!" he protested. "This is just the preliminary."

"If this is the preliminary, I'm sure as hell not sticking around for the finale! This is pure sadism! That poor bull. That horse! How can sane people *allow* this?"

"It's a ritual of manhood. It's grace under pressure. Haven't you read Hemingway?"

"Hemingway was full of shit!" Nora shouted. "He was the world's biggest phony! Ritual of manhood, my ass! Grace under pressure! What does *he* do under pressure? He grabs a gun and blows his brains out!"

"People are staring!"

"Let them stare! Get me *out* of here!"

Jim was a little gray around the gills himself. As he led her out amidst the cheering throng he confessed that he'd never actually *seen* a bullfight before himself but he'd read all about them and he'd seen *Blood and Sand* with Tyrone Power and thought it would be fun. He was holding onto her hand tightly, and suddenly he let go and rushed down a corridor and disappeared into a restroom. He rejoined her a few minutes later, looking sheepish indeed, the sombrero in his hand.

"It was those enchiladas I ate at the Market," he explained.

"Sure it was."

"What happened to the horse had nothing to do with it."

"Of course it didn't."

"Guess going to a bullfight wasn't such a bright idea."

"You've had better," she said.

"Know what I'm gonna do as soon as I get back to L.A.?"

"What's that?"

"I'm gonna burn my copy of *Death in the Afternoon*."

"I'll provide the matches," Nora told him.

Back at the hotel, Nora made arrangements to have her pottery shipped and then went up to her suite, accompanied by a still-sheepish Jim. His multicolored serape was sadly limp now and he was holding the enormous sombrero by its brim. He asked Nora if she had any plans for tonight and she said no she didn't and he asked if she would let him take her out and she asked what have you got in mind, a cockfight, and he grinned then and said he was going to make it up to her, he was going to give her a fantastic evening, dinner first and then nightclubs, wear something very, very sexy.

When he came to fetch her at eight o'clock he looked very sexy himself in his white dinner jacket, black bow tie and plaid satin cummerbund. He looked like the successful television star he was, imbued with that special Hollywood glamor. Long gone were the days of motorcycle boots and leather jackets. Jim was

one of the dearest people she knew, good-humored, bright, devastatingly attractive. He gave her a merry smile and, taking his arm from behind his back, presented her with an enormous bouquet of yellow-gold roses, the soft, velvety petals faintly tinted with pink.

"All they had downstairs," he told her. "I wanted red, but these will have to do."

"They'll do nicely," she said, touched.

"Am I forgiven the bullfight?"

"Depends."

"Depends on what?"

"On how well you feed me tonight. I'm starving, and I'm in the mood for something *very* expensive."

"The studio's paying. You can have nightingale tongue if you wish."

"Beluga caviar will do. For starters."

She placed her hands on her hips, posing. She waited. Jim said nothing. Nora frowned.

"So?" she said.

"So what?"

"So whatta-ya think?"

"About what?"

"You bastard!"

Jim grinned, eyes full of merriment. Nora was wearing the cocktail dress she had told him about earlier. The form-fitting black velvet bodice had extremely narrow sleeves and was cut quite low, the midcalf-length skirt aswirl with alternate rows of gold, white, aqua and fuchsia ruffles, much like a flamenco dancer's skirt. She looked fabulous. She looked sensational. He let her simmer for a couple of more seconds and then told her he guessed she'd do. Nora looked around for something to throw at him.

The limo whisked them to Mexico City's most exclusive, most elegant restaurant, and all eyes followed them as they were led to their table. They were a strikingly handsome couple, of course, but Nora knew it was because her gallant escort was currently one of the most recognizable celebrities around, his television series an even greater hit in its second season. The movie he had made with Diane McBain had been a critical and box office smash, here in Mexico City as well as at home and abroad. Paul Newman had best look to his laurels, fan magazines claimed.

Nora thought that Jim was much sexier than Newman and an even better actor, although she was decidedly prejudiced. Jim gave her a warm smile as they took their seats.

"This place do?" he inquired.

"In a pinch. Oh, Jesus!"

"What's the matter?"

"There's Luis Montoya, the guy I was telling you about who kept trying to make me last night."

"Where?"

"Over there by the window, sitting with that smoldering blonde in antique white lace and emeralds."

"Want me to beat him up for you?"

"She can't be his wife. She's gotta be his mistress. Why doesn't anyone give *me* emeralds like those?"

"Your day will come, babe," he promised.

"Yeah, sure," she said grumpily.

Jim ordered a bottle of Dom Perignon from the sommelier, and they studied the embossed gold menus and ordered. Classical music played discreetly in the background. Crystal chandeliers gleamed. Dark-gold carpet covered the floor, and heavy gold satin draperies hung at the windows. Look at us, Nora thought, a middle-class hooligan from Indiana and a Jewish girl from Brooklyn, mingling with the swells. Who says dreams don't come true? If Sadie could see me now she'd have a fit. Nora spread shiny beluga on a thin sliver of toast, feeling better than she'd felt in weeks. The meal was wonderful, the service impeccable, Jim the most engaging of companions. He asked her to tell him about the new novel, and she spent the next hour telling him about Andrea and Lilian and Ellen and how their stories would be altered and expanded and woven into a novel about American women living and working in another country.

"Sounds even better than *The Slipper*," Jim told her. "There's only one problem."

"What's that?"

"No part in it for me. I'm too strong to play the young diplomatic aide and too big a name to play the lifeguard, and I don't think I'd be a very convincing Norwegian explorer. It'll make a smashing movie, though, even if I'm not in it."

"Don't you have another movie lined up?"

Jim nodded. "After the success of *Roughshod*, the scripts have come pouring in. During the hiatus I'm going to make *Hellion*,

all about a temperamental young corporate lawyer in Philadel-
phia who dumps his stuffy wife and leaves her father's firm. He
opens his own office and falls in love with a luscious call girl
and then single-handedly brings down the crime syndicate responsible for her murder.''

"It's tailor-made. You'll be marvelous.''

"I figure I'll do one more season as Duke Henry and then do
feature films full time. Television has been wonderful for me
and I'm grateful for the series, but I need more variety, more
challenge. I want to be a real actor, not just a glamor boy.''

"You're already a real actor, pet,'' Nora told him, "and you're
going to be one of the greats. I've known that for years, ever
since I saw you as the Gentleman Caller in *The Glass Menagerie*
back at Claymore.''

"That seems like a lifetime ago,'' Jim said thoughtfully.

"I shudder to think of the person I was back then. A lot has
happened to all of us since those days. I guess you've read about
Julie's nominations?''

Nora nodded. "I believe it's the first time in the history of
the awards that an actress has been nominated in two categories
in the same year. If she doesn't win the best actress award for
Impulse, she's bound to win as best supporting actress for *The
Slipper*.''

"Naturally the press is making a big hoopla over it. They're
calling her a genius, hailing her as the American Bernhardt,
praising her to the skies and conveniently forgetting the stories
they ran a few weeks ago about her temperament and drinking
and such. The studio has squelched the bad press, and even
Louella has come round—they must have paid her plenty.''

"I read the column,'' Nora said dryly. "Julie's no longer difficult and temperamental. Now she's a 'perfectionist' who's 'setting a high standard for her fellow workers.' I know she's back
from Arizona now, but I haven't heard from her.''

"I saw her just before I flew down here.''

"How is she, Jim?''

"She's holding on,'' he said gravely. "She needs a long rest.
She needs one badly. I—'' Jim cut himself short, shook his head,
and then he looked at her and smiled. "Hey, we're supposed to
be having fun. You want some chocolate mousse?''

"I couldn't.''

"Coffee?''

Nora shook her head. Jim signaled the waiter and ten minutes later they were on their way to the nightclubs and the next three hours were an exciting, dizzying whirl of bright lights and brilliant colors and mariachi bands. Nora had been here for almost a month without drinking a single margarita, and Jim was appalled. He insisted she try one. He insisted she have another. At two o'clock in the morning they were in a tiny, tourist-filled dive festooned with balloons and streamers of colored paper and Nora was doing a flamenco with the slim-hipped, dark-eyed male professional and people were applauding and throwing confetti provided by the management. She was doing a creditable job with the castanets and stamping her heels with abandon. Jim applauded vigorously, and the female pro pulled him onto the floor and soon he was stamping himself, yelling "Olé!" for no particular reason. He bowed to one and all when the music stopped and then the pros taught them how to do the Mexican Hat Dance. It was a smash hit as far as the other patrons were concerned. Jim and Nora were deluged with confetti as they staggered back to their table.

"First time I've ever been the floor show," Nora said.

"You were great," he assured her.

"Thanks a lot. That's more than I can say for you."

"I was fabulous!" he protested.

"You were awful. You stomped the sombrero to smithereens."

"I did not!"

"Smithereens, and then you fell flat on your ass."

"You're a liar!"

"In front of all these wonderful people. Didn't he fall flat on his ass? See. Everyone's nodding. You gotta lot of style, Duke Henry. You're terrific with a gun and great with the girls, but a dancer you're not. Furthermore, you're gonna feel like hell in the morning."

"So?"

"So let's have one more margarita and call it a night."

"Having fun?"

"You betcha."

"It's high time," he told her.

The hotel was only four blocks away and Nora suggested they walk and they did, the limo creeping alongside at a snail's pace. Jim was singing "La Cucaracha" at the top of his voice and

Nora told him to cool it so he sang "La Cucaracha" in a whisper. Nora dismissed the limo in front of the hotel and gave the driver a generous tip and told him he had been a peach and then she linked her arm in Jim's and they went into the lobby. Jim stumbled on the rug. He didn't mean to knock over the rubber tree plant. He set it upright immediately and patted the waxy green leaves and looked very sheepish. Hell of a place to put a rubber tree plant, he muttered, right in a fellow's path. Why'd they want to do that for? Nora gave an exasperated sigh and took a firmer grip on his arm and guided him toward the stairs leading to the lower level.

"Where're we going?" he asked.

"The coffee shop is open twenty-four hours. I'm going to get you several cups, maybe some scrambled eggs and toast as well."

"Yuck!"

"Listen to me, Burke, and listen good. We're going down the stairs now. I want you to be very, very careful. I want you to hold onto my arm and hold onto the handrail, too. If you fall down, I'm going to leave you sprawling there and pretend I've never seen you in my life. Is that clear?"

"You don't have to be so bitchy about it. A person'd think I was drunk."

"A person just might," she agreed.

"You were the one drinking all those margaritas."

"Yeah, and I happen to be able to hold my liquor. Here we go. One step at a time. Watch it. Take your time. There, you're doing just fine. You're doing great."

"I'm not a baby!"

"That's a matter of opinion, love."

The coffee shop was brightly lighted and surprisingly crowded. They weren't the only ones who needed to recoup from a night on the town. Nora got Jim safely ensconced in one of the bright orange vinyl booths and he stared glumly at the cactus plant on their table and the rainbow-hued menus. A waitress in colorful native attire breezed over and gave them a big smile and Nora ordered a pot of strong black coffee. The girl looked at Jim and shook her head as if to say, "These Americans!" and hurried away. Jim slouched down on the seat and squinted his eyes against the bright lights. A spray of black locks had tumbled across his brow. His bow tie was all crooked. His elegant white

dinner jacket was badly creased. He had never looked more endearing. Nora reached across the table and smoothed the locks from his brow.

"You'll feel better after you've had some coffee," she said.

"I love her, Nora."

"I know you do, darling."

"There's no hope for me. She told me so. She said I would always have a place in her heart, but she could never love me the way I want her to love me. She said she hoped I would always be her friend."

"I'm so sorry, Jim."

"I worry about her. She—those pills they've been giving her. We both know what they are. They keep her going, she said. Metro gave 'em to Garland to keep *her* going, and look what happened to Garland. She's off 'em now, says she doesn't need 'em when she's not working, but she's as thin as an alley cat and every bit as jumpy. She's cut down on the liquor since she got back home, confines herself to white wine, but—"

Jim cut himself off, looking absolutely miserable. The waitress returned with a pot of coffee and two cups and saucers. Jim stared down at his cup as she filled it with the thick black brew.

"I make it extra strong," she said.

"Thank you," Nora told her.

"There's something else," Jim said as the waitress left. "She—she's become paranoid. I think it must be the pills. She claims someone is following her, keeping track of every move she makes. There was a man in Arizona, a guy in a pickup trunk. He was staying at the same motel and kept his eye on her, made notes on what she did, who she was with. She says the same guy followed her back to L.A., says she saw him at Farmer's Market last week. She's cracking up, Nora."

"She just needs a long rest, darling. Julie's a lot stronger than anyone gives her credit for being."

"There's no hope for me. No hope at all."

Jim drank four cups of coffee and, at Nora's insistence, ate an herb omelet and two pieces of dry toast. It was after four in the morning when they left the coffee shop. Jim looked wretched, but he was able to make it back up to the lobby without any help. He was silent as they rode up to her floor on the elevator. Nora took her room key out of her evening bag when they

reached her door. Jim sighed and took it from her and unlocked the door, and then he looked into her eyes.

"Thanks, babe," he said.

"I had a great time, Jim. I loved the margaritas, and I've always wanted to learn the Mexican Hat Dance."

"I—uh—I'm sorry I got so maudlin downstairs. I didn't mean to spoil your evening, but Julie's been on my mind and I guess— I guess I just had to talk to someone."

Nora nodded and reached up to smooth back the spray of locks that had tumbled across his brow again, and then she straightened his crooked bow tie. He shook his head, looking into her eyes again.

"You know what?"

"What?"

"You're a pretty terrific girl," he said.

"And you're a terrific guy."

"It's a shame it couldn't have been the two of us, isn't it? We would've made a great team."

"The best," she agreed.

"I love you, babe."

"I love you, too."

Jim smiled and gave her a huge hug, and Nora went on into her room. Both of them were still hung at two the next afternoon as his limo took them to the airport. The stewardess in first class asked them if they would like a drink before takeoff and Jim groaned and Nora shook her head politely. The stewardess was excited about having Jim Burke on the flight and Nora hoped she wasn't going to be a pest. Jim gripped her hand as the motors revved up and they began to move down the runway. He really *was* frightened of takeoff! He damned near broke her fingers before they were finally airborne and the plane leveled off, and then he promptly fell asleep. Some company you are, she thought bitterly.

The stewardess had bright red lips and bright red nails and wore a clinging navy blue uniform that made her look like a Barbie doll. She fluffed her blonde hair and smiled and said she thought Mr. Burke looked a bit ill.

"Mr. Burke's a bit hung," Nora said sweetly.

The stewardess took the hint and bustled away to see to the needs of other attractive men, grudgingly serving the women. Jim lolled over in his seat, resting his head on her shoulder. Her

heart swelled with affection. He was a wonderful man and she was damned lucky to have him in her life, even if he wasn't Mr. Right. Friends lasted a hell of a lot longer than lovers. Poor Jim. He wouldn't win Julie, no—Nora understood why, even if he couldn't—but one day he would meet the right girl and she would make him very happy. Hell, she thought, one day I might even meet the right man. In the meantime, who *needs* him? I've got the best friends in the world, and I've got my writing. That's what it's all about. No man could ever give me the feeling I get from pounding the keys and watching the pages pile up. This new book's gonna be fantastic. It's gonna knock 'em right off their rockers.

Nora felt a wave of elation as she thought about the book taking shape in her mind. She could hardly wait to get home and get to work on it.

18

Julie stood very, very still and told herself she was not going to crack. She was not going to scream. She was going to be calm. She was going to be pleasant. The studio had arranged everything. They were being so cooperative now, so concerned, so helpful. She had been nominated for not one but two Academy Awards and she was their Golden Girl and so they had sent the dress over here, along with the fitters, to save her a trip to the studio. The studio was paying for the dress. The studio was providing the limousine that would take her to the theater. The studio was providing her escort, a very handsome young actor who needed to have his name linked with a hot property. Property. That's what I am, she thought. I'm their property. Jesus, sweet Jesus, don't let me crack. Her heart started palpitating and she could feel the trembling in her legs and she knew it was tension, she knew it was nerves. She wasn't going to collapse.

Julie took a deep breath and willed the panic away.

They fluttered around her, two slight, fussy young men, one blond and one brown-haired, the blond Rick, the other Ralph, and Brenda, a stout, mannish woman in a tailored black suit. They pulled and tugged and pinned, treating her like a wax dummy, discussing her as though she weren't there. I wish she were taller, this skirt needs more length to flow properly. The bodice isn't dramatic enough, we need more padding. A creation

413

like this requires boobs, not a washboard. Pale oyster-gray satin overlaid with light violet chiffon aglitter with silver and violet-blue sequins. The full skirt is fine but the short puffed sleeves and heart-shaped neckline make her look like the Sweetheart of Sigma Chi. That's the look they want. Young. Fresh. Innocent. They gonna put a bow in her hair? Julie closed her eyes, her knees shaky. The dress was gorgeous, designed especially for her, and it had cost a fortune. She detested it. As they worked with their pins and their tape measures Julie looked at herself in the full-length, three-sided mirror the studio had sent over.

Who is she? She is much too thin and her face is drawn, devoid of makeup, the eyes as big as saucers, it seems. Frightened eyes. The golden-brown hair is too golden, it isn't my hair. Who is she? She is a stranger. She isn't me. Not me. I'm trapped inside her. I've got to get out. Someone has to help me. Help, she cried silently, please help me, and the fitters continued to work and chat and the telephone shrieked and she heard the crisp, efficient voice of the secretary the studio had hired to handle the calls and keep her on schedule. Yes, four o'clock, Miss Parsons, we're looking forward to seeing you.

The secretary stepped to the door. She was a spy. The studio had sent her here to spy. I'm not being paranoid. I need someone to watch after me. I need someone to help me cope with all the appointments and demands, the studio says. Helga will stay with you until after the awards ceremonies. Helga will take care of everything. You need her, Julie baby. We're watching out for you. We've got your best interests at heart. No need for you to be bothered with all those calls, all those bothersome details. Helga will keep the show running. This isn't a show, Julie thought. This is my life. Why didn't I tell them that?

"Are you almost finished?" Helga asked the fitters.

"Just a few more minutes," Brenda said.

"Miss Hammond's agent will be here to see her at eleven o'clock and after that she has to eat lunch. At two o'clock there's a photo session by the pool and at four Miss Louella Parsons will be here to do an interview."

"We've got our work to do, too, sweetie," Ralph told her.

"She's wearing this dress to the Oscars," Rick added. "It's being televised. Millions of people are going to see this dress."

"Speed it up!" Helga ordered.

Helga was tall and thin and wore brown tortoiseshell glasses

and had her drab blonde hair pulled into a tight bun on the back of her neck. In her navy blue suit and white blouse she looked like a testy Nina Foch. The phone rang again. She turned on her heel and marched briskly out of the room.

"Hate to meet her in a dark alley," Ralph said.

"I don't know," Rick replied. "Might be interesting."

"Finish that hemline," Brenda told them. "We've got to get back to the studio and work on the Barbara Rush gown and finish up the costumes for Sheree North."

"All right, sweetie," Rick told Julie a few minutes later. "You can get off the stand now. You can take off the dress."

"Mind the sequins," Ralph warned.

"Here, love," Brenda said, leading her toward the screen. "Let me help you.'

"We supposed to take the mirror back with us?" Rick inquired.

"I'm certainly not hauling it out to the van," Ralph informed him. "I'm paid to work on costumes, not do menial labor. They want it back they can get some rednecks out here to *bring* it back."

Behind the screen, Brenda helped her out of the dress and folded it carefully and placed it in a long flat box. Julie put on her white blouse and her brown wraparound skirt. She ran her fingers through her too-golden hair, and then she lighted a cigarette. The fitters left, gossiping merrily about another actress who was mysteriously gaining weight and would undoubtedly be visiting an abortionist as soon as the Powers That Be discovered she was knocked up again. Julie drew on her cigarette, the butt crackling. Helga marched back into the room.

"The studio's sending over a makeup man and a hairdresser at one," she said. "I'm afraid you won't be able to linger over lunch."

"Why?"

"I just explained, Miss Hammond."

"Why are they sending over—"

"The photo session. Parsons. They certainly can't photograph you looking like that. And we want to make a good impression on Parsons."

"Of course," Julie said. "We must kowtow to Louella."

"One of the press agents from the studio will be here to help you through the interview."

"Of course," Julie said.

"Is something wrong, Miss Hammond?"

"What could possibly be wrong?" Julie asked.

There was an edge to her voice. Helga didn't like that. Helga would undoubtedly report her to the studio. Helga can go fuck herself. Why don't I tell her that? Why do I let them do this to me? Why? I'm a human being, not a robot to be wound up with a key and set into motion.

"Marty Katzman will be here in twenty minutes," Helga told her.

"Bully for him," Julie retorted.

Helga gave her a worried look and left the room. Julie smiled. She didn't know why she was smiling. She wanted to cry. She wanted to bawl like a baby. She crushed out her cigarette and promptly lighted another one and then she wandered aimlessly through the beautiful rooms of the beautiful house with its beautiful furniture. The studio had leased the house for her and the studio had provided the furniture and the studio had hired her servants. She was a tiny fragile animal inside a luxurious shell that wasn't hers at all and she wanted out. She wanted to run away. She wanted a drink. No, she told herself. I will have one glass of white wine for lunch and one glass of wine for dinner, and that's all. I am not going to let them turn me into an alcoholic, and I am not going to let them turn me into a junkie, either. The doctor said I *needed* the tranquilizers, but I'm not going to take them. I'm not going to take anything. Not after Arizona.

Julie wandered into the spacious living room with its plush white carpet, its creamy white walls, pale blue satin drapes and glass-and-chrome tables and sofas and chairs upholstered in pale blue and pale violet satin, a set created especially for her by one of the studio decorators, everything provided, right down to the silver lamps and crystal ashtrays and the mauve-and-gray abstracts hanging on the walls. A shell. It's not mine. The liquor cabinet was white with silver trim, crystal decanters on top, bottles and glasses inside. Gin. Scotch. Vodka. Julie had discovered vodka in Arizona. It helped counteract the pills. The "vitamins." They had given her an immediate lift and she had been charged with energy, raring to go, and she did her job and then the pills turned on her and she was so edgy she wanted to scream and climb the walls and the vodka helped then. How

many bottles had she consumed there on the desert? Two dozen? Three?

Arizona had been a nightmare from the beginning. Just thinking about it made her shudder. They were staying in a sleazy motel, it was the only accommodation they could find for cast and crew, and every morning they had to climb into jeeps and drive out into the desert. Sand. Cactus. Scorpions. Blazing lights. The role was physically rigorous and demanding, mentally and emotionally demolishing, and it took every ounce of energy and stamina she had to get through each day. She was the only female in the cast. After work was over for the day, there was no one to turn to. Jeff Hunter hadn't wanted to be in the picture, either, and although he was a charming fellow and a competent actor, he had not given his all and it was difficult to play well against someone who held back and refused to give. There were minor confrontations the press blew up into a full-fledged feud. Ray Danton and Neville Brand were both pros and both played to the hilt and in their zeal they had roughed her up considerably. It was great for the camera but hell on Julie. For two solid weeks she had been terrorized by the villains, bound, gagged, brutalized, raped, and she had returned to the motel each evening a trembling, nervous wreck.

The panic attacks began. Her mouth turned dry and her heart began to palpitate and her hands shook and her legs trembled and she was terrified and the doctor told her it was just stress, there was nothing wrong with her heart and she wasn't going to collapse. He gave her vitamins to keep her going and tranquilizers to calm her down and it didn't get better, it got worse. The vodka helped. There was a liquor store two blocks from the motel and she became its best customer, walking back to the motel with a brown paper bag full of fifths of hundred-proof vodka. Oblivion in the evenings. Hangovers in the morning. Hell during the day, losing her temper, snapping at Jeff, arguing with the director, blowing her lines, acting irrational, not herself at all yet giving an inspired performance the studio agreed was her best to date. Originally slated as a B western, *Fury in Leather* was going to be released as a major picture with full studio support and promotion behind it.

Julie had first noticed the man in the pickup truck four weeks into filming. She had paid no mind at first, but every time she stepped outside he was there, watching her. He had a notebook.

He wrote things down. He had a camera. He took pictures of her. One evening Neville Brand stopped by her room to see how she was feeling. He had slapped her around all day and had twisted her arm brutally, as directed. Although the scene had been carefully choreographed for them by the stunt coordinator and Brand had tried his best not to hurt her, he feared he might have wrenched her arm. Julie asked him in for a drink. Although a sullen brute in most of his screen roles, offscreen Brand was a good-natured chap with a raucous sense of humor and much personal charm, a hardworking pro admired by all who worked with him. She confessed that her arm felt a little sore but assured him that he had given a tremendous performance, making it so much easier for her to give a convincing one herself. They had a drink and Julie stepped outside with him and Neville gave her a friendly hug before going back to his own room. There had been a flash. Neville hadn't noticed, but Julie was certain someone had taken a picture of them and she was convinced she knew who it was.

But why?

Somehow she had managed to finish the film, returning to L.A. a complete wreck, her nerves in shambles. She stopped taking the pills immediately. She knew what they were doing to her. She stopped drinking the vodka and limited herself to white wine, tapering off as much as possible. The man in the pickup truck seemed part of the nightmare of Arizona and she forgot about him completely until she took Danny to Farmer's Market for lunch and saw the same man watching her and she was terrified then and felt another panic attack building and hurried Danny through lunch and drove home as soon as possible. Jim came to visit and she told him about the man and she could tell that he thought she was being paranoid. Maybe Jim was right, Julie thought now, gazing around the sumptuous living room. Maybe I am cracking up. I'm so tired. So tired. I'm falling apart, and I don't know how I'm going to make it through the day, much less next week, next month. How am I going to make it through my meeting with Marty and the photo session and the interview with that dreadful Parsons woman without . . . I can't.

I need a drink. Just one small vodka. Just one can't hurt.

Julie started toward the liquor cabinet and she had almost opened it when she realized what she was doing. You're *not* a lush, she told herself. You're not going to let them do to you

what they did to Gail Russell. She turned and sank down onto
the plush violet sofa, trembling, thinking of the beautiful and
tragic young actress who had died last August. A sensitive and
poignant beauty with soft black hair and deep-blue eyes, Russell
had been a star during the mid-forties and early fifties, and in
an interview she had once complained she had no time to think,
to relax and take stock. The extreme pressure of her career and
the failure of her marriage to actor Guy Madison had started her
on a self-destructive downslide. An affair with costar John Wayne
had culminated in scandalous headlines when Wayne's wife, Es-
peranza, had named Russell in her divorce suit. Hollywood is
lenient on its men, hard on its women. Wayne went on to even
greater glory. With the exception of a few minor films, Russell's
career was over. Vodka was solace for her, too. When they found
her body on the floor of her hundred-and-thirty-dollar-a-month
apartment she was surrounded by empty vodka bottles. She had
apparently died of starvation. She was thirty-six years old.

Shortly before her death, Gail Russell had made a film at the
studio, *The Silent Call*. It was about a boy and his dog, Russell
playing the boy's mother. Newly arrived from New York to do
The Slipper, Julie had met her in makeup one day, a sad-eyed
ghost of her former self but still heartbreakingly lovely. "You're
not cut out for this business," Russell told her. "You're sensitive, like me, I can see it in your eyes. You feel too much, too
deeply. I did too, once." Julie had been extremely embarrassed
and uncomfortable as the actress whose movies she had seen on
television continued to stare at her with those haunted blue eyes.
"Don't let them do to you what they did to me," Russell said
in her husky alcoholic voice. Julie never saw her again. Apparently that had been her last day at the studio. She forgot about
the incident until she read about Russell's death a few weeks
later. It had upset her greatly, and she had never forgotten those
words the actress had said to her. She remembered them now,
remembered the husky voice, the sad, sad eyes.

I'm not going to let them, she vowed silently. I'm not.

I've been in Hollywood a year and a half and look at me.
Look at me. I have a heart full of love, so much love to give,
and I'm living in a beautiful shell and they wind me up and set
me into motion and I perform like a good little girl and if I don't
they slap my wrists, they threaten me with suspension. You're
not too big, sweetheart. Keep in line and do as you're told or

we show you who's boss, we put you on suspension, we put you in a western and send you to Arizona. We own you, Julie baby. We *love* you. We want you to be happy. You do exactly what we say and everything'll be peachy-keen. We know what's best for you, baby. The results prove that. Four films, two of 'em not even released yet, and you're the biggest thing in pictures.

I don't want to be the biggest thing in pictures. I don't want to *be* in pictures.

"Here you are," Helga said tersely.

Julie looked up, startled. Helga stood in the doorway, tapping her foot impatiently.

"Yes?" Julie said.

"I've been searching all over for you, Miss Hammond. Have you forgotten Mr. Katzman?"

"I'd like to," Julie retorted.

Helga arched a brow at that. "He's waiting for you in the study," she said. "He's been waiting for over ten minutes."

Let the son of a bitch wait. I know why he's here. I know what he wants me to do.

"I'll be right there," she said.

Marty Katzman was the sharpest agent in the business. Marty Katzman kindly agreed to represent her when the head of the studio recommended him. Sonia had represented her in New York, of course, but Sonia hated Hollywood and told Julie she was making a terrible mistake, leaving the theater, and Sonia washed her hands of her. Marty was short and rather dumpy and wore natty, expensive suits and black horn-rimmed glasses. He had very thick, curly black hair and an ingratiating smile that would have made a shark turn around and swim in the opposite direction. He smiled it as Julie stepped into the study. He looked askance at her lack of makeup, her old white blouse and brown skirt.

"Julie, baby, how *are* you?"

"I'm fine, Marty."

"Don't you have a photo session this afternoon?" he inquired.

"I believe I do."

"And an interview with Parsons afterwards, right?"

"Right," Julie said.

"I don't want to upset you, baby, but you look a fright. You're going to have to do something about that before they arrive. We

can't let them see you looking less than your best, particularly Parsons. It's taken a lot of persuasion to bring her around."

Fuck you, Marty.

"The studio is sending over a makeup man and a hairdresser at one," she said.

Marty looked relieved. "I worry about you, sweetheart."

"I know you do, Marty. You love me like a daughter. You've told me so more times than I can remember."

"I do, doll. You've very special to me. A lot of clients I represent, I care zilch about. You're different. You always have been. That's why I've busted my ass, watching out for you, seeing you get everything you deserve. I want what's best for you, Julie."

"It seems to me I've heard that before."

"It's true," he assured her.

"Then why did I spend eight weeks in Arizona?"

"Julie, baby, they're *wild* about that picture. They're giving it one of the most expensive promotions since *The Robe*. I've seen the rough cut. Your performance—" Marty sighed and shook his head. "Words fail me, It's another Oscar for sure."

I've never liked you, Marty. Never. I've been meek and docile all these months and I've listened to your bullshit, knowing it's bullshit, knowing you're in league with the studio, their tool. Why? What's wrong with me? Am I really the spineless little fool you all take me to be?

"You read the script they sent over?" he asked.

"I read it," she said dryly.

"A great script. Great. A fantastic part for you. They're gonna shoot it in black-and-white. Arty. A serious film, full of meaning, full of punch. The public's gonna love it, of course, but this one's gonna wow the critics as well. Pauline Kael's gonna have an orgasm in print. This one's gonna go down in the books as one of the classics."

"It's not *Citizen Kane*, Marty," Julie said. "It's the story of an uneducated young country girl who falls in love with a handsome, smooth-talking ex-con, goes on a crime spree with him, shoots a policeman during a bank robbery, is captured and ends up in the electric chair. It's pure pulp fiction, tarted up with high-flown, second-rate Clifford Odets dialogue."

"Baby!" He was aghast.

"I won't do it," she told him.

"*Elude Me, Sweet Death* is a masterpiece, greatest script I've read in all my years in this crazy business. Half the actresses in Hollywood are fighting for this part."

"*Elude Me, Sweet Death* is pretentious trash. Half the actresses in Hollywood are welcome to the part. I'd suggest Mamie Van Doren. It's the sort of thing she's been doing lately, minus the pseudointellectual dialogue."

"I can't believe I'm hearing this," Marty said.

"Believe it."

"The studio wants you for this one, doll. They had you in mind when they bought the novel and had it adapted. The whole script's been tailored to your talent, your sensitivity. We can't pass this one up, Julie. It's too important. Filming starts next month and guess who they're trying to get to costar with you. They're trying to get Newman."

"If Newman has any sense, he'll tell them to go take a flying fuck at the moon."

Marty was appalled. He was dramatically appalled, his reaction exaggerated and overdrawn, like that of a hammy old silent screen actor. Julie pulled cigarettes and lighter out of the pocket of her skirt. A short while ago when they were fitting the dress she was to wear to the Academy Awards she had been a trembling wreck, on the verge of another panic attack, and now she was absolutely calm, as calm as she had been in months. She lighted a cigarette, unconcerned about Marty's reaction.

"You've got to do this one, Julie," he said finally. His voice was very stern.

"I don't intend to."

"You've got a contract. They'll put you on suspension."

"Let them."

"Julie, baby, you're upset, and you're not thinking clearly now. I know the pressure you've been under since the nominations were announced. Everyone wants a piece of you, right? Everyone wants to jump on the bandwagon. You've been deluged with reporters and photographers and I know it's been rough, particularly after Arizona, but—"

"I'm tired, Marty."

"I know you are, doll. Believe me, I understand—"

"I need a long rest. I need to spend some time with my son. I need to breathe."

"Of course you do, baby, of course you do." His voice was

kind now, kind and reassuring. He was humoring her as he might humor a not-too-bright child. "I know what you've been through, sweetheart, and just as soon as this film is in the can I intend to see you get a—"

"I'm not doing the film, Marty."

"But—"

"You're my agent, right? You represent *me*. You take ten percent of every penny I earn. So represent me. Tell them I can't do the film because of my health. Tell them—I don't care what you tell them, Marty. You'll think of something."

"They're not going to like this, Julie."

"That's too bad."

"They'll place you on suspension, and—baby, something like that, coming at a time like this, it could do you a great deal of harm. It could influence the judges. It could cost you an Academy Award."

"I don't give a shit," she said. "If you'll excuse me now, I'm going to have lunch with my son. I haven't seen him since early this morning."

"They—"

Julie didn't wait around to hear the rest of the sentence. She left the study and went upstairs to the nursery where she found a glum Danny gazing out the window at the swimming pool in back and a bored Mrs. Anderson reading a paperback novel. Mrs. Anderson was stout and middle-aged with short dyed-blonde hair and flat brown eyes. Julie wasn't at all satisfied with her, but she had had to find someone quickly when Hannah left for New Jersey, and Mrs. Anderson was the best of the lot she'd interviewed. She had only been here a week and a half, and Danny already detested her. Mrs. Anderson would have to do until she had time to find someone better.

"Ready for lunch, darling?" she inquired.

Danny turned. He frowned. Mrs. Anderson put down her paperback and got heavily to her feet. She was wearing a white uniform. She had insisted on it herself. She felt it gave her more professional standing.

"He's been a naughty one this morning," she said. "Marked all over the bathroom walls with his Crayolas, threw his Tinker Toys and his log cabin logs all over the floor."

"We'll discuss it later, Mrs. Anderson. Come along, darling. I've asked them to set the table out on the patio by the pool. It's

a lovely day. We're going to have shrimp and avocado salad and delicious homemade rolls.''

Danny scowled. He picked up Roscoe and hugged him to his chest and moved sullenly out the door. Roscoe was the giant black-and-white panda Lund Jensen had won for him at the shooting gallery in Maine. Danny had scarcely let Roscoe out of his sight since they returned from New Hampshire almost five months ago. Julie caught up with him and they went downstairs and out to the patio. The sun was shining brightly, and it was unusually warm, spring already in the air in mid-March. The white tiles around the pool gleamed, and the blue water sparkled with silvery reflections.

"Can we go swimming after lunch?" Danny asked.

"I'm afraid not, darling. Mommy is going to be busy."

"I never get to swim. The pool's out here and it's heated and no one ever lets me go in. Why do I have to have an adult with me? Why can't I go in by myself?"

"You don't really know how to swim properly yet, darling, and the water's very deep."

"Not in the shallow end, and I have my life jacket."

"Maybe we'll go swimming later on this afternoon after I get through with my interview."

"Yeah, sure," he said. "I'll just bet."

Danny parked Roscoe in a chair, took one himself and, propping his elbows on the edge of the table, rested his chin on his fists. He looked for all the world like a miniature of Doug, with his glossy brown hair, his slate-blue eyes and that sullen mouth. Julie felt a pang as she looked at him. Danny scowled again as the servant brought out the salad and the hot rolls and two tall glasses of iced tea.

"I wanted a hot dog and chili," he said, "and a Coke."

"You love shrimp and avocado salad. It's one of your favorites."

"It's one of *your* favorites. I just eat it to be polite."

"Be polite, then."

"I wanna have lunch with Auntie Nora. She always lets me have anything I want. Last time she ordered a whole pizza just for me. With anchovies," he added.

"Auntie Nora's too busy to have you over for lunch right now. She's just started her new book and she's working night and day."

"No one has any time for me," he complained. "I might just as well run away. I could join a circus or something."

"What would you do in a circus?"

"Feed the elephants," he said, buttering a roll. "I hate that woman upstairs."

"You don't really hate her, darling."

"I do so. I miss Hannah. Why'd she have to leave for?"

"I explained it before, Danny. Hannah's brother-in-law passed away. Hannah had to go stay with her sister in New Jersey. Her sister has three little ones and her husband did not leave her much money and she's had to go to work. Hannah is taking care of the little ones."

"I didn't want her to go."

"I didn't either, darling, but it was something she had to do. She waited until I got back from Arizona to leave. We'll see Hannah again. Maybe we'll go visit her one day."

"You'll be too busy," he said. "You're always too busy to do anything. I *hate* shrimp and avocado salad."

He was surly throughout lunch and misbehaved abominably and Julie finally told him if he wasn't going to eat he could go to his room. Danny gave her a savage look, grabbed up Roscoe and trotted back into the house. My son is becoming an unruly little monster, Julie thought, and I have no one to blame but myself. He isn't really naughty. He's very, very loving, but he needs attention and I've given him precious little of that recently. Julie finished her iced tea as the sunlight sparkled on the water, worried about Danny, wondering what she was going to do with him.

He *was* becoming unmanageable, growing worse day by day, it seemed, and Julie realized that she really was to blame. She was indeed always too busy to do anything with him. He'd been left here with Hannah during all those weeks she was working in Arizona, and as soon as she got back the Academy Award nominations had been announced and she hadn't had a moment's peace. She and Danny had gone out together once, just once, to Farmer's Market, and then she had hurried him home after spotting the man from Arizona. Hannah had left for New Jersey, and that had been a trauma for him. Hannah represented security, stability, and now she was gone and he was left with nothing but a nursemaid whom he detested and a mother who barely had time to see him during the day. It isn't right, she thought. It isn't

fair. Danny means more to me than anything in this world, and . . .

Staccato footsteps sounded loudly on the tiles. Julie turned to see Helga marching briskly toward her, a prissy expression on her thin face. I don't like that woman. Why do I put up with her? Why do I put up with any of this? Why should I?

"The makeup man and the hairdresser are here," Helga announced. "They are in a bit of a hurry, so—"

"Send them away," Julie said.

"I beg your pardon?"

"Send them away. I won't be needing them. And cancel the photo session. I'm not doing it. I'm not doing the interview, either. Why should I? Why should I speak to that awful, vicious woman who's said so many terrible things about me in her column? Why should I do *any*thing I don't want to do?"

"Miss Hammond, I—I really must protest. The studio is paying me to see that you—"

"Fuck the studio," Julie said.

Helga Lundquist was visibly shaken. Her face was white, her painted red lips and brown tortoiseshells standing out in sharp contrast. It took her a moment to gather herself, and when she spoke her voice was like ice.

"I'll have to report this," she said.

"Do that, Miss Lundquist, and after you've finished making your calls I want you to leave. I don't want you in my house any longer."

Helga whirled around and marched back into the house. Julie lighted a cigarette. The studio would be furious. When Marty told them she refused to do the film and they saw she meant it, the studio would undoubtedly place her on suspension till she came round. She discovered that she didn't care one way or the other. I'm not going to have a panic attack and I'm not going to take a tranquilizer and I'm not going to have a drink. I'm going to be strong. I'm going to take charge. She smoked her cigarette and watched the sunlight reflecting on the pool. I won't let them force me to make the picture, she vowed. I need some time off. I need some time with Danny. I need some time to pull myself together. Julie sat there in the sunlight for a long time, finishing her cigarette, smoking another, and she was surprised when Helga came back outside. She was carrying her purse and a small briefcase.

"I sent the makeup man and the hairdresser away," Helga said crisply. "I canceled the photo session, and I canceled the interview. Miss Parsons was not at all happy."

"She'll get over it," Julie said.

"I'm going back to the studio now, Miss Hammond. They're not going to be at all happy, either, when I tell them what has happened. I refuse to be held responsible. I've done my best, and—"

"Good-bye, Miss Lundquist," Julie said.

Helga gave her a look and left. Julie heard a motor revving a few minutes later. She felt a sense of freedom she hadn't felt in a long time, and she sighed. No photo session. No interview. No one pushing at her, pulling at her, probing. The telephone would ring, of course, but she didn't intend to answer it. Julie stood up, brushing a wisp of hair from her temple. The rest of the day was hers. She and Danny would go swimming, and later on she would take him out for a hot dog with chili and then, perhaps, to see the revival of *Dumbo* currently playing in Bel-Air. She went inside and had just started up the stairs when the front doorbell rang.

"Damn," she said.

She didn't wait for one of the servants. She answered the door herself and she was not really surprised to see Gus Hammond standing there. He held a large manila envelope. She knew what was inside it. She knew why he was here. Everything fell into place, and she understood now. He looked older than he had looked when he came to see her in New York. He looked smaller, more wizened, a little old man with dried skin and lined face and stale blue eyes that glared at her with hatred and disgust and determination. The tailored brown suit, the tooled leather cowboy boots, the string tie and silver-and-turquoise tie holder that had seemed incongruous in New York seemed conservative here in Beverly Hills.

"You're not surprised to see me?" he asked.

"Not really," she said.

I'm not going to let this upset me. I'm not. I'm going to handle this calmly.

"Please come in, Mr. Hammond."

He stepped into the foyer, and Julie shut the door and led him into the spacious living room. Hammond glanced around with extreme distaste and then those icy blue eyes settled on her,

taking in every detail. Julie was acutely aware of her uncombed hair, her old white blouse and rumpled brown skirt. She looked like hell and she knew it and that put her on the defensive. She needed a drink badly. She wasn't going to have one. She did light another cigarette. Her hand trembled slightly as she did so.

Hammond held out the manila envelope.

"I think you'd better look at these," he said.

Julie took the envelope and opened it and pulled out a sheaf of eight by ten photographs. They were black-and-white and not very good, their poor quality emphasized by the enlargement, but they were effective nevertheless. Julie coming out of the liquor store in Arizona with hair in her eyes, wearing an old cotton dress, carrying a brown paper bag with bottles clearly visible. Julie and Neville Brand standing outside her room in what could be construed as a passionate embrace. An obviously drunk Julie climbing into one of the jeeps. Julie and one of the stuntmen. Julie and Jim out by the pool, his arms around her, her head resting on his shoulder. The man must have used a telescopic lens for that one, Julie thought. She wondered where he had been when he took it. In a neighboring yard? She glanced idly through the rest of the photographs, then stuffed them back into the envelope.

"Your man has a lot to learn about photography," she said. "I should have known he was yours. It—it never entered my mind. I thought he was some demented fan."

Hammond took the photographs from her and put them on the coffee table. Julie finished her cigarette and stubbed it out in the crystal ashtray, and she felt shaky inside, despite all her good intentions.

"What do you want, Mr. Hammond?" she asked.

"I want Danny," he said.

She just looked at him. Gus Hammond frowned.

"I'm prepared to be reasonable. I'm prepared to pay you a large amount of money in exchange for your signing an agreement permitting me to take him back to Oklahoma with me. I'll set up a trust fund for him. I'll give him the best care, the best clothes, the best schools. He'll grow up as my heir and one day he'll inherit everything I have."

Julie lighted another cigarette.

"You'll still see him, of course. My lawyer will make all the arrangements. He'll spend part of every summer with you and

some holidays, a week at Easter, for example. As I said, I'm prepared to be reasonable. I don't want a court battle any more than you do.''

Julie was trembling inside. She wanted to scream at him, to smash his face, so great was her rage, yet her voice was perfectly level and beautifully controlled.

"I think you'd better leave, Mr. Hammond."

He indicated the manila envelope. "You know what those pictures mean, don't you? They mean I've got you. They're evidence, proving beyond a shadow of a doubt that you're unfit to bring up my grandson. I've kept my eye on you just like I said I would, and when I read in that Parsons woman's column about your drinking and carrying on, I decided it was time I went into action."

"You hired a private detective. You sent him to Arizona."

"I paid him a mint, thousands of dollars, but he did a bang-up good job for me. He was very thorough. He took these photographs. He took notes, very thorough notes. I know all about your drinking and your drugs. I know all about your fucking that ugly actor in your motel room and all about your affair with that fellow who plays Duke Henry. You fucked him right here in this house with my grandson present."

"I—I really do think you'd better leave, Mr. Hammond," she said, and there was a tremor in her voice now. "I really can't be responsible for anything I might say or do if—if you continue in that vein."

"I don't want to use the evidence," Hammond said. "I'm not a complete villain. I don't want to wreck your career, make a lot of trouble. I just want my grandson, and I feel sure you'll agree to my terms."

"Get out of my house," Julie said.

"You're not going to be reasonable?"

She was silent. She was afraid to speak, afraid of what she might say to him. She knew for a fact that if she had had a gun in her hand she would have pulled the trigger without a moment's hesitation. She would have blown his brains out without the least remorse. She could understand now the urge to kill. What she felt was more than outrage, more than anger. It was like a white-hot fire blazing inside her, and yet somehow, somehow she managed to maintain some semblance of outward calm.

"I've asked you to leave," she said. "Please do. Please don't push me.

Hammond stepped closer, his eyes glittering with malice now. "I've got you, you little bitch. Don't you *realize* that?"

Something was going to snap. She could feel it. She tried her best to hold on as the white fire blazed.

"Please leave," she said quietly.

"I've got you, and if I have to I'll take you to court and *prove* you're unfit to bring up my grandson."

"I don't intend to listen to this," she said.

"I'm taking Danny back to Oklahoma with me. I'm going to give him a *decent* unbringing. You wrecked my son's life. I'm not going to stand by and let you wreck my grandson's life as well."

Julie looked at his glittering eyes and his flushed cheekbones, and she crushed out her cigarette and moved over to the liquor cabinet. She opened the door and pulled out a bottle of vodka and gripped it tightly by the neck and she wasn't Julie any more. She was someone else.

"There's not a court in this land that won't give him to me when I present my evidence!" Hammond thundered, out of control now. "I've got millions of dollars, millions, and I'll spend every one of them on lawyers if I have to, but I'm taking Danny home with me. You're a whore and a drunk and you're not going to keep him! Go fetch him for me. Right now!"

Julie slammed the side of the bottle on the edge of the liquor cabinet. The glass shattered noisily and liquor splashed in every direction and Julie was still holding the neck tightly and half a bottle with sharp, jagged edges and it made a formidable weapon, much more threatening than a knife. She would turn it in his face if she had to, she knew that. So did Gus Hammond. His face had gone white.

"I'm not a whore, Mr. Hammond," Julie said. "As it so happens, I have never slept with any other man besides Doug, but that's none of your concern. I don't have to answer your filthy allegations, nor do I have to justify myself to you. I want you to leave."

"Have you gone out of your *mind*?" he yelled.

"I'm not a whore," she repeated, "but I am a mother, and I would kill gladly to protect my son. If—if you don't leave my

house this very minute I do assure you I'll cut your fucking face off."

Was that her voice? How could she possibly sound so cool and calm when the white hot fire was blazing inside her. Hammond stared at her with an incredulous expression, his eyes wide, his face bleached of color.

"You can't intimidate me! I—"

"I mean what I said," Julie informed him.

"This will go into the report, too! I'm going to hire the best lawyers in the country. I'm going—"

Julie stepped toward him. Gus Hammond snatched up the envelope full of pictures and stumbled backwards, almost falling. He turned and hurried into the foyer and a moment later Julie heard him opening the front door and then heard it slam shut. She looked at the thin streams of vodka slipping slowly down the side of the liquor cabinet like huge tears and at the broken bottle in her hand and she was amazed. Dear God, what came over me? Richard Egan did that in his last picture, only it was in a smoke-filled bar in Honolulu, not a living room. I . . . I must have temporarily taken leave of my senses. But it worked. Julie put the broken bottle down, and her hand shook. She was shaking all over. She folded her arms around her waist, holding herself tightly. She closed her eyes.

It was several minutes before she was able to control the nervous spasms that swept over her, and then she poured herself a drink. A small one. I deserve it, she told herself. I've earned it. Julie sipped the vodka slowly, standing there in the living room. The vodka steadied her nerves. That horrible man. Those horrible pictures. Those horrible allegations. None of it is true. He isn't going to take Danny away from me. He can't. He wanted to frighten me. He thought he could frighten me into accepting his terms. You can't take a child away from his mother, not in America. Dear God. I can't deal with this now! I can't.

Julie finished her drink. She didn't pour another one. She cleaned up the mess, wiping the liquor cabinet and blotting the carpet with paper towels and dropping the shards of glass into a wastebasket. The telephone was ringing. She didn't answer it. Martha, who worked in the kitchen, and Stephen, her husband, who served and supervised the cleaning crews who came in weekly, had been instructed never to answer the phone unless requested. Neither answered it now. It rang for a good three

minutes and then stopped and started again two minutes later.
Julie stepped into the office, took it off the hook and hung it up
and then took it off the hook again, leaving it. There was no one
she wanted to talk to this afternoon.

She went upstairs, much calmer now. Danny wasn't in the
nursery. Mrs. Anderson was sitting in a comfortable chair with
her feet propped on a stool, reading her paperback. Harold Rob-
bins. She looked up as Julie stepped into the room, not at all
perturbed, making no effort to get up. She was chewing gum.
Julie felt anger welling up again. Mrs. Anderson seemed irritated that someone had had the temerity to disturb her reading.

"Where is Danny?" Julie asked sharply.

Mrs. Anderson glanced around the room. "He was here a
few minutes ago," she said.

"You were hired to look after my son, Mrs. Anderson. You
were not hired to sit around reading paperback novels."

"A person has to have *some* free time," the nursemaid
snipped.

"You can have all the free time you like," Julie retorted. "I
want you to gather up your things and get your fat ass out of
here. Immediately. You're fired. I'll send a check to the agency."

"Well! I never—"

Julie left the room. She went to Danny's bedroom. He wasn't
there, nor was he in any of the rooms upstairs. He was probably
in a corner somewhere, sulking because she wouldn't let him go
swimming by herself. Swimming. The panic hit her all at once
and Julie froze on the stairs, paralyzed, her heart beating like a
trip-hammer. Her skin seemed to have turned to ice. Danny had
defied her several times of late, but surely he wouldn't . . . surely
he knew how dangerous . . . She heard his voice then, coming
from the distance, calling her.

"Mommy! Mommy! Mommy!"

Julie literally flew down the stairs and raced down the hall
and through the sitting room and out the open French windows
and onto the patio, but to her it seemed as though she were
moving in slow motion. She saw the gleaming white tiles and
the sparkling blue water and Roscoe was sitting in one of the
deck chairs and Danny was in the deep end of the pool, splashing and kicking, flailing his arms, crying for her. He was wearing his bright orange life jacket, thank God he was wearing his
life jacket, but his little head kept bobbing under nevertheless

because of his struggles. Julie kicked off her shoes and ran across the patio and dove into the water, all in an instant, and then she really did move in slow motion, under the water, everything blurry and shiny, silver and blue, two pudgy little legs and a blob of bright orange visible to her right, several yards away. She kicked and propelled herself forward, surfacing beside him and clutching him to her.

She swam to the steps, pulling Danny along with her. She climbed out of the water and gathered him into her arms and sank down onto one of the chairs and sobbed hysterically, holding him tightly. She sobbed and sobbed, without restraint, her whole body trembling violently. Danny gazed at her with wide, startled blue eyes. He had never seen his mommy like this before. It frightened him. Her hair was all wet and plastered to her head and long snaky tendrils covered her forehead and eyes. Danny gently smoothed them back and saw the tears brimming over her lashes and felt her body trembling all over. He scooted up in her lap and wound his arms around her neck and rested his cheek against hers. Several minutes went by before her body stopped trembling and the tears stopped spilling. She grew very, very still.

"It's all right, Mommy," he said. "I just drifted."

"My baby," she whispered.

"I had my life jacket on," he explained. "I wudn't hurt. I was just kinda scared."

"I know, darling."

She held him close, shaken to the core by what had happened. It was her fault. She knew that. Maybe Gus Hammond was right. Maybe she wasn't fit to bring him up. Her arms tightened around him and the tears welled again. It isn't me, she told herself. It's this town. It's Hollywood. It's this business. I . . . I don't have Carol's strength, her drive. I don't have her need to be a star. Being a star means everything to Carol. It means nothing to me. I don't belong here. I never have.

"You mad at me, Mommy?" Danny asked.

She shook her head, holding him close.

"Hadn't you better get ready for them picture-taking people?"

"They're not coming. I—Mommy canceled everything."

"You're not gonna be too busy for me?" he inquired.

"I—I'm not ever going to be too busy for you again, precious.

I promise. We—you and I are going to—we're going to go away for while. We're going to take a vacation, just the two of us.''

Danny sat up, his eyes wide again.

"We're gonna leave Hollywood?''

Julie nodded, smoothing the damp locks from his brow.

"But—what about your mah-caddy-me award?''

"That isn't important,'' she told him. "It doesn't matter at all. You're the only thing that matters to me, darling.''

"Where're we gonna go?''

"I—I'm not sure.''

"Could we go see Lund, Mommy?''

"I don't know, Danny. Lund is—I'm sure he's very busy, and he might not want us to—''

"Sure he would!'' Danny exclaimed. "Lund *loves* us. Lund didn't want us to leave. That'd be great, seeing Lund again. It'd be the bestest thing I would think of. Let's go call him, Mommy. Let's go call him right now.''

Danny jumped down and took her hand and pulled her to her feet, his face all aglow. Julie had rarely seen him so elated. She let him lead her into the house. She felt elation herself at the thought of seeing Lund again. It would be good for Danny, and . . . she refused to allow herself to think beyond that. As soon as they had dried off and changed into fresh clothes she would place the call.

19

The Beverly Hills Hotel was huge and pink and gaudy, the sky a brilliant blue as Nora cruised up the palm-tree-lined drive five days later. She and Carol had just returned from driving Lund, Danny and Julie to the airport, and both agreed that a drink— or several—was called for. Carol suggested the Polo Lounge, and somehow it seemed appropriate. Nora stopped the car and a doorman opened the car door for Carol and helped her out and a good-looking young car jockey performed the same service for Nora. She surrendered her car keys with some reluctance.

"Mind the fenders, love," she told him. "I know it's not much, but it happens to be all I've got."

The youth grinned at her and promised he would take good care of her car and see she got it back in perfect condition.

"Bet this is the first time he's ever parked a lowly Thunderbird," Nora told Carol. "He's used to Rolls and Mercedes and the occasional Bentley. Do I look all right in this dress? You sure they're not gonna take one look and throw me out?"

"Stop playing the hick," Carol scolded. "You've had lunch here dozens of times."

"Yeah, and I've never gotten used to it. Do you think we might see some real live movie stars?"

Carol gave her a look of mock exasperation and they stepped into the elegant lobby. Nora was wearing a gold-and-tan striped

sundress—it was like summer today—and Carol looked cool in pale beige. People stared discreetly as they entered the Polo Lounge. It's this knockout body of mine, Nora told herself, this gorgeous face. The fact that Carol's an international star has nothing to do with it. As the maître d' prepared to seat them at one of the much-coveted banquettes, Carol politely asked if it would be possible for them to be seated outside on the patio. No problem whatsoever. Hell, he would've tossed Darryl F. Zanuck out on his ass in order to make room for Carol. They were seated at a choice table under the Brazilian pepper trees, surrounded by tan, blond, beautiful people who all looked as if they had just stepped out of a bandbox. Carol waved to Sylvia Wallace, who was lunching nearby with Jorja Curtwright, the former actress married to screenwriter Sidney Sheldon and one of the great ladies of Beverly Hills, Carol informed Nora.

"I've met Jorja," Nora said. "She's Hollywood's most gracious hostess, a renowned interior decorator as well."

Mrs. Sheldon looked up, spied Nora and smiled warmly. Nora smiled back and lifted her water glass to her.

"Want some lunch?" Carol inquired.

"You treating?"

"Naturally."

"Something light, then. I really came here to drink."

Carol ordered a bottle of chilled Pinot Chardonnay, Royal squab and some beluga malossol caviar. Nora made another wisecrack. Both of them were sad, both of them trying valiantly not to show it. Sunlight filtering through the leaves of the pepper trees made dancing patterns of light and shadow over the tabletop.

"Jesus," Nora said. "I'm going to miss her."

"So am I," Carol told her, "but she seems to be in very good hands. I fell in love with Lund."

"Me, too. I hate to admit it, but I was tempted to bang Julie over the head with some heavy object and run off with him myself. Not only is the man absolutely gorgeous, he's intelligent and level-headed and tremendously efficient as well. Julie phoned him and tried to act casual but after a few minutes she broke down and started crying and told him about Gus Hammond and the studio and all the pressures she's been under, and Lund told her to stay put. He took the first plane to L.A., arriving the next morning. Then he simply took charge."

Their wine arrived, and as the waiter was uncorking it and pouring, Nora thought about the past five days. Julie had called the studio and calmly informed them that she was breaking her contract and leaving Hollywood for good and all hell had broken loose. The press went wild, Julie's "defection" making headlines all over the country. Parsons had penned a scathing column in which she pointed out that the studio had invested a huge fortune in building Julie up and now all those hundreds of thousands of dollars were a total loss because of Julie's "rank ingratitude." That was the kindest thing she wrote, and she ended her column with a stern warning to Shirley Jones and Diane Baker and other up-and-coming young actresses, telling them they'd best be grateful for all Hollywood had done for them as there were hundreds of girls waiting out there to take their places if they didn't toe the line. Louella made no mention of those millions of dollars Julie's films had made and would continue to make for the studio. Fox was rushing the last two out just as soon as possible in order to capitalize on the notoriety.

"To Julie," Carol said, lifting her glass.

"To Julie."

They drank, and then Nora sighed.

"She'll never work in this town again, of course."

"She doesn't want to," Carol pointed out. "The theater has always been Julie's first love. If and when she feels the urge to act again, New York is just a short train ride from South Medford. If the right part came along, I feel sure Lund would be very supportive."

"I know he would. She looked radiant at the airport, didn't she?"

"So did Danny. I've never seen him so happy."

"Did-ja see him stick his tongue out at all the photographers while Lund was fending off the press? That kid's something else. I—uh—I guess this blows the Oscars for her, too."

Carol nodded. "Rumor has it that *The Miracle Worker* is going to make a grand sweep now, Anne Bancroft for best actress, Patty Duke for best supporting actress. I—I feel certain Julie would have taken home at least one of those awards if this hadn't happened."

"She didn't get an Oscar," Nora said, "but she got her happy ending. I'd say that's a pretty good trade-off."

"So would I," Carol agreed.

"I'll tell you one thing, love—Julie's gonna be a helluva lot happier than you or I will ever be. She's lucky. She isn't cursed with driving ambition and a burning desire to scale the heights. She has exactly what she's always wanted."

"I—I almost envy her," Carol said wistfully.

Nora gave her a sharp look. "Don't bullshit me, Martin. You wouldn't give it all up for *any* man, and you bloody well know it."

"I don't suppose I would," Carol confessed.

"Neither would I. It was different with Julie. Julie got the slipper, all right, but it never really fit."

Nora took another sip of the deliciously cool wine. The waiter brought the caviar along with minced onion, chopped-up boiled egg and a tray arranged with thin slivers of toast. Carol watched with a thoughtful look in her eyes as Nora heaped caviar onto one of the slivers.

"You know," she said, "it's funny about the slipper. All three of us grew up believing in the myth. We all had the dream and we all got the slipper and I—I suppose we all expected to live happily ever after. They tell you about the slipper but—they don't tell you about the sacrifices you have to make. They don't tell you about the hardships and the heartaches. They don't tell you there *is* no happily ever after."

"This is it," Nora informed her.

"I suppose it is."

"Pretty damn grim, isn't it? Caviar. Pinot Chardonnay. You an internationally famous film star, me a best-selling novelist. I may start bawling any minute now."

Carol had to smile. "I may, too."

"I *love* being a best-selling novelist," Nora said.

"And I love being an internationally famous film star."

"Eat your heart out, world. We've got it made. Who *needs* Mr. Right?"

"Who indeed?"

"I've got my work, and this new novel I'm doing is fabulous—it's gonna knock 'em dead. Ross has already turned down half a million bucks from Simon and Schuster, he believes we can get more with a complete manuscript in hand, and film rights are gonna go through the ceiling. Every morning when I wake up I can hardly wait to get to my typewriter."

"I feel the same way about reporting for work."

"So there you are," Nora said.

They drank their wine and nibbled on caviar, and then the waiter brought their Royal squab. He refilled their wineglasses. Nora gave him a winning smile. The leaves of the pepper trees rustled faintly in the breeze, casting more dancing patterns of sunlight and shadow, and all around them was the low hum of cultivated voices and the tinkle of ice cubes.

"I read about Lolly Dougherty's death," Nora remarked. "I imagine Blake was pretty torn up about it."

"He was," Carol said.

"You've seen him?"

"Night before last. We discussed a film project he wants me to do this fall. He'd sent me the script some time ago—it's wonderful. *Remember Dennie Lane.* I'm definitely going to do it."

"Blake Dougherty is a very handsome man."

"He is indeed."

"I imagine he could use a lot of comforting just now."

"Eat your squab, Nora."

"Who *knows* what the future might bring? Maybe there's someone out there for me, too."

"Maybe there is."

"It isn't as though either of us is over the hill. I'm just twenty-five years old—barely out of the cradle—and there's still plenty of time. Mr. Right could be just around the corner. Just think, Carol, we might both end up having it *all.*"

"It's possible," Carol agreed.

"In the meantime, I'm having the time of my life."

"So am I."

"Let's drink to the future," Nora said.

"Let's."

"And to Mr. Right—wherever he might be."

"Why not?"

They exchanged a look. Both of them smiled.

"In fact, love, if you don't think it'll break you, you might just order another bottle."

About the Author

JENNIFER WILDE lives in Texas in a three-story, octagon-shaped red brick house filled with books, paintings, antiques, and an old manual typewriter on which another bestseller is currently being written.

PEACH'S
MONSTER
COMPENDIUM

the enemy!
TAP

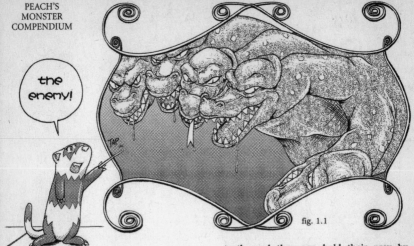

fig. 1.1

Handra

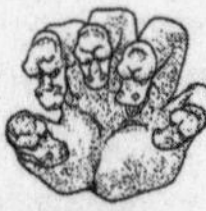

As young kits, we are taught by our mommy-ferrets about the terrifying monster of ferret lore: the Handra! We are warned that this five-headed reptilian beast snatches up bad ferrets and takes them away, never to be seen again. My littermates and I didn't really believe in them, but all the same, we strived to be good little ferrets...just in case. But the truth is the Handra is more than just a mythological beast-it is real! And it snatches up all ferrets, good or bad!

Having been captured by the creature personally, I speak from experience when I say the Handras are cruel, controlling, unfriendly, and selfish! They seem to take great pleasure in keeping a large stable of prisoners under their control, then pitting these captives against each other in battle. They watch from the sidelines and reward the winner with treats.

Handras also seem to enjoy taking on these prisoners in one-on-one combat. I myself have been forced to fight them on numerous occasions. Handras are very strong! They can use their massive frame to push and prod. Worse, they have a powerful bite with sharp teeth, and they can hold their prey by coiling their multiple heads into a constricting grip. Their defense, however, is surprisingly weak. Their thin, furless hide offers little protection from a ferret's bite and they are quick to retreat if attacked head-on.

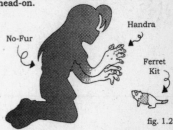

Handra
No-Fur
Ferret
Kit

fig. 1.2

It was originally believed that Handras were an independent and free roaming entity. However, we have recently discovered that the Handras are in fact part of a much larger monster: the No-Fur! To date, very little is known about the No-Fur, but we are undergoing studies to learn more. I personally believe that the key to defending against the Handra will come from a deeper understanding of the No-Fur.

see you next book!

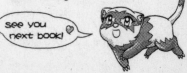

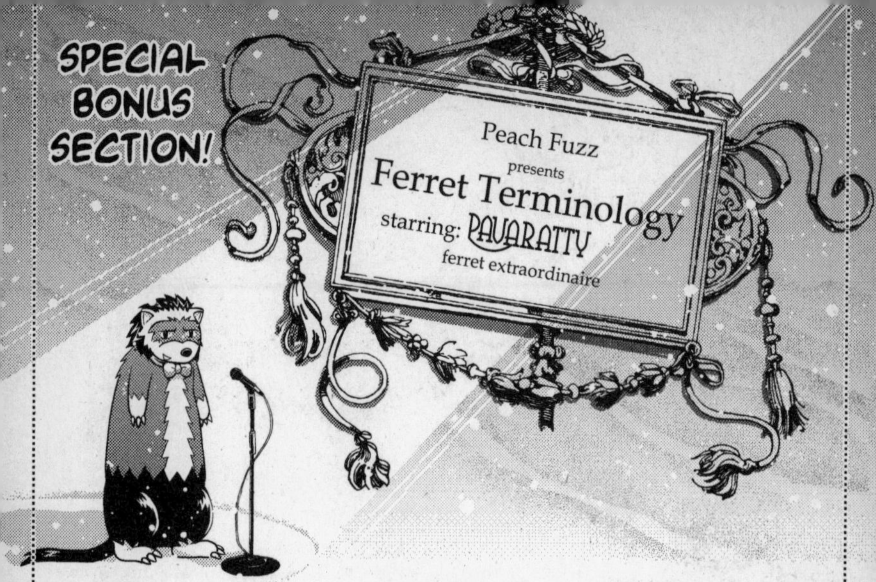
SPECIAL BONUS SECTION!
Peach Fuzz
presents
Ferret Terminology
starring: PAVARATTY
ferret extraordinaire

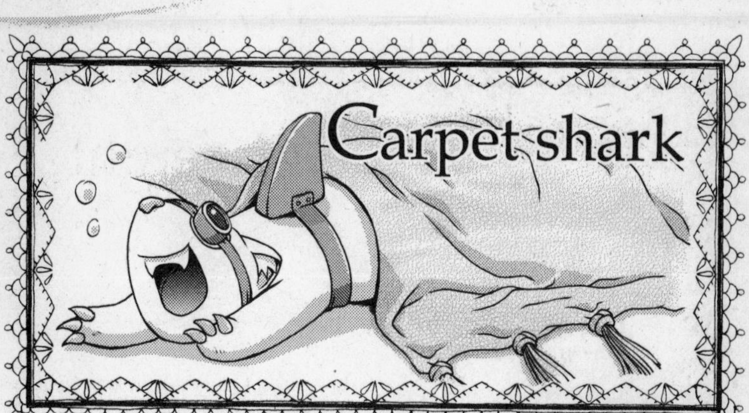
Carpet shark

A common nickname given to ferrets due to their dominance over the carpet...not to mention a mouthful of sharp teeth.

The act of swimming and zigzagging under a throw rug. May involve a surprise attack in which the ferret leaps out from under the rug at its unsuspecting prey.

Please be careful not to step on any suspicious rug bulges! There could be a ferret underneath!

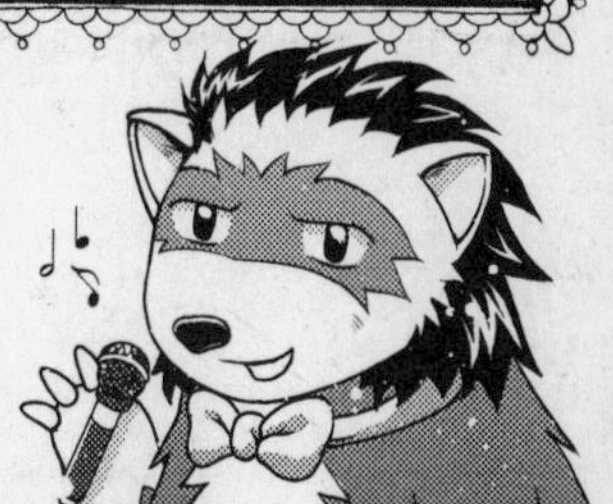

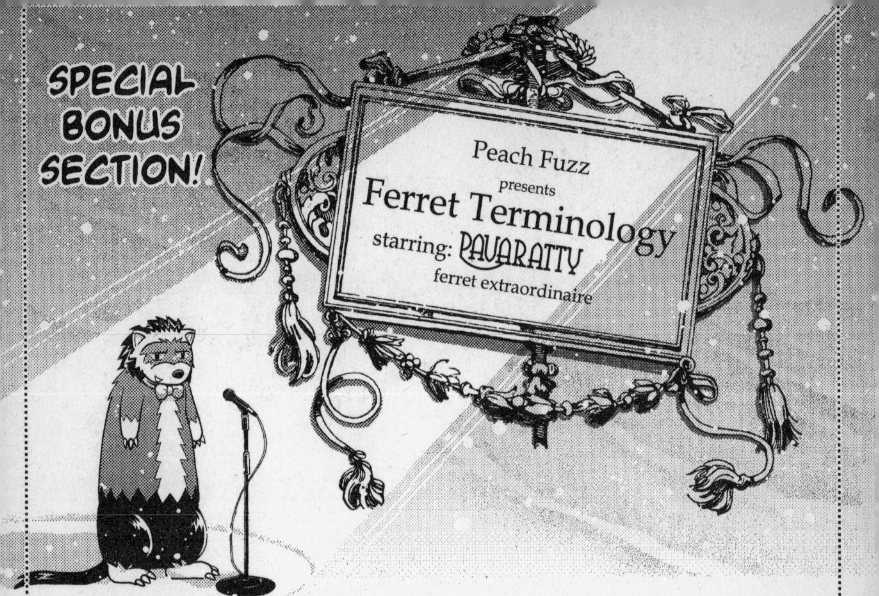
SPECIAL BONUS SECTION!
Peach Fuzz
presents
Ferret Terminology
starring: PAVARATTY
ferret extraordinaire

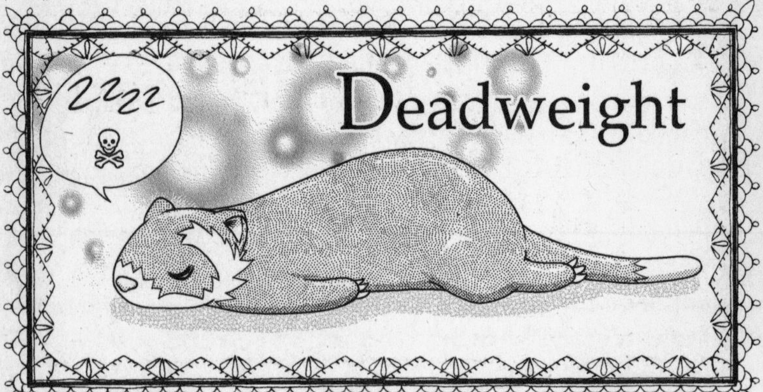
Deadweight
ZZZZ

One of a ferret's favorite activities is sleeping, which they tend to spend about 20 hours a day doing. This is because they require a lot of energy when playing.

As Peach demonstrated in chapter two, ferrets can sometimes sleep so deeply that they can be almost impossible to wake.

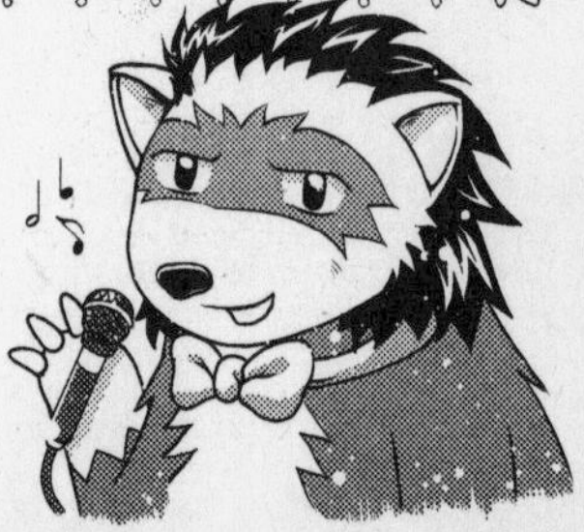

In the next volume of

Peach Fuzz

No way! The exciting day of "Show and Tell" in Amanda's class has arrived! Amanda *finally* has the chance to show off her fuzzy friend Peach to the school. But because some girls have to have anything that's popular, Amanda's classmate Kim gets a ferret of her own. But all ferrets are not created equal and, when personalities totally clash, Peach makes the new ferret her arch enemy! And Amanda, who for once is not feeling invisible to the other kids, takes the school's new obsession with ferrets a step too far and gets the attention of the meanest bullies on campus! Will Peach defeat her new foe? Will Amanda *ever* feel like she fits in at school? Find out in *Peach Fuzz* Volume 2!

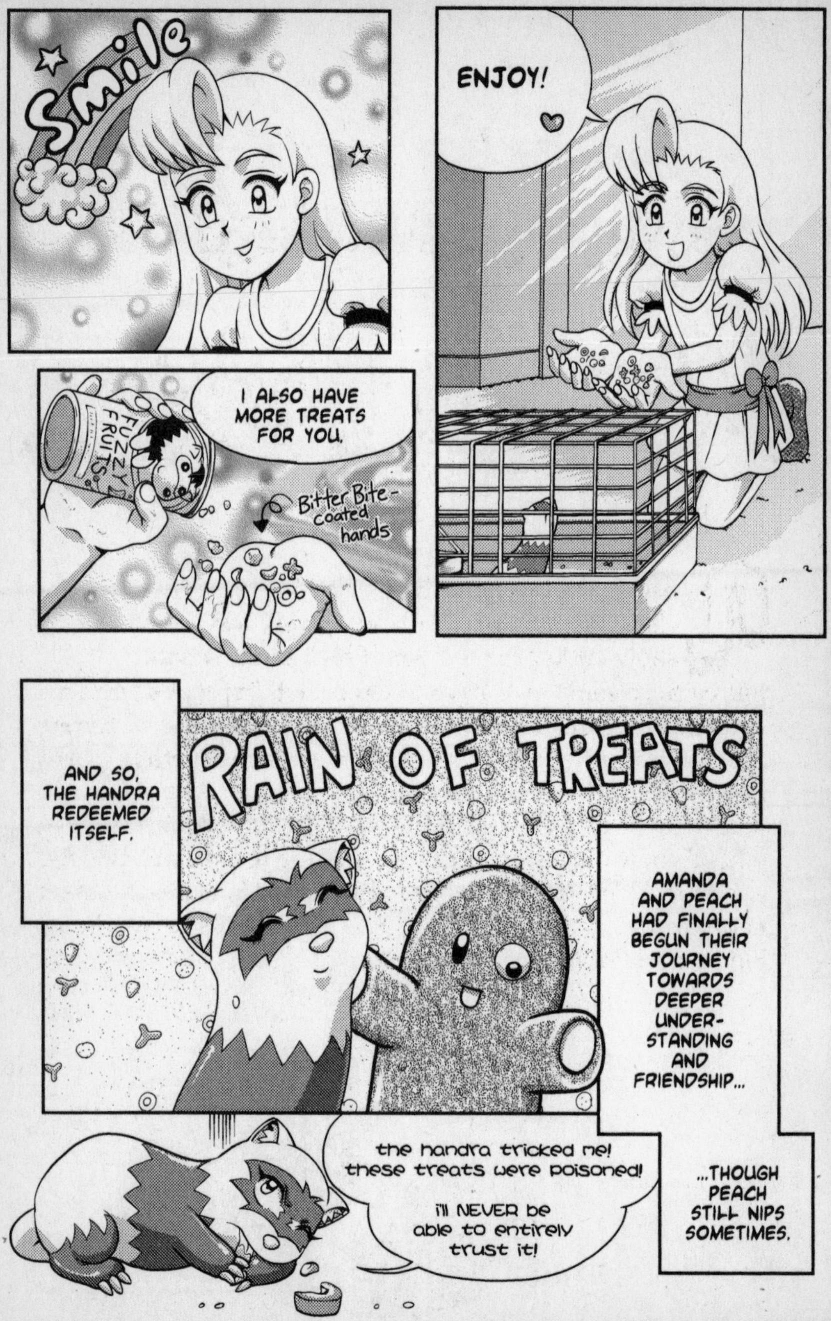
Smile
I ALSO HAVE MORE TREATS FOR YOU.
FUZZY FRUITS
Bitter Bite-coated hands
ENJOY!
AND SO, THE HANDRA REDEEMED ITSELF.
RAIN OF TREATS
AMANDA AND PEACH HAD FINALLY BEGUN THEIR JOURNEY TOWARDS DEEPER UNDER-STANDING AND FRIENDSHIP...
the handra tricked me! these treats were poisoned!
i'll NEVER be able to entirely trust it!
...THOUGH PEACH STILL NIPS SOMETIMES.

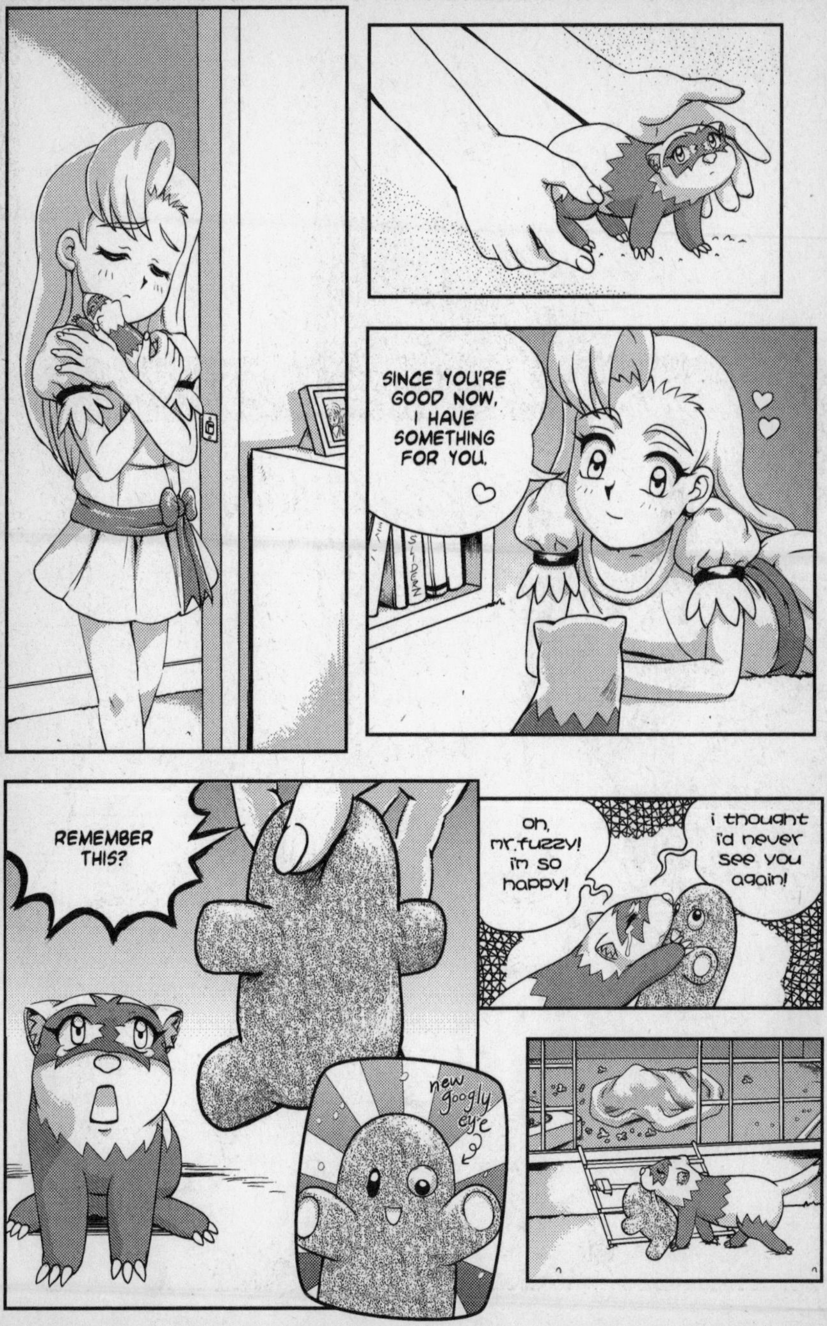
SINCE YOU'RE GOOD NOW, I HAVE SOMETHING FOR YOU.
REMEMBER THIS?
new googly eye
oh, mr.fuzzy! i'm so happy!
i thought i'd never see you again!

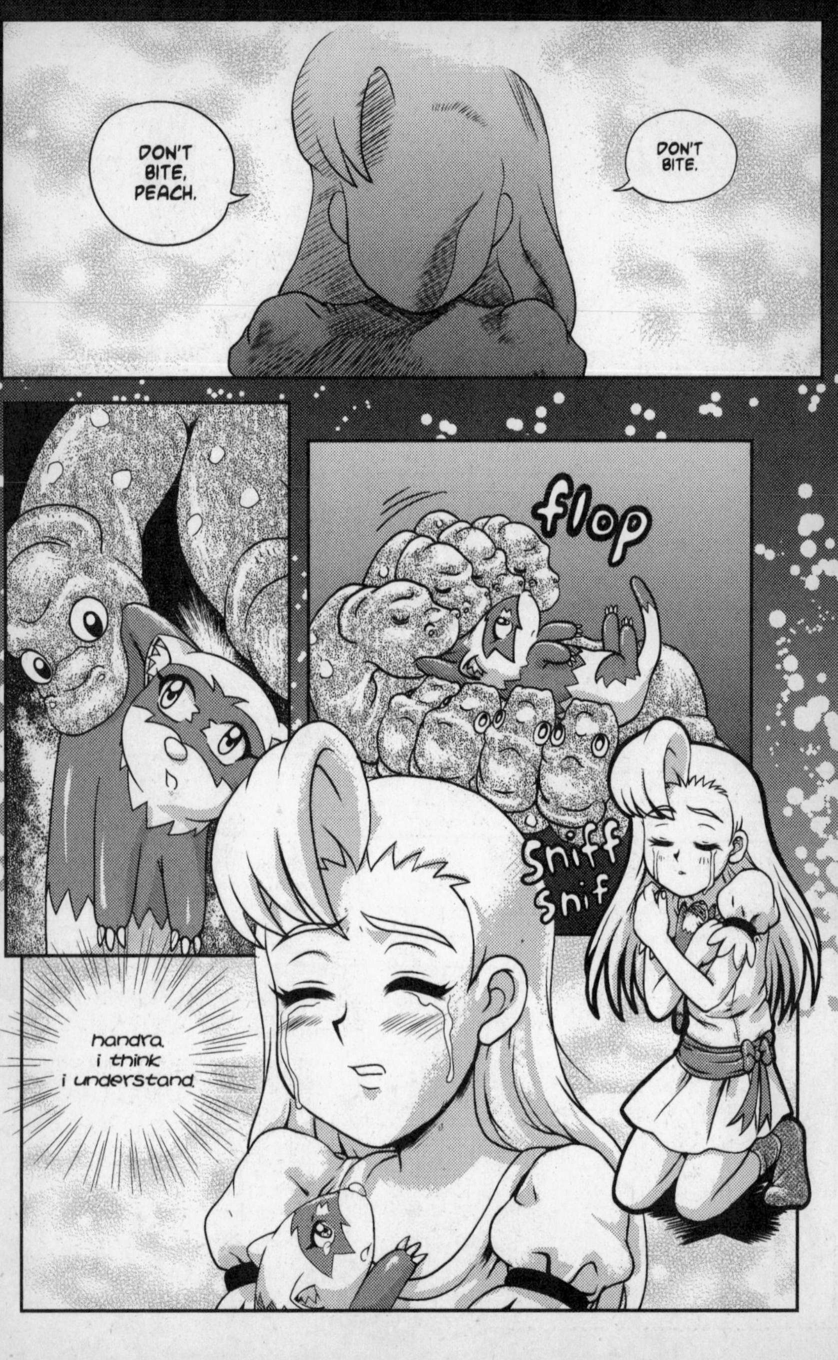
DON'T BITE, PEACH.
DON'T BITE.
flop
sniff snif
handra, i think i understand.

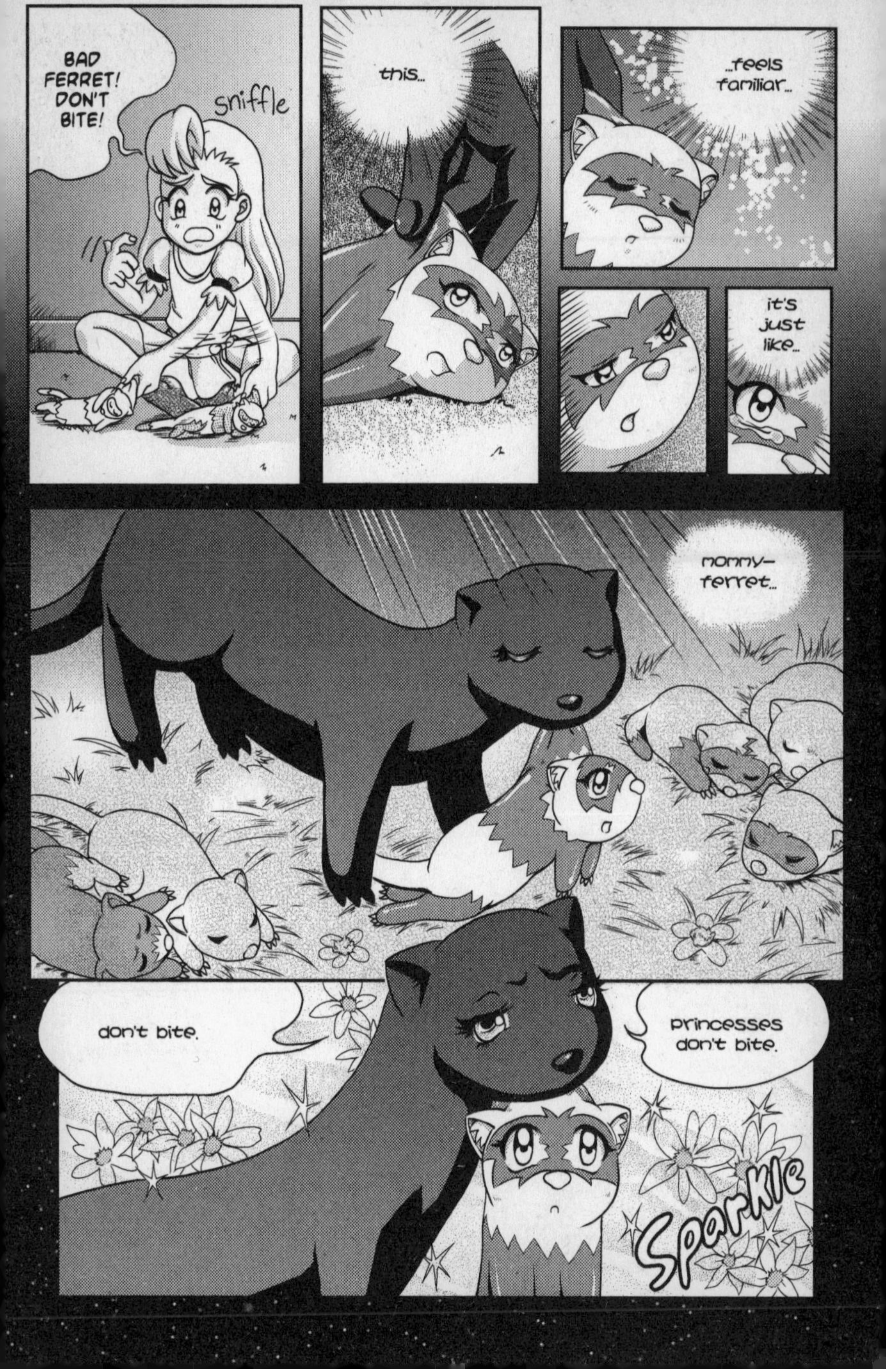
BAD FERRET! DON'T BITE!
sniffle
this...
...feels familiar...
it's just like...
mommy-ferret...
don't bite.
princesses don't bite.
Sparkle

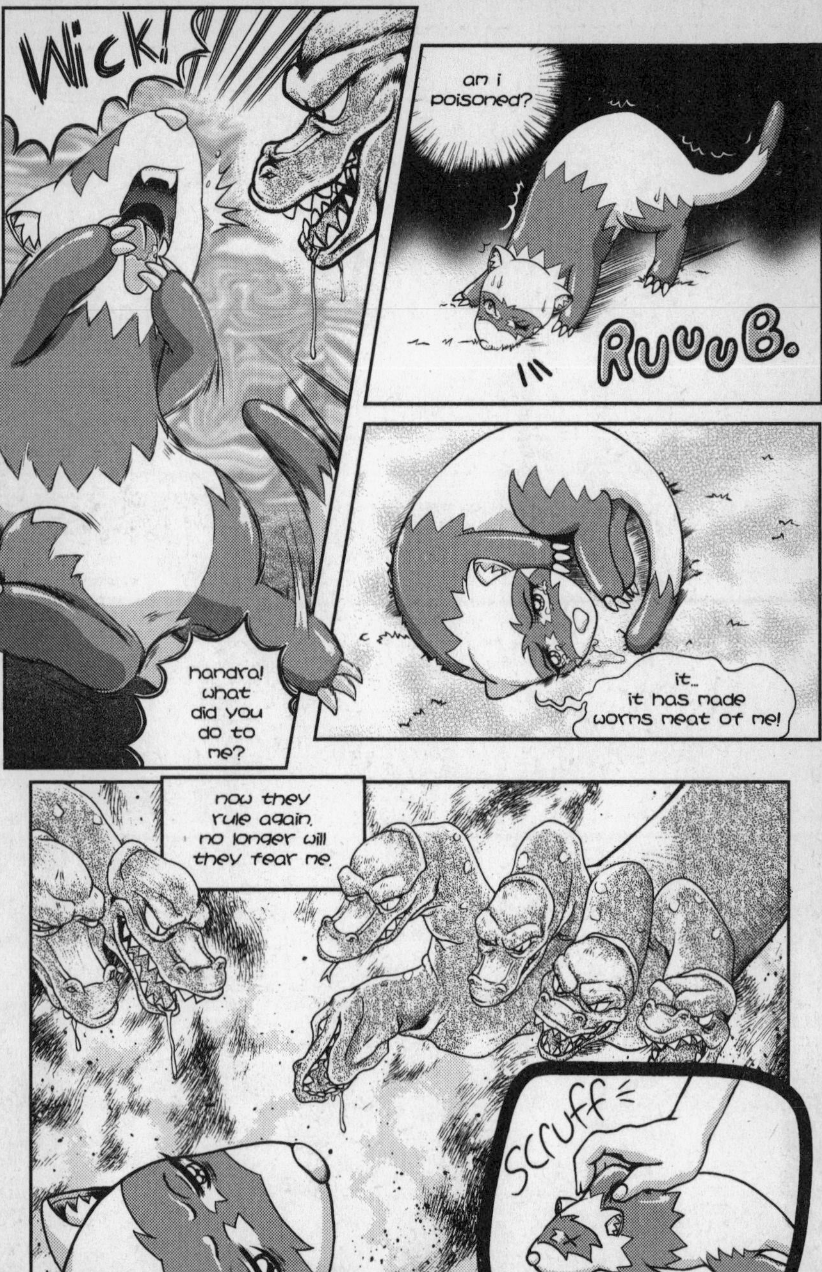
Wick!
handra! what did you do to me?
am i poisoned?
RUUUB.
it... it has made worms meat of me!
now they rule again. no longer will they fear me.
scruff

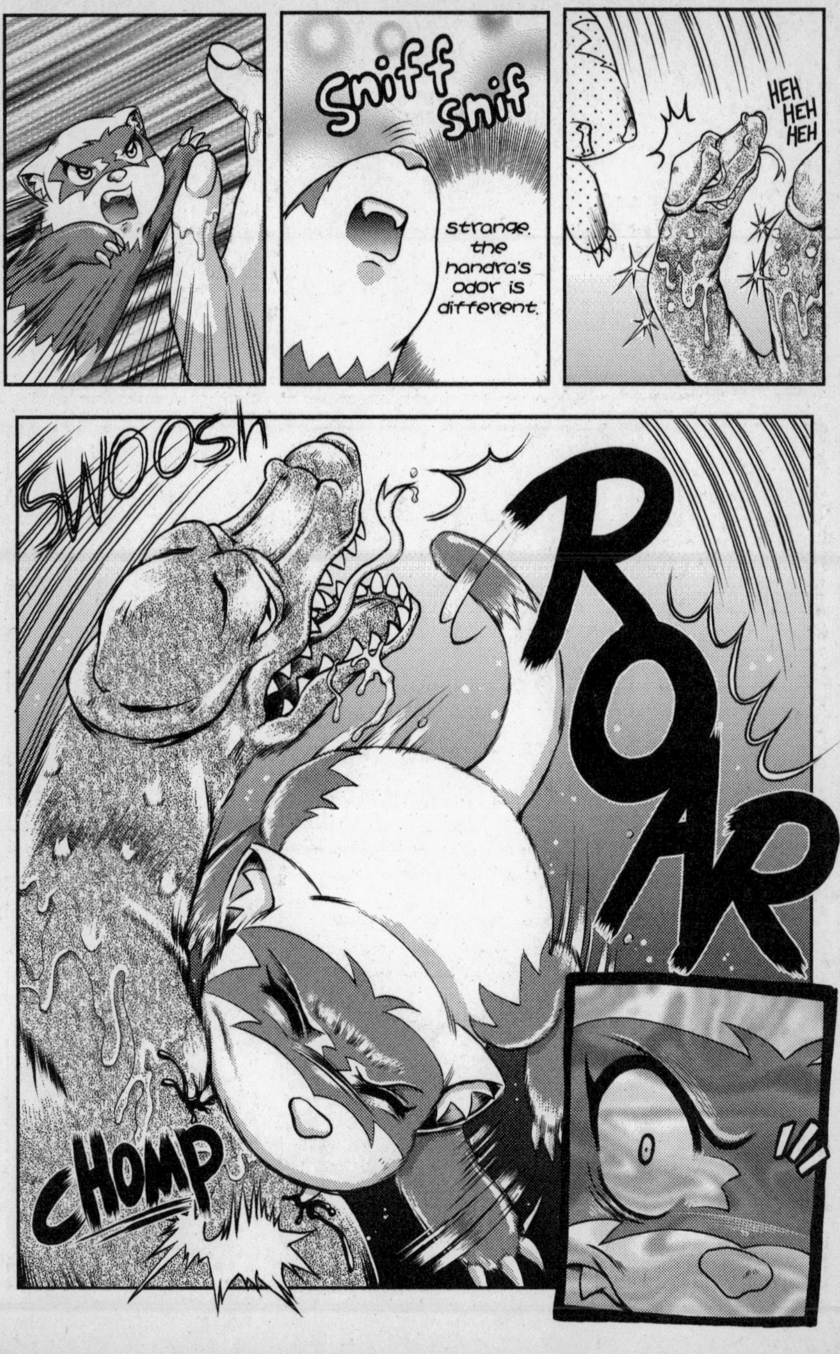
Sniff snif
strange. the handra's odor is different.
HEH HEH HEH
SWOOSH
ROAR
CHOMP

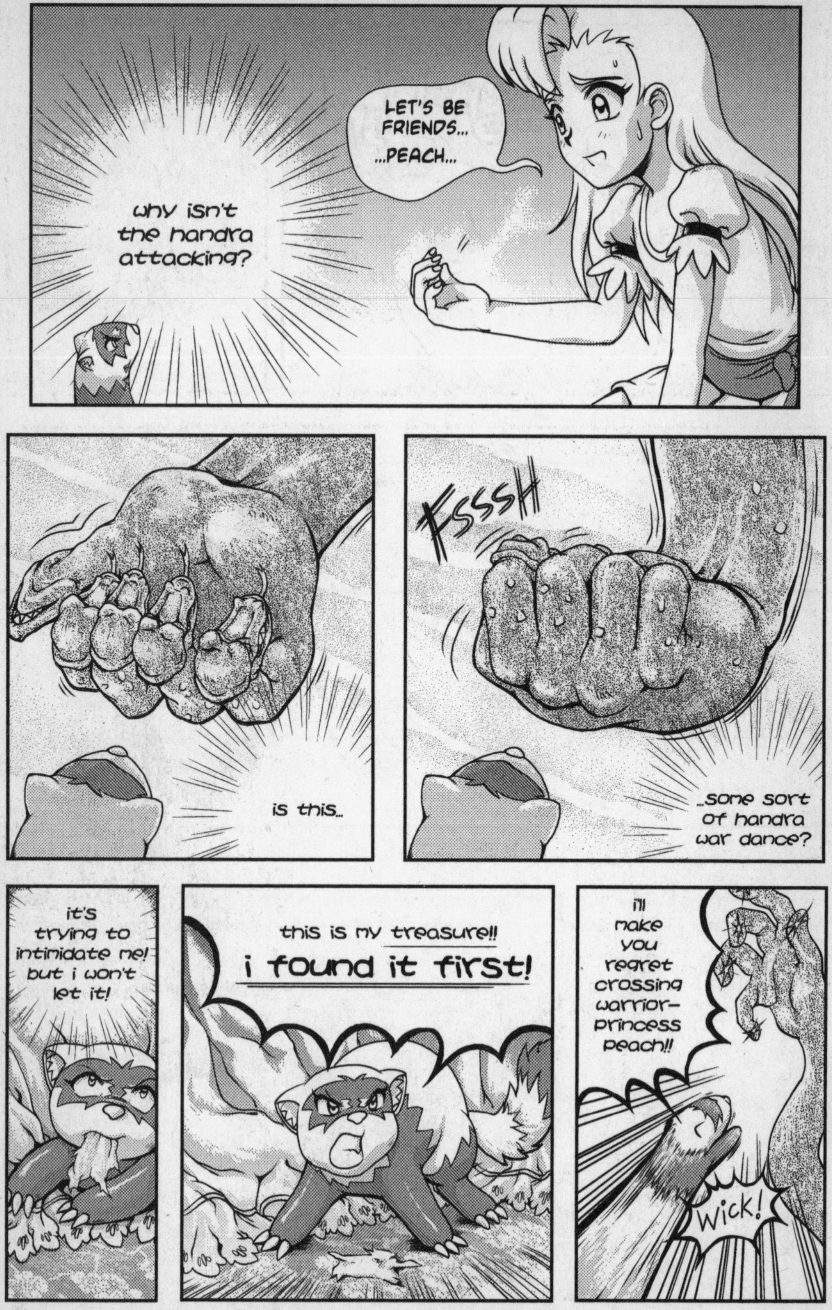
LET'S BE FRIENDS... ...PEACH...
why isn't the handra attacking?
is this...
FSSSH
...some sort of handra war dance?
it's trying to intimidate me! but i won't let it!
this is my treasure!! i found it first!
i'll make you regret crossing warrior-princess peach!!
WICK!

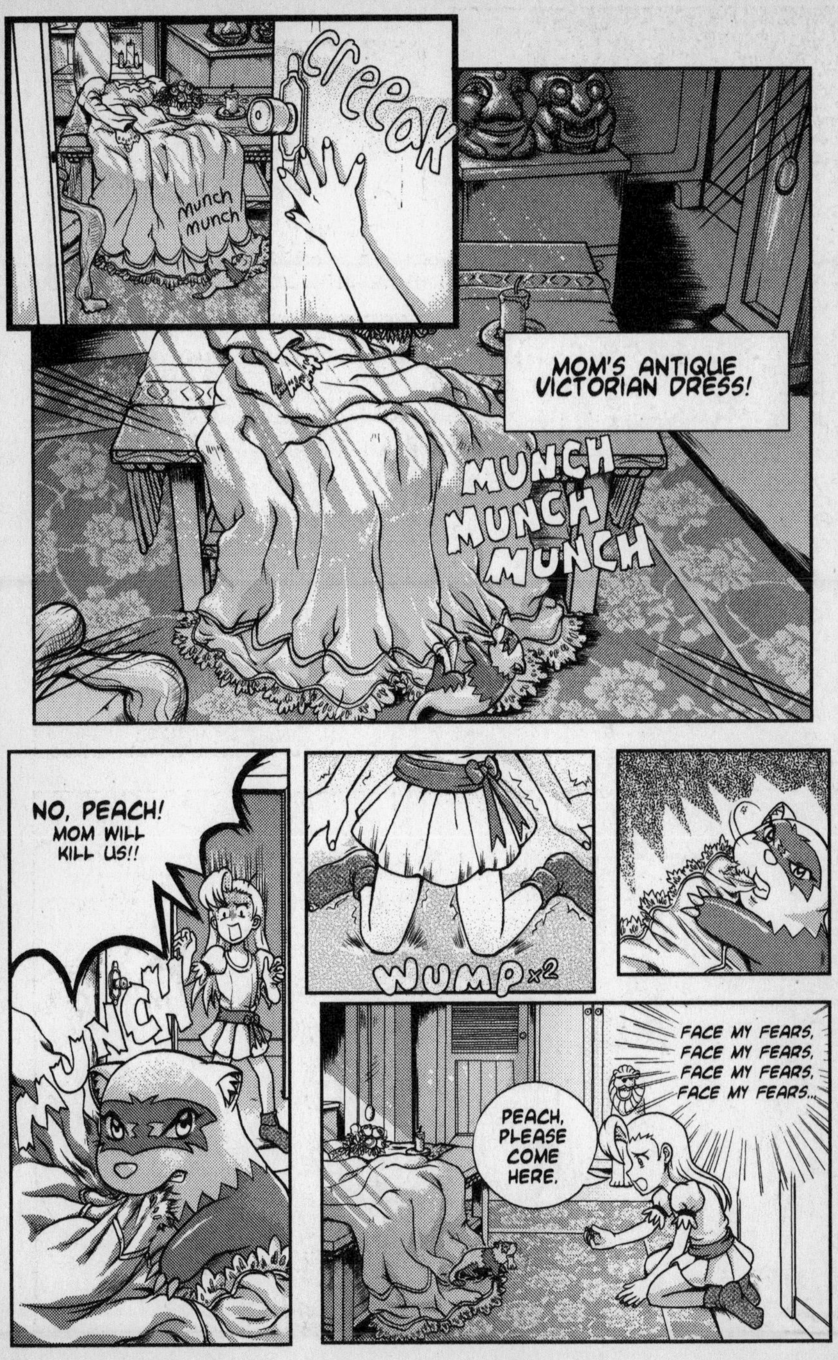
munch munch
creeeak
MOM'S ANTIQUE VICTORIAN DRESS!
MUNCH MUNCH MUNCH
NO, PEACH!
MOM WILL KILL US!!
MUNCH
WUMP x2
FACE MY FEARS, FACE MY FEARS, FACE MY FEARS, FACE MY FEARS...
PEACH, PLEASE COME HERE.

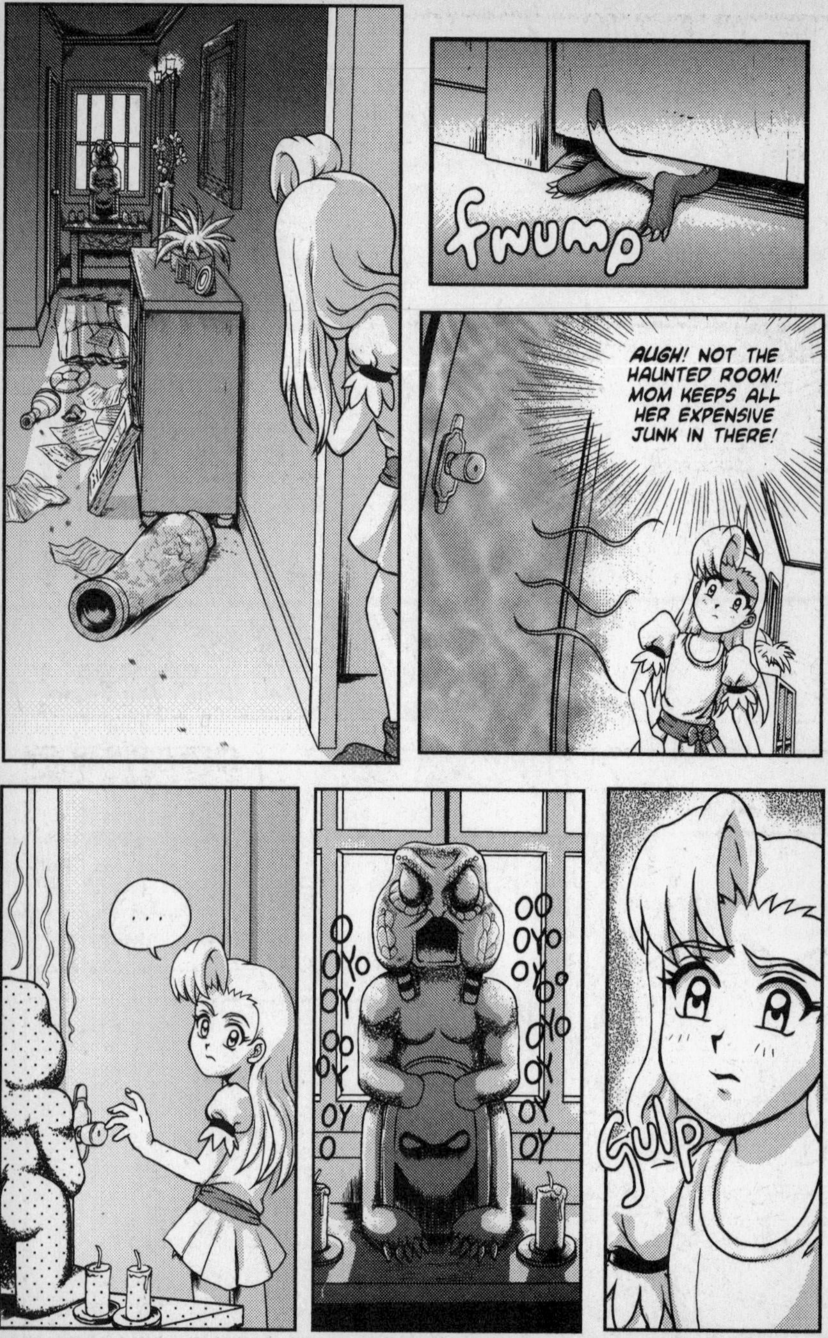
fwump
AUGH! NOT THE HAUNTED ROOM! MOM KEEPS ALL HER EXPENSIVE JUNK IN THERE!
...
OYO OY OYO OY
Gulp

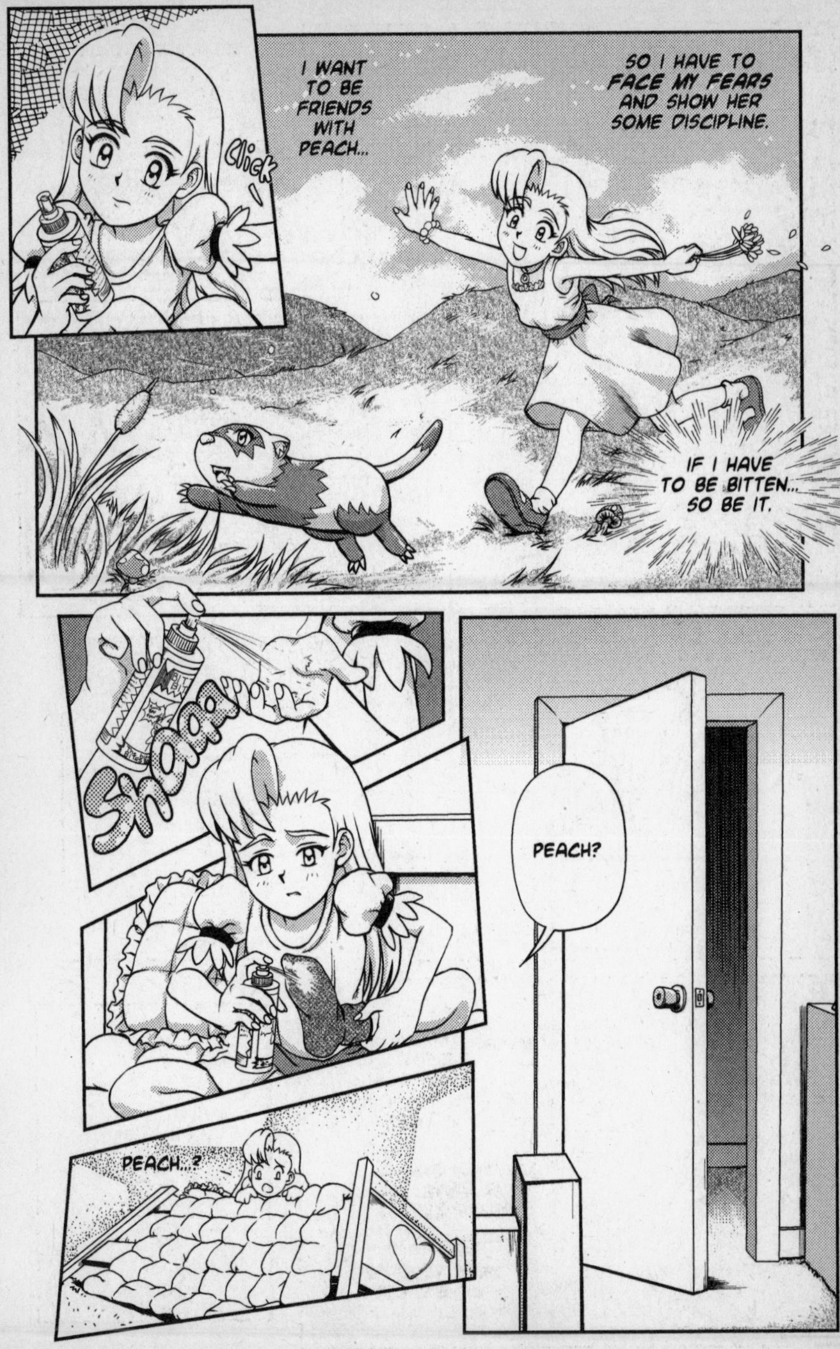
Click
I WANT TO BE FRIENDS WITH PEACH...
SO I HAVE TO FACE MY FEARS AND SHOW HER SOME DISCIPLINE.
IF I HAVE TO BE BITTEN... SO BE IT.
Shaaa
PEACH...?
PEACH?

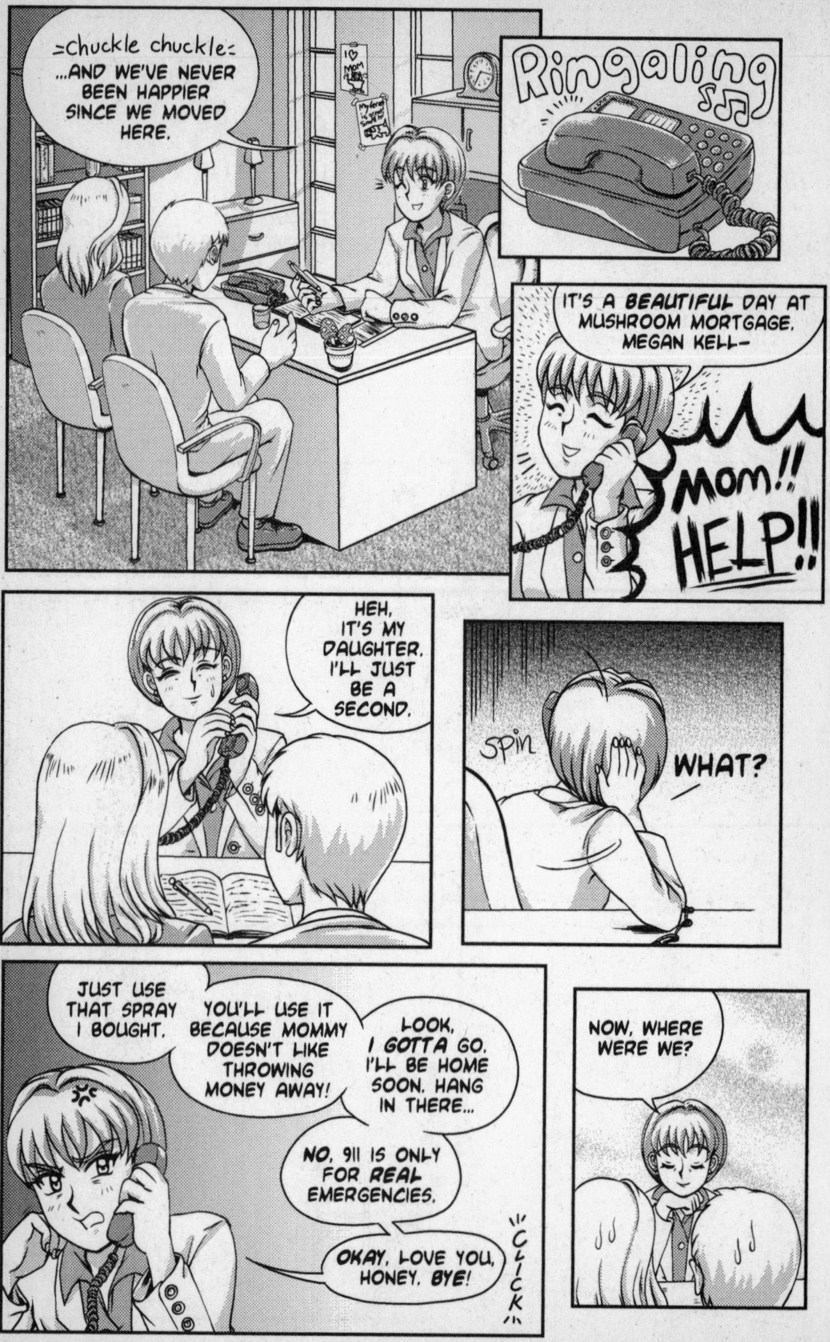
=chuckle chuckle=
...AND WE'VE NEVER BEEN HAPPIER SINCE WE MOVED HERE.
Ringaling
IT'S A BEAUTIFUL DAY AT MUSHROOM MORTGAGE. MEGAN KELL–
MOM!! HELP!!
HEH, IT'S MY DAUGHTER. I'LL JUST BE A SECOND.
SPIN
WHAT?
JUST USE THAT SPRAY I BOUGHT.
YOU'LL USE IT BECAUSE MOMMY DOESN'T LIKE THROWING MONEY AWAY!
LOOK, I GOTTA GO. I'LL BE HOME SOON. HANG IN THERE...
NO, 911 IS ONLY FOR REAL EMERGENCIES.
OKAY, LOVE YOU, HONEY. BYE!
CLICK
NOW, WHERE WERE WE?

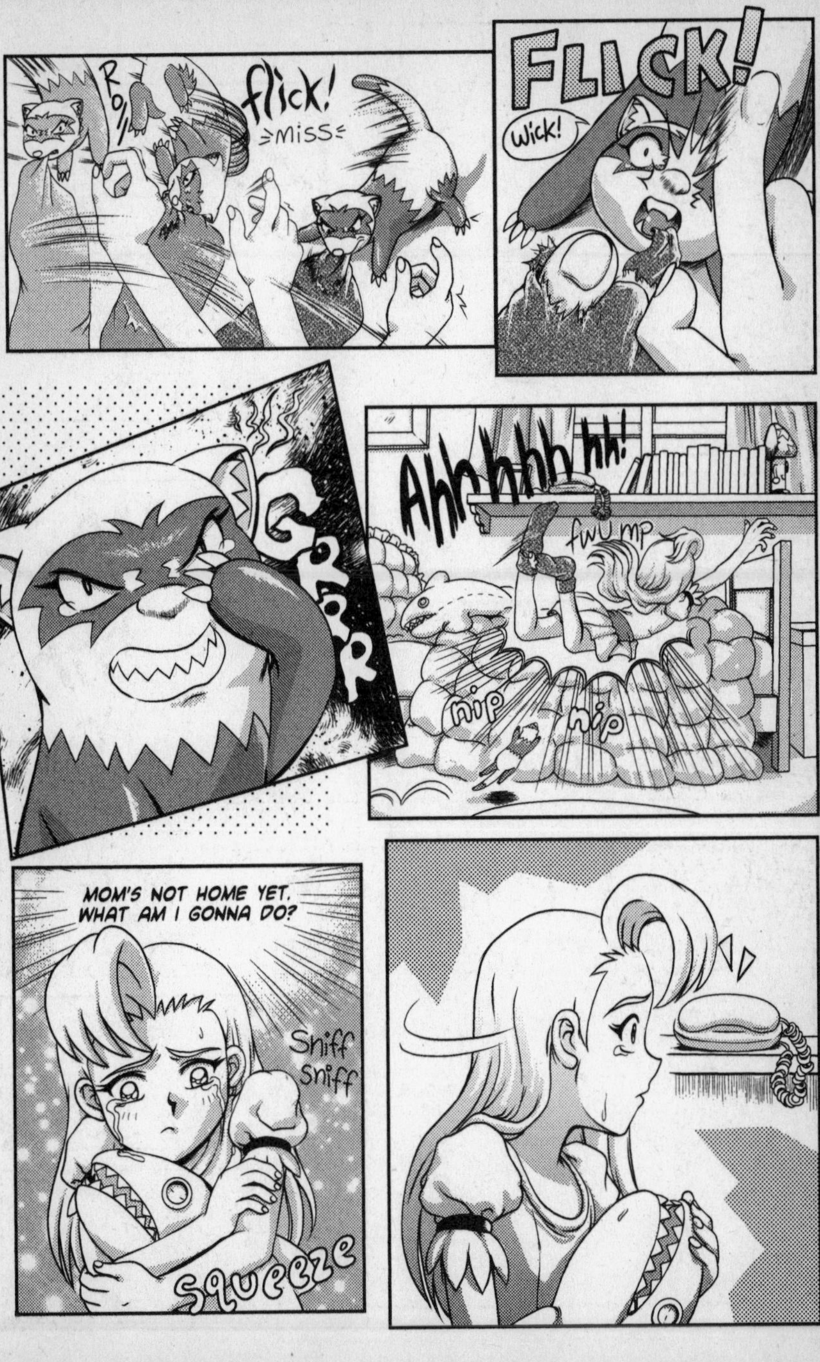
Roll
flick!
MISS
FLICK!
wick!
Grrrr
Ahhhhhhhh!
fwump
nip
nip
MOM'S NOT HOME YET. WHAT AM I GONNA DO?
Sniff
Sniff
Squeeze

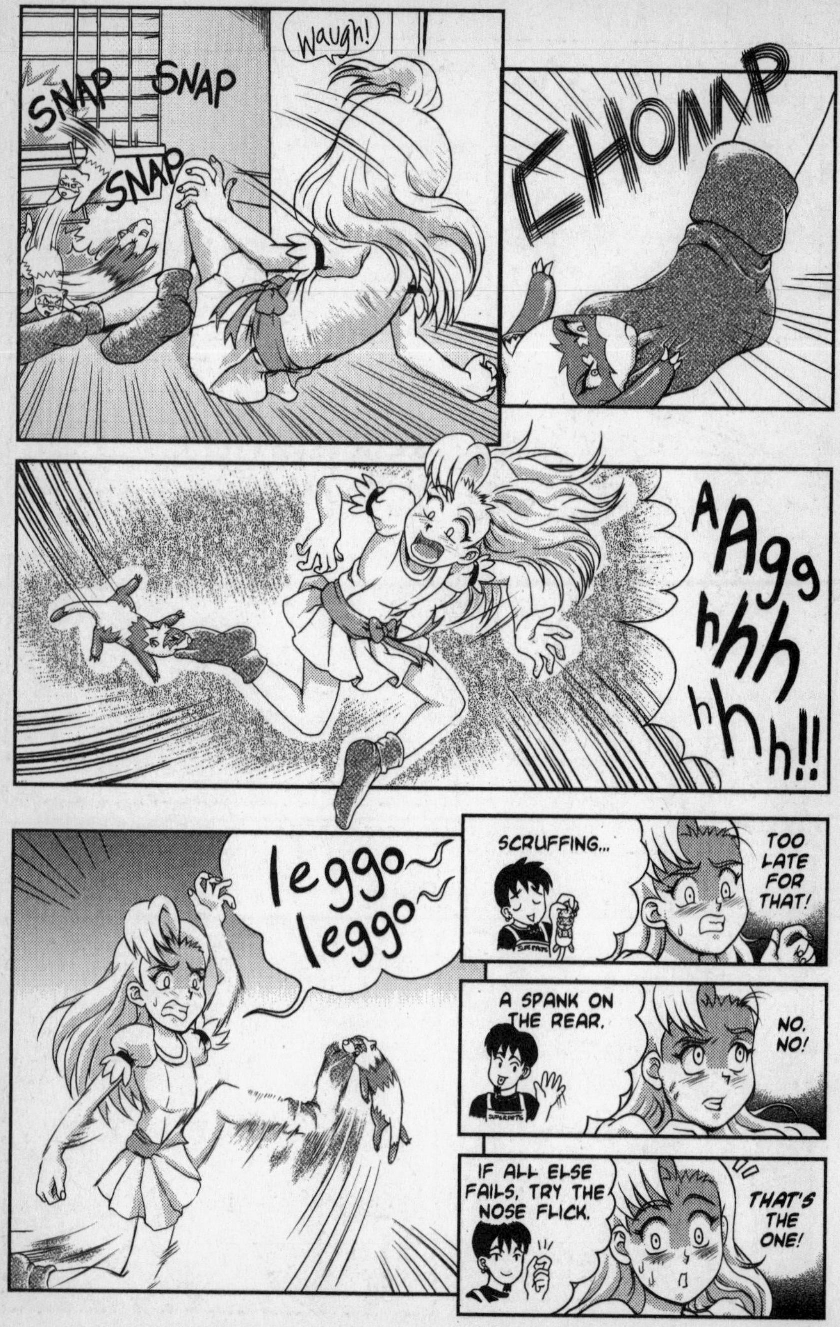
SNAP SNAP
SNAP
Waugh!
CHOMP
AAgghhhhhh!!
leggo~ leggo~
SCRUFFING...
TOO LATE FOR THAT!
A SPANK ON THE REAR.
NO. NO!
IF ALL ELSE FAILS, TRY THE NOSE FLICK.
THAT'S THE ONE!

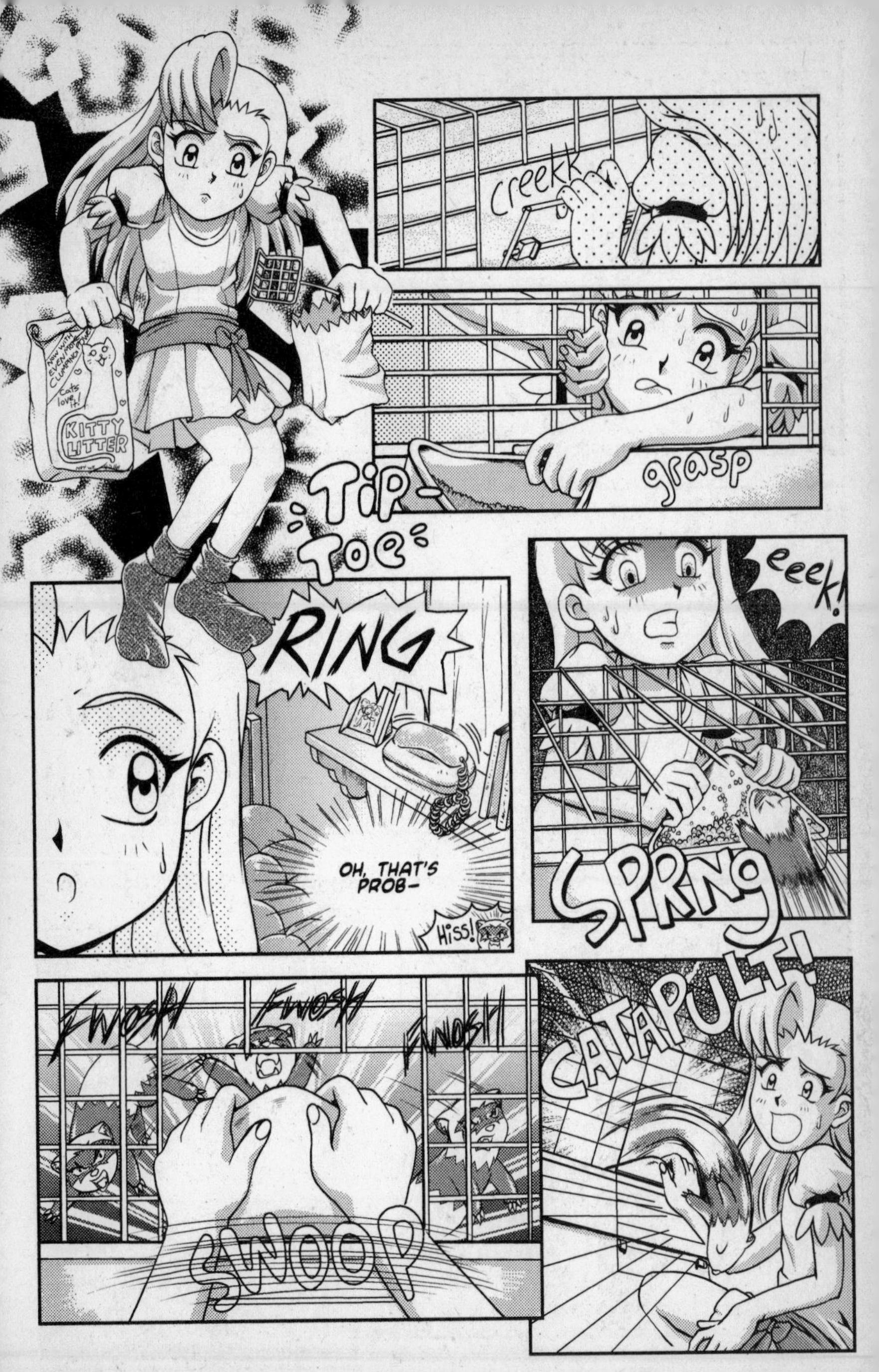
KITTY LITTER
Cats love it!
creekk
grasp
Tip-Toe
RING
OH, THAT'S PROB-
Hiss!
eeek!
SPRNG
FWOSH
FWOSH
FWOSH
SWOOP
CATAPULT!

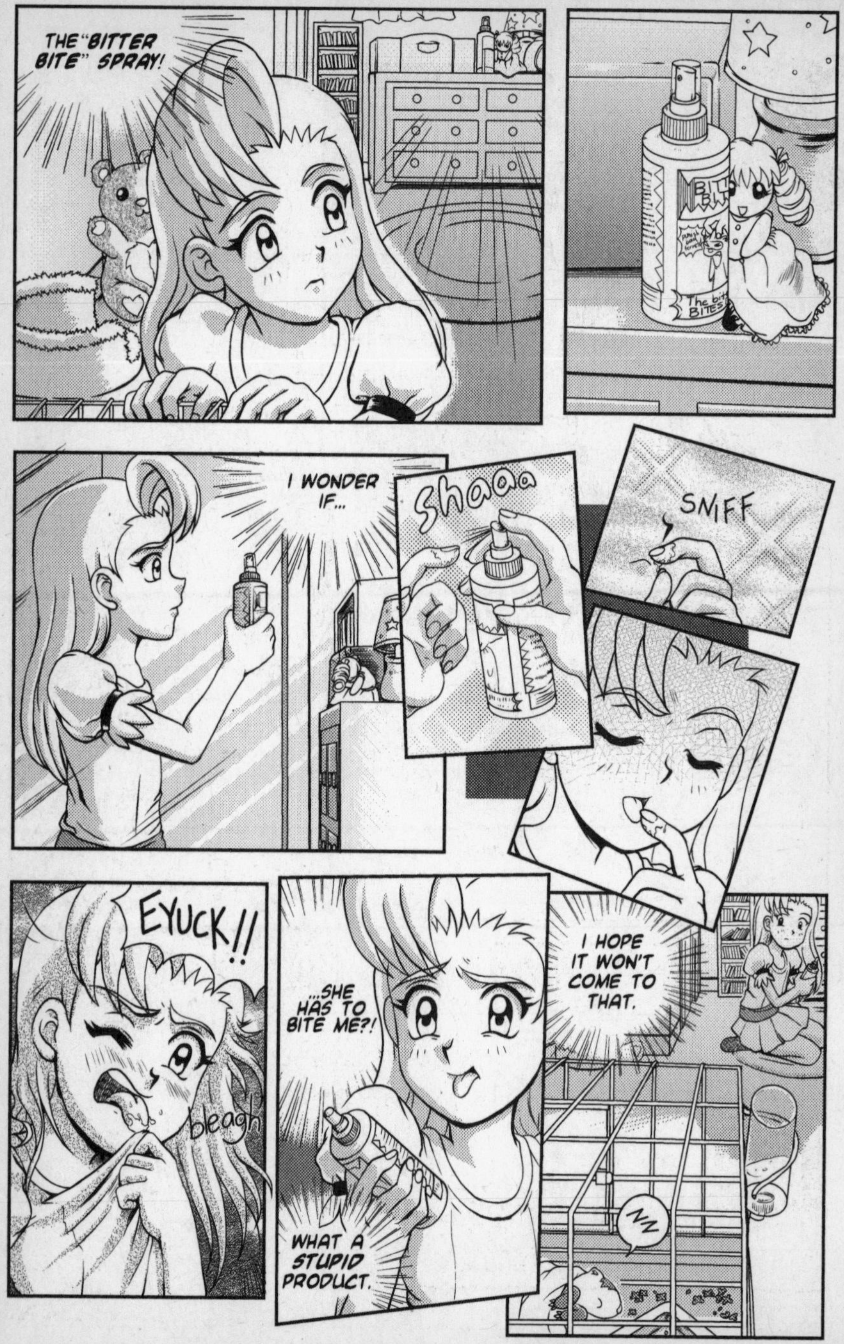

THE "BITTER BITE" SPRAY!
I WONDER IF...
Shaaa
SNIFF
EYUCK!!
bleagh
...SHE HAS TO BITE ME?!
WHAT A STUPID PRODUCT.
I HOPE IT WON'T COME TO THAT.

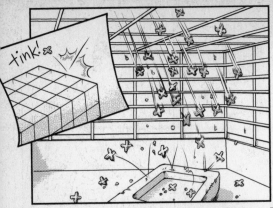

tink!

Doink!

CHOMP

CHOMP

ROAR!

Fwoosh

SHE USED TO BE SO GENTLE. WHAT HAPPENED TO HER?

TOK

OH YUUUUUCK! THE LITTER BOX IS FULL.

BUT IF I TRY TO CLEAN IT NOW, PEACH WILL TAKE OFF A FINGER.

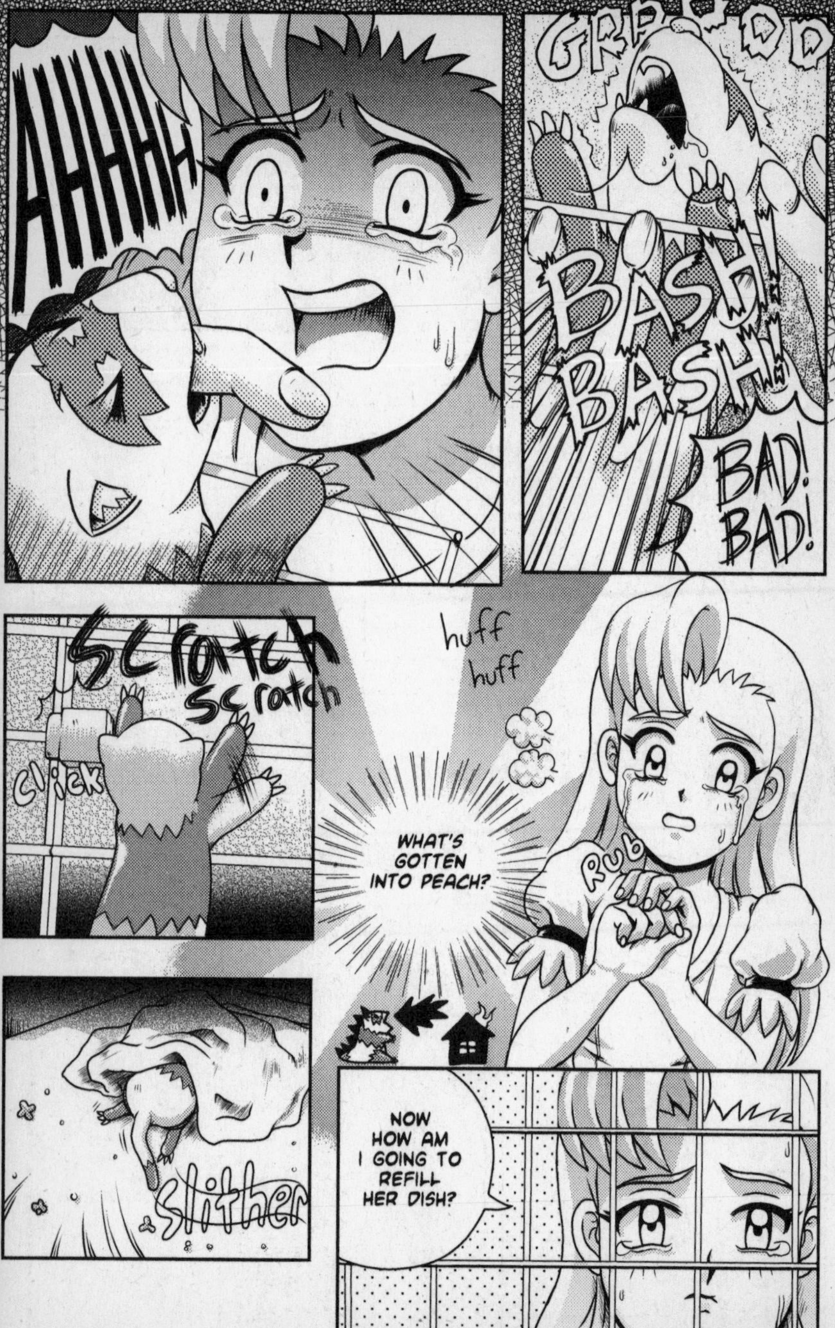
GRROOD
BASH! BASH!
BAD! BAD!
AHHHH
huff huff
WHAT'S GOTTEN INTO PEACH?
Rub
scratch scratch
click
slither
NOW HOW AM I GOING TO REFILL HER DISH?

WAIT 'TIL YOU SEE! "AUNTIE" KIM HELPED ME WITH IT. ♥

WHOA, YOU'VE BEEN BUSY.

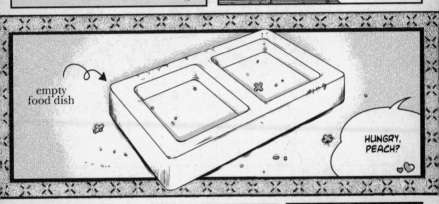

empty food dish

HUNGRY, PEACH? ♥♥

"FUZZY FARM FEED" COMING RIGHT UP!

click

gleam

fwoosh

CHOMP

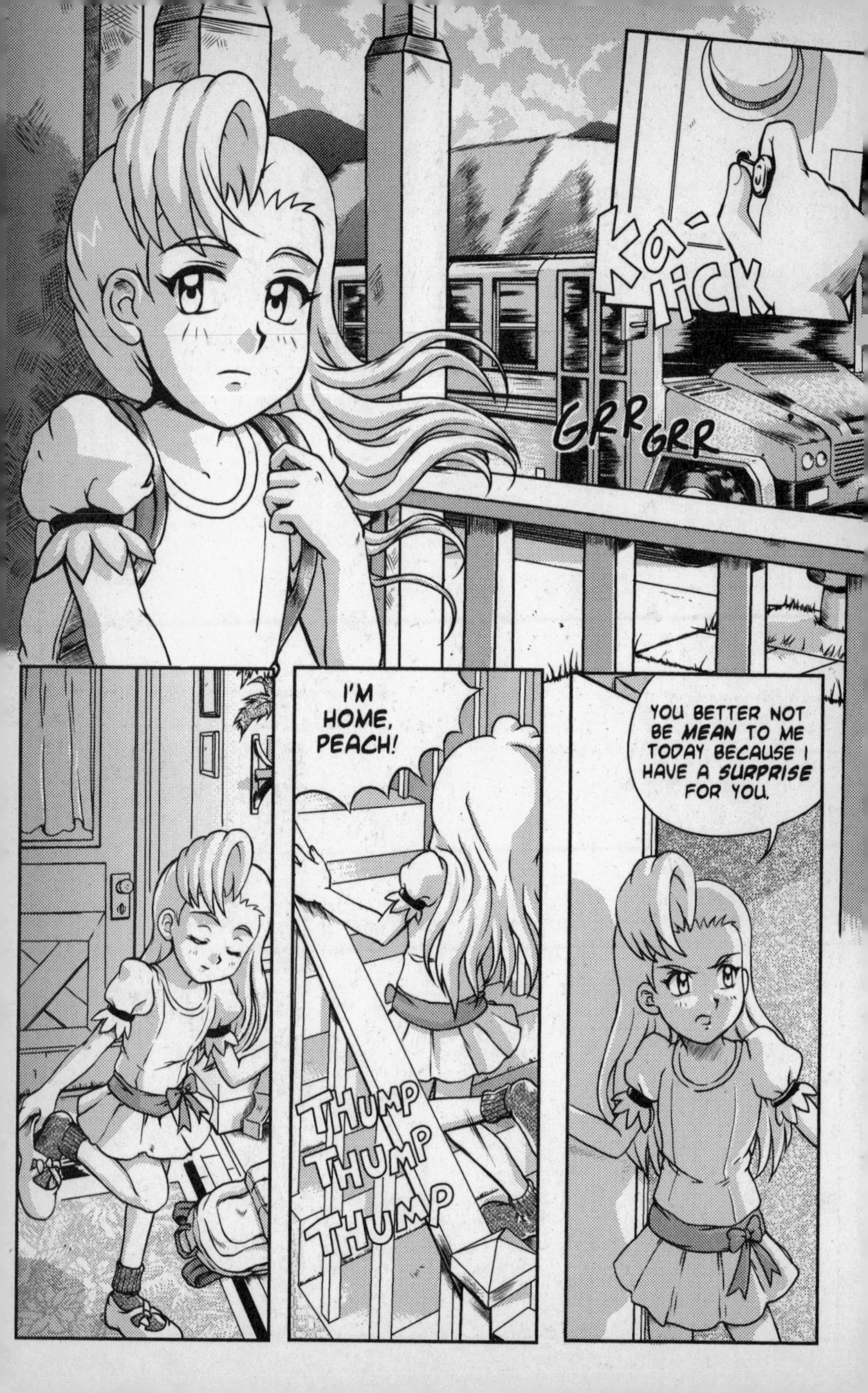
GRR GRR
KA-LICK
I'M HOME, PEACH!
THUMP THUMP THUMP
YOU BETTER NOT BE MEAN TO ME TODAY BECAUSE I HAVE A SURPRISE FOR YOU.

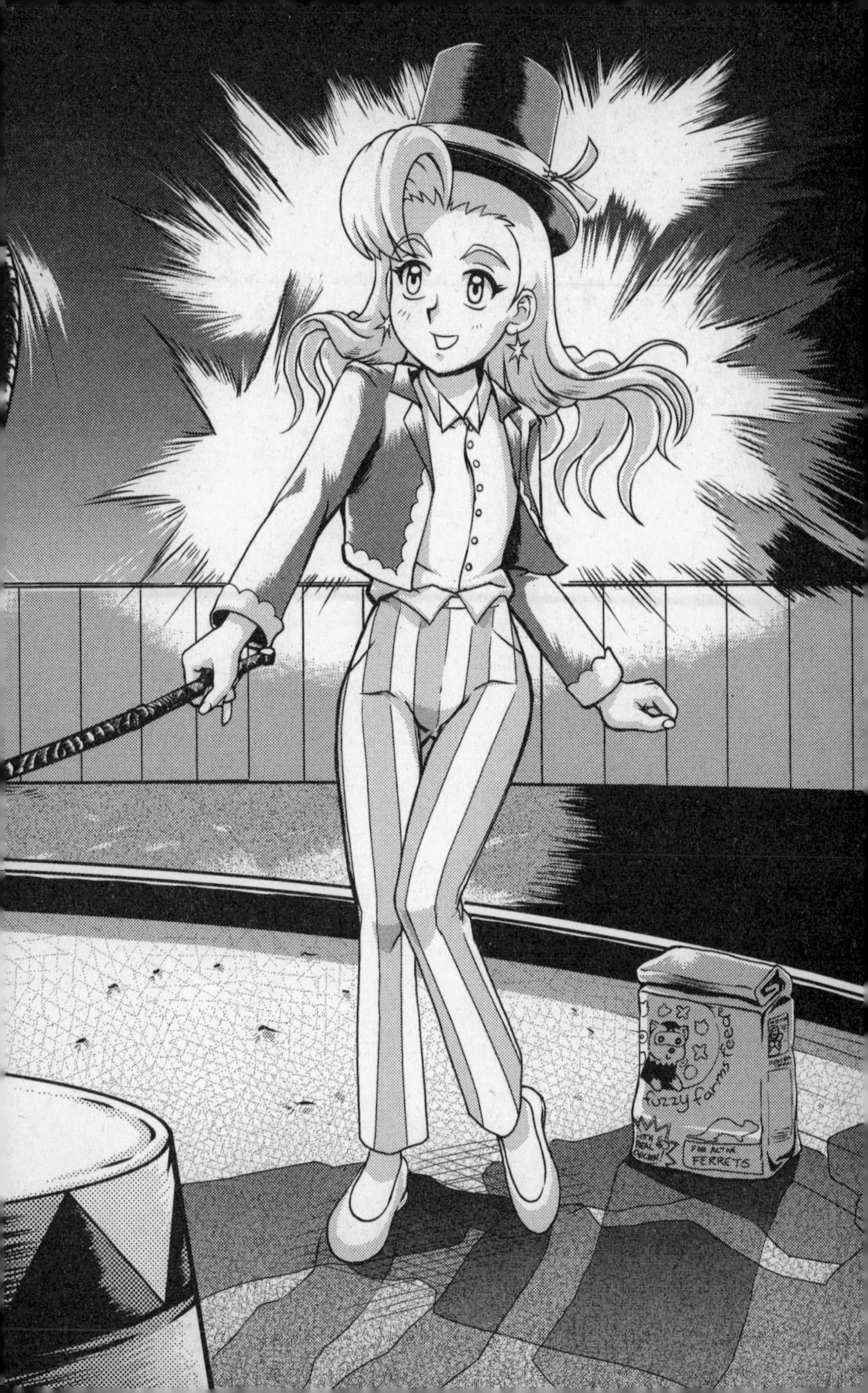
fuzzy farms feed
WITH REAL CHICKEN!
FOR ACTIVE FERRETS

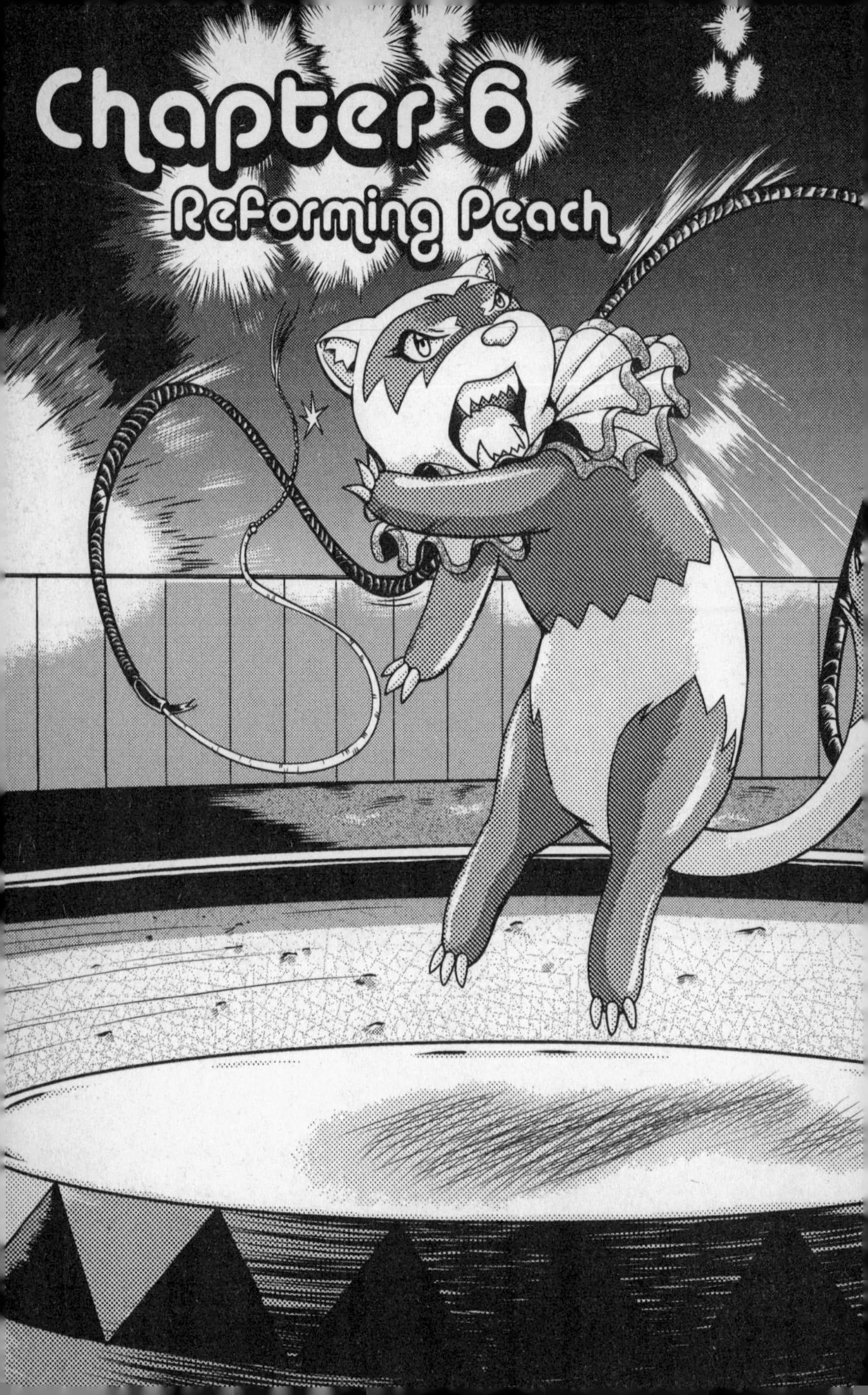
Chapter 6
Reforming Peach

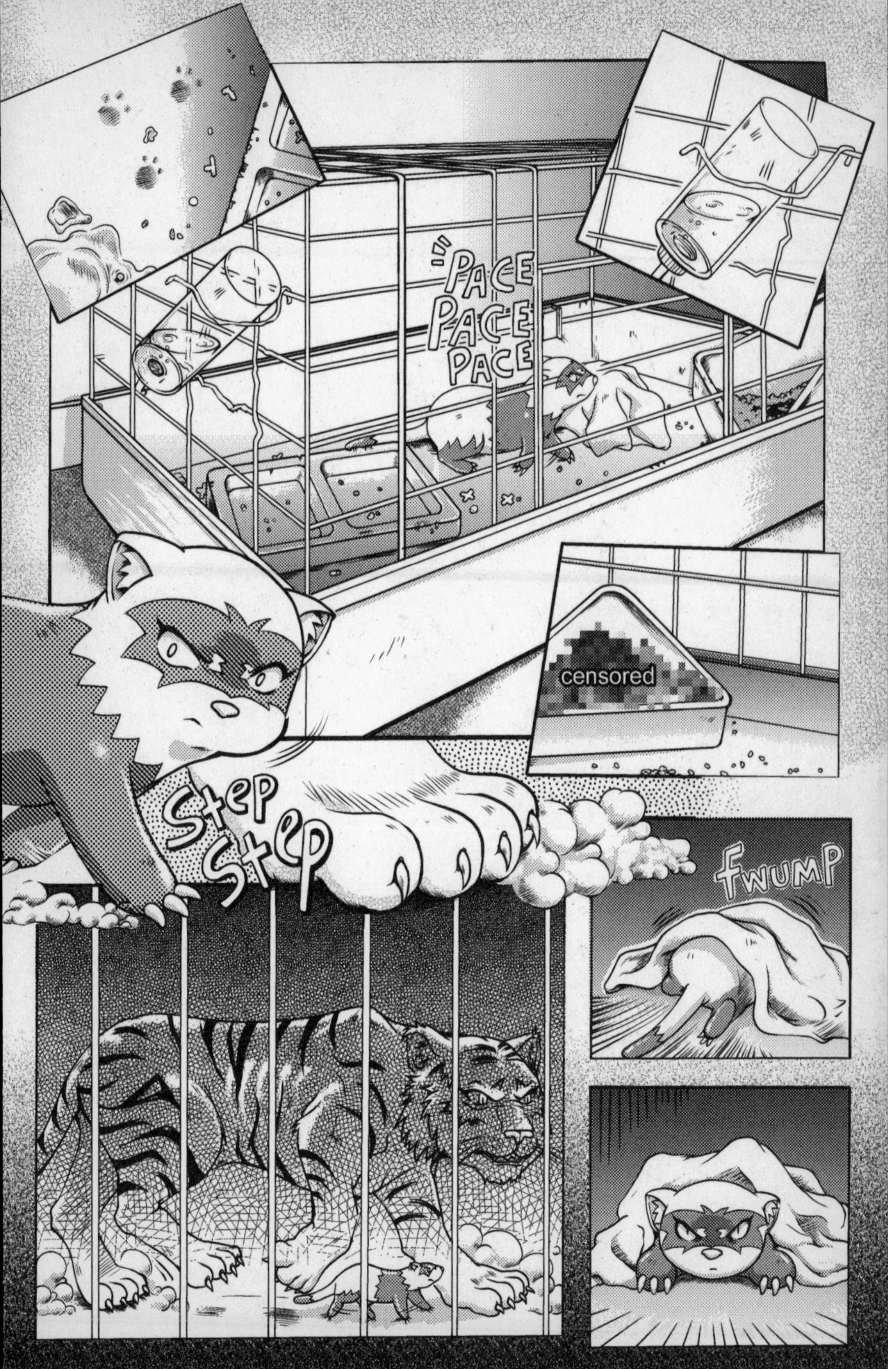
PACE
PACE
PACE
censored
Step
Step
FWUMP

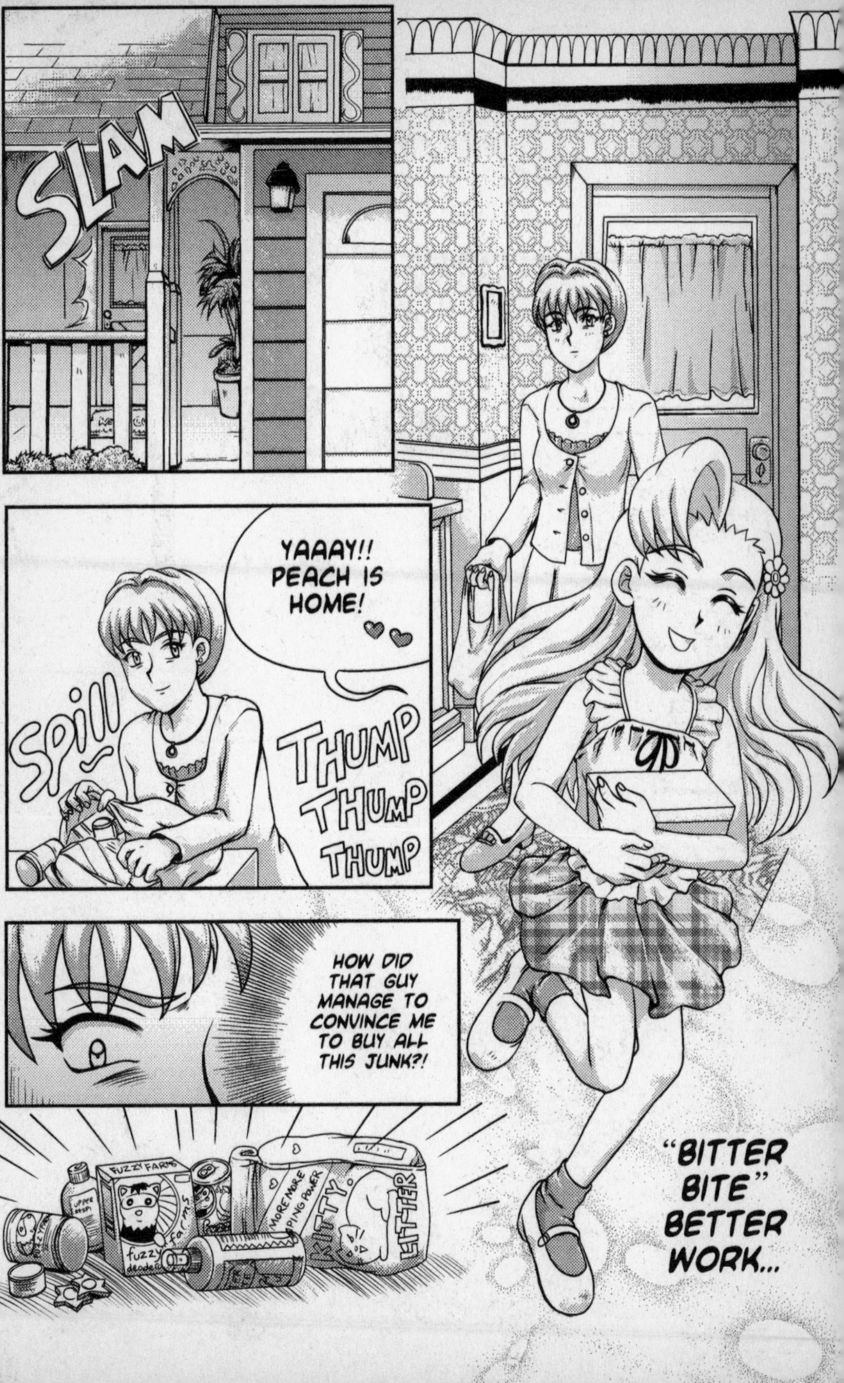
SLAM
YAAAY!! PEACH IS HOME!
Spill
THUMP THUMP THUMP
HOW DID THAT GUY MANAGE TO CONVINCE ME TO BUY ALL THIS JUNK?!
FUZZY FARMS
KITTY LITTER
"BITTER BITE" BETTER WORK...

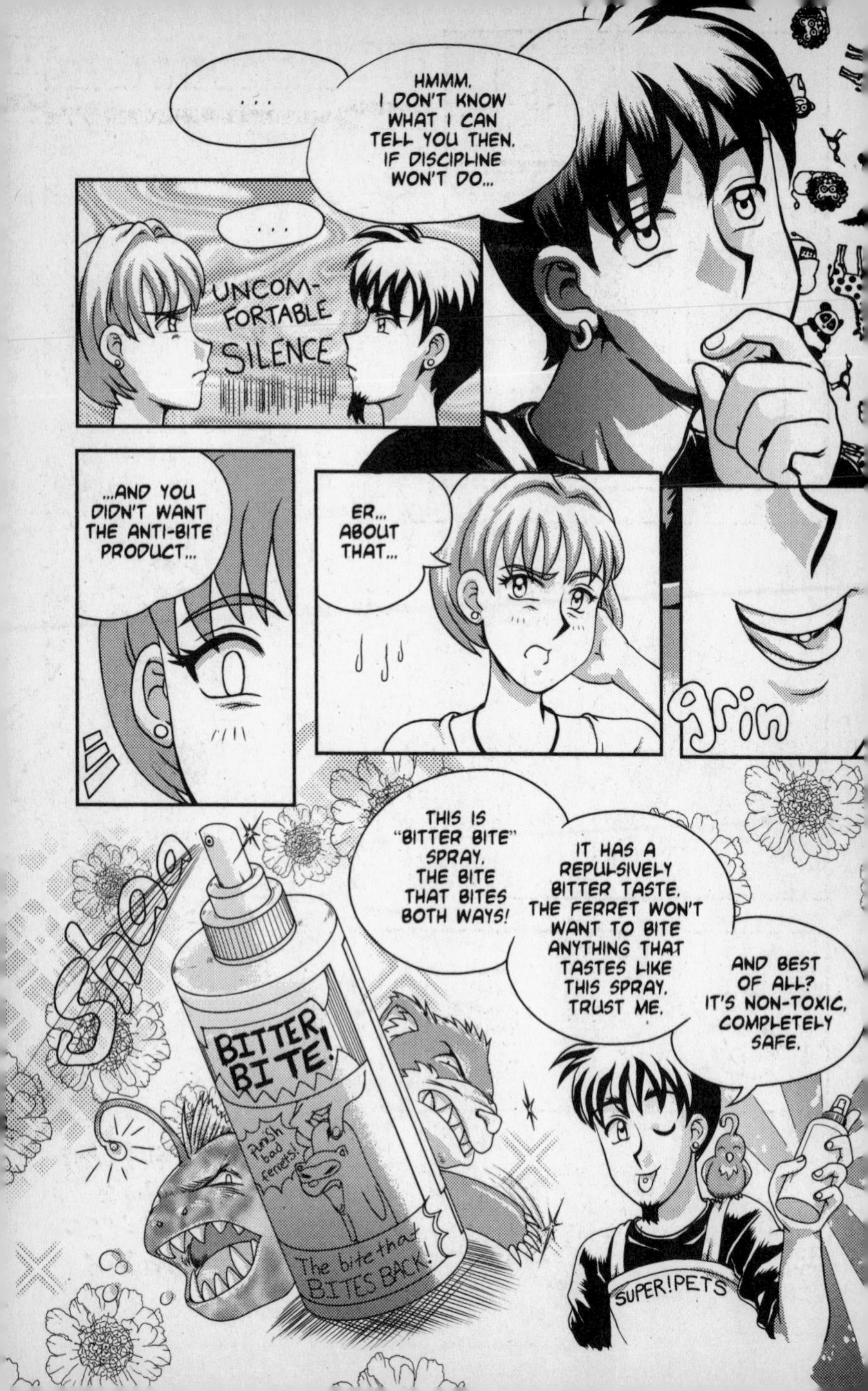
...
HMMM. I DON'T KNOW WHAT I CAN TELL YOU THEN. IF DISCIPLINE WON'T DO...
...
UNCOM-FORTABLE SILENCE
...AND YOU DIDN'T WANT THE ANTI-BITE PRODUCT...
ER... ABOUT THAT...
grin
THIS IS "BITTER BITE" SPRAY. THE BITE THAT BITES BOTH WAYS!
IT HAS A REPULSIVELY BITTER TASTE. THE FERRET WON'T WANT TO BITE ANYTHING THAT TASTES LIKE THIS SPRAY. TRUST ME.
AND BEST OF ALL? IT'S NON-TOXIC. COMPLETELY SAFE.
BITTER BITE!
Punish bad ferrets!
The bite that BITES BACK!
SUPER!PETS

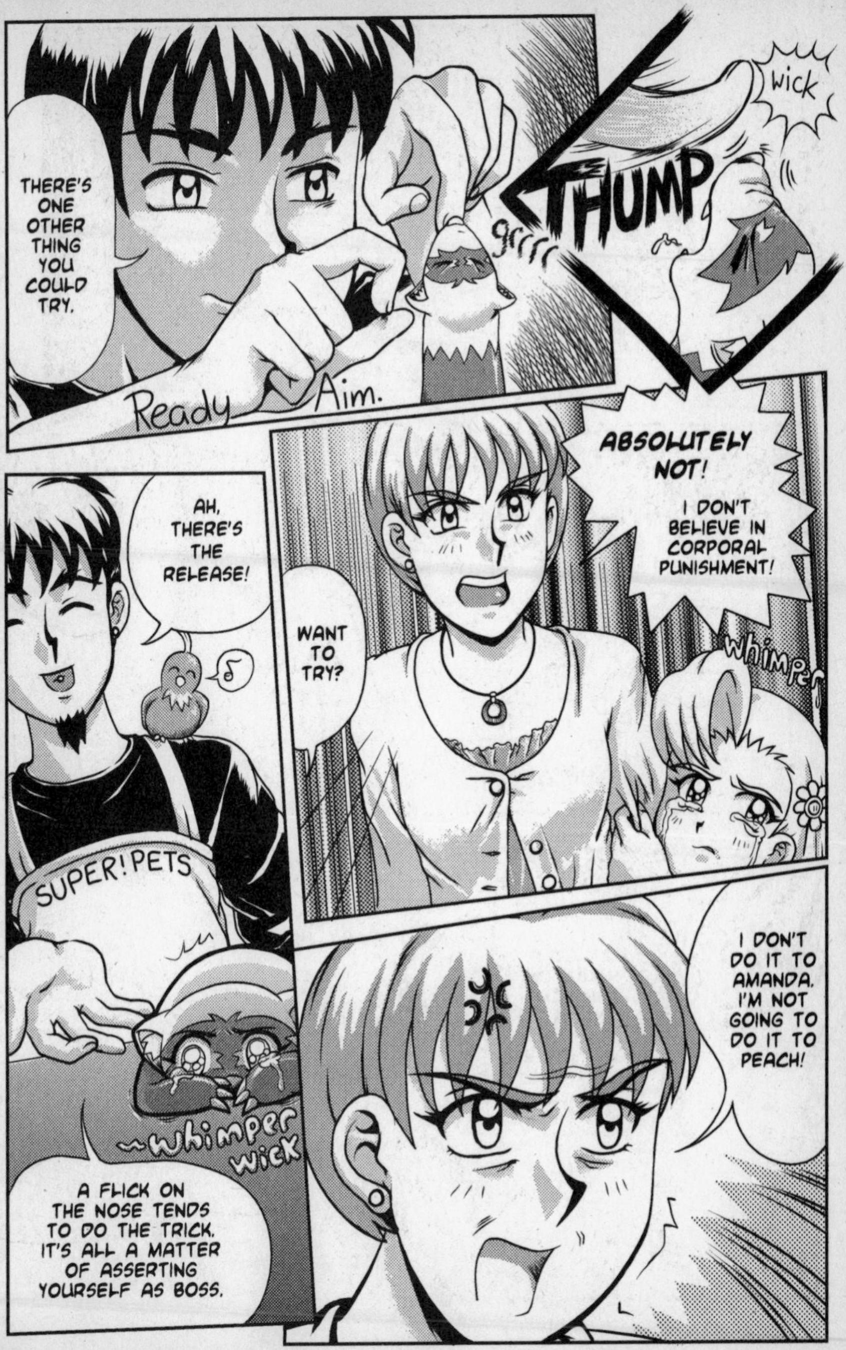
THERE'S ONE OTHER THING YOU COULD TRY.
Ready
Aim.
grrr
THUMP
wick
AH, THERE'S THE RELEASE!
SUPER!PETS
~whimper
wick
A FLICK ON THE NOSE TENDS TO DO THE TRICK. IT'S ALL A MATTER OF ASSERTING YOURSELF AS BOSS.
WANT TO TRY?
ABSOLUTELY NOT!
I DON'T BELIEVE IN CORPORAL PUNISHMENT!
whimper
I DON'T DO IT TO AMANDA. I'M NOT GOING TO DO IT TO PEACH!

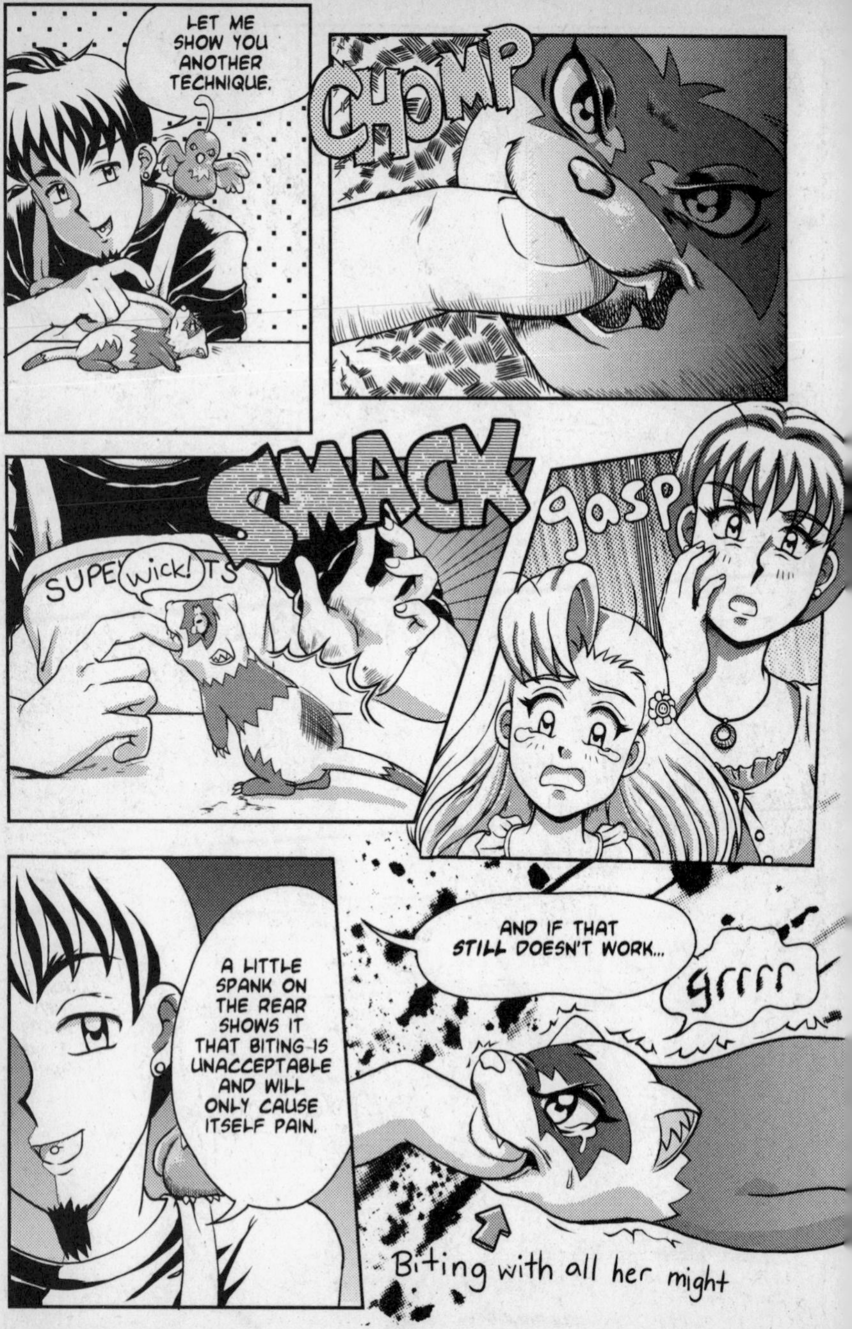
LET ME SHOW YOU ANOTHER TECHNIQUE.
CHOMP
SMACK
wick!
gasp
A LITTLE SPANK ON THE REAR SHOWS IT THAT BITING IS UNACCEPTABLE AND WILL ONLY CAUSE ITSELF PAIN.
AND IF THAT STILL DOESN'T WORK...
grrrr
Biting with all her might

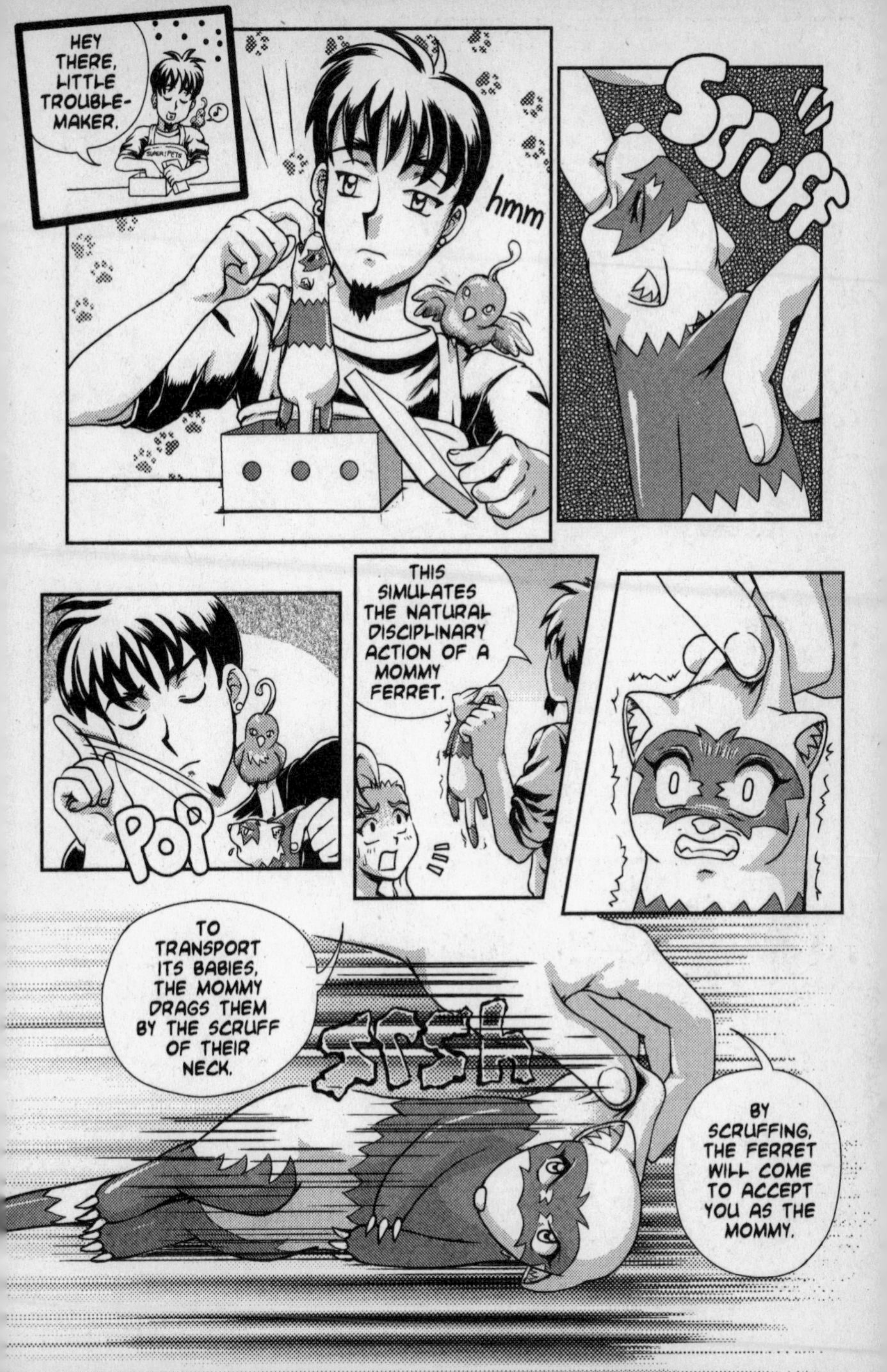
HEY THERE, LITTLE TROUBLE-MAKER.
SUPER PETS
hmm
SCRUFF
POP
THIS SIMULATES THE NATURAL DISCIPLINARY ACTION OF A MOMMY FERRET.
TO TRANSPORT ITS BABIES, THE MOMMY DRAGS THEM BY THE SCRUFF OF THEIR NECK.
BY SCRUFFING, THE FERRET WILL COME TO ACCEPT YOU AS THE MOMMY.

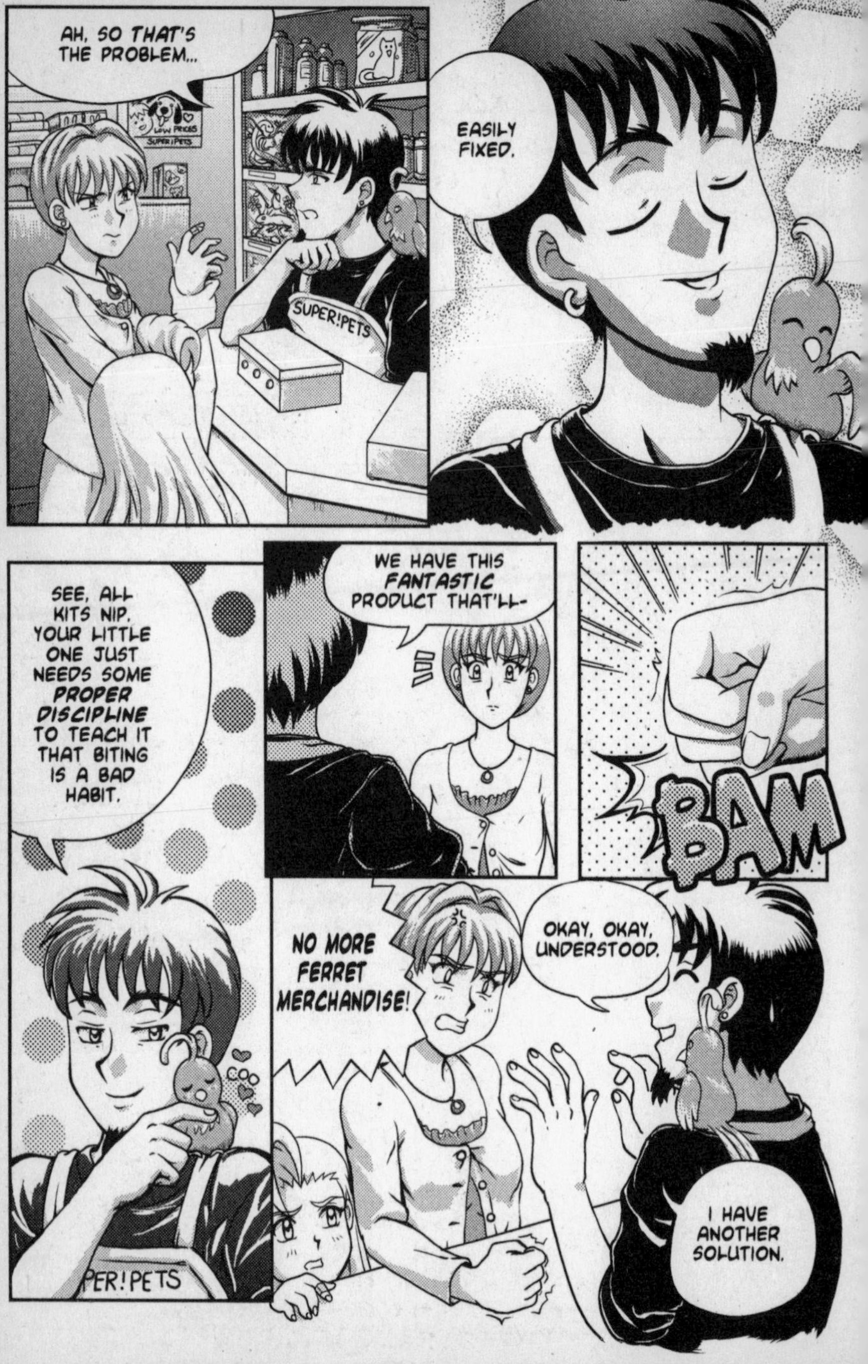
AH, SO *THAT'S* THE PROBLEM...
LOW PRICES
SUPER!PETS
SUPER!PETS
EASILY FIXED.
SEE, ALL KITS NIP. YOUR LITTLE ONE JUST NEEDS SOME *PROPER DISCIPLINE* TO TEACH IT THAT BITING IS A BAD HABIT.
COO
PER!PETS
WE HAVE THIS *FANTASTIC* PRODUCT THAT'LL-
BAM
NO MORE FERRET MERCHANDISE!
OKAY, OKAY, UNDERSTOOD.
I HAVE ANOTHER SOLUTION.

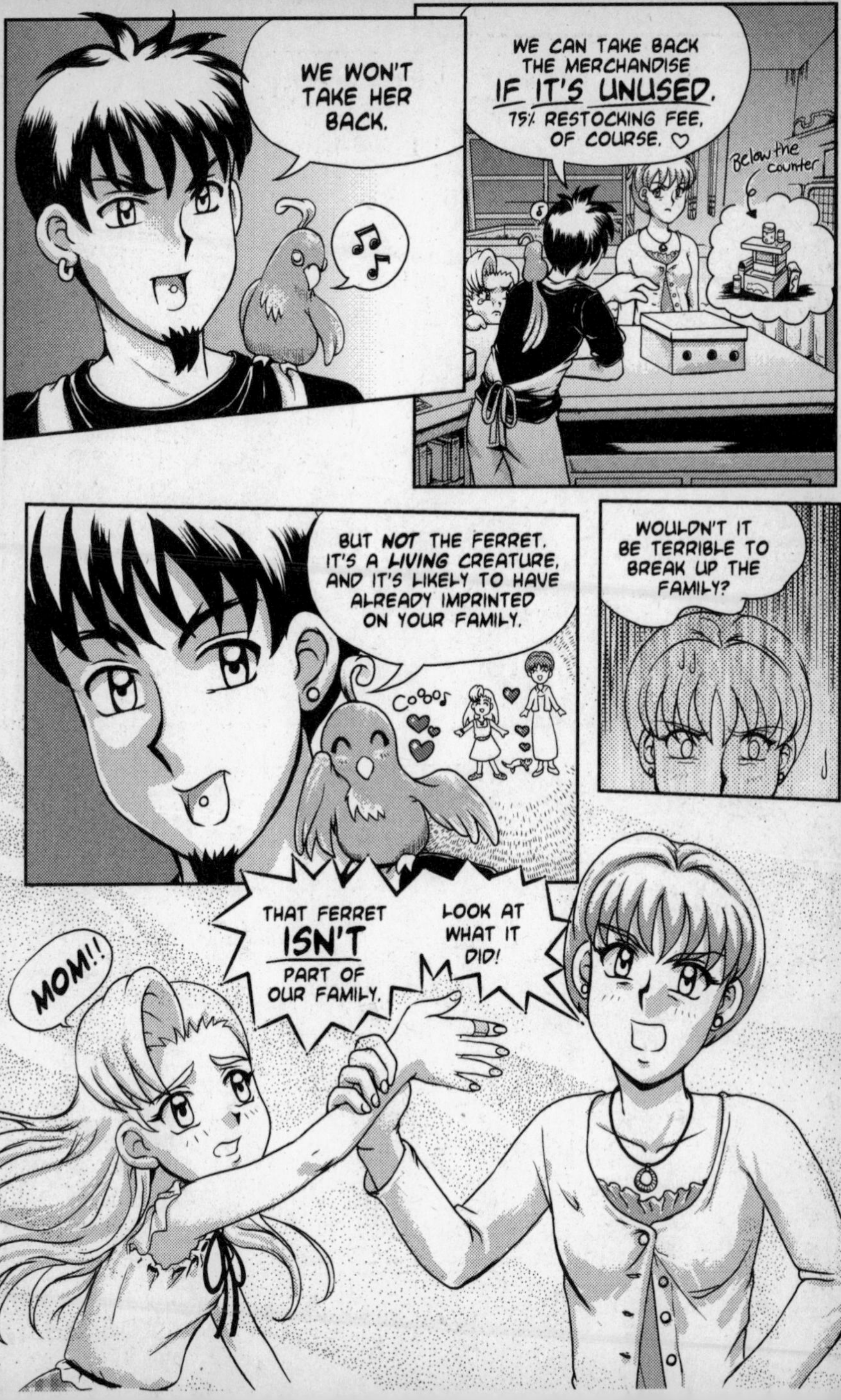
WE WON'T TAKE HER BACK.
WE CAN TAKE BACK THE MERCHANDISE IF IT'S UNUSED. 75% RESTOCKING FEE, OF COURSE. ♡
Below the counter
BUT NOT THE FERRET. IT'S A LIVING CREATURE, AND IT'S LIKELY TO HAVE ALREADY IMPRINTED ON YOUR FAMILY.
Cooo
WOULDN'T IT BE TERRIBLE TO BREAK UP THE FAMILY?
MOM!!
THAT FERRET ISN'T PART OF OUR FAMILY.
LOOK AT WHAT IT DID!

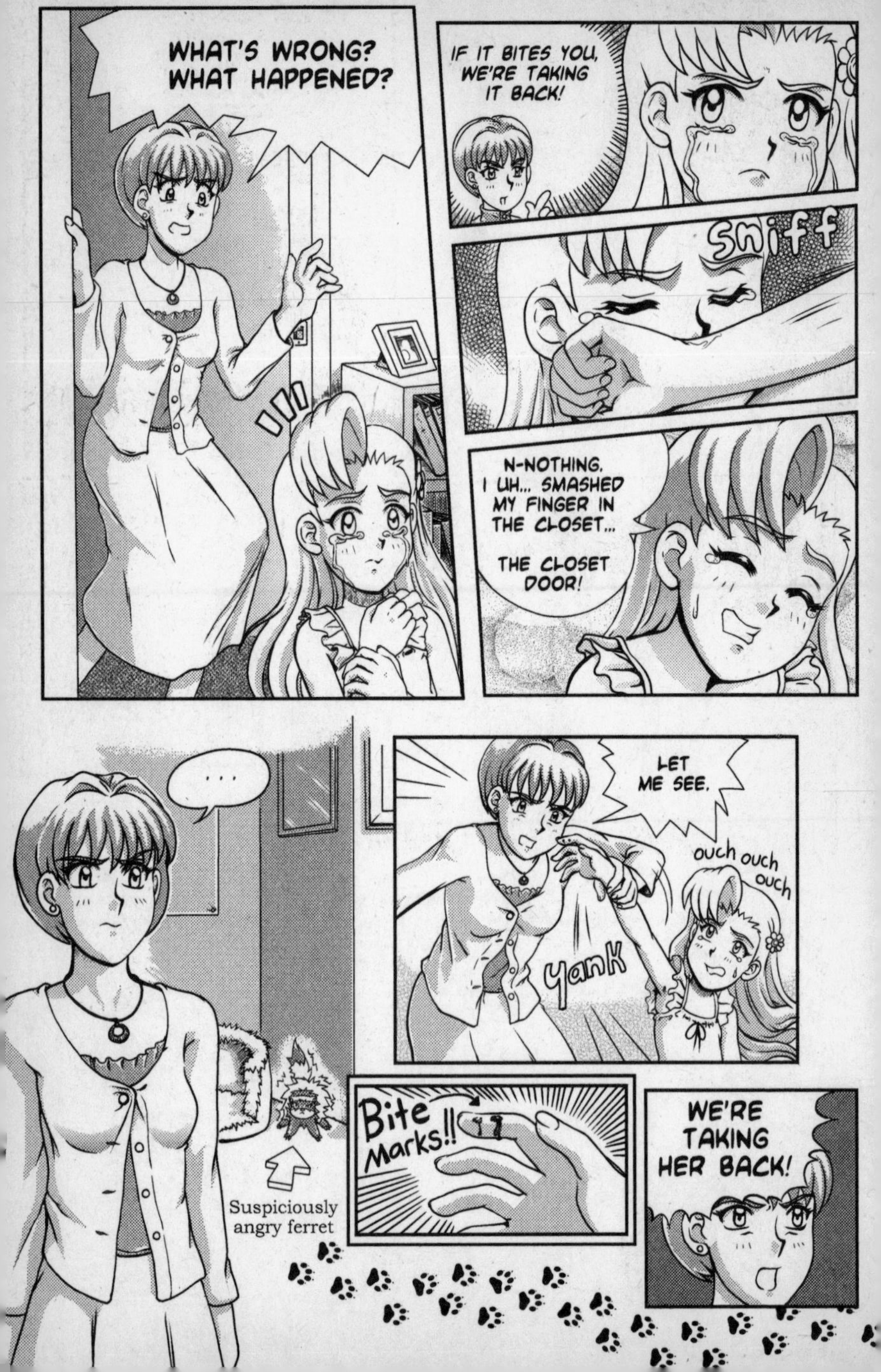
WHAT'S WRONG? WHAT HAPPENED?
IF IT BITES YOU, WE'RE TAKING IT BACK!
Sniff
N-NOTHING. I UH... SMASHED MY FINGER IN THE CLOSET...
THE CLOSET DOOR!
...
Suspiciously angry ferret
LET ME SEE.
ouch ouch ouch
yank
Bite Marks!!
WE'RE TAKING HER BACK!

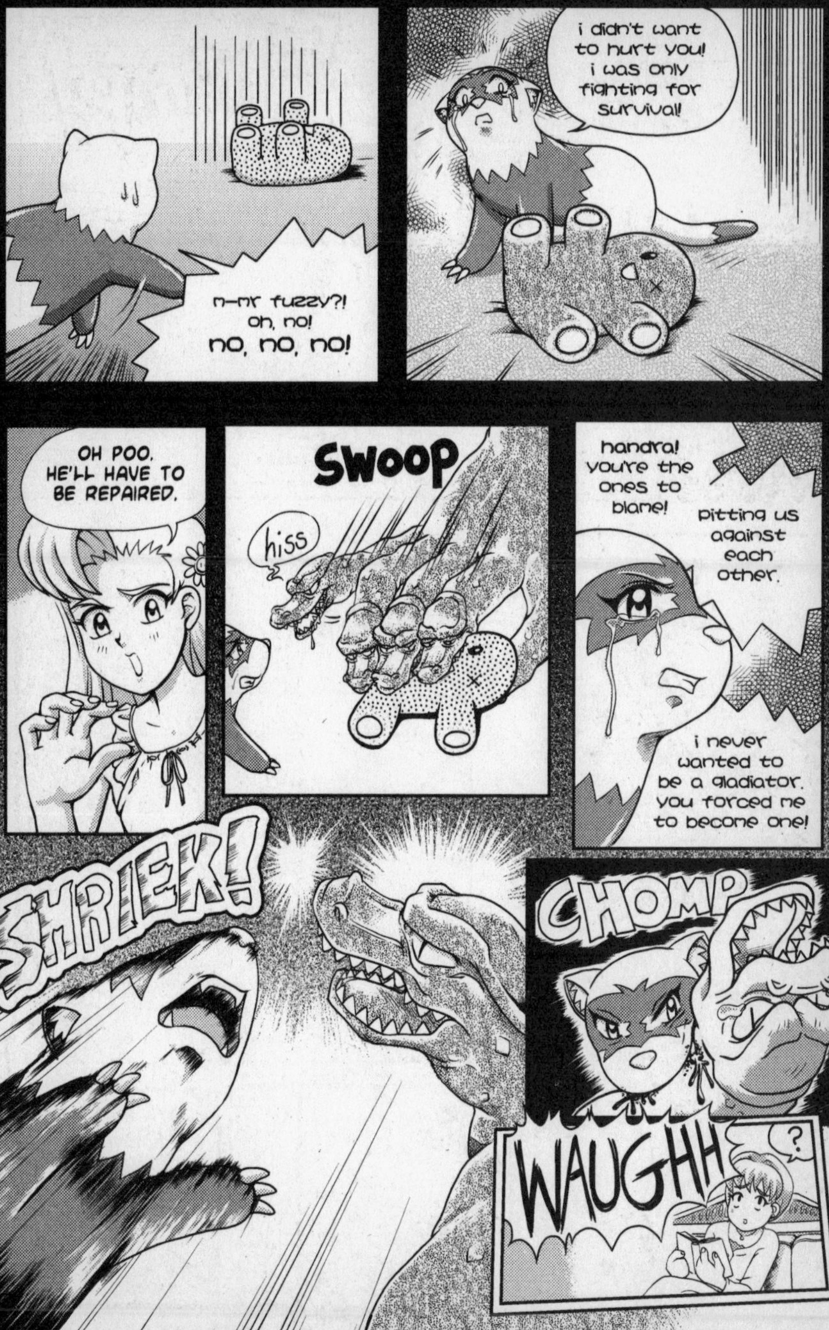
m-mr fuzzy?!
oh, no!
no, no, no!
i didn't want to hurt you! i was only fighting for survival!
OH POO. HE'LL HAVE TO BE REPAIRED.
SWOOP
hiss
handra! you're the ones to blame!
pitting us against each other.
i never wanted to be a gladiator. you forced me to becone one!
SHRIEK!
CHOMP
WAUGHH
?

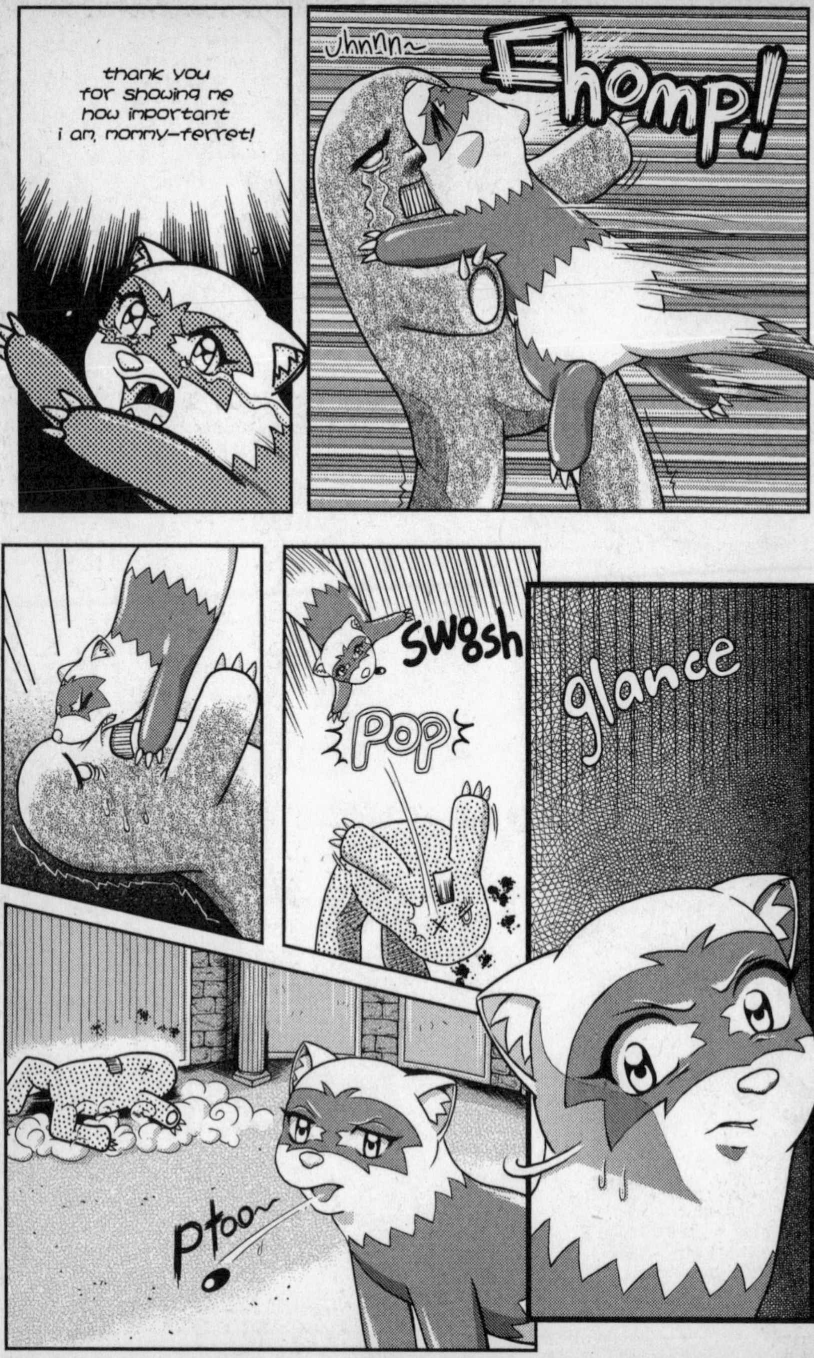
thank you for showing me how important i am, mommy-ferret!
Jhnnn~
Chomp!
swosh
POP
glance
ptoo~

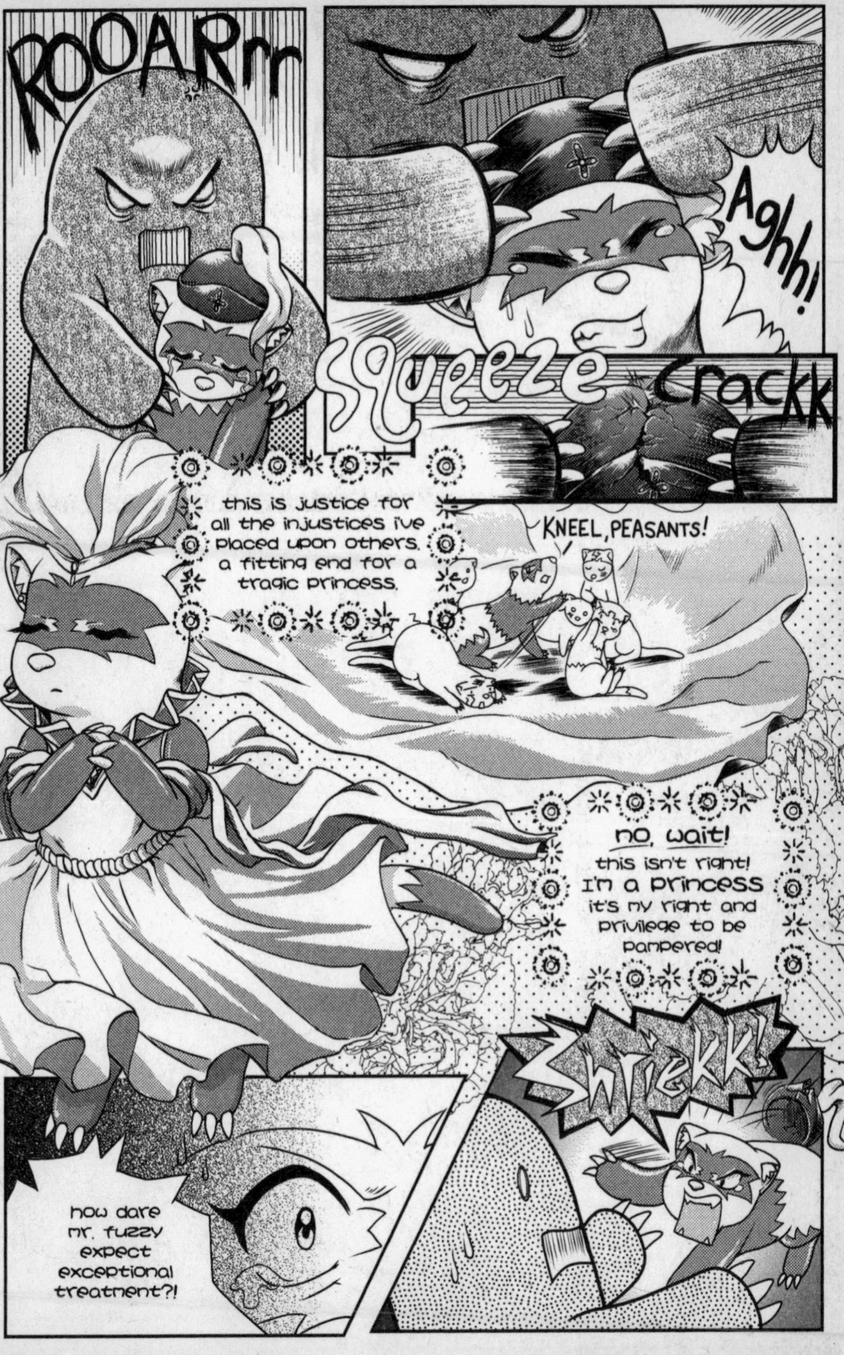
ROOARrr
Aghh!
squeeze
Crackk
this is justice for all the injustices i've placed upon others. a fitting end for a tragic princess.
KNEEL, PEASANTS!
no, wait!
this isn't right! I'm a princess it's my right and privilege to be pampered!
how dare mr. fuzzy expect exceptional treatment?!
Zhriekk!

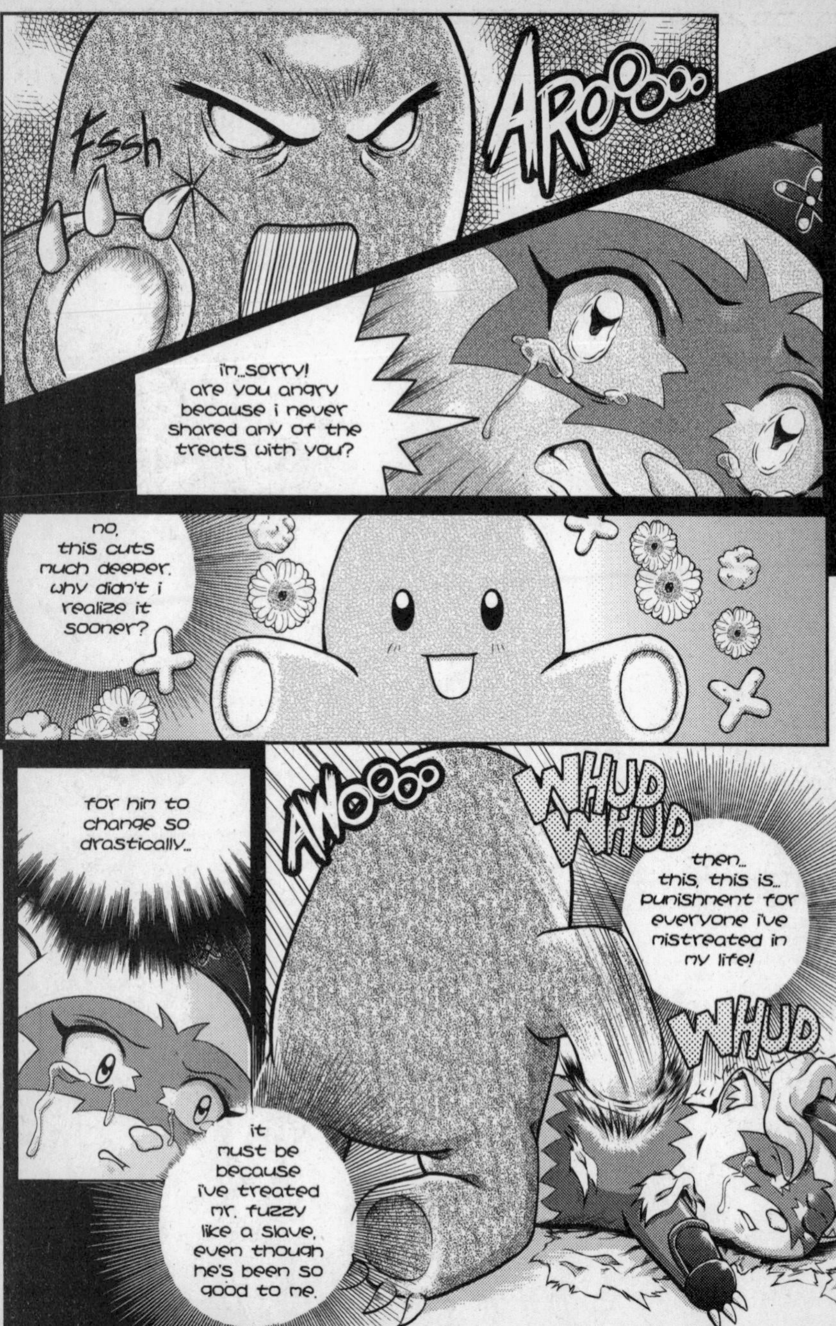
Fssh
AROOooo
i'm..sorry! are you angry because i never shared any of the treats with you?
no, this cuts much deeper. why didn't i realize it sooner?
for him to change so drastically...
it must be because i've treated mr. fuzzy like a slave, even though he's been so good to me.
AWOOooo
WHUD WHUD
then... this, this is... punishment for everyone i've mistreated in my life!
WHUD

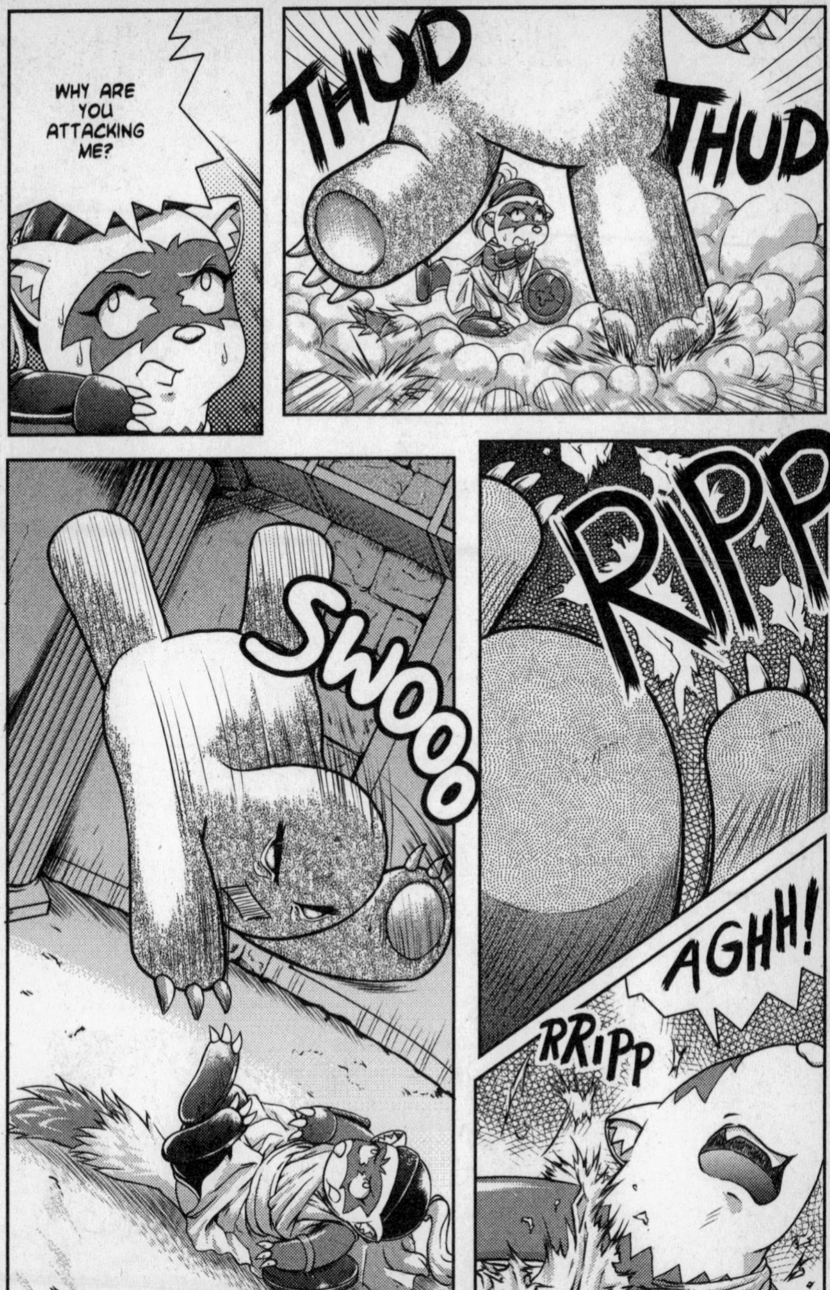
WHY ARE YOU ATTACKING ME?
THUD
THUD
SWOOO
RIPP
RRIPP
AGHH!

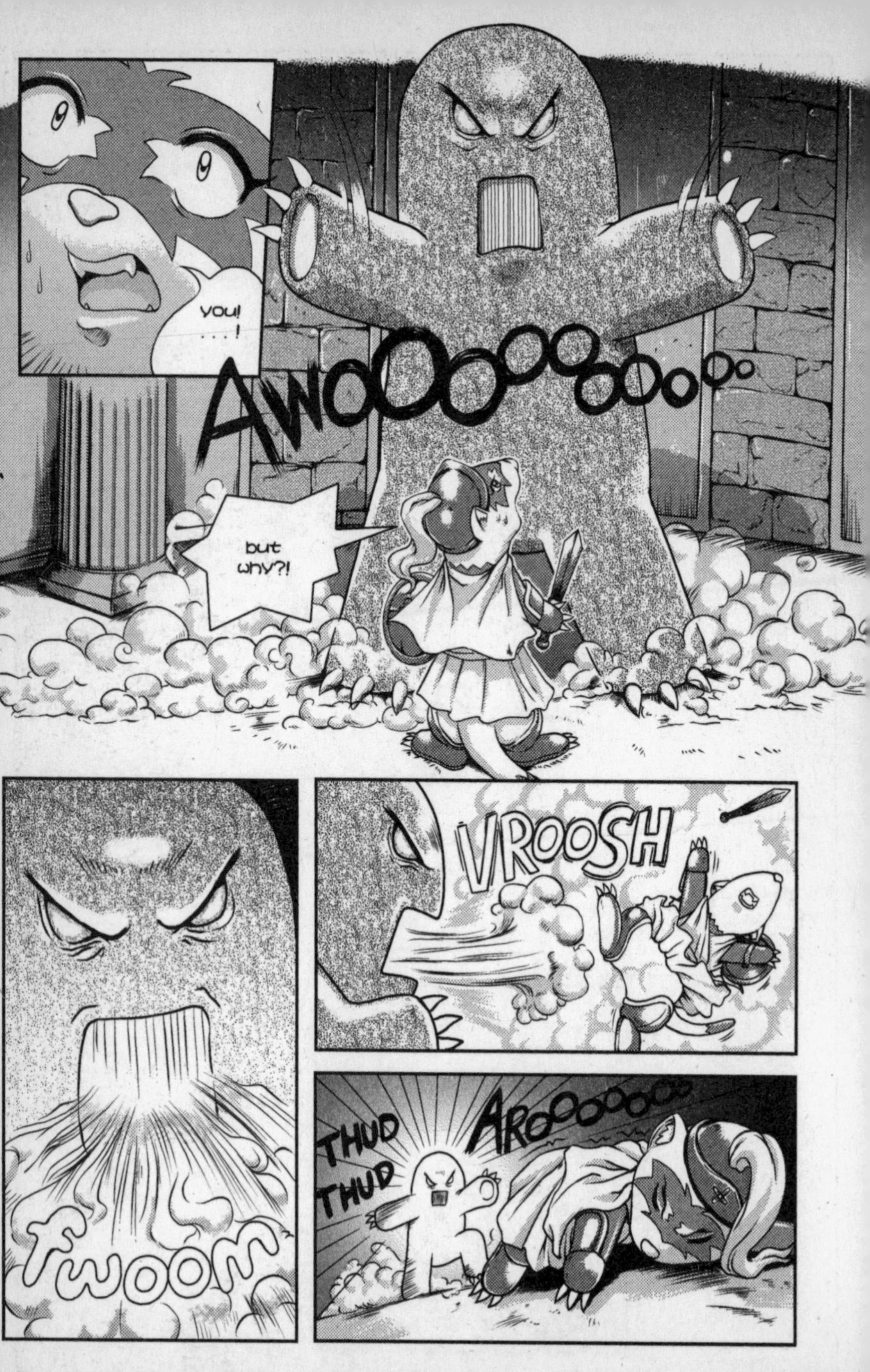
you!
. . . !
AWOOOOOOOOOO
but why?!
fwoom
VROOSH
THUD
THUD
AROOOOOOO

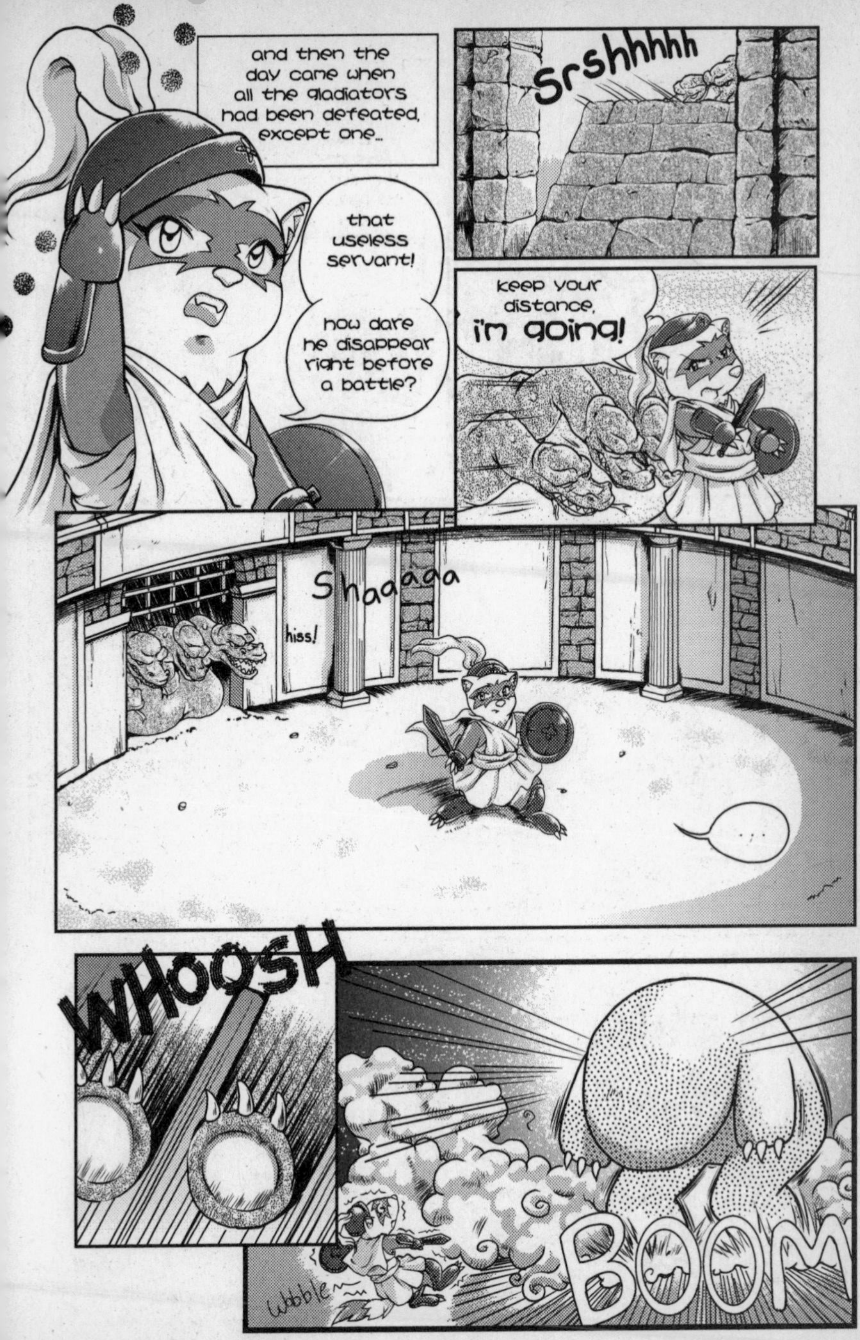
and then the day came when all the gladiators had been defeated, except one...
that useless servant!
how dare he disappear right before a battle?
Srshhhhh
keep your distance, i'm going!
Shaaaaa
hiss!
...
WHOOSH
?
BOOM
Wobble

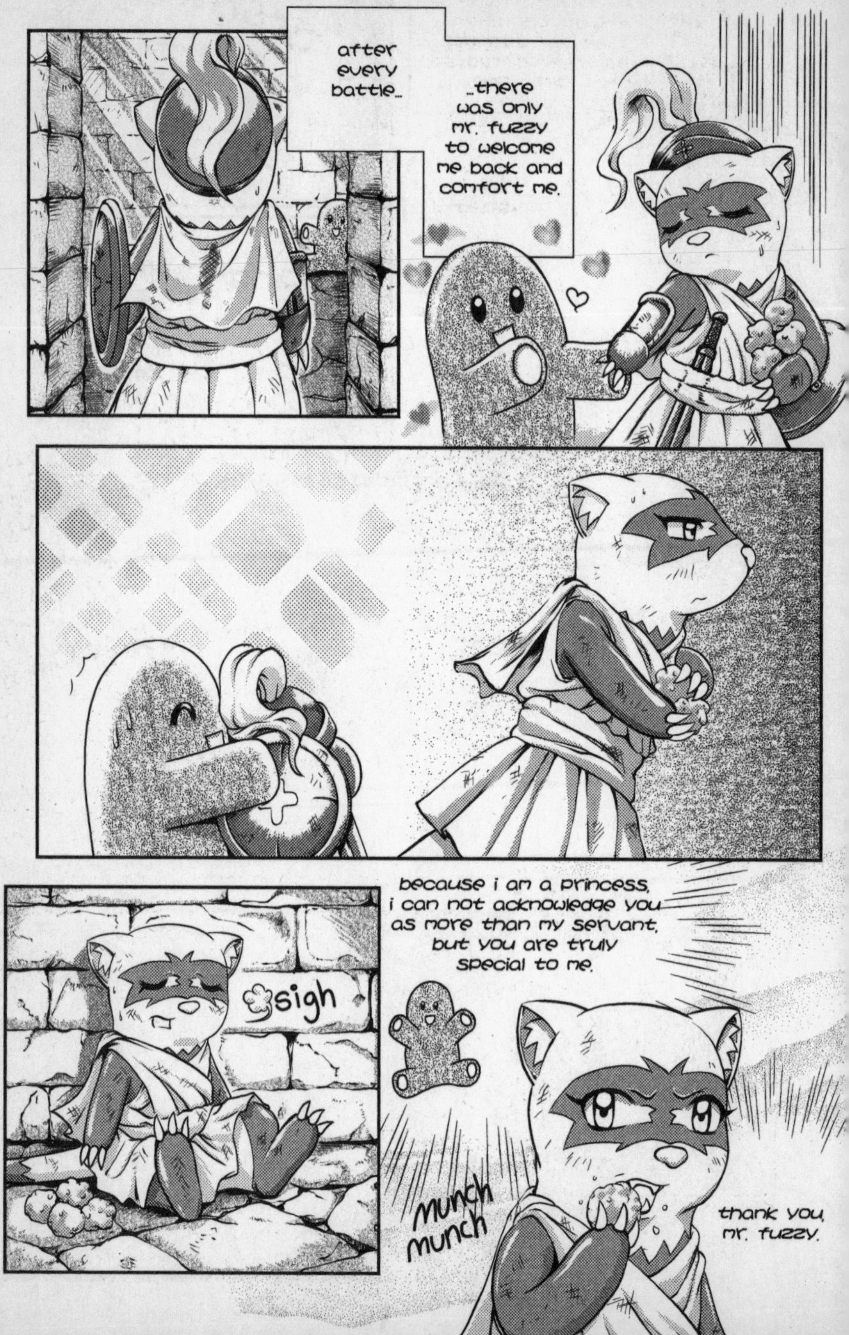
after every battle...
...there was only mr. fuzzy to welcome me back and comfort me.
sigh
because i am a princess, i can not acknowledge you as more than my servant, but you are truly special to me.
munch munch
thank you, mr. fuzzy.

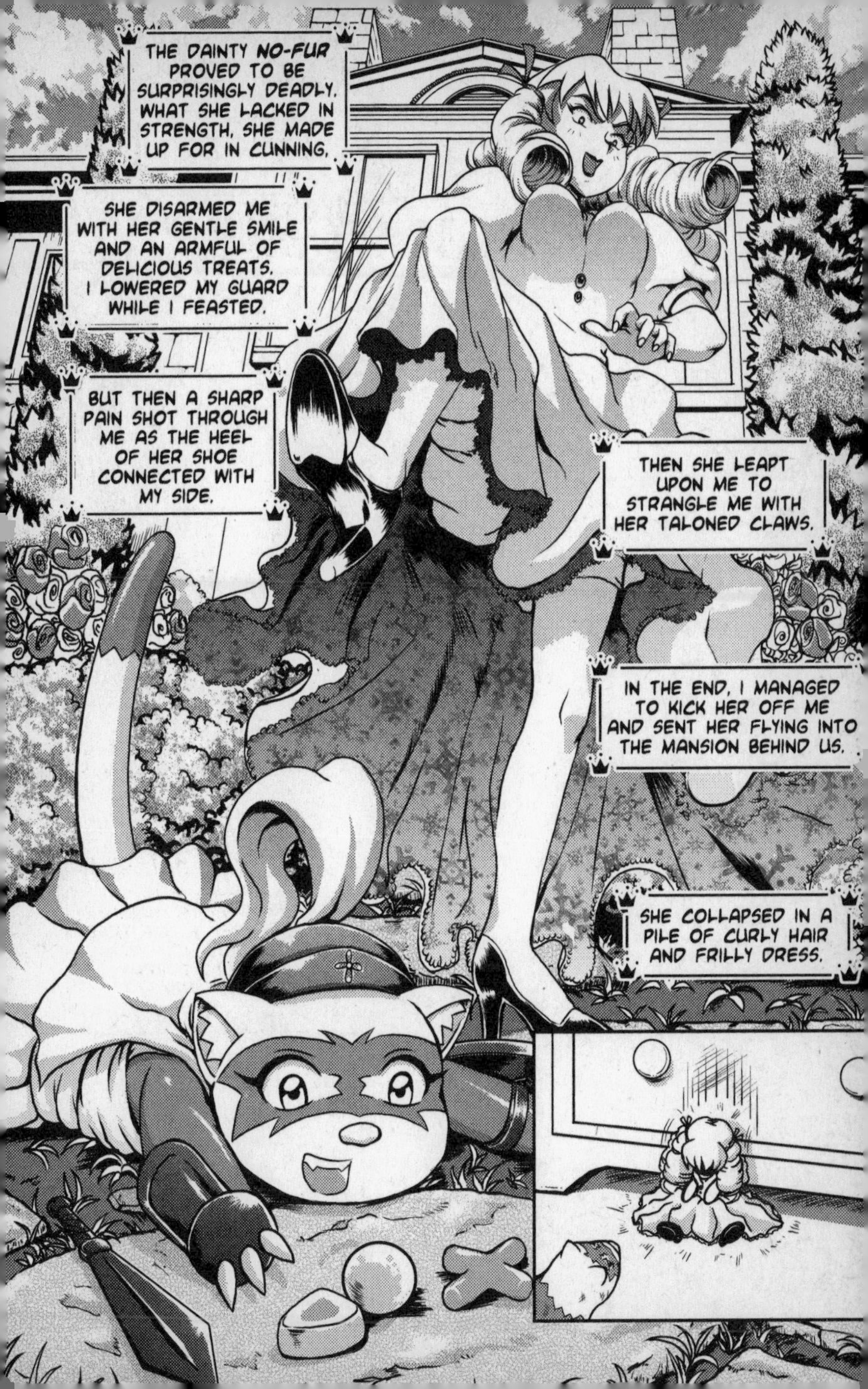
THE DAINTY NO-FUR PROVED TO BE SURPRISINGLY DEADLY. WHAT SHE LACKED IN STRENGTH, SHE MADE UP FOR IN CUNNING.
SHE DISARMED ME WITH HER GENTLE SMILE AND AN ARMFUL OF DELICIOUS TREATS. I LOWERED MY GUARD WHILE I FEASTED.
BUT THEN A SHARP PAIN SHOT THROUGH ME AS THE HEEL OF HER SHOE CONNECTED WITH MY SIDE.
THEN SHE LEAPT UPON ME TO STRANGLE ME WITH HER TALONED CLAWS.
IN THE END, I MANAGED TO KICK HER OFF ME AND SENT HER FLYING INTO THE MANSION BEHIND US.
SHE COLLAPSED IN A PILE OF CURLY HAIR AND FRILLY DRESS.

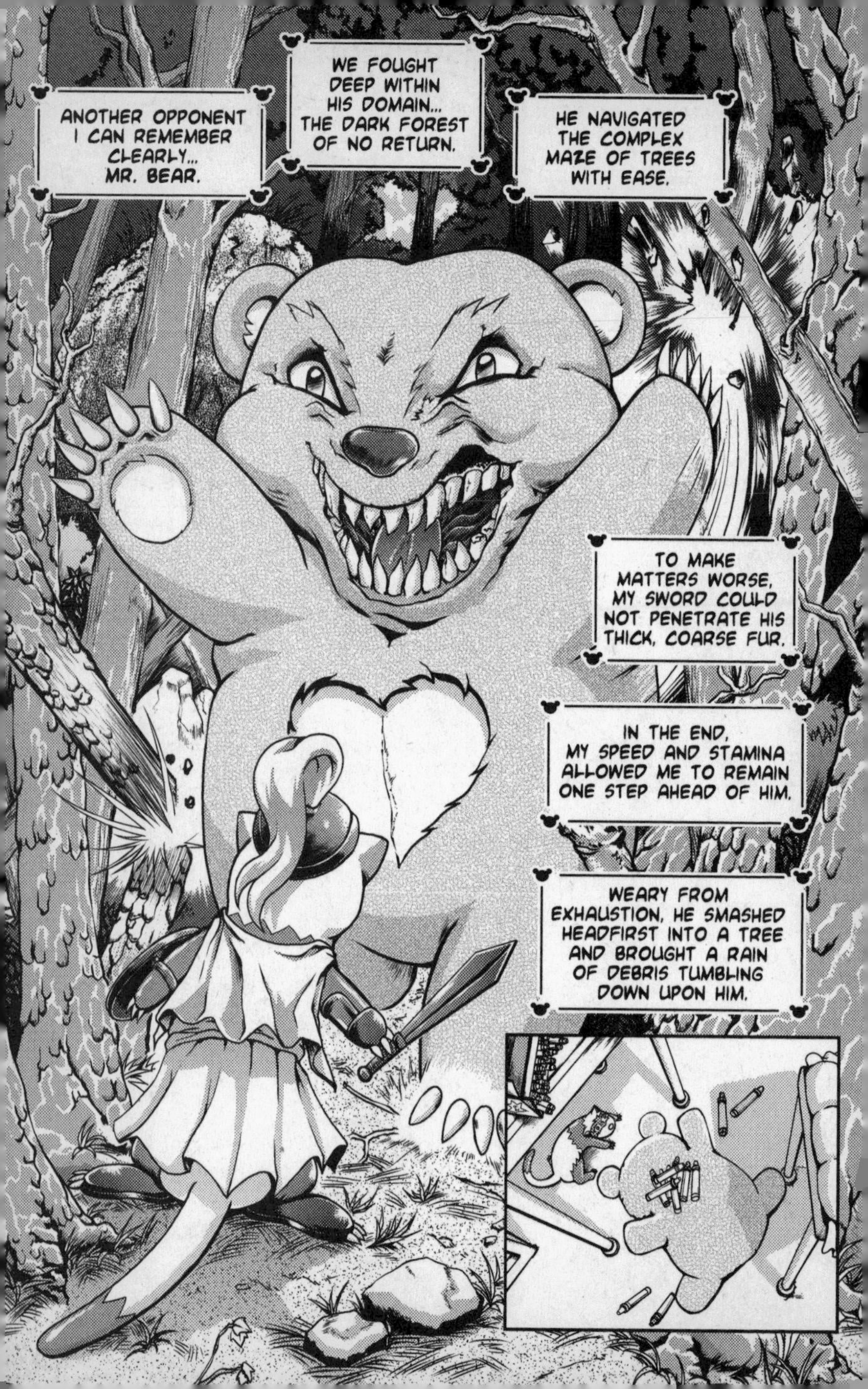
ANOTHER OPPONENT I CAN REMEMBER CLEARLY... MR. BEAR.
WE FOUGHT DEEP WITHIN HIS DOMAIN... THE DARK FOREST OF NO RETURN.
HE NAVIGATED THE COMPLEX MAZE OF TREES WITH EASE.
TO MAKE MATTERS WORSE, MY SWORD COULD NOT PENETRATE HIS THICK, COARSE FUR.
IN THE END, MY SPEED AND STAMINA ALLOWED ME TO REMAIN ONE STEP AHEAD OF HIM.
WEARY FROM EXHAUSTION, HE SMASHED HEADFIRST INTO A TREE AND BROUGHT A RAIN OF DEBRIS TUMBLING DOWN UPON HIM.

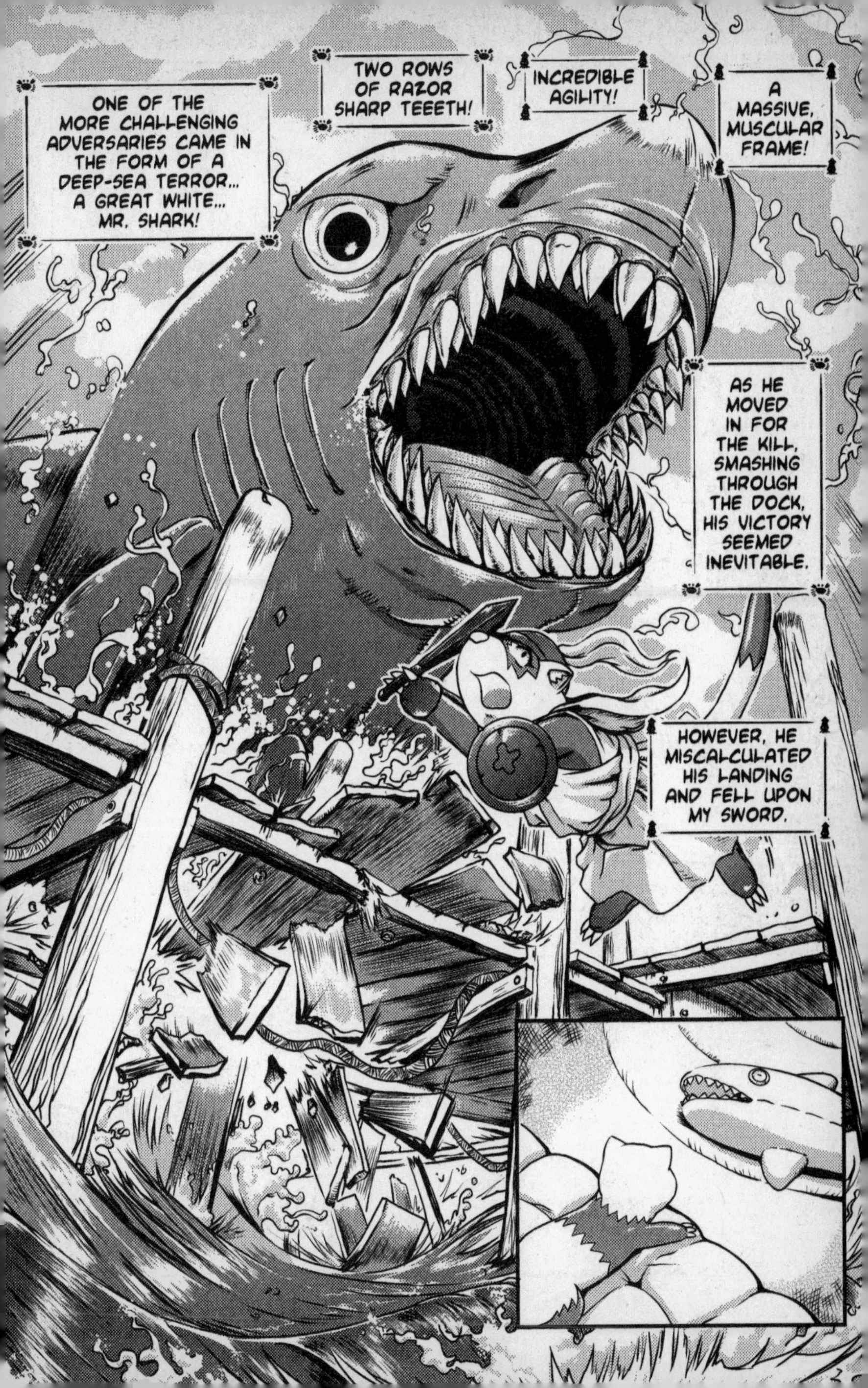
ONE OF THE MORE CHALLENGING ADVERSARIES CAME IN THE FORM OF A DEEP-SEA TERROR... A GREAT WHITE... MR. SHARK!
TWO ROWS OF RAZOR SHARP TEEETH!
INCREDIBLE AGILITY!
A MASSIVE, MUSCULAR FRAME!
AS HE MOVED IN FOR THE KILL, SMASHING THROUGH THE DOCK, HIS VICTORY SEEMED INEVITABLE.
HOWEVER, HE MISCALCULATED HIS LANDING AND FELL UPON MY SWORD.

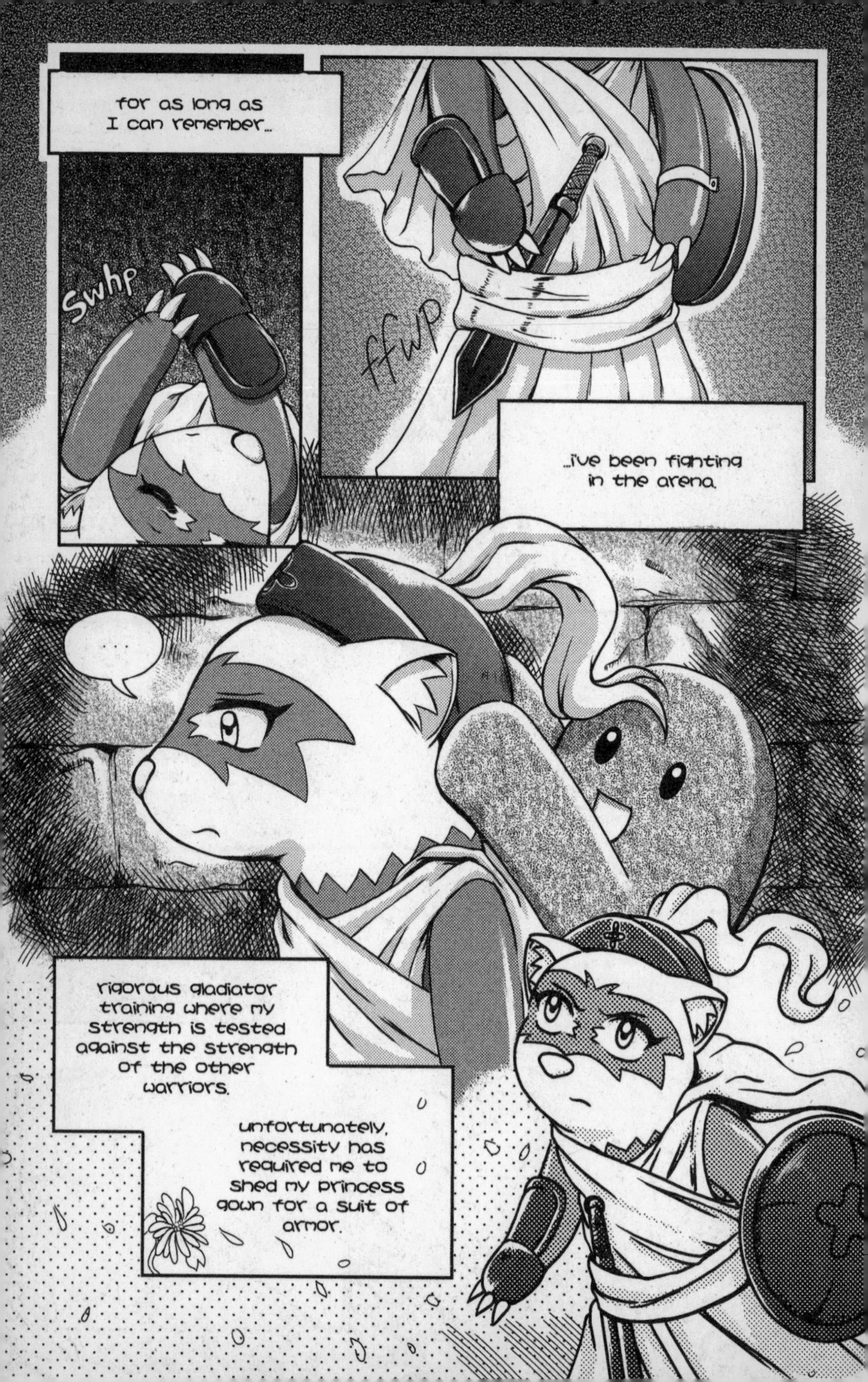
for as long as I can remember...
Swhp
ffwp
...i've been fighting in the arena.
. . .
rigorous gladiator training where my strength is tested against the strength of the other warriors.
unfortunately, necessity has required me to shed my princess gown for a suit of armor.

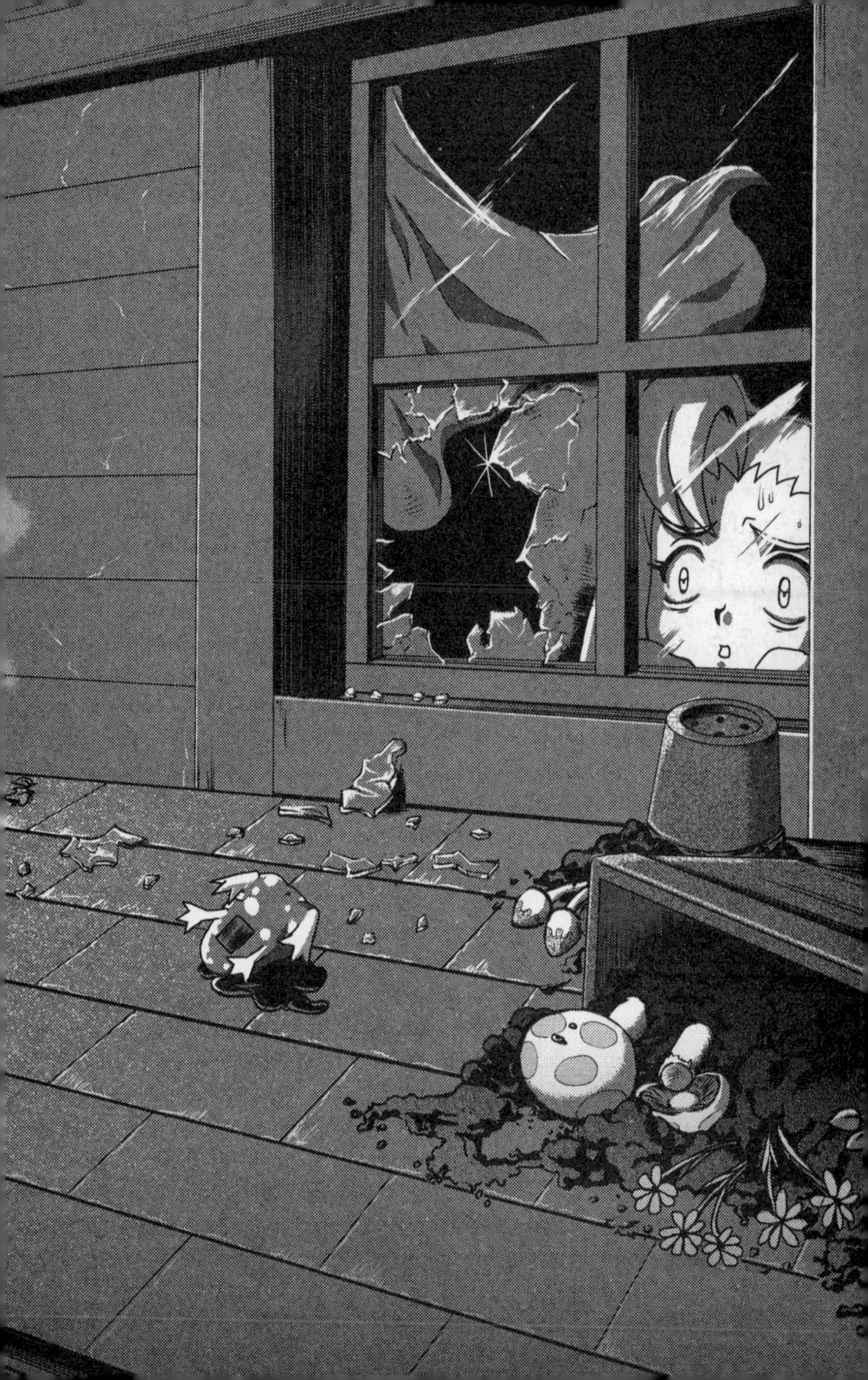

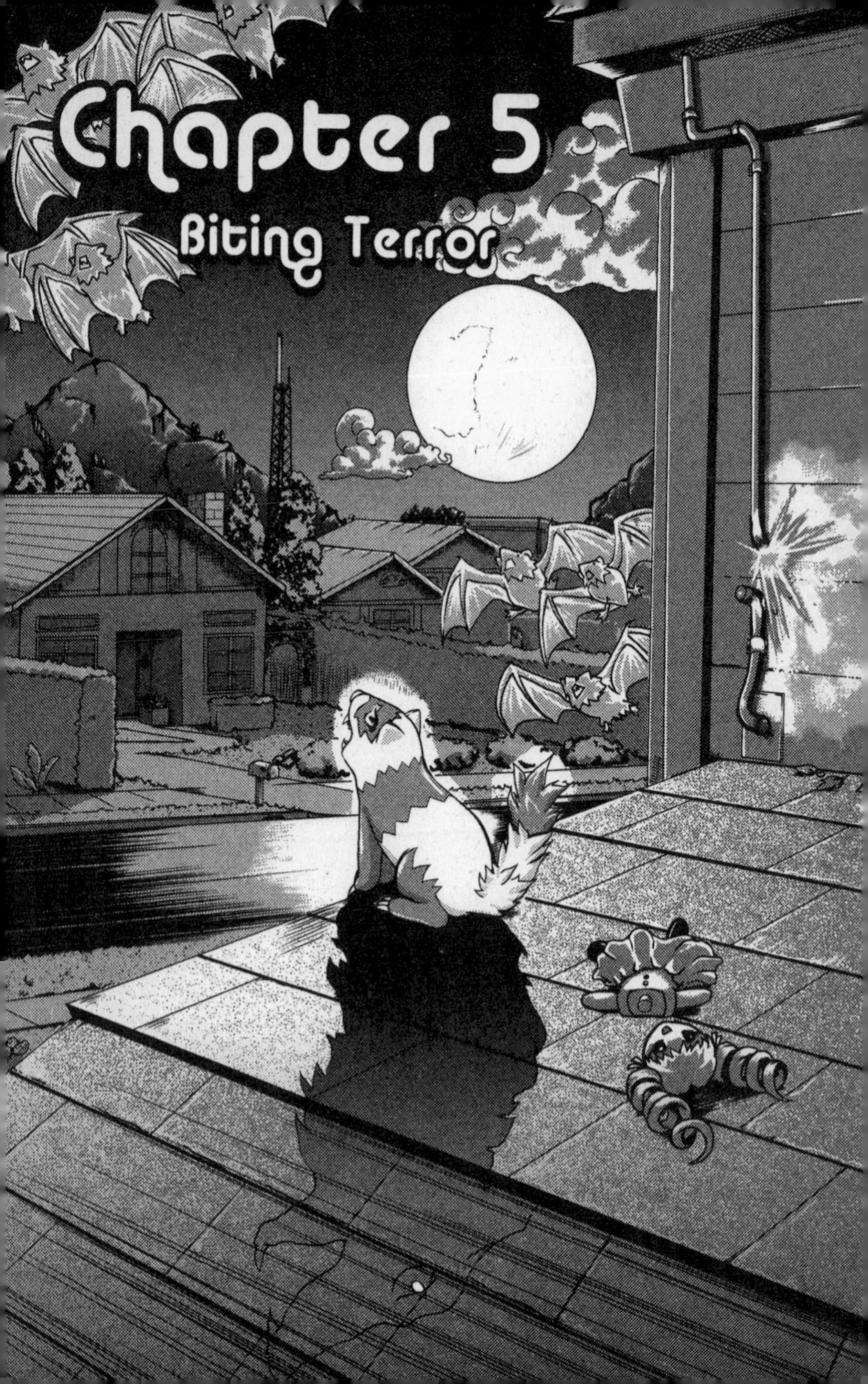
Chapter 5
Biting Terror

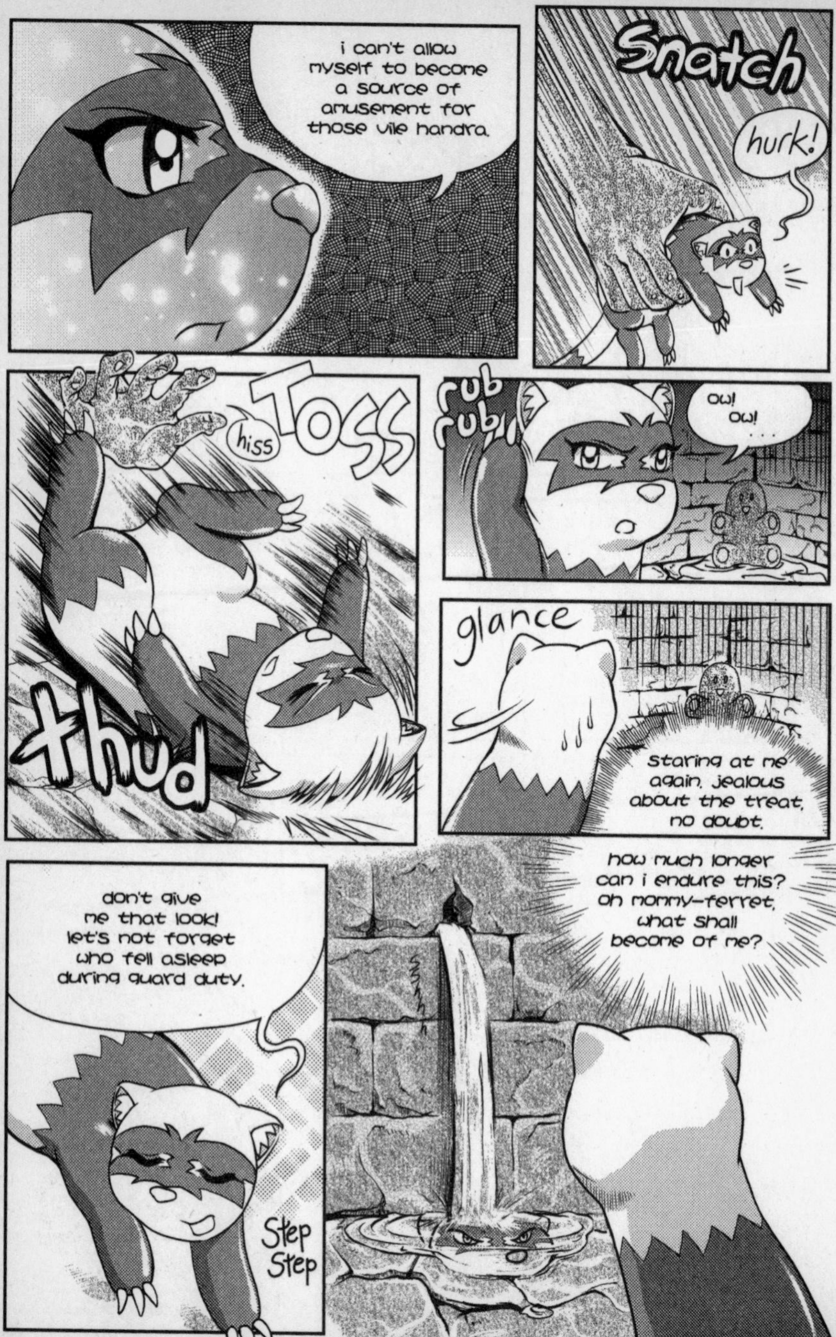

i can't allow myself to become a source of amusement for those vile handra.
Snatch
hurk!
hiss
Toss
thud
rub rub
ow! ow! . . .
glance
staring at me again, jealous about the treat, no doubt.
don't give me that look! let's not forget who fell asleep during guard duty.
Step Step
how much longer can i endure this? oh mommy-ferret, what shall become of me?

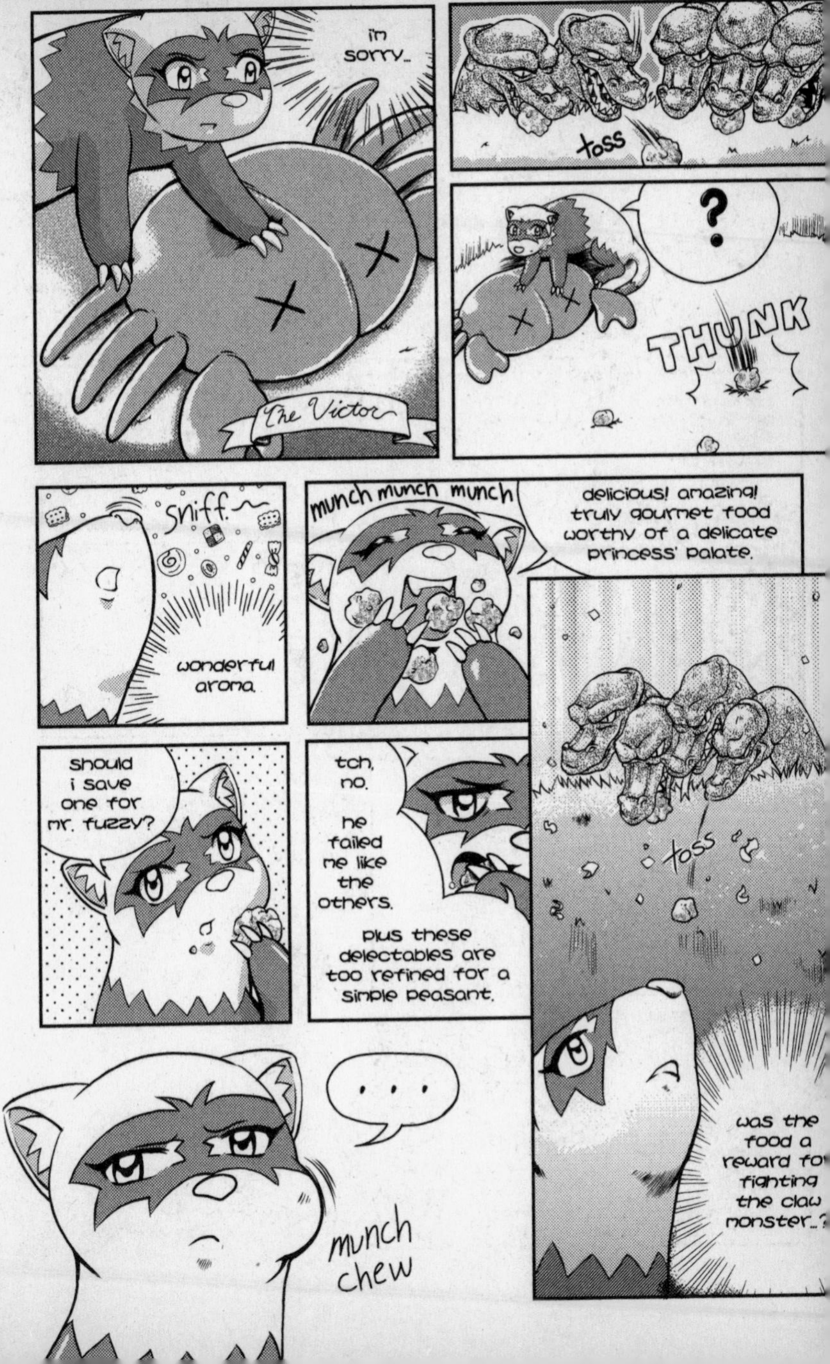
i'm sorry...
The Victor
toss
?
THUNK
sniff
wonderful aroma.
munch munch munch
delicious! amazing! truly gourmet food worthy of a delicate princess' palate.
should i save one for mr. fuzzy?
tch, no.
he failed me like the others.
plus these delectables are too refined for a simple peasant.
toss
was the food a reward fo fighting the claw monster...?
. . .
munch chew

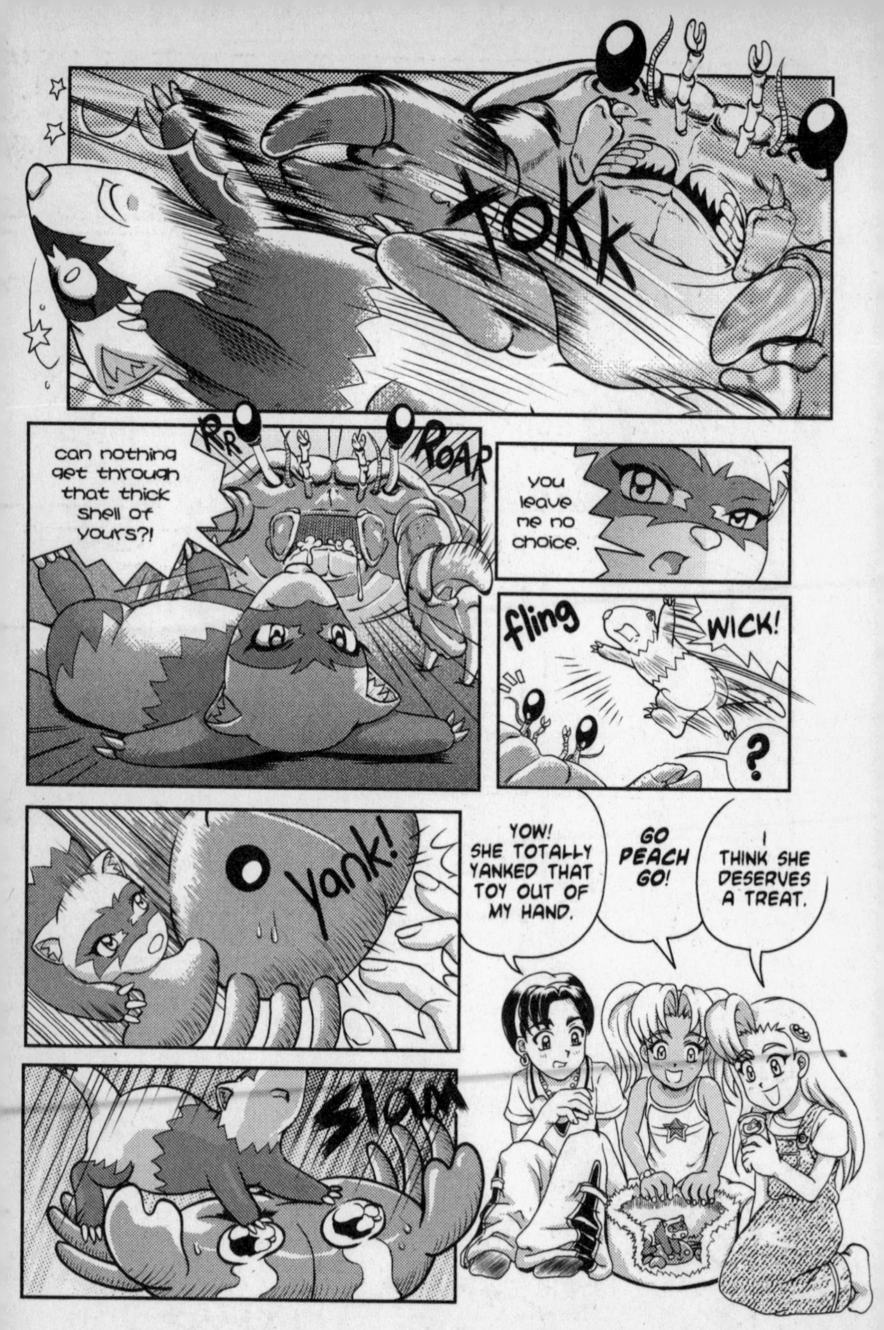
TOKK
RR
ROAR
can nothing get through that thick shell of yours?!
you leave me no choice.
fling
WICK!
?
yank!
YOW! SHE TOTALLY YANKED THAT TOY OUT OF MY HAND.
GO PEACH GO!
I THINK SHE DESERVES A TREAT.
SLAM

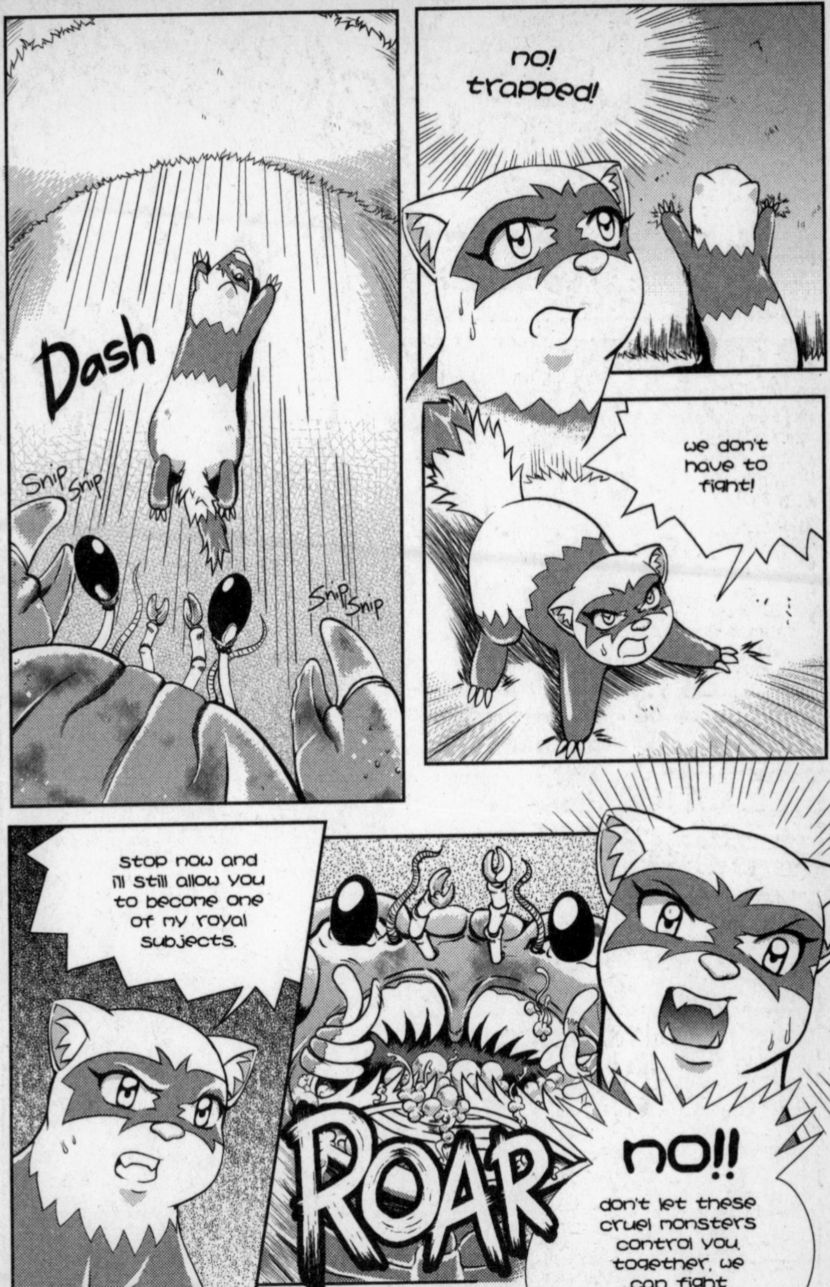
Dash
Snip Snip
Snip Snip
no! trapped!
we don't have to fight!
stop now and i'll still allow you to become one of my royal subjects.
ROAR
no!!
don't let these cruel monsters control you. together, we can fight against them!

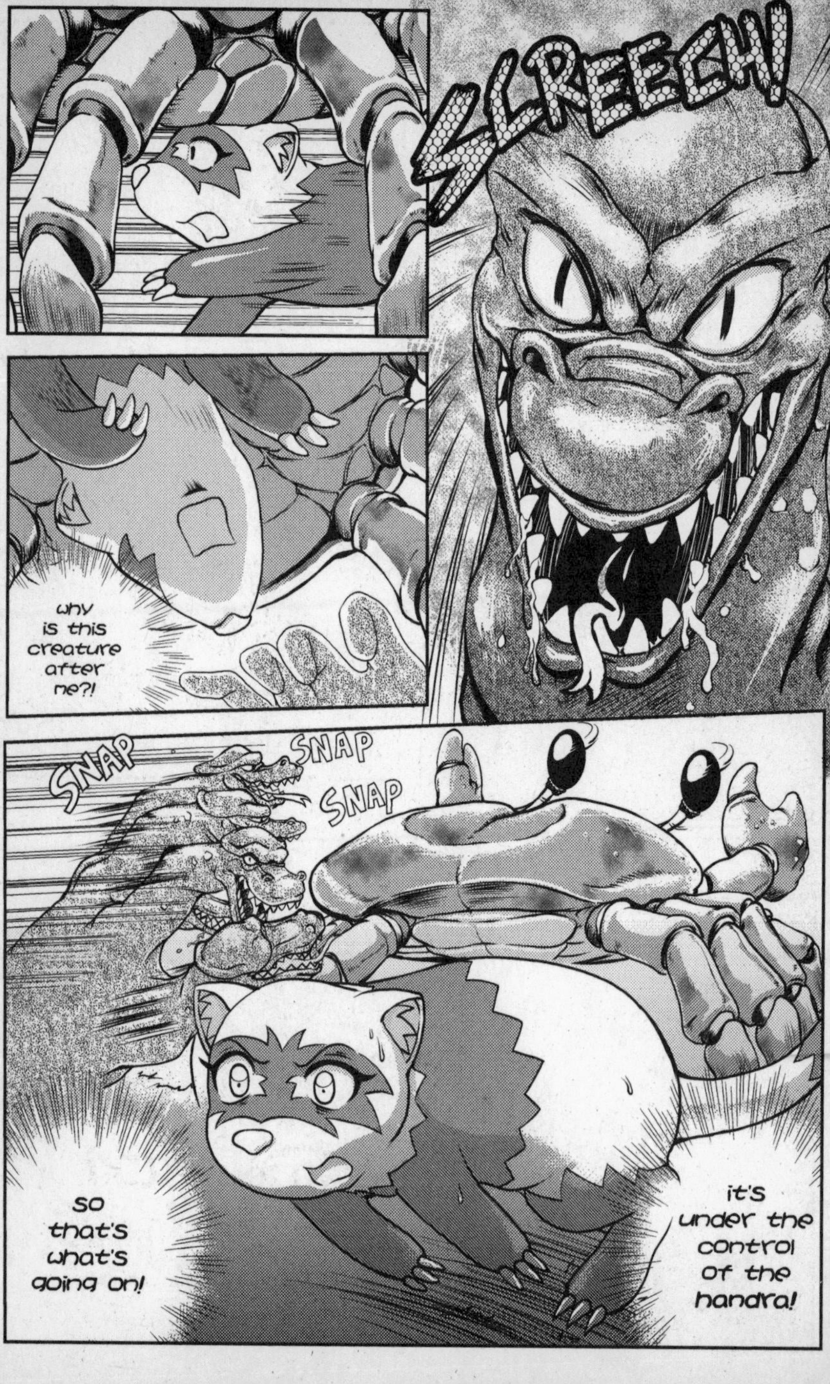
why is this creature after me?!
SCREECH!
SNAP
SNAP
SNAP
so that's what's going on!
it's under the control of the handra!

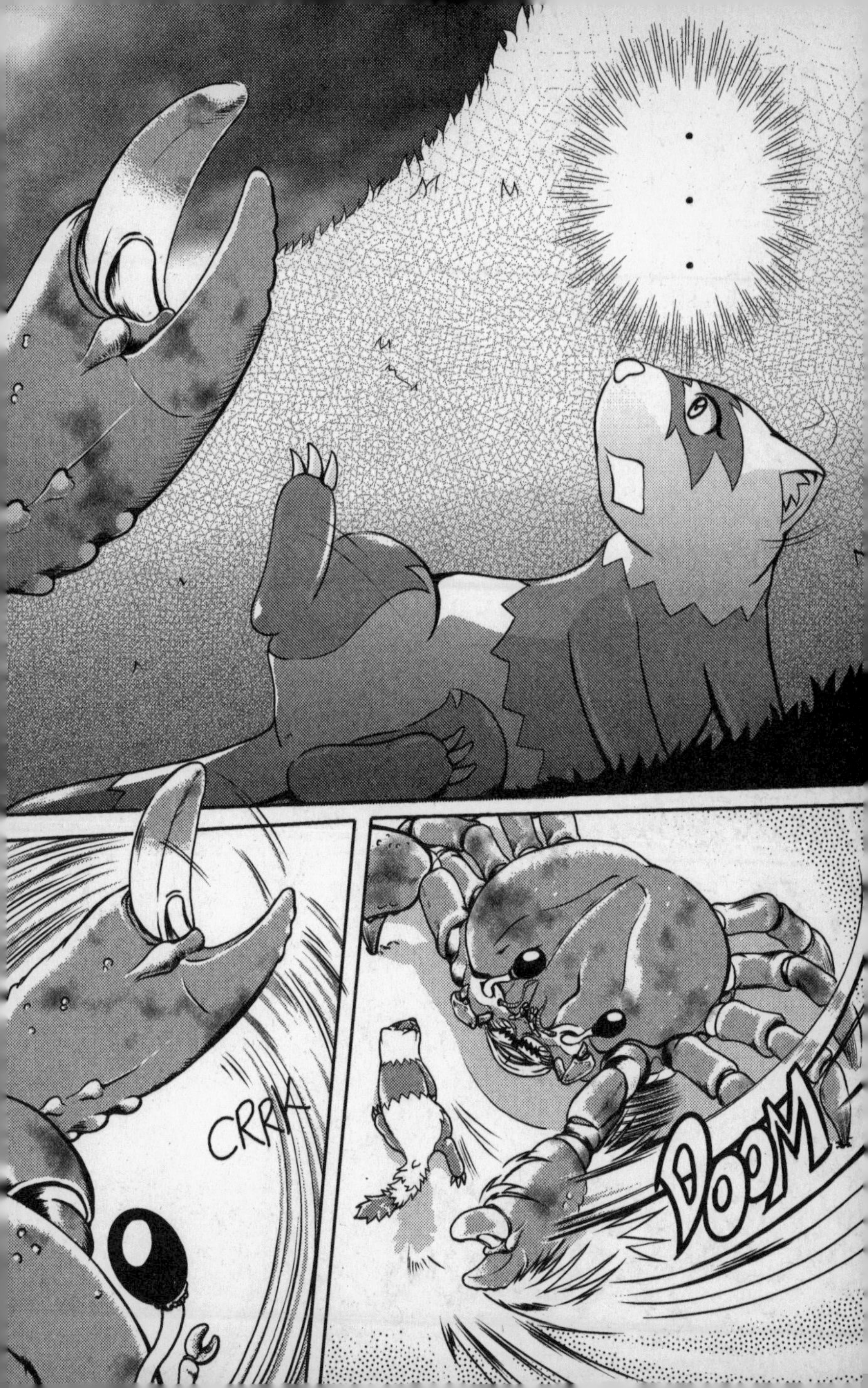
...
CRRA
DOOM

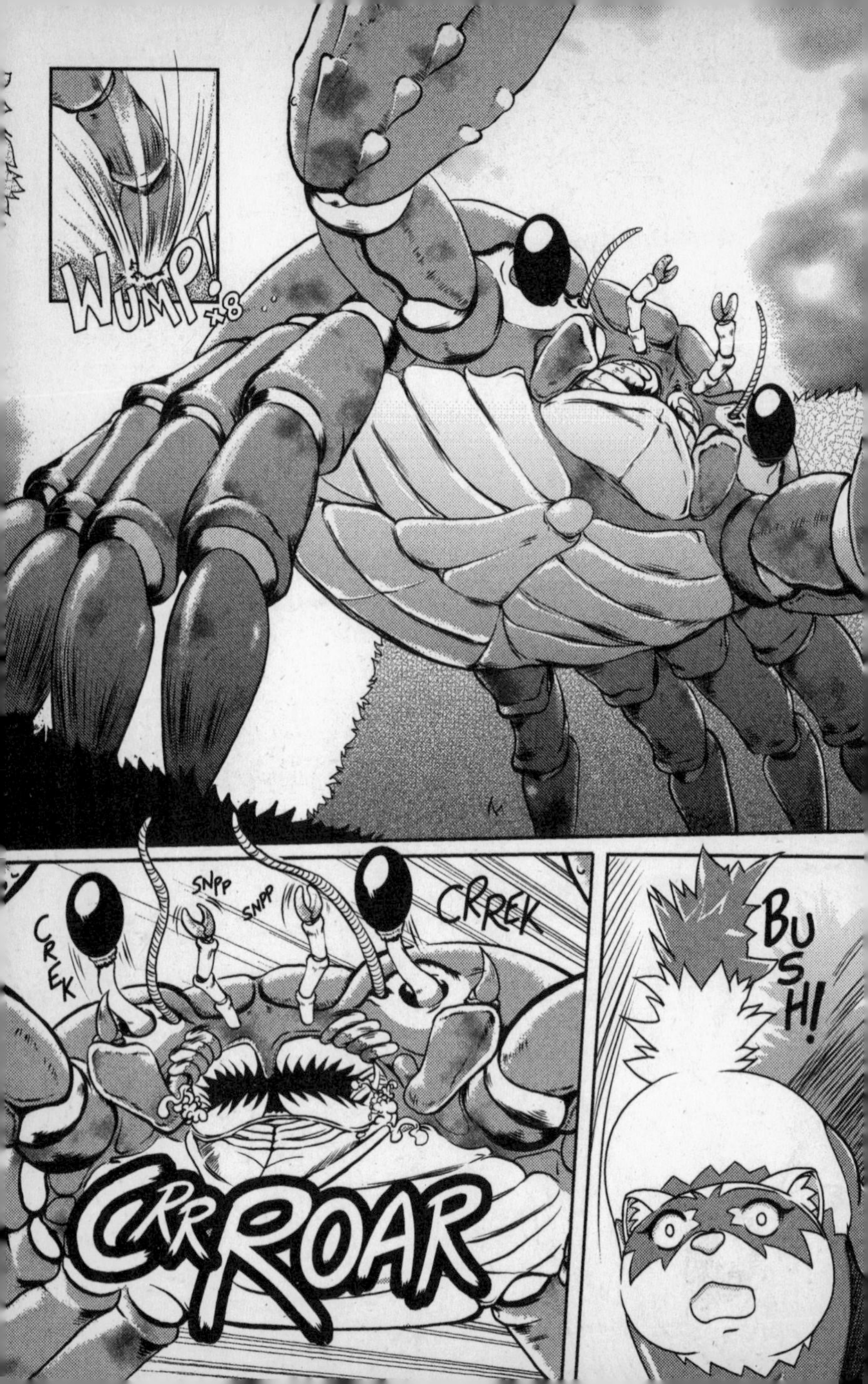
WUMP! x8
BUSH!
CRREK
SNPP
SNPP
CREK
CRRROAR

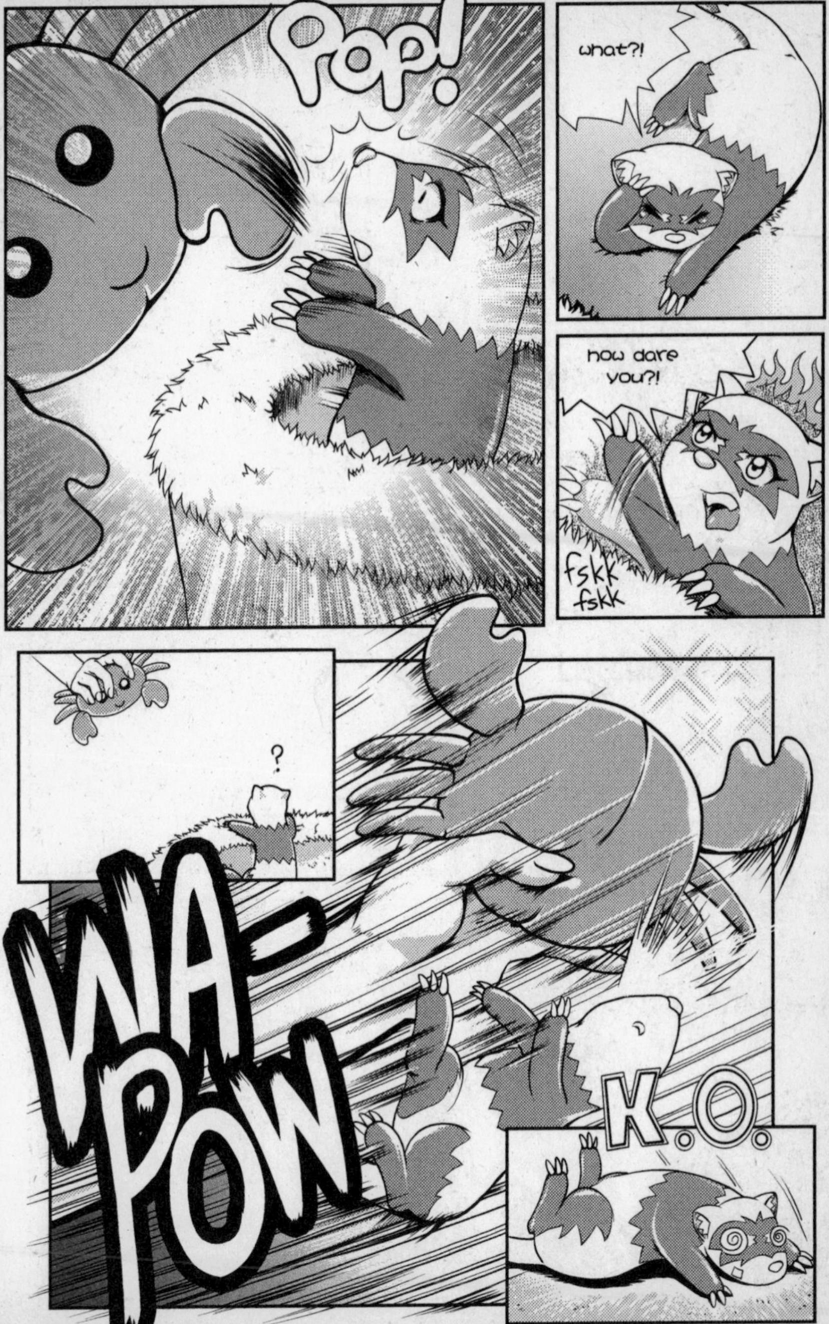
Pop!
what?!
how dare you?!
fskk fskk
?
WA-POW
K.O.

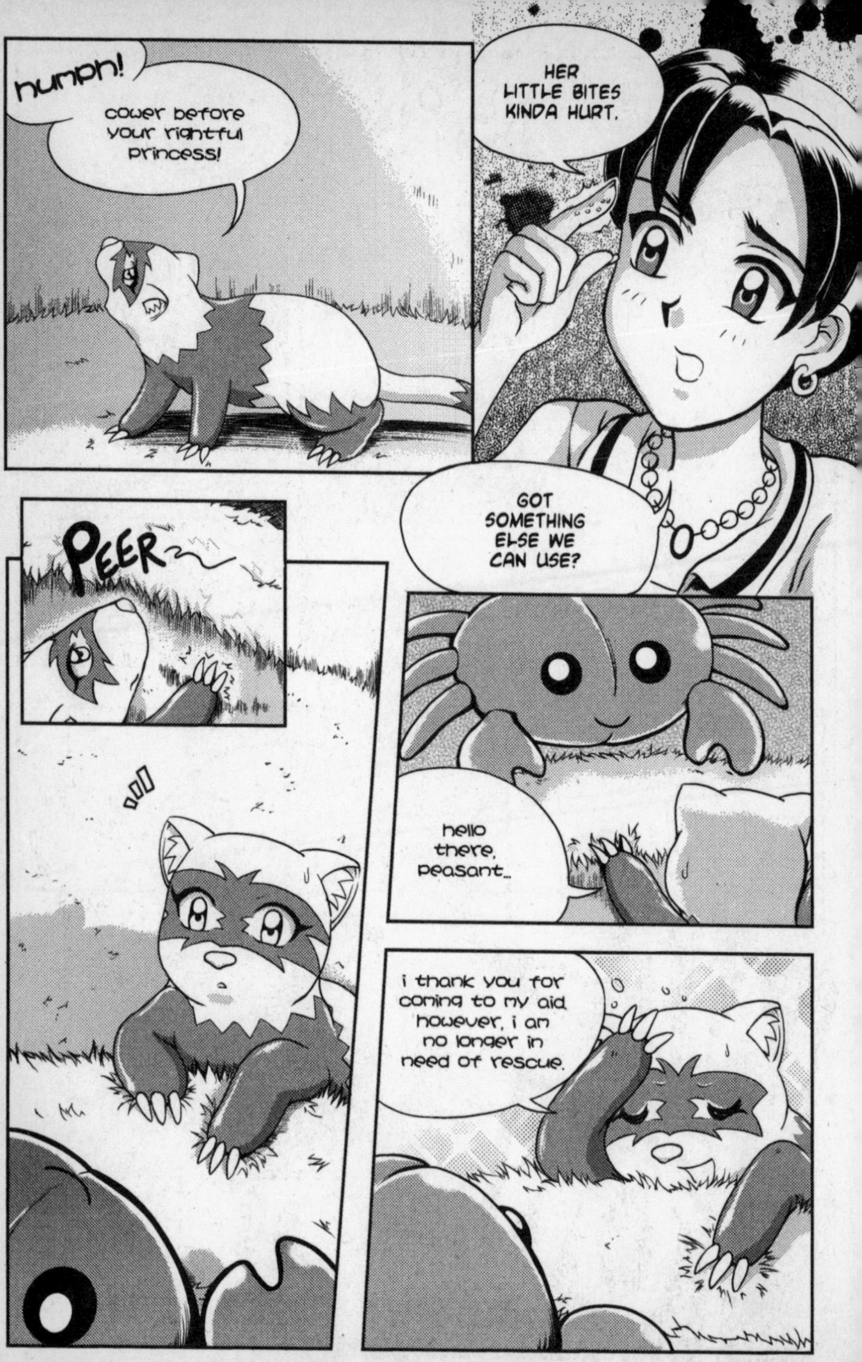
humph!
cower before your rightful princess!
HER LITTLE BITES KINDA HURT.
GOT SOMETHING ELSE WE CAN USE?
PEER
!!
hello there, peasant...
i thank you for coming to my aid. however, i am no longer in need of rescue.

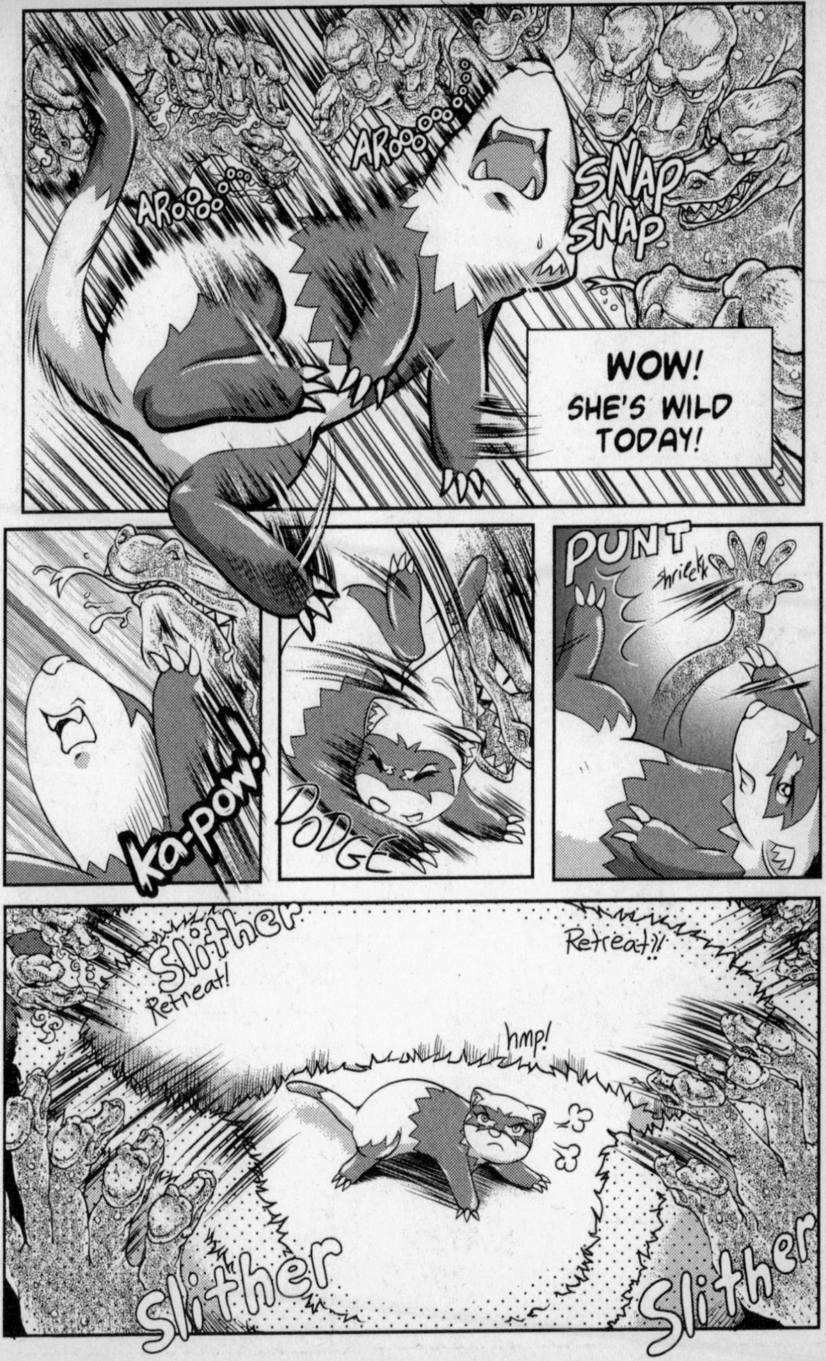

AROOOOO
AROOOOOOOOO
SNAP SNAP
WOW! SHE'S WILD TODAY!
KA-POW!
DODGE
PUNT
shrieekk
Slither
Retreat!
Retreat!!
hmp!
Slither
Slither

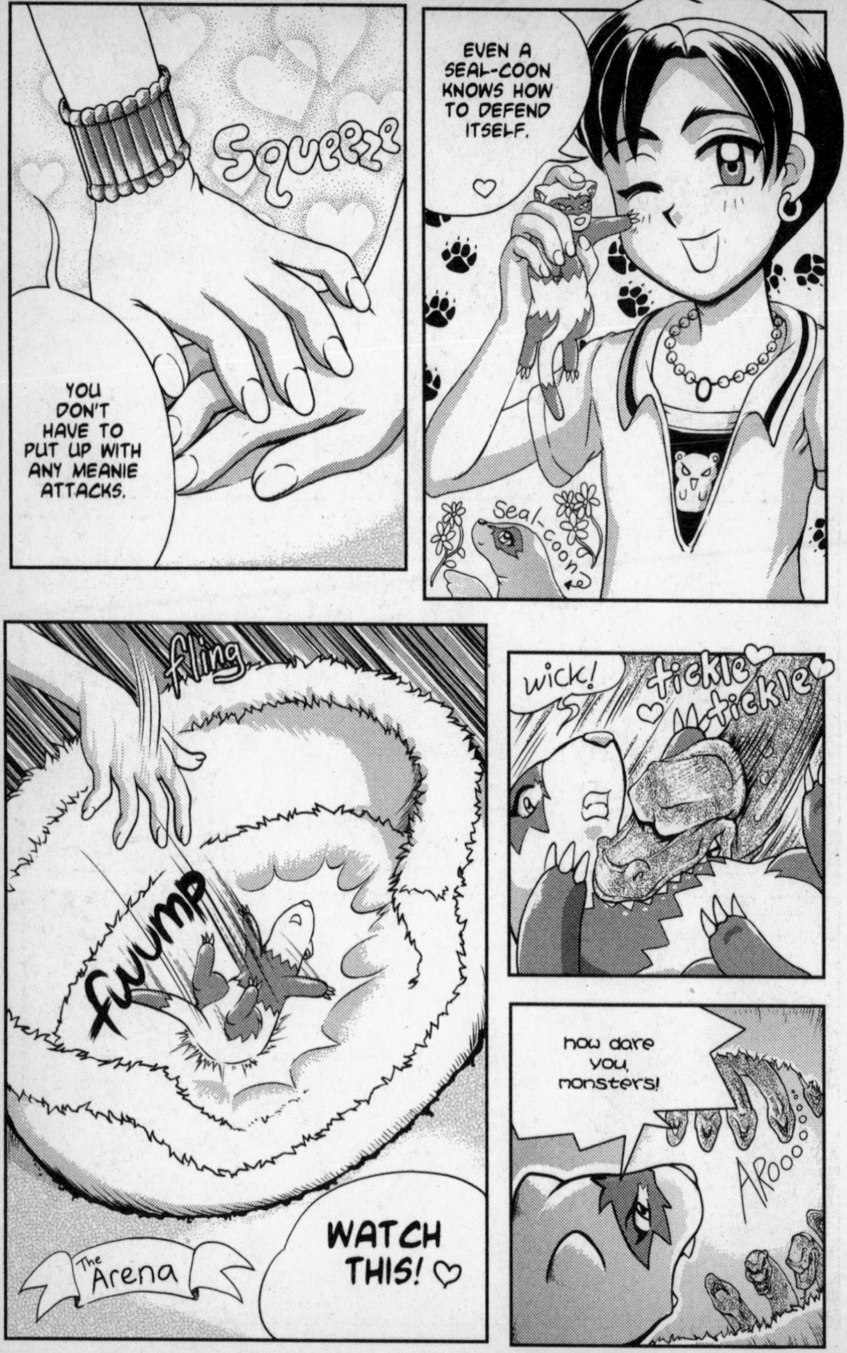

EVEN A SEAL-COON KNOWS HOW TO DEFEND ITSELF.
Seal-coon
Squeeze
YOU DON'T HAVE TO PUT UP WITH ANY MEANIE ATTACKS.
wick!
tickle tickle
how dare you, monsters!
AROooo
fling
fwump
WATCH THIS!
The Arena

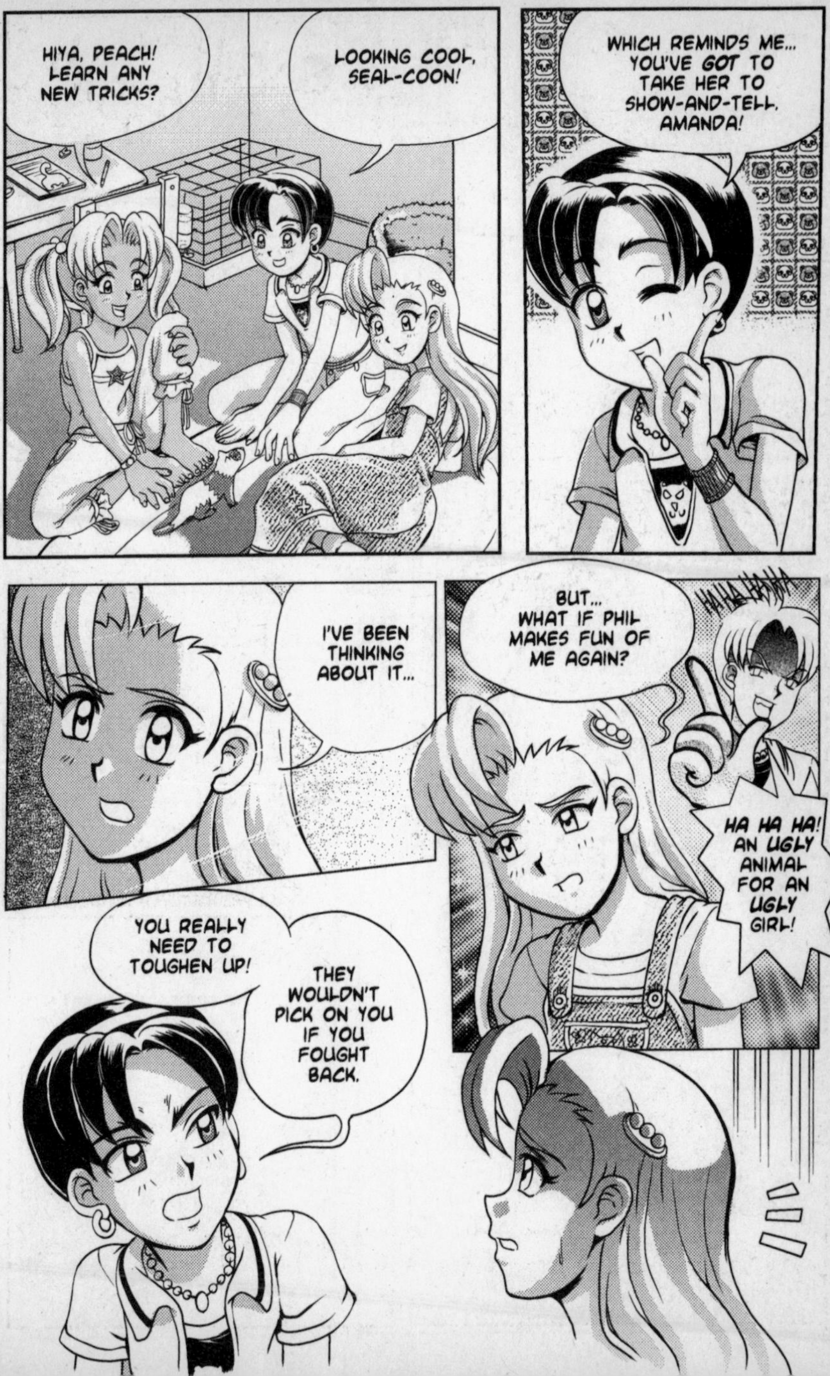
HIYA, PEACH! LEARN ANY NEW TRICKS?
LOOKING COOL, SEAL-COON!
WHICH REMINDS ME... YOU'VE GOT TO TAKE HER TO SHOW-AND-TELL, AMANDA!
I'VE BEEN THINKING ABOUT IT...
BUT... WHAT IF PHIL MAKES FUN OF ME AGAIN?
HA HA HA HA
HA HA HA! AN UGLY ANIMAL FOR AN UGLY GIRL!
YOU REALLY NEED TO TOUGHEN UP!
THEY WOULDN'T PICK ON YOU IF YOU FOUGHT BACK.

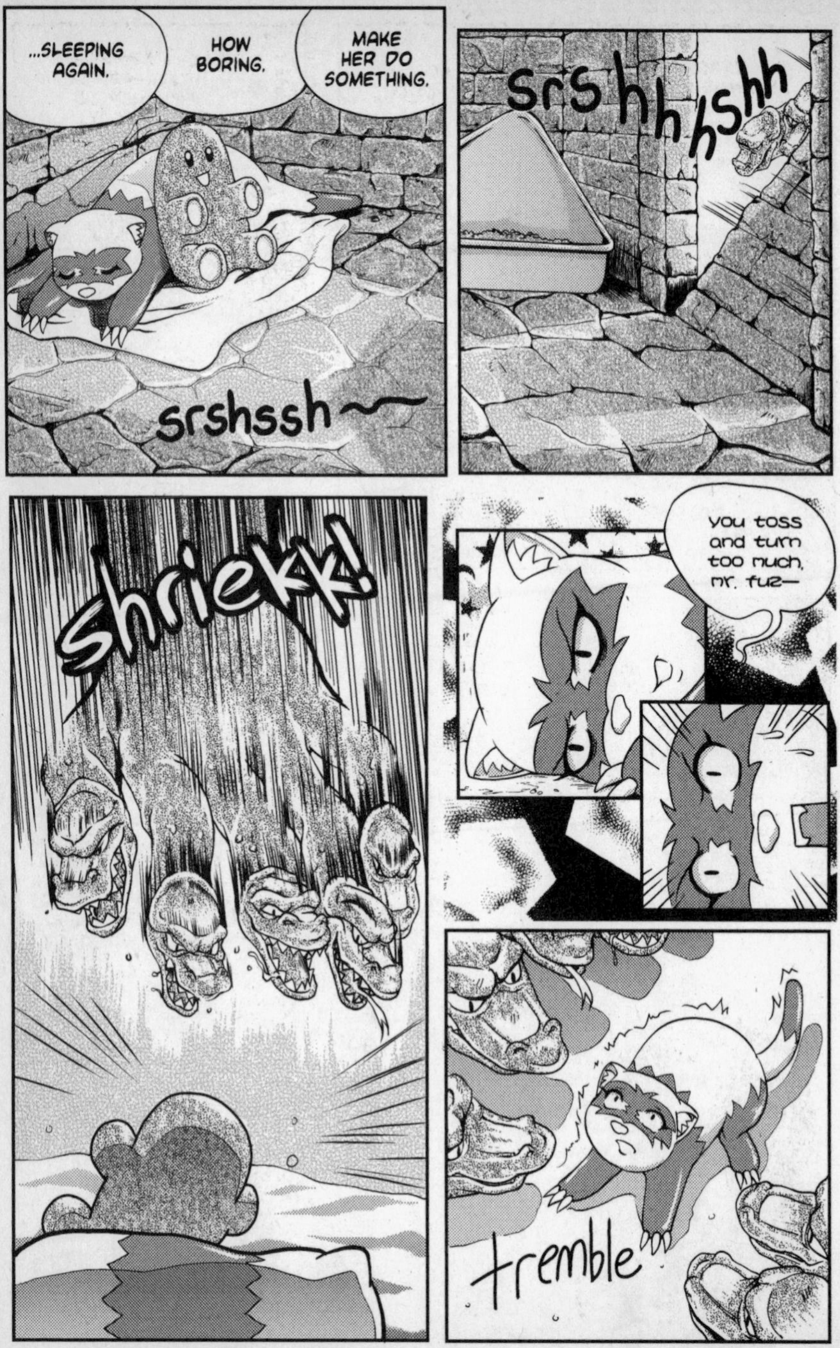
...SLEEPING AGAIN.
HOW BORING.
MAKE HER DO SOMETHING.
srshssh~~
srshhhshh
shriekk!
you toss and turn too much, mr. fuz—
tremble

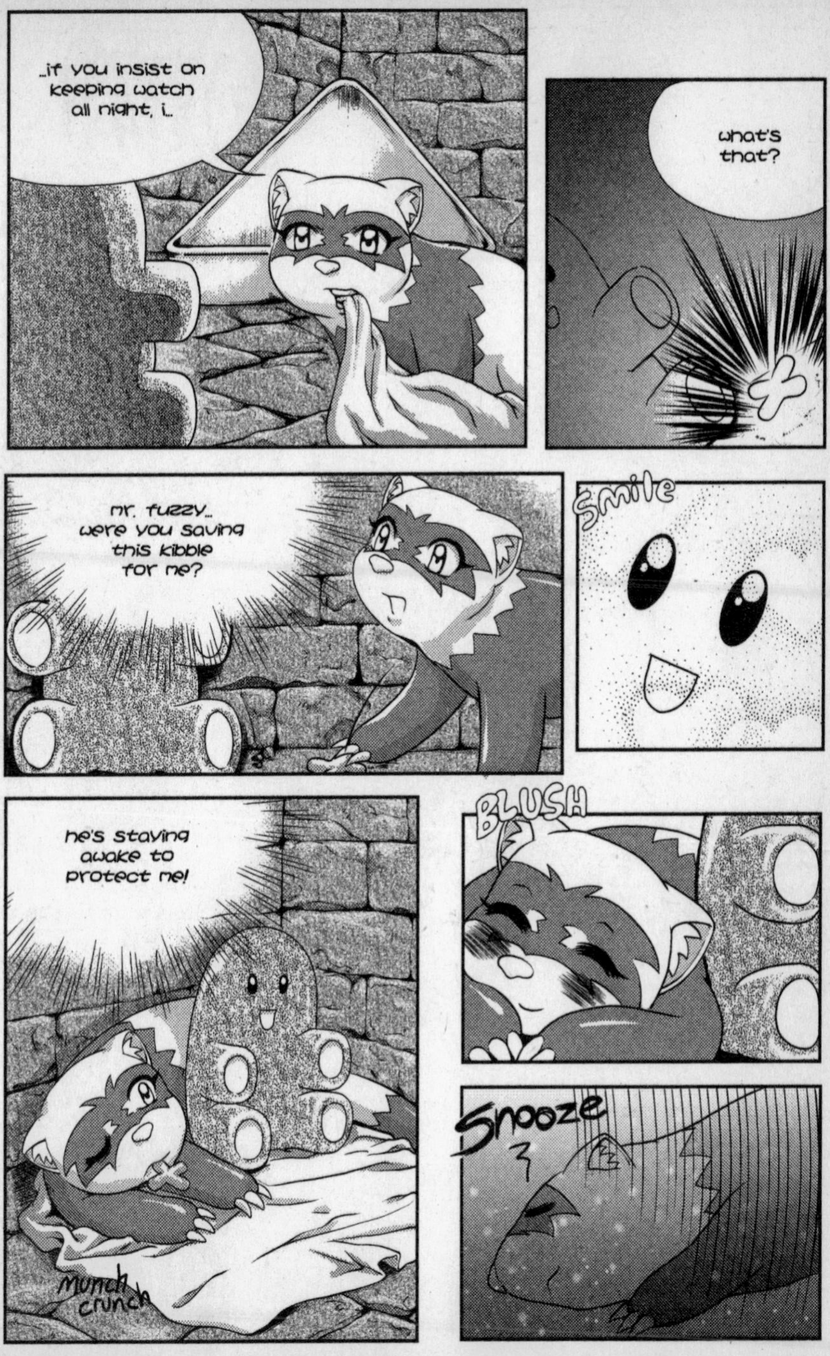
..if you insist on keeping watch all night, i..
what's that?
mr. fuzzy.. were you saving this kibble for me?
Smile
he's staying awake to protect me!
Munch crunch
BLUSH
Snooze

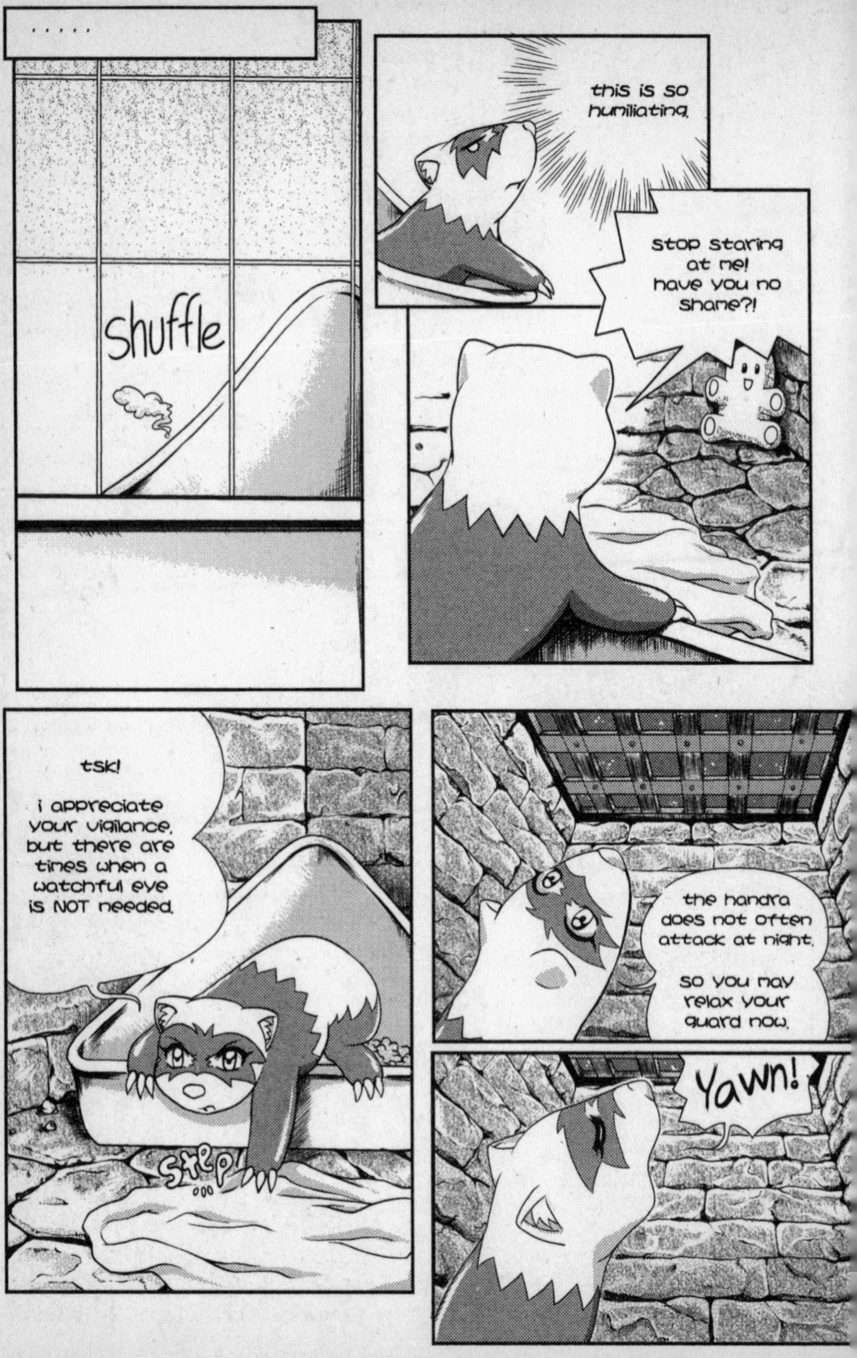
. . . . .
shuffle
this is so humiliating.
stop staring at me! have you no shame?!
tsk!
i appreciate your vigilance, but there are times when a watchful eye is NOT needed.
step
the handra does not often attack at night.
so you may relax your guard now.
Yawn!

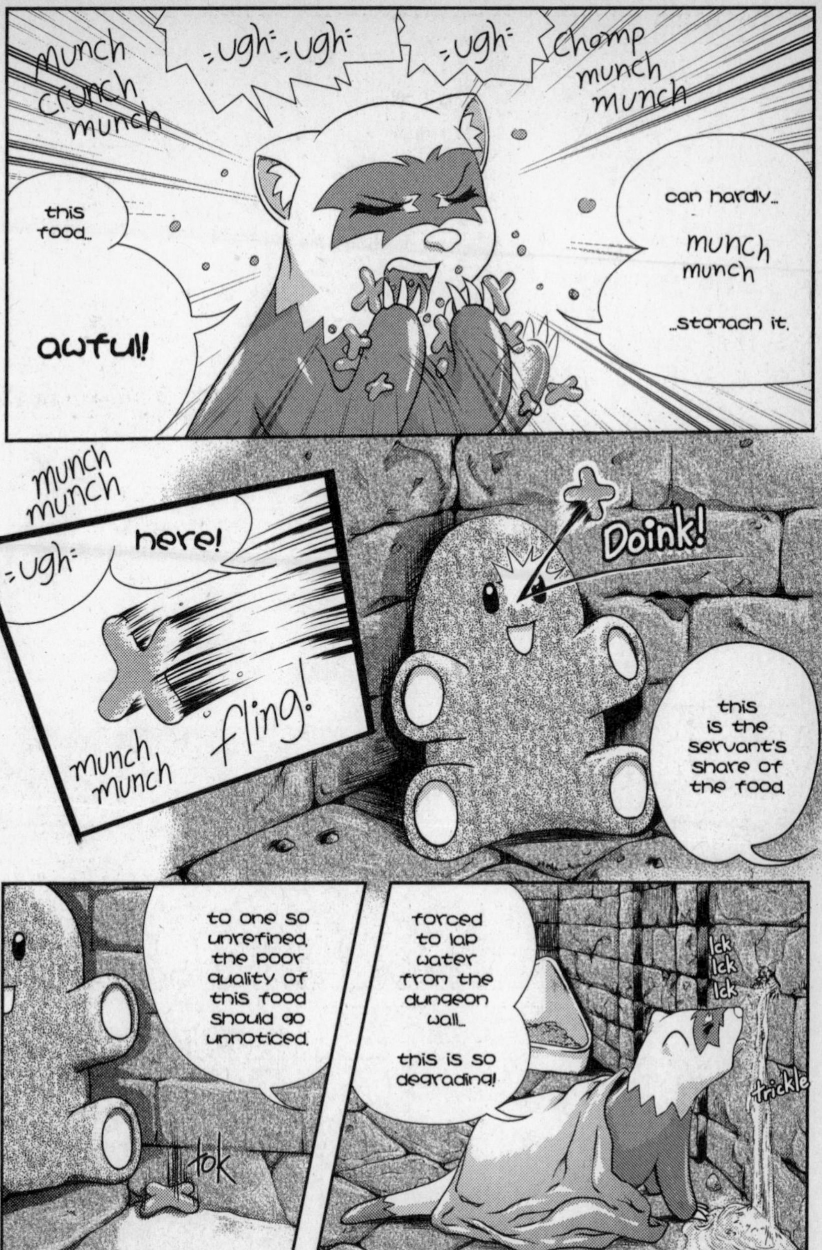
munch crunch munch
=ugh= =ugh=
=ugh=
chomp munch munch
this food...
awful!
can hardly...
munch munch
...stomach it.
munch munch
=ugh=
here!
fling!
munch munch
Doink!
this is the servant's share of the food.
to one so unrefined, the poor quality of this food should go unnoticed.
tok
forced to lap water from the dungeon wall...
this is so degrading!
lck lck lck
trickle

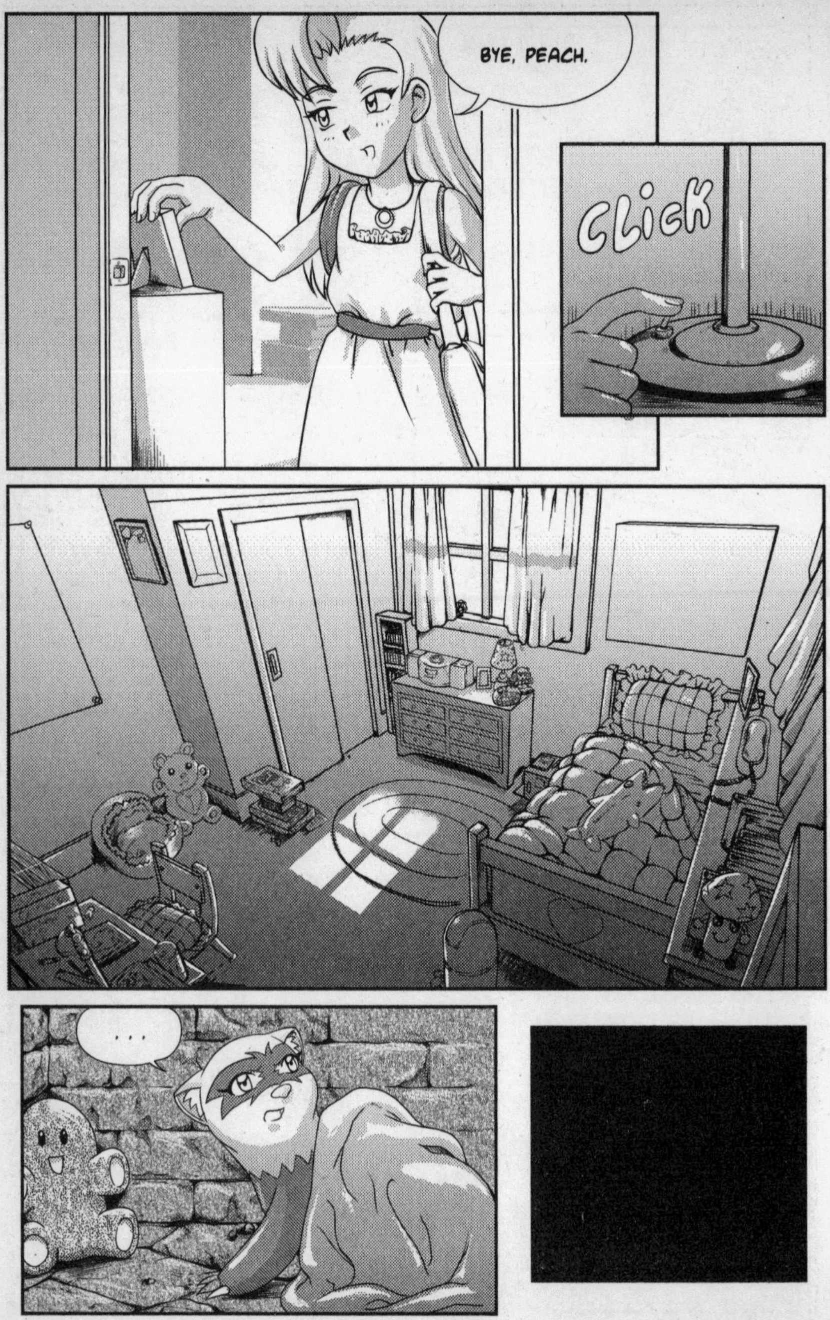
CLICK
BYE, PEACH.
. . .

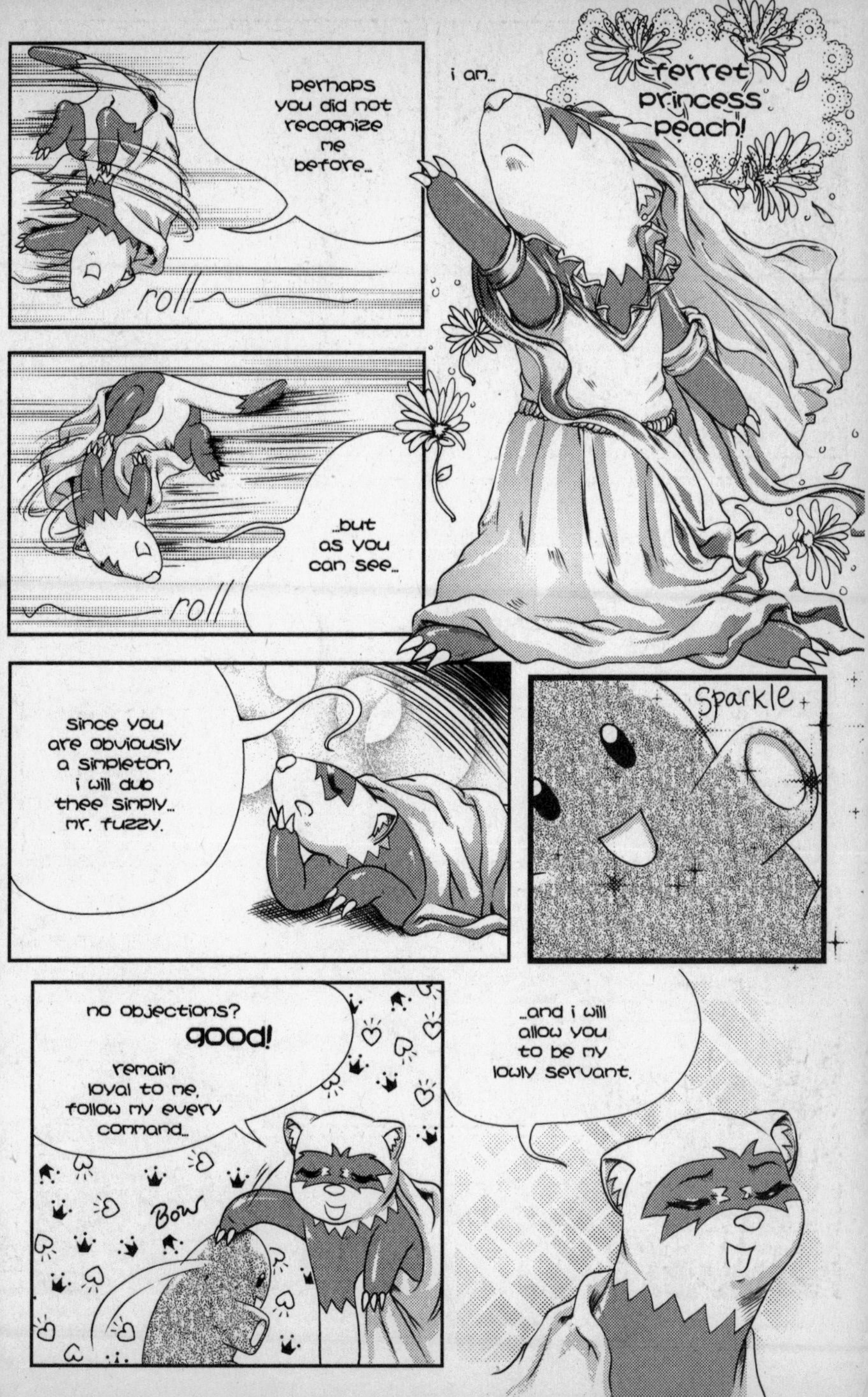
perhaps you did not recognize me before...
roll
...but as you can see...
roll
i am...
ferret princess peach!
since you are obviously a simpleton, i will dub thee simply... mr. fuzzy.
Sparkle
no objections? good!
remain loyal to me, follow my every command...
Bow
...and i will allow you to be my lowly servant.

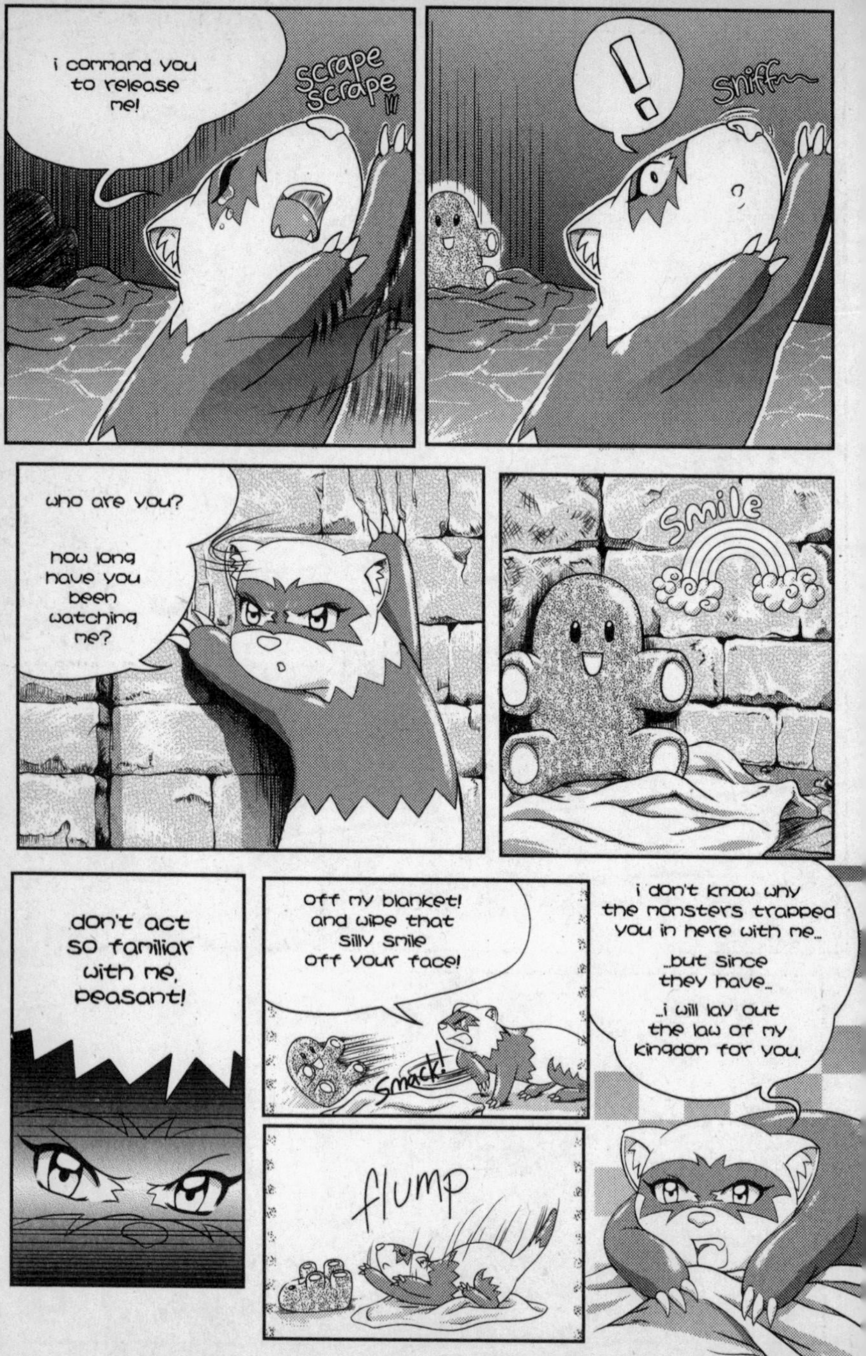
i command you to release me!
scrape scrape
!
Sniff~
who are you?
how long have you been watching me?
Smile
don't act so familiar with me, peasant!
off my blanket! and wipe that silly smile off your face!
Smack!
flump
i don't know why the monsters trapped you in here with me...
...but since they have...
...i will lay out the law of my kingdom for you.

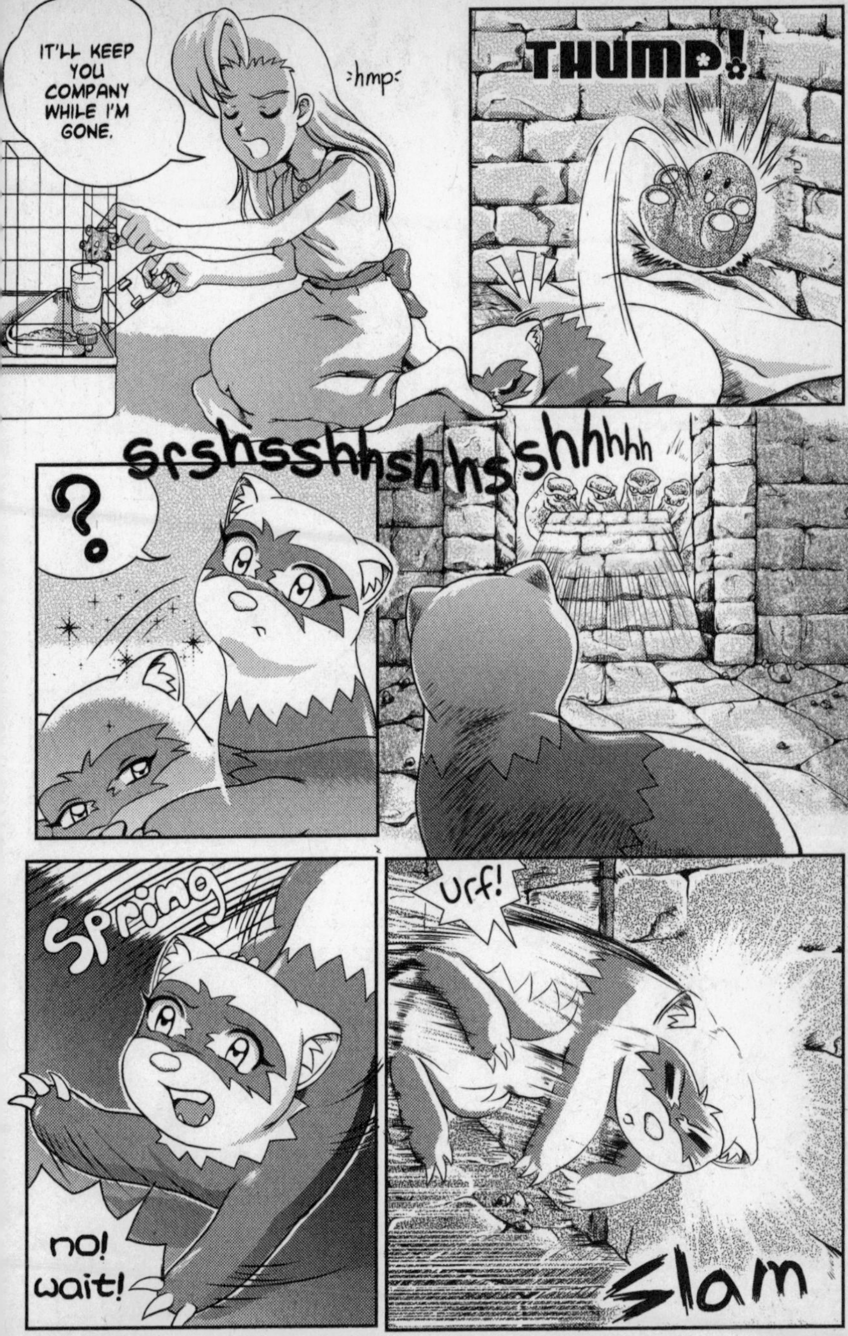
IT'LL KEEP YOU COMPANY WHILE I'M GONE.
:hmp:
THUMP!
srshsshhshhsshhhh
?
Spring
no! wait!
Urf!
Slam

thump
Thump
THUMP

cla..
chk

BAM

tok

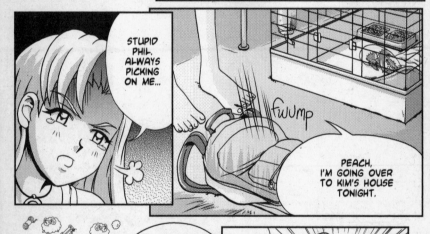

STUPID PHIL. ALWAYS PICKING ON ME...

fwump

PEACH, I'M GOING OVER TO KIM'S HOUSE TONIGHT.

fwp

NOT THAT *YOU'D* NOTICE SINCE YOU'RE *ALWAYS* SLEEPING.

rustle rustle

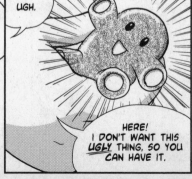

UGH.

HERE! I DON'T WANT THIS *UGLY* THING, SO YOU CAN HAVE IT.

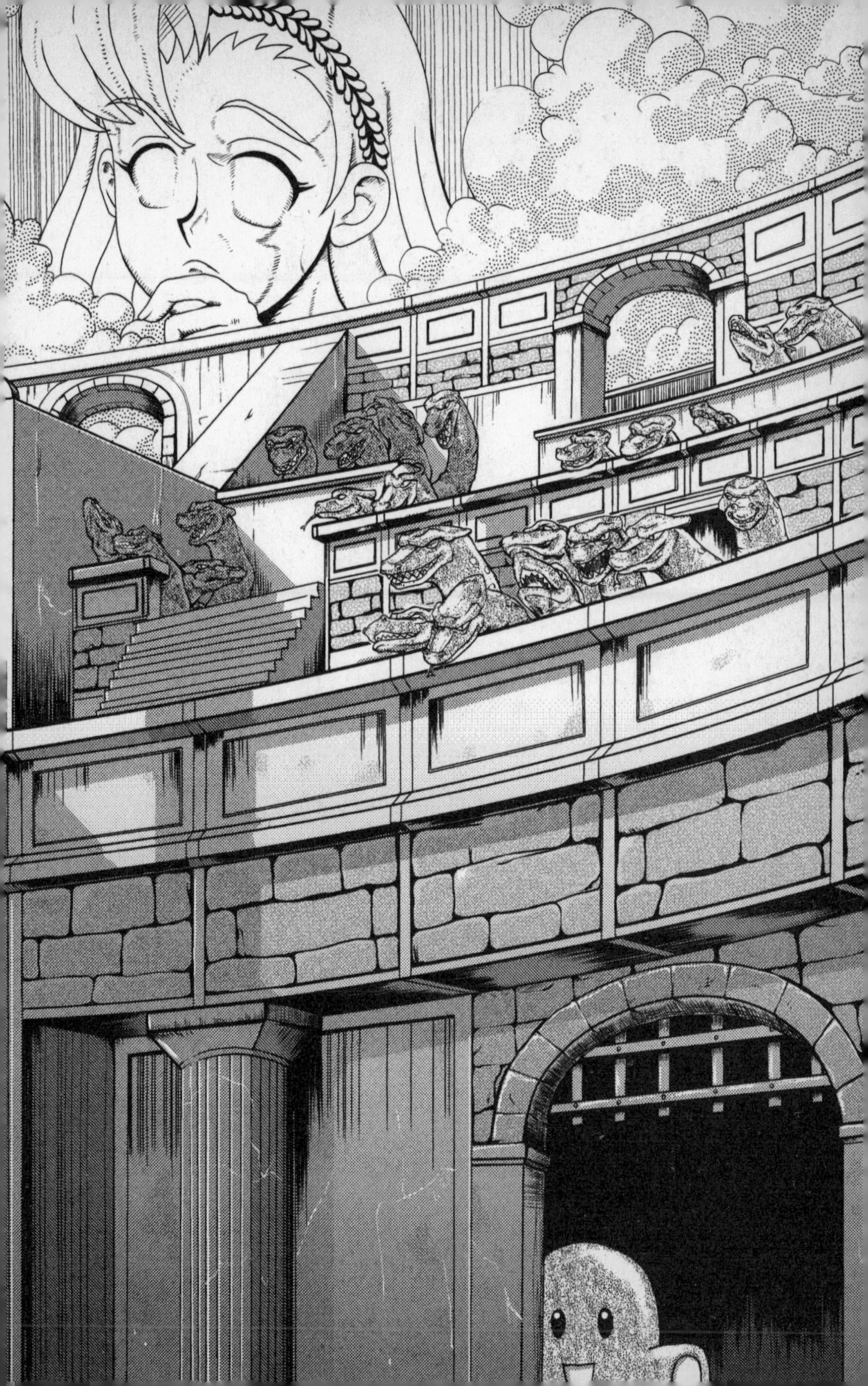

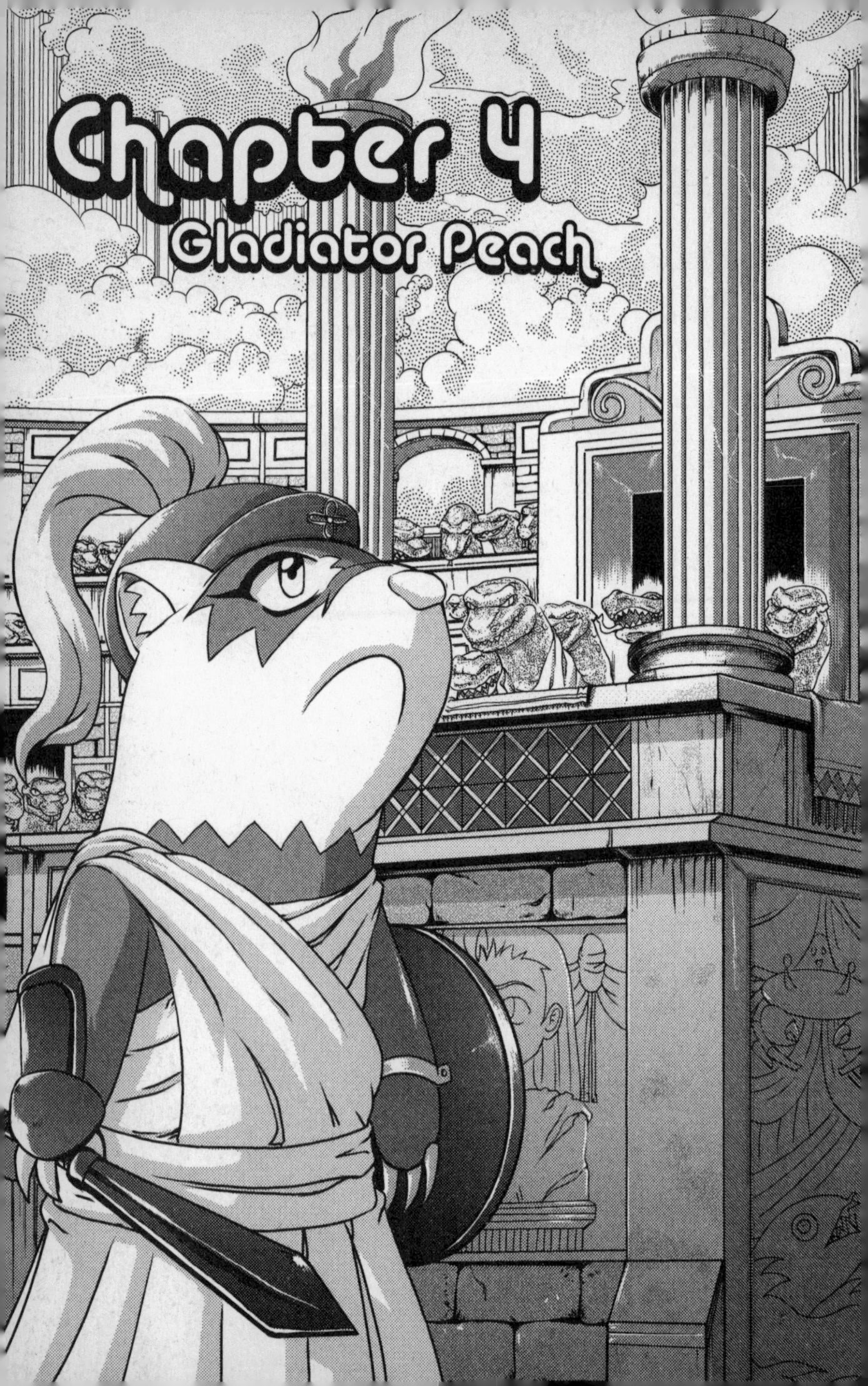
Chapter 4
Gladiator Peach

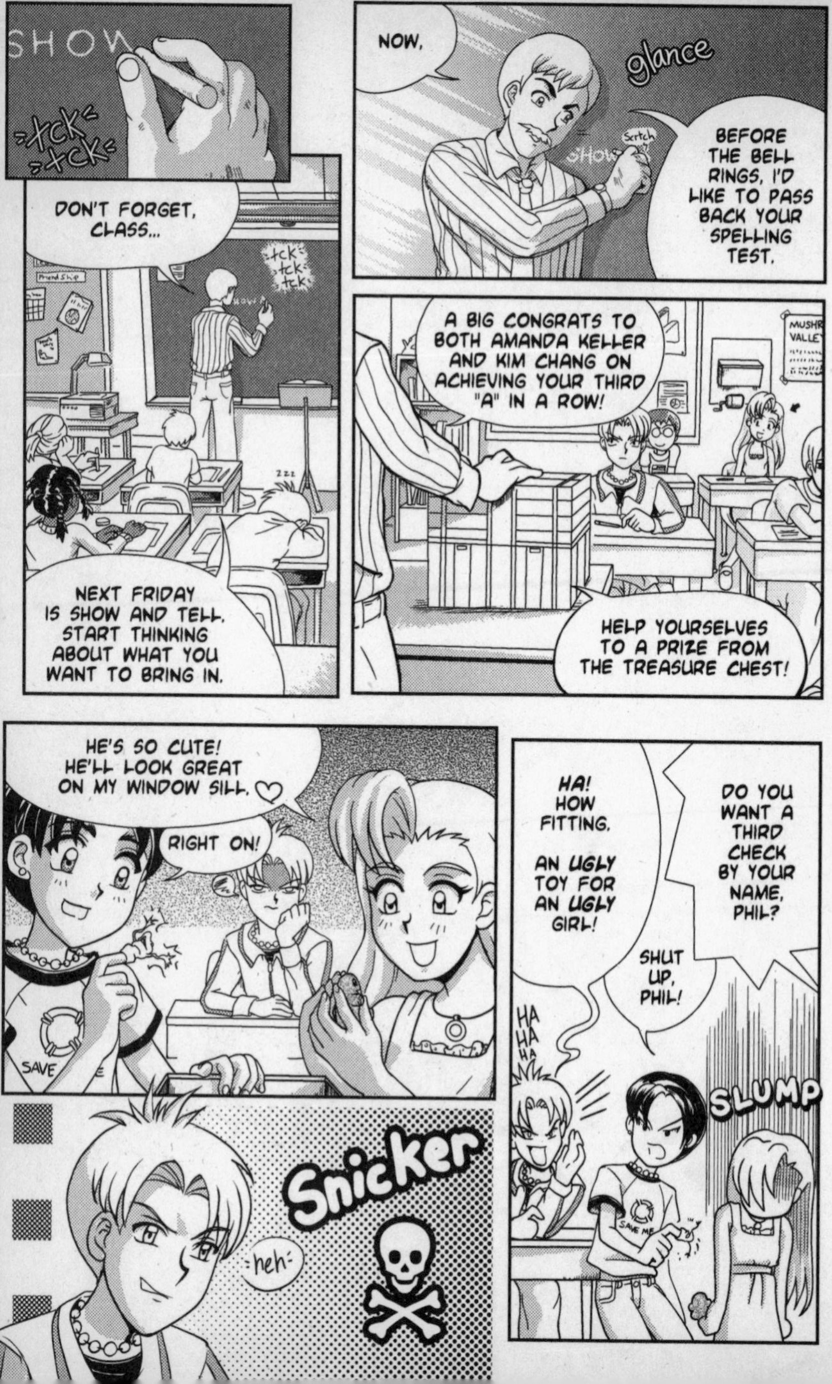
SHOW
tck tck
DON'T FORGET, CLASS...
tck tck tck
zzz
NEXT FRIDAY IS SHOW AND TELL. START THINKING ABOUT WHAT YOU WANT TO BRING IN.
NOW,
glance
Scrtch
SHOW
BEFORE THE BELL RINGS, I'D LIKE TO PASS BACK YOUR SPELLING TEST.
A BIG CONGRATS TO BOTH AMANDA KELLER AND KIM CHANG ON ACHIEVING YOUR THIRD "A" IN A ROW!
HELP YOURSELVES TO A PRIZE FROM THE TREASURE CHEST!
HE'S SO CUTE! HE'LL LOOK GREAT ON MY WINDOW SILL.
RIGHT ON!
SAVE
Snicker
heh
HA! HOW FITTING.
AN UGLY TOY FOR AN UGLY GIRL!
HA HA HA
SHUT UP, PHIL!
DO YOU WANT A THIRD CHECK BY YOUR NAME, PHIL?
SLUMP
SAVE ME

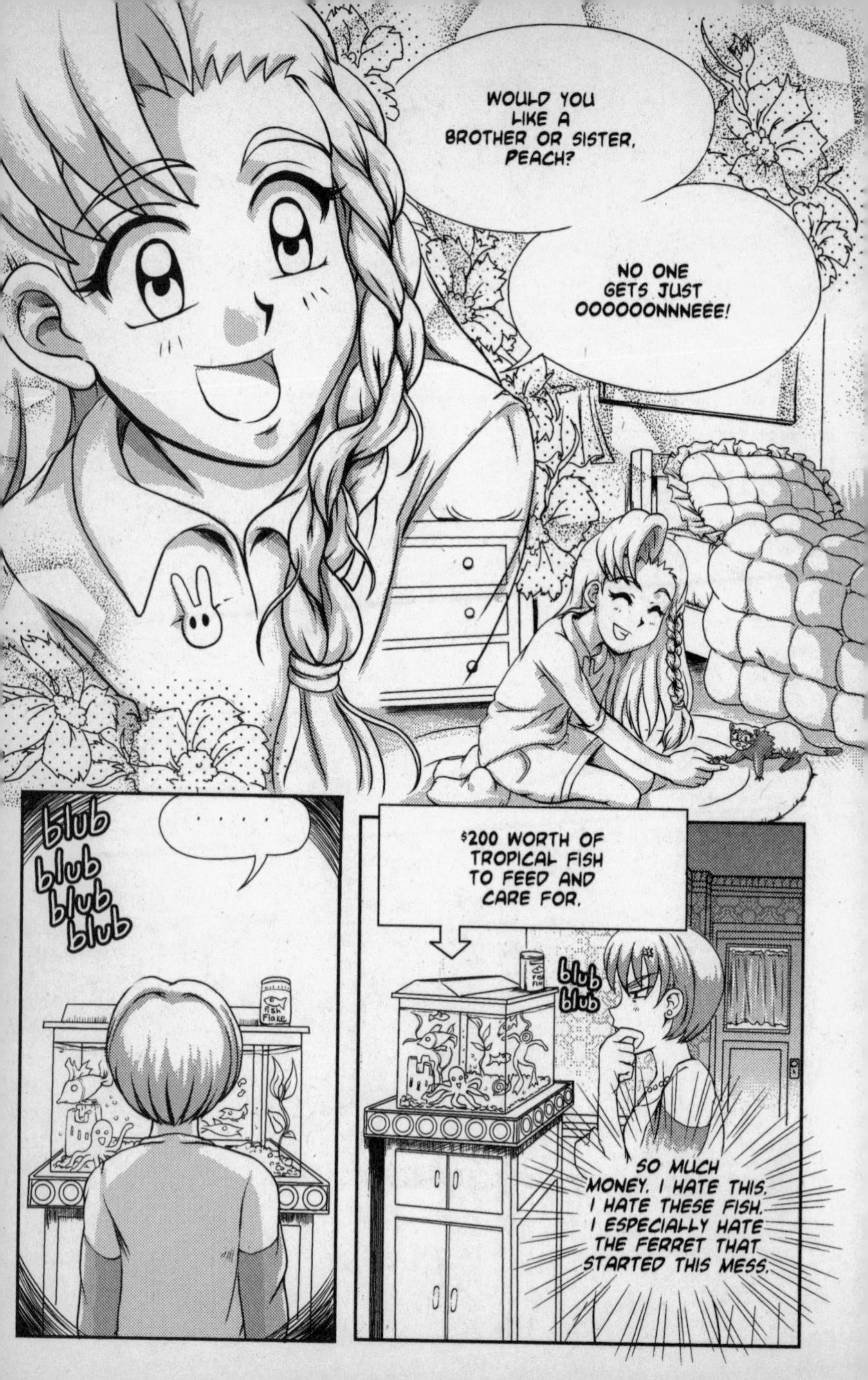
WOULD YOU LIKE A BROTHER OR SISTER, PEACH?
NO ONE GETS JUST OOOOOONNNEEE!
blub blub blub blub
. . . .
Fish Flake
$200 WORTH OF TROPICAL FISH TO FEED AND CARE FOR.
blub blub
SO MUCH MONEY. I HATE THIS. I HATE THESE FISH. I ESPECIALLY HATE THE FERRET THAT STARTED THIS MESS.

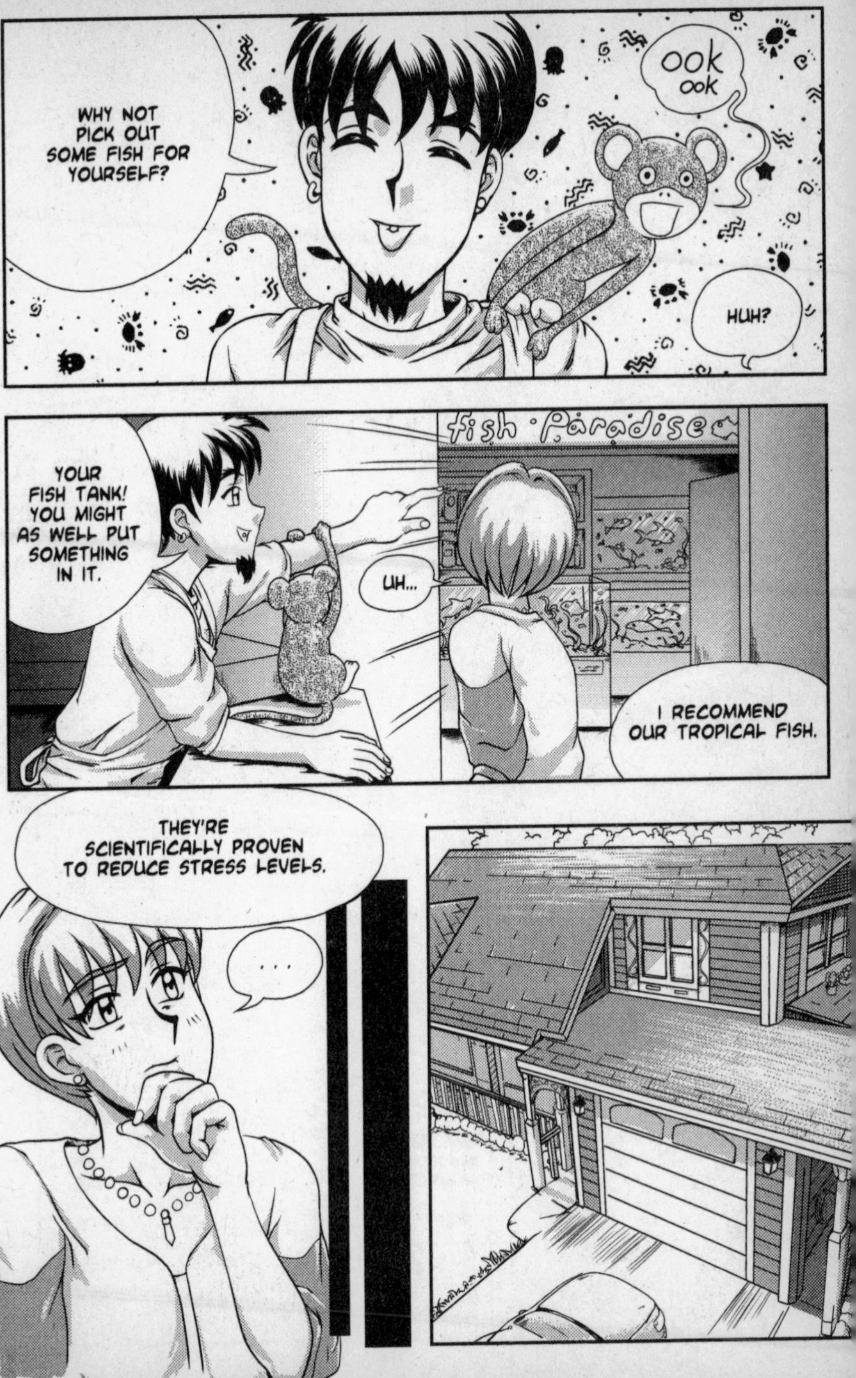
WHY NOT PICK OUT SOME FISH FOR YOURSELF?
ook ook
HUH?
YOUR FISH TANK! YOU MIGHT AS WELL PUT SOMETHING IN IT.
fish ·Paradise
UH...
I RECOMMEND OUR TROPICAL FISH.
THEY'RE SCIENTIFICALLY PROVEN TO REDUCE STRESS LEVELS.
. . .

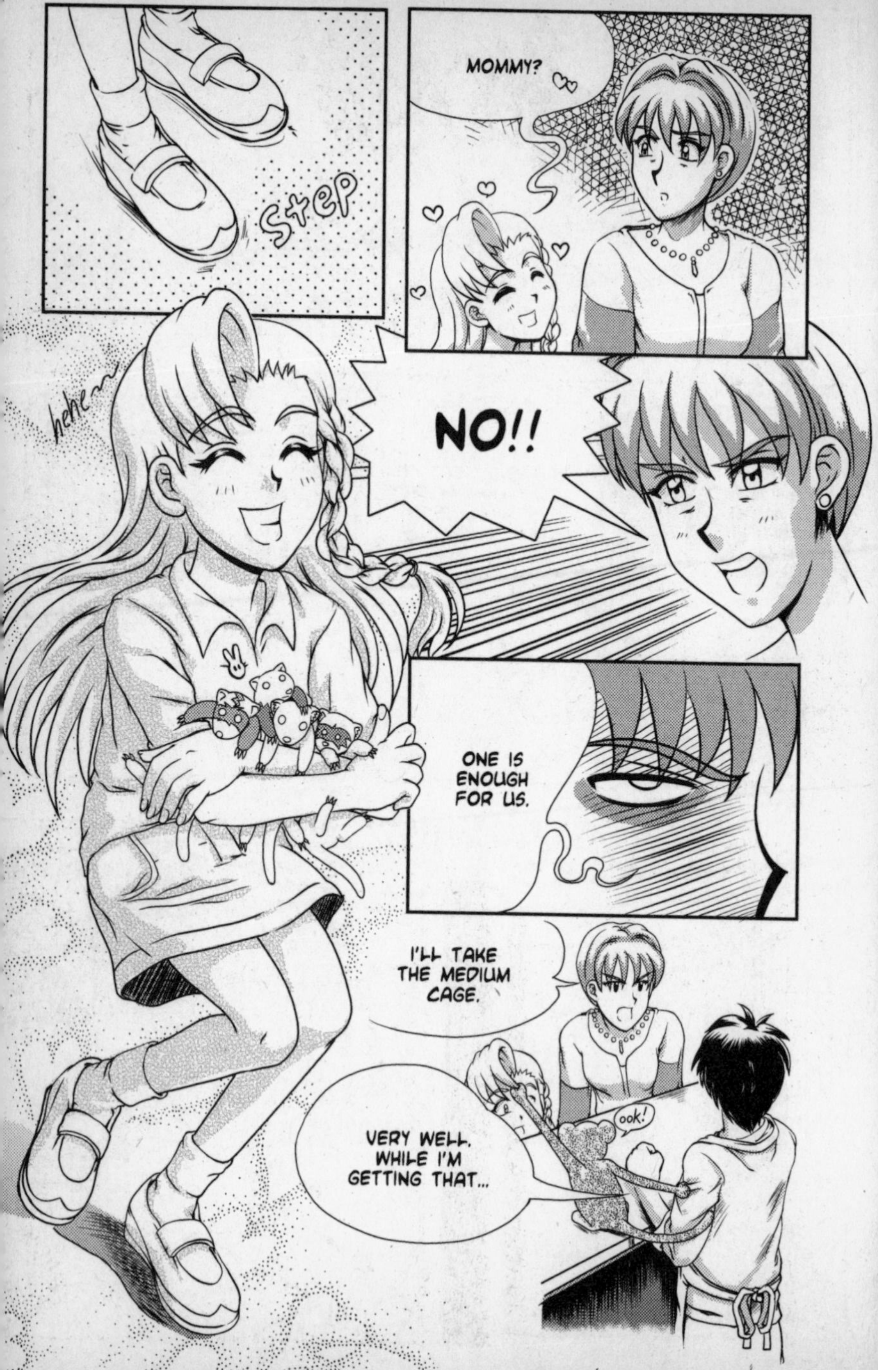
step
MOMMY?
hehe~
NO!!
ONE IS ENOUGH FOR US.
I'LL TAKE THE MEDIUM CAGE.
ook!
VERY WELL. WHILE I'M GETTING THAT...

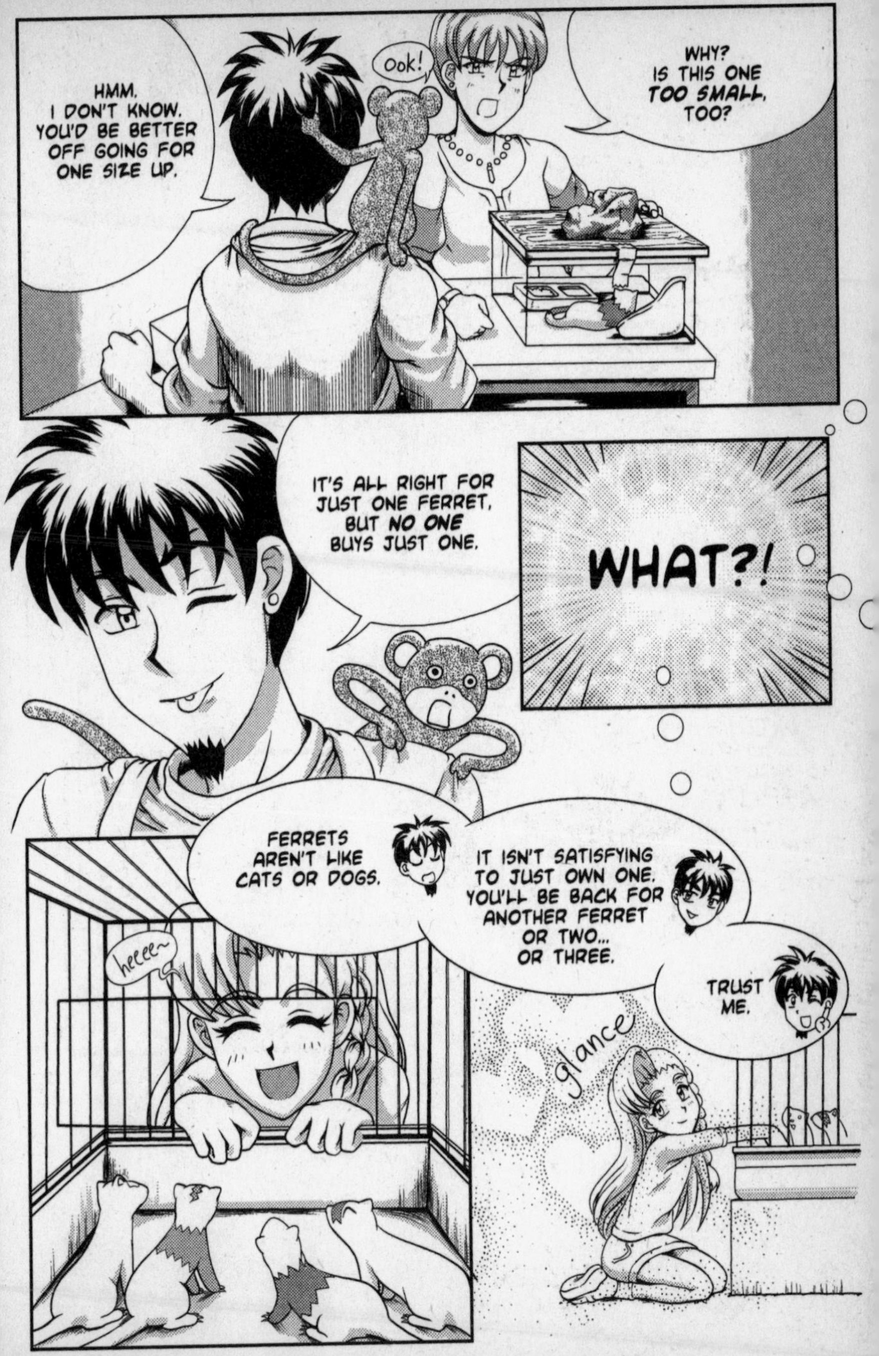
HMM. I DON'T KNOW. YOU'D BE BETTER OFF GOING FOR ONE SIZE UP.
Ook!
WHY? IS THIS ONE TOO SMALL, TOO?
IT'S ALL RIGHT FOR JUST ONE FERRET, BUT NO ONE BUYS JUST ONE.
WHAT?!
FERRETS AREN'T LIKE CATS OR DOGS.
IT ISN'T SATISFYING TO JUST OWN ONE. YOU'LL BE BACK FOR ANOTHER FERRET OR TWO... OR THREE.
TRUST ME.
heeee~
glance

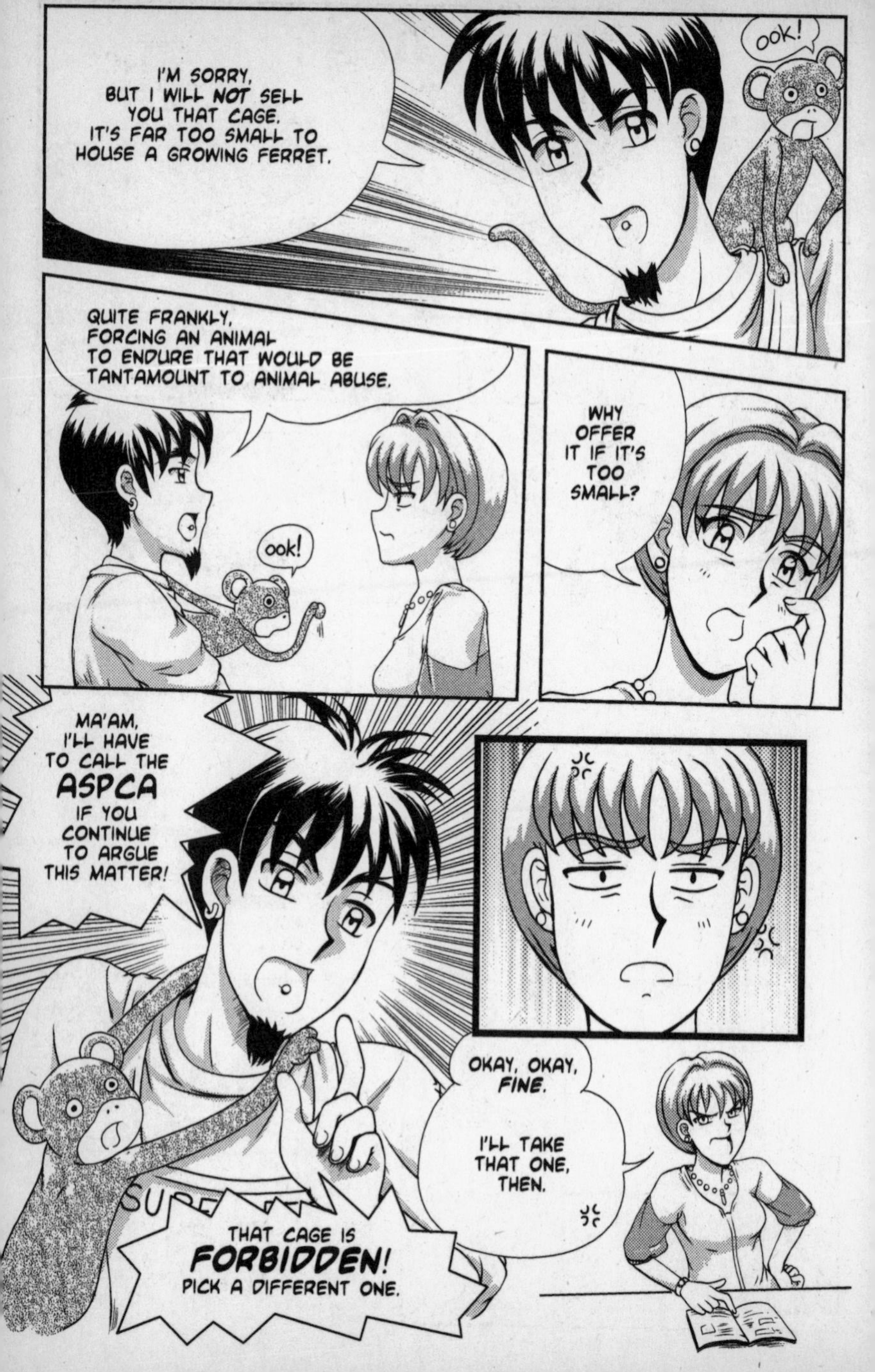
I'M SORRY, BUT I WILL NOT SELL YOU THAT CAGE. IT'S FAR TOO SMALL TO HOUSE A GROWING FERRET.
OOK!
QUITE FRANKLY, FORCING AN ANIMAL TO ENDURE THAT WOULD BE TANTAMOUNT TO ANIMAL ABUSE.
OOK!
WHY OFFER IT IF IT'S TOO SMALL?
MA'AM, I'LL HAVE TO CALL THE ASPCA IF YOU CONTINUE TO ARGUE THIS MATTER!
THAT CAGE IS FORBIDDEN! PICK A DIFFERENT ONE.
OKAY, OKAY, FINE.
I'LL TAKE THAT ONE, THEN.

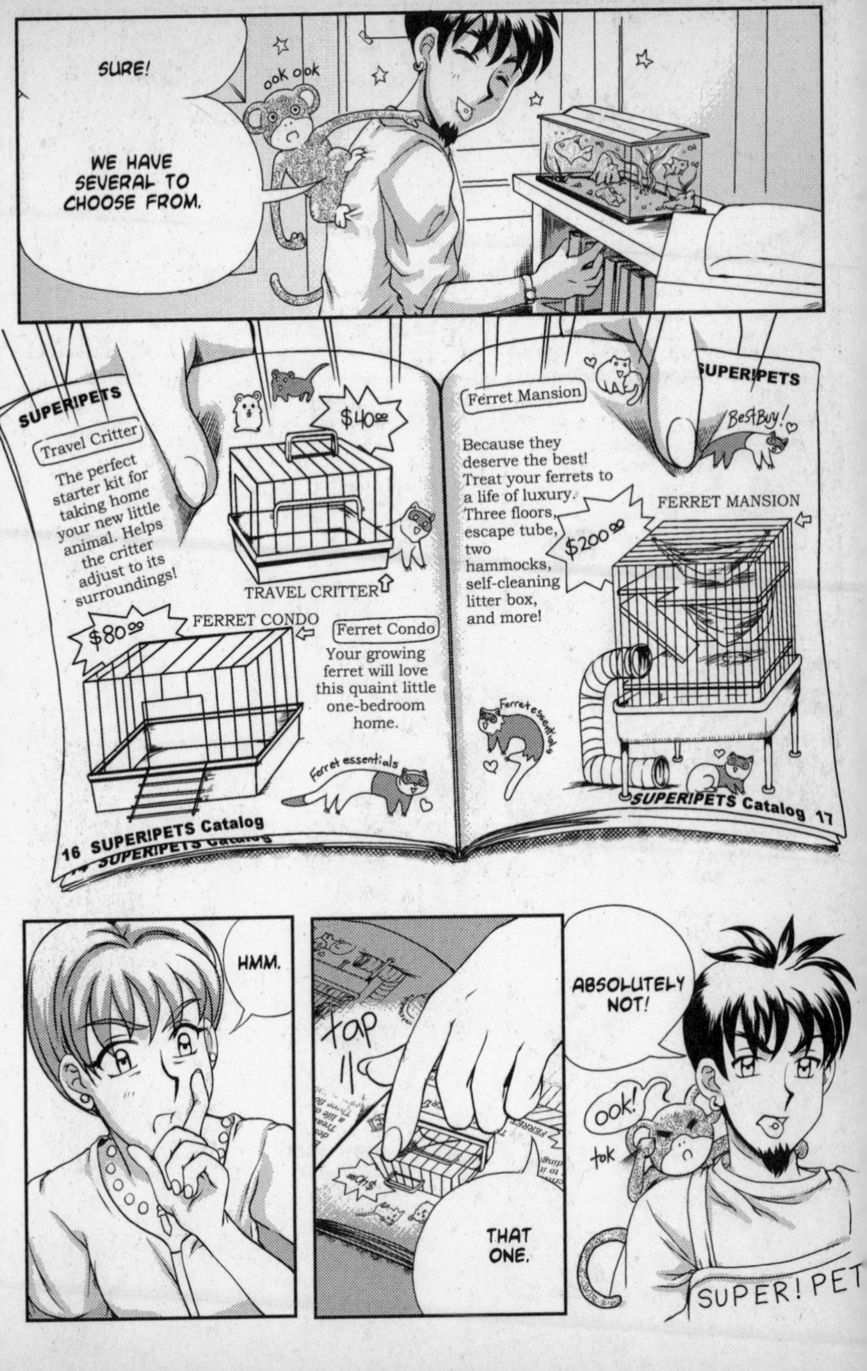
SURE!
ook ook
WE HAVE SEVERAL TO CHOOSE FROM.
SUPER!PETS
Travel Critter
The perfect starter kit for taking home your new little animal. Helps the critter adjust to its surroundings!
$40.00
TRAVEL CRITTER
$80.00
FERRET CONDO
Ferret Condo
Your growing ferret will love this quaint little one-bedroom home.
Ferret essentials
16 SUPER!PETS Catalog
Ferret Mansion
Because they deserve the best! Treat your ferrets to a life of luxury. Three floors, escape tube, two hammocks, self-cleaning litter box, and more!
SUPER!PETS
Best Buy!
FERRET MANSION
$200.00
Ferret essentials
SUPER!PETS Catalog 17
HMM.
tap
THAT ONE.
ABSOLUTELY NOT!
ook!
tok
SUPER! PET

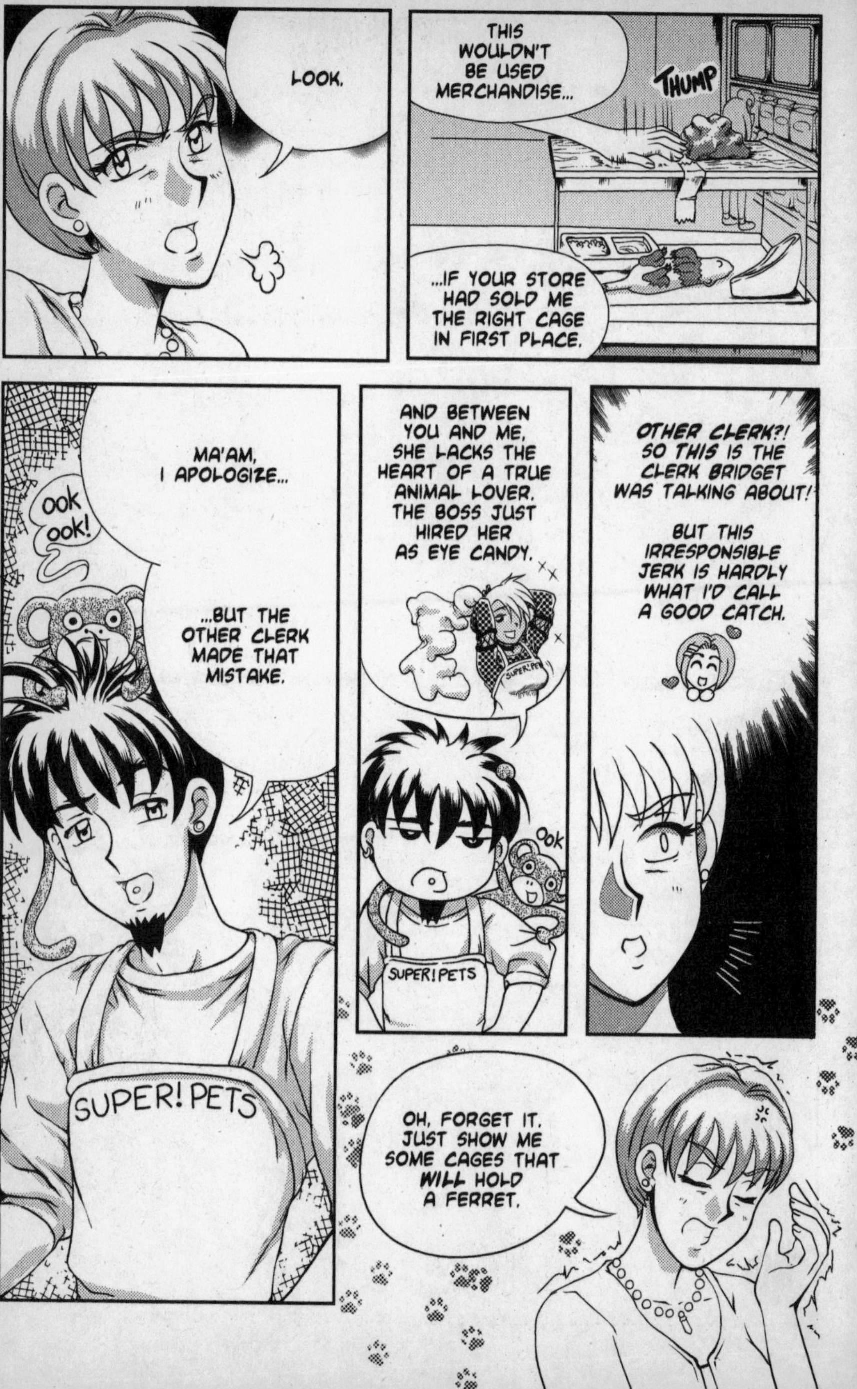
LOOK.
THIS WOULDN'T BE USED MERCHANDISE...
THUMP
...IF YOUR STORE HAD SOLD ME THE RIGHT CAGE IN FIRST PLACE.
MA'AM, I APOLOGIZE...
OOK OOK!
...BUT THE OTHER CLERK MADE THAT MISTAKE.
SUPER! PETS
AND BETWEEN YOU AND ME, SHE LACKS THE HEART OF A TRUE ANIMAL LOVER. THE BOSS JUST HIRED HER AS EYE CANDY.
SUPER! PETS
OOK
SUPER! PETS
OTHER CLERK?! SO THIS IS THE CLERK BRIDGET WAS TALKING ABOUT!
BUT THIS IRRESPONSIBLE JERK IS HARDLY WHAT I'D CALL A GOOD CATCH.
OH, FORGET IT. JUST SHOW ME SOME CAGES THAT WILL HOLD A FERRET.

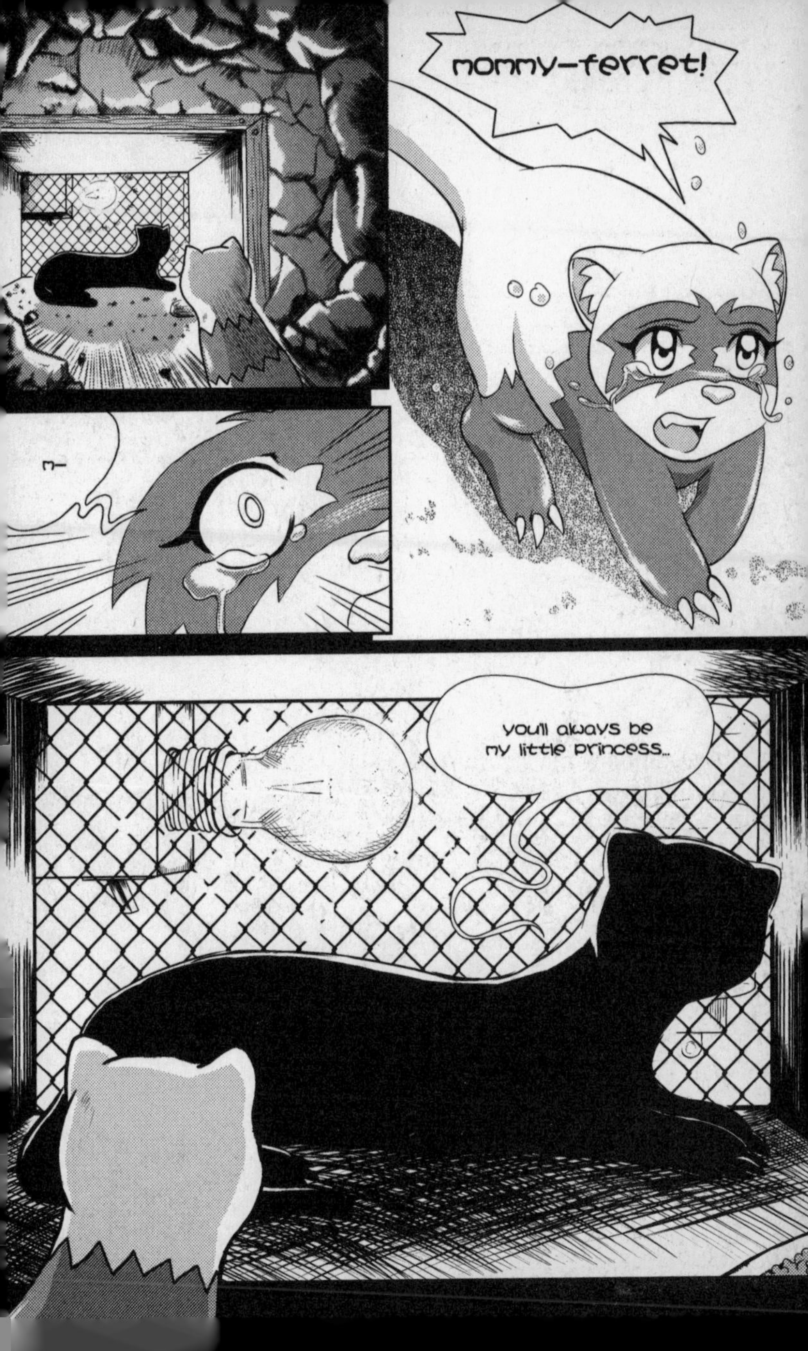
mommy-ferret!
you'll always be my little princess...

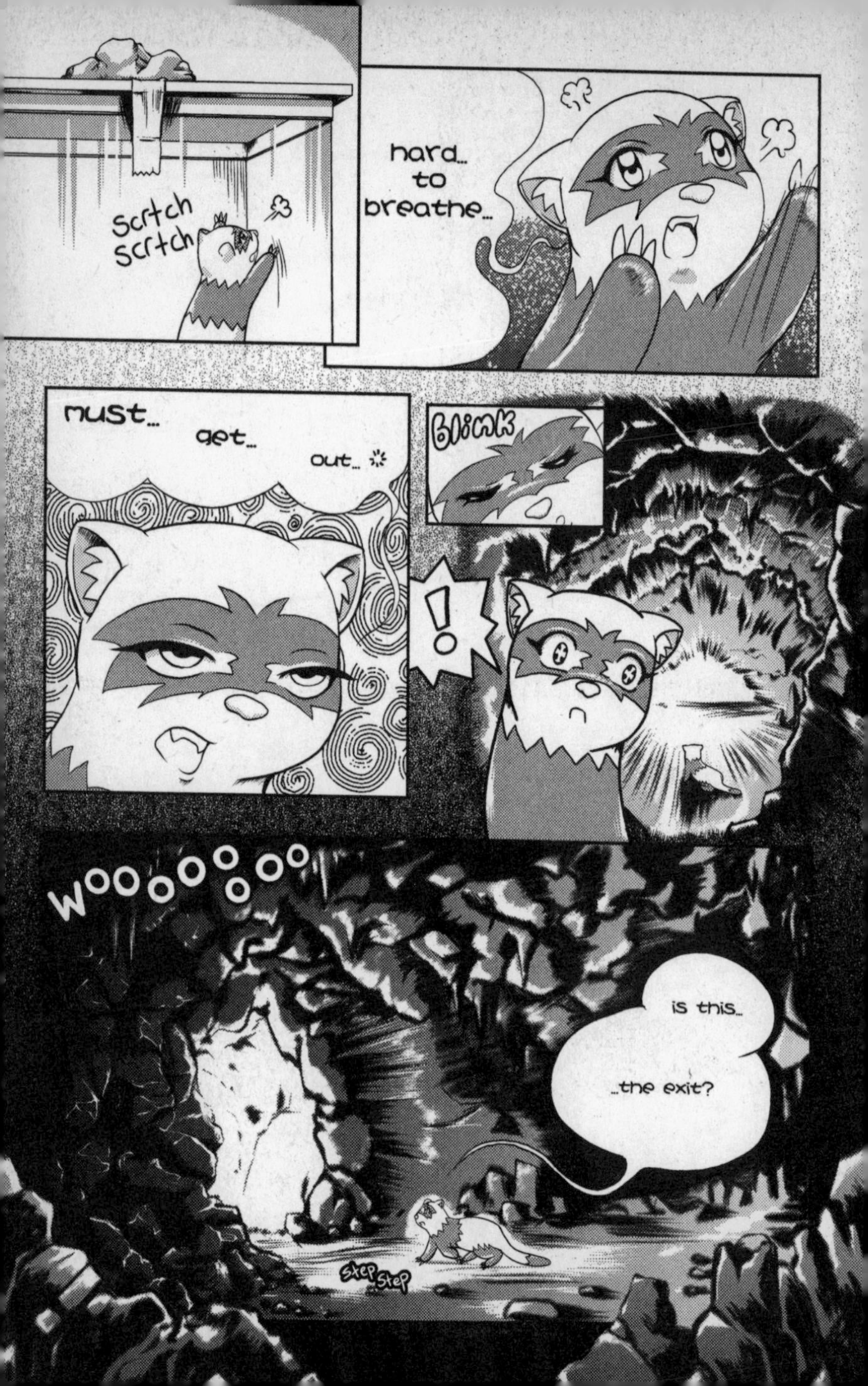
scrtch scrtch
hard... to breathe...
must... get... out...
BLINK
!
WOOOOOOOO
is this...
...the exit?
step step

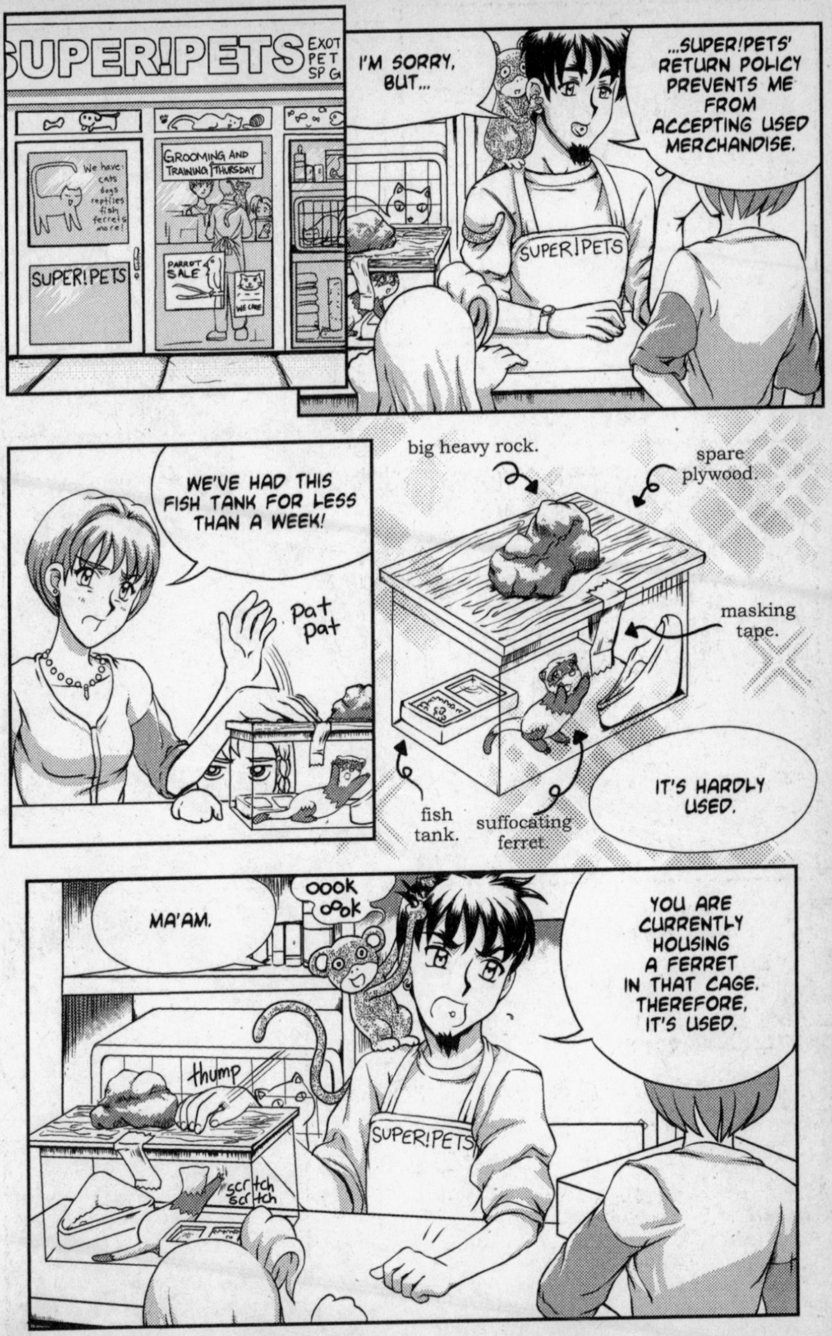
SUPER!PETS EXOT PET SP G
We have: cats dogs reptiles fish ferrets more!
SUPER!PETS
GROOMING AND TRAINING THURSDAY
PARROT SALE
WE CARE
I'M SORRY, BUT...
...SUPER!PETS' RETURN POLICY PREVENTS ME FROM ACCEPTING USED MERCHANDISE.
SUPER!PETS
WE'VE HAD THIS FISH TANK FOR LESS THAN A WEEK!
Pat pat
big heavy rock.
spare plywood.
masking tape.
fish tank.
suffocating ferret.
IT'S HARDLY USED.
MA'AM.
oook oook
YOU ARE CURRENTLY HOUSING A FERRET IN THAT CAGE. THEREFORE, IT'S USED.
thump
SUPER!PETS
scrtch scrtch

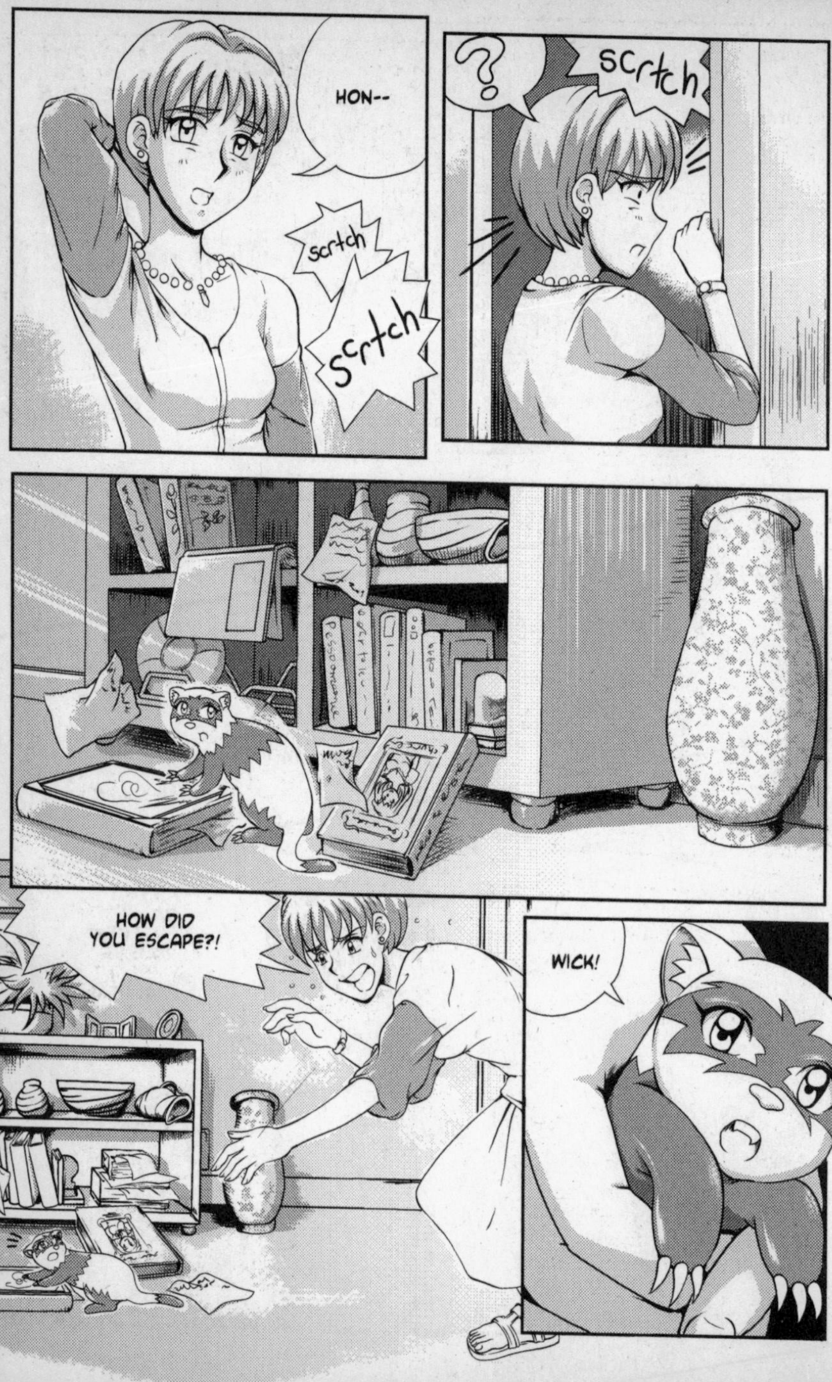
HON--
scrtch
scrtch
?
scrtch
HOW DID YOU ESCAPE?!
WICK!

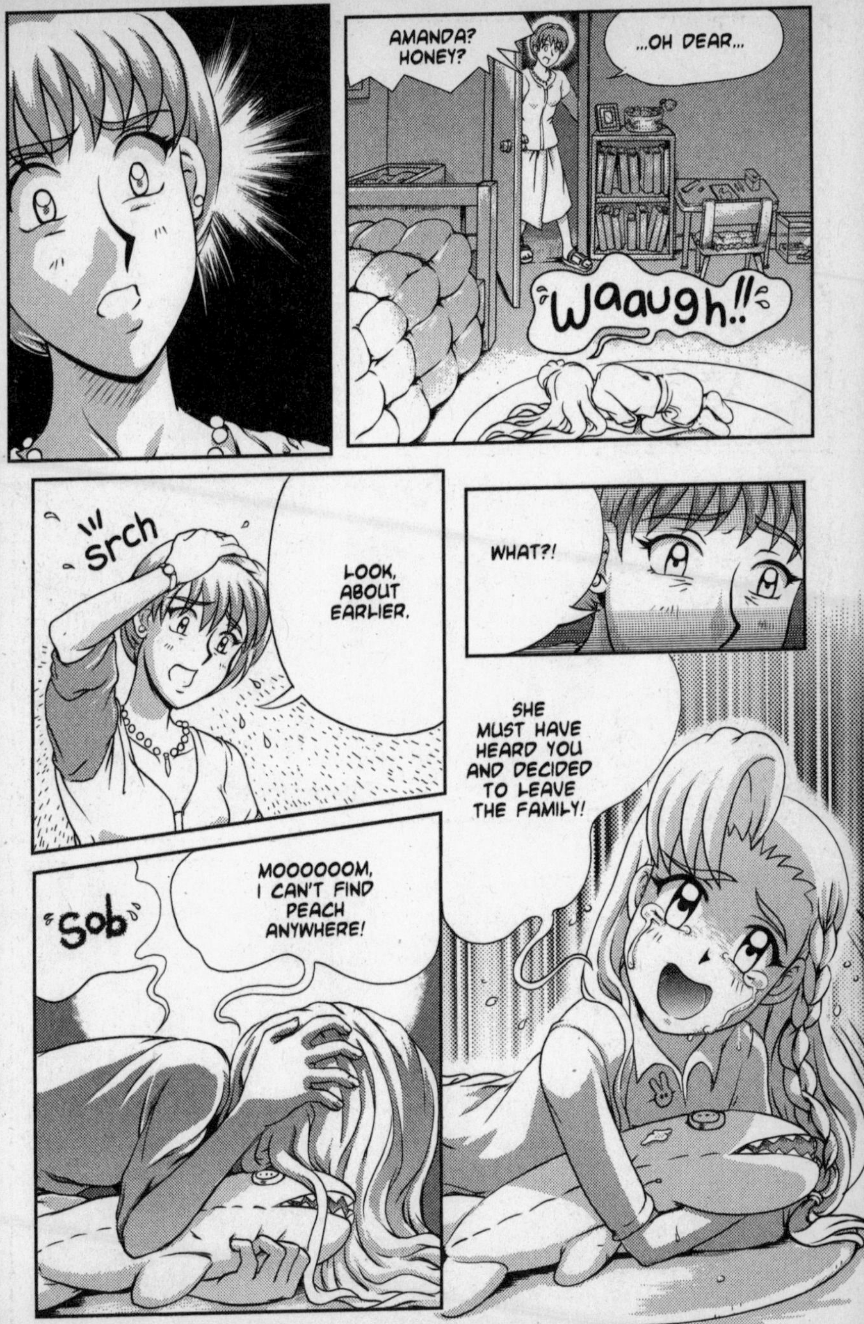
AMANDA? HONEY?
...OH DEAR...
Waaugh!!
WHAT?!
srch
LOOK, ABOUT EARLIER.
SHE MUST HAVE HEARD YOU AND DECIDED TO LEAVE THE FAMILY!
Sob
MOOOOOOM, I CAN'T FIND PEACH ANYWHERE!

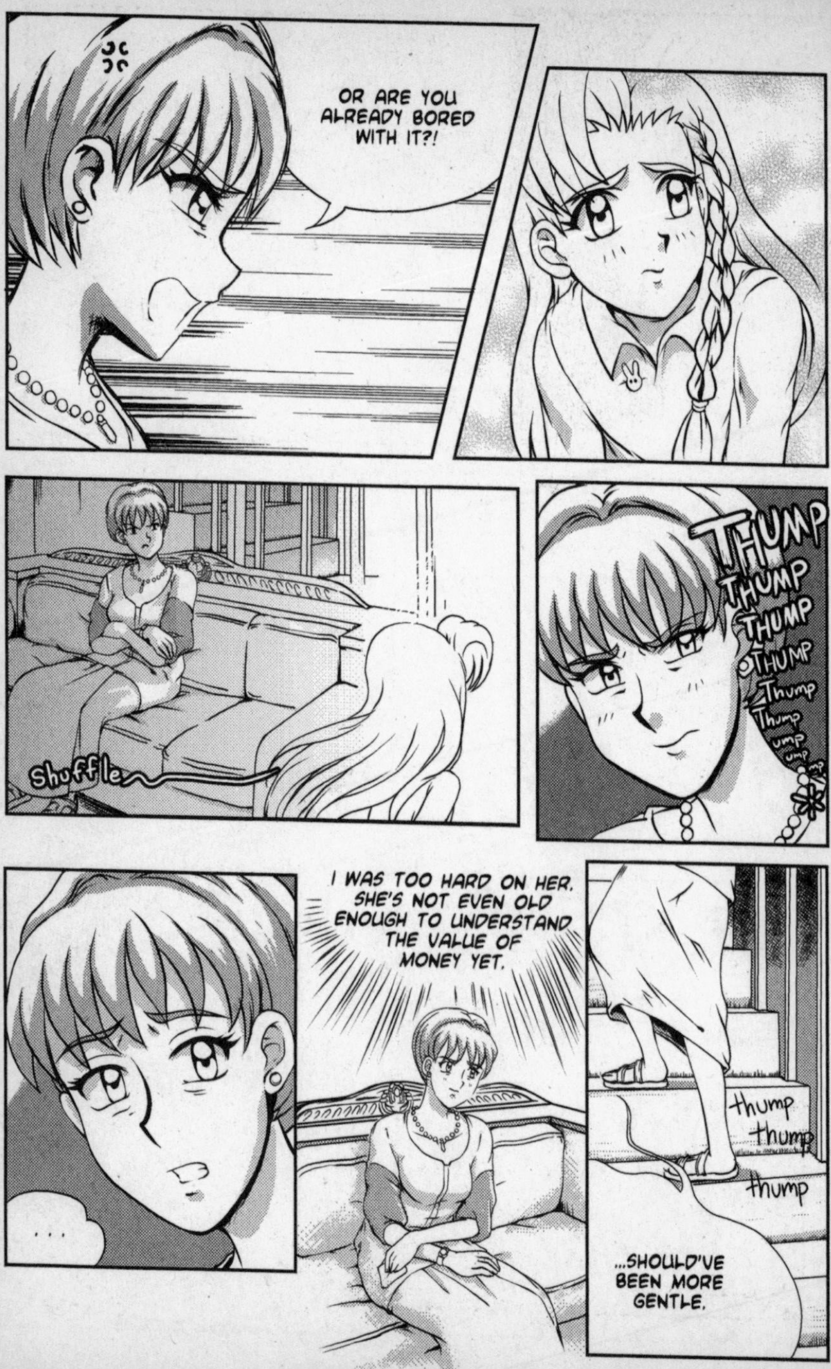
OR ARE YOU ALREADY BORED WITH IT?!
Shuffle~
THUMP THUMP THUMP THUMP Thump Thump ump ump
...
I WAS TOO HARD ON HER. SHE'S NOT EVEN OLD ENOUGH TO UNDERSTAND THE VALUE OF MONEY YET.
thump thump thump
...SHOULD'VE BEEN MORE GENTLE.

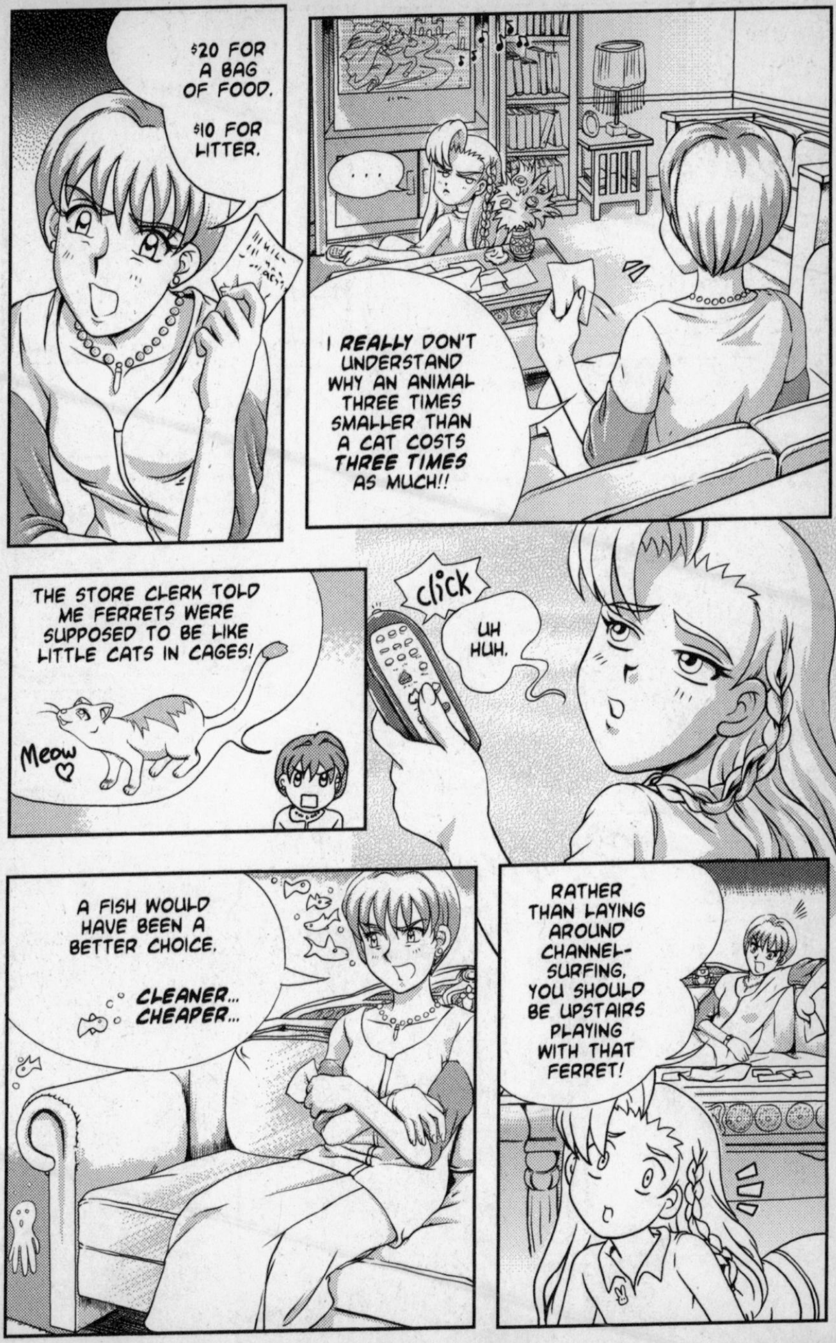
$20 FOR A BAG OF FOOD.
$10 FOR LITTER.
...
I *REALLY* DON'T UNDERSTAND WHY AN ANIMAL THREE TIMES SMALLER THAN A CAT COSTS *THREE TIMES* AS MUCH!!
THE STORE CLERK TOLD ME FERRETS WERE SUPPOSED TO BE LIKE LITTLE CATS IN CAGES!
Meow ♡
click
UH HUH.
A FISH WOULD HAVE BEEN A BETTER CHOICE.
CLEANER... CHEAPER...
RATHER THAN LAYING AROUND CHANNEL-SURFING, YOU SHOULD BE UPSTAIRS PLAYING WITH THAT FERRET!

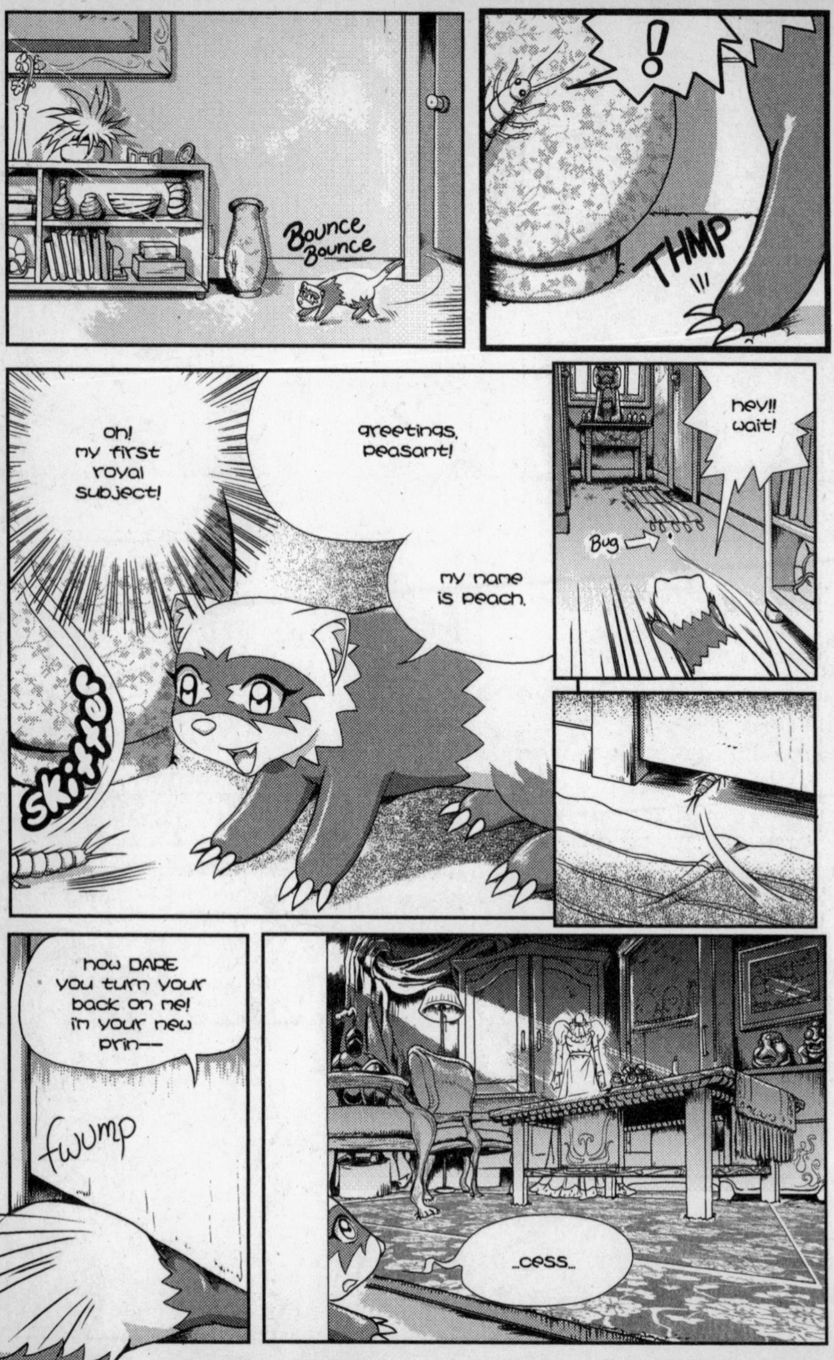

Bounce Bounce
!
THMP
skitter
oh! my first royal subject!
greetings, peasant!
my name is peach.
hey!! wait!
Bug
how DARE you turn your back on me! i'm your new prin--
fwump
...cess...

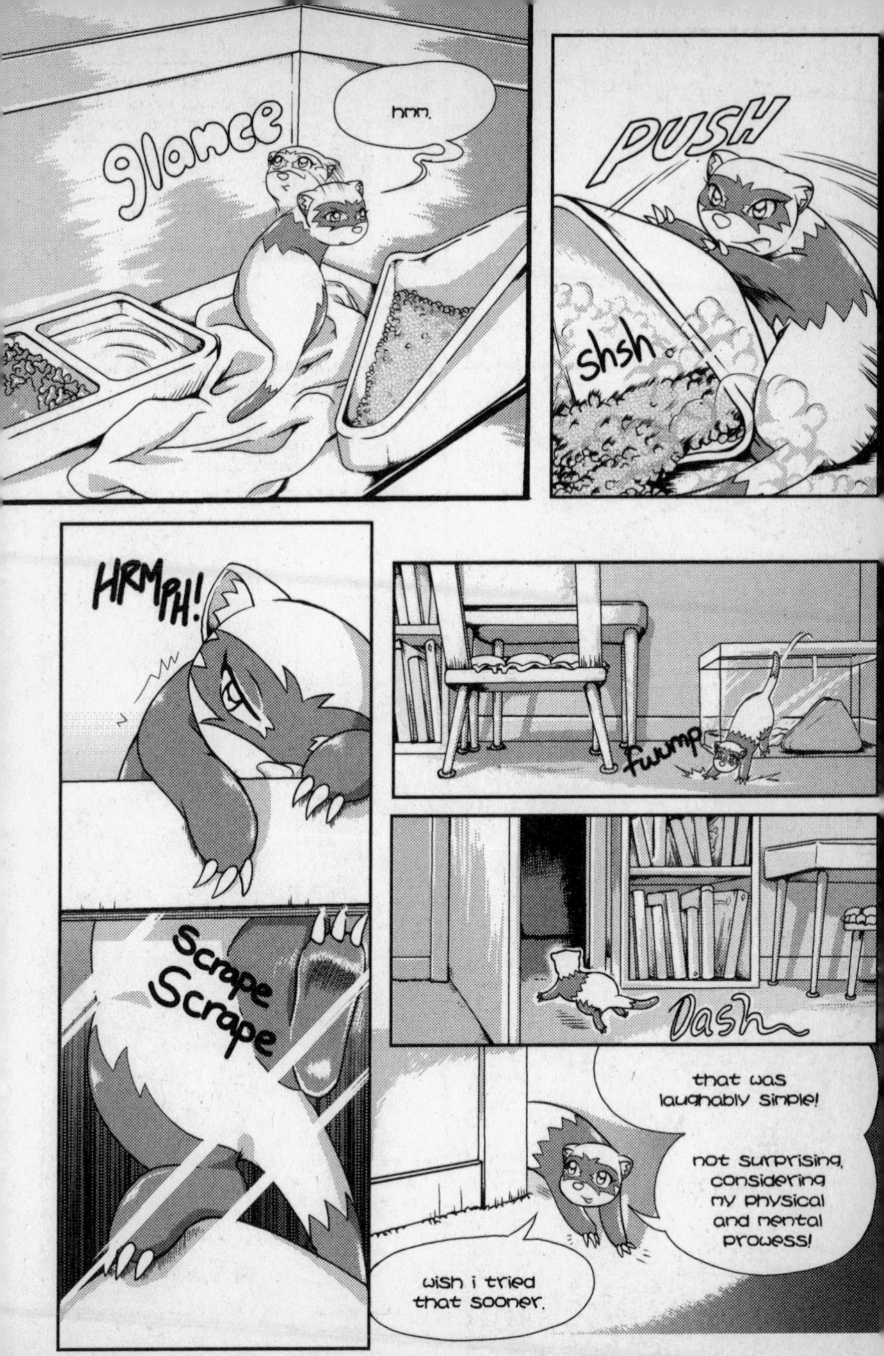
glance
hmm.
PUSH
shsh
HRMPH!
Scrape
Scrape
fwump
Dash
that was laughably simple!
not surprising, considering my physical and mental prowess!
wish i tried that sooner.

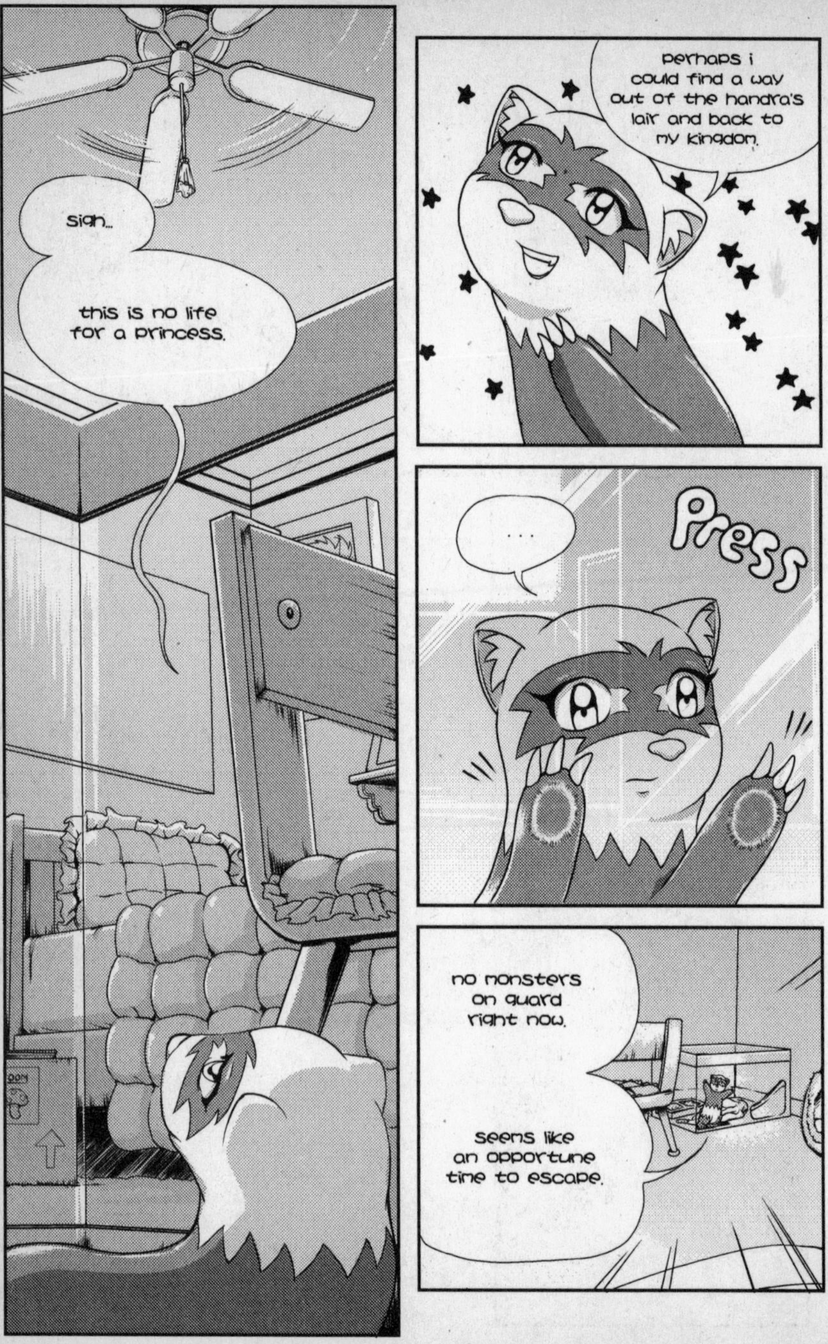
sigh...
this is no life for a princess.
perhaps i could find a way out of the handra's lair and back to my kingdom.
...
Press
no monsters on guard right now.
seems like an opportune time to escape.

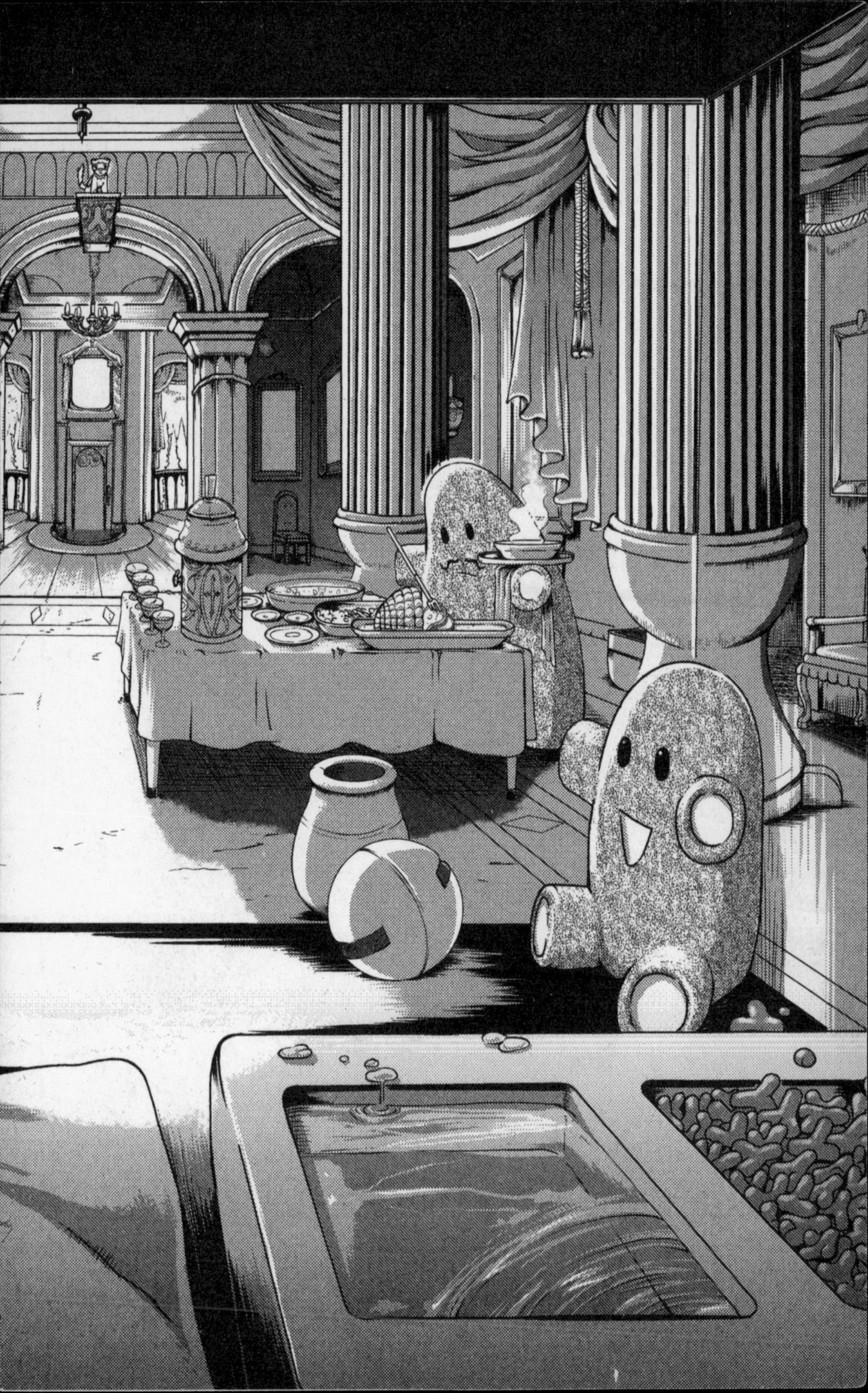

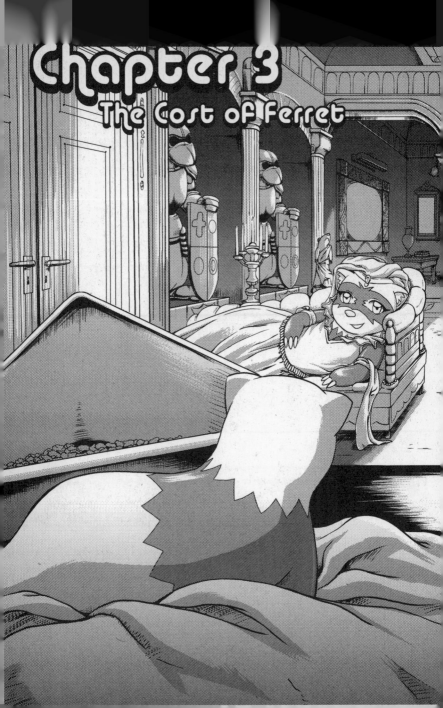

Chapter 3
The Cost of Ferret

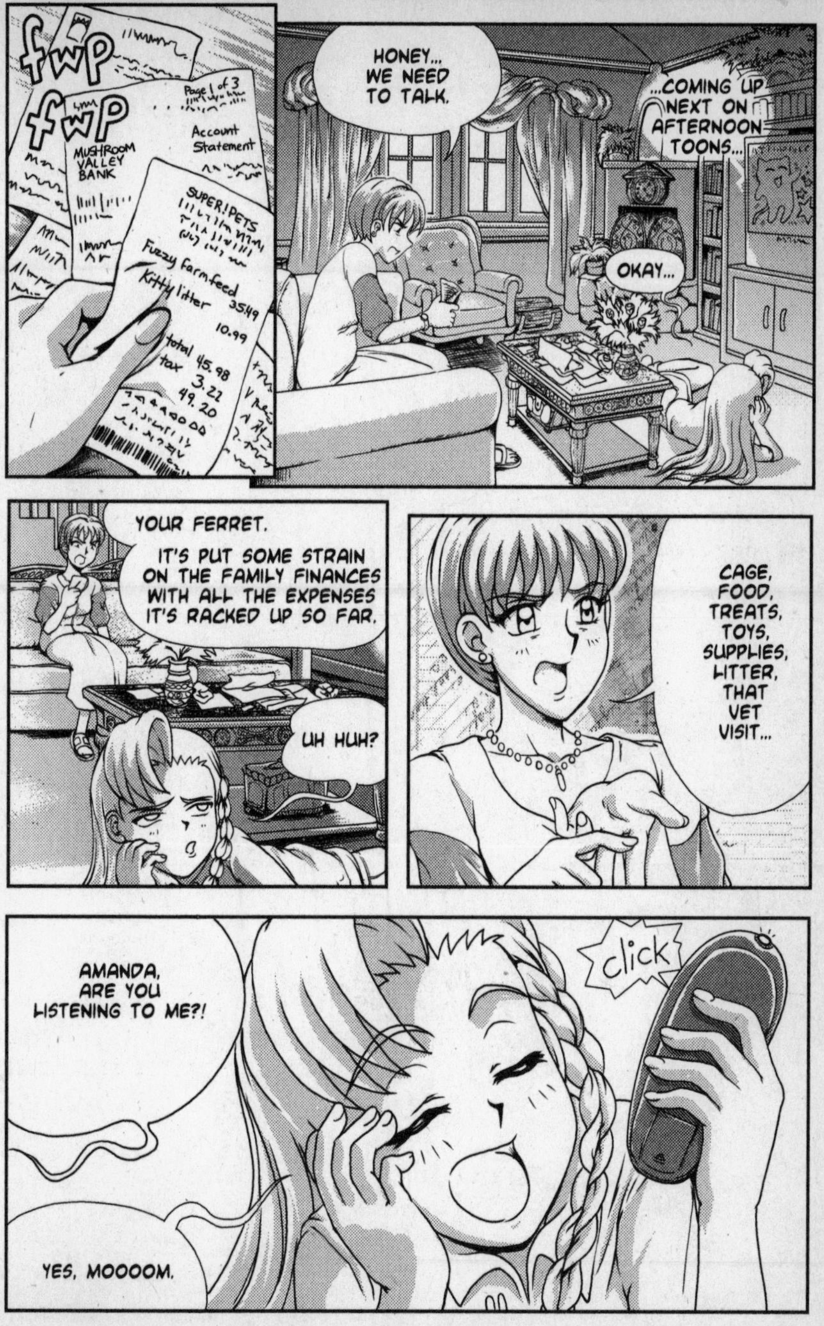
fwp
fwp
Page 1 of 3
Account Statement
MUSHROOM VALLEY BANK
SUPER!PETS
Fuzzy farm feed 35.49
Kitty litter 10.99
total 45.98
tax 3.22
49.20
HONEY... WE NEED TO TALK.
...COMING UP NEXT ON AFTERNOON TOONS...
OKAY...
YOUR FERRET.
IT'S PUT SOME STRAIN ON THE FAMILY FINANCES WITH ALL THE EXPENSES IT'S RACKED UP SO FAR.
UH HUH?
CAGE, FOOD, TREATS, TOYS, SUPPLIES, LITTER, THAT VET VISIT...
AMANDA, ARE YOU LISTENING TO ME?!
click
YES, MOOOM.

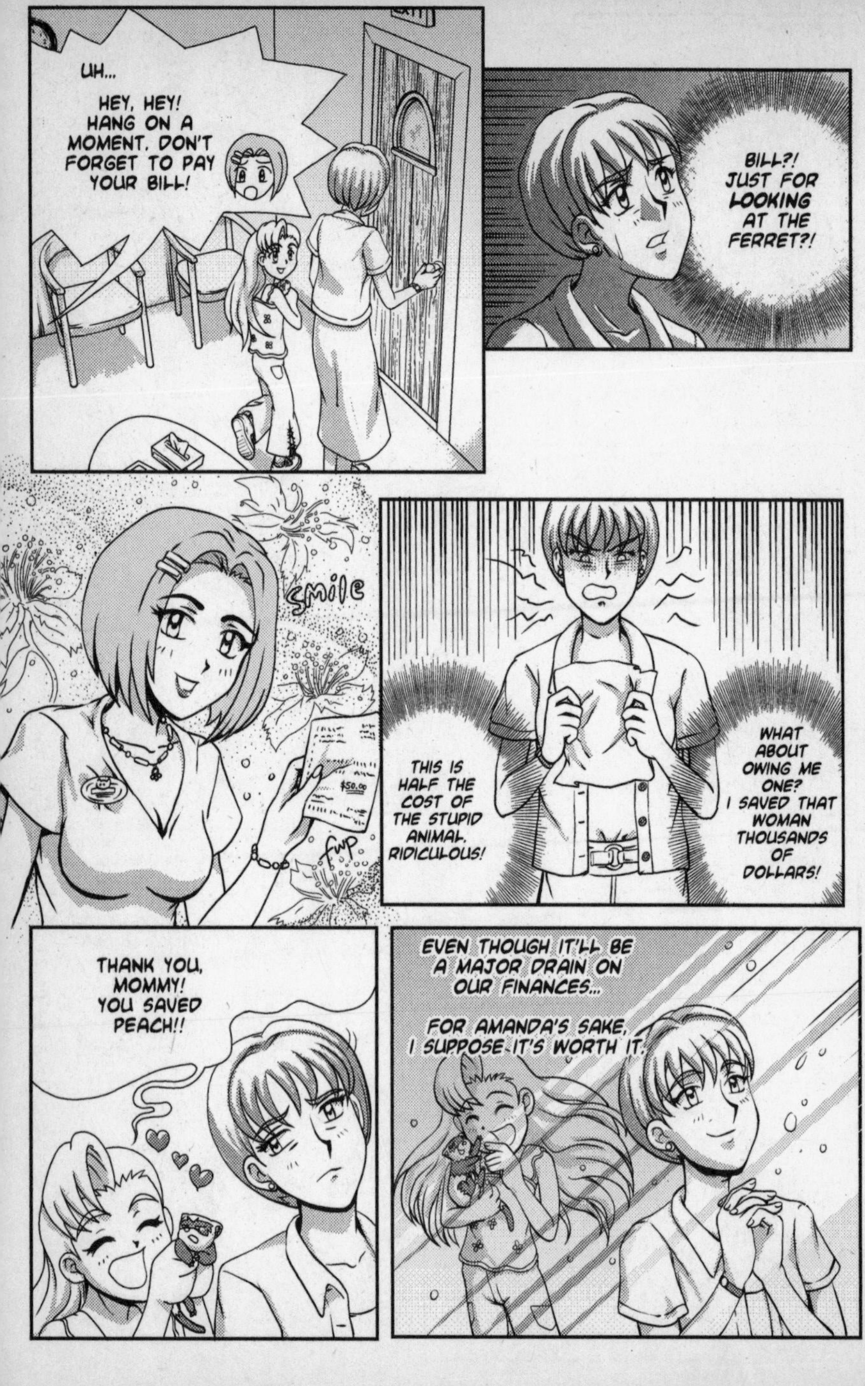
UH...
HEY, HEY! HANG ON A MOMENT. DON'T FORGET TO PAY YOUR BILL!
BILL?! JUST FOR LOOKING AT THE FERRET?!
smile
$50.00
fwp
THIS IS HALF THE COST OF THE STUPID ANIMAL. RIDICULOUS!
WHAT ABOUT OWING ME ONE? I SAVED THAT WOMAN THOUSANDS OF DOLLARS!
THANK YOU, MOMMY! YOU SAVED PEACH!!
EVEN THOUGH IT'LL BE A MAJOR DRAIN ON OUR FINANCES...
FOR AMANDA'S SAKE, I SUPPOSE IT'S WORTH IT.

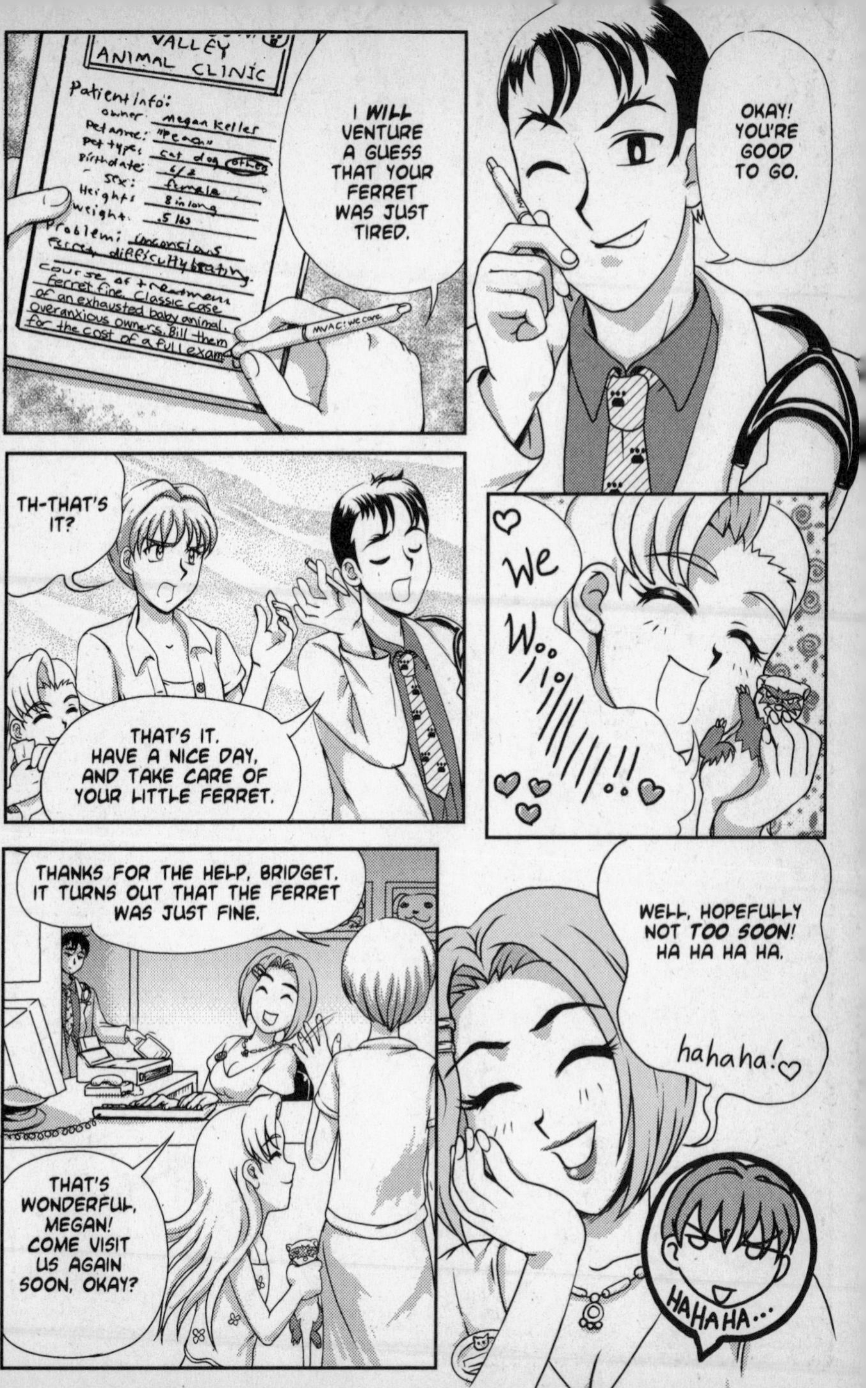
VALLEY ANIMAL CLINIC
Patient Info:
owner: Megan Keller
Pet name: "Peach"
pet type: cat dog other
Birthdate: 6/2
sex: female
Height: 8 in long
weight: .5 lbs
Problem: unconscious ferret, difficulty breathing
course of treatment: Ferret fine. Classic case of an exhausted baby animal. Overanxious owners. Bill them for the cost of a full exam
MVAC: we care
I WILL VENTURE A GUESS THAT YOUR FERRET WAS JUST TIRED.
OKAY! YOU'RE GOOD TO GO.
TH-THAT'S IT?
THAT'S IT. HAVE A NICE DAY, AND TAKE CARE OF YOUR LITTLE FERRET.
We Wooo!!
THANKS FOR THE HELP, BRIDGET. IT TURNS OUT THAT THE FERRET WAS JUST FINE.
THAT'S WONDERFUL, MEGAN! COME VISIT US AGAIN SOON, OKAY?
WELL, HOPEFULLY NOT TOO SOON! HA HA HA HA.
hahaha!
HAHAHA...

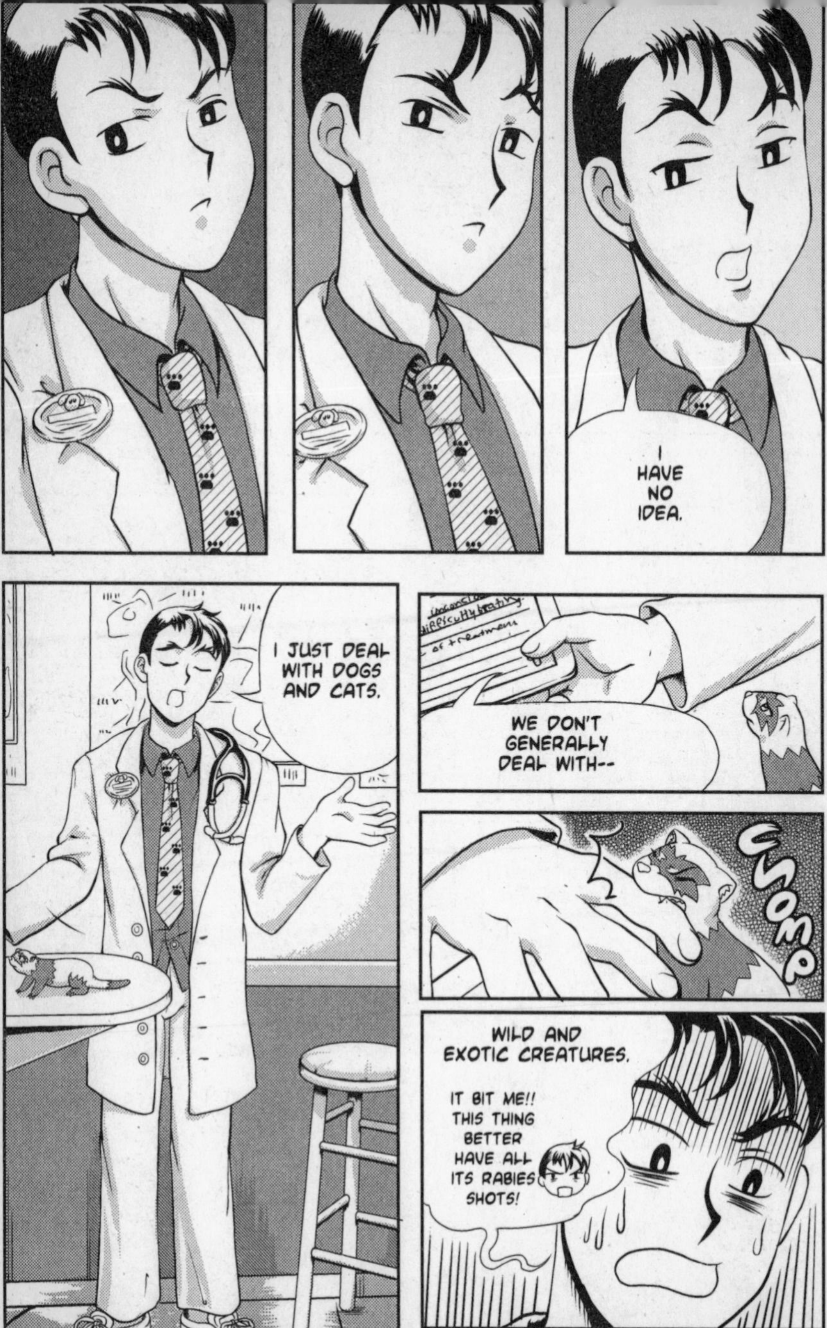
I HAVE NO IDEA.
I JUST DEAL WITH DOGS AND CATS.
WE DON'T GENERALLY DEAL WITH--
CHOMP
WILD AND EXOTIC CREATURES.
IT BIT ME!! THIS THING BETTER HAVE ALL ITS RABIES SHOTS!

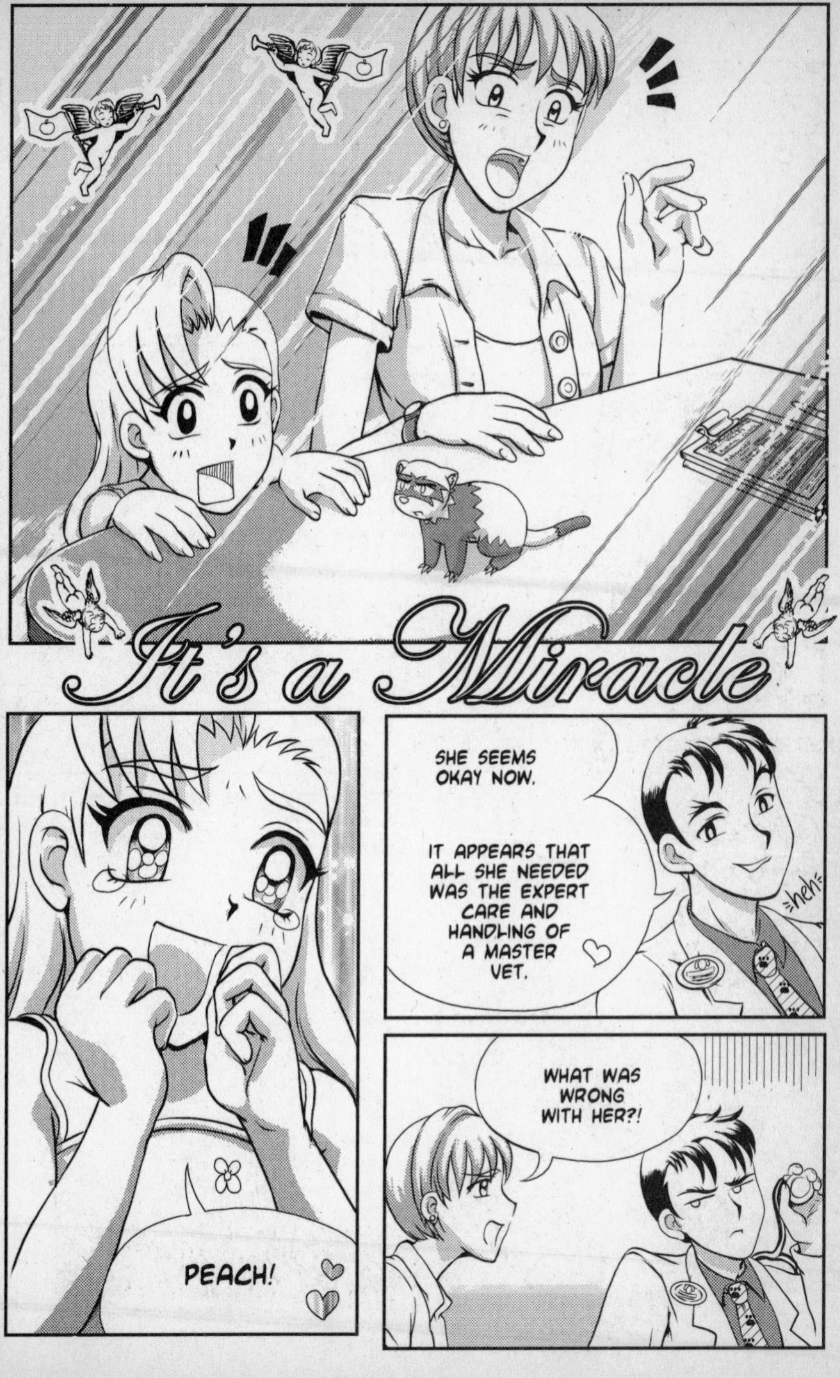
It's a Miracle
SHE SEEMS OKAY NOW.
IT APPEARS THAT ALL SHE NEEDED WAS THE EXPERT CARE AND HANDLING OF A MASTER VET.
heh
WHAT WAS WRONG WITH HER?!
PEACH!

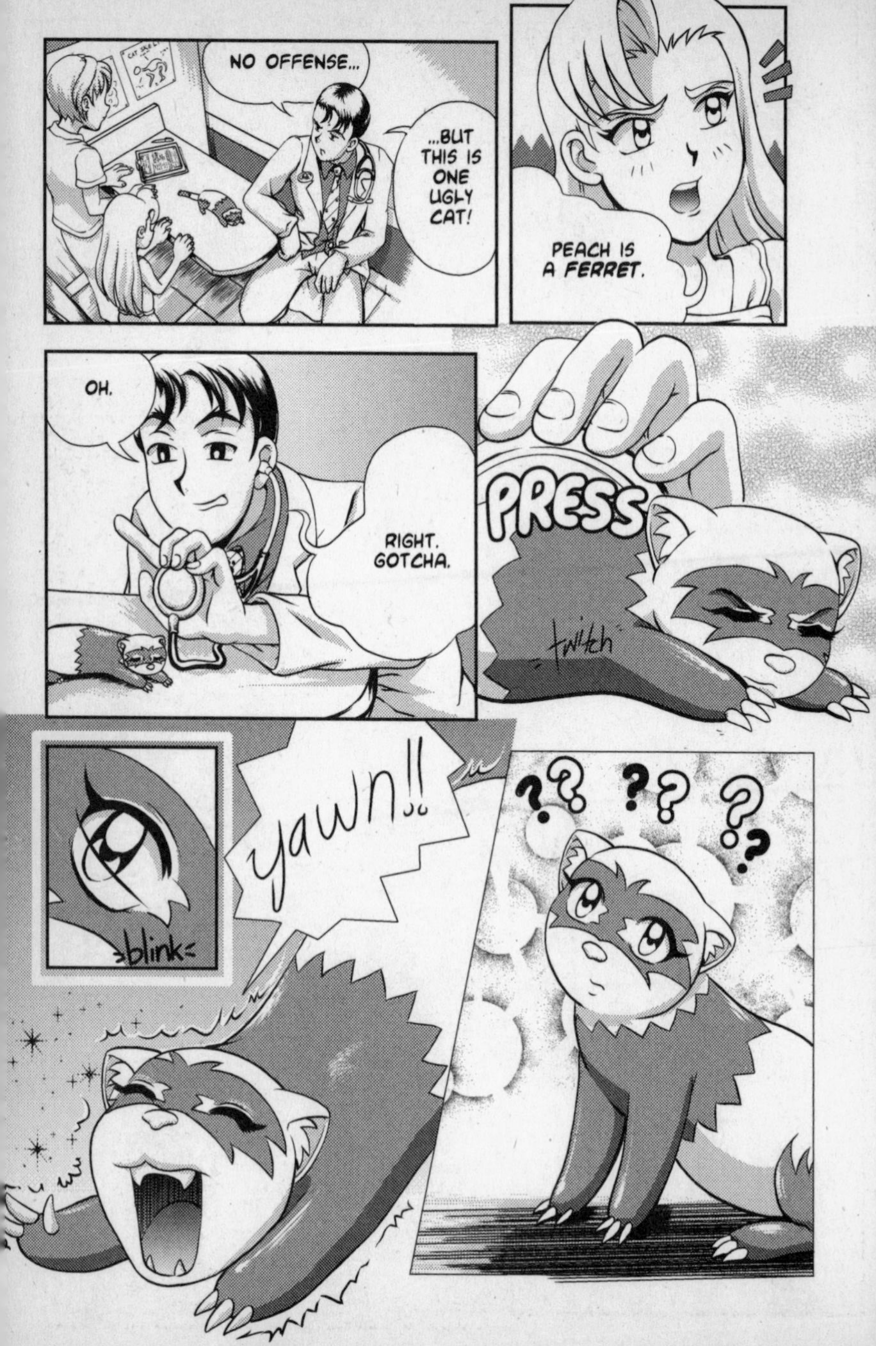
NO OFFENSE...
...BUT THIS IS ONE UGLY CAT!
PEACH IS A FERRET.
OH.
RIGHT. GOTCHA.
PRESS
twitch
blink
yawn!!
?? ?? ??

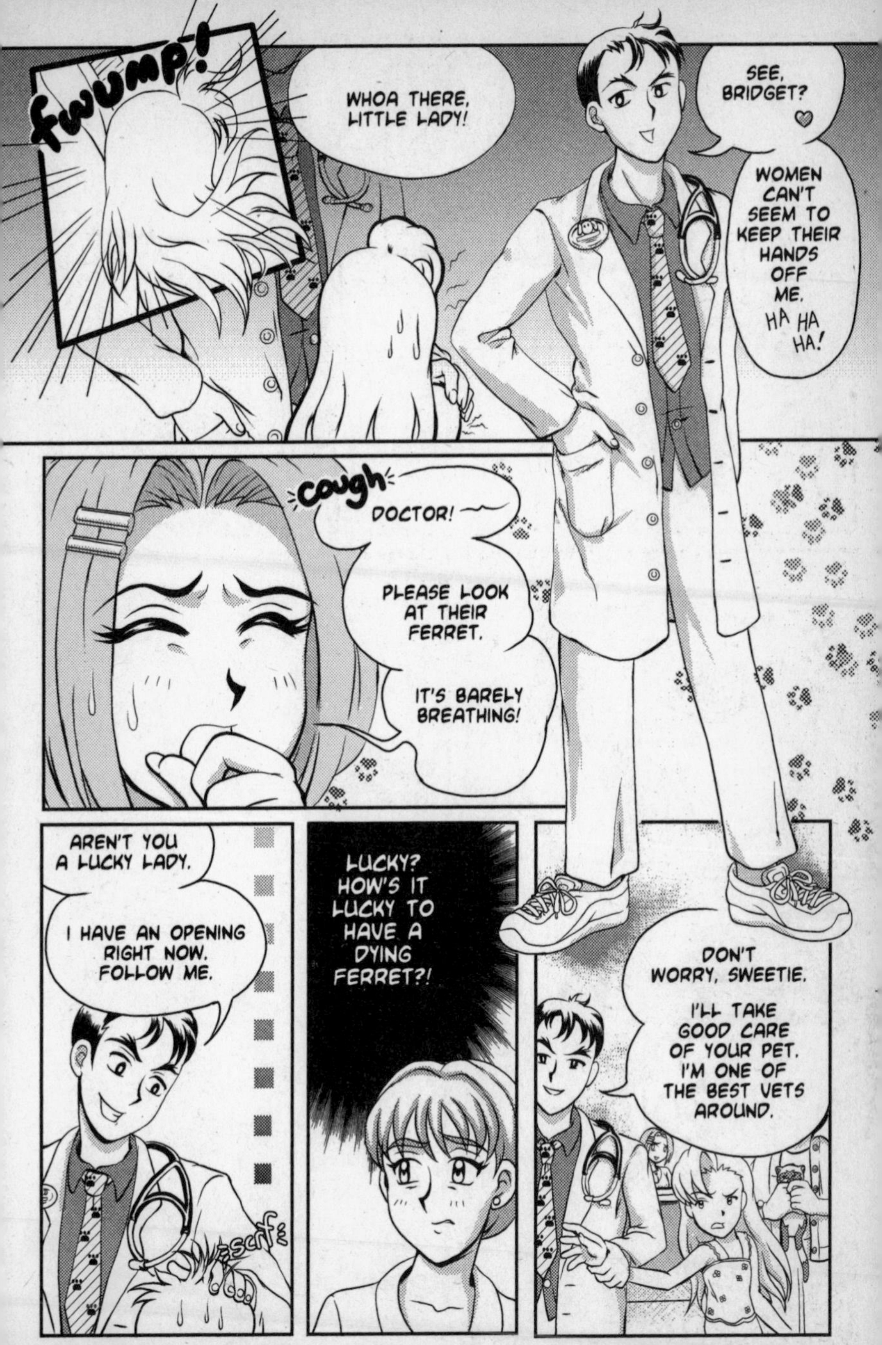
fwump!
WHOA THERE, LITTLE LADY!
SEE, BRIDGET? ♡
WOMEN CAN'T SEEM TO KEEP THEIR HANDS OFF ME. HA HA HA!
cough
DOCTOR!
PLEASE LOOK AT THEIR FERRET.
IT'S BARELY BREATHING!
AREN'T YOU A LUCKY LADY.
I HAVE AN OPENING RIGHT NOW. FOLLOW ME.
scrf
LUCKY? HOW'S IT LUCKY TO HAVE A DYING FERRET?!
DON'T WORRY, SWEETIE.
I'LL TAKE GOOD CARE OF YOUR PET. I'M ONE OF THE BEST VETS AROUND.

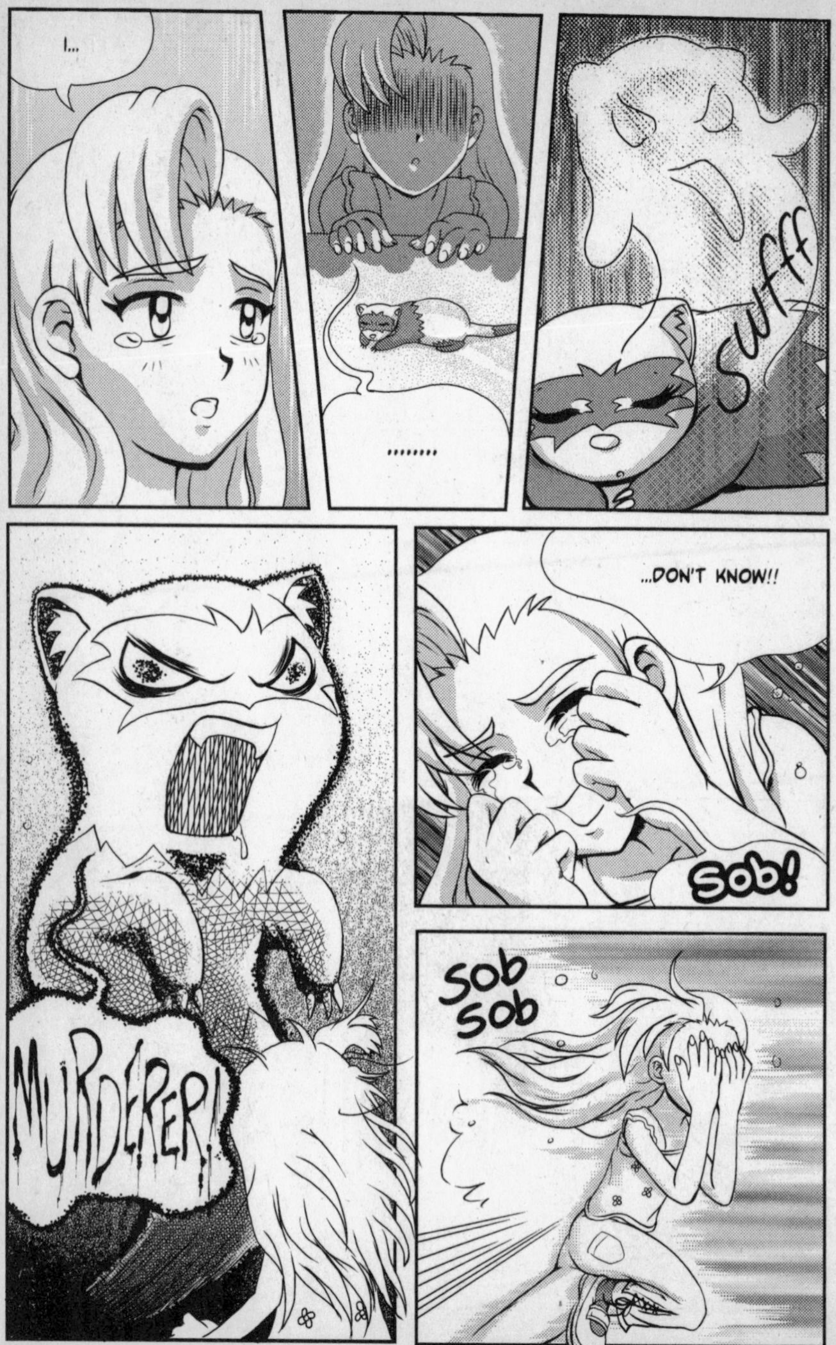
I...
....
SUFFF
MURDERER!
...DON'T KNOW!!
Sob!
Sob
Sob

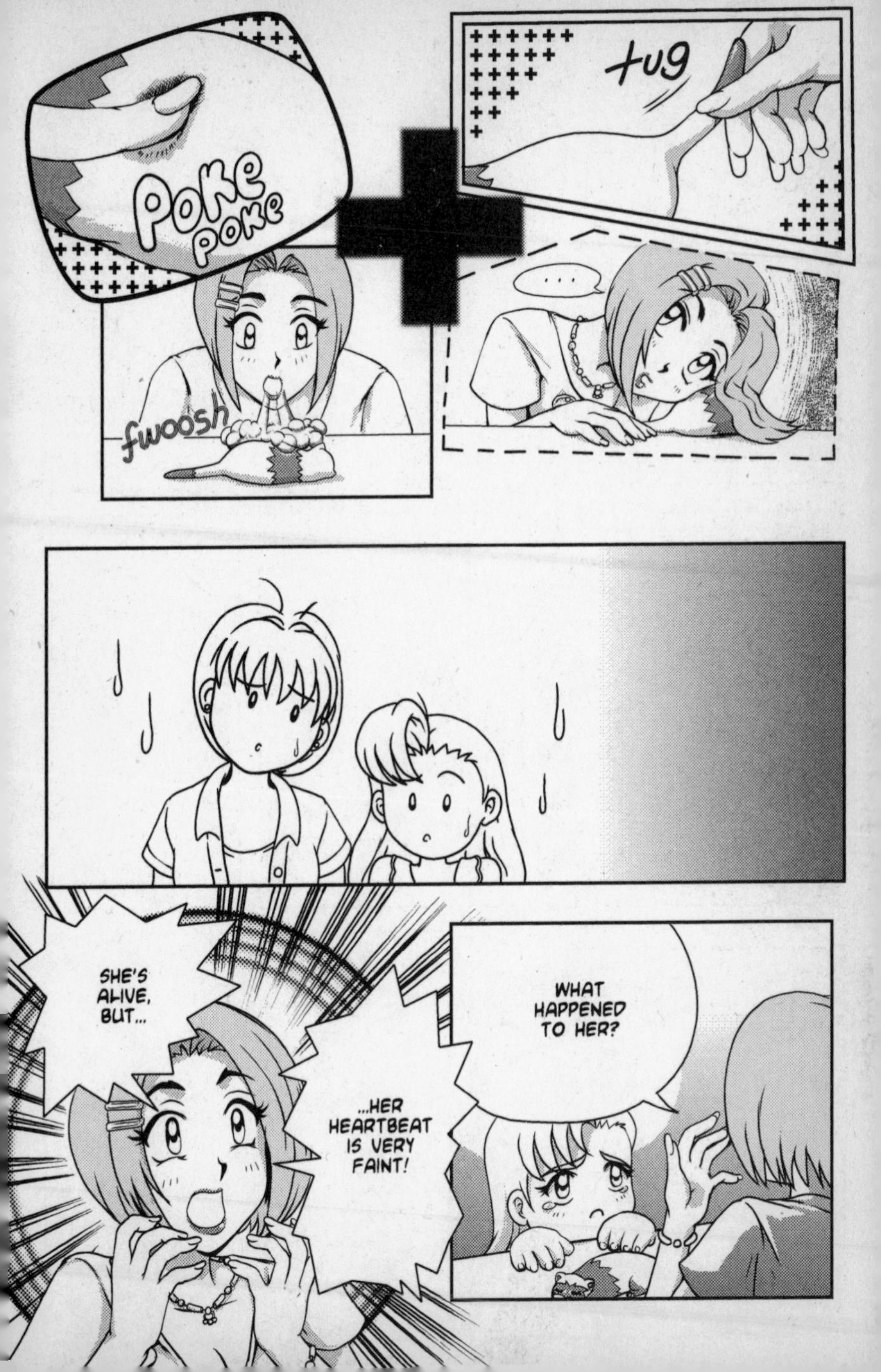
tug
Poke poke
...
fwoosh
WHAT HAPPENED TO HER?
SHE'S ALIVE, BUT...
...HER HEARTBEAT IS VERY FAINT!

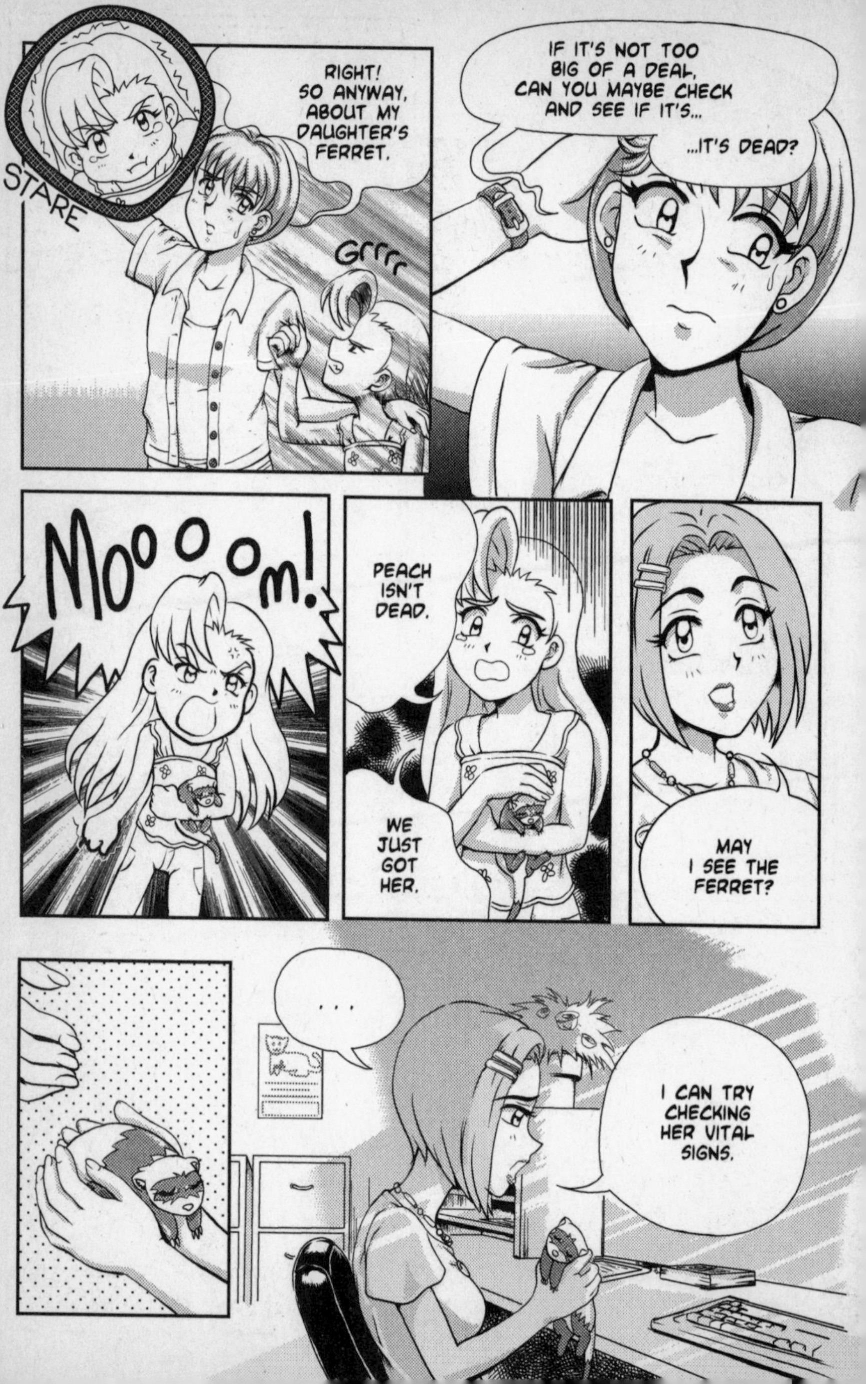
STARE
RIGHT! SO ANYWAY, ABOUT MY DAUGHTER'S FERRET.
Grrrr
IF IT'S NOT TOO BIG OF A DEAL, CAN YOU MAYBE CHECK AND SEE IF IT'S...
...IT'S DEAD?
Mooo o om!
PEACH ISN'T DEAD.
WE JUST GOT HER.
MAY I SEE THE FERRET?
. . .
I CAN TRY CHECKING HER VITAL SIGNS.

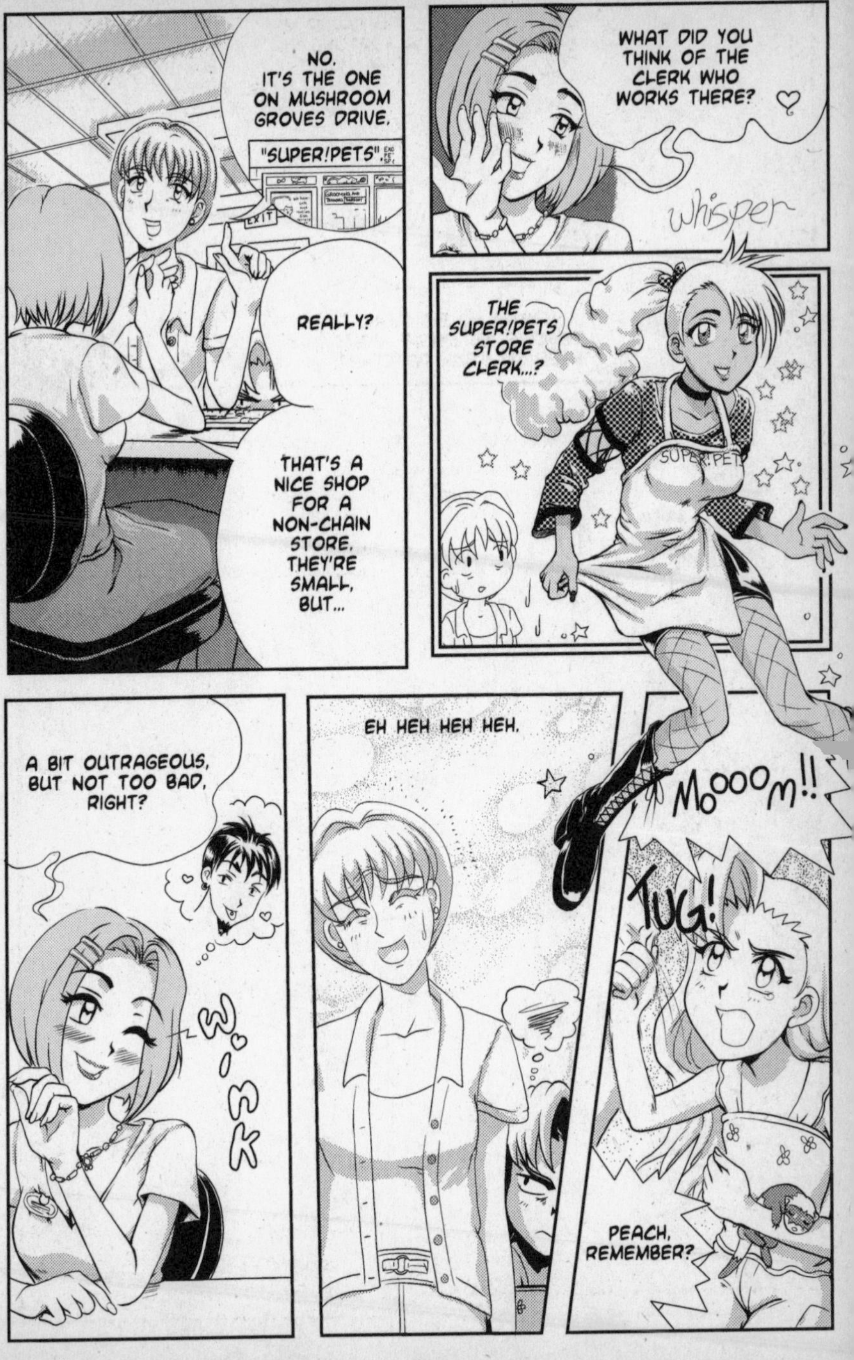

NO. IT'S THE ONE ON MUSHROOM GROVES DRIVE.
"SUPER!PETS".
EXIT
REALLY?
THAT'S A NICE SHOP FOR A NON-CHAIN STORE. THEY'RE SMALL, BUT...
WHAT DID YOU THINK OF THE CLERK WHO WORKS THERE?
whisper
THE SUPER!PETS STORE CLERK...?
SUPER!PET
A BIT OUTRAGEOUS, BUT NOT TOO BAD, RIGHT?
Wink
EH HEH HEH HEH.
MoOOOm!!
TUG!
PEACH, REMEMBER?

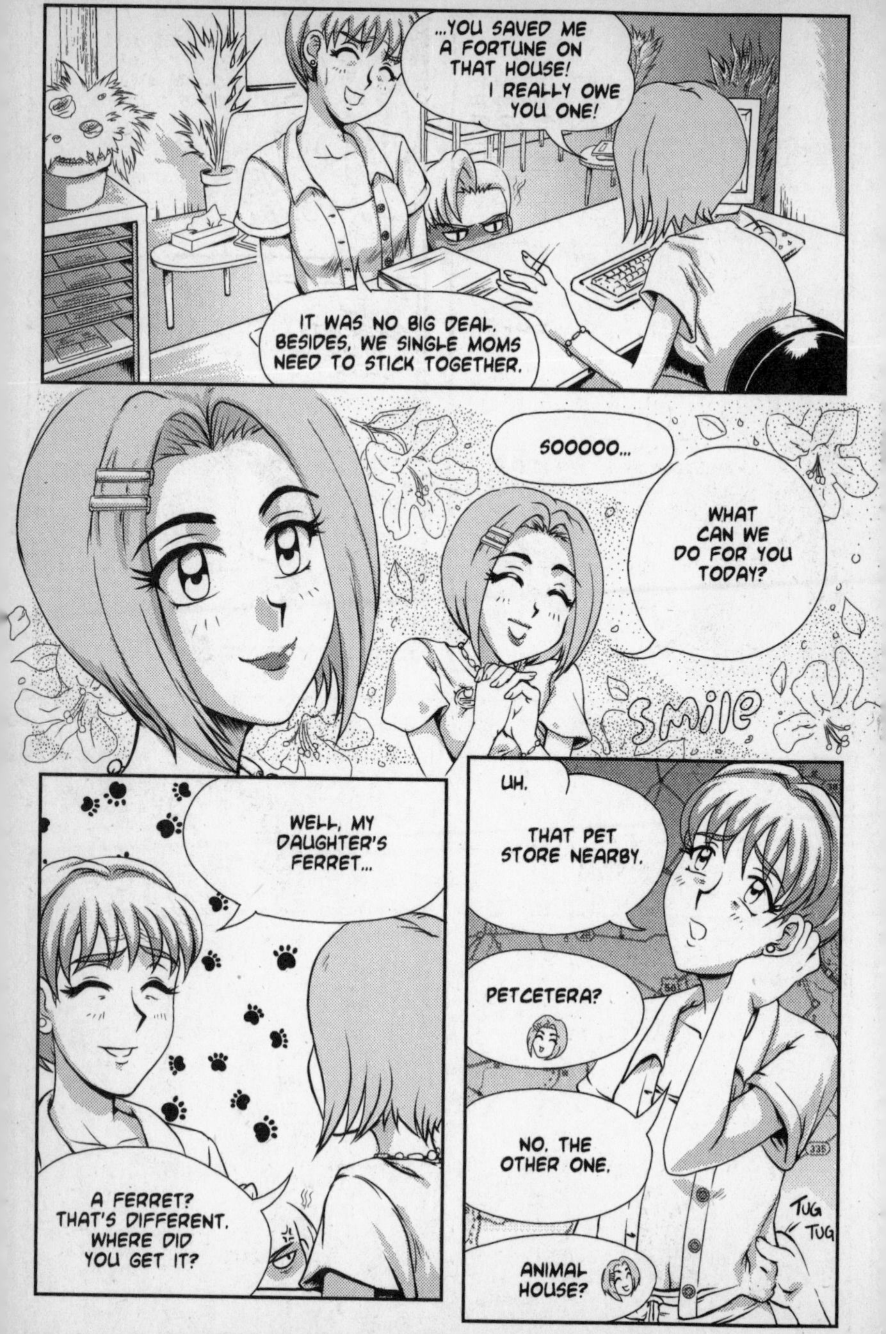
...YOU SAVED ME A FORTUNE ON THAT HOUSE! I REALLY OWE YOU ONE!
IT WAS NO BIG DEAL. BESIDES, WE SINGLE MOMS NEED TO STICK TOGETHER.
SOOOOO...
WHAT CAN WE DO FOR YOU TODAY?
smile
WELL, MY DAUGHTER'S FERRET...
A FERRET? THAT'S DIFFERENT. WHERE DID YOU GET IT?
UH.
THAT PET STORE NEARBY.
PETCETERA?
NO. THE OTHER ONE.
TUG TUG
ANIMAL HOUSE?

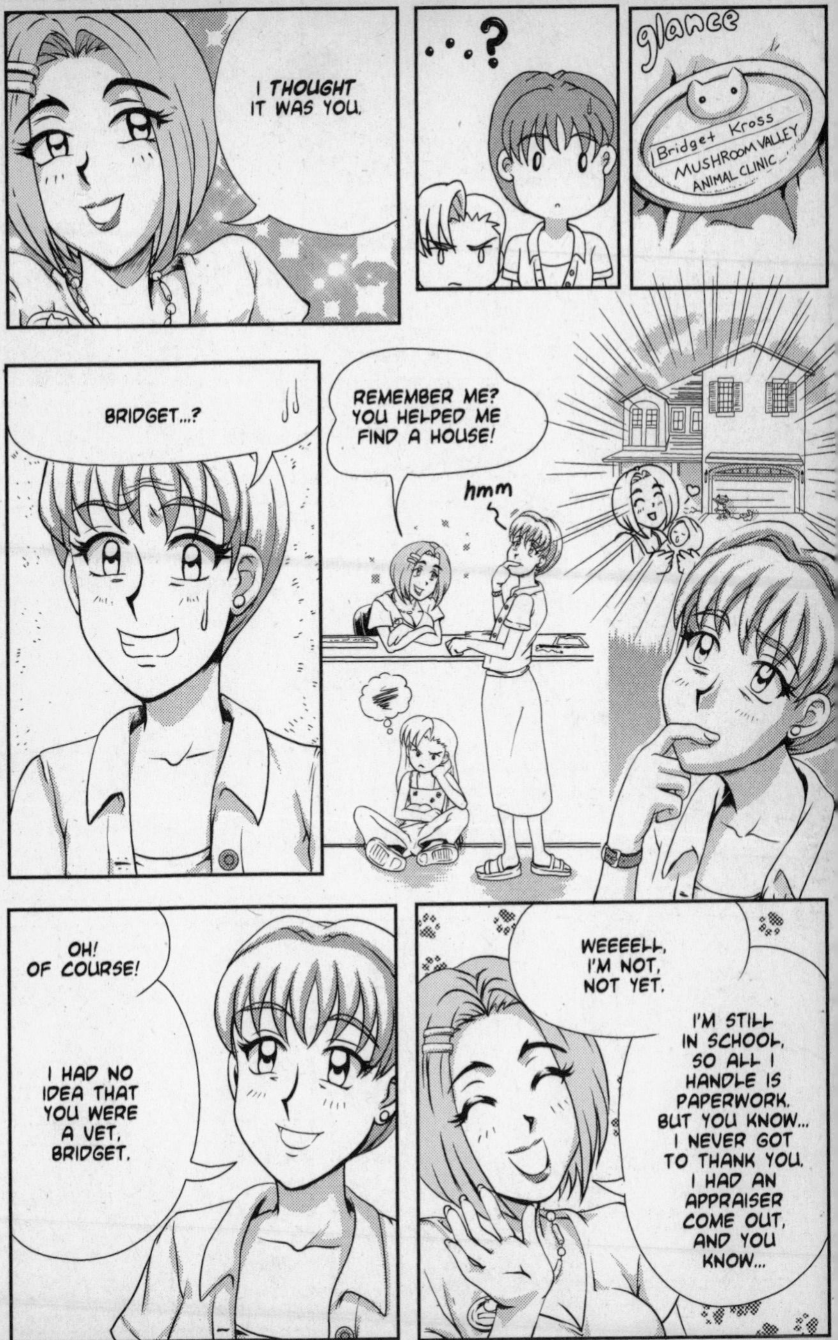
I THOUGHT IT WAS YOU.
...?
glance
Bridget Kross
MUSHROOM VALLEY ANIMAL CLINIC
BRIDGET...?
REMEMBER ME? YOU HELPED ME FIND A HOUSE!
hmm
OH! OF COURSE!
I HAD NO IDEA THAT YOU WERE A VET, BRIDGET.
WEEEELL, I'M NOT, NOT YET.
I'M STILL IN SCHOOL, SO ALL I HANDLE IS PAPERWORK. BUT YOU KNOW... I NEVER GOT TO THANK YOU. I HAD AN APPRAISER COME OUT, AND YOU KNOW...

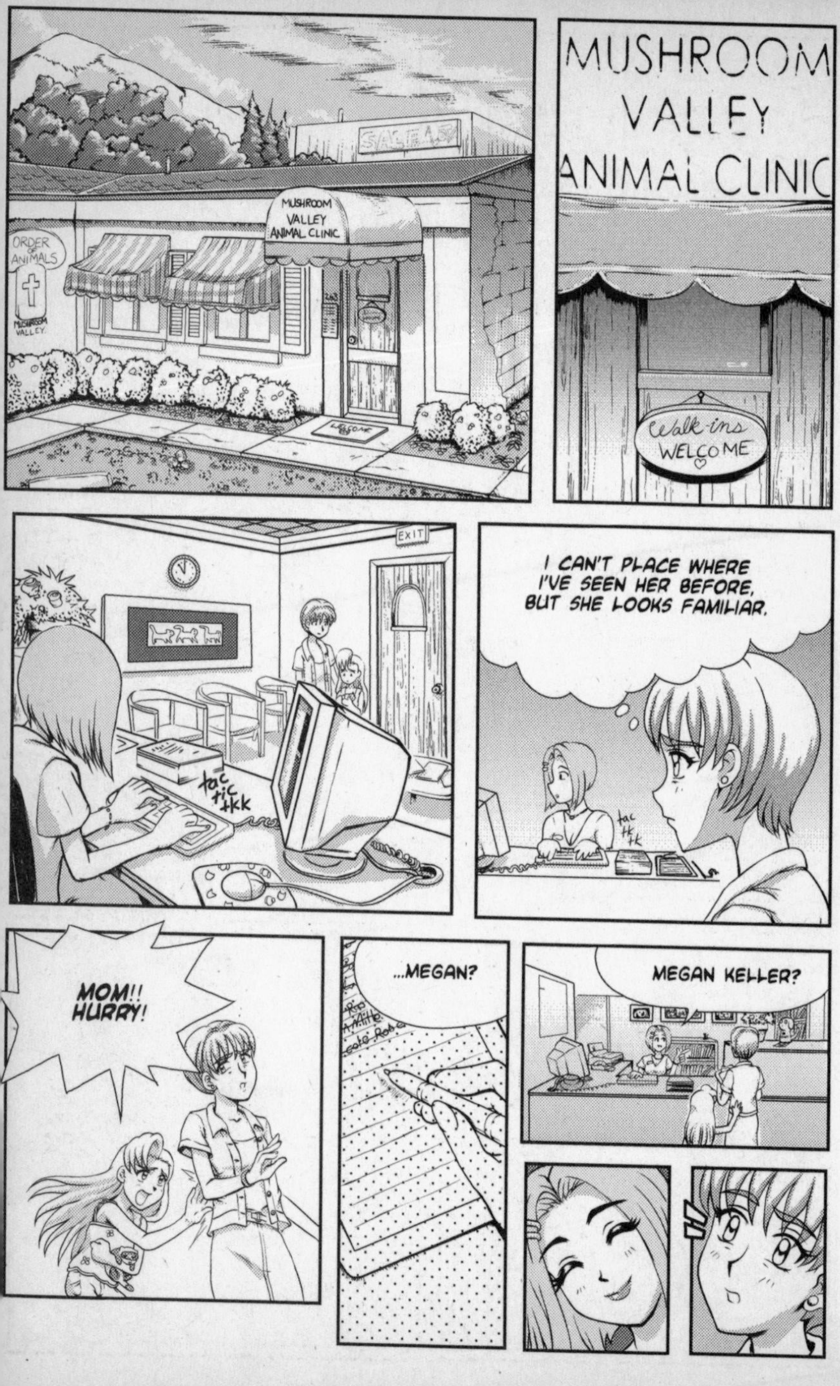
MUSHROOM VALLEY ANIMAL CLINIC
ORDER OF ANIMALS
MUSHROOM VALLEY
WELCOME
MUSHROOM VALLEY ANIMAL CLINIC
Walk-ins WELCOME
EXIT
tac tic tkk
I CAN'T PLACE WHERE I'VE SEEN HER BEFORE, BUT SHE LOOKS FAMILIAR.
tac tk tk
MOM!! HURRY!
...MEGAN?
MEGAN KELLER?

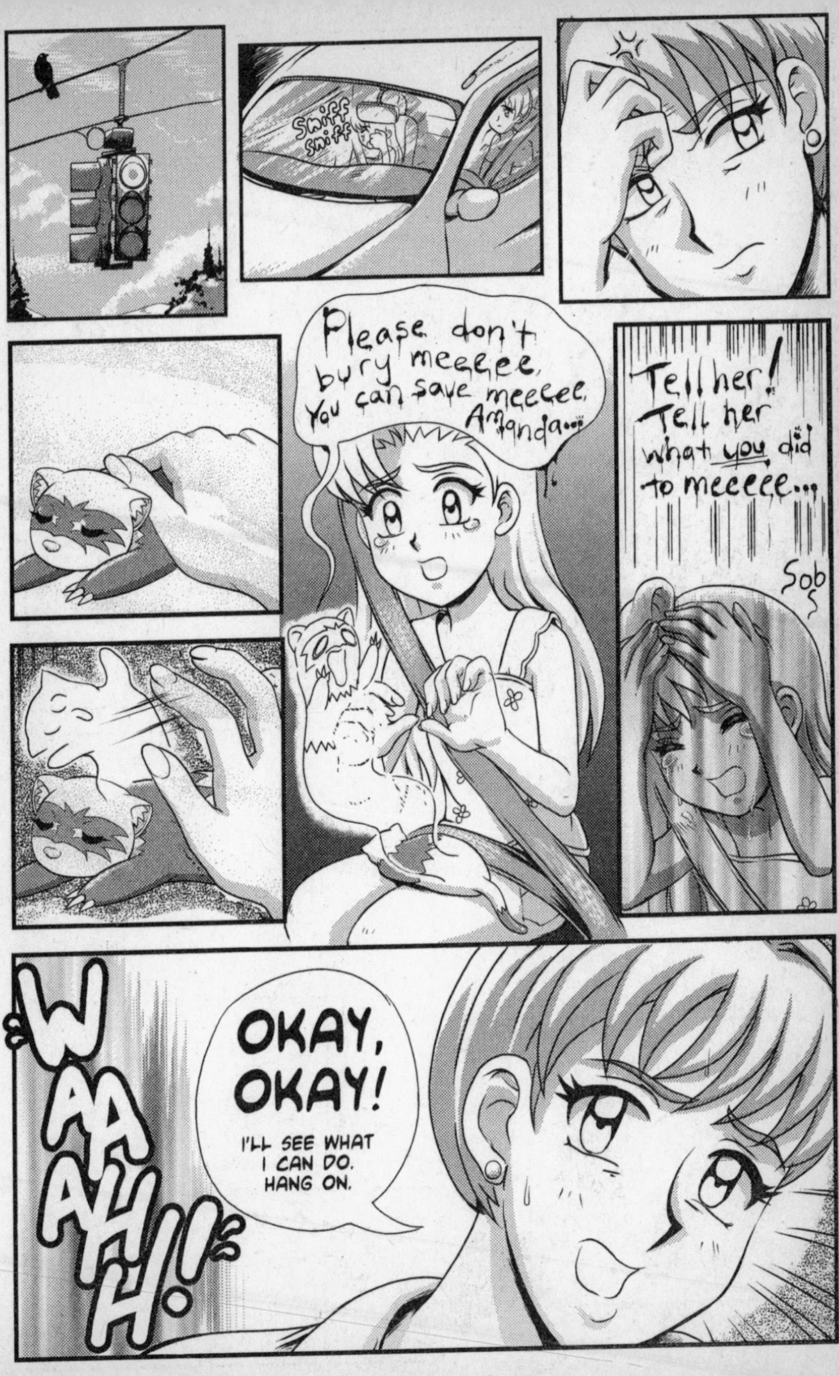

Sniff sniff
Please don't bury meeeee, You can save meeeee, Amanda...
Tell her! Tell her what you did to meeeee...
Sob
WAAAHH!
OKAY, OKAY!
I'LL SEE WHAT I CAN DO. HANG ON.

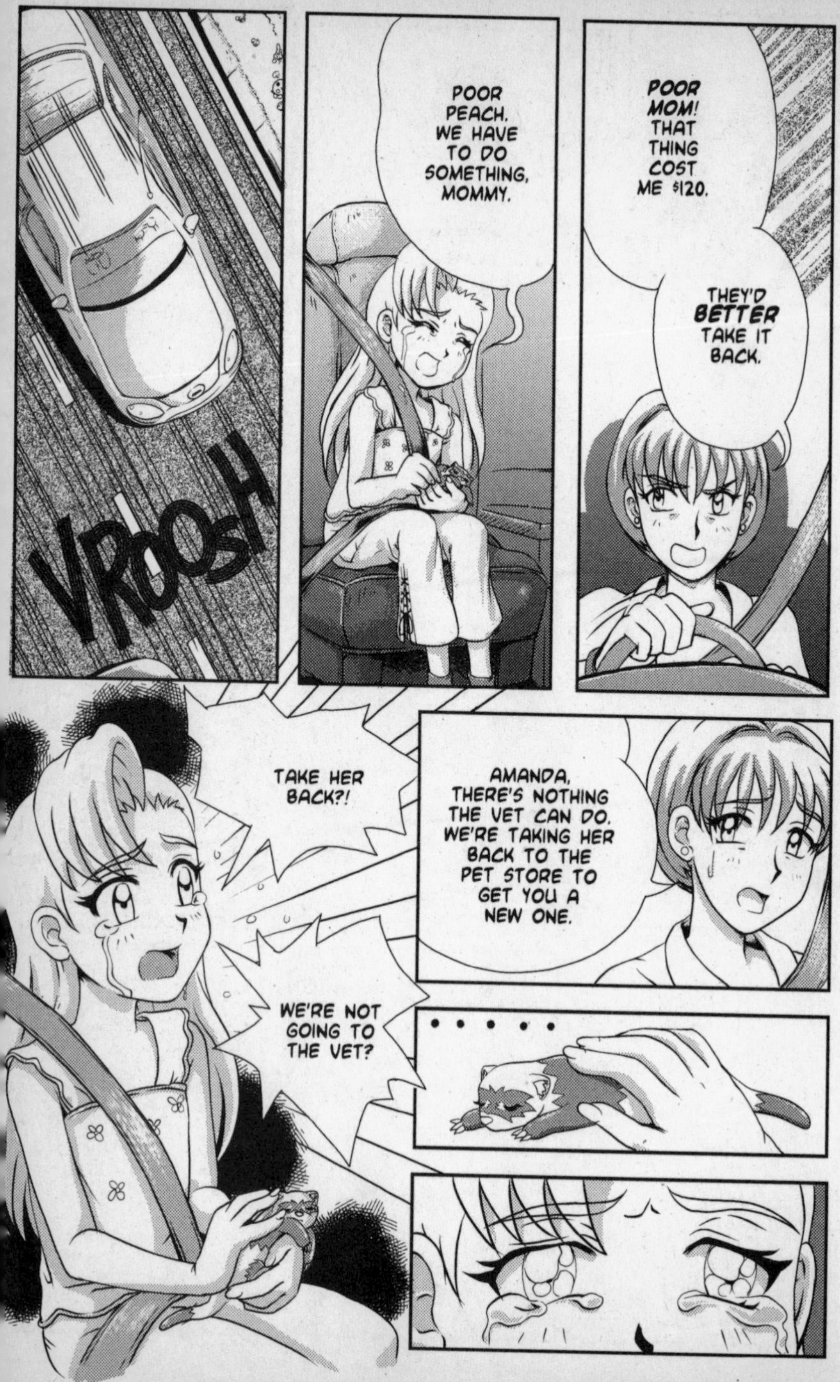
VROOSH
POOR PEACH. WE HAVE TO DO SOMETHING, MOMMY.
POOR MOM! THAT THING COST ME $120.
THEY'D BETTER TAKE IT BACK.
TAKE HER BACK?!
WE'RE NOT GOING TO THE VET?
AMANDA, THERE'S NOTHING THE VET CAN DO. WE'RE TAKING HER BACK TO THE PET STORE TO GET YOU A NEW ONE.
• • • • •

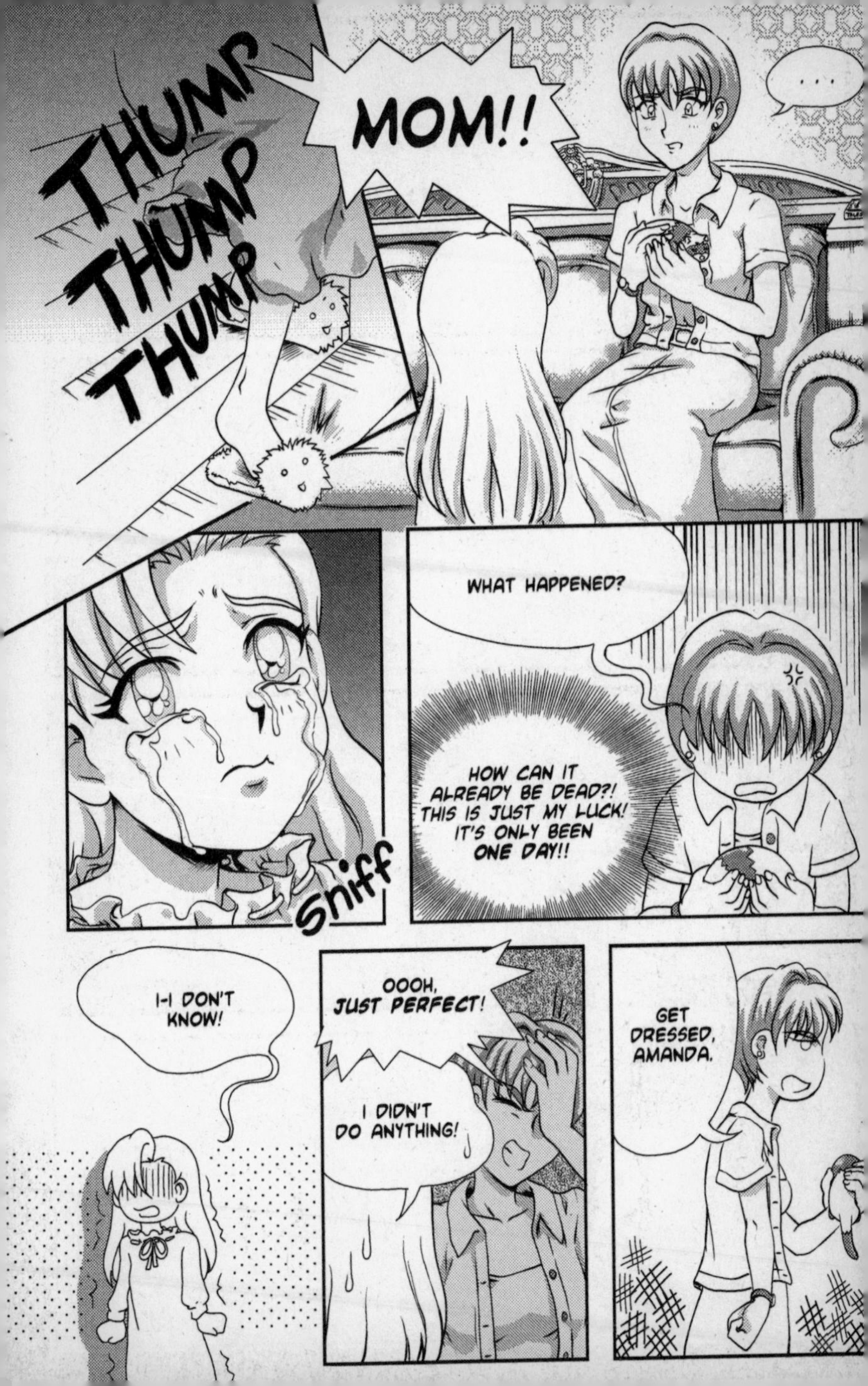
THUMP THUMP THUMP
MOM!!
...
Sniff
WHAT HAPPENED?
HOW CAN IT ALREADY BE DEAD?! THIS IS JUST MY LUCK! IT'S ONLY BEEN ONE DAY!!
I-I DON'T KNOW!
OOOH, JUST PERFECT!
I DIDN'T DO ANYTHING!
GET DRESSED, AMANDA.

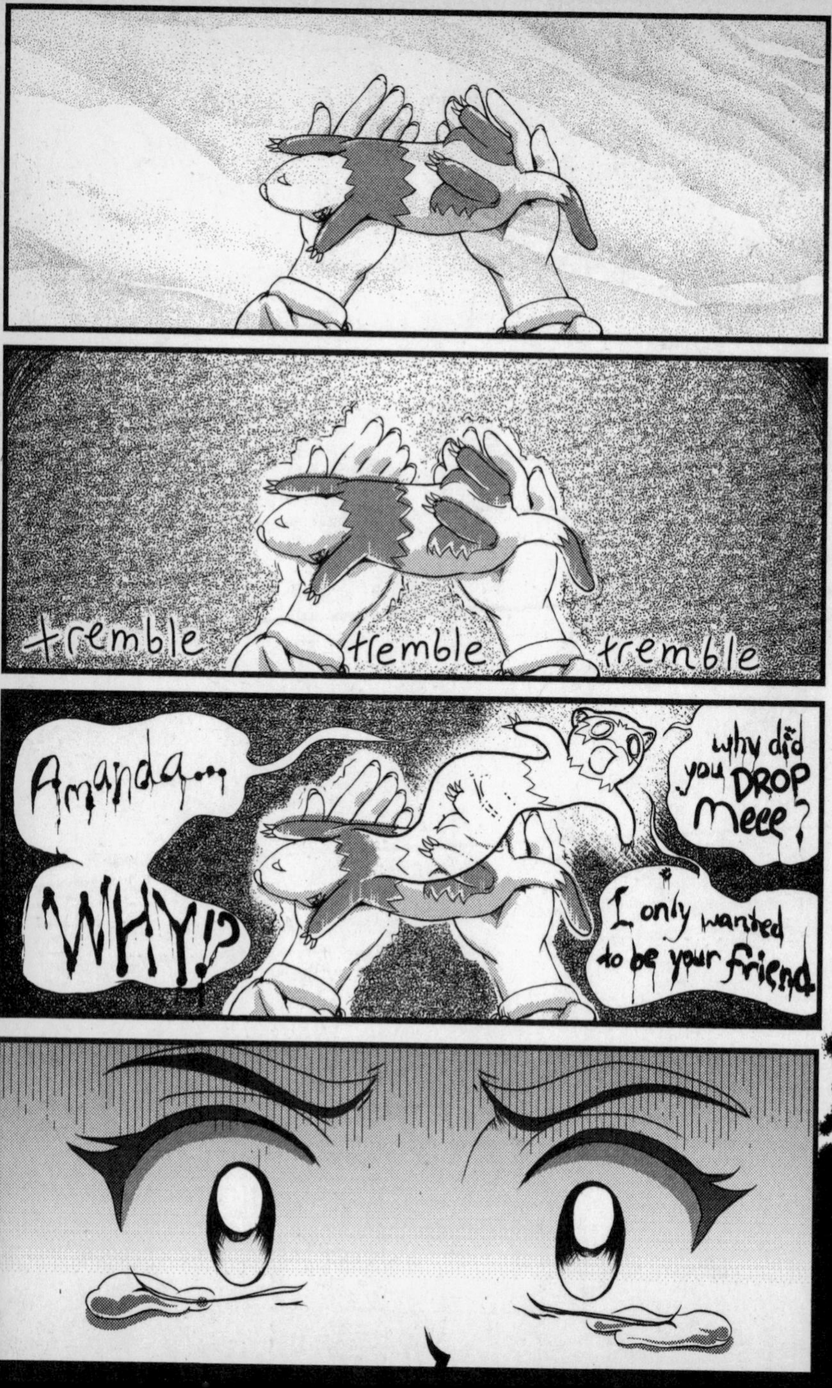
tremble tremble tremble
why did you DROP meee?
Amanda...
WHY!?
I only wanted to be your friend

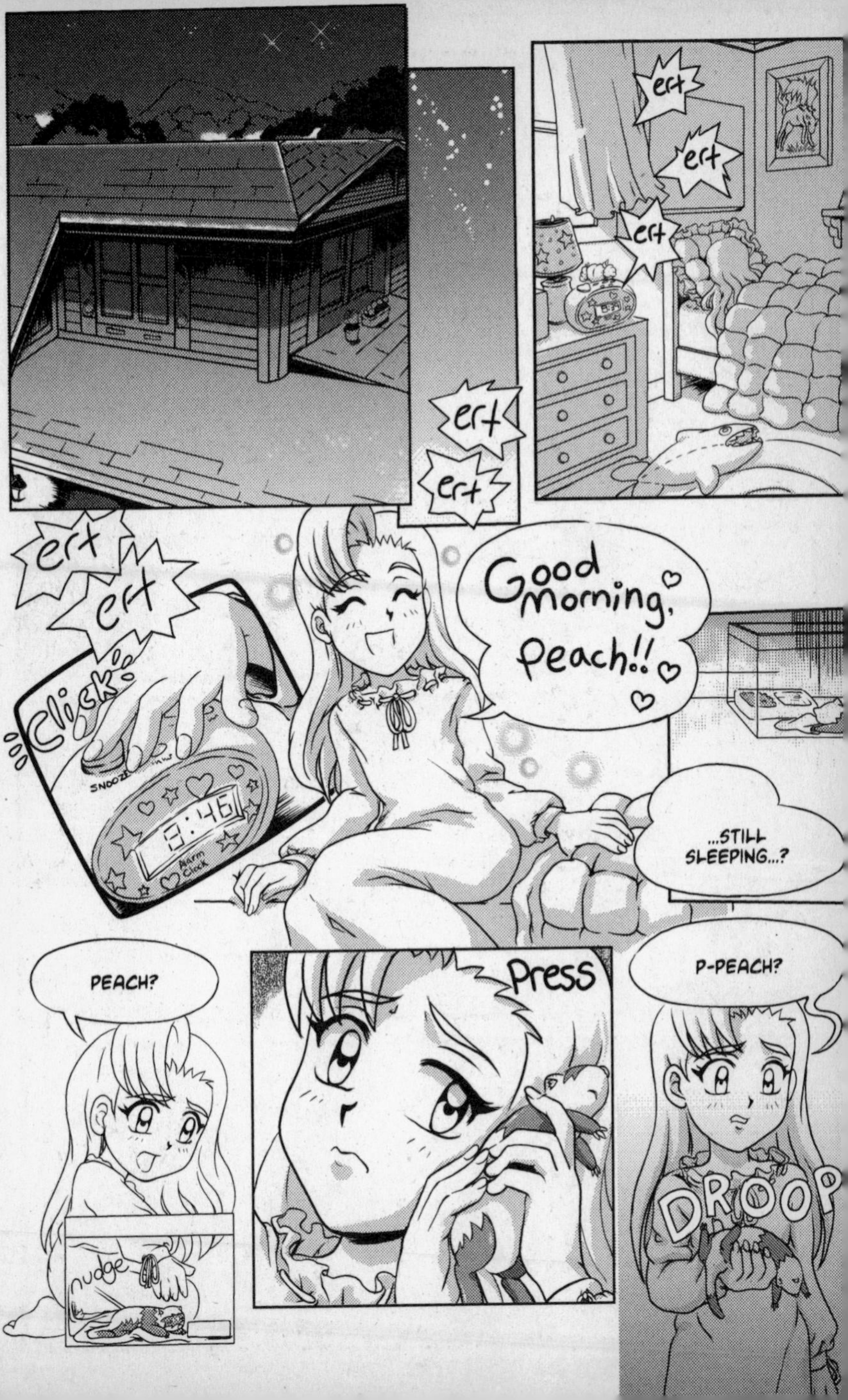
ert
ert
ert
ert
ert
ert
ert
Click
SNOOZE
8:46
Alarm Clock
Good Morning, Peach!!
...STILL SLEEPING...?
PEACH?
nudge
Press
P-PEACH?
DROOP

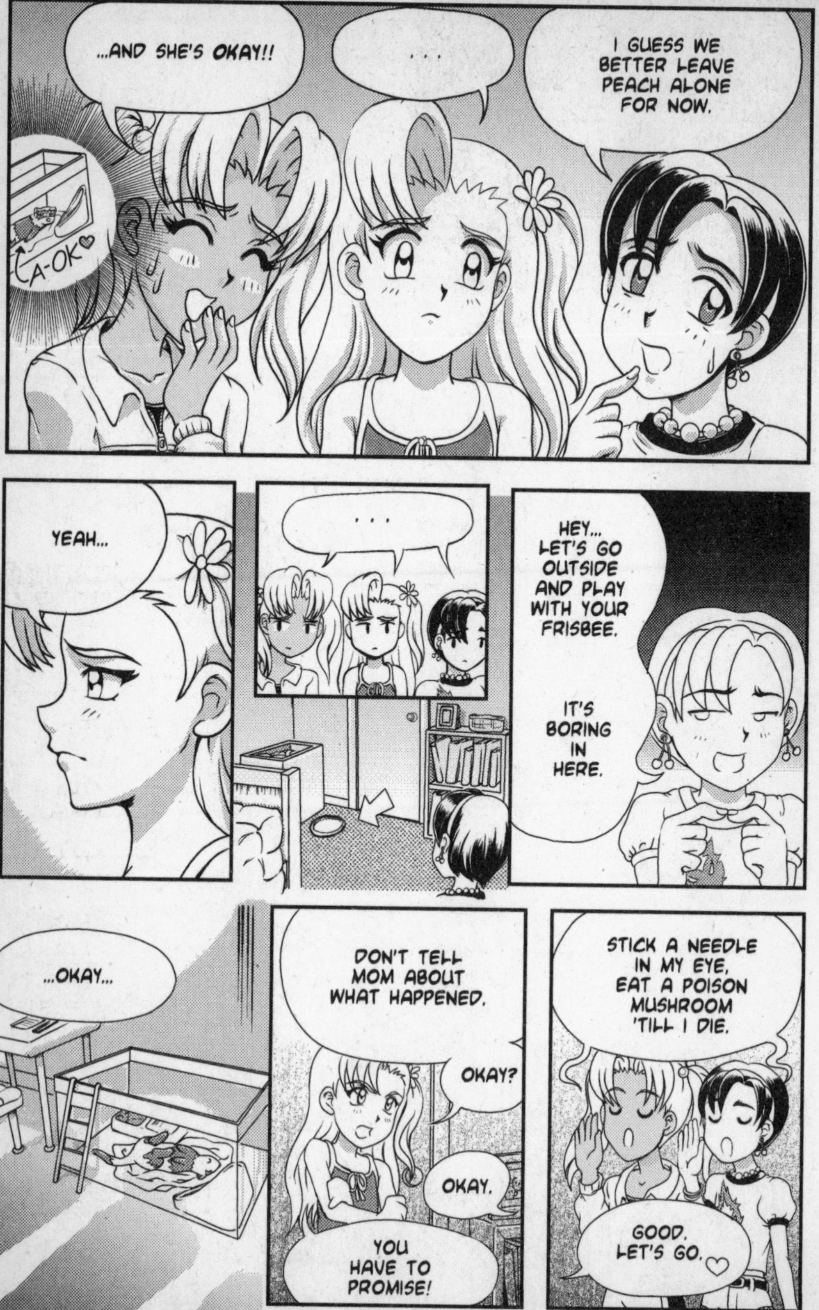
...AND SHE'S OKAY!!
A-OK
. . .
I GUESS WE BETTER LEAVE PEACH ALONE FOR NOW.
YEAH...
. . .
HEY... LET'S GO OUTSIDE AND PLAY WITH YOUR FRISBEE.
IT'S BORING IN HERE.
...OKAY...
DON'T TELL MOM ABOUT WHAT HAPPENED.
OKAY?
OKAY.
YOU HAVE TO PROMISE!
STICK A NEEDLE IN MY EYE, EAT A POISON MUSHROOM 'TILL I DIE.
GOOD. LET'S GO. ♡

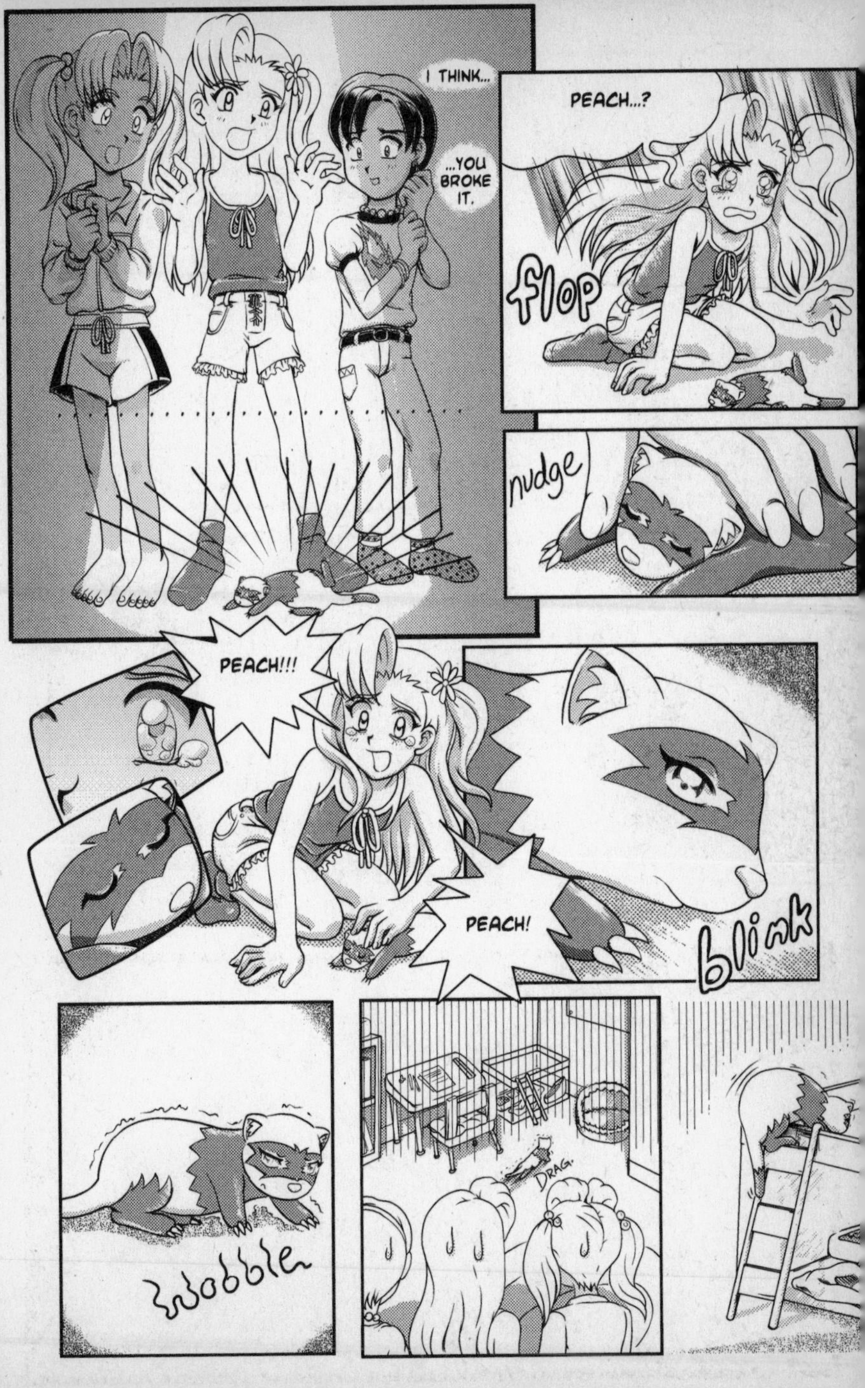
I THINK...
...YOU BROKE IT.
PEACH...?
flop
nudge
PEACH!!!
PEACH!
blink
wobble
DRAG.

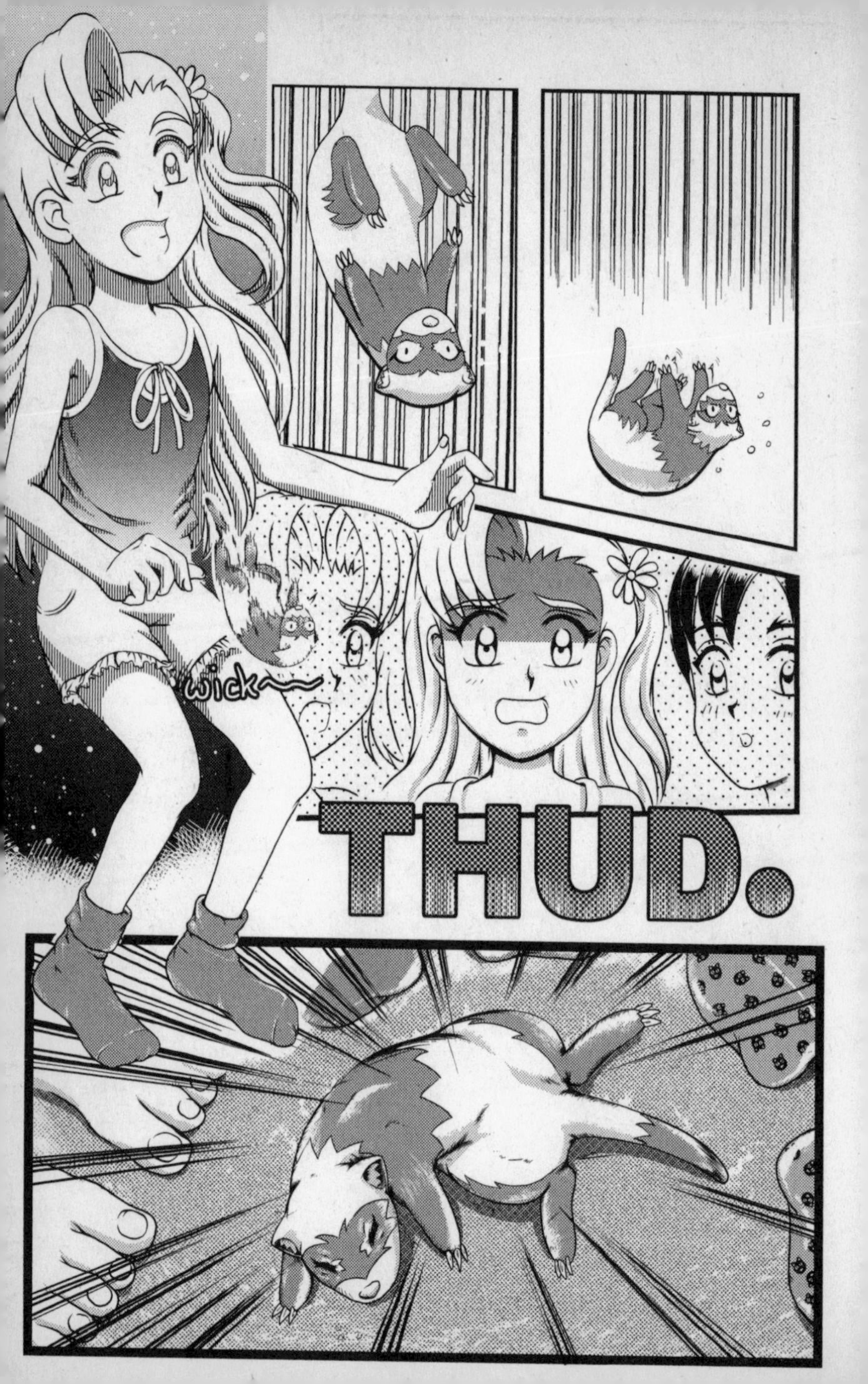
wick~~~
THUD.

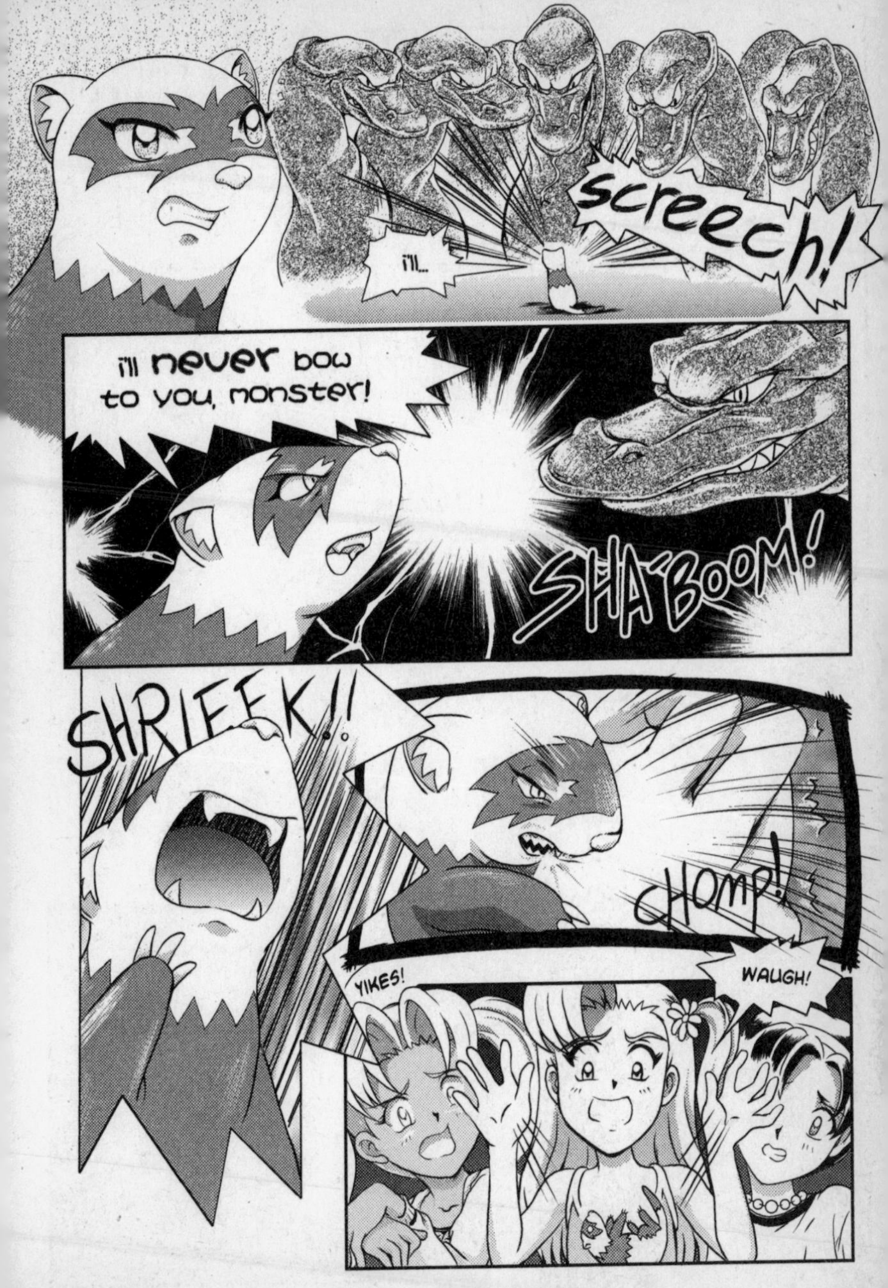
SCREECH!
I'LL..
I'LL NEVER BOW TO YOU, MONSTER!
SHA-BOOM!
CHOMP!
WAUGH!
YIKES!
SHRIEEK!!

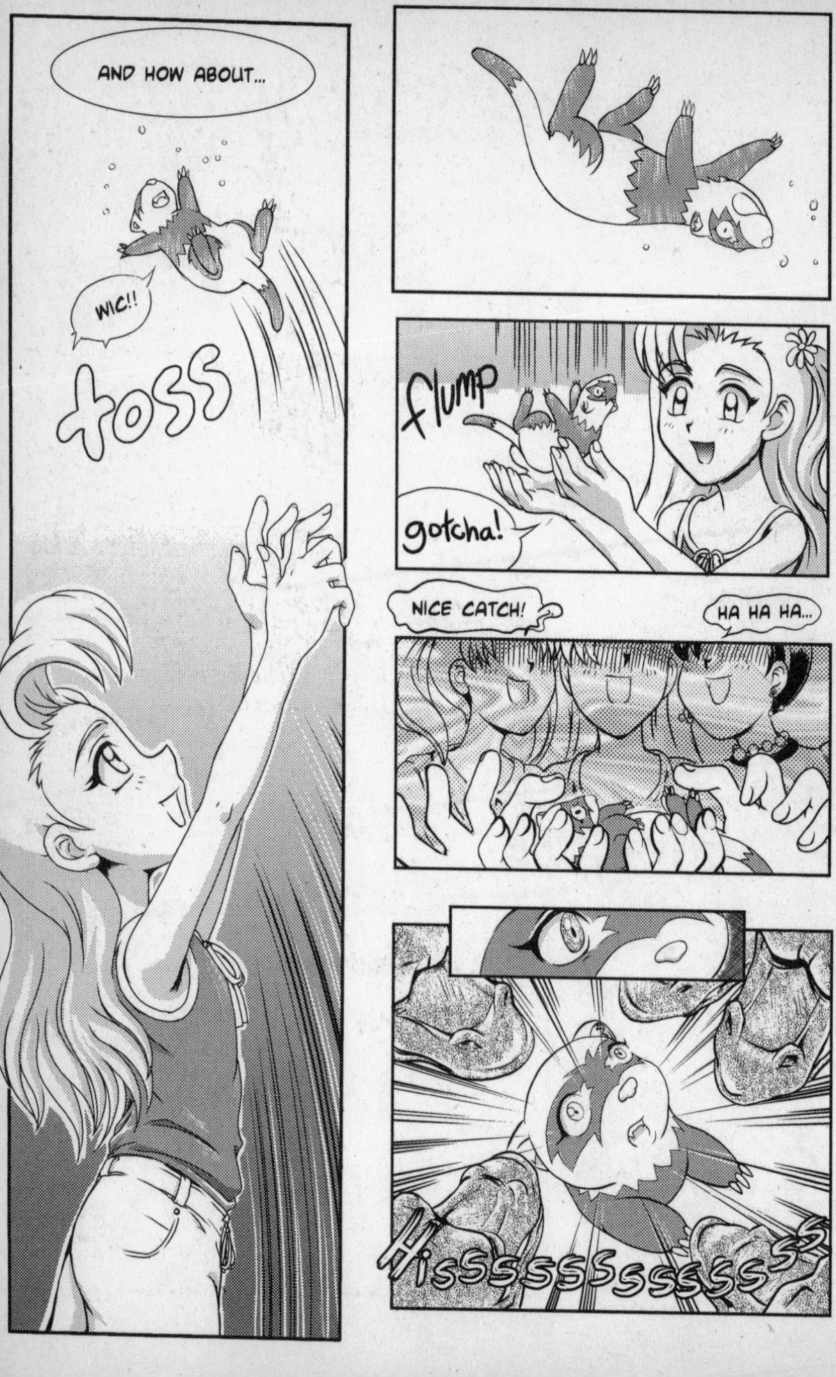
AND HOW ABOUT...
WIC!!
toss
flump
gotcha!
NICE CATCH!
HA HA HA...
HisSSSSSSSSSSSS

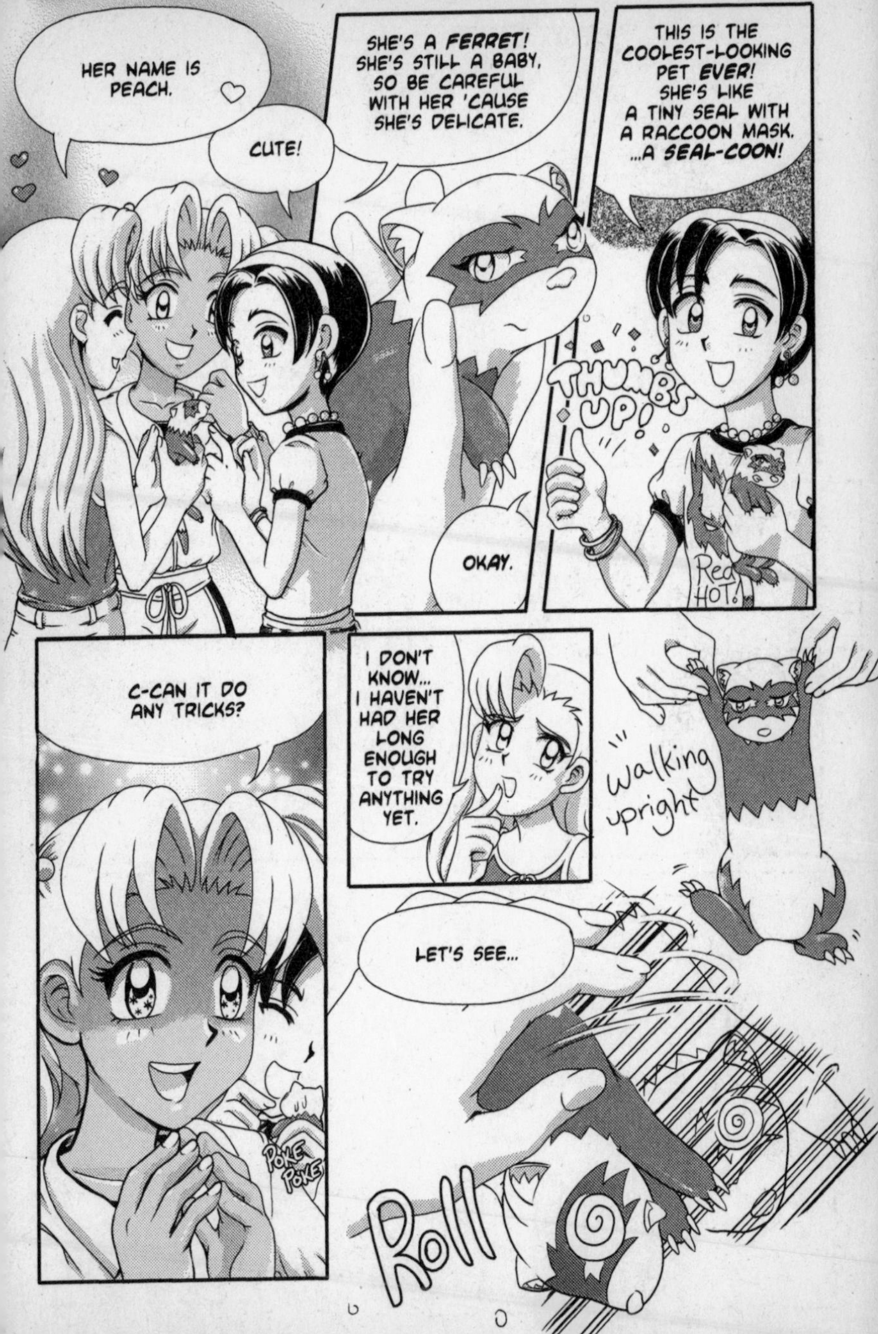
HER NAME IS PEACH.
CUTE!
SHE'S A FERRET! SHE'S STILL A BABY, SO BE CAREFUL WITH HER 'CAUSE SHE'S DELICATE.
OKAY.
THIS IS THE COOLEST-LOOKING PET EVER! SHE'S LIKE A TINY SEAL WITH A RACCOON MASK. ...A SEAL-COON!
THUMBS UP!
Red HOT!
C-CAN IT DO ANY TRICKS?
POKE POKE
I DON'T KNOW... I HAVEN'T HAD HER LONG ENOUGH TO TRY ANYTHING YET.
walking upright
LET'S SEE...
Roll

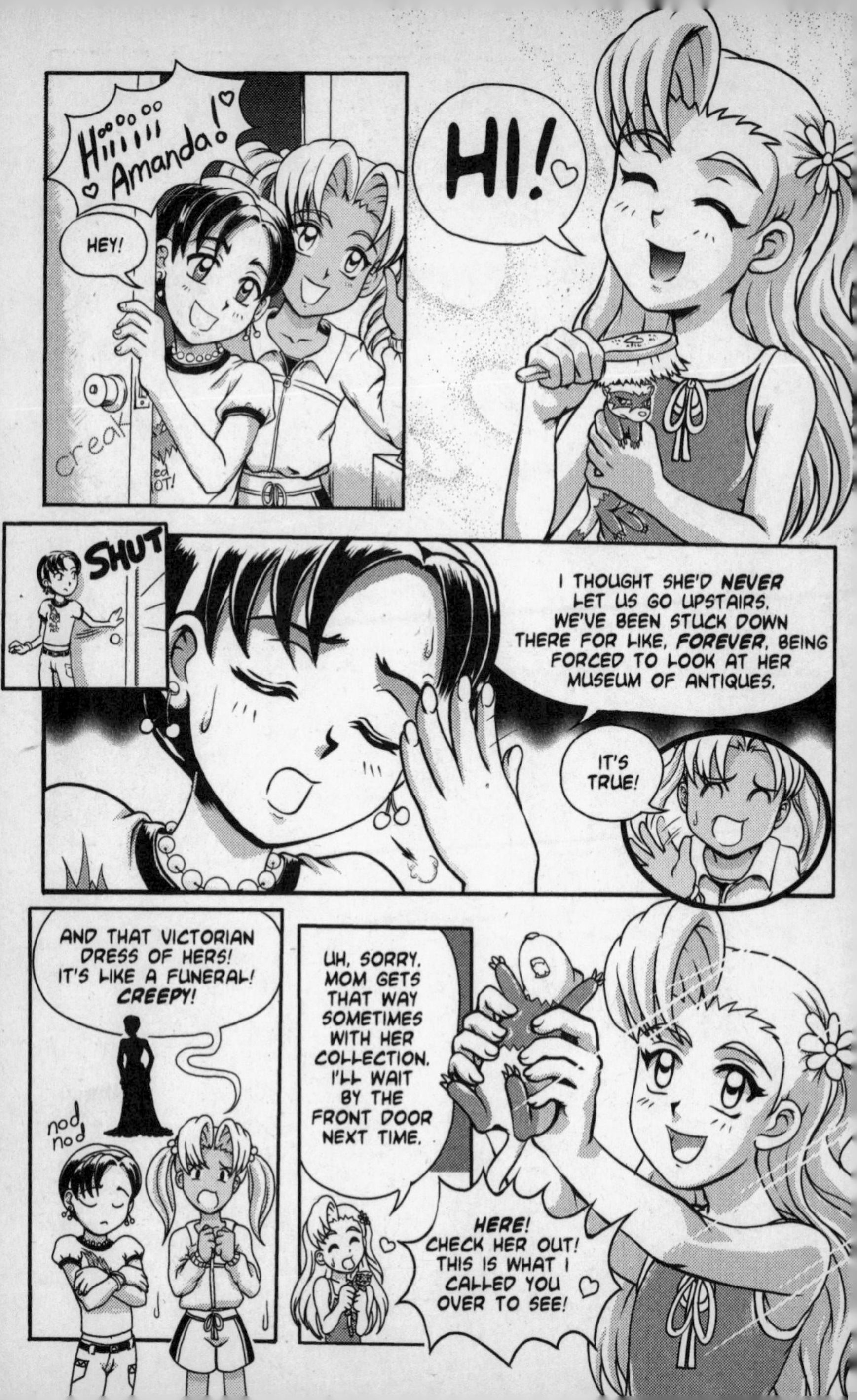
Hiiiiii Amanda!
HEY!
creak
HI!
SHUT
I THOUGHT SHE'D NEVER LET US GO UPSTAIRS. WE'VE BEEN STUCK DOWN THERE FOR LIKE, FOREVER, BEING FORCED TO LOOK AT HER MUSEUM OF ANTIQUES.
IT'S TRUE!
AND THAT VICTORIAN DRESS OF HERS! IT'S LIKE A FUNERAL! CREEPY!
nod nod
UH, SORRY. MOM GETS THAT WAY SOMETIMES WITH HER COLLECTION. I'LL WAIT BY THE FRONT DOOR NEXT TIME.
HERE! CHECK HER OUT! THIS IS WHAT I CALLED YOU OVER TO SEE!

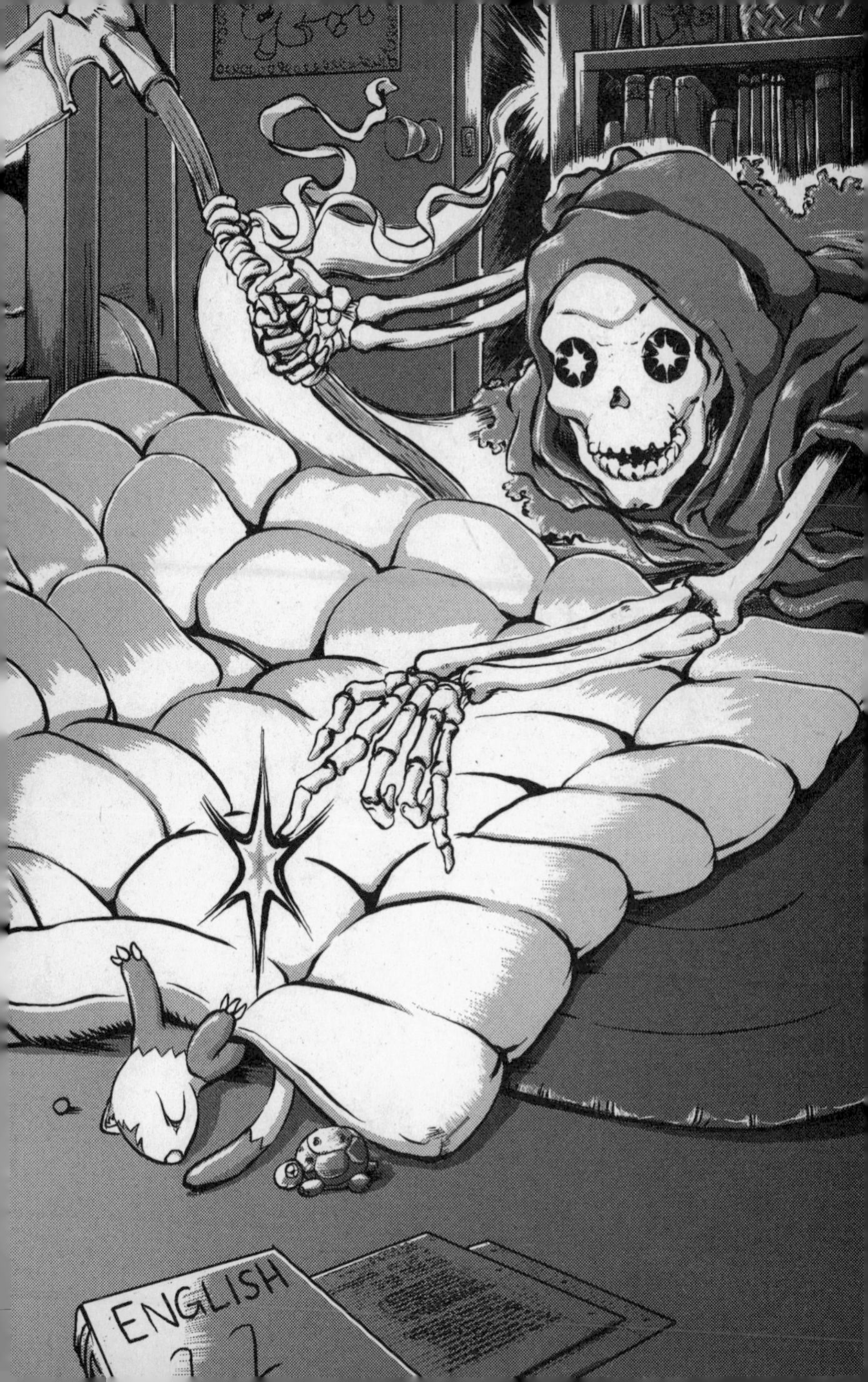
ENGLISH

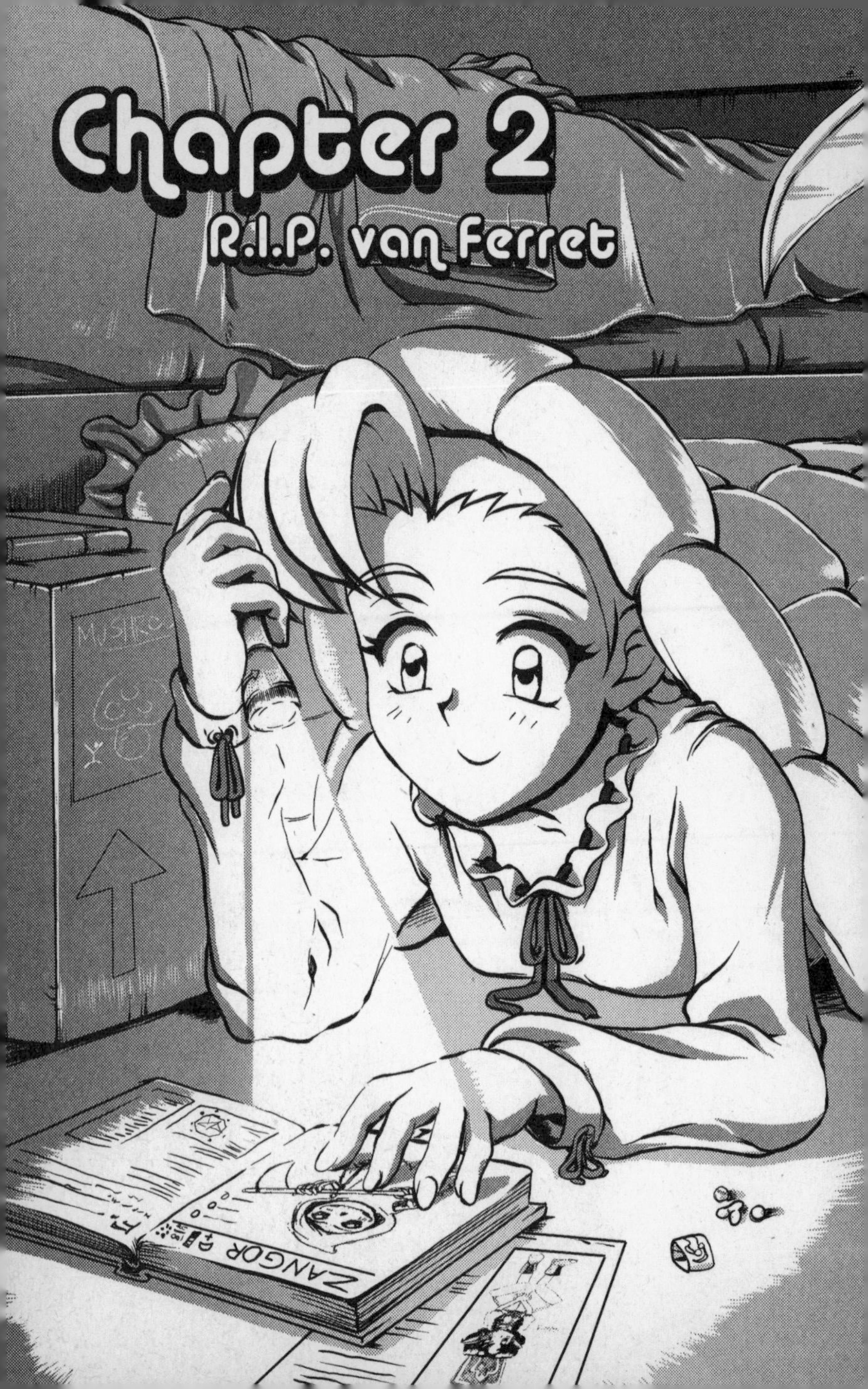
Chapter 2
R.I.P. van Ferret
ZANGOR

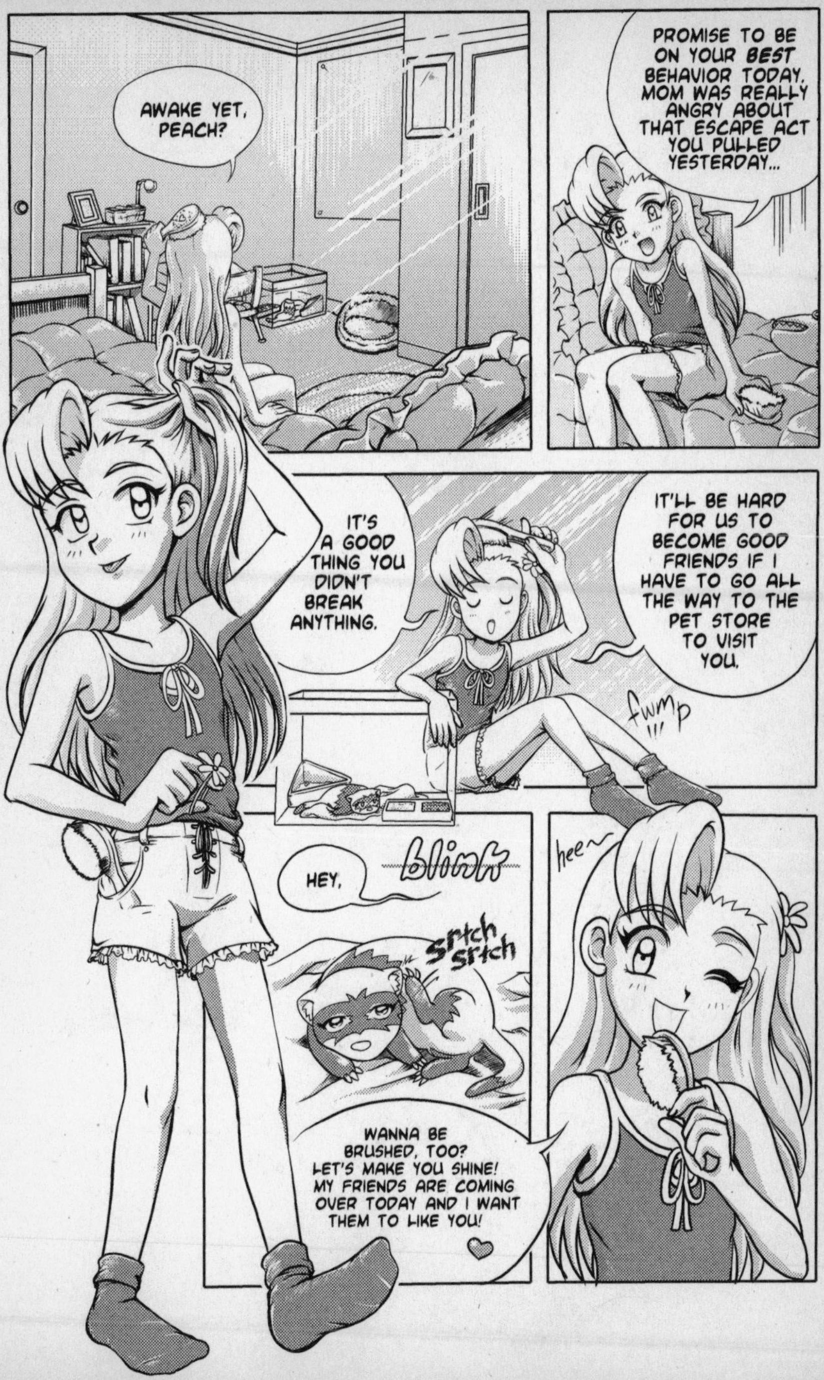
AWAKE YET, PEACH?
PROMISE TO BE ON YOUR BEST BEHAVIOR TODAY. MOM WAS REALLY ANGRY ABOUT THAT ESCAPE ACT YOU PULLED YESTERDAY...
IT'S A GOOD THING YOU DIDN'T BREAK ANYTHING.
IT'LL BE HARD FOR US TO BECOME GOOD FRIENDS IF I HAVE TO GO ALL THE WAY TO THE PET STORE TO VISIT YOU.
fwmp !!!
HEY,
blink
srtch srtch
WANNA BE BRUSHED, TOO? LET'S MAKE YOU SHINE! MY FRIENDS ARE COMING OVER TODAY AND I WANT THEM TO LIKE YOU!
hee~

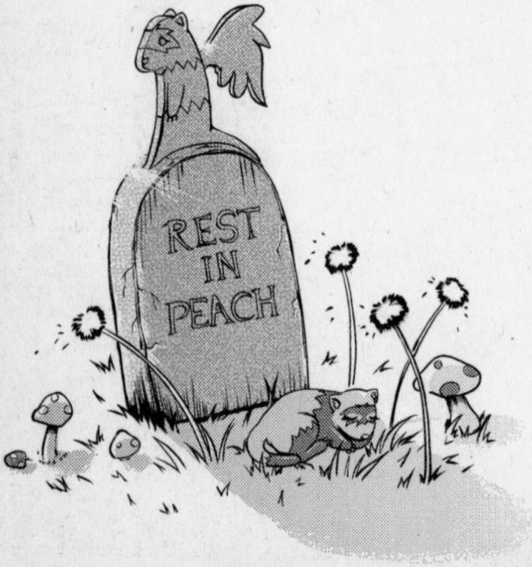
REST
IN
PEACH

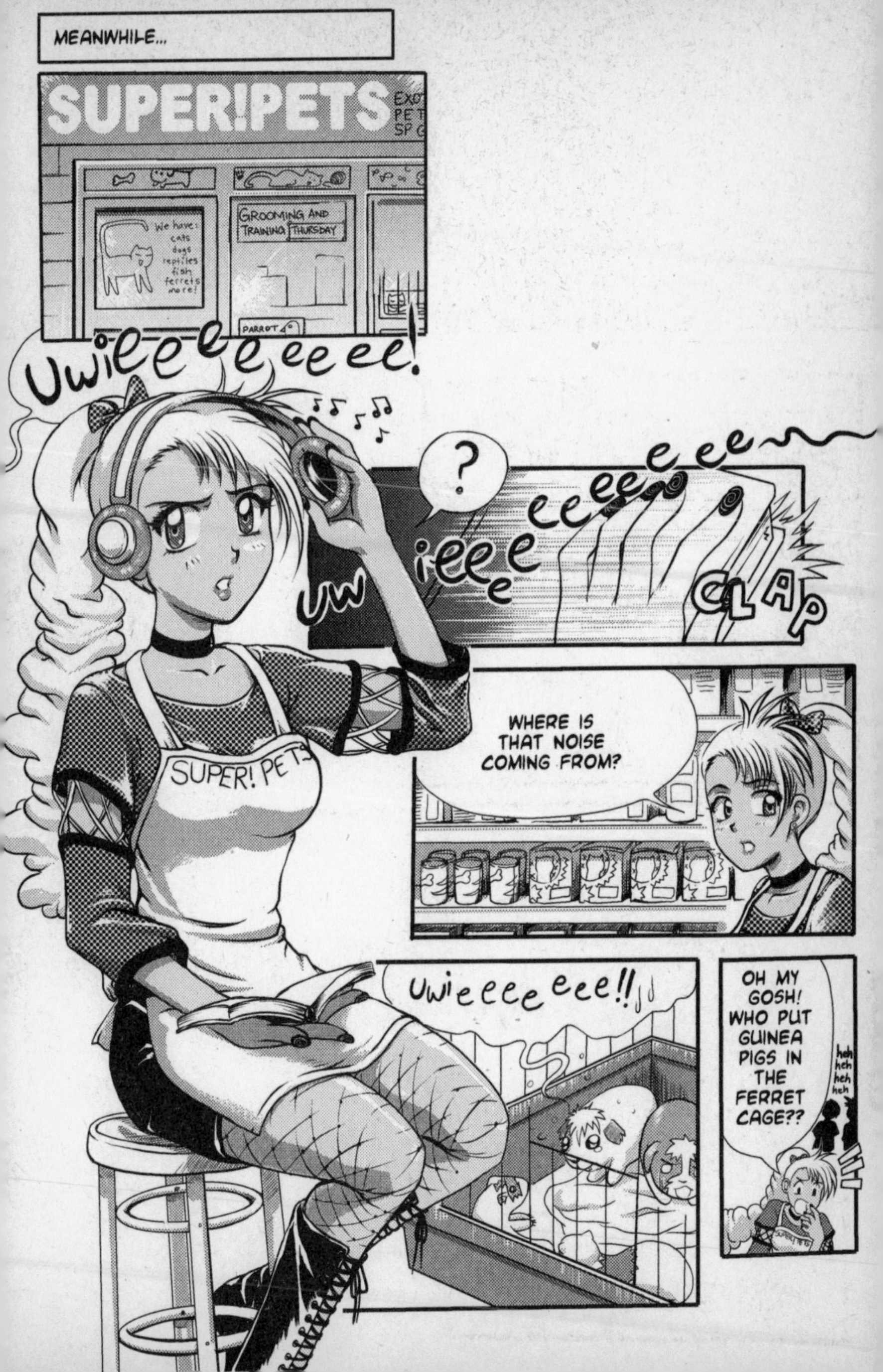

MEANWHILE...
SUPER!PETS
GROOMING AND TRAINING THURSDAY
We have: cats dogs reptiles fish ferrets more!
PARROT
Uwileeleeeeel!
?
Uwileeeeeeeeeeeee~
CLAP
SUPER! PETS
WHERE IS THAT NOISE COMING FROM?
Uwieeeeeee!!
OH MY GOSH! WHO PUT GUINEA PIGS IN THE FERRET CAGE??
heh heh heh heh

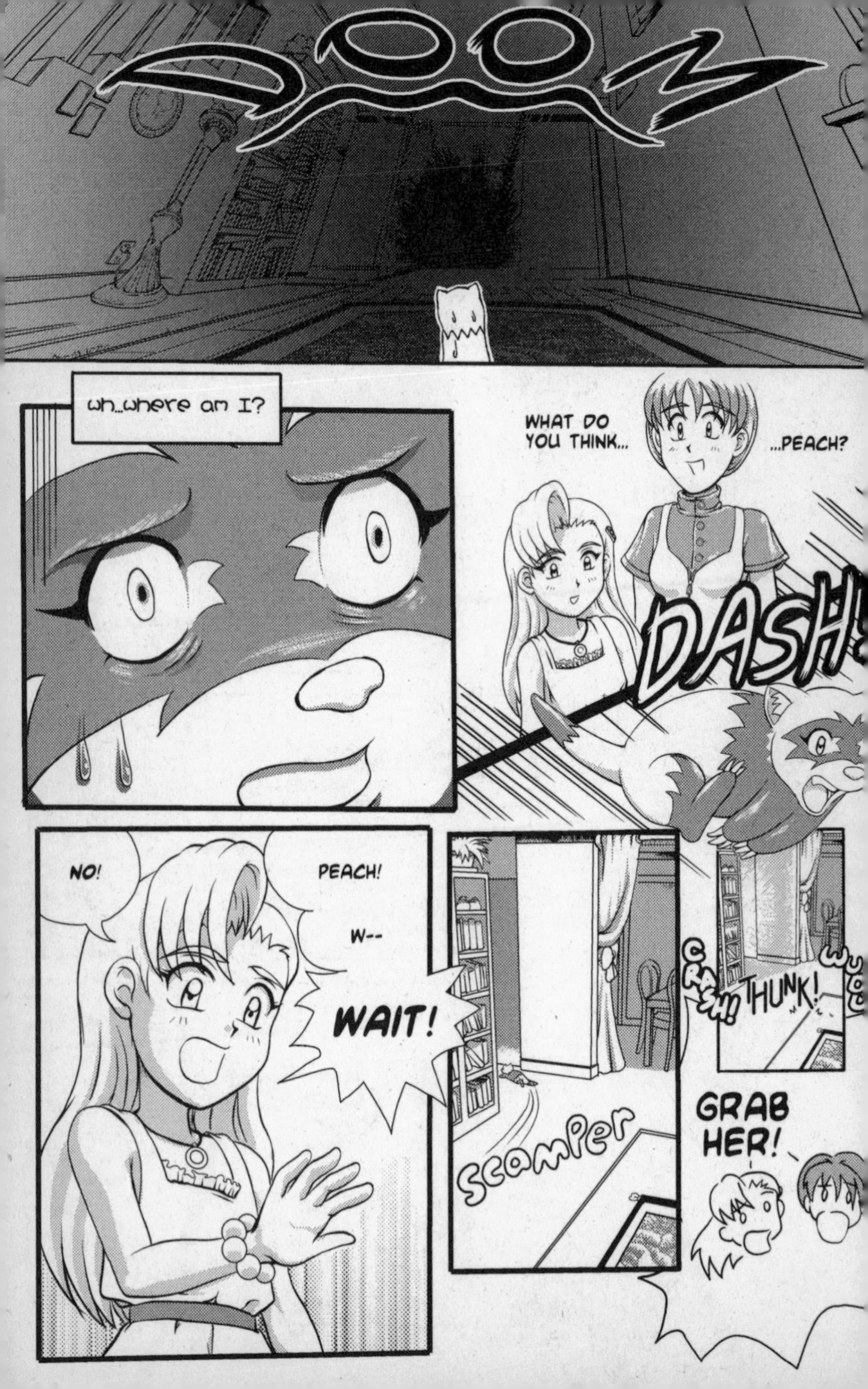
DOOM
wh..where am I?
WHAT DO YOU THINK...
...PEACH?
DASH
NO!
PEACH!
W--
WAIT!
scamper
CRASH!
THUNK!
GRAB HER!

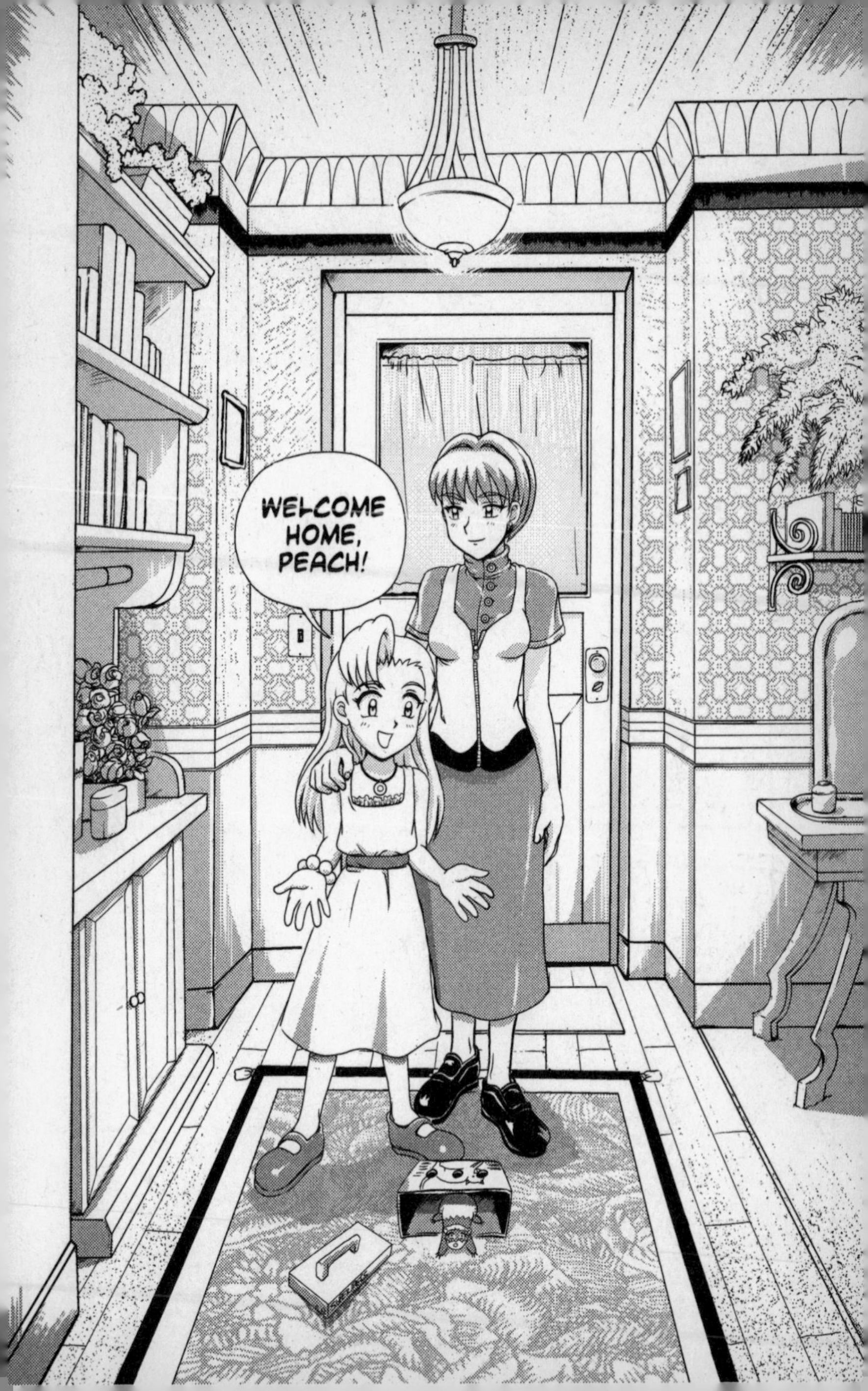
WELCOME HOME, PEACH!

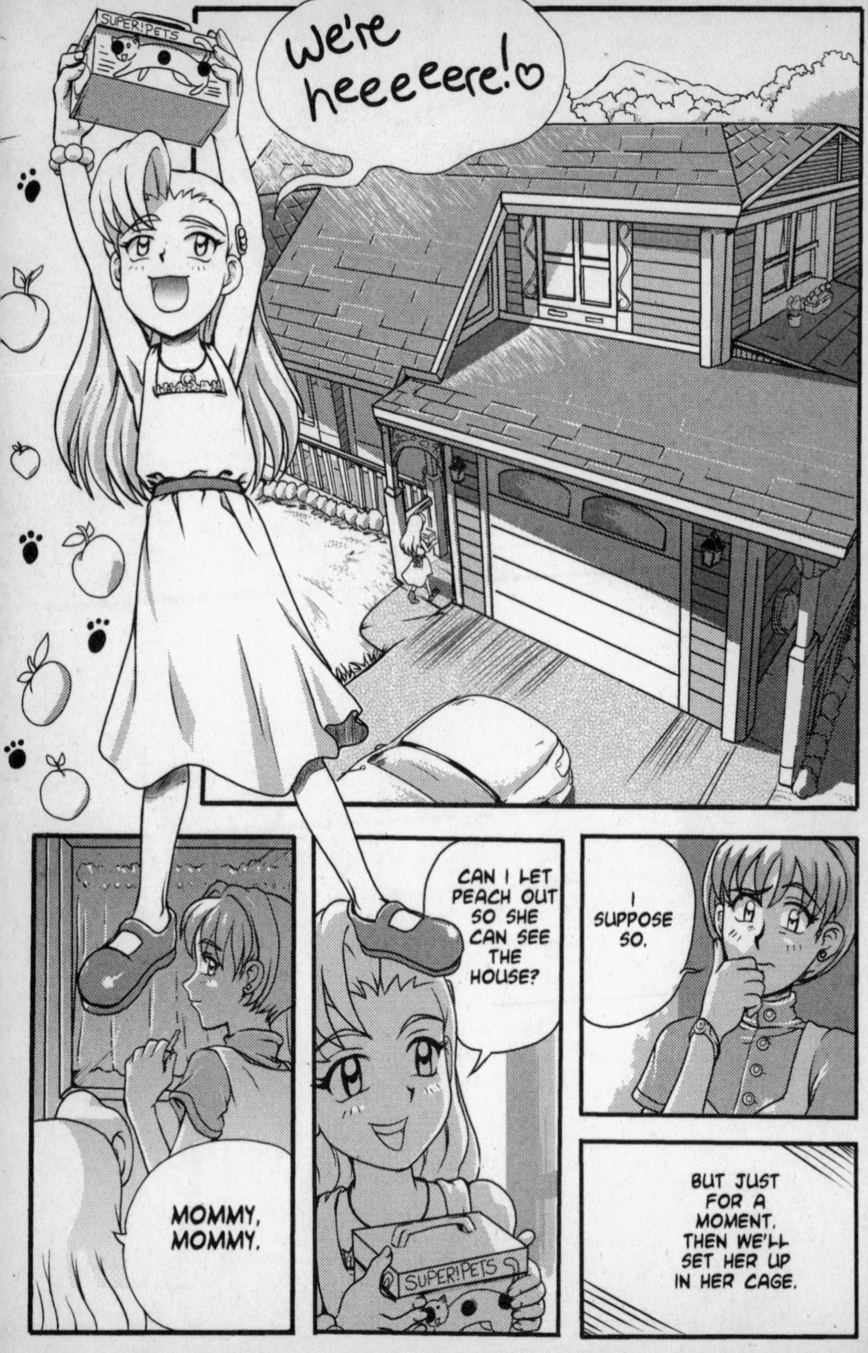
We're heeeeere!♡
SUPER!PETS
MOMMY, MOMMY.
CAN I LET PEACH OUT SO SHE CAN SEE THE HOUSE?
SUPER!PETS
I SUPPOSE SO.
BUT JUST FOR A MOMENT. THEN WE'LL SET HER UP IN HER CAGE.

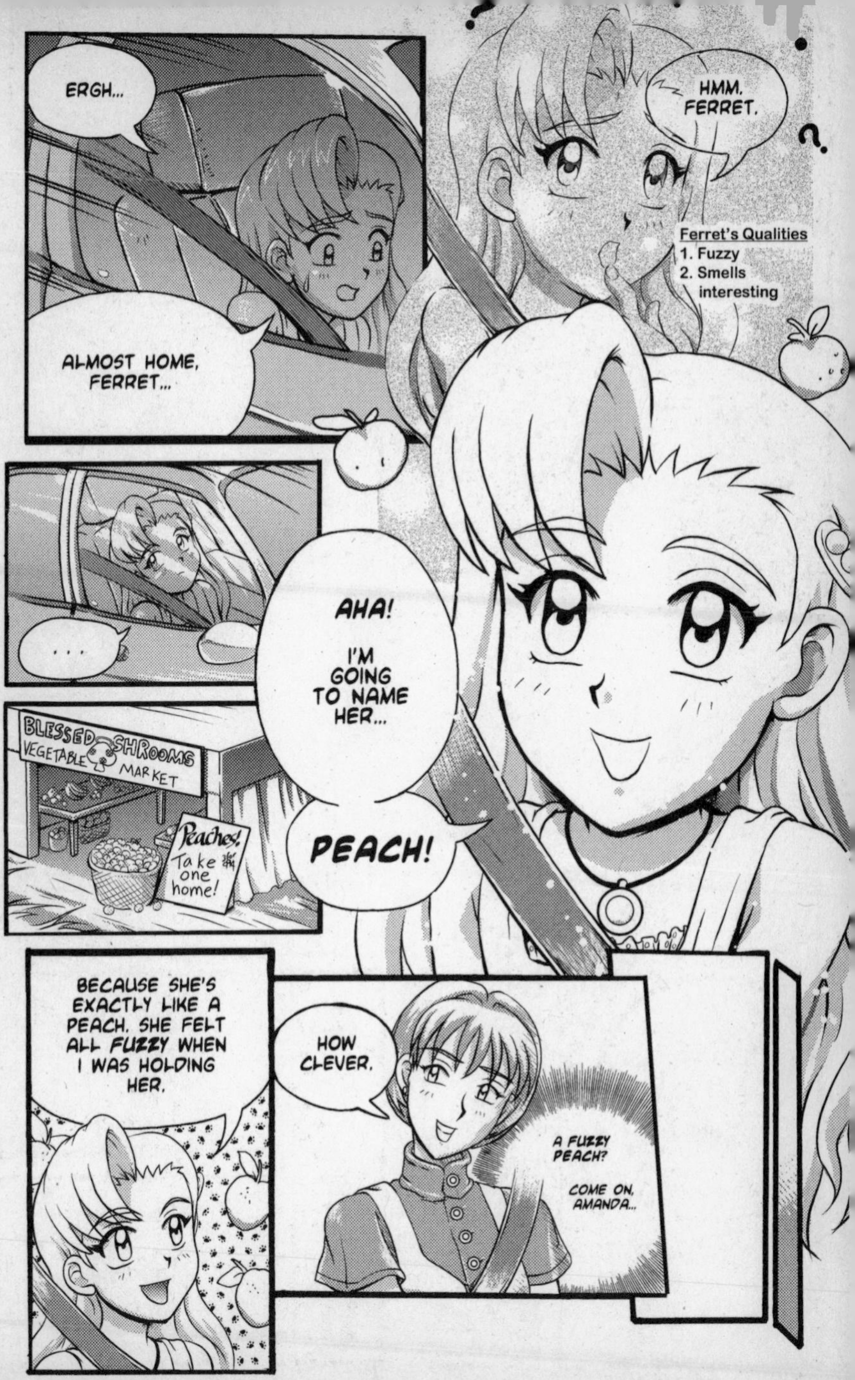
ERGH...
ALMOST HOME, FERRET...
HMM. FERRET.
Ferret's Qualities
1. Fuzzy
2. Smells interesting
...
BLESSED SHROOMS VEGETABLE MARKET
Peaches! Take one home!
AHA! I'M GOING TO NAME HER...
PEACH!
BECAUSE SHE'S EXACTLY LIKE A PEACH. SHE FELT ALL FUZZY WHEN I WAS HOLDING HER.
HOW CLEVER.
A FUZZY PEACH?
COME ON, AMANDA...

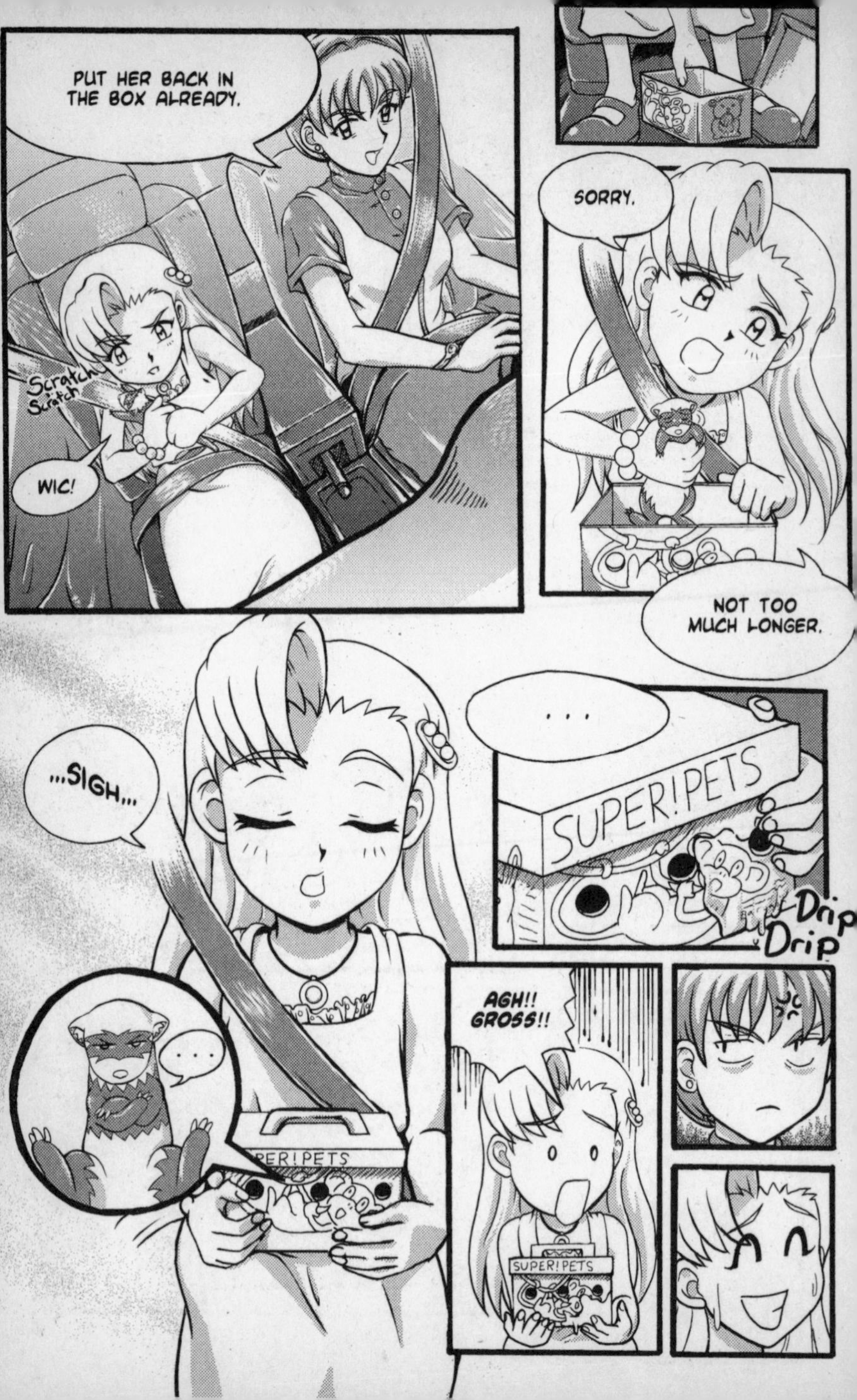
PUT HER BACK IN THE BOX ALREADY.
Scratch Scratch
WIC!
SORRY.
NOT TOO MUCH LONGER.
...SIGH...
. . .
SUPER!PETS
. . .
SUPER!PETS
Drip Drip
AGH!! GROSS!!
SUPER!PETS

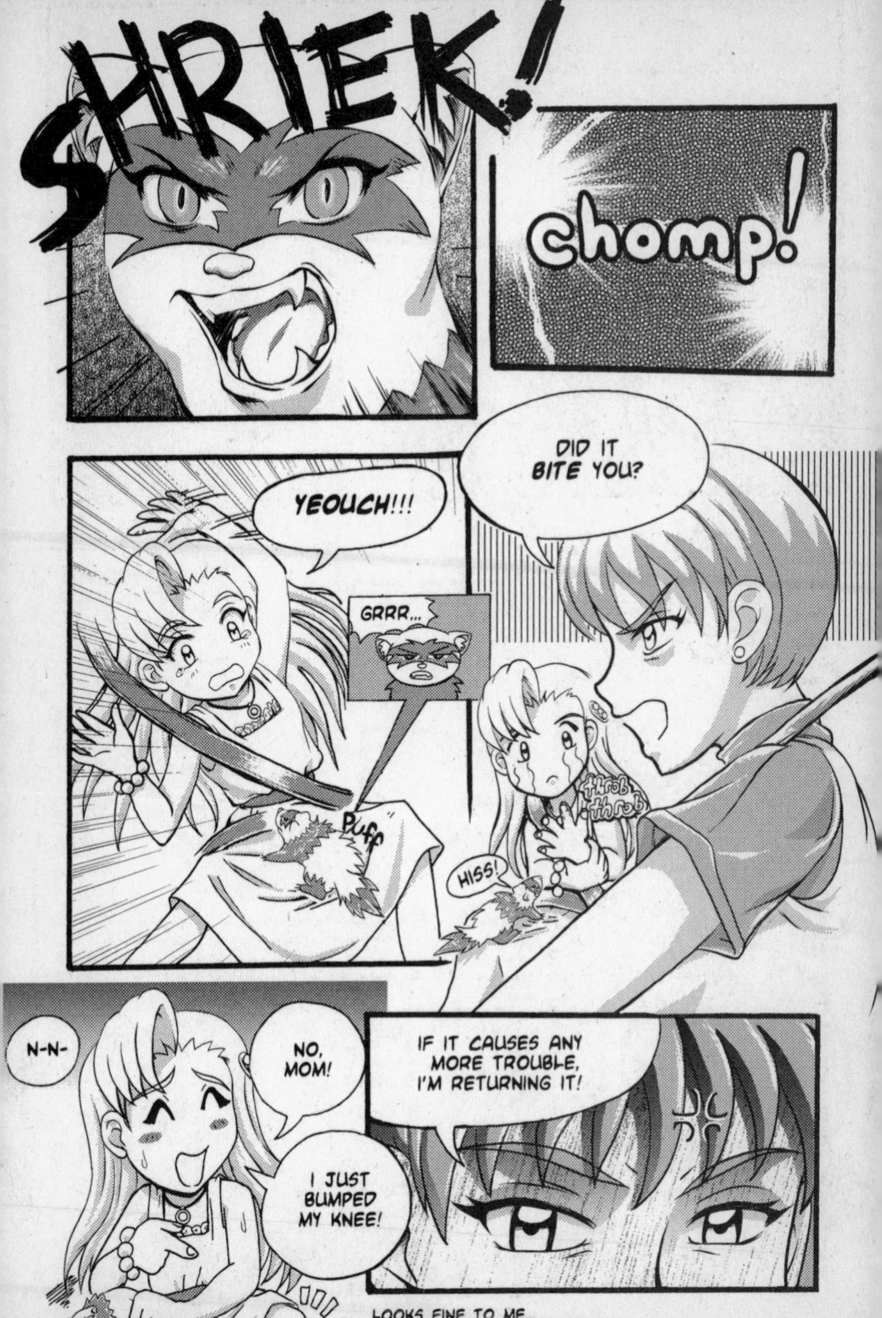
SHRIEK!
chomp!
YEOUCH!!!
GRRR...
Puff
DID IT BITE YOU?
throb throb
HISS!
N-N-
NO, MOM!
I JUST BUMPED MY KNEE!
IF IT CAUSES ANY MORE TROUBLE, I'M RETURNING IT!
LOOKS FINE TO ME...

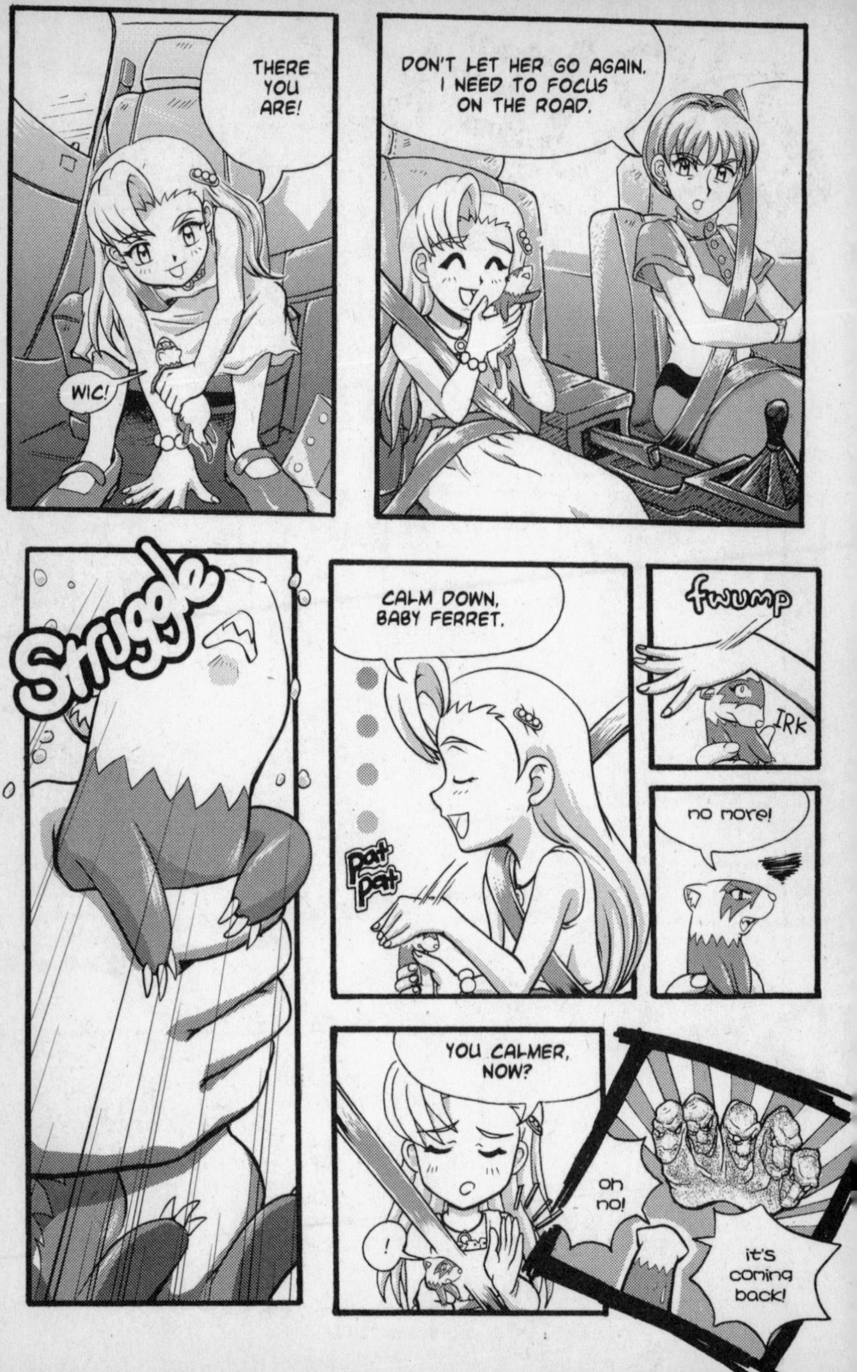
THERE YOU ARE!
WIC!
DON'T LET HER GO AGAIN. I NEED TO FOCUS ON THE ROAD.
Struggle
CALM DOWN, BABY FERRET.
pat pat
fwump
IRK
no more!
YOU CALMER, NOW?
!
oh no!
it's coming back!

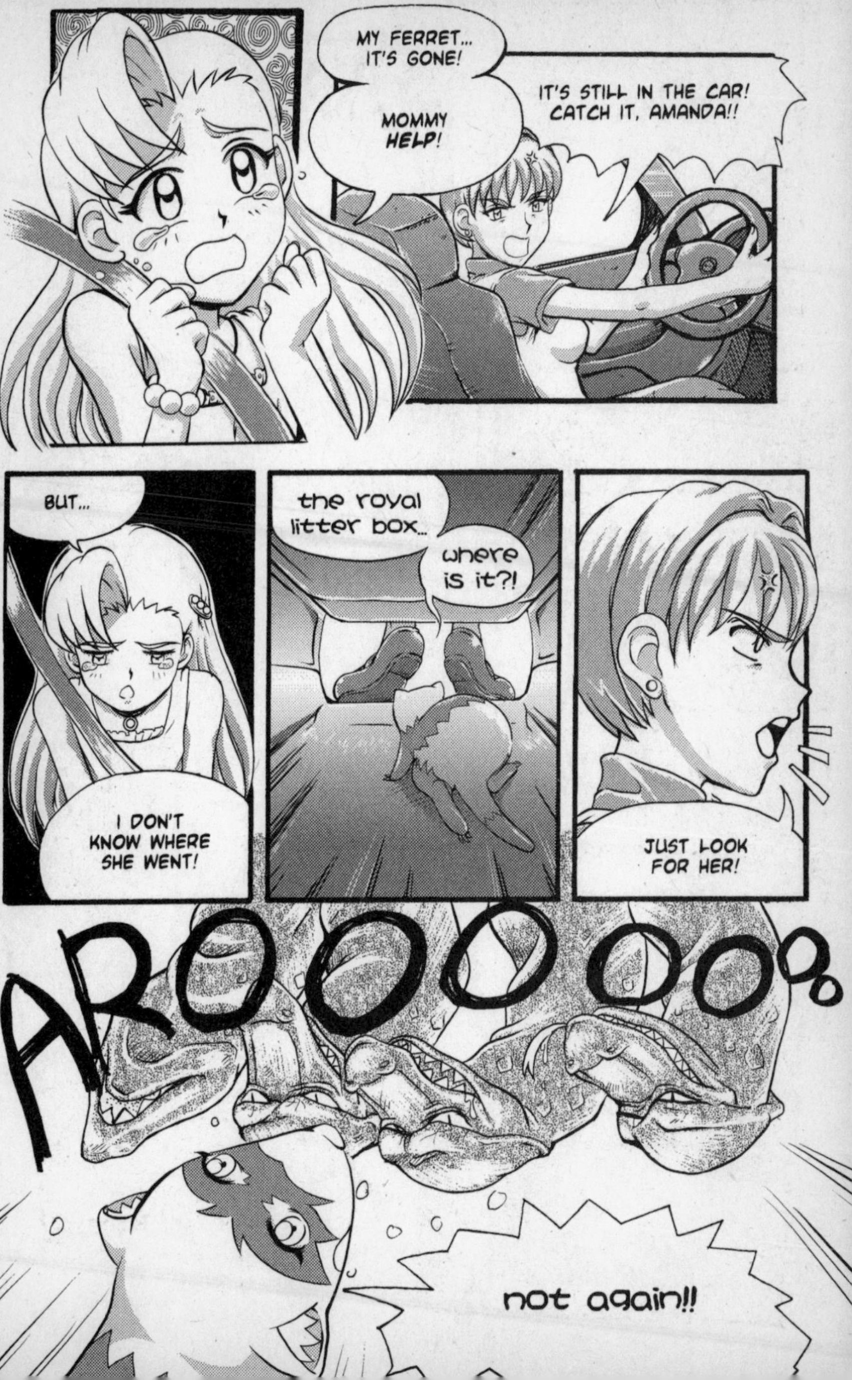
MY FERRET... IT'S GONE!
MOMMY HELP!
IT'S STILL IN THE CAR! CATCH IT, AMANDA!!
BUT...
I DON'T KNOW WHERE SHE WENT!
the royal litter box...
where is it?!
JUST LOOK FOR HER!
AROOOOOo
not again!!

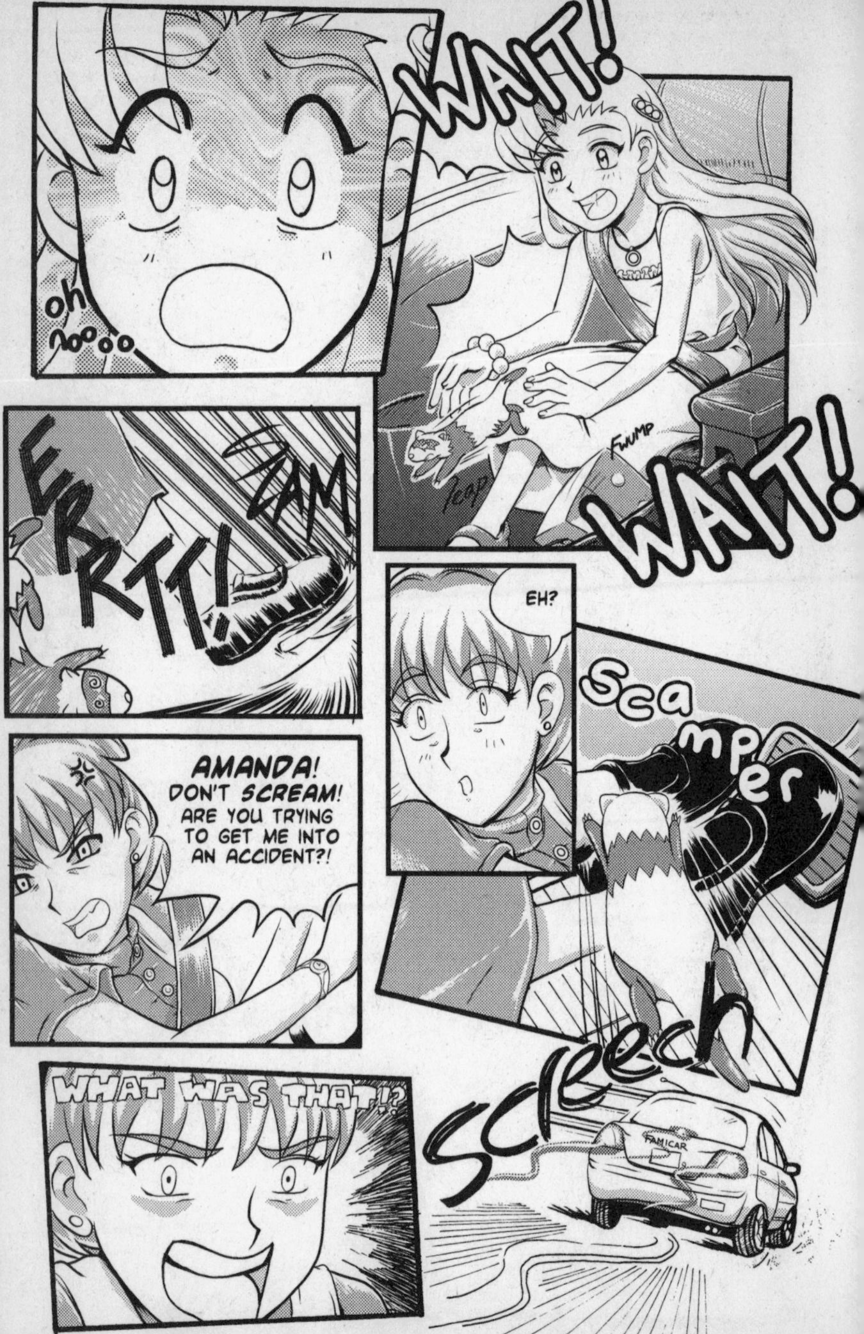
WAIT!
fwump
leap
WAIT!
oh nooooo
EH?
Scamper
ERRTT!
SLAM
AMANDA! DON'T SCREAM! ARE YOU TRYING TO GET ME INTO AN ACCIDENT?!
SCREECH
FAMICAR
WHAT WAS THAT!?

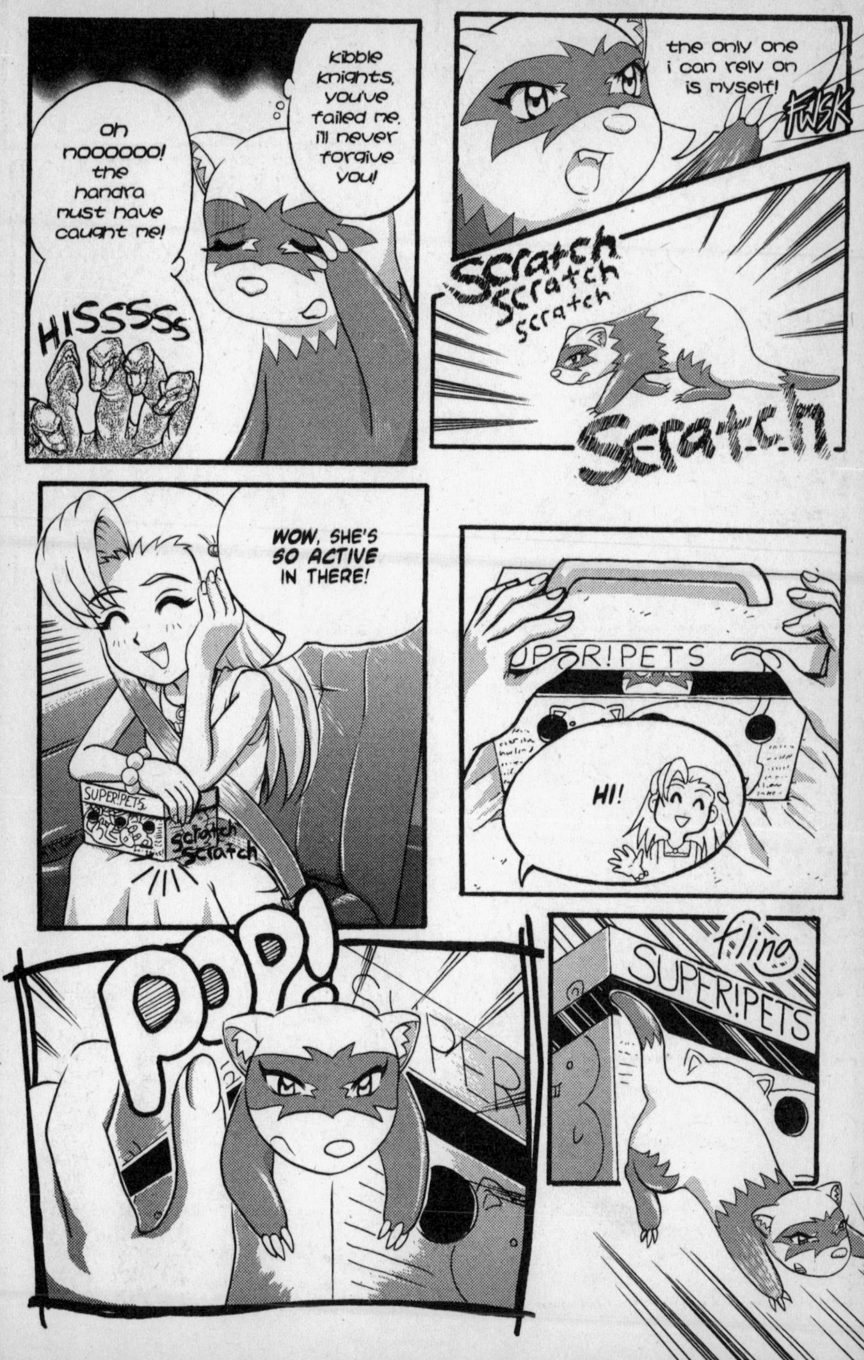
oh noooooo! the handra must have caught me!
kibble knights, you've failed me. i'll never forgive you!
HISSSSs
the only one i can rely on is myself!
FWSK
Scratch
Scratch
Scratch
Scratch
WOW, SHE'S SO ACTIVE IN THERE!
SUPER!PETS
Scratch Scratch
SUPER!PETS
HI!
POP!
fling
SUPER!PETS

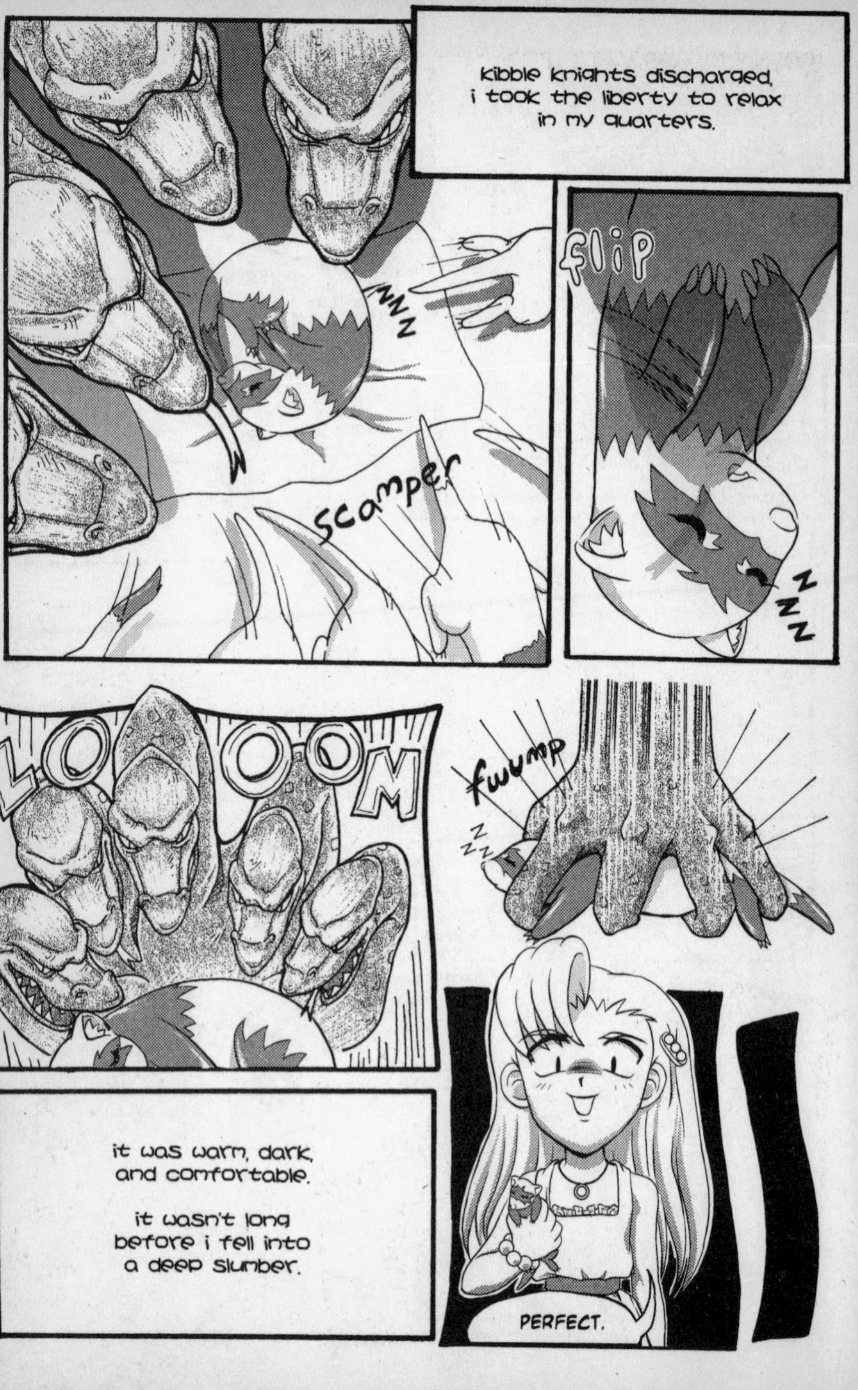
kibble knights discharged,
i took the liberty to relax
in my quarters.
ZZZ
scamper
flip
ZZZ
LOOOOM
fwump
ZZZ
it was warm, dark,
and comfortable.
it wasn't long
before i fell into
a deep slumber.
PERFECT.

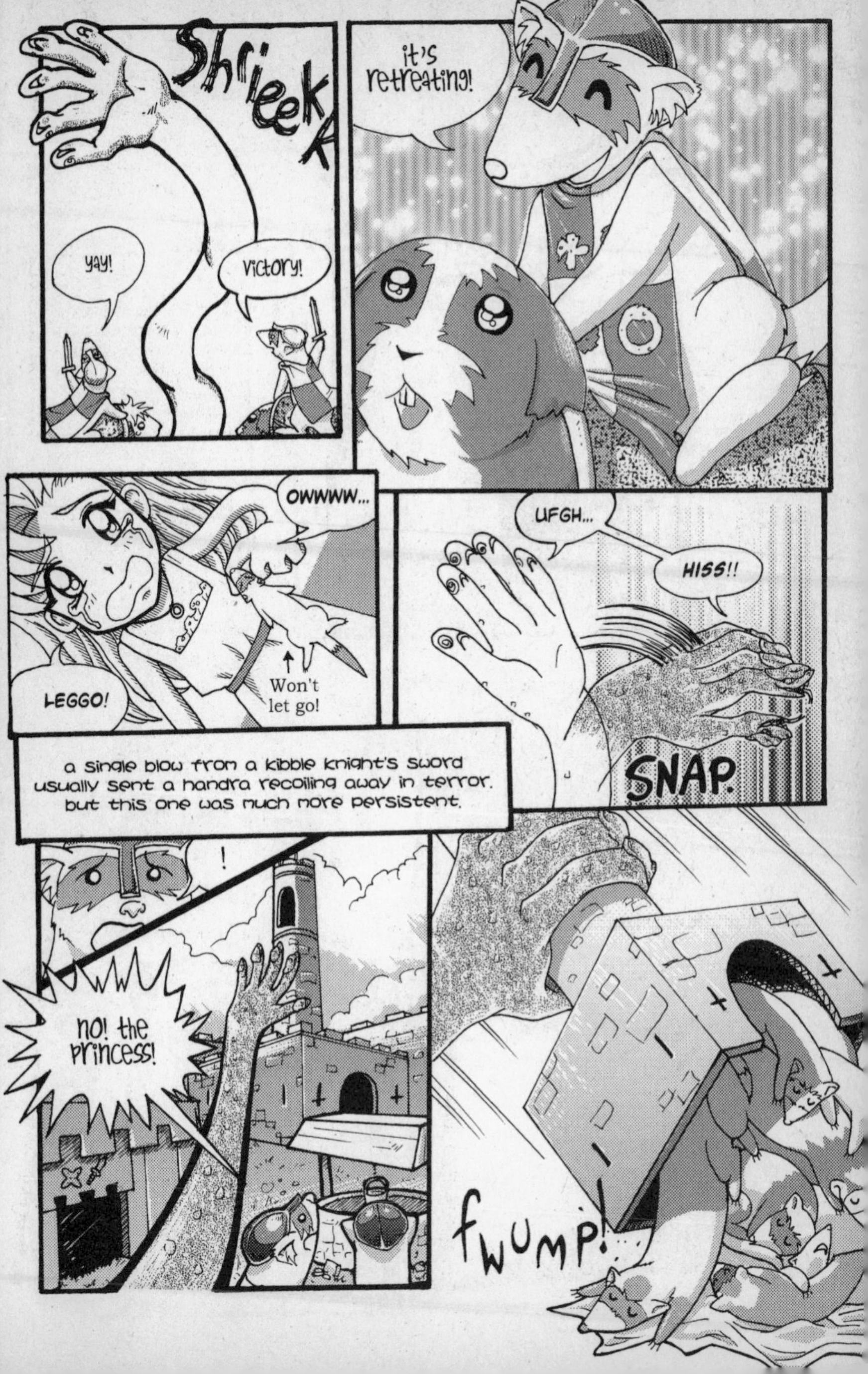
Shrieeek
yay!
Victory!
it's retreating!
OWWWW...
LEGGO!
Won't let go!
UFGH...
HISS!!
SNAP.
a single blow from a kibble knight's sword usually sent a handra recoiling away in terror. but this one was much more persistent.
!
no! the princess!
fwump!

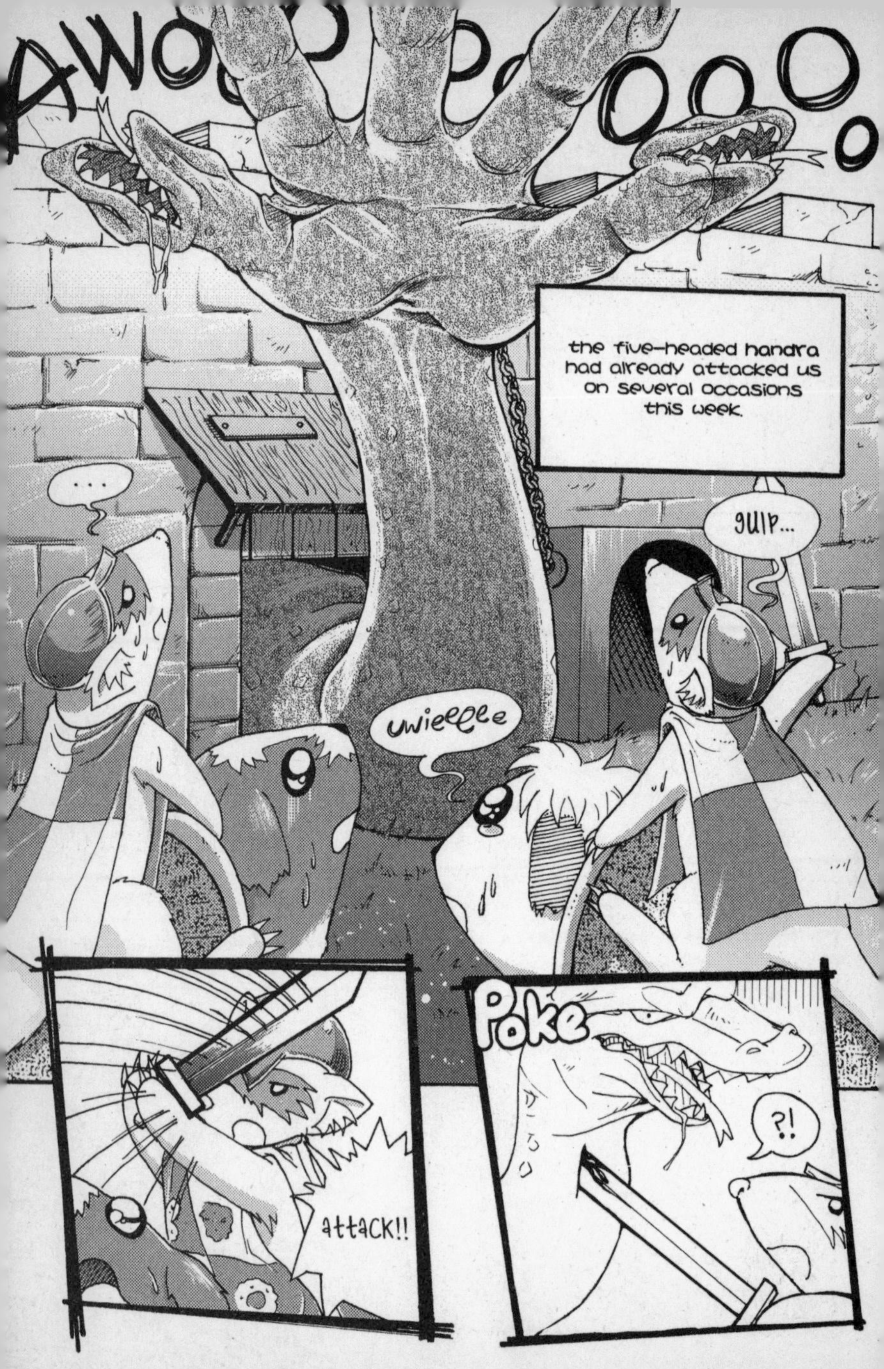
AWOOOOOOOO
the five-headed handra had already attacked us on several occasions this week.
...
gulp...
uwiellle
attack!!
Poke
?!

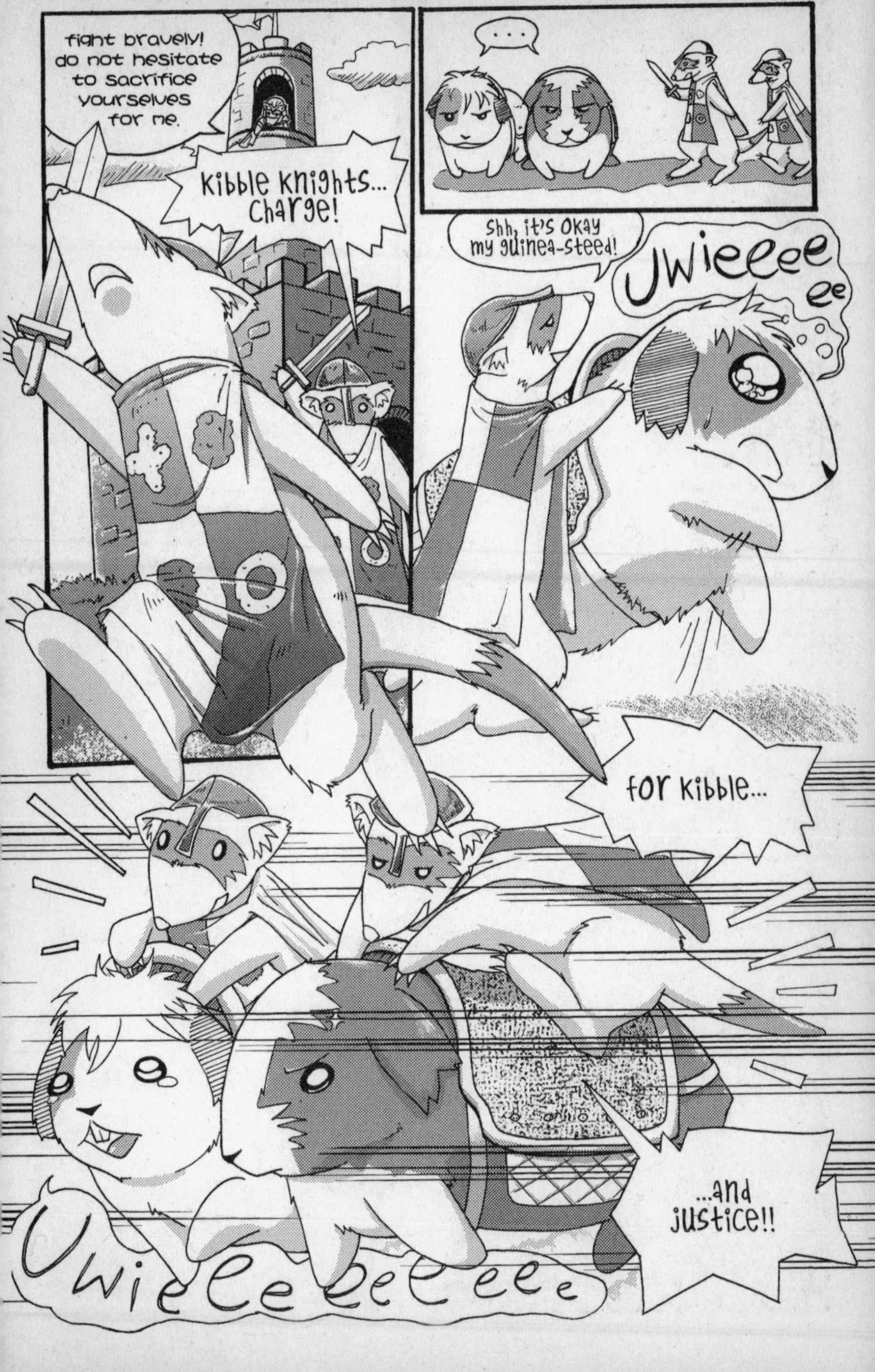
fight bravely! do not hesitate to sacrifice yourselves for me.
Kibble Knights... Charge!
...
Shh, it's Okay my guinea-steed!
Uwieeeee
for kibble...
...and justice!!
Uwieleeeleee

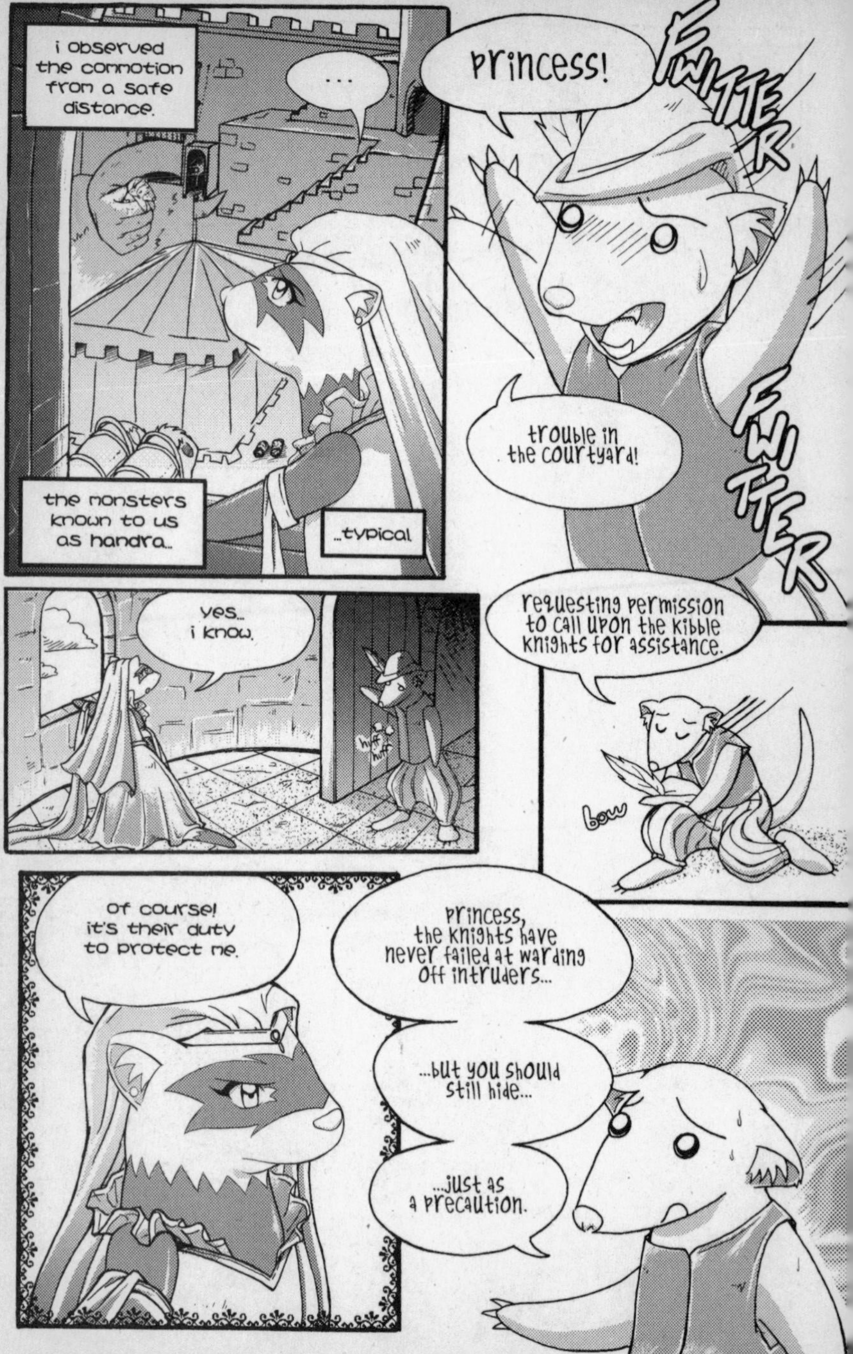
i observed the commotion from a safe distance.
...
the monsters known to us as handra...
...typical.
princess!
FWITTER
trouble in the courtyard!
FWITTER
yes... i know.
huff huff
requesting permission to call upon the kibble knights for assistance.
bow
of course! it's their duty to protect me.
princess, the knights have never failed at warding off intruders...
...but you should still hide...
...just as a precaution.

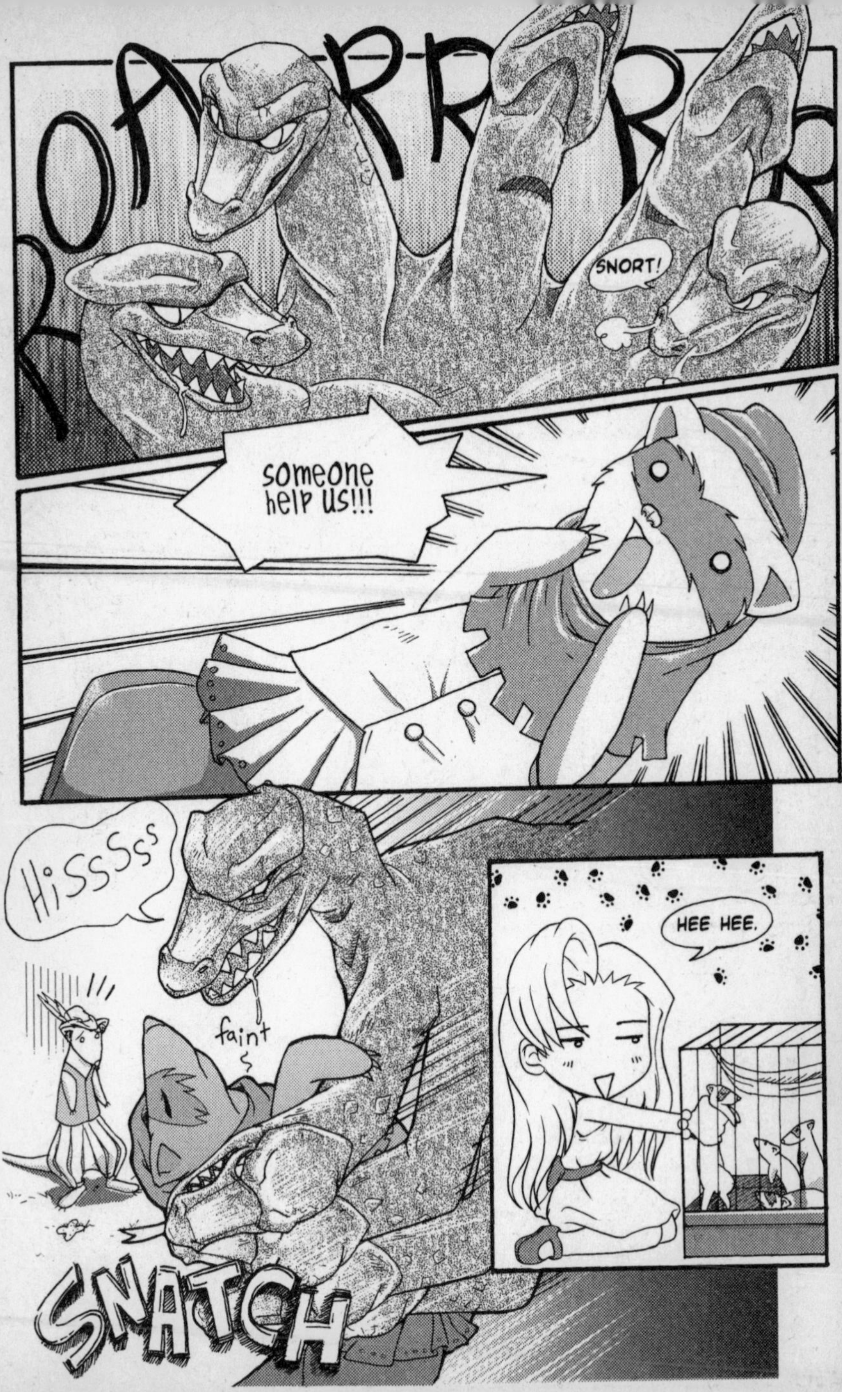
ROARRRRR
SNORT!
someone help us!!!
HiSsSsS
faint
SNATCH
HEE HEE.

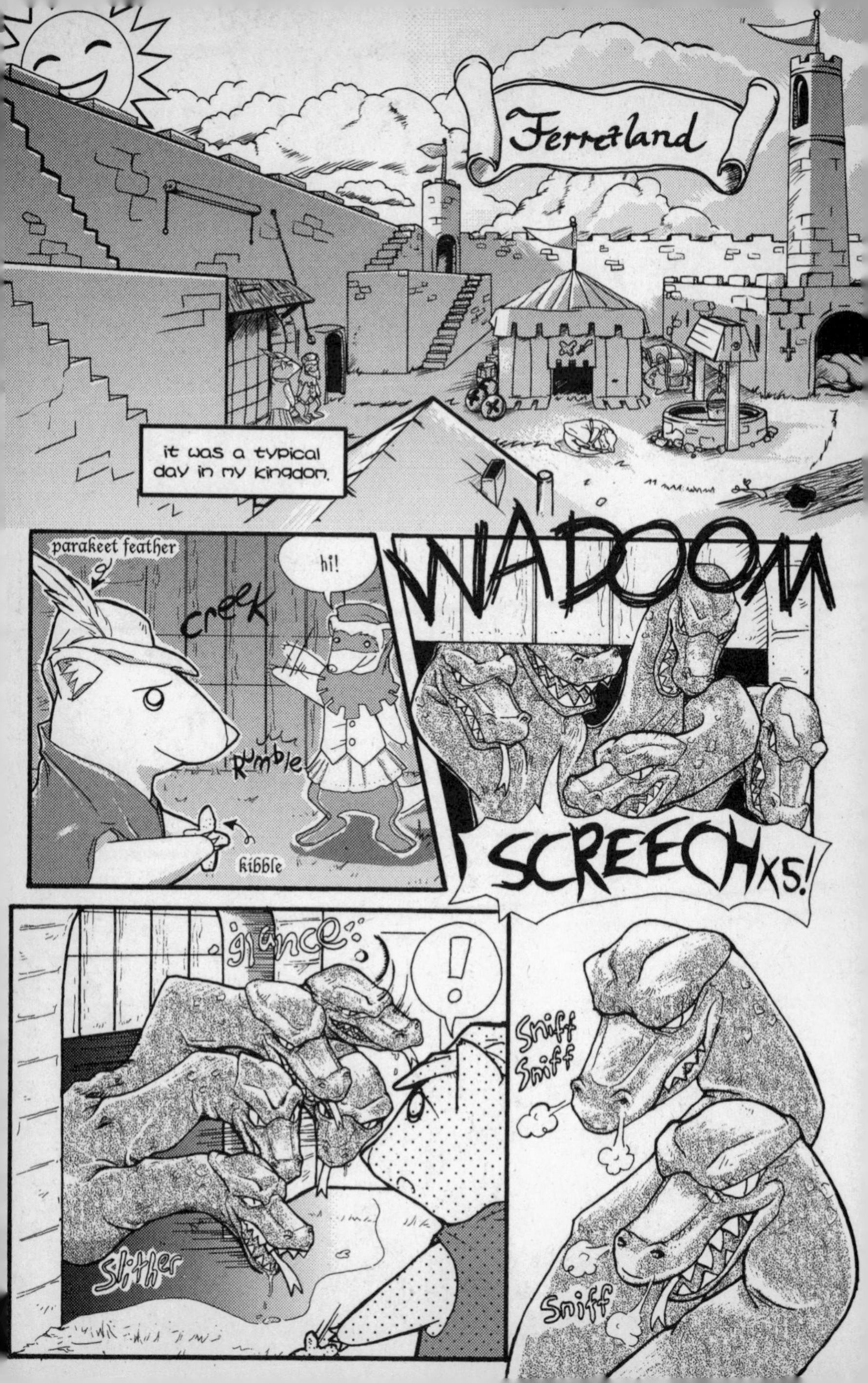
Ferretland
it was a typical day in my kingdom.
parakeet feather
creek
hi!
rumble
kibble
WADOOM
SCREECH x5!
glance
!
slither
Sniff Sniff
Sniff

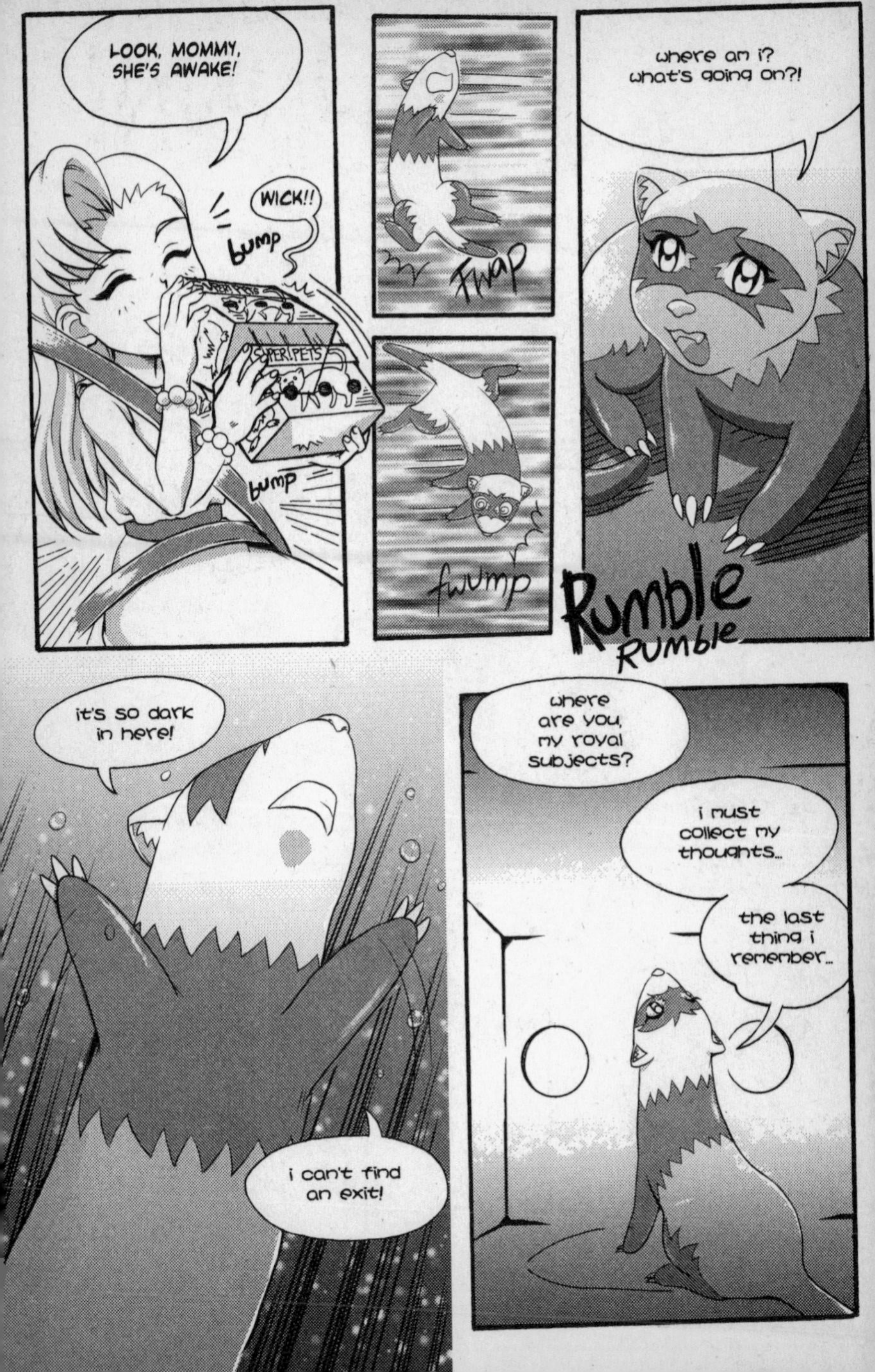
LOOK, MOMMY, SHE'S AWAKE!
WICK!!
bump
SUPER PETS
SUPER PETS
bump
Fwap
fwump
where am i? what's going on?!
Rumble
Rumble
it's so dark in here!
i can't find an exit!
where are you, my royal subjects?
i must collect my thoughts...
the last thing i remember...

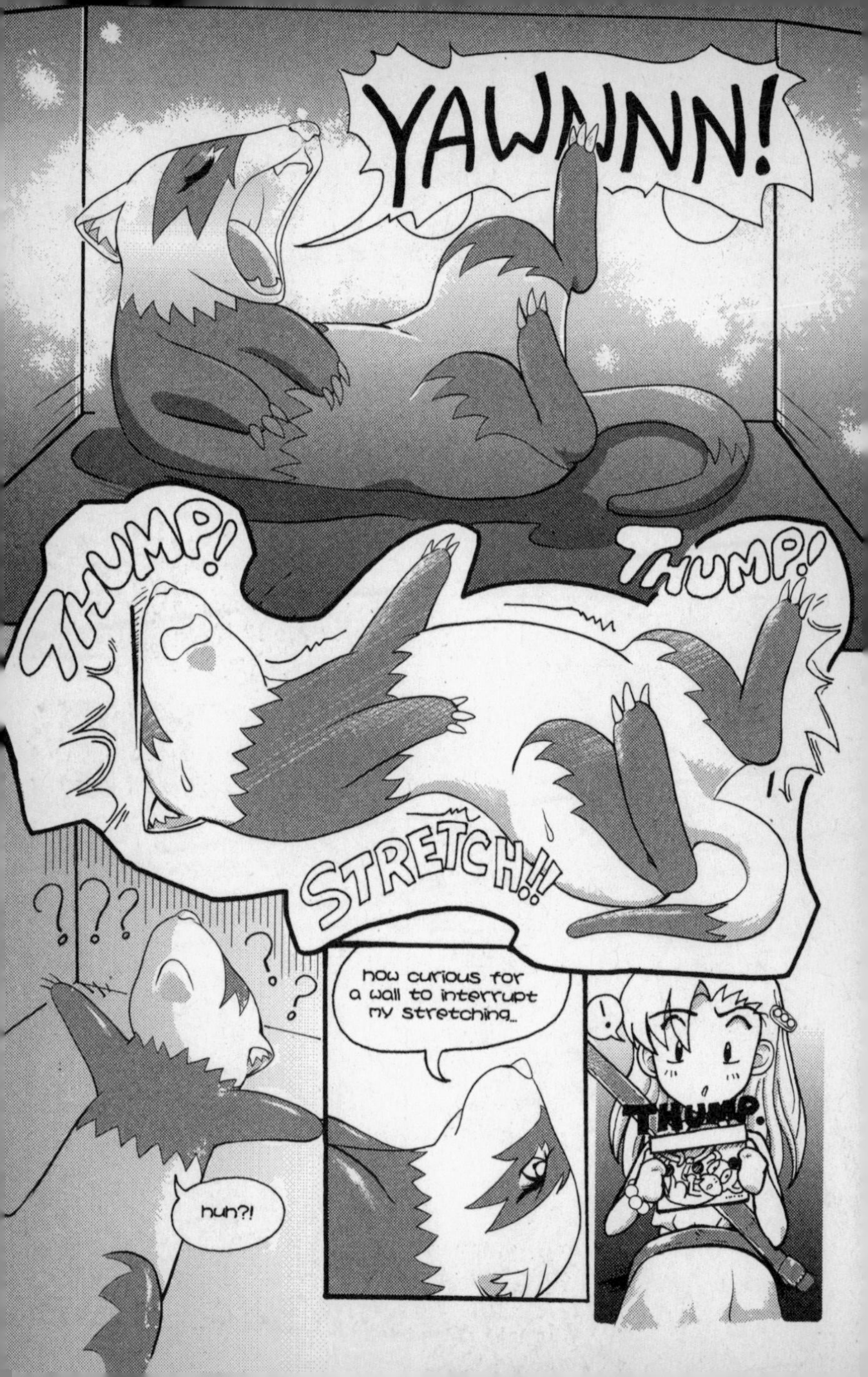
YAWNNN!
THUMP!
THUMP!
STRETCH!!
!
THUMP.
how curious for a wall to interrupt my stretching...
???
??
huh?!

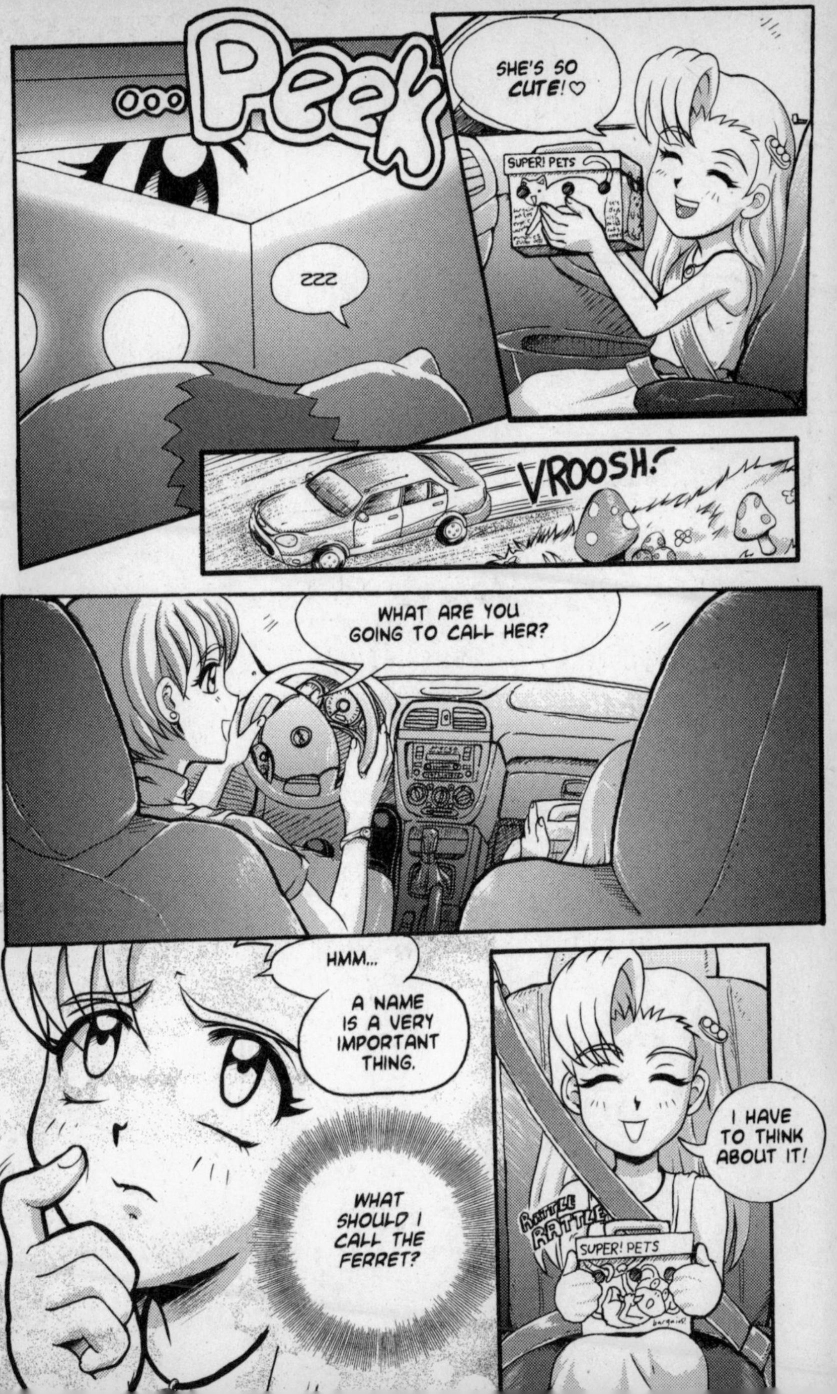

...Peek
ZZZ
SHE'S SO CUTE! ♡
SUPER! PETS
VROOSH!
WHAT ARE YOU GOING TO CALL HER?
HMM...
A NAME IS A VERY IMPORTANT THING.
WHAT SHOULD I CALL THE FERRET?
I HAVE TO THINK ABOUT IT!
RATTLE RATTLE
SUPER! PETS

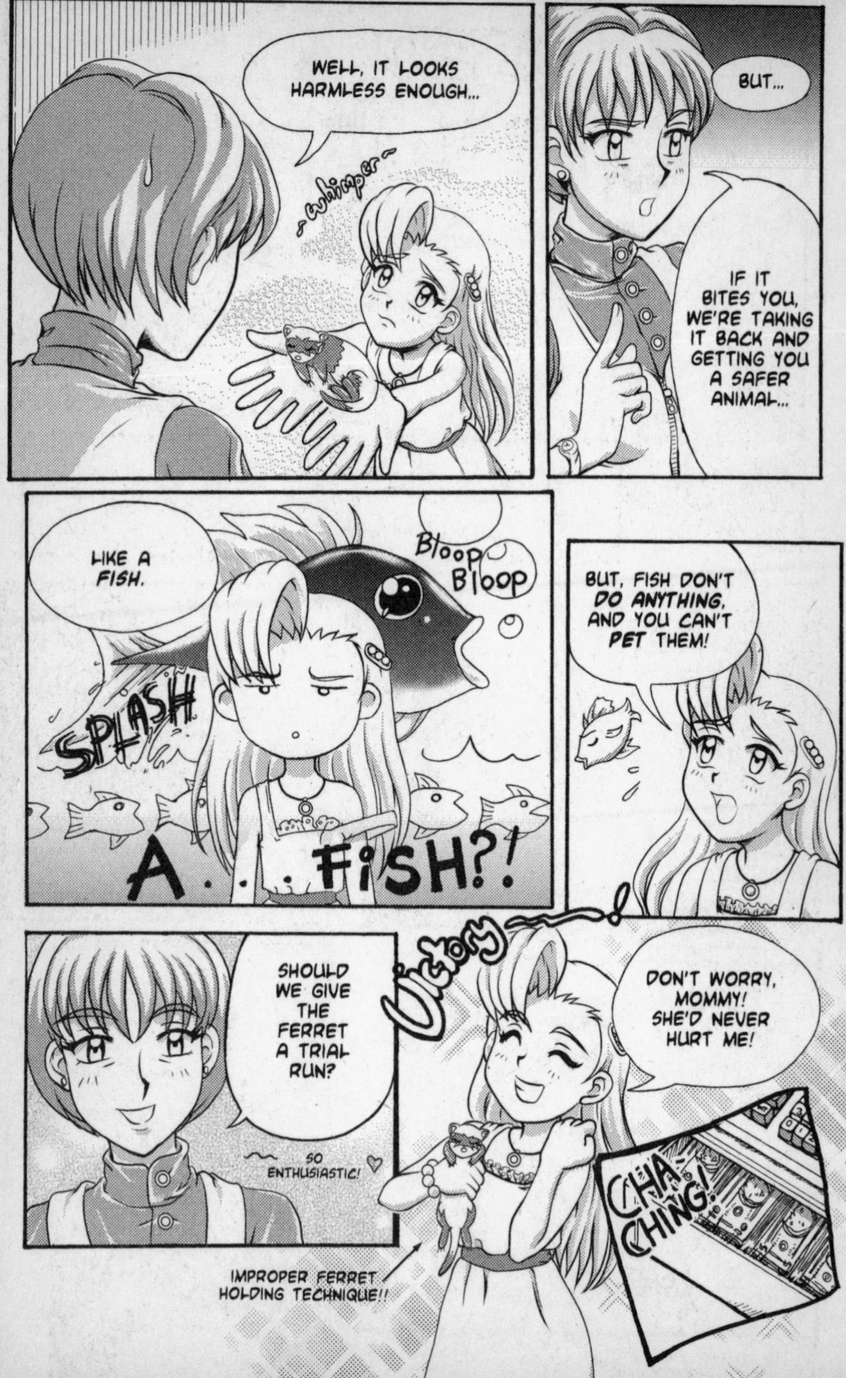
WELL, IT LOOKS HARMLESS ENOUGH...
~whimper~
BUT...
IF IT BITES YOU, WE'RE TAKING IT BACK AND GETTING YOU A SAFER ANIMAL...
LIKE A FISH.
SPLASH
Bloop Bloop
A... FISH?!
BUT, FISH DON'T DO ANYTHING, AND YOU CAN'T PET THEM!
SHOULD WE GIVE THE FERRET A TRIAL RUN?
~ SO ENTHUSIASTIC! ♡
Victory
DON'T WORRY, MOMMY! SHE'D NEVER HURT ME!
CHA-CHING!
IMPROPER FERRET HOLDING TECHNIQUE!!

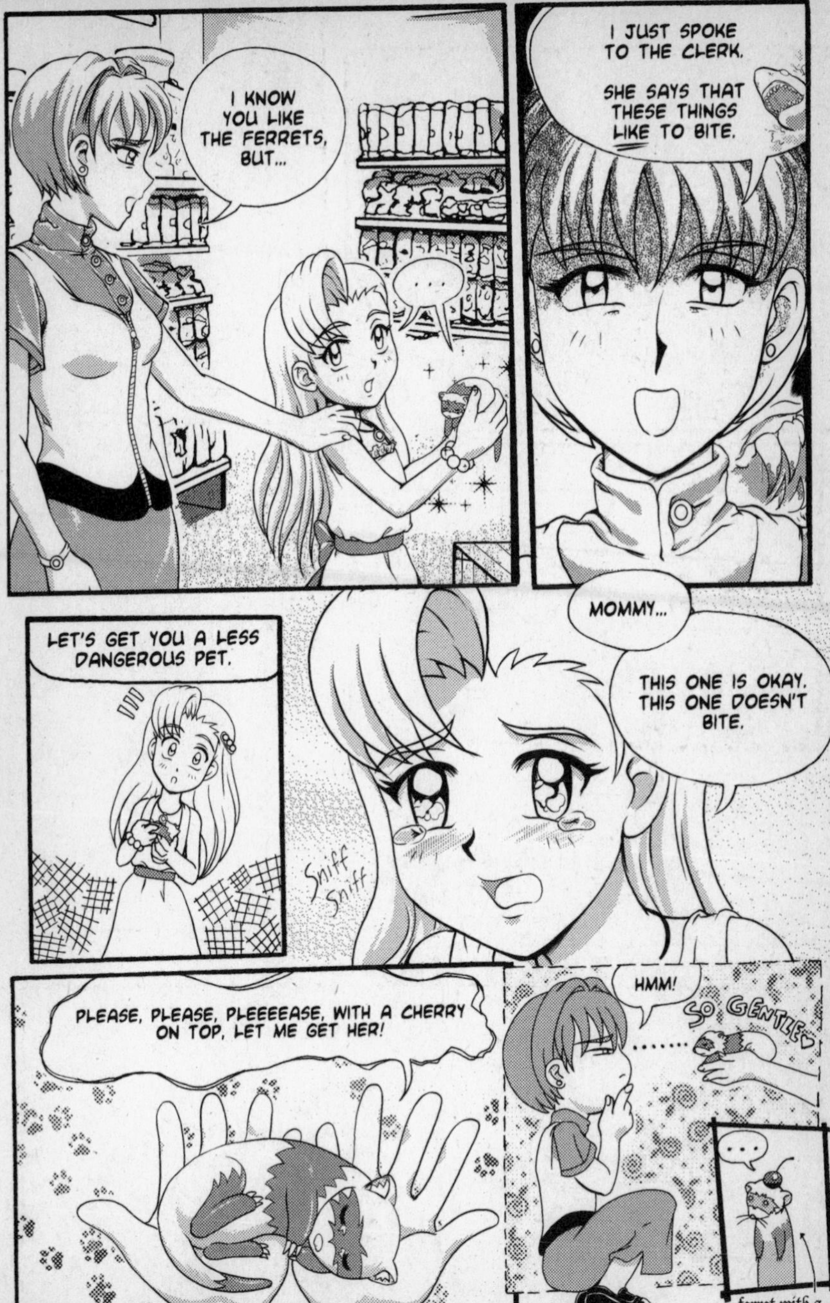
I KNOW YOU LIKE THE FERRETS, BUT...
...
I JUST SPOKE TO THE CLERK.
SHE SAYS THAT THESE THINGS LIKE TO BITE.
LET'S GET YOU A LESS DANGEROUS PET.
MOMMY...
THIS ONE IS OKAY. THIS ONE DOESN'T BITE.
Sniff Sniff
PLEASE, PLEASE, PLEEEEASE, WITH A CHERRY ON TOP, LET ME GET HER!
HMM!
....
SO GENTLE
...
ferret with a cherry on top

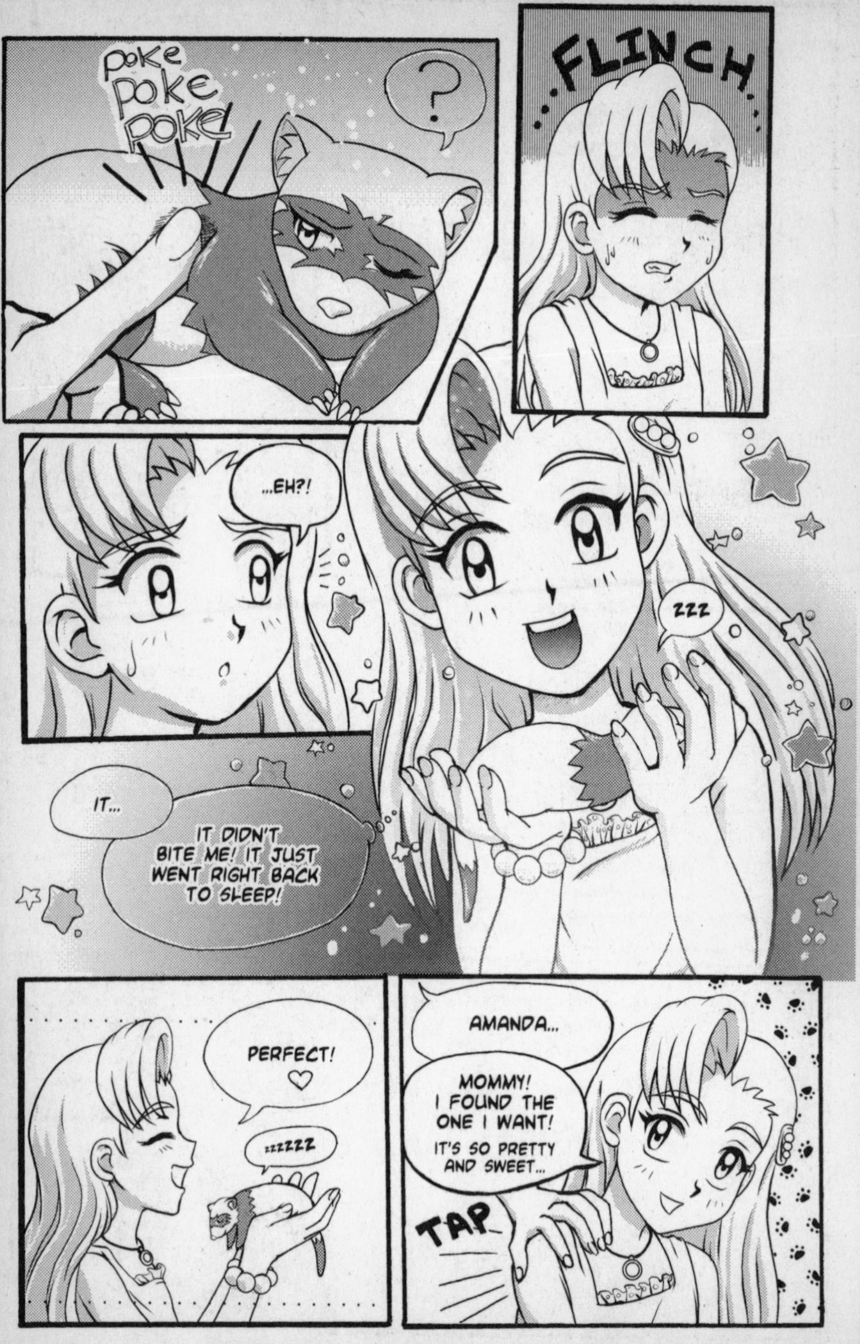
POKE POKE POKE
?
FLINCH
...EH?!
ZZZ
IT...
IT DIDN'T BITE ME! IT JUST WENT RIGHT BACK TO SLEEP!
PERFECT! ♡
zzzZZZ
AMANDA...
MOMMY! I FOUND THE ONE I WANT! IT'S SO PRETTY AND SWEET...
TAP

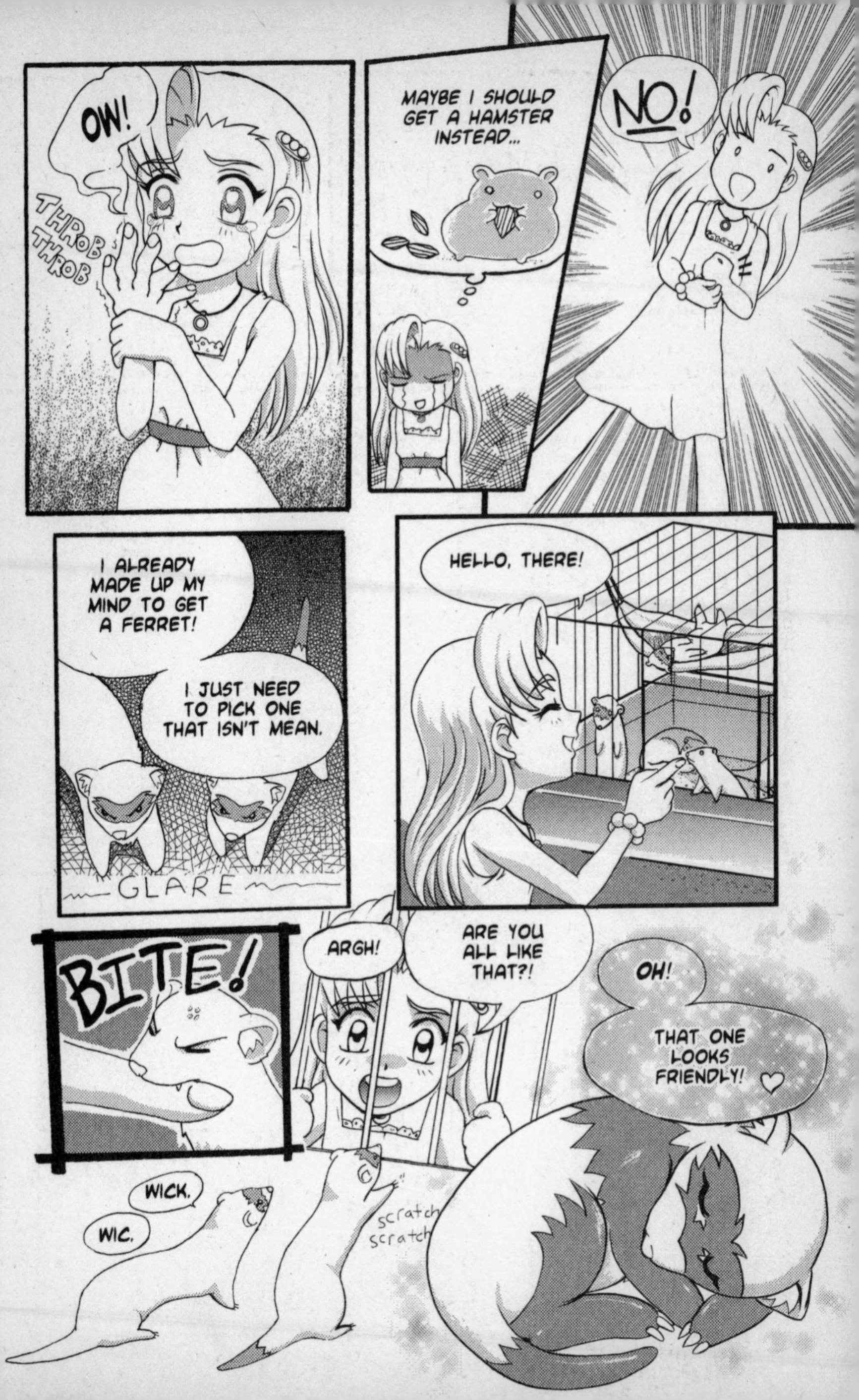
OW!
THROB THROB
MAYBE I SHOULD GET A HAMSTER INSTEAD...
NO!
I ALREADY MADE UP MY MIND TO GET A FERRET!
I JUST NEED TO PICK ONE THAT ISN'T MEAN.
GLARE
HELLO, THERE!
BITE!
ARGH!
ARE YOU ALL LIKE THAT?!
OH!
THAT ONE LOOKS FRIENDLY!
WICK.
WIC.
scratch scratch

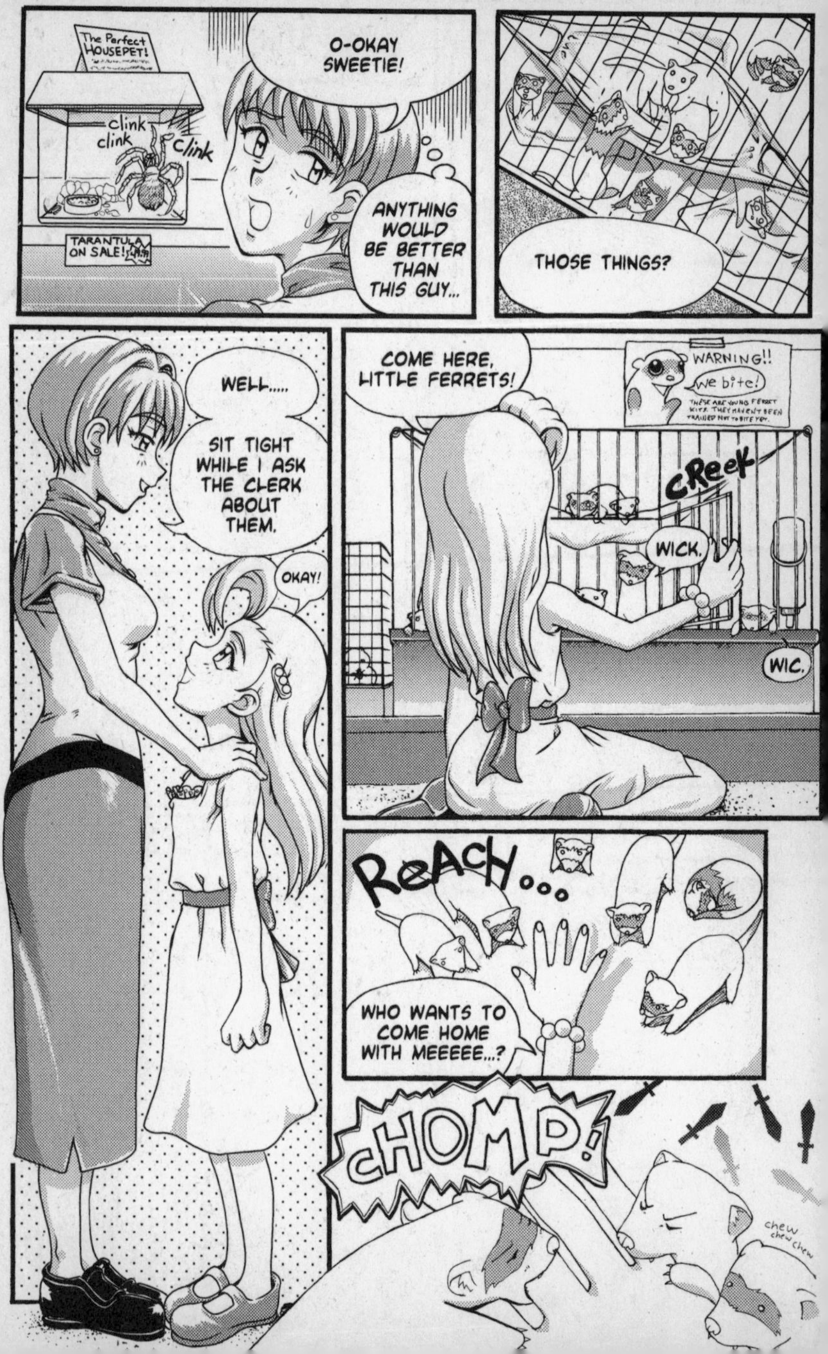
The Perfect HOUSEPET!
clink
clink
clink
TARANTULA ON SALE!
O-OKAY SWEETIE!
ANYTHING WOULD BE BETTER THAN THIS GUY...
THOSE THINGS?
WELL.....
SIT TIGHT WHILE I ASK THE CLERK ABOUT THEM.
OKAY!
COME HERE, LITTLE FERRETS!
WARNING!!
We bite!
THESE ARE YOUNG FERRET KITS. THEY HAVEN'T BEEN TRAINED NOT TO BITE YET.
CReek
WICK.
WIC.
ReACH...
WHO WANTS TO COME HOME WITH MEEEEE...?
CHOMP!
chew chew chew

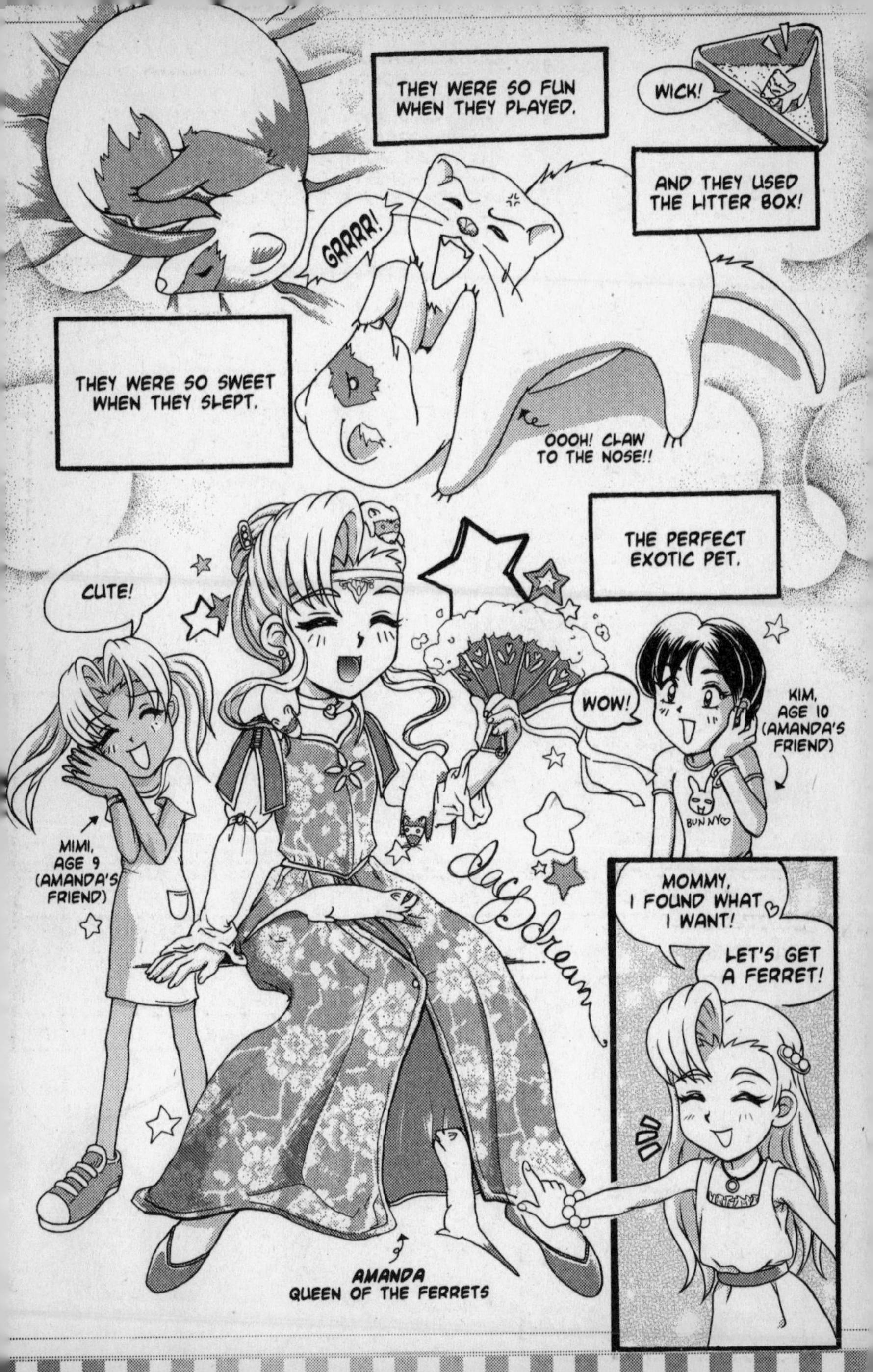
THEY WERE SO SWEET WHEN THEY SLEPT.
THEY WERE SO FUN WHEN THEY PLAYED.
GRRRR!
OOOH! CLAW TO THE NOSE!!
WICK!
AND THEY USED THE LITTER BOX!
THE PERFECT EXOTIC PET.
CUTE!
MIMI, AGE 9 (AMANDA'S FRIEND)
DAYDREAM
AMANDA QUEEN OF THE FERRETS
WOW!
KIM, AGE 10 (AMANDA'S FRIEND)
BUNNY
MOMMY, I FOUND WHAT I WANT!
LET'S GET A FERRET!

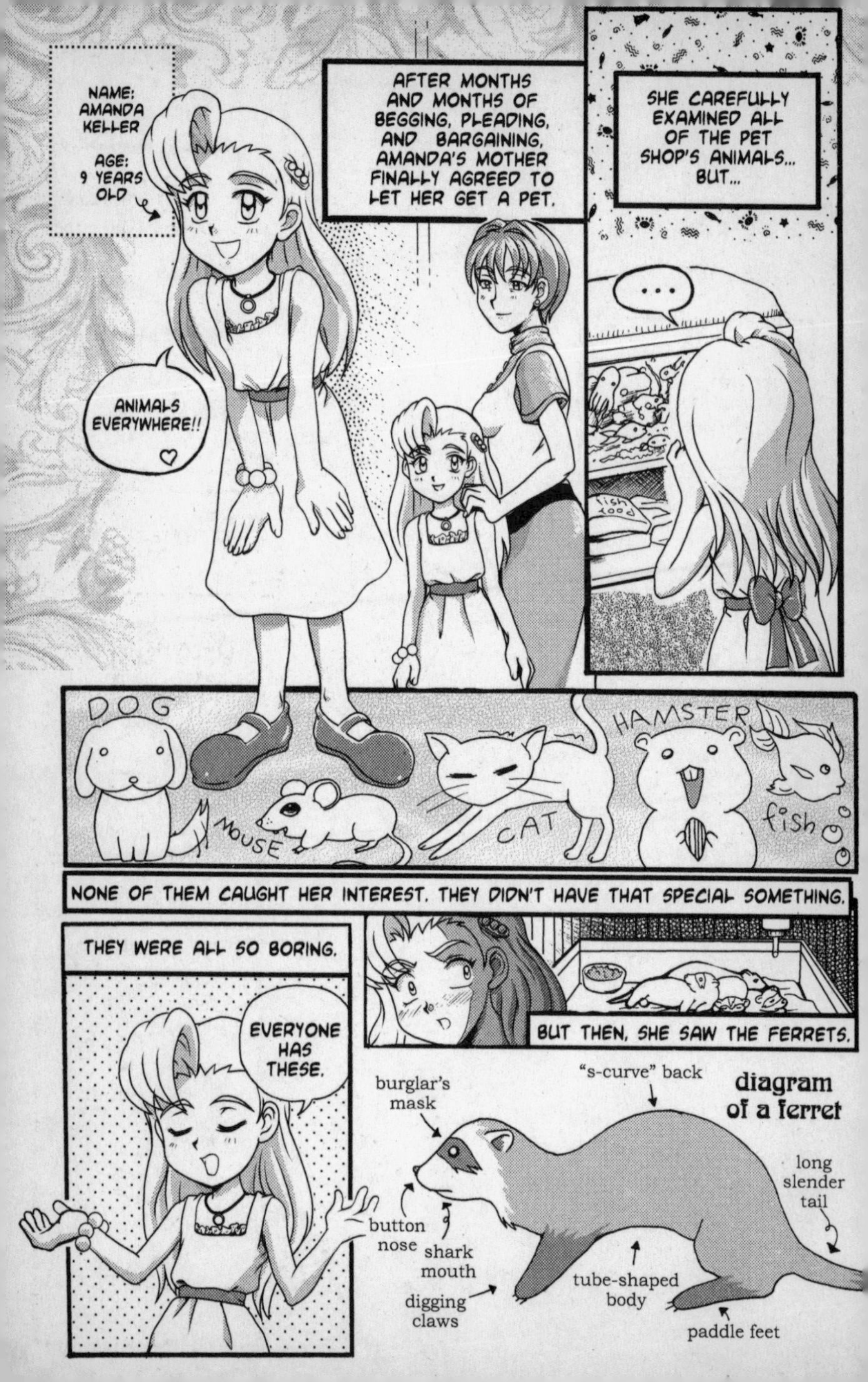
NAME: AMANDA KELLER
AGE: 9 YEARS OLD
ANIMALS EVERYWHERE!! ♡
AFTER MONTHS AND MONTHS OF BEGGING, PLEADING, AND BARGAINING, AMANDA'S MOTHER FINALLY AGREED TO LET HER GET A PET.
SHE CAREFULLY EXAMINED ALL OF THE PET SHOP'S ANIMALS... BUT...
...
DOG
MOUSE
CAT
HAMSTER
fish
NONE OF THEM CAUGHT HER INTEREST. THEY DIDN'T HAVE THAT SPECIAL SOMETHING.
THEY WERE ALL SO BORING.
EVERYONE HAS THESE.
BUT THEN, SHE SAW THE FERRETS.
diagram of a ferret
burglar's mask
"s-curve" back
long slender tail
button nose
shark mouth
digging claws
tube-shaped body
paddle feet

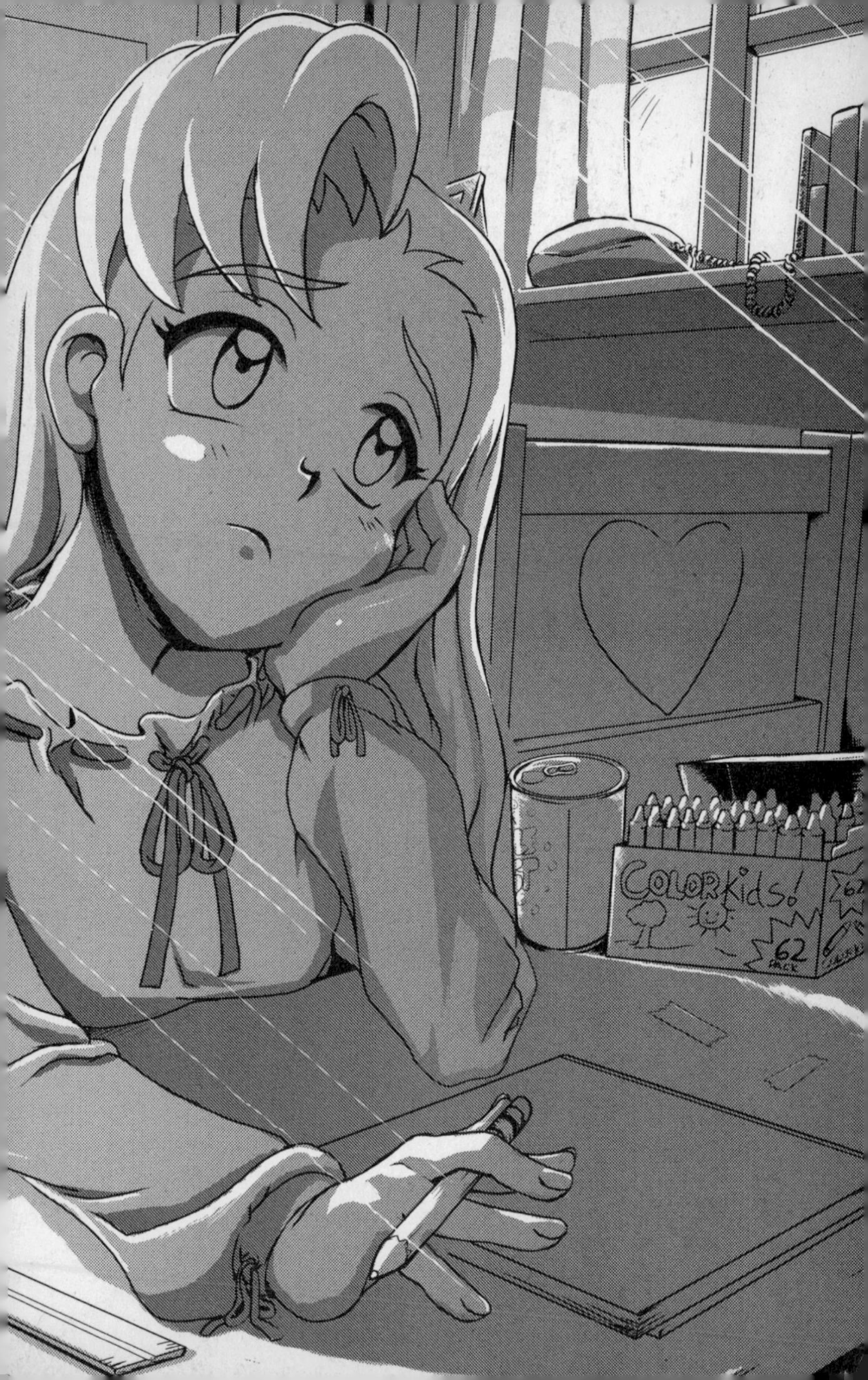
COLOR Kids!
62
PACK

Chapter 1
First encounter

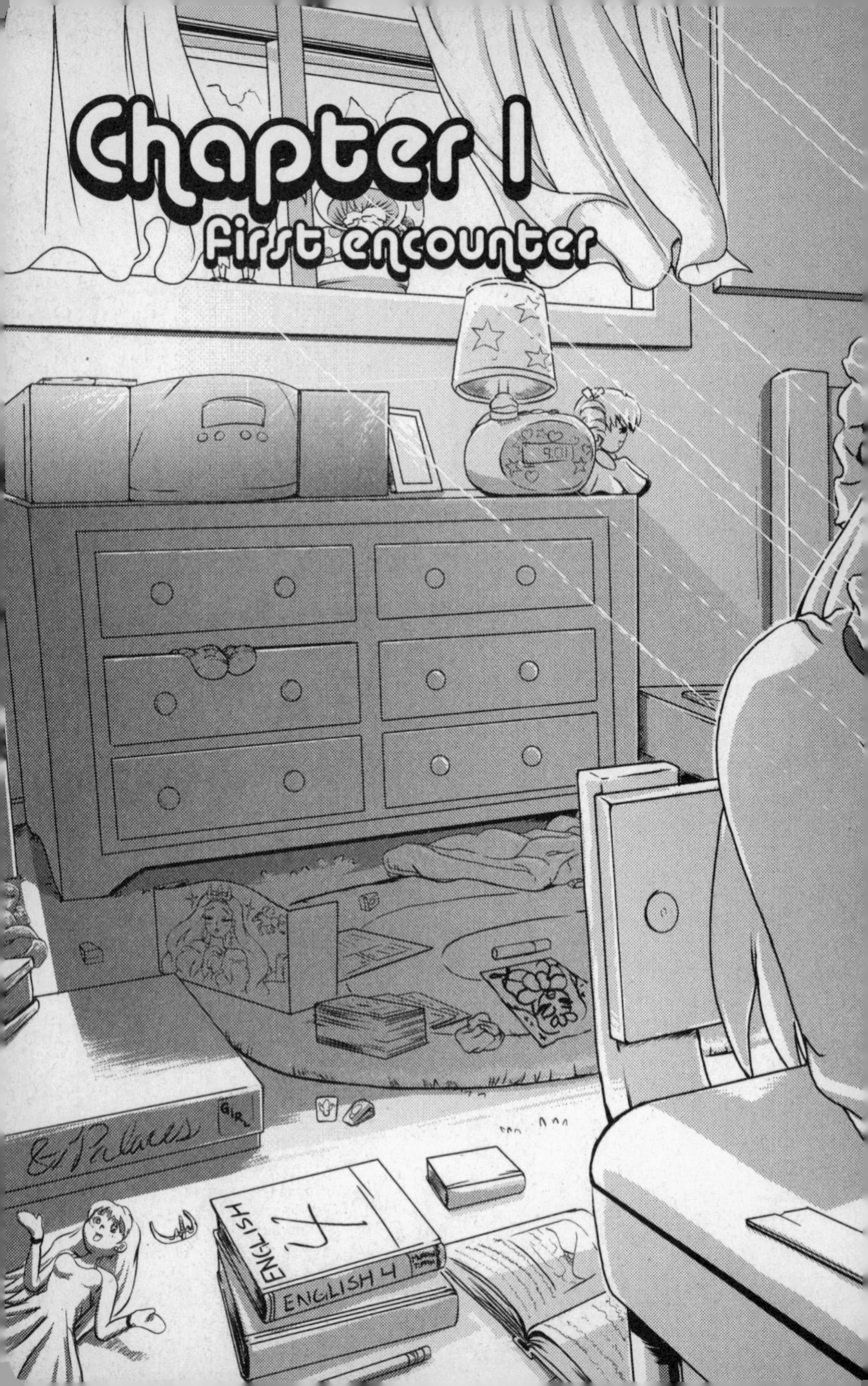
ENGLISH
ENGLISH 4

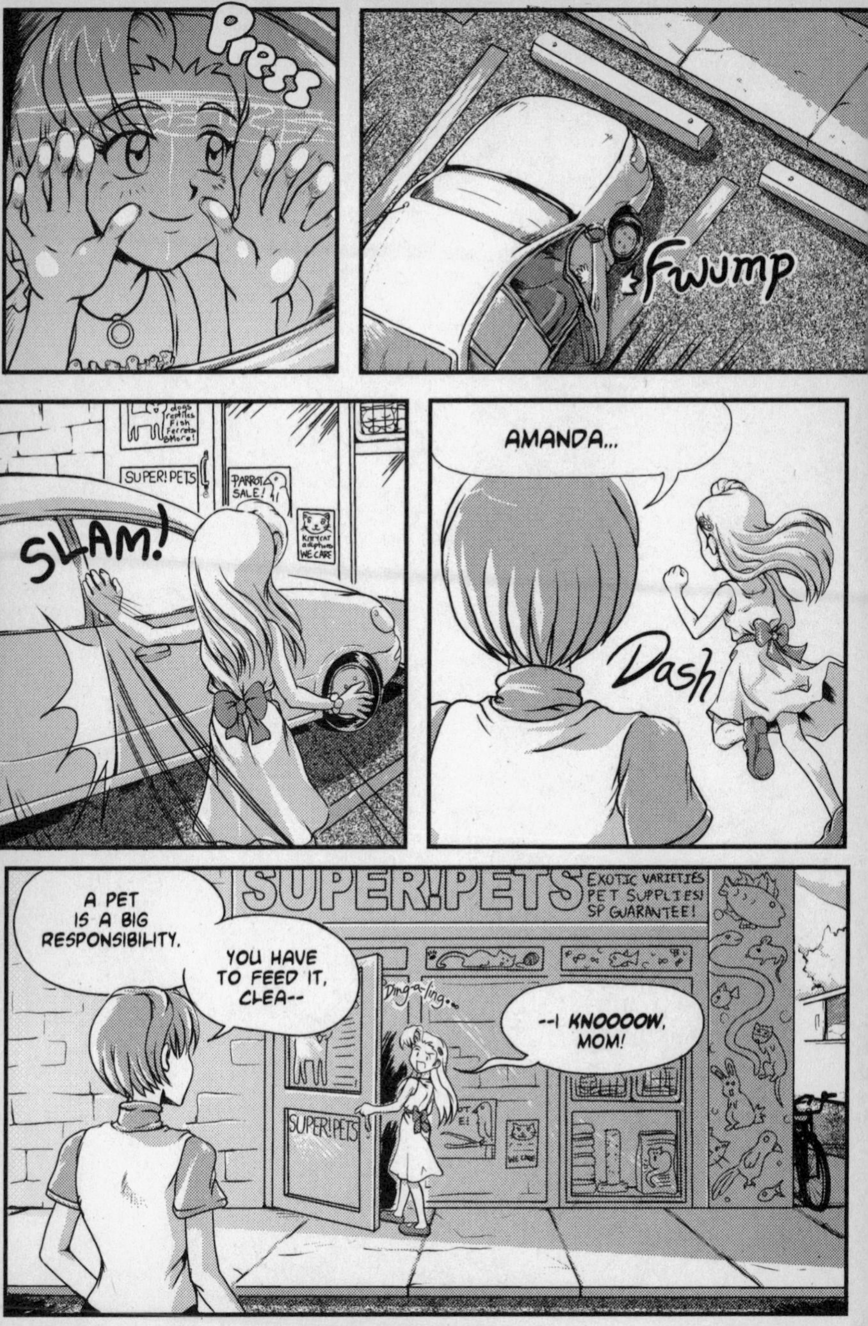
Press
Fwump
SUPER!PETS
PARROT SALE!
WE CARE
SLAM!
AMANDA...
Dash
SUPER!PETS
EXOTIC VARIETIES
PET SUPPLIES!
SP GUARANTEE!
A PET IS A BIG RESPONSIBILITY.
YOU HAVE TO FEED IT, CLEA--
Ding-a-ling...
--I KNOOOOW, MOM!
SUPER!PETS

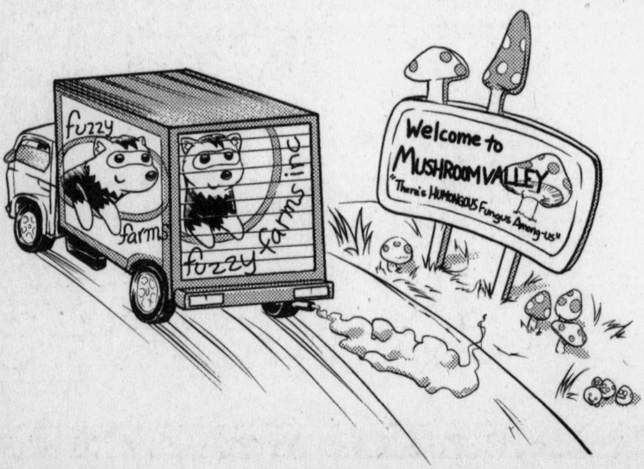
Welcome to
MUSHROOM VALLEY
"There's HUMONGOUS Fungus Among-us"
fuzzy farms
fuzzy farms inc

Table of Contents

Peach Fuzz Vol. 1
created by Lindsay Cibos and Jared Hodges

Production Artist - James Dashiell
Cover Design - Raymond Makowski

Editor - Carol Fox
Digital Imaging Manager - Chris Buford
Production Managers - Jennifer Miller and Mutsumi Miyazaki
Managing Editor - Lindsey Johnston
VP of Production - Ron Klamert
Publisher and E.I.C. - Mike Kiley
President and C.O.O. - John Parker
C.E.O. - Stuart Levy

A  Manga

TOKYOPOP Inc.
5900 Wilshire Blvd. Suite 2000
Los Angeles, CA 90036

E-mail: info@TOKYOPOP.com
Come visit us online at www.TOKYOPOP.com

ISBN: 1-59816-486-4

First TOKYOPOP printing: December 2005
10 9 8 7 6 5 4 3 2 1
Printed in the USA

Peach Fuzz

by

Lindsay Cibos
and
Jared Hodges

HAMBURG // LONDON // LOS ANGELES // TOKYO